American Heritage®

☆ ILLUSTRATED HISTORY OF ☆

THE PRESIDENTS

AmericanHeritage®

☆ ILLUSTRATED HISTORY OF ☆

THE PRESIDENTS

MICHAEL BESCHLOSS

GENERAL EDITOR

A BYRON PREISS BOOK

CROWN PUBLISHERS • NEW YORK

Published by Crown Publishers, New York, New York. Member of the Crown Publishing Group.

Random House, Inc. New York, Toronto, London, Sydney, Auckland
www.randomhouse.com

CROWN is a trademark and the Crown colophon is a registered trademark of Random House, Inc.

Printed in the United States of America

A Byron Preiss Book

Picture Research: Valerie Cope
Design: Gilda Hannah
Editor: Renée Zuckerbrot
Associate Editor: Valerie Cope

Library of Congress Cataloging-in-Publication Data
    The American Heritage illustrated history of the presidents / Michael Beschloss, general editor.—1st ed.
        p. cm
    Includes index
    1. Presidents—United States—History. 2. Presidents—United States—History—Pictorial works. 3. United States—Politics and government. 4. Presidents—United States—Biography. I. Beschloss, Michael R.
E176.1 .A6515 2000
973'.09'9—dc21
[B]   99-462173

ISBN 0-8129-3249-8

10 9 8 7 6 5 4 3 2 1

Revised and Updated Edition

☆ CONTENTS ☆

AmericanHeritage®

☆ ILLUSTRATED HISTORY OF ☆

THE PRESIDENTS

☆ INTRODUCTION ☆

BY MICHAEL BESCHLOSS

The first president of the United States I ever saw was Richard Nixon, during his 1960 campaign against John Kennedy. At the age of four, I am told, I was held up in the air as the future president's motorcade sped down the Lincoln Highway in Illinois, where I lived. That fall, Nixon was promising Americans that if they made him president, "your children and grandchildren won't grow up under Communism." To drive home his point, the Nixon campaign wanted his parade routes lined by small girls and boys. I was one of those.

My fascination with presidents grew. At the age of six, when I watched on television as John Glenn became the first American to orbit the earth, I was struck when one of the commentators said that Glenn was putting his life in danger to advance President Kennedy's dream that Americans get to the moon by the end of the decade. Later that year, I saw Kennedy tell us on television that he would risk nuclear war to get Soviet missiles out of Cuba. Knowing how neighboring towns were sometimes demolished by tornadoes, I wondered whether mine (population forty-six hundred) would be leveled by a nuclear attack.

Three years later, I kept on seeing, or so I thought, the same picture, day after day, week after week, on the flag-emblazoned front page of the *Chicago Tribune*. The image was of a smiling Lyndon Johnson signing a bill, with members of Congress clustered behind him. Only later did I understand that it only looked like the same picture, and that Johnson was enacting the most substantial body of social legislation in history. That year—1965—LBJ also began his first major escalation of the conflict in Vietnam. My fifth-grade teacher gravely told our class, "You boys and girls may not realize it yet, but your country is at war."

It would have been difficult for any American who grew up during the 1960s—the Cold War confrontations, the struggle for civil rights, the Great Society, Vietnam, the race to the moon—to escape the notion that a president loomed, almost physically, over the lives of every American. I presumed at the time that this must have been true for most of American history. Only much later, as an historian, did I come to understand how sharp were the ebbs and flows of presidential power—and of the quality of the men who have served in America's highest office. In this book you will discover those forty-one men in the context of their times, rendered by some of our most accomplished historians—their traumas and joys, their public words and private struggles as they all helped to shape the American story.

You will read of stirring displays of presidential leadership that continue to affect us today: George Washington inventing key elements of our political system, Andrew Jackson battling the Bank of the United States, Abraham Lincoln binding the Union,

Theodore Roosevelt and Woodrow Wilson involving the government more than ever before in our economic affairs and expanding our role among nations, Franklin Roosevelt rescuing our society and the world, Harry Truman improvising the means that would defeat the Soviet empire, Ronald Reagan seeking to end the Cold War.

What makes these achievements all the more spectacular is that our presidents have all operated under a Constitution that did not grant them unilateral power. This was not accidental. On the cusp of independence the founders of the new American republic did not wish to endow the presidency with powers that might lead to some new American version of the British monarchy they had fought so hard to shake off.

This book illuminates the contrast between the limited powers of the office and the acts of presidential leadership that have driven so much of our history. You will see how frequently, thanks to the American system, our people have managed to choose leaders who have had the character to alter public opinion, the vision to spot public dangers and opportunities, and the skills to get Congress, citizens, and sometimes the world to share their view of the way things should be.

More than anyone else, George Washington demonstrated how the strictures of the Constitution would be translated into actual power. The old hero recognized, as Robert Rutland shows in this book, that he was setting one precedent after another—his refusal to be called "His Mightiness" or "His Elective Majesty," his diplomacy, his efforts to fashion a legal structure for the new land, his demonstration, in putting down the Whiskey Rebellion, that the United States was able and willing "to support our government and laws," his refusal to accept a third term.

It was left to John Adams to follow the adored and groundbreaking leader who had stood above partisan-

ship to navigate grave crises with France and with Alexander Hamilton. Adams was the first president to live in the Executive Mansion. He understood the potential of the white stone house as a unifying symbol of the new democracy, writing his famous prayer that heaven "bestow the best of Blessings on this House and all that shall hereafter inhabit it" and that "none but honest and wise men ever rule under its roof."

The quintet of presidents who followed Adams suggested that his prayer had been heard: Thomas Jefferson, who demanded "a government rigorously frugal and simple" and had the foresight to double the size of the new nation with the Louisiana Purchase; James Madison, who took the country through the War of 1812 and helped establish the United States as a world power; James Monroe, who fashioned an enduring foreign policy doctrine; John Quincy Adams, who set out the need for a national system of roads and canals, thoughtful regulation of national resources, and government aid to education; Andrew Jackson, who expanded the powers of the office, waged war against the notion of a national bank, expunged the national debt, and became a people's hero.

For the next quarter-century, with the exception of James Polk, who pursued American expansion and revived the independent treasury, the candlepower of the presidency dimmed. Martin Van Buren struggled against the Panic of 1837. William Henry Harrison died after a month in office. John Tyler, "His Accidency," established the expectation that presidents-by-succession assumed the office in full and annexed Texas, but was ultimately expelled by his own party. Zachary Taylor, Millard Fillmore, and Franklin Pierce were among the weakest leaders ever to serve as president.

The final president before the Civil War, James Buchanan, embodied the failure that shadowed the reputations of his seven immediate predecessors: Each had tried to paper over the deepening issue of slavery that divided the American people, endangered the Union, and threatened to make a mockery of the American notion of democracy.

Few historians would disagree that Abraham Lincoln was our greatest president. What better demonstration could there be of the American idea that anyone can become president than a boy who sprang from "the short and simple annals of the poor" with a year and a half of sporadic formal education; who mastered Euclid, the Bible, Shakespeare, and Blackstone; made himself the natural leader of almost any community he entered; and then went on to confront the issue of slavery and save the Union with a costly and complicated war?

The end of the Civil War, which had seen Lincoln expand the powers of his job to prevail over the Confederacy, might have opened the way to a new era of strong presidents. It did not. The most severe crisis of the Union was over and as Reconstruction unfolded, the Congress, Supreme Court, and the American people were eager to whittle the presidency back to more human scale.

It was in 1888 that the widely read British scholar and diplomat James Bryce wrote "Why Great Men Are Not Chosen Presidents." Andrew Johnson had been impeached. Ulysses Grant's administration had grown entangled in scandal and economic crisis. Although Rutherford Hayes helped to restore the office after the tremors of Johnson and Grant, he was constrained by his failure to win the popular vote and his pledge to serve merely a single term. James Garfield was murdered after a half-year in office. Chester Arthur and Benjamin Harrison were only too happy to allow Congress to take the driver's seat. Although Grover Cleveland aspired to strengthen the presidency, he was frustrated in many of his public ambitions. As you read about these presidents, you might well ask yourself whether America could have

been a greater country during this era had it benefited from stronger executive leadership—or was this a period in which the nation, after the greatest crisis in its history, had to lick its wounds and consolidate?

Then, on the eve of the twentieth century, the wheel turned again. With the Spanish-American War and his dispatch of five thousand Americans to fight the Boxers in China, William McKinley heralded America's new role as a world power. Theodore Roosevelt and, after the William Howard Taft interlude, Woodrow Wilson expanded presidential power over foreign policy and our economic life. The presidencies of Warren Harding and Calvin Coolidge were largely a rebuke to the powerful presidency, but as John Milton Cooper, Jr., and Lewis L. Gould suggest in this book, Herbert Hoover—far more than most people understood at the time—was a forerunner of the dramatic surge in presidential authority that began in 1933.

Franklin Roosevelt launched the longest period of sustained presidential command in our history. The American epoch from the early 1930s until the start of the 1990s was dominated by what the historian Arthur Schlesinger, Jr., has called the "imperial Presidency." When FDR took the oath, the nation was in such desperate economic straits that many members of Congress and influential columnists like Walter Lippmann were almost begging him to seize more power and tinker with ways out of the national mess. Roosevelt would have been stultified to be president in a time that did not allow such potential for leadership. He was only too happy to oblige, sending new domestic programs through Congress that were so far-reaching that the Supreme Court struck some of them down.

Nevertheless, what Congress gave Roosevelt in the domestic arena, it withheld in foreign and military affairs. Despite the president's growing suspicion that the nation might have to wage a war against totalitarians in Germany, Japan, Italy, and their allies, an isolationist Congress mired him in legislation that gave him little leeway. In 1937, backed by three-quarters of Americans (according to one reputable survey), Congress almost passed an amendment requiring that, except in case of invasion, "the authority of Congress to declare war shall not become effective until confirmed by a majority of all votes cast in a Nation-wide referendum."

Pearl Harbor removed the shackles on presidential power in foreign and military affairs. After the Japanese attack, the American people and Congress handed Roosevelt authority to fight World War II that far exceeded anything he had amassed in the 1930s. Leading the Allies into battle, forging an industrial "arsenal of democracy" on the home front, FDR was as near to being a king of the world as any president would ever be.

When the war ended in 1945, there was every expectation that presidential power would recede, just as it had after the Civil War and World War I. But with its air of a clear and immediate danger, the Cold War gave Harry Truman and those leaders who followed him power in foreign affairs that neared that of a president fighting a hot war. Especially during showdowns like the Berlin blockade of 1948 and the Cuban Missile Crisis, many Americans felt that literally one human being was shielding them against a worldwide threat. Congress was often willing to give presidents the benefit of the doubt. The House and Senate let Truman fight in Korea without a congressional war declaration, just as they later let Eisenhower, Kennedy, Johnson, and Nixon do in Vietnam.

In domestic affairs, Americans seemed willing if not eager to continue the flow of national power to Washington that had begun with the New Deal and continued as Americans on the home front girded to win World War II. The imperial presidents were happy to exploit congressional deference that stemmed from the Cold War danger to get contro-

versial domestic programs passed. Eisenhower justified his highway and education programs by saying they were essential for national defense. When Kennedy wished to shoot for the moon—a program that had little direct military value and in fact took resources away from more important military ventures—he reasoned that Americans needed the added prestige and would have to command outer space in order to win the struggle with the Soviet Union.

The strong presidency of the twentieth century also gained power by acquiring new symbols, mystique, and ways to influence the public that it had never had before. In the absence of kings and queens, Americans had always wanted to hold up presidents of special stature like George Washington and Abraham Lincoln as examples for their children. But after World War II, the office was provided with new theatrical props.

When Truman's aides advised him that the presidential aura was a valuable asset in fighting the Cold War, he authorized them to design a new presidential flag and mount a presidential seal on his lectern wherever he spoke. Kennedy had the presidential plane—once blandly labeled MILITARY AIR TRANSPORT SERVICE—repainted by the industrial designer Raymond Loewy (who also designed radios and kitchen blenders) in regal blue and white with the sweeping legend UNITED STATES OF AMERICA. The image of *Air Force One* was so potent that when Gerald Ford's campaign against Jimmy Carter was flagging, Ford's handlers had him deliver a televised campaign speech from aboard the plane, engines screaming as it hurtled through azure skies, because they thought it would make Ford seem more "presidential." Other presidents handed out presidential cufflinks, golf balls, and boxes of M&M's emblazoned with their signatures.

The mass media of mid-twentieth century America made certain that every American knew about their leaders' tastes in dress, cinema, and food. JFK started a craze for two-button suits. His refusal to wear hats (he thought they made his cheeks look too fat) threatened to ruin the hat industry. Besieged by desperate hat moguls, Kennedy was persuaded to at least carry a hat during public ceremonies like airport greetings and military parades. Richard Nixon's well-publicized obsession with *Patton* helped make the film a winner at the box office. Ronald Reagan, after spurring the national consumption of jelly beans, launched the literary success of an obscure insurance agent named Tom Clancy by praising Clancy's first thriller, *The Hunt for Red October.*

Presidents of the eighteenth and nineteenth century had had to address the public through newspapers or handbills. But when presidents of the mid-twentieth century had something to say, they needed merely to call the three major television networks (there were only three) and almost every American watching the tube would be confronted with a presidential speech or press conference. When you saw the presidential seal dissolve into JFK talking about Cuba or Nixon about Cambodia, you knew it was something important and you usually watched.

Another way presidents seized power for themselves during this period was in no way public. These were the illicit abuses of presidential power that constituted a scarlet thread in the underside of the presidential carpet. Members of Ulysses Grant's and Warren Harding's entourages may have exploited the presidency to line their pockets, but twentieth-century agencies like the Bureau of Internal Revenue (later the Internal Revenue Service) and the Federal Bureau of Investigation gave presidents and their aides new opportunities to secretly intimidate or thwart—sometimes under the guise of national security—their political enemies.

When Senator Huey Long threatened Franklin Roosevelt's reelection, federal tax agents were sent to Louisiana to dredge up compromising information that could be used to discredit him. Dwight Eisenhower's chief aide, Sherman Adams, asked the FBI for damaging evidence on Democratic senators that could be used to embarrass them. Under Kennedy, the telephones of presidential critics were tapped and their tax returns, including those of Richard Nixon and his mother, were audited. These misdeeds expanded presidential influence. If you were a Washington columnist whose private life might look tawdry in an FBI file or who had cheated on your income taxes, you might have thought twice before incurring the wrath of a sitting president.

When Nixon came to the White House, he dramatically expanded such practices, abusing the FBI, IRS, and Central Intelligence Agency, devising secret funds for burglary and blackmail. After the Watergate scandal burst open and Nixon's malfeasance was exposed, he complained that he had merely followed his predecessors' custom—and that besides, just as Lincoln had suspended the writ of habeas corpus during the Civil War and just as Franklin Roosevelt had cut the corners of American neutrality laws to secretly aid the British, he too was a wartime president, waging a struggle in Vietnam that, he noted, other presidents had started.

In the wake of Nixon's scandal, Americans, happily, succeeded in yanking most of the scarlet thread from underneath the presidential tapestry. Rules for presidential dealings with agencies like the IRS, CIA, and FBI were implicitly or statutorily tightened. The congressional opposition and a new watchdog press leaped at any public hint of abuse.

In the last decade of the twentieth century, the foundations of the strong presidency cracked. In December 1991, when the Soviet Union dissolved and the Cold War ended once and for all, George Bush found that his influence not only in foreign affairs but also domestic policy shrank almost overnight. Americans wanted a stop to the era of Big Government, as Bill Clinton acknowledged in his 1996 State of the Union, and one of the chief casualties was the strong presidency. What better symbol was there of Big Government than imperial presidents such as Franklin Roosevelt and Johnson and Nixon—and Reagan, who expanded the federal budget? In the absence of an overwhelming foreign or domestic crisis that seemed to cry out for executive leadership, Congress stopped acceding so often to presidential will as it had during the Great Depression, World War II, and the Cold War. There was the prospect that the clock might be turned back to the post-Civil War period, when speakers of the House and Senate majority leaders often dictated to presidents and were sometimes better known and more influential than the men in the White House.

By the end of the twentieth century, the belief that presidents were well-intentioned and told the truth, the idealism and trust that endowed presidents such as Theodore and Franklin Roosevelt, Eisenhower and Kennedy with so much of their public impact had been drained away. After presidential deceptions over the Bay of Pigs and Vietnam as well as the Watergate, Iran-contra, and Monica Lewinsky scandals, Americans (especially the young) were much more skeptical about what they heard from the White House. And in the age of round-the-clock television news and the Internet, presidents would have to compete for airtime with Madonna and O. J. Simpson. Whatever distance and majesty had once surrounded leaders such as FDR and JFK had given way to revelations about presidential underwear.

At the dawn of the twenty-first century, as I write, we are therefore in a period in which it will be very difficult for presidents to exercise strong leadership in the absence of some all-encompassing crisis like the Civil War or the Great Depression—or the election of some leader with such extraordinary stature and political skills that he or she can overcome the ebbing authority of the office.

America does not always need a strong presidency. As the Civil War historian Bruce Catton wrote in his foreword to the last edition of this book, in 1968, "If the story of the Presidents proves nothing else, it testifies to the enormous stability of the office itself and of the nation that devised it." Sometimes we are better off without presidents who overreach. But at critical moments, the absence of that distinctive presidential voice and of the executive power to push foot-dragging public officials and skeptical citizens to think anew or make vital sacrifices can endanger the country. What if there had been no Washington to unite the new nation, no Lincoln to save the Union, no FDR to lead Americans through the Great Depression and prepare us for World War II?

Few historians today would argue that Washington, Lincoln, and Franklin Roosevelt belong anywhere but at the top of the presidential ladder. But for most of the other presidents, the metaphor should be not ladder but stock exchange. Presidential reputations are constantly fluctuating—some much more than others —as we discover new information about them from letters, diaries, secret memoranda, tape recordings, and other sources, and as we see them in more distant hindsight, the phenomenon that the historian Barbara Tuchman so vividly called the "lantern on the stern."

Since the last edition of this volume, for instance, scholars and other Americans have gained new appreciation for such presidents as Polk, Coolidge, and Eisenhower. The pages of this book reflect the current state of scholarship on each of our forty-one leaders.

As a child, I thought that historians ranked presidents on a grand roll call of greatness, whose order never changed. When President Kennedy was assassinated, I was certain that JFK should go straight to the top. On pale-blue-lined grammar school paper, I scrawled a letter to his successor, Lyndon Johnson, saying, "You could get some large carving firm to carve his head in the Mount Rushmore Memorial of South Dakota." I got back a typed letter on White House stationery signed in blue ink by LBJ's devoted secretary Juanita Roberts, saying that her boss had asked her to thank me for sharing my idea "to honor the late President Kennedy." (When I showed the letter to friends at the local hockey rink, they insisted that it was a forgery.)

As an eight-year-old, I could not know that LBJ, had he read this boy's letter, would not have welcomed my advice. Already feeling enveloped by Kennedy's shadow, he privately believed that JFK was a "Joe College man" of minor accomplishment but that Ivy League historians would stack the deck in Kennedy's favor. As for himself, until Johnson died in 1973, disparaged for his rough-hewn style and his war in Vietnam, he insisted that those same historians would have no wish or ability to understand him. But a quarter-century later, as this book affirms, Johnson's reputation is sharply on the upswing.

The LBJ surge is a superb example of what makes the history of the American presidents so mesmerizing. Like a rushing river drawing force and direction from unforeseen new currents and streams, what we think and write about the leaders who have gone before is never final and is always changing.

George Washington's granite profile stands at the front of the presidential monument at Mount Rushmore, and with good reason. Washington—the commander of the tattered colonial army, chairman of the Constitutional Convention, first president of the United States—was indisputably, as General Henry "Light-Horse Harry" Lee eulogized him, "first in war, first in peace, and first in the hearts of his countrymen." Despite their political differences, Thomas Jefferson gave credit to Washington for almost single-handedly creating the nation by winning the Revolutionary War and then guiding the shaky republic for eight years.

No man so experienced in commanding an army and running a nation can escape criticism, but Washington came close. America would not be satisfied with the realities—glorious though they were—of Washington's life. The people wanted a flawless hero. Washington "was destined to a stature in death," writes the historian Daniel Boorstin, "which he had never attained in life. . . . A deification which in European history might have required centuries was accomplished here in decades."

The first president of the United States was born in Virginia's Westmoreland County, in a brick farmhouse, on February 11, 1732 (or February 22, according to the modern calendar adopted in 1752). His father was Augustine Washington, a moderately successful planter. Augustine's second wife, Mary Ball Washington, was the mother of George and his three brothers—Samuel, John Augustine, and Charles—and two sisters, Elizabeth and Mildred. George also had two half brothers, Lawrence and Augustine, Jr., and a half sister, Jane.

Attended from birth by slaves, George was first brought by his parents some forty miles up the Potomac River to a 2,500-acre tract named Epsewasson (later called Mount Vernon) and in 1738 to a smaller plot, Ferry Farm, on the Rappahannock River. When he was eleven his father died, and thereafter Mary Washington's eldest child escaped her watchful eye whenever he could, fleeing to visit relatives and friends.

Washington's education was rudimentary. He was tutored by private schoolmasters, as was common in plantation society, and received a good dose of mathematics and geometry that would be useful when the lad became a surveyor. Early on, Washington came across a copy of a French book of maxims—*The Rules of Civility*—translated into English as a "commonplace book." As to manners, the work warned: "bedew no man's face with Spittle, approaching too near." As for rules of life, the book advised: "Labour to keep alive in your breast that spark of celestial fire known as conscience." Young Washington copied these morsels in his own commonplace book and recalled them throughout his life.

In 1751 George accompanied Lawrence Washington to Barbados, where his half brother, ill with tuberculosis, hoped to regain his health. There, George contracted the smallpox that pock-marked his face permanently but left him immune to the disease that later ravaged his Continental Army. In the following year, Lawrence died.

Washington began his military career in 1752, after his mother forbade his plan for service in the Royal Navy. Instead, he was commissioned a major in the militia and appointed adjutant of the southern district of Virginia. In the fall of 1753 Governor Robert Dinwiddie charged Washington with delivering to the French at Fort Le Boeuf, three hundred miles away in the Ohio Valley, a royal ultimatum to cease fortifications and settlements there "within His Majesty's Dominions." Washington left on his mission on November 15. He stopped on the way to survey the site of a projected fort and, at Logstown on the north bank of the Ohio, urged the Indians, unsuccessfully, to accept the British as benign big brothers. Proceeding to Le Boeuf, he found the

Valentine Green's 1783 engraving of General George Washington, after a painting by John Trumbull.

A dainty portrait-in-miniature of Martha Washington was painted on ivory by Charles Willson Peale, then worn by Washington in a gold neckpiece while he served as commander in chief until the war ended.

French adamant and cocky in their rejection of Britain's claims.

The defiant reply of the French confirmed Governor Dinwiddie's conviction that British holdings in the Ohio Valley must be defended. Commissioned a lieutenant colonel by Dinwiddie in 1754, Washington was ordered to secure the site of the Ohio Company's fort, which was being built at the junction of the Allegheny and Monongahela rivers. En route he learned that the site had fallen to the French (they named it Fort Duquesne) and that enemy troops were advancing toward him in strength. Washington entrenched an abandoned post, which he named Fort Necessity. It was "badly sited," notes the historian Esmond Wright, "in an open, swampy hollow over which a nearby hill gave a commanding view." (This was the first of several less-than-brilliant maneuvers that would leave Washington open to criticism by future military historians.) On July 3, facing a superior force, Washington surrendered.

As an aide-de-camp, Washington then accompanied General Edward Braddock on the ill-fated expedition to Fort Duquesne in 1755 that ended in disaster for nearly everybody but Washington. In the ambush that started the French and Indian War, Washington himself had two horses killed beneath him, and four bullets pierced his coat before he organized a retreat. Washington's official report was published in London, and with rhetorical flourish the unharmed young commander noted how ricocheting musket balls had whizzed around him. King George II is said to have heard of Washington's bravado and guessed that the young colonial had never been in a real fight.

Returning to Virginia, Washington was promoted to colonel and became commander in chief of the Virginia militia. He was thus called upon, at twenty-three, to defend the colony's three hundred-mile frontier from an expected French and Indian attack. But inadequate troops and provisions, limited authority, and a royal governor who denied him permission to seize Fort Duquesne (the key position in the West), made his task impossible. When even his right to command was challenged by an officer of the Maryland militia who held a royal commission, Washington rode all the way from Williamsburg to Boston to ask Governor William Shirley, the acting commander in chief of British forces in North America, to confirm his rank. In Boston the proud young colonel was told that his rank was indeed valid, but only when no British regulars were present.

For more than two years Washington doggedly defended Virginia's frontier with badly equipped, poorly paid militiamen. Then, in 1758, a British force under General John Forbes was assigned to march on Fort Duquesne. Washington was selected to serve as Forbes's acting brigadier, and when the French abandoned and burned the fort, the main objective of his strategy for Virginia's defense was achieved. Disappointed when no commission in the king's army was forthcoming, Washington eventually resigned his commission and retired to sixteen years as a prosperous Virginia planter.

Washington's marriage to the widow Martha Dandridge Custis on January 6, 1759, vastly increased his fortune. Plump and appealing, and reputedly the richest widow in the colony, Martha Washington added six thousand acres to George's five thousand and 150 slaves to his 49. She also provided him with a town house in the capital at Williamsburg along with Daniel Custis's two children, John Parke Custis and Martha Parke Custis (who died at seventeen). George called little Martha "Patsy," while his wife, twenty-seven at the time of the marriage, called George (her junior by one year) her "Old Man." That their marriage was based primarily on romantic love is unlikely, but their affections grew steadily.

Resigned to civilian life, he settled down with Martha at Mount Vernon and became a dutiful vestryman and church warden, tobacco planter, land broker, speculator, and surveyor. Now one of the richest men in Virginia, Washington—in the historian Shelby Little's words—"took up his duties as a Burgess, was publicly thanked for his great services to his country, and drafted a law to prevent hogs running at large in Winchester."

Farming became his passion. He read treatises on crops, manure, and animal husbandry. Washington's attitude toward his black slaves reflected the notions of reigning plantation owners of his time: Slaves were property, efficient or not. Slowly his viewpoint changed. Although he owned more slaves than he probably needed, he refused to sell them without their permission. Failing to see the similarities between the tyranny of slavery and the alleged tyranny of Britain

BIOGRAPHICAL FACTS

BIRTH: Pope's Creek, Westmoreland County, Va., Feb. 22, 1732

ANCESTRY: English

FATHER: Augustine Washington; b. Westmoreland County, Va., 1694; d. King George County, Va., Apr. 23, 1743

FATHER'S OCCUPATION: Planter

MOTHER: Mary Ball Washington; b. Lancaster County, Va., 1708; d. near Fredericksburg, Va., Aug. 25, 1789

BROTHERS: Samuel (1734–1781); John Augustine (1736–1787); Charles (1738–1799)

SISTERS: Elizabeth (1733–1797); Mildred (1739–1740)

HALF BROTHERS: Lawrence (1718–1752); Augustine, Jr. (1720–1762)

HALF SISTER: Jane (1722–1735)

MARRIAGE: Kent County, Va., Jan. 6, 1759

WIFE: Martha Dandridge Custis; b. New Kent County, Va., June 21, 1731; d. Mount Vernon, Va., May 22, 1802

CHILDREN: John Parke Custis; Martha "Patsy" Parke Custis

RELIGIOUS AFFILIATION: Episcopalian

EDUCATION: Private family tutor

OCCUPATIONS BEFORE PRESIDENCY: Surveyor; soldier; planter; land broker

MILITARY SERVICE: Virginia militia (1752–1758); commander in chief of Continental Army (1775–1783)

PREPRESIDENTIAL OFFICES: Member of Virginia House of Burgesses; justice of Fairfax County; delegate to First and Second Continental Congresses; president of Constitutional Convention

AGE AT INAUGURATION: 57

OCCUPATION AFTER PRESIDENCY: Planter

DEATH: Mount Vernon, Va., Dec. 14, 1799

PLACE OF BURIAL: Mount Vernon, Va.

toward her colonies, Washington opposed freeing slaves who were content with their masters. Such action, he argued, would lead to "discontent on one side and resentment on the other."

By 1774 Washington had begun to participate actively in America's burgeoning economic and political revolution. He had opposed the obnoxious Stamp Act—Parliament's first and ill-timed effort to impose a colonial levy—and favored boycotts of British goods in retaliation. Angered by Britain's closing of the port of Boston (in reaction to the Boston Tea Party), he was present with Jefferson at the Raleigh Tavern in Williamsburg on May 27, 1774, after the royal governor had dissolved the rebellious House of Burgesses. At this meeting the Virginia legislators issued a vote of sympathy with their New England brothers, appointed delegates to a Virginia convention that would select representatives to a Continental Congress, and passed a resolution stating that an attack on one of the colonies would be considered an attack on all. Later that year Washington was chosen to attend the First Continental Congress in Philadelphia, where he sat silently, his sword at his side.

Washington was appointed a delegate to the Second Continental Congress in May 1775. The battles at Lexington and Concord in April had led to a siege of the British troops in Boston, and Washington was nominated as commander in chief of a proposed Continental Army. He was elected unanimously. In assuming the post, Washington was humbly magnanimous: "Though I am truly sensible of the high honor done me in this appointment, yet I feel great distress from a consciousness that my abilities and military experience may not be equal to the extensive and important trust." But he would accede to congressional will, do his plain duty, and "exert every power I possess in the service for support of the glorious cause." Refusing a salary, he asked only that Congress bear his expenses.

Washington took command of his army on the outskirts of Boston on July 3, 1775. Lack of ammunition and cannons, however, delayed his first major move until March 1776 when he fortified Dorchester Heights, placing the British fleet in Boston Harbor under threat of bombardment. The British evacuated the city on March 17, and Washington led his troops southward to New York City, where, he correctly believed, the enemy would next strike.

In New York, Washington had 20,000 ill-trained troops. With them, he was expected to beat back a combined British assault force—then gathering at Staten Island—of some 32,000 crack redcoats under General William Howe and more than 30 war vessels and 400 transports under Sir William's brother, Admiral Richard Howe.

On July 4, 1776, Congress proclaimed in the Declaration of Independence that the colonies were free of the Crown under "the Laws of Nature and of Nature's God." But in August the brothers Howe moved in to seize control of New York Harbor and both the East and Hudson rivers. Facing encirclement, Washington dispatched 5,000 men to Brooklyn Heights, maintaining the rest of his forces in Manhattan. General Howe defeated the Americans in the Battle of Long Island, inflicting 1,500 casualties. Admiral Howe then sailed up the East River, cutting Washington's forces in two. On August 29 Washington crossed the East River and withdrew the rest of his Long Island troops to the island of Manhattan.

Plagued by desertions, Washington's forces dwindled, while British ranks swelled. In September, Howe struck again in a massive landing at Kip's Bay in Manhattan, and facing no opposition from the terrified and retreating Americans, he forced Washington north to Harlem Heights. When the Continental Congress rejected his proposal to burn New York City, Washington stationed 7,500 men to guard the Hudson at both Fort Washington on the New York shore and Fort Lee on the New Jersey side. He then eluded Howe's advance up the East River by retreating to White Plains in October. Attacked there, Washington retreated again.

By dividing his forces, Washington courted disaster. Fort Washington surrendered, and two days later Fort Lee fell. Left with just 5,000 men, Washington retreated through New Jersey and crossed the Delaware River into Pennsylvania. The British, now in firm control of New York City and most of New Jersey, sent a portion of their forces to pursue him, garrisoning finally at Trenton and Bordentown.

But now Washington moved with daring. On Christmas night, 1776, he and his men rowed silently across the icy Delaware to attack the sleeping encampment of British mercenaries at Trenton. The attack, in which some nine hundred Hessians (hired by George III) were taken prisoner, showed Washington's ability to spring hope and reverse American morale.

Ultimately the British pulled back to New York, and Washington set up winter quarters in Morristown, New Jersey. For their part, the British now resolved on a major new strategy: a thrust from Lake Champlain in the north to secure New England and New York, and to keep Washington busy on two fronts. But at Saratoga 6,000 British troops under General John Burgoyne were defeated by some 17,000 Continentals led by General Horatio Gates. Saratoga was a turning point in the war, for the victory convinced French leaders the Americans could win, and vital aid from Paris followed.

The troops under Washington, however, faced a new period of despair. Howe, instead of coming to the aid of Burgoyne on Gates's southern flank, had chosen to take Philadelphia. Washington, with 10,500 troops, marched south to meet Howe's 15,000 redcoats at Brandywine Creek on September 11, 1777. The Americans suffered another defeat but made an orderly retreat across the Schuylkill River. Howe entered Philadelphia on September 26. A week later, in a daring but unsuccessful assault, Washington attacked Howe's encampment at Germantown, Pennsylvania, and lost 1,000 more men. He then retired for the winter at Valley Forge, some twenty miles outside Philadelphia.

It was a black season for General Washington.

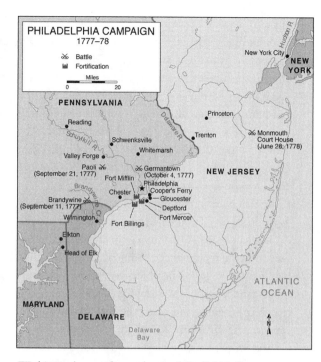

Washington's ragged army harassed the British from bases near Philadelphia during 1777 and 1778. Several bloody losses convinced the British that New York was a better place for their headquarters, and they evacuated the Pennsylvania stronghold in June 1778.

Valley Forge was, he said, "a dreary kind of place, and uncomfortably provided." This was a vast understatement. His men faced bitter cold and frost without shoes or blankets, and they were forced to drink soup "full of burnt leaves and dirt." Before the winter was over, 3,000 of Washington's 9,000 men had deserted.

In May 1778 General Howe was replaced by Sir Henry Clinton, who abandoned Philadelphia in June 1778 to march back through New Jersey toward New York. Washington, in pursuit, met the British on June 28 at Monmouth, New Jersey, and held the field after angrily quashing a precipitate retreat of American forces under General Charles Lee. The British used one of Washington's treasured tactics—withdrawal by night (to New York). Monmouth was the last major battle in the North.

Content with their snug fortress on Manhattan, the British shifted their strategy. Invasion of the Carolinas became a top priority. Charleston fell, and the Southern states were threatened by a formidable army led by Lord Cornwallis. After a series of hard-fought battles in the Carolinas in the first half of 1781, Cornwallis brought his full force into Virginia at Yorktown on the first day of August.

In the North, Washington's 9,000 Continentals were joined by 7,800 French troops under the Comte de Rochambeau. A combined operation with the French naval commander Admiral de Grasse was planned for August. The objective: to trap Cornwallis by land and sea. Washington planned the long march to Virginia, and when the French and American armies arrived in Yorktown, Cornwallis found himself outnumbered two to one. He surrendered on October 19, 1781. Yorktown was the last major military engagement of the war, but the cautious Washington kept a small army together until rumors of a peace treaty were confirmed.

How did this American Cincinnatus win against such overwhelming odds? According to Esmond Wright, "the explanation is not that Washington won [the war] but that Britain lost it, and to the terrain rather than to the enemy." But General Washington won on many positive counts. He had unassailable and unflinching courage when it was needed most; the worst conditions brought out his best qualities as a leader of men and a daring strategist. He believed in the "glorious cause" of America and, in the darkest moments, could envision its future greatness. Contemporary descriptions prove that he possessed charisma, the magnetic aura of leadership that moves others to extraordinary effort.

Washington himself set April 19, 1783, the eighth anniversary of the Battle of Lexington, as the date of formal cessation of hostilities with England. Not until November did he enter New York in triumph, welcomed by fireworks and waving flags. But the long wait had been interrupted in June, when Washington wrote what he probably believed to be his last public gesture, a kind of farewell statement to the nation. This document, "Circular Letter to the Governors of All the States," was a heartfelt message—a plea to his fellow Americans to clutch and hold the liberty they had finally won on the battlefield. Noting the nation's great potential, Washington informed each of the states that if the experiment in democracy failed, only Americans could be blamed. "This is the time of their political probation," he wrote, ". . . this is the moment to establish or ruin their national Character for ever." He warned that an unstable union would enable European states to divide and conquer the country. To secure a more durable union, he advocated four "Pillars on which the glorious Fabrick of our Independency and National Character must be supported." These were "1st. An indissoluble Union of the States under an Federal Head. 2dly. A sacred regard to Public Justice. 3dly. The adoption of a proper Peace Establishment, and 4thly. The prevalence of that pacific and friendly Disposition, among the People of the United States, which will induce them to forget their local prejudices and policies, to make those mutual concessions which are requisite to the general prosperity, and in some instances, to sacrifice their individual advantages to the interest of the Community."

Washington returned to Mount Vernon on Christmas Eve, 1783. There he stayed, switching his crops from tobacco to wheat, building grist mills, and breeding mules and superb riding horses. At this time, the new nation languished in a troubled peace. The Articles of Confederation—which provided a weak national government with an empty treasury—were no match for the strong-armed state politicians who jealously guarded their own coffers. Time and again the Congress showed its ineptitude at governing the new nation. The huge war debt, much of it owed to foreign creditors, became a national embarrassment. Lacking a power to tax, the struggling nation was almost bankrupt.

By the winter of 1786–87 matters came to a head. Desperate men flouted the law, cash was scarce, and even the smallest taxes on marginal farms went unpaid. Finally, a half-hearted resistance movement surfaced in western Massachusetts (Shays's Rebellion), where debt-pressed farmers routed sheriffs and defied authorities. In Rhode Island farmer-lawmakers passed laws forcing creditors to accept depreciated paper money.

These events galvanized Washington's wartime comrade in arms Henry Knox into action. Knox wrote Washington a hysterical letter, depicting Captain Daniel Shays's ragtag farmers as mutineers. "A rebellion of 10,000 men against our governments would indisputably secure encouragement from Canada," Knox told Washington. Alarmed, Washington saw "Combustibles in every state" that needed only a spark to ignite a general uprising across the land. General "Light-Horse Harry" Lee told Washington that anarchy was just around the corner.

Washington answered Lee: "You talk . . . of employing influence to appease the tumults in Massachusetts. I know not where that influence is to be found . . . Influence is no government. Let us have one by which our lives, liberties, and properties will be secured, or let us know the worst at once." Meanwhile, Virginia legislator James Madison was hoping to force action by calling for a national convention to meet in Philadelphia to revise the Articles of Confederation, and he needed Washington's help. Washington admitted the situation was critical but was reluctant to take an active role.

Yet all was not lost. Madison did usher the call for a general convention through the Virginia legislature and persuaded Washington that his attendance was vital. "Duty" was the key word, so Washington changed his mind and became one of the fifty-five delegates sent by twelve states (Rhode Island refused to send any representatives). Fortunately, once word leaked out that Washington was to be present, some of the most talented public men in the United States accepted their appointments as delegates, including Gouverneur Morris, George Mason, Alexander Hamilton, James Wilson, and Oliver Ellsworth.

Thirty-nine delegates stayed at their task in the summer of 1787. Washington was elected as president of the Constitutional Convention; he then turned the gavel over to chairmen who oversaw daily committee meetings that carried the business of nation-building forward. Madison's Virginia Plan became the working blueprint for a national government with three branches (executive, legislative, and judicial) that had the power to tax, carry on foreign affairs, and insure the domestic tranquility of the struggling republic. From May 25 to September 17 they labored—Washington appears to have spoken only once (concerning the representation ratio in the House of Representatives)—and then he signed both the document and the covering letter which carried the finished Constitution to the states for ratification.

On September 18, 1787, the Federalists—delegates who believed in a strong centralized government—were confident that the sufficient number of states would readily adopt the new Constitution (nine states were necessary for the Constitution to become operative). Except for a few states'-rights defenders such as George Clinton of New York and Patrick Henry of Virginia, most public men agreed that the Articles of Confederation had to be abandoned. On the other hand some citizens, called Anti-Federalists in the campaign for ratification, wanted a few alterations, plus the addition of a bill of rights. Ultimately the moderates had their way. For the key states, beginning in Massachusetts, Federalists conceded that a bill of rights would be added once the new government was in place. James Madison made certain that this campaign pledge was honored.

Supporters of the Constitution promoted the idea that Washington was going to be the first president, once the document had been ratified. James Monroe, an Anti-Federalist from Virginia, told a friend "Washington's name carried the day." And so it was in state after state, until the magic nine had acted.

Here was something new in world history, and more of a revolution than the war that had preceded it: Freely elected men were meeting and writing a fundamental law, then going to the people again to elect a head of state. Never before had such a reliance upon a broad electorate been witnessed. For century upon century military prowess, brute force, and royal intrigue were the avenues to power until the Founding Fathers suggested another method: trust in the people. As the historian Robert Dallek notes, Washington's role as the first president gave the Constitution "instant credibility. . . . Washington's presence as a unifying force was essential." Moreover, Washington "served as a permanent exemplar toward which the country would aspire throughout its history." Washington was unanimously elected president by the first electoral college in February 1789. According to the Constitution, the candidate who came in second place in the electoral college became vice president. Hence John Adams of Massachusetts provided the northern half of the first balanced national ticket.

On April 16 Washington left his plantation for the nation's temporary capital, New York City. Despite his assurance that he had no "wish beyond that of living and dying an honest man on my own farm," he was now called, at the age of fifty-seven, to lead a great experiment in democracy. He assumed the presidency with no less foreboding than pride: "My movements to the chair of government," he said, "will be accompanied by feelings not unlike those of a culprit, who is going to the place of his execution." He had the comfort of knowing, however, that a hopeful, united nation stood by his side.

The president-elect was besieged by public applause, parades, and celebrations in a triumphant march from Mount Vernon northward. In New York, on April 30, 1789, Washington rode to Federal Hall on, at the corner of Wall and Nassau streets, for the nation's first presidential inauguration. An expectant crowd massed in the streets, looking up to the canopied portico, awaiting their champion. Church bells pealed their welcome.

Then Washington appeared, majestic and tall, dressed in brown broadcloth and white silk stockings, his dress sword at his side. Robert Livingston, Chancellor of New York, lifted the Bible to administer the oath, which the commander in chief repeated, according to a newspaper account, with "devout fervency." Now president of the United States, Washington bowed to kiss the Bible. Then Chancellor Livingston said: "It is done," and shouted, "Long live George Washington, President of the United States." Washington and the other dignitaries then attended services at St. Paul's Anglican Church. At dusk the crowd was treated to a fireworks display featuring an illuminated transparency of the president. The streets were so packed that Washington had to walk back to his new quarters after a happy but tiring day.

President and Mrs. Washington went about the business of creating an executive office and setting up a household, all in the same building. Tobias Lear (a wartime aide) was chosen as Washington's personal secretary and organized the president's schedule. Washington tried to make it clear that, as in the days when he was a general, he would accept no salary but take only expenses. Soon Congress balked at that arrangement and appropriated an annual salary of $25,000. Magnanimous as his gesture seemed, Washington was strapped for cash and would have been hard-pressed without his federal income, for he had to support a large entourage of slaves, pay rent on his New York quarters, maintain a social calendar involving much food and drink, and keep a fine carriage and full stable of twelve to eighteen horses. His hay

The newly elected president was inaugurated on April 30, 1789, on the balcony of Federal Hall, as illustrated in Montbaron and Gautschi's engraving. Cheering citizens at the corner of Wall and Nassau streets hailed the beginning of Washington's eight-year tenure as president.

bills were enormous. When his mother complained in 1787 that he was not helping her, he wrote with some chagrin: "I take the first safe conveyance to send you 15 Guineas which believe me is all I have. . . . I have demands upon me for more than 500L three hundred and forty odd of which is due for tax . . . and I know not where, or when I shall receive one shilling with which to pay it." Constantly disappointed by the declining revenue from his farms, Washington needed cash.

The president's first official duty, once he took the oath of office, had been to address the people. Reported by the newspapers, the speech was Washington's earliest precedent-setting endeavor. In fact, from 1789 until the end of the nineteenth century, the presidential inaugural address was reported verbatim in the American press and was considered, along with the State of the Union message, one of the major news stories of the year. To both houses of Congress,

assembled in the Senate chamber, Washington delivered the first such message. Invoking God's aid, he expressed the hope that "no local prejudices or attachments, no separate views nor party animosities, will misdirect the comprehensive and equal eye" that ought to govern the nation above sectional interests. Liberty and "the republican model of government," he said, are "finally staked on the experiment entrusted to the hands of the American people."

Washington wished to be a president above politics, above sectionalism, and, indeed, above all controversy. The president's only attempt to appear in person before the Senate became a tempest-in-a-teapot affair, involving his advice on an Indian treaty. Senator William Maclay claimed an immediate vote was improper. "This defeats every purpose of my coming here," the president huffed. Washington never returned. That incident in itself became a precedent followed by all his successors; presidents would nego-

called him "an old mutton head," and even Jefferson said on one occasion, "Curse on his virtues, they have undone his country." Later, though, Jefferson had to admit Washington was in a class by himself.

Eventually the critics would form a phalanx that bothered Washington more than he cared to admit. Meanwhile, Congress debated what to call the new chief executive. The Senate, harried by what Jefferson called its "monarchist" faction, debated the merits of grand-sounding titles. The suggestions now seem ludicrous—"His Elective Majesty," "His Elective Highness," "His Highness, the President of the United States and Protector of the Rights of the Same," even "His Mightiness." A more rational House of Representatives settled the matter, after Madison asserted that high-sounding titles were out of place in the republic and would "diminish the true dignity of the first magistrate himself." The chief executive would be styled, with elegant simplicity, "President of the United States."

Similarly, when Congress debated the design of coins, some members thought Washington's profile would be fitting. Madison and the congressmen moving in opposition to the Federalist "monarchy men" insisted this smacked of the practice in England where George III's countenance was stamped on all royal coins. After some desultory debate, Congress decided the coins should not bear the likeness of a living American but rather an artist's version of the goddess of Liberty and the date. This policy, too, became a permanent fixture.

Washington was acutely conscious of his immense power in setting precedents. If he made the wrong appointments as chief executive, he feared he "might perhaps raise a flame of opposition that could not easily, if ever, be extinguished. . . ." He believed that government officials should be appointed on the basis of abilities, residence, and "former merits and sufferings in the service." They should also be, he insisted, "just and candid men who are disposed to measure matters

tiate treaties and then bring them to the Senate as faits accomplis, still to be ratified or rejected.

Washington avoided all direct personal advocacy or involvement in congressional legislation and limited his messages to Congress to broad and optimistic homilies. But his hope of remaining completely above the fray was dashed by the inevitable rise of political parties—Federalist and Democratic-Republican—during his second administration. Exasperated with Washington's sometimes glacial aloofness, John Adams

on a Continental Scale." In a bid for national unity, he appointed both Federalists and the opposition, with evident regard for geographic balance.

At length, the First Congress got down to business and passed laws creating a cabinet of executive officers and a federal court system. The departments of cabinet rank were designated as state, treasury, and war; the offices of postmaster general and attorney general were created but not at cabinet rank, perhaps to hold down costs. As his secretary of state, Washington appointed Thomas Jefferson of Virginia, newly arrived home after serving as the American minister to France. Two officers who had served with Washington during the war gained the other appointments. New York's Alexander Hamilton, Washington's former aide-de-camp and a major author of *The Federalist*, became secretary of the treasury. Henry Knox of Massachusetts, his chief of artillery in the Revolution, was named secretary of war. Washington appointed Samuel Osgood of Massachusetts as postmaster general. For his attorney general, Edmund Randolph, another of Washington's aides-de-camp and a prime mover in Virginia's ratification of the Constitution, was appointed.

Washington believed that "the Constitution of the United States, and the laws made under it, must mark the line of [his] official conduct. . . ." He would, he wrote, neither stretch presidential powers "nor relax from them in any instance whatever, unless imperious circumstances shd. render the measure indispensable." Nevertheless, Washington had no qualms about asserting firm presidential authority in areas where the Constitution was silent or gray. The document said nothing about a cabinet of appointed officers, but Congress took care of that oversight. Nor did the Constitution say anything about the president's right to proclaim neutrality (clearly a negative corollary to the power of Congress to declare war), but Washington nonetheless did so during the Franco-British war. Personally, as well as through sub-ordinates, he was a strong president, asserting executive priority as the occasion demanded and as the law, positively or tacitly, allowed.

Of Washington's methods as chief executive, Jefferson later said: "His mind . . . was slow in operation . . . but sure in conclusion. . . . Hearing all suggestions, he selected whatever was best . . . [but was] slow in readjustment." Neither hatred nor friendship, Jefferson added, could bias his decisions. In other words, Washington was deliberate, fair-minded, and eager to hear all sides of a political question. Once Washington made a decision, there was no hand-wringing about the soundness of his position.

Deferential to Congress, Washington believed that a bill should be vetoed only if it were clearly unconstitutional. Early on, Washington sought advice from Jefferson, Hamilton, and James Madison (floor leader in the House of Representatives) regarding the constitutionality of a measure passed by Congress. He had a rigid sense of the nation's tripartite system of checks and balances, but he had equal regard for his own presidential prerogatives. When in 1796 an angry House of Representatives demanded that the president submit for its investigation all executive instructions and papers relating to John Jay's controversial pro-British treaty with England, Washington reminded the House that its assent to this—or any—treaty was not legally required.

In a nation with no experience in strong elected executives, he worked slowly toward a presidential balance of dignity and candor. The world was watching this bold experiment in self-government—a chief executive chosen by a free election—and a skeptical European intelligentsia thought it bound to fail. Washington realized his every move was being monitored, and he believed that the president must in his "public character . . . maintain the dignity of Office, without subjecting himself to the imputation of superciliousness."

This same conviction, reinforced by Washington's

own patrician experience as a Virginia landowner, dictated a substantial degree of ritual pomp. Washington had no hesitation in forcing respect for the presidency among European observers by moving through the capital in a yellow chariot adorned with gilded cupids and his personal coat of arms. The executive mansion was staffed by fourteen white servants and seven slaves. After listening to advice from his vice president and a few Virginia friends now in federal service, Washington decided to hold public levees twice a week. In the newspapers he announced that he would accept no invitations to private dinner parties, but instead invited the public to one-hour social sessions. Any suitably dressed male was welcome at the Tuesday reception, while ladies could take tea with Mrs. Washington on Fridays.

Thus Washington established another precedent that still holds. The home of the president was open to the people who had chosen him, but on a fixed schedule. The only president not to live in the White House, Washington had determined how the people would regard the official residence long before a spade of earth had been turned to start its construction.

Not all Americans were delighted by this display of executive elegance. The acerbic Senator Maclay attended levees regularly but could not enjoy them wholeheartedly. He bowed to the president and in his diary noted that the affairs were innocent but "certainly anti-republican." Maclay and other back-country lawmakers regarded the splendor as a harbinger of an aristocracy that had no place in classless America.

With social calls kept to a minimum, President Washington devoted his time to pressing executive duties. He assigned the organization of the nation's basic financial structure to Alexander Hamilton, whose importance in the administration became second only to Washington's. Hamilton moved with swift efficiency to build his new system. In a deal with Jefferson and Madison—the eventual leaders of the Democratic-Republican party—he agreed to support the location of the new national capital on the Potomac River, closer to the South. In return, the Virginians agreed to approve of the federal government's assumption of state debts. Hamilton also proposed that new bonds be issued, covering the federal debt at full value, and that a portion of the government's revenue be set aside regularly for payment of interest and principal. Five years later Jefferson was determined to halt Hamilton's influence, and out of the Federalist-approved, pro-British Jay's Treaty imbroglio, the two-party system emerged.

As the nineteenth century neared, Hamilton's system was ready-made for the prosperity that followed during that period of expansion and technological change. There was a price to be paid, however. The chief tenets of Jefferson's political philosophy were low taxes and small government, and Hamilton would have no part of such limitations. In 1789 the French Revolution became a pivotal test for the young nation, for Hamilton's goal was an alliance with Great Britain and a financial program designed along British lines. Jefferson's followers hailed the fall of the Bastille and what followed—the rise of the French Republic—while Hamilton and the Federalists were horror-stricken. True, Lafayette sent Washington the key to the fallen citadel as a symbol of Franco-American unity; and Democratic-Republican societies sprang up in villages and towns where the French revolutionaries' uprising was applauded and tricolored cockades were worn. Meanwhile, Hamilton secretly informed a British agent that the United States would find a way out of its 1778 Franco-American Alliance. Hamilton's cause was helped by the execution of Louis XVI and Marie Antoinette, whereupon American ardor for the revolutionists quickly cooled.

In 1791 Hamilton suggested that the federal government form a corporation—the Bank of the United States—to issue banknotes backed by gold and silver, and to serve as the main depository of government funds (in effect, the financial agent of the Treasury). The bank was to be a corporation technically supervised by the government but actually run by directors representing private stockholders. When agrarians and states' righters cried out against "financial and political tyranny," questioning the constitutional right of Congress to charter a bank, Hamilton replied that this right was inherent in its power to tax, to regulate trade, and to defend the nation. In 1791 Washington signed the bill chartering the bank. Also under Hamilton's aegis, a decimally based currency was adopted, an excise tax was imposed on whiskey, and a protective tariff was adopted to favor domestic goods.

The Jeffersonians were incensed. Jefferson himself chose to resign over what he regarded as a flagrant collusion of financial and political oligarchies. Washington urged an end to both Hamilton's and Jefferson's "wounding suspicions and irritable charges,"

ALEXANDER HAMILTON

He was a revolutionary who considered the frame of the government he revolted against "the best in the world"; he was admired as a political philosopher—the brilliant advocate of strong central rule—and was hated as the high-handed, egocentric party boss, even by many who shared his political beliefs.

This was Alexander Hamilton—next to the president, the dominant figure of Washington's administration. Born of a common-law marriage in the Caribbean in 1755 or 1757, Hamilton came to New York in 1772 for an education. At King's College (later Columbia University), he became a leader of the unrest that led to the Revolution. While serving as an officer under General Washington, he began to develop his theories of democratic rule and to campaign for a convention to enlarge the powers of the federal government. To survive, Hamilton thought, the nation would have to be what it was not under the Articles of Confederation—firmly united, with the separatist tendencies of the states kept in check, able to defend itself against attack, and dependable in economic matters. Hamilton favored government support of American commerce and the encouragement of an educated, well-to-do ruling class, whose interests would be closely tied to interests of the nation.

Many of his aristocratic ideas, drawn from the British model, clashed with strong republican sentiments in the states. His plan for government did not attract support at the Constitutional Convention in 1787, and at the end of that long conclave he admitted (according to James Madison) that "No man's ideas were more remote [from the final draft of the Constitution] than his own were known to be." Even so, he pleaded for its unanimous approval by the delegates, and then went home to begin writing, with the help of Madison and John Jay, arguments in favor of ratification—the *Federalist* papers. He believed that the new Constitution, imperfect though it might be, offered a viable alternative to the "anarchy and convulsion" he saw rapidly engulfing the Confederation.

Appointed secretary of the treasury by Washington in 1789, he continued to strengthen the federal powers. At his insistence, the United States assumed full responsibility for its own Revolutionary debts and for the war debts of the states. This served to unite the wealthy creditor class behind the central government and to stabilize the economy. With an excise on whiskey, he confirmed the government's right to levy internal taxes. Perhaps most important, his arguments in favor of the creation of a national bank—the doctrine of implied powers—gave the Constitution the flexibility it would need to cope with the changing demands of passing decades.

He left Washington's cabinet and practiced law in New York until 1804, when he was killed in a duel with his archenemy, Aaron Burr.

which had now reached a state of public vituperation. In 1792, however, both men agreed that only Washington's decision to accept a second term could even temporarily bridge the widening schism; Washington was unanimously reelected by the electoral college.

The temper of the new federal government was tested by three events during Washington's second administration: the celebrated Whiskey Rebellion; the machinations of the French minister, Edmond Genêt; and the fierce public storm over John Jay's treaty with England. In July 1794 Washington was challenged by defiant whiskey distillers in western Pennsylvania who abhorred the Federalist excise tax on their product. (It was difficult and expensive for farmers to transport corn to market, but when distilled, whiskey became an easily movable cash crop—and their chief source of income.) They terrorized excise agents, forced troops guarding the chief excise inspector to surrender, and threatened to march on Pittsburgh. Alarmed that the revolt might spread, Washington called for some fifteen thousand state militiamen to check the insurgents and thus proved that the United States was "able [and] willing to support our government and laws." He and Hamilton both rode out to review the militia. In fact there was little opposition to this demonstration of executive strength.

Revolutionary France and its conflict with England remained as divisive an issue as Hamilton's fiscal programs. Washington's own policy was a formal and circumspect neutrality, despite French and British attacks on Yankee ships and the British impressment of American seamen. But the tension was heightened in 1793 by the arrival in the United States of a new French minister, Citizen Edmond Genêt, who recruited American money and volunteers for the French armies. Playing on American antipathy toward Britain, the flamboyant Genêt harangued the populace, hiring and arming United States privateers to prey on British ships and return them as prizes to American ports. "Ten thousand people in the streets of Philadelphia," said John Adams, "day after day

A contemporary engraving, attributed to Frederick Kemmelmeyer, shows Washington reviewing the troops, with Alexander Hamilton alongside. Farmers in western Pennsylvania resented the tax on whiskey imposed by the federal government. In the summer of 1794 President Washington, alarmed by riots that intimidated federal tax collectors, called for a sizable militia to disperse the angry crowds. The so-called Whiskey Rebellion ended quickly, its chief offenders later pardoned by Washington.

threatened to drag Washington out of his house, and effect a revolution in the Government, or compel it to declare war in favor of the French revolution. . . ."

Washington and Hamilton, unmoved by the anti-British sentiment, were enraged by Genêt's activities. And when he threatened to appeal directly to the people for support, over Washington's head, even Jefferson, the Francophile, was upset. Washington demanded the minister's recall, but Genêt, fearful of returning to France (now controlled by extremists), appealed for and was granted asylum in the United States.

Despite Washington's firm declaration of neutrality, the British continued to impress American seamen and to search United States ships on the pretext of hunting for deserters. They continued to occupy military posts they had promised to abandon, and to incite the Indians to harass the Western frontier. The Maine-Canada boundary was also in dispute, as was the exclusion of American ships from West Indian trade.

To settle these issues, Washington sent the staunch Federalist John Jay to London in April 1794. The contents of Jay's Treaty were not made public until March 1795. Britain agreed to abandon the frontier military posts by 1796, to refer the Maine boundary dispute to a commission, and to negotiate Yankee ship-seizure claims, but she made no concession on neutral trading rights, impressment, or the pre-war debts owed to British merchants. Moreover, the United States was denied the right to export forest and farm products to the West Indies.

The public and press exploded in wrath. Hamilton was personally threatened by mobs in the streets. Jefferson watched from afar as newspapers no longer spared Washington from personal abuse. Their intemperate attacks on the treaty were really aimed at the president, Washington claimed, and in "such exaggerated and indecent terms as could scarcely be applied to a Nero, a notorious defaulter, or even to a common pickpocket."

JOHN JAY

First chief justice of the United States, the cultured and diligent John Jay—born in New York City in 1745—was a noted lawyer and a member of both Continental Congresses. He served as minister to Spain from 1780 to 1782, and then participated in the peace talks in Paris, ending the Revolutionary War. His insistence that the American commissioners be regarded as representatives of the United States, not of the "Colonies," delayed the negotiations and may have cost the United States possession of Canada, which the British might have been willing to cede in exchange for an early end to the war. Jay also shared responsibility with John Adams for suing for peace without consultation with France. The final treaty was signed in September 1783, and Jay returned home early the next year to serve as secretary of foreign affairs. An advocate of a strong central government, he wrote five *Federalist* papers. He was named chief justice by President Washington and went to England in 1794 to cope with the threat of a new war. His success was limited, for the treaty bearing his name did not include British recognition of American neutrality rights. He returned to New York to find himself elected governor, and held that office for six years, retiring to private life at the age of fifty-five. Twenty-eight years later, Jay died in Bedford, New York.

Only Washington's personal prestige enabled him to withstand the assault. He signed the treaty in August 1795. But the opposition was now out in the open, and although Washington was firm in deciding to step down at the end of his second term, a clear-cut battle for the presidency was imminent. In the interim, there was much shuffling of the cabinet. Hamilton resigned and was replaced by Oliver Wolcott. Knox quit and was succeeded by Timothy Pickering. Democratic newspapers protested the strong Federalist makeup, which caused Washington to respond that he would never allow a man in his cabinet "whose political tenets are adverse to the measures which the general government are pursuing." To bring dissenters into his official family, Washington added, "would be a sort of political suicide."

Washington was able to end his administration on a high note. He signed the popular Pinckney Treaty with Spain in 1795, which recognized American navigation rights on the Mississippi River and the right to export from New Orleans duty-free for a period of three years. As he contemplated a farewell charge to the nation, Washington must have realized how much he had accomplished. As Robert Dallek notes: "In every respect, his presidency was . . . a learning exercise for himself and the country." A weary president told advisers to prepare a final speech as his valediction.

In fact, Washington had asked Madison to write a farewell speech when he thought about retiring in 1792. Madison, who held a familiar role as Washington's speechwriter, complied. But changed circumstances led the president to stay on for a second term, so he had filed away Madison's handiwork. In May 1796 he sent Hamilton the Madison draft for comments. Hamilton produced a graceful plea for Americans to avoid entangling alliances with European powers: "The nation which indulges toward another an habitual hatred or an habitual fondness is in some degree a slave." Washington liked Hamilton's strike at political parties, too, and kept his warning that in a republic such evidences of factionalism only promoted "a spirit of revenge." In the revised draft Washington also warned against maintaining a large standing army, and insisted that in a strong Union there was no need for "overgrown military establishments." Washington had added a wistful note: "I anticipate with pleasing expectation that retreat, in which I promise myself to realize, without alloy, the sweet enjoyment of partaking, in the midst of my fellow-citizens, the benign influence of good Laws under a free Government—the ever favourite object of my heart." Now it was time for President and Mrs. Washington to go. Washington's last official act was to attend the inauguration of his successor, John Adams. Two days later the Washingtons gave a farewell dinner party, and on March 9 they climbed into a carriage, said their goodbyes, and left for Virginia.

Washington had put his stamp on the American presidency forever. "It was no easy task," writes the

---

SECOND ADMINISTRATION

INAUGURATION: Mar. 4, 1793; Federal Hall, Philadelphia
VICE PRESIDENT: John Adams
SECRETARY OF STATE: Thomas Jefferson;
   Edmund Randolph (from Jan. 2, 1794);
   Timothy Pickering (from Aug. 20, 1795)
SECRETARY OF THE TREASURY: Alexander Hamilton;
   Oliver Wolcott, Jr. (from Feb. 2, 1795)
SECRETARY OF WAR: Henry Knox;
   Timothy Pickering (from Dec. 10, 1795);
   James McHenry (from Feb. 6, 1796)
ATTORNEY GENERAL: Edmund Randolph;
   William Bradford (from Jan. 29, 1794);
   Charles Lee (from Dec. 10, 1795)
POSTMASTER GENERAL: Timothy Pickering;
   Joseph Habersham (from Feb. 25, 1795)
SUPREME COURT APPOINTMENTS: William Paterson
   (1793); John Rutledge, chief justice (1795); Samuel
   Chase (1796); Oliver Ellsworth, chief justice (1796)
3RD CONGRESS (Dec. 2, 1793–Mar. 3, 1795):
   SENATE: 17 Federalists; 13 Democratic-Republicans
   HOUSE: 57 Democratic-Republicans; 48 Federalists
4TH CONGRESS (Dec. 7, 1795–Mar. 3, 1797):
   SENATE: 19 Federalists; 13 Democratic-Republicans
   HOUSE: 54 Federalists; 52 Democratic-Republicans
STATE ADMITTED: Tennessee (1796)

ELECTION OF 1792

CANDIDATES	ELECTORAL VOTE
George Washington	132
John Adams	77
George Clinton	50
Thomas Jefferson	4
Aaron Burr	1

A lithograph by Régenier, ca. 1853, based on a painting by Junius Brutus Stearns, depicts George Washington in the fields at Mount Vernon. He made daily rounds on horseback and tried to switch from labor-intensive tobacco crops to wheat and other grains.

historian Clinton Rossiter, "to be the first occupant of a mistrusted office under a dubious Constitution." No doubt Washington made the government of the United States work as only he, a national hero, could. He built the peace on which nationhood was based; he presided over the formulation of its legal structure; he nurtured and governed when the nation suffered its birth pangs. As Rossiter said, "He fulfilled the hopes of the friends of the Constitution and spiked the fears of its critics."

In retirement Washington was content "to make, and sell, a little flour. . . . To repair houses going fast to ruin. . . . To amuse myself in agriculture and rural pursuits. . . . Now and then to meet friends I esteem. . . ." But his retirement was not entirely pastoral. President Adams, alarmed by declining relations with France, named Washington commander of a provisional army on alert. Fortunately, Adams ignored his advisers' recommendations and kept the war hawks at bay.

But most of Washington's days at Mount Vernon were spent living the life of the planter and landowner, as he began his "diurnal course with the sun." At night, he said, he felt "tired and disinclined" to write

or read. Besides, he concluded, he might soon be "looking into [the] Domesday Book."

On Saturday, December 14, 1799, Washington, suffering from a tracheal infection, was bled repeatedly, and prepared to pay "the debt which we all must pay." "I am not afraid to go," he told his doctors. Within hours, the silence at Mount Vernon was broken by sighs and tearful reactions to the sad announcement. "The general is gone." Blackbordered newspapers soon carried the doleful news to every corner of the republic.

No eulogy seemed to say it all. The historian Richard Norton Smith concluded: "Washington forced a world more accustomed to Caesars than Cincinnatus to revise its definition of greatness. His legacy of integrity and strength will be with the American people forever." In a sense, the America heading into the twenty-first century is Hamilton's creation—a thriving industrial-capitalistic powerhouse. But if Hamilton was the head, Washington was the heart of the first presidency and arguably our best chief executive between 1789 and 2000.

—*WILSON SULLIVAN,*
revised by ROBERT A. RUTLAND

John Adams was not born into the First Family of the United States; he founded it. Although his Puritan ancestors were active in local affairs, the Adamses of Massachusetts remained typical colonial farmers until John and Susanna Boylston Adams of Braintree parish had their first son. In this Adams, born on October 30, 1735, there developed a brilliance of intellect and a uniqueness of character that he passed to his children and their progeny. But if character separated John Adams from his forefathers and distinguished his descendants, it also forbade rapport between the Adamses and the American people, to whose service they were totally devoted.

That John Adams became president at all is one more tribute to the Founding Fathers of the United States: it is doubtful that he could progress very far in modern politics. Early in his career, when he began to devote himself to the cause of American independence, he maintained a legalistic posture high above the issues in which his fellow patriots were emotionally involved. He was haughty, condescending, self-righteous, short-tempered, and cantankerous throughout his life.

Sometimes Adams was so aloof that even the people with whom he joined forces were not always sure he was on their side. Yet they were delighted when he was, for he was incorruptible and extraordinarily intelligent, and he had the courage to stand by his convictions at any cost.

Another facet of Adams's character was introspectiveness. He could be unusually objective about himself: The self-portraiture in his diary might have been written by a disinterested party. He called himself "puffy, vain, conceited." He wrote that vanity was his "cardinal folly," and often his contemporaries paid tribute to his perceptiveness by agreeing with him.

While his offspring appear to have inherited the Adams character, John Adams had to develop it. In his youth he much preferred farm chores to schoolwork, and though he studied Latin his real interest was agriculture (which remained his hobby for life). His family had provided a model for him: his uncle Joseph Adams, a Harvard graduate who had been a schoolmaster and then a clergyman of some stature. Thus in 1751, at the age of sixteen, Adams entered Harvard.

After graduating, Adams was employed as master of the grammar school in Worcester, Massachusetts. From the outset, teaching stubborn youths was at best barely tolerable for him. As a schoolmaster Adams was soft-spoken and introverted, almost shy. The boys—there were fifty of them in his class, ranging in age from five to fifteen—at first behaved with some restraint, testing him, making certain that a wolf was not hidden beneath the sheepskin. Before long the pupils had the measure of their master and took the upper hand. They were to Adams "little runtlings, just capable of lisping A, B, C, and troubling the master"; the classroom became for him a "school of affliction." Yet the apparent alternative, the ministry, seemed no less depressing. Adams was bathed in gloom until the summer of 1756, when he began finding nightly retreat in the law offices of James Putnam. After two years of reading in Putnam's office, Adams quit teaching, passed the bar examination, and began practicing law in Braintree.

In order to observe the methods of more experienced lawyers, Adams attended trials throughout the surrounding counties. One of the attorneys he greatly admired was the fiery James Otis of Boston, advocate general of the colonial vice admiralty court. When, early in 1761, Otis resigned his office to argue the colonial case against the Writs of Assistance before the chief justice of Massachusetts, Adams attended the hearing. The experience changed his life.

The Writs of Assistance were legal permits giving inspectors the right to enter and search any ship, warehouse, or private home where smuggled goods were thought to be hidden. Although colonial courts

John Adams, whom some senators called "His Rotundity" behind his back, in an undated painting by John Frazer Andrews.

had long been empowered to issue writs, it had not often been necessary or prudent to do so. After the French and Indian War, however, Parliament confronted a huge national debt at home while colonial prosperity had never been healthier, especially in Massachusetts. Pressure from England for better enforcement of the taxes on imports caused the courts to issue the unpopular writs.

It was difficult enough to suddenly enforce a long-ignored law, but to complicate matters further for England, on October 25, 1760, King George II died. Traditionally, all writs automatically expired six months after the death of a monarch; according to Otis, the English decision not to withdraw the writs was in opposition to British law. Moreover, Otis added emotionally, enforcement of the writs was a violation of an Englishman's established right to freedom from an invasion of his own home. In America, as in England, everyman's home was his castle.

Sixty years later John Adams would write that in the council chamber where Otis spoke "the child Independence was born." Adams's diary of the time makes only passing mention of the speech, but retrospective drama was characteristic of Adams's writing. Beneath the cold, intellectual facade, under the detachment and pomposity, was a John Adams who was more romantic than he ever would have admitted. He fell in and out of love as often as a schoolgirl. He cherished the ladies, pampered them, and left them untouched—by him anyway—on their pedestals. An early sweetheart, Hannah Quincy, tempered her affection for him because she thought no ordinary woman could ever return the immeasurable quantity of love that John Adams had in him to give. On his part Adams longed for a wife and family, but he was cautious, and he proposed marriage only to Abigail Smith. They were married in 1764.

Hannah Quincy had been right: Abigail Smith Adams was no ordinary woman. She read more than a lady was supposed to; she was smarter than a woman ought to have been; and she spoke out when convention called for feminine silence. She was the perfect wife for Adams, for she managed to keep the cold, impersonal statesman out of the home and the devoted family man in it. She humored his hypochondria and made light of his constant premonitions of an early death. Adams did not emerge as a public figure until after his marriage. True, the national issues were growing in intensity, but he still had elements of the timid schoolmaster in him. As the Americans began to resist orders from Whitehall and a browbeating Parliament, these traits disappeared.

For one thing, he began to spend more time with his cousin Samuel. A bankrupt businessman, patriot, teacher, rabble-rouser—depending on who was describing him—Sam Adams was in 1764 a Boston tax collector who resented the taxes he was supposed to collect. Thirteen years older than John, Sam had the vision to look beyond the superficiality of individual incidents to the larger issues that were dividing Crown and colonies. Although John Adams would remain considerably more cautious than his cousin, he too began to view each dispute as part of a whole.

The Stamp Act of 1765 provides a case in point. The surface issue was censorship: Because the act would require the colonials to purchase stamps for every printed document, from wills to playing cards, from insurance policies to newspapers, the royal officials could refuse to sell stamps for material they regarded as unfavorable. But the real issue, as it had been with the Writs of Assistance, was taxation without representation, since no American sat in Parliament. When word came that the obnoxious act had been passed, angered colonials swung into action. The militant Sons of Liberty stormed and wrecked the home of Massachusetts-born Lieutenant Governor Thomas Hutchinson, and Sam Adams organized a blockade of the customhouse to prevent the stamps from being distributed. John Adams wrote a series of brilliant articles for the Boston *Gazette*, condemning the act purely on legal grounds. He turned for premises to British law, claiming that it was "inconsistent with the spirit of the common law and of the essential fundamental principles of the British constitution that we should be subject to any tax imposed by the British Parliament; because we are not represented in that assembly in any sense." When a Massachusetts colonial legislature was called to meet in October, he wrote a list of recommendations for the Braintree delegate. To his surprise, forty towns in Massachusetts adopted as their own his "Braintree Instructions." In short order, John Adams was a man with a reputation.

But John Adams was no radical. The law-flaunting Sons of Liberty were not his heroes. To oppose an unjust law in court, to petition, to call a congress—these were legal rights; but to react with vigilante vandalism was beyond the law. Such was John Adams's position until the courts were suddenly closed. The government's reasoning was clear enough: All legal documents had to be stamped; the colonials would not permit distribution of the stamps; therefore the business of the law could no longer proceed. Shaken from his perch, Adams saw the weakness in his commitment to legality. How does one employ legal channels when the channels are closed? Even after the Stamp Act was repealed and the courts reopened, Adams was troubled: The Crown had closed the courts once and could do so again.

Although he remained a moderate, favoring legal petition as the first weapon of protest, Adams no longer equated forceful resistance with treason. He grew closer to Sam Adams and James Otis; and when he refused the governor's appointment to the lucrative post in the admiralty court, he was acknowledged by the people of Boston as a patriot (albeit a stuffy one).

In a typical reaction, Adams placed his political career on the block after the events of March 5, 1770, when a squad of soldiers under the command of Captain Thomas Preston paraded past a crowd of rowdy

BIOGRAPHICAL FACTS

BIRTH: Braintree (Quincy), Mass., Oct. 30, 1735
ANCESTRY: English
FATHER: John Adams; b. Quincy, Mass., Jan. 28, 1691; d. Quincy, Mass., May 25, 1761
FATHER'S OCCUPATIONS: Farmer
MOTHER: Susanna Boylston Adams; b. Brookline, Mass., Mar. 5, 1709; d. Quincy, Mass., Apr. 17, 1797
BROTHERS: Peter Boylston (1738–1823); Elihu (1741–1776)
MARRIAGE: Weymouth, Mass., Oct. 25, 1764
WIFE: Abigail Smith; b. Weymouth, Mass., Nov. 22, 1744; d. Quincy, Mass., Oct. 28, 1818
CHILDREN: Abigail Amelia (1765–1813); John Quincy (1767–1848); Susanna (1768–1770); Charles (1770–1800); Thomas Boylston (1772–1832)
RELIGIOUS AFFILIATION: Unitarian
EDUCATION: Attended private schools; Harvard (B.A., 1755)
OCCUPATIONS BEFORE PRESIDENCY: Teacher; lawyer
PREPRESIDENTIAL OFFICES: Member of Massachusetts legislature; delegate to First and Second Continental Congresses; member of Provincial Congress of Massachusetts; delegate to Massachusetts Constitutional Convention; commissioner to France; minister to the Netherlands and England; U.S. vice president
AGE AT INAUGURATION: 61
OCCUPATION AFTER PRESIDENCY: Writer
DEATH: Quincy, Mass., July 4, 1826
PLACE OF BURIAL: First Unitarian Church, Quincy, Mass.

Bostonians. During the customary exchange of insults, the crowd became a mob; stones were thrown, shots were fired, five civilians were killed and several injured. Outraged, Sam Adams and his friends demanded a trial for perpetrators of the Boston Massacre. When no other Boston lawyer would agree to defend the soldiers involved, John Adams announced that he would serve as the defense counsel.

Before the trial began, Adams was persuaded to become a candidate for the provincial legislature. Having no confidence in the judgment of the people, he was sure that the defender of British soldiers could not possibly win; but he entered the race anyway and, much to his surprise, won by the considerable ratio of 4 to 1. Though the people who elected him admired his courage in standing forward for the defendants, they were not prepared for Adams's success in court. Captain Preston was acquitted, two of the soldiers were convicted of minor infractions and given light sentences, and the rest were exonerated.

Adams was ostracized: The Sons of Liberty called him a deserter, the patriot press turned against him, and, perhaps most painful of all, Sam Adams wrote a series of articles signed VINDEX, which implied collusion in the redcoats' defense. To make matters worse, the royalists (often called Tories) began wooing John Adams, assuming that he had come over to their side. Touchy and hurt by the Tories' solicitations, Adams reacted in typical fashion: He packed up and went back to Braintree. "Farewell politics," he wrote in his diary.

Adams's "permanent" farewell lasted for two and a half years. Then, late in 1772, Parliament introduced reforms to provincial courts. Some letters by Thomas Hutchinson, which proved that the courts had been rigged previously and that the new "reforms" were calculated to make the courts entirely subordinate to the Crown, were intercepted by Benjamin Franklin and sent to Sam Adams, who published them. On January 4, 1773, the first of a series of eight long articles decrying the situation appeared in the Boston *Gazette* over the signature of John Adams, a clear demonstration that Adams was a patriot after all.

In May the legislature nominated him to sit in the upper chamber of the House of Representatives; when the governor vetoed his name, Adams was back in the patriot camp with good credentials.

In the autumn of 1773, the much-scarred umbilical cord between Crown and colonies was stretched to the breaking point. Three years earlier, Parliament had repealed most of the duties on colonial imports imposed by the Townshend Acts but had left the tax on tea. The colonists had evaded the tax by smuggling tea from the Netherlands, while bales of tea rotted in London warehouses. Now the East India Company, heavily indebted to the government, was nearly bankrupt, and Parliament awarded it exclusive right to the sale of tea in the American colonies.

This was the last straw for the colonials; they would not have their economy ruined by parliamentary favors that created British monopolies in American markets. On the evening of December 16, 1773, the merchant ship *Dartmouth*, first of three tea-bearing vessels to dock in Boston Harbor, was the site of a ransacking mission led by a group of Indian-disguised Bostonians, who summarily tossed the cargo overboard. The action spread to the other ships when they arrived. This time John Adams approved.

The ministers of George III responded to the Boston Tea Party by passing the Intolerable Acts, which closed Boston Harbor and appointed a military governor for Massachusetts. Mainly directed at New England, the implications of the acts were clear throughout the colonies, and in Philadelphia, on September 5, 1774, the First Continental Congress convened in protest. John Adams, a delegate from Massachusetts, labored for passage of the Suffolk Resolves (named for Boston's county), which advocated outright resistance to the Intolerable Acts. The resolves were accepted, and Adams returned home, recognized as one of the most influential men in the province.

From 1774 onward, Adams was a leader in the Continental Congress with a hand in nearly every vital decision. In 1775 he urged that regionalism be sacrificed for the good of all the colonies, that each state contribute to a single continental army, and that George Washington be commander of that army. He served on the committee that drew up the Declaration of Independence and, when it was attacked by moderates, was its foremost defender. He favored a union of states into a single government and actively backed the Articles of Confederation, which created a United States of America and remained in force until the Constitution was ratified in 1788.

Past forty, pale, and rotund, Adams was not cut out for soldiering and never was tempted to go into the field. Diplomacy, an endeavor he hardly understood, became his passion after his first appointment to a French mission in 1778 and again two years later. Priggish Yankee that he was, Adams got along with neither Benjamin Franklin, the American minister, nor Charles Vergennes, the French foreign minister. In The Hague, however, Adams successfully negotiated a large loan in 1782. Then he returned to France, where with Franklin and John Jay on September 3, 1783, he signed the Treaty of Paris, ending the Revolutionary War. Two years later he became the first American minister to the Court of St. James.

Adams was a proud, aggressive, uncompromising defender of American interests, but in London he found himself up against a blank wall. The English hierarchy was convinced that the feeble young republic would not last. Thus almost every American attempt to establish friendship and commercial relations with England was received coldly. In 1788, after three frustrating years in London, Adams asked to be recalled.

When he arrived home a new government was being formed under the recently ratified Constitution. Adams believed—and he was by no means alone in his belief—that the vice presidency belonged to him almost as automatically as the presidency did to George Washington; but while the general was elected unanimously, Adams won with a plurality of only 34 out of 69 electoral votes. The widely distributed balloting was engineered by Alexander Hamilton, who thereby planted the seeds of a feud from which neither man would profit.

Adams's first attempts to interpret and define the responsibilities of the vice presidency were not distinguished. His concern with petty details amused the senators, and when consulted by President Washington he was only too eager to give advice—much of it bad. He pondered whether he should be his own man or the president's, whether he should be an independent statesman in the Senate, over which he presided, or an impartial monitor. He asked the Senate for advice: Should he address the chamber standing or sitting?

Who cares? thought Senator William Maclay, a rugged Pennsylvania lawyer, advocate of democratic

The American-born artist Benjamin West never completed his painting of the peace commission that signed the Treaty of Paris in 1783, ending the War for Independence, because a British signer had died. The American diplomats were John Jay (far left), John Adams (seated), and Benjamin Franklin (center).

BENJAMIN FRANKLIN

He was seventy years old, and though he had "retired" almost three decades before, Benjamin Franklin found himself clomping down the ship's ramp onto French soil on behalf of his country. He had come to ask for help—for support and money—and all his talk about what France might gain from American independence would be just so much salesmanship; nevertheless, the French were delighted to see him. They displayed his portrait in shop windows, stamped his image on coins and jewelry, held banquets in his honor. When John Adams arrived two years later, in 1778, he was astonished. Franklin's reputation, he noted, was so universal that "there was scarcely a peasant or a citizen, a valet de chambre, coachman or footman, a lady's chambermaid or a scullion in a kitchen who was not familiar with it, and who did not consider him a friend to human kind."

Europe had known Franklin for a long time. *Poor Richard's Almanack* had been translated into French, his scientific experiments widely duplicated, and even the great Mozart had composed an adagio for the armonica, a musical instrument of Franklin's invention. But France held a special admiration for the Philadelphian, for while he suited their romantic portrait of the wise and simple American, he also belonged alongside Voltaire and Defoe and Montesquieu in the Age of Enlightenment, that international phenomenon which France thought purely French.

Franklin was wise but by no account simple, and he was perfectly willing to accept the role in which the French had cast him. Before long, John Adams grew impatient with Franklin; Adams had come to

deal in diplomacy, not to participate in "continual dissipation," nor to dress like a Daniel Boone and recite homespun aphorisms. Openly critical of his colleague, he deplored the Franklin-led commission, its waste and inefficiency, and he was recalled. What John Adams had neglected to consider was that Benjamin Franklin was accomplishing a great deal.

Adams could not even enjoy the luxury of being alone with his resentment during the voyage home; instead, he was accompanied by a French official gushing admiration for Franklin. At one point the jealous Yankee erupted. "It is universally believed in France, England and all of Europe," Adams said, "that his electric wand has accomplished this Revolution. But nothing is more groundless. He has done very little."

Adams returned to Europe in 1780 and negotiated a Dutch loan large enough to reduce American dependency on France. This proved valuable during the Paris peace negotiations, for Franklin had in fact become overly acquiescent to French plans to participate in the talks. France would be better served by a continuing war between the United States and Great Britain than by American independence; thus Adams and the third American commissioner, John Jay, overruled Franklin's efforts to have the French present at the parleys. The treaty was concluded in 1783 with a minimum of French interference. Franklin irritated Adams even after his death in 1790. While the aura around Franklin's name grew, John Adams insisted that he had been "the vainest man and the falsest character I have ever met." Adams tended to overstate, particularly in his estimate of men and events.

simplicity, and keeper of the personal journal that gives us our most complete glimpse into the early years of the Senate. Adams was fond of official titles, without which, he thought, "governments cannot be

raised nor supported." He was all for calling the president something grand, like "His Highness, the President of the United States and Protector of the Rights of the Same." In amusement, Maclay wrote that

Adams "may go and dream about titles, for he will get none." Maclay and his side prevailed. But behind Adams's back, some senators did acquiesce in the vice president's affection for titles by informally awarding him one: His Rotundity.

With the matter of titles settled against him, Adams, according to Maclay, continued to infuriate the Senate with his condescension. Before debate on any issue could begin, the vice president insisted on addressing the chamber with a lecture on the constitutional responsibilities of the Senate. Presiding over Senate debates, he was arbitrary and prejudiced in his decisions regarding who could or could not participate. Before a vote, like a schoolmaster talking to children, Adams would summarize the issue and unhesitatingly instruct the senators how to vote.

By philosophy Adams was soon aligned with the Federalists. An outgrowth of the struggle for ratification of the Constitution, the Federalist party supported a strong central government that would be affiliated with the banker-merchant forces behind the Constitution. Alexander Hamilton was the group's idol, and in Washington's cabinet he was persuasive. Adams was not in the Federalists' inner circle, but he shared their distrust of the masses and he acknowledged a "natural division [between] the gentlemen and the simple men." By temperament he was clearly not a party man. However opinionated he might have been, he was not faithful to ideological dogma.

For all his faults, Adams tried to see both sides of an issue. Hamilton seems to have gathered as much, and throughout Washington's first administration, he looked for signs of the vice president's unreliability. As Senate president, Adams had broken twenty tie votes, all in accordance with the position of Washington, who more often than not sided with the high-flying Federalists. Therefore Hamilton had no grounds on which to oppose Adams, but he disliked the man personally and saw Adams as a stumbling block to his own ambition.

In 1792 Adams stood for reelection because he too was ambitious. Adams wanted to be president and convinced himself that he deserved the office, owing to his long public career and his service during the late war. In his second term in the second office, he had less to do—there were fewer tie votes—and he came to despise the job, particularly after Hamilton became Washington's right-hand man. Once he had been a mover of events, a great debater, a figure in controversy; now he was a loyal, passive observer. To Abigail he wrote, "My country has in its wisdom contrived for me the most insignificant office that ever the invention of man contrived or his imagination conceived."

The election of 1796 was the first "dogfight" election for the presidency. The Constitution had made no provisions for parties, and candidates were selected by state legislatures and an informal caucus held by congressional insiders. Candidates for the presidency and vice presidency were all listed on a ballot that did not differentiate between the offices. In many states there was no direct vote on the presidency, and state legislators most often made the final choice for presidential electors. The electoral college convened early in the new year, well before the inauguration scheduled for March 4. There each elector voted twice, and the highest and next-highest vote getters became president and vice president. The Federalists in 1796 clumsily nominated Adams and Thomas Pinckney, while the opposition (known informally as the Democratic-Republicans) worked to elect Thomas Jefferson and Aaron Burr.

Convinced he would never be able to control Adams, Hamilton quietly worked for the election of Pinckney as president. Hamilton's own power to control the election, however, was less than he had estimated, and his plan backfired. Adams won, but he barely edged out Jefferson by a mere three votes. Thus a Federalist president would be paired with a vice president from the opposition forces. There was constitutional trouble ahead, as the election of 1800 soon proved.

The circumstances in which Adams took office could hardly have been worse. In the first place, he succeeded the beloved Washington. It was no easy task to follow the father of his country, and it became even more difficult when men in his own party served as Hamilton's henchmen. To Adams it seemed unfair that he should have to wallow in the muck of party politics, unlike Washington who had for the most part been able to maintain a nonpartisan stance on most public issues. But wallow he did. Unlike Washington, Adams had no adoring electors ready to trust his judgment implicitly. Ever since the bitter fight over ratifying Jay's Treaty, public opinion was more polarized, and Adams, the ungainly intellectual, could find no support from the idolizing masses.

Adams's first and perhaps biggest mistake was to appoint a cabinet composed of Hamilton's friends. Thus spies in his official family reported regularly to Hamilton, who was now a practicing lawyer in New York. Adams was further saddled with Jefferson. Philosophically, the two men were worlds apart. Although the vice president tried to start their official business on a friendly tone, the administrative harmony could not last.

Initially, by taking Jefferson into his confidence, Adams hoped that they could labor together effectively. But a gap soon developed between them. Jefferson had read articles by Adams condemning some aspects of the French Revolution, an event Jefferson had witnessed firsthand and greatly admired. In short order, Jefferson labeled Adams a monarchist as he perceived that Hamilton was trying to become the president de facto. Adams's able son, John Quincy Adams, had written answers to the Jefferson-endorsed works of Thomas Paine; when reissued, the articles were erroneously attributed to the elder Adams, thus widening the gap.

At the outset, before the crisis with France intensified, their mutual desire to avoid war might have succeeded in closing the rift to some extent. But after Jefferson, on the grounds that the vice president was part of the legislative branch of the government and could not participate in executive discussions, refused to go to France as a special envoy, they seldom saw each other. They were further estranged after passage of the partisan Alien and Sedition Acts, aimed at crushing the Democratic-Republicans into oblivion. By the end of 1799 Adams and Jefferson were barely on speaking terms.

Adams also tried to work with Alexander Hamilton, but that proved impossible. Hamilton simply could not rid himself of the notion that every political compromise revealed Adams's untrustworthiness. A cycle developed: The president would give an inch, Hamilton would take a foot, and Adams the next time would give nothing at all. Adams's persistence and courage could take the form of either stubborn inflexibility or admirable determination— depending on whom he was dealing with—but on the surface he retained that old air of diffidence that Hamilton detested. The Adams-Hamilton conflict marred the whole of the administration and eventually wrecked the political future of Adams, Hamilton, and the Federalist party.

Adams inherited the foreign crisis that had baffled Washington's administration. Great Britain waged war against the French with a naval force that could blockade Napoleon's European stronghold. The pro-British Federalists suffered, almost in silence, while the Democratic-Republicans wanted to aid France in support of old ties going back to the Revolutionary War. American commerce was a growing part of the nation's prosperity, and Yankee shippers were crushed between the Royal Navy and the roving French maritime forces. Hence, the crisis with France was the principal issue of Adams's administration.

For his part, Adams was not sympathetic to the French revolutionists, but he had long been biased against Great Britain; so he immediately became a man in the middle. By nature, the Federalists favored aristocratic England; and increasingly the French thought the United States had turned pro-British after Jay's Treaty was ratified. In some respects, the French were right, and the Federalist-dominated Congress did little to contradict their impression. In France, citizens with pro-American sympathies were imprisoned; the French assumed that every American vessel was bound toward a British port, and thus fair game for seizure.

Federalists in Congress rattled the saber, and probably would have voted for war if Adams had sent them a belligerent message. But Adams wanted to avoid a fight. When he dispatched General Charles

THOMAS PINCKNEY

Because John Adams's relationship with the Federalist party was more an alliance than allegiance, Alexander Hamilton tried to arrange the election so that the vice presidential candidate, Thomas Pinckney, would be elected president. Hamilton, however, was not always a perceptive judge of men, and Pinckney later proved less faithful to the party than Adams: He was an advocate of states' rights; he not only opposed Hamilton's efforts to have war declared with France, but he was against Adams's military buildup during the crisis; and as a congressman from South Carolina, he voted against the Sedition Act. Born in Charleston in 1750, Pinckney was raised and educated in England, graduating from Oxford. He returned to South Carolina and became an officer in the militia in 1775. After the Revolution, he was appointed minister to Great Britain and he served until 1795, when he was sent to Spain to negotiate a settlement of U.S.–Spanish borders in North America. Returning home a year later, he probably would have won the vice presidency but for Hamilton's meddling. When the New England electors heard that Hamilton was trying to secure more votes for Pinckney than for Adams, they cast their votes for Adams and Jefferson, and Pinckney received only fifty-nine votes. After two terms in Congress (1797–1801), he quit politics and devoted his life to agriculture until his death in 1828.

Cotesworth Pinckney to Paris to see what could be done about stopping French harassment of American ships, Talleyrand, the French foreign minister, refused to see the emissary. The Federalists were poised for battle, and the president urged an increase in the strength of the armed forces.

Determined to negotiate before firing, however, Adams tried diplomacy again, dispatching two other diplomats to join Pinckney in Paris. Talleyrand sent a trio of his own to meet them under a cloak of carefully contrived secrecy. In confidential undertones, the French agents said that Talleyrand would listen favorably to any American proposal if the United States would offer a huge loan to France and make Talleyrand's attentions worth his while. Bribery was part of the game in European diplomacy, but the naive Americans were offended. Informed of the attempted blackmail, Adams sent the diplomats' report to Congress, but for the names of the French agents, he substituted the initials X, Y, and Z. Gleeful Federalists in Congress released the report to the public, which became infected with what Jefferson called the "XYZ fever," a political malady to be cured by war. Always anti-French, Hamilton provided ammunition for the militant attitude, and declared in a newspaper essay that any defender of France was "a fool, a madman, or a traitor."

He implied, of course, that John Adams was one or all of these. Although the president was in favor of preparedness—he signed military appropriations and urged George Washington to resume command of the armed services—he was not himself stricken with XYZ fever. Still determined to negotiate, he insisted on Talleyrand's assurance that representatives of the United States would be treated with courtesy in Paris. Thoroughly embarrassed by the furor that the XYZ Affair had caused, the French minister agreed, reasoning that further hostility toward the United States would simply provide England with a further ally. Another American minister to the French Republic

was dispatched (over the objections of Hamilton, who later pressured Adams into changing the delegation to a mission of three, two of whom were his pals). French and American warships had traded blows, Yankee blood had been spilled, and war appeared likely.

French diplomacy and American hardheadedness collided, but with happy results. The quasi war with France ended without growing any hotter after the Treaty of Morfontaine was signed on September 30, 1800. Soon friendlier relations between the United States and France were restored. Disgusted Federalists condemned Adams, the peacemaker who preferred plowshares to battleships. The settlement had great personal value for Adams, who soon after its conclusion composed his own epitaph: "Here lies John Adams, who took upon himself the responsibility of the peace with France in the year 1800."

The Federalist party was badly shaken by the XYZ Affair. Hamilton had expected that congressional passage of military bills would inspire France to declare war, thereby discrediting the pro-French Republicans. That, of course, had not worked. Moreover, the Republican press had called the whole affair a hoax, insinuating that the diplomats whose report had fostered the XYZ fever had made themselves unavailable to conciliation. Adams received blows from both sides, from the Federalists for not going to war with France and from the Republicans for stimulating panic by promoting a huge military budget.

In 1798 the Federalist majority tried to utilize the national enthusiasm for war to silence their critics; they sponsored and passed the Alien and Sedition Acts. During the height of the French crisis, Frenchmen in America were widely assumed to favor their homeland, while many non-French Europeans were known to sympathize with the principles of the French Revolution. Forgetting—or choosing to ignore—the similarity between the French and the American struggles for independence, the Federalists first passed the Naturalization Act, raising the period

This contemporary cartoon depicts three American diplomats rejecting a French effort to obtain a bribe in the notorious XYZ Affair. (The code name for the French agents who proposed the offer were X, Y, and Z.) Trying to avert war, President John Adams had sent these three diplomats to Paris to negotiate a settlement with France.

of residency required for American citizenship to fourteen years. Then came the Alien Act, which gave the president power to expel all foreigners he considered dangerous, and the Alien Enemies Act, which gave him the right to deport or imprison any native of a nation at war with the United States. Finally, the Sedition Act forbade "insurrection, riot, unlawful assembly" and prescribed fines and jail terms for "false, scandalous and malicious writing" about the president, Congress, or the nation. By subsequent actions the intent of the legislation was clear, for Federalists enforced the acts as a means of silencing opponents.

Closing their ranks against what they considered an assault on freedom of speech and the press, the Democrats declared that the Alien and Sedition Acts were violations of constitutionally guaranteed rights. State courts were urged to disregard the acts, and many did. In federal district courts, however, Democratic editors and one congressman were found guilty and heavily fined or sent to prison. In Vermont, Congressman Matthew Lyon was found guilty of disparaging the president, fined $5,000 in gold, and sent to

jail. The case became a Democratic *cause célèbre* and cast an unfavorable light on the bewildered Federalists.

The passage of the Alien and Sedition Acts was a large nail in Adams's political coffin. He applauded their intent because the acts conformed with his political philosophy, and he signed them willingly, thus losing what little Republican admiration his stand on France had won him. In practice, however, Adams was inclined to ignore the obnoxious acts. In fact, Hamilton himself had grave doubts about the constitutionality of the Alien and Sedition Acts, but he could not resist the opportunity to abuse Adams for his leniency. When the president failed to deport Joseph Priestly, an English radical whose outspoken advocacy of the French Revolution had scandalized the Federalists, and when he pardoned John Fries, who had been condemned to death for leading a violent Pennsylvania uprising against the war taxes approved by Congress in 1798, Hamilton wrote *Letter Concerning the Public Conduct and Character of John Adams*. Dealing mostly with the president's handling of the French crisis, the document was too obscure to be understood by the general public and too illogical to impress the nation's leaders. Nonetheless, Hamilton's pet Federalists saw to it that the diatribe was printed in their newspapers, with disastrous results for Adams.

His administration had been stormy, but Adams was cautiously optimistic about winning the second term he so desperately wanted. He had purged his cabinet of two Hamiltonian spies, his generosity regarding the Alien and Sedition Acts defendants had by and large compensated for his earlier unpopular support of the acts, and the peace with France had

George Washington and architect James Hoban survey the progress of construction of the executive mansion during a 1798 inspection trip, as depicted in a painting by N. C. Wyeth. Even though Washington selected the site and style of the building, President John Adams was the first occupant of the White House.

deprived the Democrats of a monumental issue. But when Hamilton's letter was published, Adams's optimism was dissipated, for if the document was an almost meaningless hodgepodge of unreadable rhetoric, it was also a crystal-clear statement that the Federalists were deeply divided. The letter irritated even Charles Pinckney, the Federalists' "vice presidential" candidate in 1800, who, to his credit, announced that he would not be a party to a plan to divert votes from Adams.

Meanwhile, the White House, though far from finished, was ready for occupancy. Abigail was ill, and Adams arrived from Philadelphia without her. On November 1, 1800, Adams became the first chief executive to sleep in the building. Reflecting on the potential of the Executive Mansion (as it was officially called until the twentieth century) as a symbol of the affections of Americans, he composed a prayer that Franklin Delano Roosevelt later had carved on the mantel of the State Dining Room: "I pray Heaven to bestow the best of Blessings on this House and all that shall hereafter inhabit it. May none but honest and wise men ever rule under this roof." When Mrs. Adams finally arrived, she hung a clothesline and a Gilbert Stuart portrait of George Washington; the outcome of the election would determine what else she would do.

In the 1800 campaign, according to prevailing protocol, neither Adams nor the two Democrats—Jefferson and Burr—went out on the hustings. Friends and supporters, would-be officeholders and bitter castoffs did the campaigning at rallies and through newspaper endorsements. The political showdown proved that the middle Atlantic states were crucial, and the powerful New York machine turned out to be decisive. Jefferson and Burr were ahead of the Federalist ticket and headed for a showdown in the House of Representatives in February 1801. Meanwhile, Adams was a lame duck. The Federalist party was also discredited.

What caused the Federalists to fall so rapidly in public esteem? "By scorning the popular intelligence and behaving as though politics was a matter of preaching wisdom to the untutored masses," historian John C. Miller notes, "the Federalists condemned themselves not only to defeat in the election of 1800 but to [eventual] extinction as a party." The president himself had no trouble at all placing the blame for his defeat: "Mr. Hamilton has carried his eggs to a fine market," he wrote. "The very two men of all the world that he was most jealous of are now placed over him." In a letter to a friend Adams confided that his defeat was a good thing, as he expected to die soon. His last official act was the appointment of John Marshall as chief justice of the United States.

Disappointed and bitter, Adams did not die soon. He left Washington by stagecoach on the morning of Jefferson's inauguration, conspicuously absenting himself from it. Retiring to Quincy (formerly Braintree), Massachusetts, he became a farmer, insisting that he had not been so cheerful "since some sin to me unknown involved me in politics." He gathered together his diaries and started work on an autobiography.

Adams grew mellow and eventually regretted his break with Jefferson. In January 1812 Adams sent a genial, conciliatory letter to Monticello. "I wish you Sir many happy New Years and that you may enter the next and many succeeding Years with as animating Prospects for the Public as those at present before Us." He signed it "Friend," and Jefferson—by what was almost return mail in those days—wrote back on January 21: "A letter from you calls up recollections very dear to my mind. It carries me back to the times when, beset with difficulties and dangers, we were fellow laborers in the same cause, struggling for what is most valuable to man, his right of self-government." The two ex-presidents thus began an extensive correspondence, exchanging ideas about current affairs from time to time, but devoting themselves mainly to nostalgic reminiscences or philosophical bantering. Jefferson shared Adams's misery when Abigail died of typhoid in 1818, and his joy when John Quincy Adams was elected president of the United States.

John Adams died at ninety-one, appropriately, the Fourth of July, 1826, the fiftieth anniversary of the Declaration of Independence. His last words were "Jefferson still survives." But Jefferson in fact did not. He had died at Monticello several hours earlier.

—DAVID JACOBS, *revised by* ROBERT RUTLAND

THOMAS JEFFERSON

RENAISSANCE LEADER

If great men reach their niche in history through one or two magnificent accomplishments, then Thomas Jefferson stands in the first rank of presidents because his career was a succession of triumphs. Starting in 1774 as a talented local politician, Jefferson went on to serve in the Continental Congress, as the American minister to France, the governor of Virginia, the first secretary of state, the second vice president, and, for two remarkable terms, the third president of the United States. John F. Kennedy once described a group of Nobel Prize winners, dining in the executive mansion, as "the most extraordinary collection of talent . . . that has ever been gathered together at the White House—with the possible exception of when Thomas Jefferson dined alone."

Sandwiched in with these accomplishments, Jefferson also made his mark as author of the Declaration of Independence and as the cofounder of the Democratic party. And in 1854 the Republican party chose their name to honor Jefferson's commitment to the proposition "that all men are created equal." If one more jewel is allowed in the crown, recall that Jefferson wanted to be remembered as the founding father of the University of Virginia. On his epitaph, he listed his Statute of Religious Freedom (passed in Virginia in 1786), but he omitted from his tombstone the fact that he was also president of the United States.

The range of the man's involvements and skills was remarkable. Preeminently a statesman and politician, he was also an adept writer, lawyer, farmer, naturalist, architect, musician, linguist, classicist, philosopher, scientist, geographer, surveyor, botanist, ethnologist, and paleontologist. He was interested in everything, from the origin of the rainbow to the habitat of the wild turkey, from fossils and Newtonian physics to calculus, Anglo-Saxon grammar, and the condition of blacks in Santo Domingo.

Books he treasured, and his private library was one of the best ever assembled in the fledgling nation. "I cannot live without books," he said, and eventually his personal collection became the nucleus of one of the world's greatest libraries, the Library of Congress. Jefferson not only collected books, he read them with an unquenchable appetite—Cicero in Latin, Plato in Greek, Montesquieu in French, Cervantes in Spanish.

What Mount Vernon was to Washington, Monticello was to Jefferson. Wherever he was—in France or Philadelphia, among scholars or kings—he was always eager to return to Albemarle County, Virginia, and his mountaintop mansion. His spirits lifted when he beheld "a leg of a rainbow plunge down" to the nearby Rivanna River. Jefferson confessed he was more interested in the first budding of trees at Monticello than in public business at the highest levels.

His departure from his "country" (as he always called Virginia) to make his entrance into politics was no less than epochal for the United States. "Jefferson's was to be the leading mind of the first age of our national life," the historian Daniel Boorstin concludes, "and therefore in a powerful position for shaping the American intellectual character."

Thomas Jefferson was born, one of ten children, on April 13, 1743, midway through the reign of George II. His birthplace was the family estate known as Shadwell, in Goochland (now Albemarle) County in the foothills of the Blue Ridge mountains. His parents were Peter Jefferson, a prosperous tobacco plantation owner and surveyor, and Jane Randolph Jefferson, the daughter of one of Virginia's first families, descended from English and Scottish nobility, "to which," Jefferson would wryly add in old age, "let everyone ascribe the . . . merit he chooses."

The young boy's education was entrusted to tutors. From his earliest schooling Jefferson acquired the rudiments of Latin, Greek, and French. After Peter Jefferson died in 1757, Jefferson was taken under the wing of Reverend James Maury, whom Jefferson described as a "correct classical scholar," and under whose guid-

Thomas Jefferson—Renaissance man and advocate of liberty—in a portrait painted by Rembrandt Peale in 1800.

ance he mastered several languages and was introduced to natural philosophy and geology.

Eventually, Jefferson was ready to move beyond home tutoring. Early in 1760, when he was seventeen and wanted to see the world, he asked his guardian for permission to attend the College of William and Mary, in Williamsburg. "By going to the College," he reasoned, "I shall get a more universal Acquaintance, which may hereafter be serviceable to me; & I suppose I can pursue my studies in the Greek & Latin as well there as here, & likewise learn something of the Mathematics."

In Williamsburg the teenage student met and became a dinner companion of George Wythe, one of Virginia's leading jurists, and Lieutenant Governor Francis Fauquier. In this heady company Jefferson reveled, and probably learned more from their dinner conversation than he did in the classroom.

Jefferson graduated from William and Mary in April 1762 and became an apprentice in Wythe's Williamsburg office. As a reader he continued to rub elbows with some of the colony's leading public men, particularly when Williamsburg came alive during the annual sessions of the colonial assembly. Jefferson was admitted to the bar in 1767; two years later he was elected to the House of Burgesses from Albemarle County.

On January 1, 1772, Jefferson married a well-to-do widow, Martha Wayles Skelton, in the Anglican rite, and their honeymoon began in a snowstorm. He was twenty-eight, she twenty-three. Martha was pretty, graceful, and high-spirited. A year after the marriage, her father died, leaving her 40,000 acres of land and 135 slaves. Unfortunately she and her husband also inherited a large debt, which accounted in part for Jefferson's subsequent financial troubles.

Moving into the still uncompleted Monticello (construction had begun in 1769), the newlyweds were at first restricted to Jefferson's one-room bachelor quarters. When a suitable room was ready, they moved into Monticello proper, where Martha Jefferson was to bear Thomas six children, of whom only Martha "Patsy" and Maria "Polly" lived to maturity. Throughout marriage, Mrs. Jefferson was wracked by chronic miscarriages that contributed to her ill health.

Jefferson doted on his children, worried about his wife, and plunged into politics. When relations between England and her colonies worsened, he sided with the burgesses who favored resistance to royal edicts. As a speaker Jefferson was mediocre, but in committees he was often the spokesman for the growing group of radicals. On March 12, 1773, Jefferson and other truculent burgesses drafted resolutions creating an official Committee of Correspondence. This group would be empowered to contact and coordinate resistance to Parliament's laws affecting the colonies.

The closing of the port of Boston in 1774 was a bombshell. Throughout the thirteen colonies the reaction created a unity that brought offers of aid to Boston and stiffened the patriots' resolve. Jefferson championed a proclamation calling for a symbolic fast day to protest the British tyranny in Massachusetts. When the angered governor of Virginia, the Earl of Dunmore, responded by dissolving the House of Burgesses, Jefferson and his fellow rebels met on May 27, 1774, at the Raleigh Tavern, declaring that "an attack on any one colony should be considered as an attack on the whole." They also agreed that Virginia's counties should elect delegates to a convention that would select representatives to the Continental Congress.

Lord Dunmore was now a prisoner in his own Governor's Palace. Albemarle County chose Jefferson as its delegate to the Virginia convention, but dysentery prevented him from attending. He drafted, however, an eloquent protest against royal policy: *A Summary View of the Rights of British America.* Jefferson's case against the mother country was rejected by hesitant Virginians as too bold, but when it appeared in pamphlet form the essay made Jefferson a major spokesman for the resistance movement.

Addressed directly to George III, *A Summary View* is a classic of political advocacy and polemic. Jefferson's argument against the Crown was based not merely on evident commercial and political injustice, but also on the natural rights of Englishmen themselves—inherent and irrevocable rights that the king would not have dared to contravene in his own country. "Kings," he reminded George III, "are the servants, not the proprietors of the people." Denying all parliamentary authority over the American states, Jefferson informed the sovereign that the colonies' initial submission to him had been voluntary, clearly implying that what had been freely given could also, in tyranny, be withdrawn.

Jefferson pleaded for the rights of Americans to trade freely in international commerce, contrary to the crippling mercantilist system England practiced. He further called for an end to taxation of a people not represented in Parliament by a single vote, and he ridiculed the idea that 160,000 electors in Britain should tyrannize some four million British-Americans through a capricious Parliament. Clearly, in 1774 the villain in the controversy was for Americans a corrupt Parliament, not a bumbling king. Still hoping for conciliation, Jefferson held out an olive branch, but despotic rule was unacceptable. "The whole art of government consists in the art of being honest," Jefferson wrote, encapsulating perhaps the best advice ever offered to public servants.

A Summary View hit the colonies—and Europe—with tremendous force. As its author, Jefferson was promptly proscribed by Parliament in a bill of attainder, still another violation of British law.

In the summer of 1775 he was elected to serve again at the Second Continental Congress. By this time, the fighting at Lexington and Concord was history. "This accident," Jefferson said, "has cut off any hope of reconciliation." At the Congress, Jefferson

made no speeches but served on two committees. Because both his wife and daughter were ill, Jefferson returned to Monticello in December of 1775. He found Virginia enraged by Lord Dunmore's punitive

---

BIOGRAPHICAL FACTS

BIRTH: Goochland (Albemarle) County, Va., Apr. 13, 1743

ANCESTRY: Welsh and Scotch-English

FATHER: Peter Jefferson; b. Chesterfield County, Va., Feb. 29, 1708; d. Albemarle County, Va., Aug. 17, 1757

FATHER'S OCCUPATIONS: Planter; surveyor

MOTHER: Jane Randolph Jefferson; b. London, England, Feb. 9, 1720; d. Albemarle County, Va., Mar. 31, 1776

BROTHERS: Peter Field (b. and d. 1748); Unnamed (b. and d. 1750); Randolph (1755–1815)

SISTERS: Jane (1740–1765); Mary (1741–1760); Elizabeth (1744–1774); Martha (1746–1811); Lucy (1752–1784); Anna Scott (1755–?)

MARRIAGE: Charles City County, Va., Jan. 1, 1772

WIFE: Martha Wayles Skelton; b. Charles City County, Va., Oct. 19, 1748; d. Charlottesville, Va., Sept. 6, 1782

CHILDREN: Martha "Patsy" (1772–1836); Jane (1774–1775); Unnamed son (b. and d. 1777); Maria "Polly" (1778–1804); Lucy Elizabeth (1780–1781); Lucy Elizabeth (1782–1785)

RELIGIOUS AFFILIATION: None

EDUCATION: Private tutoring; country day school; College of William and Mary (1762)

OCCUPATIONS BEFORE PRESIDENCY: Planter; lawyer; writer; philosopher; scientist; architect

PREPRESIDENTIAL OFFICES: Member of Virginia House of Burgesses; county lieutenant; county surveyor; delegate to Second Continental Congress; member of Virginia House of Delegates; governor of Virginia; commissioner to France; minister to France; secretary of state; U.S. vice president

AGE AT INAUGURATION: 57

OCCUPATIONS AFTER PRESIDENCY: Planter; writer; educator

DEATH: Charlottesville, Va., July 4, 1826

PLACE OF BURIAL: Monticello, Charlottesville, Va.

burning of Norfolk in January 1776. Saddened by the death of his mother and suffering from his periodic migraine headaches, Jefferson did not return to Philadelphia until May. Less than one month later, on June 7, the Virginian Richard Henry Lee rose to propose a resolution that would change forever the course of world history. Be it resolved, Lee declared, "That these United Colonies are and of right ought to be free and independent states, that they are absolved from all allegiance to the British crown, and that all political connection between them and the state of Great Britain is and ought to be, totally dissolved."

Within a month, the Continental Congress accepted Lee's premise and declared the United States of America an independent nation. As a rebel state, America could not expect aid from abroad. France yearned for revenge over the French and Indian War, but would not help the resisting British colony. An opposing nation, yes; a petulant colony, no. Every delegate at the Continental Congress knew the difference.

Congress, delaying its vote on the Lee resolution until July 1, appointed a committee of five to draft a formal Declaration of Independence: Jefferson, John Adams of Massachusetts, Benjamin Franklin of Pennsylvania, Roger Sherman of Connecticut, and Robert R. Livingston of New York. The committee, deferring to the thirty-three-year-old Jefferson's established skill as a writer and advocate (he had just completed the preamble for a proposed Virginia constitution), delegated him to draft the Declaration. From June 11 to June 28 he worked on it, polishing, changing, rewriting. After amendments by Adams and Franklin were incorporated, the committee submitted the document to Congress on June 28, 1776.

Jefferson's original draft contained more than 1,800 words. Congress expunged 460 of them, including a stunning condemnation of slavery, as Jefferson sat mute and hurt. Boldly defiant of the doubters, the eminent Adams defended the document, word by word. Gradually the moderates retreated. On July 2 the Declaration was issued; it was made public two days later, on July 4, 1776. The search for nationhood had ended, and the United States of America took its place among the world powers. The nascent nation was off to a wobbly start, but there was no turning back. Dissenters and Torries (those still loyal to King George III) skedaddled for cover.

The Declaration was more than an ideological statement of American aspirations. Jefferson's work expressed a newly won consensus of American thought; his words inspired it, and committed it to a universal principle of freedom for all mankind. Jefferson's document epitomized the eighteenth century's faith in human reason and contempt for unearned authority. Human rights were an indissoluble birthright given by God and therefore inalienable. And first among these were the rights of "life, liberty, and the pursuit of happiness." Government's only just function was to secure and advance these rights; when a government ceased to perform this function, it was the duty of its citizens to rebel and form another group based on justice and compassion.

His major task completed, Jefferson remained in Congress for the first debates on the Articles of Confederation, and then left for Monticello in September of 1776. There was, after all, much revolutionary work to be done at home in Virginia. On October 7 Jefferson entered the newly designated House of Delegates, where he remained until 1779. In the House, Jefferson spearheaded the program to recodify royal law into a civil and criminal code for Virginia. Of 126 reform bills he sired, at least 100 passed. The law of primogeniture and entails was abolished. The laws dealing with crime and punishment were revised. Although his bill to establish a system of general education failed to pass, it remained a model for future laws.

In 1779 Jefferson introduced the Act for Establishing Religious Freedom, which was too radical for

In 1817 artist John Trumbull re-created the signing of the Declaration of Independence. Thomas Jefferson's draft was altered in committee, but its main points were retained and presented to the Continental Congress. Its acceptance cut the final ties between Great Britain and the thirteen rebellious colonies.

the majority. This classic bill guaranteed that "no man shall be compelled to frequent or support any religious worship, place, or ministry whatsoever," and that "all men shall be free to profess, and by argument to maintain, their opinions in matters of religion, and that the same shall in nowise diminish, enlarge, or affect their civil capacities." Jefferson reasoned that "our civil rights have no dependence on our religious opinions, more than our opinions in physics or geometry," and that official attempts to impose an established state religion breed only hypocrisy and corruption of the very faith they purport to espouse. Although not a churchgoer, Jefferson described him-

self as "a real Christian," subscribing to the ethics of Jesus, if not the metaphysics of Christianity. (His bill was reintroduced by James Madison and became law in 1786.)

On June 1, 1779, Jefferson succeeded Patrick Henry as wartime governor of Virginia. From the start, his administration was beset by ills. Objectively, Jefferson was plagued by an inadequate militia and by border harassments by Indians. Fear of an impending British invasion, for which Virginians were unprepared, pervaded the state. Subjectively, Jefferson was less effective as an executive than as a seer, committeeman, and draftsman. He eschewed, even in war, the use of illegal or arbitrary executive means toward just ends. When Britain finally invaded Virginia in force, as his term ended, Jefferson favored his replacement by a military governor, and retreated to his home. On June 4, 1781, the British pursued him to Monticello. Forewarned, Jefferson barely escaped and fled to Poplar Forest, a summer cottage some one hundred miles southward.

An angered House of Delegates, prodded by the overzealous Patrick Henry, ordered an inquiry into Jefferson's conduct as governor and his alleged failure to organize an adequate militia. A more clement House, in December 1781, absolved him of guilt.

On September 6, 1782, Jefferson's wife died. Although he had been determined never to return to politics, the loneliness of his mansion now caused him "to seek relief from personal woe in public activity." He doted on his two daughters and plunged back into politics. In June of 1783 he was elected a delegate to the Continental Congress, where his legislative proposals were formidable. He suggested the adoption of the dollar as the nation's monetary unit, subdivided into tenths and hundredths—a measure finally approved during Washington's presidency. Equally far-reaching was Jefferson's Plan of Government for the Western Territory (the core of the later Northwest Ordinance of 1787), in which he successfully advocated the exclusion of slavery in all territories north of the Ohio River.

During this period Jefferson became a legislative workhorse. He drew up a scheme for the final peace treaty with Great Britain and prepared a report that would establish procedure in the drafting of commercial agreements with other nations.

In May 1784 Jefferson was sent to France to assist Franklin and Adams in the preparation of consular treaties. A year later he was named Franklin's successor as minister to France, a post he held until October of 1789. Franklin's homespun wit and forthrightness had won the heart of Paris; Jefferson evaded comparisons by insisting that he had come not to replace Franklin but only to succeed him. As minister, Jefferson presented America's republican case with erudition and dexterity, hailed France tactfully as a counterpoise to a common British antagonist, and negotiated a consular convention.

"On France itself," writes the biographer Nathan Schachner, "Jefferson was of two minds. He envied the French their architecture, sculpture, painting, and music; but nothing else. Fresh from the spaciousness of America, where institutions, no matter how far behind the ideal, at least were liberal and progressive, where the people walked with an independent air and poverty [among citizens] was practically unknown, the swarming alleys of Paris, the contrast between resplendent Court and the hopeless masses . . . filled him with a sense of horror." To see the world, Jefferson would say, is to love America all the more.

In a sense, Jefferson never really left home; his eye was ever on Virginia. While in France he designed the buildings for the new state capital at Richmond, worked on further plans for his beloved Monticello, and heard the glad news that his Act for Establishing Religious Freedom finally had passed the Virginia legislature. From Paris, too, reviewing the newly adopted Constitution by mail with his friend James Madison, he insisted on the prompt inclusion of a bill of rights.

Despite official United States neutrality in France's revolution, Jefferson was patently sympathetic with the more moderate revolutionists, who were at once the source of his diplomatic data and contacts and the object of his special concern. He proposed to the Marquis de Lafayette a new charter for France, and to Lafayette's aunt, Madame de Tessé, a procedural form for the French Assembly of Notables. In later years Jefferson would maintain that every cultivated and traveled man would prefer France as a principal alternative to his own country.

On his return from Europe in 1789, Jefferson had clearly developed his basic philosophy, modified at least marginally by the French revolutionary experience. He had, above all, a confirmed and unbridled faith in America, viewing it in biblical terms as a promised land. But America's abundance and promise, Jefferson argued in 1789, were no cause for pride. The United States, he said, must "show by example the sufficiency of human reason for the care of human affairs and that the will of the majority, the Natural Law of every society, is the only sure guardian of the rights of man."

Impressed by the ideology of the Enlightenment, Jefferson shared its faith in reason, science, and human perfectibility. "We believed," he would say in retrospect in 1823, "that man was a rational animal, endowed by nature with rights and with an innate sense of justice . . . that he could be restrained from wrong and protected in right, by moderate powers confided to persons of his own choice, and held to their duties by dependence on his own will." He believed also in the superiority of agrarian virtue, unsullied by industry and commerce. "Those who labor in the earth," Jefferson had written in his *Notes on the State of Virginia*, "are the chosen people of God." Urging American reliance on the products of Europe, already hopelessly corrupted by factories, he turned with contempt on the urban community in the United States: "The mobs of great cities add just so much to the support of pure government, as sores do to the strength of the human body."

Appointed by President Washington in December 1789 as the first secretary of state, Jefferson arrived in New York City to assume his duties in March 1790. It was a difficult tenure. Although he collaborated with Hamilton on the federal government's assumption of state debts, in exchange for Hamilton's concession that the new national capital be located on the banks of the Potomac, he was distressed to see Washington espouse Hamilton's plan for a central Bank of the United States—to Jefferson an insidious concentration of wealth. As an agrarian, he regarded banks as parasitic. With Washington's mounting interest in Hamilton's advice, Jefferson planned his own resignation as a gesture of protest.

Unhappy over Hamilton's leading role in the administration, Jefferson asked to retire at the end of 1792. He was persuaded by the president to stay on at least another year to avoid overt dissension within the government. During this period his coinage and monetary system was adopted with Hamilton's approval, and Jefferson had to deal with a major political problem—the French appointment of Citizen Edmond Genêt as minister to the United States. Jefferson said in 1793 that rather than see the French Revolution fail he "would . . . have seen half the earth desolated." But when Genêt, despite America's officially stated neutrality in the Franco-British conflict, "spoke of going over President Washington's head" in direct appeal to the American people for assistance against England, Jefferson was nonplussed. He recommended Genêt's prompt expulsion.

Disappointed by France and still frustrated by Hamilton, Jefferson was now determined to resign and held Washington to the earlier promise to let him go at the end of 1793. On January 16, 1794, Jefferson was back at Monticello. His retirement would be brief, however. In 1796 the Republicans, incensed by the terms of Jay's Treaty, nominated Jefferson and Aaron Burr to oppose John Adams in his bid for the presidency. Jefferson lost the election to Adams by three electoral votes, thus becoming vice president for four more years of Federalist frustration. But Jefferson was clearly the spokesman for a new political force in the young republic: the Democratic-Republican party.

Sentiment against the Federalists became frenetic with the passage of the Alien and Sedition Acts, which Republicans viewed as an odious attempt to silence or intimidate all opposition. "Against us," Jefferson wrote, "are . . . all the officers of the government, all who want to be officers, all timid men who prefer the calm of despotism to the boisterous sea of liberty." The Alien and Sedition Acts, he told Madison in June of 1800, were "so palpably in the teeth of the Constitution as to show they [the Federalists] mean to pay no respect to it."

To counter federal power and reassert the states' rights to political freedom, Jefferson secretly prepared and friends pushed through the Kentucky legislature (and Madison through Virginia's) a series of resolutions declaring the Alien and Sedition Acts unconstitutional. In Kentucky, Jefferson's resolves presented a radical solution for unconstitutional acts of Congress. "Where powers are assumed which have not been delegated," he said, "a nullification of the act is the rightful remedy."

In 1800 Jefferson was nominated by the Republicans for the presidency of the United States. His running mate was Aaron Burr; his opponents, John Adams, seeking reelection, and Charles Pinckney. Jefferson's basic concept of the federal role, as he approached the election, was presented in a lucid letter of 1799 to Elbridge Gerry. Jefferson knew his letter would be circulated, and in effect he was presenting a political agenda for the Republicans.

Its hallmarks were thrift in government and freedom for the individual. "I am for preserving to the States," the candidate wrote, "the powers not yielded by them to the Union. . . . I am not for transferring all the powers of the States to the General Government, and all those of that government to the executive branch." He said he preferred "a government rigorously frugal and simple," its savings promptly applied to discharging the national debt, its attitude firmly fixed against bureaucracy based on spoils. Dismissing a standing army as a coercive menace to liberty, and urging a navy limited to coastal patrol, he endorsed a strong militia as adequate to maintaining the social order, short of invasion. He urged free trade with all.

Despite five years of duty in France, Jefferson advocated "little or no diplomatic establishment" and opposed foreign alliances. In another assault on the Alien and Sedition Acts, he declared himself "against all violations of the Constitution to silence by force and not by reason the complaints or criticisms, just or unjust, of our citizens against the conduct of their agents." In light of Jefferson's conduct as president, these statements take on ironic significance: Although he did cut the American diplomatic corps to the bone, he was to reverse or abridge all the rest of what was, in effect, a party platform. A generation later, Democrats would hail Jefferson's 1799 principles as a still-valid political statement.

But now he faced a vicious campaign, as Federalist editors denounced Jefferson as "the Jacobin anti-Christ" who would destroy the republic. In their party councils, however, the Federalists were badly split, as Hamilton and his faction warred openly with Adams. Hamilton raged against Jefferson, determined to prevent that "atheist in religion, and a fanatic in politics, from getting possession of the helm of state." But Hamilton, gambling to finesse Adams's ouster, tried to swing Federalist support to an alternative candidate.

Publicly, of course, no candidate could speak out. Thus the campaign became a newspaper and pamphlet war. Jefferson was attacked as a drunkard, the libertine father of numerous mulattoes, and an atheist. "Our churches will be prostrated," insisted the *New England Palladium*. "There is scarcely a possibility," added the *Connecticut Courant*, "that we shall escape a Civil War. Murder, robbery, rape, adultery, and incest will be openly taught and practiced." Jefferson complained about "the artillery of the press" but kept silent in public.

While there was a definite understanding among the Republican party managers that Jefferson was running for the presidency and Burr for the vice presidency, the method of voting demanded that state electors cast votes for two men, without distinguishing between their choices for the first and second offices. When Jefferson and Burr received the same number of votes, obviously something had gone wrong (New York partisans had reneged on their deal and stayed with Burr). Burr played a watching game instead of bowing out gracefully. The election was thus thrust into a seething Federalist-controlled House of Representatives. The tie was not broken until thirty-six ballots had been cast, and then only because Hamilton, hating Jefferson less than he hated Burr, swung the Federalist vote in Jefferson's favor.

President at fifty-seven, Jefferson was the first chief executive inaugurated in Washington, D.C.; he was sworn in, ironically, by the arch-Federalist, Chief Justice John Marshall, who had been a lame-duck appointment made by Adams in the closing weeks of his administration.

Jefferson, conscious that he had forged the nation's first viable opposition party, offered appeasement to old enemies but not to Burr. In a noble inaugural address, Jefferson urged conciliation and an end to sectionalism, and tried to set at rest the fear that he planned a new revolution. "We are all republicans," he said; "we are all federalists." Hailing "a rising nation, spread over a wise and fruitful land . . . advancing rapidly to destinies beyond the reach of mortal eye," Jefferson asked an end to political bitterness. "Every difference of opinion," he said, "is not a difference of principle. We have called by different names brethren of the same principle." It was a candid appeal for practical consensus toward shared ends. Jefferson promised "a wise and frugal government, which shall restrain men from injuring one another, [but] which shall leave them otherwise free to regulate their own pursuits."

Jefferson (yet to be unveiled as the author of the Kentucky Resolutions, with their hint of nullification) turned to those who had threatened secession in the North. "If there be any among us who would wish to dissolve this Union or to change its republican form, let them stand undisturbed as monuments of the safety with which error of opinion may

Federalist cartoonists had a field day depicting Jefferson as a presidential candidate in 1800. From courthouse steps and pulpits, the Virginian was denounced as an atheist in league with the devil, who would try to pull down the young republic that Washington and Adams had so carefully constructed.

be tolerated where reason is left free to combat it."

His oath sworn, President Jefferson moved to make good on his promises. With a majority in the new Congress eager to follow his bidding, Jefferson pushed hard a reform agenda. The Federalist excise tax and Judiciary Act were repealed, several of Adams's midnight judgeship appointments were declared null and

one of Adams's midnight appointees, who then sued; but Marshall managed both to chastise the administration for its defiance, and to declare that the law creating the office was invalid.

Jefferson's first major foreign crisis began in 1801. European commercial powers—and the United States—had long paid Africa's Barbary Coast pirates annual bribes to protect their vessels from raids. When the pasha of Tripoli demanded that America increase its payments, the United States refused, and the pasha declared war. Jefferson ordered the small American fleet to the Mediterranean. In 1804 Tripolitans took the American warship *Philadelphia*, which had run aground, and United States frigates bombarded Tripoli. His purpose, Jefferson said, was to bludgeon "the Barbarians of Tripoli to the desire of peace on proper terms by the sufferings of war." Later, William Eaton, the American consul at Tunis, marched with a small force from Libya to the Tripolitan town of Derna and seized it. A treaty favorable to the United States was signed in 1805, but the troubles continued.

The major achievement of Jefferson's presidency was the Louisiana Purchase, which doubled the size of the United States. By the Treaty of San Ildefonso in 1800, Spain had ceded to France its rights to the port of New Orleans and, by extension, to the Mississippi River and the vast province of Louisiana. Realizing that free navigation of the Mississippi and the use of New Orleans for storage were crucial to the commerce of the nation, and fearful of new French territorial designs in the West, Jefferson moved to purchase New Orleans in 1803. Given two million dollars by Congress to use for that purpose, he dispatched James Monroe to Paris to join Robert Livingston, who was already negotiating with Napoleon.

The emperor was strapped for cash. Livingston was delighted to learn that Napoleon was willing to offer more than just New Orleans. "They ask of me only one town in Louisiana," the dictator declared,

void, and victims of the Alien and Sedition Acts were pardoned. By 1803 a political patronage balance had been deftly restored. Federalist tidewaiters and postmasters were not removed wholesale, however.

One stumbling block was the belated Supreme Court decision of 1803 in *Marbury v. Madison*, where John Marshall's colleagues joined him to declare an act of Congress unconstitutional and therefore void. Secretary of State Madison had refused a commission to

"but I already consider the colony as entirely lost." By the time Monroe arrived, France had ceded to the United States the vast continental slice of land from the Mississippi to the Rockies for fifteen million dollars. Aware that his ministers had far exceeded their congressional instructions and constitutional authority, Jefferson decided nevertheless to confront a special session of Congress with the accomplished fact. The Senate and House authorized the purchase, and Jefferson signed the treaty with France on October 20, 1803.

Jefferson's first presidential term was also distinguished by his commissioning of the Lewis and Clark expedition to map the Missouri River and to increase American knowledge of the unchartered West. The expedition, begun in May 1804, concluded when Meriwether Lewis reported to the president on January 10, 1807. The pathfinders named major western streams to honor the president and his cabinet—hence the Jefferson, Madison, and Gallatin rivers became embedded in the region's history—and for the first time the myth of an easy northwest passage to the Pacific was shattered.

Jefferson, meanwhile, had projected a presidential image wholly new to official Washington. While he served French food—to the chagrin of chauvinists—he also abolished the levee, a starchy ritualistic reception favored by both Presidents Washington and Adams, and maintained in the White House the informality of Monticello. Anthony Merry, Britain's minister, spoke in 1804 of Jefferson's "yarn stockings and slippers down at the heels," describing his general appearance as "very much like that of a tall, large-boned farmer."

Without question, the diffident patrician had become the hero of America's common man. Jefferson's achievement in gaining this stature was, the biographer Dumas Malone writes, owing "to his identification of himself with causes for which time was fighting. . . . His unchallenged leadership was due,

not to self-assertiveness and imperiousness of will, but to the fact that circumstance had made him a symbolic figure, and that to an acute intelligence and unceasing industry he joined a dauntless and contagious faith."

Jefferson's first term had been a triumph, but the

Journals kept by Meriwether Lewis and William Clark provided information on everything from Indian dialects to the species of fish— including salmon—found in Western waters. Jefferson had sent the two men on an expedition that took them into the uncharted territory between the Rockies and the Pacific coast.

outbreak of war between France and England heralded trouble ahead for neutral America. Against only token opposition by the Federalists, Jefferson sought and decisively won reelection as president in 1804. Burr, who had killed Hamilton in a duel in July, was replaced as Jefferson's running mate by New York's governor, George Clinton.

In 1806 the United States was confronted with naval harassment by both Britain and France, who blockaded each other's ports, seized American ships, and impressed American seamen. Jefferson responded with less belligerence than he had shown toward Tripoli: He overtly rejected war with either European power. Though angered in 1807 by Britain's attack on the United States frigate *Chesapeake* and the capture of its crew on the grounds that four of the sailors were British deserters, Jefferson still refused to tarnish his administration with war. His solution was an embargo, terminating all foreign commerce with the United States.

The embargo not only failed to reverse British and French naval policy, but called down the wrath of the nation's commercial and shipping interests on Jefferson's head. "A whole people," thundered Josiah Quincy, "is laboring under a most grievous oppression. All the business of the nation is deranged. . . . All its industry stagnant." Farmers accepted the lower prices their products received on a shrinking market, but shipowners and merchants howled, and smuggling in the inlets of New England increased dramatically.

"The embargo," writes the historian Leonard Levy, "begun as a means of coercing and starving England and France into respect for American rights, rapidly became an instrument of coercion against American citizens. To avoid foreign war, Jefferson inadvertently made domestic war." The regular army, which Jefferson had opposed, was increased, and the United States Navy and militia were ordered to enforce the embargo by capturing smugglers. "Congress," the president insisted, "must legalize all *means* which may be necessary to obtain its *end*."

A federal judge in Charleston, himself appointed by Jefferson, attacked the Embargo Act as "an unsanctioned encroachment upon individual liberty." Senator Samuel White of Delaware charged that it put "the whole country under military law," and permitted unwarranted search, seizure, and arrest on the merest suspicion of intent to export. "To this day," Levy concludes, the embargo "remains the most repressive and unconstitutional legislation ever enacted by Congress in time of peace."

SECOND ADMINISTRATION

INAUGURATION: Mar. 4, 1805; Senate Chamber, Washington, D.C.
VICE PRESIDENT: George Clinton
SECRETARY OF STATE: James Madison
SECRETARY OF THE TREASURY: Albert Gallatin
SECRETARY OF WAR: Henry Dearborn
ATTORNEY GENERAL: John Breckinridge; Caesar A. Rodney (from Jan. 20, 1807)
POSTMASTER GENERAL: Gideon Granger
SECRETARY OF THE NAVY: Robert Smith
SUPREME COURT APPOINTMENTS: Brockholst Livingston (1806); Thomas Todd (1807)
9TH CONGRESS (Dec. 2, 1805–Mar. 3, 1807):
    SENATE: 27 Democratic-Republicans; 7 Federalists
    HOUSE: 116 Democratic-Republicans; 25 Federalists
10TH CONGRESS (Oct. 26, 1807–Mar. 3, 1809):
    SENATE: 28 Democratic-Republicans; 6 Federalists
    HOUSE: 118 Democratic-Republicans; 24 Federalists

ELECTION OF 1804

(The Twelfth Amendment, ratified in September, 1804, provided for separate voting for president and vice president, and precluded a repetition of the Jefferson-Burr tie of 1800.)

CANDIDATES	ELECTORAL VOTE
Thomas Jefferson (Democratic-Republican)	162
Charles C. Pinckney (Federalist)	14

By February 21, 1809, Jefferson stood aside as Congress lifted the embargo against all but French and British shipping, and lifted it entirely by March 3, 1809. In the Senate, Jefferson's nominee for a diplomatic post in Russia was rejected unanimously. Indeed, for the last six months of his presidency, Jefferson decided to swim with the tide of hostility generated in Congress. It was left to Madison, the historian Stuart Gerry Brown notes, "to develop a better policy if he could, or else go to war."

Jefferson's second term was marred by still another major departure from civil liberties. Former Vice President Aaron Burr, who had tried unsuccessfully to lead a revolt of Western states (possibly intending to unite them with Mexico, with himself as emperor of a new kingdom), was tried for treason and acquitted by a federal court under Chief Justice John Marshall. Before the verdict was in, Jefferson made it clear that he thought Burr should be found guilty. It was a grave departure from Jefferson's usual code of fairness, but Burr's acquittal settled the matter.

Jefferson's eight years in office left reminders of his executive strengths. Like John Adams, he never vetoed an act of Congress; and unlike most presidents before and since, he kept the same cabinet through two terms. His less-than-splendid second term notwithstanding, many urged Jefferson to seek a third and derail the two-term tradition laid down by Washington. Jefferson declined, however. In his eyes, the presidency had been "a splendid misery," bringing "nothing but unceasing drudgery and daily loss of friends." He took his time leaving the White House, knowing that his successor—James Madison—was in no hurry to move in.

In retirement at sixty-six, Jefferson became "Old Sachem," the Sage of Monticello. "I resume with delight," he wrote in 1810, "the character and pursuits for which nature designed me. I talk of ploughs and harrows, of seeding and harvesting, with my neighbors, and of politics, too, if they choose . . . and

feel, at length, the blessing of being free to say and do what I please." Old correspondence was renewed. "I have given up newspapers in exchange for Tacitus and Thucydides," he wrote to John Adams in 1812 after their eleven-year silence.

Up at dawn, Jefferson's routine at Monticello was strict. He wrote and read until breakfast, then he rode six or eight miles on horseback each day, overseeing his lands and farms. He supervised his gristmill, nail factory, and furniture shop; built a dumbwaiter and weather vanes; and delighted in spoiling his beloved great-grandchildren. When British troops destroyed the Library of Congress in 1814, Jefferson offered his personal library to the nation for a token of its cost. After some partisan wrangling, the House of Representatives voted 81 to 71 to pay Jefferson $23,950 for ten wagon loads of 6,497 books. The money was used to reduce his burdensome debt.

At times, Jefferson's hospitality was overtaxed by hordes of visitors, some political and some merely curious. In the wake of the Panic of 1819, land values in Virginia plunged. Tragically, Jefferson's debts forced him to consider a lottery with Monticello as the first prize, but the plan miscarried. When word spread of his near bankruptcy, concerned friends throughout the nation raised almost sixteen thousand dollars to bail him out of debt. The gesture failed, but bought enough time to keep Monticello as Jefferson's haven and refuge.

He found time to advise Presidents Madison and Monroe when they asked. But his primary interest in retirement was the founding of the University of Virginia. He was involved in the selection of its professors, its library books, its curriculum. He designed its buildings and directly supervised their construction. And he presented at the founding of this early state-supported university a classic definition of academic freedom: "This institution," he said, "will be based on the illimitable freedom of the human mind. For here we are not afraid to follow truth wherever it may lead, nor to tolerate any error so long as reason is left free to combat it."

In retirement, too, Jefferson refined and enlarged his philosophy of freedom. He refused to look back to past authority. "Some men," he wrote, "look at constitutions with sanctimonious reverence, and deem them like the ark of the covenant, too sacred to be touched. . . . Laws and institutions must go hand in hand with the progress of the human mind."

Jefferson retained a vibrant and undiminished faith in democracy. "The only orthodox object . . . of government," he wrote in 1812, "is to secure the greatest degree of happiness possible to the general mass."

Where else, he reasoned, will we "find the origin of *just* powers, if not in the majority of the society?" But although he asserted that the will of the majority prevail, he was equally insistent that the rights of the minority must be protected. He also retained his faith in the exemplary mission of America. In the Revolution, he maintained, we were not "acting for ourselves alone, but for the whole human race. The event of our experiment is to show whether man can be trusted with self-government."

In his final years Jefferson held to conservative concepts of federal and state power. Despite his own unorthodox acts as chief executive, he insisted that he

JOHN MARSHALL

John Marshall provided the judicial force that gave permanence to Alexander Hamilton's vision of a strong national government. In so doing, Marshall became the sworn enemy of his distant kinsman, Thomas Jefferson, and created a judicial bulwark for the Constitution that still stands firmly in place.

Born in northern Virginia in 1755, Marshall had little formal schooling. He spent a mere six weeks studying the law, and rose rapidly in legal circles through his acumen and powers of concentration. In a society where legal tangles over debts and land titles enshrouded courtrooms, Marshall became the foremost lawyer in Richmond and a Federalist leader at the 1788 ratifying convention, where he joined James Madison in routing Anti-Federalist opponents to win approval for the Constitution at a critical moment. Thereafter, his standing in Federalist circles was impeccable.

Marshall avoided public service again until he was appointed to join the American commission sent to France in 1797 by President Adams to settle troublesome differences. The mission turned into the famous XYZ Affair, which exposed French duplicity and Yankee fortitude; Marshall himself

gained further esteem for his solid integrity, and soon became one of John Adams's most trusted political allies. He served briefly as secretary of state, and then became chief justice of the United States in 1801.

Marshall began his long tenure as the Federalist party itself began to fade. In the *Marbury v. Madison* decision, the Marshall court established the right of the high court to declare acts of Congress unconstitutional, and thus made itself the final arbiter on all constitutional issues. Marshall presided at the treason trial of Aaron Burr, and with Burr's acquittal Marshall again proved he was unwilling to allow Jefferson's efforts for executive intrusion in the regular course of legal matters. A furious Jefferson denounced Marshall's legal "twistifications," but could not undo the chief justice's pronouncements, which rose to 1,106 precedent-setting cases.

During Marshall's thirty-four years on the bench he hammered out decisions that established the national government's supremacy and consistently restricted the powers of state governments, but after 1803 he never again would declare an act of Congress unconstitutional.

was opposed to "a very energetic government" as "always oppressive." The states, he maintained, were "the wisest conservative power ever contrived by man."

Jefferson opposed a strong Supreme Court—especially under Federalist control—with judicial reviewing that could overturn acts passed by an elected Congress and signed by an elected president. "The great object of my fear," he wrote in 1821, "is the Federal Judiciary." He cited the Court's potential reign as an oligarchy, insisting that the Constitution had "erected no such single tribunal," independent of "the will of the nation." In the long run, as Jefferson probably suspected, Chief Justice John Marshall may have been more of a force in the nation's history than the Sage of Monticello.

Forced by events to modify soaring theory in searing practice, Jefferson left behind a rich but paradoxical heritage. Conservatives have admired his opposition to "energetic government," his defense of states' rights, his opposition to the Supreme Court, his frugality with public funds, and his patrician good sense. Liberals have applauded his vigorous use of executive power, his defense of minorities, his commitment to civil liberties, and his defiance of precedent.

Over generations, Jefferson's reputation has soared and ebbed. His flaws have provided controversy through two centuries. Local gossip turned into a national scandal early in Jefferson's first administration and still carries reverberations today. In 1802 a frustrated office seeker, James Callender, turned down by Jefferson in his bid for the Richmond postmaster's job, broke the story in a local newspaper that Jefferson had had a long liaison with a slave. Jefferson refused to give the rumor credence, but over the years the allegations concerning Sally Hemings and her offspring in the Monticello slave quarters persisted.

A best-selling book in 1974 revived the saucy

Facing bankruptcy after the Panic of 1819, Jefferson decided to raise funds from a public lottery where the prize would be his mountaintop home, Monticello. The lottery scheme failed, leaving Jefferson in dire financial straits during his last years.

gossip with convincing circumstantial evidence, and in 1998 a study of DNA chromosomes in the Jeffersonian lineage seemed to confirm the matter. Skeptics still endure, however, as does the rumor. As Jefferson's biographer, Dumas Malone, notes, Callender "gave the world the Sally story," and it has challenged and titillated ever since.

On July 4, 1826, the fiftieth anniversary of the Declaration of Independence, the third president of the United States died just a few hours before his old friend John Adams. He had fought to stay alive for that day, awakening on the third of July in delirium to mutter instructions that the Virginia Committee of Safety must be warned of the British approach. Shortly before his death, Jefferson wrote his last and strongest formula for liberty. Urging that America remain to the world "the signal of arousing men to burst [their] chains," he said: "The mass of mankind has not been born with saddles on their backs, nor a favored few, booted and spurred, ready to ride them legitimately, by the Grace of God."

—*WILSON SULLIVAN*,
revised by ROBERT A. RUTLAND

JAMES MADISON

THE NATION BUILDER

In any era that valued robust looks, James Madison would not rank high. Standing five feet four inches tall, prematurely bald, and with a squeaky voice, his physical appearance belied a brilliant mind. But as father of the Constitution, congressman, cofounder of the Democratic-Republican party, secretary of state, and president, James Madison was, and remains, a giant in the history of the United States. President John F. Kennedy once said, "James Madison is our most underrated president."

During all his years in public life, his peers had to quiet down when Madison rose to speak. But what he had to say was usually worth hearing. A bookish man, most at ease in his library, he was nonetheless a good conversationalist—knowledgeable, of course, but witty, earthy, and satirical too. He might have preferred a discussion of Greek philosophy with his friend Thomas Jefferson, but he was quite capable of making small talk with his wife's guests and charming them with his ingratiating smile and wry jests.

Born in his maternal grandmother's home, at Port Conway, Virginia, on March 16, 1751, he was, like Washington and Jefferson, a scion of the powerful planter aristocracy. James Madison, Sr., built and named his family seat, Montpelier, a two-story frame house where James was reared as the firstborn of a growing family. His mother taught him to read and write, and his father, a justice of the peace, imparted by example the obligations to community service that the planter class assumed.

At the age of eleven, Madison was sent to a school run by the Scotsman Donald Robertson, who spoke English and other languages with so pronounced a burr that young Madison joked about having to learn "Scottish French."

In 1769 Madison enrolled in the College of New Jersey (Princeton University) where he began to understand the Virginian conception that one owed his patriotic allegiance to his native province—his "country." In the same way, Princeton's theological broad-mindedness and avowed tolerance of religious dissent confirmed Madison's conviction that no sect could claim a privileged place in any society.

Madison was a dedicated student, a natural scholar who retained and applied what he learned. Most of his fellow students were headed for careers in law or the church. Madison was not sure of his career plans. As his own hard taskmaster, he studied Locke, Hume, Montesquieu, and other political philosophers. Accounts of history, particularly of the English Revolution, were relished. And when the time came, he, like Jefferson and other contemporaries, would apply their Whiggish philosophies to the reality of the American situation. John Locke held that every just nation exists as a compact between the government and the governed: Should one party violate the compact, the other is entitled to react in any way deemed necessary to secure its rights. Investigating the machinery of free government, Baron de Montesquieu (Charles-Louis de Secondat) concluded that maintenance of freedom depended on a separation of executive, legislative, and judicial powers so that each could check and balance the others. Hume spoke out for an extended republic where reason prevailed.

After receiving his bachelor's degree in 1771, Madison briefly considered becoming a minister, and he remained at Princeton for another year to study Hebrew and ethics. He returned to Virginia, still in doubt about his future, but found a brief fling at reading law boring. Nominally an Anglican in St. Thomas's parish, Madison was not much of a churchgoer, and a ministerial life held no appeal. He seemed destined, therefore, to learn how to run a plantation and eventually become the master of Montpelier.

Madison's studies and extracurricular interests had weakened his physical condition, and his deteriorated health left him tense, depressed, and without enthusiasm for plantation life.

James Madison's fierce dedication to creating a working federal government belied his small stature and soft-spoken nature. Portrait by Gilbert Stuart, ca. 1805–1807.

Then came the Revolution. The struggle with Great Britain created opportunities for heroics, and gave Madison a chance to move in heady circles. American independence was to James Madison a great moral and philosophical cause but also a strength-building, restorative tonic. Too weak to carry a musket, he shouldered the burdens of statesmanship.

On January 2, 1775, Madison was present at the meeting of the Orange County Committee of Safety, where his father was elected chairman of the local group that would run things on an ad hoc basis. Family connections meant everything. Seventeen months later the younger Madison was chosen as a delegate to the Virginia Convention of 1776, which within a month's time made two crucial decisions: On May 15 it instructed the Virginia delegates in the Continental Congress to declare for independence from Great Britain, and on June 12 it passed the Virginia Declaration of Rights, which established fundamental guarantees of personal liberty and later became the model for the Bill of Rights.

Although the chief draftsman of the Virginia Declaration of Rights was George Mason, Madison prompted a subtle but important change in the wording of one key passage. While Mason's draft called for "toleration" of religious dissent, Madison prevailed on the Convention to broaden the passage's reach by declaring that "all men are equally entitled to the free exercise of religion, according to the dictates of conscience." The change had enormous implications.

With a free government in place after July 1776, Madison expected to serve in the Virginia House of Delegates. His scruples got in the way of an easy election, as he declined to offer voters in Orange County with the customary swig of brandy at the voting tables. After his defeat, he vowed never to lose again or—more bluntly—to pay for a barrel or two of brandy. It was the only election Madison would ever lose.

Madison was the youngest delegate to the Continental Congress, which carried on the war effort and, after many delays, in 1781 established through the Articles of Confederation a government for the United States of America. Under the makeshift government there was no national judiciary or chief executive officer; Congress was the sole branch with any muscle. Madison was keenly aware that the Articles were imperfect, but they served as a stopgap until the war was won and peace established. The Articles provided for no real leadership, however; and because the power to tax, regulate commerce, and raise armies had been left to the states, the national government was impotent. Congress could recommend financial allocations, for example, but all the individual states had to approve all taxation laws. So the national treasury was bare, foreign debts went unpaid, and the republic's future looked bleak.

Forced out of Congress by the three-term rule, Madison returned to Virginia and was promptly sent to the House of Delegates. There he undertook passage of several key bills written by Jefferson in 1779–1780 but left since to languish. At the behest of Jefferson (then in France, serving as the American minister), Madison introduced a bill providing for complete separation of the Anglican Church from its ties with the state and banning any future connection between the state and all religious institutions. Patrick Henry, a powerful state legislator, was committed to some form of state aid for "teachers of the Christian religion." As long as Henry was in the legislature, Jefferson's bill could make no progress despite Madison's backing.

Meanwhile, the national government was powerless to repay its war debt or quell civil disturbances. The worst news came when farmers in western Massachusetts stopped foreclosures on delinquent farms and sent the sheriffs packing. The makeshift band of tax protesters was led by Daniel Shays, a war veteran and reluctant rebel. "Anarchy and confusion!" cried the Bostonians who spread the alarm. The fracas ended with little fanfare, but the incident was a catalyst for public men such as Madison, who realized the Articles of Confederation had to be replaced with a national government that had the power to tax and provide a financial system for the growing nation.

Working through the state legislature, Madison took advantage of the absence of Patrick Henry (who was now governor) to push to passage the bill establishing religious freedom. On the national scene, Madison first tried to sound the alarm for the ailing Confederation at the Annapolis Convention in 1786, but poor attendance caused this effort to fail. A call for a more general convention, backed by Alexander Hamilton of New York and by Madison was duly issued. With the reluctant consent of George Washington to attend such a meeting, Madison beseeched all the states to send delegates to Philadelphia for a May meeting to consider ways and means of "revising" the Articles of Confederation. It was a ruse, of course, the real motive being to scrap the Articles and come up with a totally new plan.

Madison led the Virginia delegates in an early caucus when they arrived in Philadelphia before the formal meeting convened. From these informal gatherings, Madison created a plan that had three branches of government (legislative, judicial, and executive), and a Congress empowered with broad powers to tax, declare war, and pass laws for "the general welfare." This plan became the blueprint for a constitution.

After some delays, on May 25, 1787, the Federal Convention converged in Philadelphia. Attracted by the chance to serve with Washington, the brightest and best legal talent in the country gathered, ready for drastic reforms. Among the fifty-five delegates were men who wanted broad, almost authoritarian power to be conferred on a central government. Many supported retention of state sovereignty and wanted to close the loopholes of the Articles of Confederation; most delegates occupied positions somewhere between these poles. A few, such as Hamilton, were

BIOGRAPHICAL FACTS

BIRTH: Port Conway, Va., Mar. 16, 1751

ANCESTRY: English

FATHER: James Madison; b. Mar. 27, 1723; d. Feb. 27, 1801

FATHER'S OCCUPATIONS: Justice of the peace; vestryman; farmer

MOTHER: Eleanor Conway Madison; b. Jan. 9, 1731; d. Feb. 11, 1829

BROTHERS: Francis (1753–?); Ambrose (1755–1793); William (1762–1843); Reuben (1771–1775)

SISTERS: Nelly (1760–1802); Sarah (1764–?); Elizabeth (1768–1775); Frances (1774–?)

MARRIAGE: Harewood, Va., Sept. 15, 1794

WIFE: Dorothea "Dolley" Payne Todd; b. Guilford County, N.C., May 20, 1768; d. Washington, D.C., July 12, 1849

CHILDREN: None

RELIGIOUS AFFILIATION: Episcopalian

EDUCATION: Private tutors; attended Donald Robertson's school; College of New Jersey (Princeton), (B.A., 1771); one year postgraduate study at Princeton

OCCUPATION BEFORE PRESIDENCY: Politician

PREPRESIDENTIAL OFFICES: Member of Orange County Committee of Safety; delegate to the Virginia Convention; member of Virginia Legislature; member of Virginia Executive Council; delegate to Continental Congress; delegate to Annapolis Convention; delegate to Constitutional Convention; member of the Virginia Ratification Convention; U.S. congressman; secretary of state

AGE AT INAUGURATION: 57

OCCUPATIONS AFTER PRESIDENCY: Planter; writer; university rector; state legislator; presidential advisor

DEATH: Montpelier, Va., June 28, 1836

PLACE OF BURIAL: Montpelier, Va.

ready to imitate the British constitution and might have even favored a monarchy.

From the outset, Convention sessions were held behind closed doors so that delegates could speak freely without public disclosure of their remarks. The official record gave only the outcome of votes on various motions; but Madison kept his own notes on the principal proceedings, setting down each night his impression of the preceding day's business. His own speeches were among the most significant: Madison was ready for radical reforms and was eager to curb the powers of state legislatures. With an eye cocked toward Montesquieu's advice, Madison and the other delegates wanted a republic based on representation and the rule of law. For Madison, this could come about only if a strong federal government was the result of their deliberations.

That the president, Congress, and Supreme Court would form the three branches of the government was agreed upon with comparatively little dispute, but the composition of the legislature did not so easily emerge from the debates. Madison's Virginia Plan, which came out of the caucus, suggested representation proportionate to population. Delegates from the small states balked and finally supported the New Jersey Plan, which retained the Confederation system of one state, one vote. Finally, Connecticut delegates proposed an acceptable compromise, which incorporated both plans in a two-chambered legislature. But another problem remained: Since the Convention had decided to apportion the House of Representatives on the basis of total population (as opposed to number of voters), the Southerners grew restive and claimed that slaves should be counted, while the Northern delegates maintained that slaves should not be counted at all. Again, there was a compromise, as the Convention agreed that five slaves would be equal to three freemen in congressional apportionment.

Thirty-nine delegates signed the Constitution on September 17, 1787, and soon the entire document was printed in newspapers up and down the Atlantic coastline. Each state had to ratify it for the Union to survive, but the Constitution would become effective after nine states gave their approval to the new document. After an initial round of easy victories, friends of the Constitution struggled to reach the needed ninth state. Early on, the lack of a bill of rights was seen to give opponents of the Constitution a strong talking point. Madison had his ear to the ground and realized another concession must be made.

At the Virginia Ratification Convention in June 1788, Madison acknowledged that a bill of rights ought to be added to the Constitution. To fend off criticism, he promised to press at the earliest opportunity for a series of amendments protecting individual freedom. The vote was close, but Madison and his allies won, thus guaranteeing a trial of the new Constitution. True to his word, he later led the fight for the Bill of Rights after defeating James Monroe for a seat in the First Congress.

Along with Hamilton and John Jay, Madison contributed to a series of articles that during 1787 and 1788 appeared in the New York press over the signature "Publius." Aimed at voters in New York, the series was popular with friends of the Constitution everywhere, and was a campaign tract published as the *Federalist* papers. In time it became a primer for students of constitutional government. In one essay Madison explained why men must accept the rule of law, pointing out that "If men were angels, no government would be necessary." Americans were not angels, he wrote, but they did believe in a republican form of government. That was the promise of the Constitution.

Madison moved into the House of Representatives with assurance. The new government needed revenue, the president needed a cabinet, and an army was needed to protect the frontier. Madison tackled all the problems with dedication, and also advised Washington as the president moved cautiously in setting precedents for future chief executives. During his four terms in Congress, Madison watched as the Federalist party formed behind Hamilton, but he was no party man in the early going. Instead, he was the floor leader for important legislation.

When other congressmen seemed indifferent to

promises for a bill of rights, Madison served notice and forced a vote. Ten of his original fourteen proposed amendments survived the ratification process and earned him praise for his persistence when the Bill of Rights was finally adopted in December 1791.

During this time, Madison's friendship with Secretary of State Jefferson grew into a working relationship. They viewed the Federalist party, developed by Hamilton until it was the leading force in Congress, as a threat to the agrarian republic they envisioned. With the outbreak of the French Revolution, political forces in America took sides. Madison was a leading opponent of Jay's Treaty, which polarized political opinion in 1795. Working behind the scenes, Jefferson and Madison created a viable political party out of the Democratic-Republican societies Hamilton detested as "Frenchified" dissenters.

Tired of partisan bickering, Madison left Congress but went back to the Virginia legislature. There he pushed through Jefferson's bill establishing religious freedom, after his anonymous pamphlet attacked the established church as an antirepublican device that denied citizens a freedom of choice and worship. During the stormy administration of John Adams, Madison denounced the Alien and Sedition Acts as unconstitutional displays of political vengeance. At Jefferson's urging he wrote the Virginia Resolutions, which assumed states could ignore a law they deemed unconstitutional.

When Jefferson entered the White House in 1801, Madison became his secretary of state. Although the conduct of foreign affairs during his eight years in the cabinet was of lasting significance, little credit goes to Madison, for Jefferson chose to act as his own secretary of state. But if Madison's achievements in the Jefferson administration were not significant, the fact remains that the administration avoided outright war with Britain and France. A congressional caucus nominated Madison to succeed Jefferson, and no real

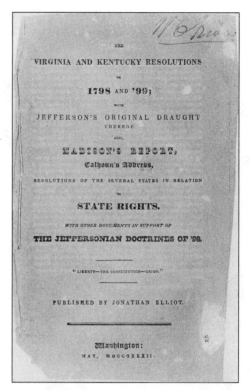

To counter the obnoxious Alien and Sedition Acts, Jefferson and Madison wrote the Virginia and Kentucky Resolutions, in which they insisted that states might choose to ignore unconstitutional acts of Congress.

opposition appeared. From the moment Jefferson said he would not serve a third term, Madison's candidacy was accepted, and he went on to defeat the Federalist Charles Cotesworth Pinckney by an electoral vote of 122 to 47.

James Madison was a different kind of president than his predecessor. He suffered from effects of the policy of drift that had characterized Jefferson's final year in office. Madison was trying to mend fences with a Congress that was looking for trouble. Intimidated by a Senate clique, he kept Albert Gallatin at the Treasury Department instead of making him secretary of state. In general, his cabinet appointments were mediocre as Madison tried to balance geography with party loyalty, and wound up with only one trustworthy person: Gallatin. Madison had dreams of whittling down the national debt, as Gallatin had done between 1802 and 1809. Congress, however, was more concerned with cutting taxes than with debt reduction. Not until Andrew Jackson became president would the debt be erased to realize the Jeffersonian dream.

Socially, Madison was more successful. His wife, Dolley, was used to being in the White House where she had often served as Jefferson's hostess. Vivacious and talkative, Dolley Madison was a counterbalance for her shy husband. (Madison had married Mrs. Dolley Payne Todd, a widow, on September 15, 1794, just three months after he had written a letter to a mutual acquaintance, Aaron Burr, asking him to arrange a meeting.) As first lady, Mrs. Madison entertained on a lavish scale, dazzling Washington with formal dinners and the lively spontaneity of her private parties.

The gaiety of the state social functions did not, however, reflect the atmosphere of Madison's administration. Like the three chief executives before him, the president found himself deeply involved in issues connected with European wars. England's Orders in Council assumed for British ships the right to stop and search neutral, specifically American, vessels suspected of bearing contraband, and Napoleon declared that any American ship that permitted itself to be boarded by the British would be considered fair game for French guns.

The one issue that cut deepest into the young nation's pride was the impressment of American sailors. British naval officers dismissed the validity of naturalization papers and, on boarding American ships, pressed into service any sailor who acted suspiciously or spoke or looked like an Englishman. Jefferson's embargo had been no solution to the problem, for it evaded international confrontation at the expense of national self-respect. Acknowledged as a failure, the Embargo Act was repealed in 1809, three days before Madison's inauguration, to be replaced by the Nonintercourse Act, which reopened trade with all nations except France and England, and gave the president authority to restore trade whenever either or both belligerents withdrew their edicts against American shipping.

Neither England nor France took the bait. In 1810, out of frustration, Congress desperately passed Macon's Bill No. 2, which restored trade with the warring powers and gave them until March 3, 1811, to revoke their edicts. Should one of the powers acquiesce, the president could declare a ninety-day suspension of trade with the other, and if its decrees were not withdrawn in that time, America would revive the Nonintercourse Act against the offending nation. Calculated to play France and England against each other, the bill in reality gave them a year to trade with the United States and to harass American ships with impunity.

The country was sharply divided in its sympathies. New England Federalists were, as usual, anti-French and eager to revive the shipping trade; the Republicans—especially those in the South and West—remained in an anti-English mood. Ironically, despite the fact that the growing rallying cry for war was "free trade and sailors' rights," shippers in the Northeast were quite unready for war. They blamed Republican incompetence for their troubles rather than the British, and they were earning enough profit from the ships that penetrated the blockade to make up for their losses. The Westerners, on the other hand, were itching for a showdown with England. Led by Henry Clay of Kentucky, these "war hawks" talked about national pride, but they also thought about national expansion and looked longingly to Canada and West Florida as future members of the Union. Boasting Kentuckians said Canada could be conquered in two weeks.

While the United States waited for French and English replies to Macon's Bill, the nation prospered from the increased customs receipts resulting from the resumption of trade. Prosperity hung by a thread, however, because the charter of the Bank of the United States was due to expire on March 4, 1811. As Madison's biographer, Irving Brant, points out, the president was a victim of a "lifelong unwillingness to make a public display of political inconsistency." With war a possibility, and with the country's money interests so obviously opposed to a stand against the probable enemy, Madison needed the bank and wanted it

rechartered; but he was reluctant to take a public stand. When the Senate voted 17 to 17 on recharter, Vice President George Clinton broke the tie with a negative vote. As the bank went out of existence, a banking crisis erupted, and farm prices slid. Soon an economic recession spread throughout the Union.

In December 1810, after agreeing to honor American shipping rights (thereby compelling America to declare nonintercourse with England), Napoleon sequestered all American ships in French ports and declared all ports in the French alliance closed to American trade. With sly logic, the emperor claimed that his actions were designed to compel Britain to revoke its Orders in Council.

The intended effects of Macon's Bill had backfired, leaving Madison caught in a diplomatic trap. Great Britain, meanwhile, claimed that France had not in fact revoked its decrees (which was so); and Madison's enemies insisted that France was the enemy, not England. In truth, Madison had been tricked by Napoleon, but he stubbornly hoped for a saving gesture from London. The president held firm and demanded repeal of the Orders in Council. Faced with serious economic problems at home, the British prime minister, Spencer Perceval, finally decided to endorse repeal, but was assassinated before he could act. The dispatch ship *Hornet*, which was sent on a diplomatic mission, came home from England empty-handed.

Within days Madison bowed to the inevitable, and the United States declared war. On June 1, President Madison had sent Congress a list of "the spectacle of injuries and indignities which have been heaped on our country." Deploring the fact that "our moderation and conciliation have had no other effect than to encourage perseverance and to enlarge pretentions," Madison placed the decision of "opposing force . . . in defense of national rights" into the hands of Congress. When news of the repeal of the Orders in Council came, it was too little, and too late, for the country was in a warlike mood. That is, most of the country—but not New England.

Indeed, the nation was not united, as was evident from the congressional war vote—79 to 49 in the House, 19 to 13 in the Senate. To a degree, the division would prevail throughout the War of 1812. Although it had wanted war, Congress was sluggish about voting funds to increase the size of the Army and Navy; and just as the frontier states prepared for battle, the New England states came together in refusing to send troops or money for the conflict. In the Northeast, governors would not allow their state militias to join the national Army, and as Madison had feared, Bostonian financiers refused to grant loans for the war effort.

To add to Madison's woes, the military phase of the war started badly. Detroit, supposedly an American stronghold, surrendered to a combined British-Indian force without a shot fired. Incompetent generals blustered on the Canadian border and achieved more blunders than victories. The capture of York (later Toronto) and its burning by the Yankee troops only infuriated the Canadians, who called for retribution, and got it. The Royal Navy bottled up the tiny U.S. Navy on the Atlantic, and the only cheering came for Americans when the naval hero James Lawrence shouted, "Don't give up the ship!" during an engagement on Lake Erie.

As the first wartime president, Madison had his hands full. While Gallatin found ways to raise money by discounting treasury bonds, Madison kept looking for a competent general (a struggle known by most presidents thereafter). The war was the central issue in the presidential election of 1812; although five out of six New England states voted for New York's DeWitt Clinton, Madison won a second term.

The Federalists could not defeat Madison at the polls, but they derisively called the fight "Mr. Madison's War," and kept their powder extra dry. In fact, the dissenters were proving that America was a free country—a citizen could denounce the war and the president, and yet nobody was thrown in jail or knocked on the head. So it was indeed "a free country" where free speech was alive. While the historian Bradford Perkins writes that Madison "seemed to drift rather than to direct policy" during the prelude to war, the biographer Irving Brant said that Madison encouraged the war movement in order to make his bid for peace from a position of strength, but that he was sabotaged by the Federalists, whose "active support of Great Britain and vituperation of their own government as . . . imbecile . . . created a dual delusion which poured on London in two lines of communication."

Madison may have been out of his depth as commander in chief, but he finally fired his unworthy secretary of war and was determined not to run. Just enough pride lived on from the American victories on the Great Lakes to keep morale from dipping, and Madison probably hoped that somehow New England would reverse its course and become a patriotic part of the Union. And on September 10, 1813, Commodore Oliver Hazard Perry had some New Englanders among his crew when the Americans won the Battle of Lake Erie. "We have met the enemy and they are ours," he reported to public jubilation.

After American troops halted British advances in the Northwest, the war was stalemated. But in the summer of 1814, with Napoleon exiled to Elba, Great Britain was able to turn its full attention to the United States. In August a combined force of British marines with Royal Navy support landed at Chesapeake Bay and headed for the capital. After scattering the American militia at Bladensburg, Maryland, they proceeded to Washington.

On the morning of August 24, as the sound of cannon neared, Dolley Madison remained in the White House waiting for the president, who was meeting his commanders at the nearby Navy Yard. Finally aware that the British would soon be on the doorstep, she supervised the removal of Gilbert Stu-

Artist J. Bowers depicts the stout American defense of Baltimore in 1814, which inspired Francis Scott Key to write "The Star-Spangled Banner."

art's portrait of George Washington, and wrote a desperate letter to her sister: "Mr. Madison comes not; may God protect him! Two messengers covered with dust come to bid me fly; but I wait for him." She received a note from Madison, suggesting that she flee to their rendezvous in Virginia. Soon most of the public buildings in Washington were in flames, but the scorching ended after a British powder magazine exploded and a rainstorm damped the troops' ardor. Later, the blackened walls of the Executive Mansion were repainted, thus leading the public to refer to the "White House"—a nickname formalized when Theodore Roosevelt chose to have it printed on his official stationery.

The British then moved on to Baltimore, a city situated behind a hilly peninsula that creates a bottleneck in Chesapeake Bay. As the British ships sailed near the peninsula, they were held off by the guns of Fort McHenry and by militia sharpshooters. Through the night of September 13 the British bombarded the fort. At dawn, Francis Scott Key, aboard an American dispatch boat, observed that the flag still flew.

The battle at Baltimore and the American victory at Plattsburgh, New York, strengthened the position of the American commission at Ghent, in Belgium, where the belligerents were trying to negotiate a peace. Napoleon's final defeat left the British feeling easier, almost magnanimous. On Christmas Eve, 1814, the Treaty of Ghent was signed, and the two nations returned to the pre-war situation. Neither side had won, or lost. American sea rights were not guaranteed, but with Napoleon gone, the impressment issue was moot. And Canada remained British, more loyal to the Crown than ever before. Tragically, the last battle was waged after the peace had been made: On January 8, 1815, General Jackson defeated the British at New Orleans.

Cocky Federalists had held a meeting at Hartford to prepare an ultimatum for the president. Their emissaries reached Washington as the news from Ghent took the charred capital by storm. Amid the huzzahing and gleeful parade in front of the Octagon House (the temporary home of the president), the Federalists discreetly withdrew. Congressmen who had talked about moving the capital inland drew catcalls and no votes. Madison denounced such an idea as cowardly, and the nation approved.

More good news came with Jackson's victory in

New Orleans. In Washington the *National Intelligencer* bespoke the administration's sense of triumph, and newspapers across the country repeated the welcome tidings. When the implications of the peace treaty sunk in, Congress reacted with a fresh will and the president seemed invigorated. Gallatin, always an acute observer, returned from the peace table with a changed view of his adopted nation. "The war," he wrote, "has renewed and reinstated the national feelings and character which the Revolution had given, and which were daily lessened. The people have now more general objects of attachment with which their pride and political opinions are connected." The people "are more American; they feel and act more as a nation; and I hope the permanency of the Union is thereby better secured." The war had brought the widow's weeds and a huge national debt, but after the War of 1812 the United States was on its way to becoming a major power in the world community.

James Madison himself emerged from the war with enhanced prestige and with little political opposition. Regarded in the popular imagination as the little president who had tolerated no nonsense from the world's strongest empire, he was also thought of by Americans as the architect of victory even though neither side had won.

Warning Congress not to revoke abruptly all war measures, Madison abandoned his faithfulness to consistency. The author of the Virginia Resolutions, which had asserted the rights of states, now denounced states' rights as subversive to the Constitution; and the onetime foe of the Bank of the United States decided, in 1816, to support its reestablishment. There were, however, some limits to Madison's flexibility. Although he went before Congress and urged the institution of "a comprehensive system of roads and canals, such as will have the effect of drawing more closely together every part of our country," he vetoed an internal improvements bill. A constitutional amendment, he believed—not a mere piece of legislation—was needed.

At the end of his second term, in 1817, the president and his wife returned to Montpelier, their Virginia home. There James Madison assumed the role of gentleman farmer, and Dolley continued playing hostess to the gentry. After several years in retirement, however, Madison again began taking active part in the affairs of his state and nation. In 1826 he succeeded Jefferson as rector of the University of Virginia. As a delegate to the Virginia Constitutional

---

SECOND ADMINISTRATION

INAUGURATION: Mar. 4, 1813; House of Representatives, Washington, D.C.

VICE PRESIDENT: Elbridge Gerry

SECRETARY OF STATE: James Monroe

SECRETARY OF THE TREASURY: Albert Gallatin; William Jones, secretary of the Navy, performed Treasury duties (from Apr. 21, 1813 to Feb. 9, 1814, while Gallatin was in Europe seeking a resolution to the War of 1812); George W. Campbell (from Feb. 9, 1814); Alexander J. Dallas (from Oct. 14, 1814); William H. Crawford (from Oct. 22, 1816)

SECRETARY OF WAR: John Armstrong; James Monroe (from Oct. 1, 1814); William H. Crawford (from Aug. 8, 1815); George Graham (from Oct. 22, 1816)

ATTORNEY GENERAL: William Pinkney; Richard Rush (from Feb. 11, 1814)

POSTMASTER GENERAL: Gideon Granger; Return J. Meigs, Jr. (from Apr. 11, 1814)

SECRETARY OF THE NAVY: William Jones; Benjamin W. Crowninshield (from Jan. 16, 1815)

13TH CONGRESS (May 24, 1813–Mar. 3, 1815):
  SENATE: 28 Democratic-Republicans; 8 Federalists
  HOUSE: 112 Democratic-Republicans; 68 Federalists

14TH CONGRESS (Dec. 4, 1815–Mar. 3, 1817):
  SENATE: 26 Democratic-Republicans; 12 Federalists
  HOUSE: 117 Democratic-Republicans; 65 Federalists

ELECTION OF 1812

CANDIDATES	ELECTORAL VOTE
James Madison (Democratic-Republican)	128
DeWitt Clinton (Fusion)	89

DOLLEY

When Dolley Madison made her entrance into Long's Hotel for the inaugural ball of 1809, characteristically dressed in pale velvet, plumed turban, and pearls, she confirmed a friend's earlier appraisal of her as "all dignity, grace and ability." More somber was her husband James, whose face already reflected the cares of his new office. Certainly not among those cares was the running of the executive mansion: That was Dolley's bailiwick, as it had been when she served as hostess for widower Thomas Jefferson. Her cheerful informality had complemented Jefferson's domestic simplicity, but now that she was actually living in the manor to which she had become accustomed, Dolley intensified the social schedule. The first lady's weekly receptions and "drawing rooms," her teas, lawn parties, and dinners, belied her Quaker upbringing, and a few detractors noted that Dolley took snuff and was "said to rouge"; but her career as a hostess and grande dame, spanning nearly half a century, was a spectacularly popular one. Her aplomb at official functions often was a political asset to her reticent husband, and in crises she could display a cool common sense: Among the few things she saved before the British burned the executive mansion in 1814 were some vital state documents and Gilbert Stuart's portrait of George Washington. Dolley faithfully nursed James Madison through his retirement at Montpelier, and when he died in 1836, she became a widow for the second time (her first husband, John Todd, had died of yellow fever in 1793). Although financial troubles plagued her for the rest of her life, Dolley maintained her poise: As a contemporary described Dolley's extraordinary quality, "'Tis not her form, 'tis not her face, it is the woman altogether."

Convention of 1829, he protested the disproportionate power of the eastern slaveholders in the state legislature. Throughout Monroe's two presidential terms, Madison wrote newspaper articles defending the administrations' decisions and served as foreign policy adviser. He continued to work for the gradual abolishment of slavery; he wrote his autobiography; and he edited his journal of the Federal Convention.

Madison's small frame was frail, but his mind remained alert to the end. On June 27, 1836, he spent several hours dictating a letter. He dismissed with a wave of the hand well-intentioned suggestions that he ought to keep healthy until July 4, as had Adams and Jefferson. The next morning breakfast was brought to him in bed, but he could not swallow.

When his niece asked him what was wrong, he replied, "Nothing more than a change of *mind*, my dear." And then, according to his servant, James Madison "ceased breathing as quietly as the snuff of a candle goes out."

Perhaps Kennedy was too generous in calling Madison an underrated president. By any criteria, however, he was a great statesman. Most presidents probably would be pleased to be remembered for just one solid accomplishment. Madison left his imprint on the Constitution, the Bill of Rights, and the presidency. And the Union he loved as much as his precious Dolley is still his living monument.

—*VINCENT BURANELLI,*
revised by ROBERT A. RUTLAND

Two and a half months after he had become president, in May 1817, James Monroe left Washington, D.C., for a tour of the middle and northern United States. His announced purpose was to inspect the federal shipyards, forts, and frontier outposts, but he also was hopeful that his appearance would restore the national unity damaged by the recent war. Monroe soon discovered that the trip was succeeding beyond his hopes: Roadsides and riverbanks were filled with people anxious to have a glimpse of him, and cheering crowds greeted his arrival at state capitals. "In principal towns," he wrote to Thomas Jefferson, "the whole population has been in motion, and in a manner to produce the greatest degree of excitement possible."

Monroe, repeating the tour that George Washington had taken, proved once again the public curiosity for a glimpse of the president. After journeying through the Middle Atlantic States, Monroe swung into New England, the last stronghold of the Federalist party. As the third consecutive Democratic-Republican president, Monroe had lost only Connecticut and Massachusetts in the 1816 election, but any misgivings he held were soon abandoned. On July 12, 1817, the Boston *Columbian Centinel* noted Monroe's visit with a prophetic heading: ERA OF GOOD FEELINGS. These sentiments from Benjamin Russell, editor of the newspaper and once the high priest of the Federalist party, spoke volumes about the return of prosperity to New England. "During the late Presidential Jubilee many persons have met at festive boards, in pleasant converse, whom party politics had long severed," Russell reported. "We recur with pleasure to all the circumstances which attended the demonstration of good feelings."

Perhaps Russell was a bit too optimistic, for some of his Federalist friends did not join in the celebrating. But peace and prosperity will do wonders for any politician, and the Era of Good Feelings label became fastened both to the Monroe administration and to the president personally. His support extended from the masses to many former political adversaries—including the *Columbian Centinel*, which in earlier times had been the organ voice of the Federalist party and a traditional foe of the Democratic-Republicans.

A devoted party man, Monroe found himself a personification of the nonpartisan hero, credited with all the good but rarely blamed for the ills of his two terms. Even John Quincy Adams—who rather than say anything nice about anybody could usually be counted on to say nothing at all—wrote that the Monroe years would "be looked back to as the golden age of this republic."

The times were right for James Monroe to assume the presidency. In his inaugural address he said, "the United States have flourished beyond example. Their citizens individually have been happy and the nation prosperous. . . . The sentiment in the mind of every citizen is national strength. It ought therefore to be cherished." Americans agreed: The success of their Revolution, of their experiment with republicanism, of their military engagements—most recently the War of 1812—had buoyed their spirits and bolstered their national pride, unity, and ambition. Shipyards hummed with activity, there was a rage for building turnpikes and canals, and farm prices held steady. A nationalistic generation, born under the American flag, was confident it could handle the problems expansion would raise.

Even so, Americans looked for leadership and example to the fathers of their independence. Washington was dead, Adams and Jefferson were old, and Madison had stepped down; but there was Monroe. He too was from Virginia, and if he had not forged the Revolution he had at least helped to wage it; besides, he looked the part. Not yet sixty, he stood tall, angular, erect, his features large and chiseled, his blue-gray eyes at once penetrating and kind, and

Rembrandt Peale captured the kindness and strength of President Monroe in this portrait set against the backdrop of the Capitol, ca. 1824-1825.

those who knew both men said he bore an unmistakable resemblance to George Washington. Monroe would be the last president to wear small clothes (snug knee breeches) or to powder his graying hair. He was also the last president from among the Founding Fathers—those men who either fought or governed during the American Revolution and its aftermath.

The first Monroes were landowning farmers, neither rich nor poor, not quite aristocratic but wholly respectable in Virginia's complex social hierarchy. James Monroe, the oldest of five children, was born in Westmoreland County on April 28, 1758. He probably became a patriot at an early age, for his father was an admirer of Patrick Henry and an occasional petitioner for colonial causes, and his mother's brother, Judge Joseph Jones, was a close friend to Washington, Jefferson, and Madison. With his neighbor and classmate John Marshall (future chief justice of the United States), Monroe walked several miles a day to and from the school of Parson Archibald Campbell, reputedly "a disciplinarian of the sternest type. . . ."

In 1774, at the age of sixteen, Monroe was sent to Williamsburg to acquire at William and Mary College the education and polish required of a Virginia gentleman. Before the year was out, his father died, but Judge Jones paid the bills to keep Monroe in school. Neither time nor place, however, was conducive to scholarship. Then the capital of Virginia, Williamsburg was a center of colonial discontent. As resistance to the Crown mounted, Monroe began drilling with student-formed military companies, and in 1775 he received a lieutenant's commission in the 3d Virginia Regiment.

In August 1776 Congress ordered a number of state regiments, the Virginia 3d among them, to New York for service under General Washington's command. By the time the Virginians arrived the city had been lost to the British, and Washington was holed up at Harlem Heights. Most of Monroe's earliest experiences with the Continental Army were devoted to retreating, the successful defense of White Plains being an exception. As November brought winter down the Hudson, Washington took his fast-shrinking army across it, through New Jersey, and across the Delaware River into Pennsylvania. Despite the diminished condition of his troops and supplies, the general decided to recross the Delaware. On Christmas night, while the Hessian mercenaries who occupied Trenton slept, the Americans penetrated the city. It was daylight when the Hessians realized what was happening. As they mobilized, Monroe led a column of troops in a victorious race to the arsenal. During the action Monroe was severely wounded, and he needed two months in convalescence to regain his strength.

Monroe, not yet nineteen, was promoted to captain, but enlistments were so few that there were not enough men for the formation of a company for him to command. In August 1777 he became an aide to Lord Stirling, Major General William Alexander. On September 11, after the rout at Brandywine Creek, Monroe tended the wounds of the French officer Lafayette, and the two soldiers became lifetime friends. Then Monroe participated in the abortive American attack of Germantown and was promoted to major.

In 1779, when the war shifted south, Monroe returned home, anxious to defend his state. In one of his rare letters of recommendation, General Washington wrote to the Virginia legislature suggesting that the major be given a command in the militia. "In every instance," the general wrote, Monroe "maintained the reputation of a brave, active, and sensible officer." Once again, however, he was a victim of the manpower shortage, and he received the commission but no command.

Advising Monroe to take advantage of the lull in fighting, Judge Jones suggested that he study with Thomas Jefferson, who, though he was then governor of Virginia, still accepted a number of law students. Jones arranged the introduction, Washington's letter provided the best of recommendations, and Monroe spent two years with the governor. They established a friendship that lasted, despite strains and struggles, until Jefferson's death in 1826.

It was easy to be friendly to James Monroe. "He is a man," said Jefferson, "whose soul might be turned wrong side outwards without discovering a blemish to the world." Jefferson believed both of his young friends, Madison and Monroe, were headed for greatness. Excessively candid, not in the least pretentious, and seldom discouraged for long, Monroe was trustworthy. Moreover, he disdained grudges and retained his friends even through profound political disagreements. His political limitations were often simply misplaced expressions of his personal qualities. He could be overgenerous, honest to the point of naïveté, and indiscreet.

He entered politics in 1782 as a member of the Virginia legislature and a year later was elected to the Continental Congress. In both state and national affairs he eventually distinguished himself as a Jeffersonian agrarian-liberal, strongly sectionalist, a foe of centralized government, and a champion of frontier development. He made two trips "through the wilderness," and once seriously, though unofficially, suggested that the United States think about convincing Britain to relinquish Canada. As a member of the Virginia Convention of 1788, he originally opposed the Constitution on the grounds that it assigned too much power to the federal government. As for slavery, when a vote on some aspect of the issue came up, he absented himself.

Probably at Patrick Henry's urging, Monroe ran for Congress in 1788 but lost to his friendly rival, James Madison. In 1790, however, the Virginia legislature elected him to the United States Senate. During his four years in the Senate he was—with Jefferson's advice, Madison's cooperation, and Aaron

---

BIOGRAPHICAL FACTS

BIRTH: Westmoreland County, Va., Apr. 28, 1758

ANCESTRY: Scotch

FATHER: Spence Monroe; b. Westmoreland Country, Va.; d. Westmoreland County, Va. ,1774

FATHER'S OCCUPATION: Farmer

MOTHER: Elizabeth Jones Monroe; b. King George Country, Va.; d. Unknown

BROTHERS: Andrew (1763–1826); Joseph Jones (1764–1824); Spence (?–?)

SISTER: Elizabeth (?–?)

MARRIAGE: New York, N.Y., Feb. 16, 1786

WIFE: Elizabeth Kortright; b. New York, N.Y., June 30, 1768; d. Oak Hill, Va., Sept. 23, 1830

CHILDREN: Eliza (1786–1840); Maria Hester (1804–1850)

RELIGIOUS AFFILIATION: Episcopalian

EDUCATION: Parson Archibald Campbell's school; attended College of William and Mary

OCCUPATIONS BEFORE PRESIDENCY: Lawyer, writer

MILITARY SERVICE: Officer in 3d Virginia Regiment and Continental Army (1775–1779)

PREPRESIDENTIAL OFFICES: Military commissioner for Southern Army; member of Virginia Legislature; member of Governor Jefferson's Council; member of Virginia House of Delegates; delegate to Continental Congress; member of Virginia Assembly; U.S. senator; minister to France; minister to England; governor of Virginia; secretary of state; secretary of war

AGE AT INAUGURATION: 58

OCCUPATION AFTER PRESIDENCY: Writer

DEATH: New York, N.Y., July 4, 1831

PLACE OF BURIAL: Hollywood Cemetery, Richmond, Va.

Burr's political expertise—instrumental in organizing opposition to the Federalist policies directed by Alexander Hamilton. The result was a consolidation of Anti-Federalist factions that became, in 1795–96, the Democratic-Republican party.

In 1794 relations between the United States and France were beginning to worsen. Gouverneur Morris, the American minister to France, was a Federalist of aristocratic inclinations, hardly sympathetic to revolutionary France, whose government demanded his recall. At the same time, John Jay was in England negotiating a treaty, and the French were upset lest the United States become allied to Great Britain. To soothe the French, President Washington appointed Monroe to succeed Morris. When he arrived in Paris, Monroe addressed the National Convention. Calling France "our ally and friend," he praised "the fortitude, magnanimity and heroic valor of her troops . . . the wisdom and firmness of her councils," and assured his audience that Jay would not weaken the relationship between the United States and France.

Across the Channel, the English read of Monroe's laudatory speech and found it disagreeable. Washington thought it not "well devised," and Secretary of State Edmund Randolph wrote the minister, reminding him to cultivate French friendship "with zeal, proportioned to the value we set upon it." Then, late in 1794, Monroe managed to secure the release of controversial Thomas Paine, the Revolutionary War pamphleteer, from a Paris jail. Paine had been thrown into prison for his opposition to the execution of King Louis XVI. Upon his release Paine soon launched an attack on Washington, accusing the president of having been too fearful to intervene on his behalf. Washington probably did not applaud Monroe's generosity toward the old patriot.

But Monroe's usefulness abroad had lapsed. The French were angered by the terms of Jay's pro-British treaty, and Monroe's apology did not sit well with Washington, who thought that a minister's responsibility was to defend his government's policy. In December 1796 Monroe was recalled.

Back in America, a distressed Monroe demanded without success that Washington make public the reasons for his recall. He wrote an ill-advised, damning attack on the general, which was not published until Washington had left office. Adams employed the treatise in his propaganda campaign against the French, reminding Americans of the fine send-off the French

had given Monroe—"a disgraced minister." Hurt and angry, Monroe kept the issue alive, published the unfortunate paper, and probably lost Washington's esteem in a bad bargain.

Monroe came out of the incident looking like a spoiled child, but he recovered. National sentiment was increasingly Republican, and he found that his experience in France had gained him more in recognition than it had cost him in popularity. Washington, however, remained bitter—not without cause —about Monroe's attack. One December night in 1799, returning home from a walk in the snow, Washington was informed that James Monroe had just been elected governor of Virginia. Without changing his wet clothes, Washington sat before the fire mulling the news.

Twice elected governor of Virginia, in 1803 Monroe agreed to give diplomacy another try when President Jefferson asked him to return to France to negotiate a treaty for free navigation of the Mississippi River. Before Monroe arrived in Paris, however, Robert Livingston had made the Louisiana Purchase, and so Monroe was directed to Madrid with orders to acquire Spanish Florida. When Spain refused to sell, Jefferson instructed him to go to London to see what could be done concerning tension caused by the high-handed Royal Navy in dealing with American vessels. Impressment of American sailors was the burning issue.

Excessively eager to make a deal, Monroe signed on December 31, 1806, a treaty that did not mention impressment. Jefferson was so disappointed, he never sent the treaty to the Senate, but he wanted to recognize Monroe's record in the foreign service. Although Jefferson offered Monroe the governorship of the Louisiana Territory, "the second office in the United States in importance," the president misjudged Monroe's sense of shame. Monroe refused the office and returned home in 1807.

The next year, when James Madison was elected

Constantino Brumidi's 1875 painting shows the American diplomats James Monroe and Robert R. Livingston closing the Louisiana Purchase with the seated French minister, Charles-Maurice de Talleyrand-Périgord. In truth, Monroe was on his way to Paris when Livingston and Talleyrand-Périgord finalized their negotiations. The deal has been called the biggest real estate bargain in history, for it transferred a vast trans-Mississippi region to the United States for pennies per acre.

president, Monroe hoped for a cabinet post but was once again offered the governorship of Louisiana, and again Monroe refused.

Monroe's public career resumed in 1810, when he was reelected to the Virginia legislature, but a coolness developed between Madison and Monroe. In 1811 he again became governor, and less than three months after taking office, Monroe was approached by President Madison, who patched their friendship and asked the governor to become secretary of state, replacing the inept Robert Smith. Monroe showed administrative skills by creating an orderly, smooth-functioning agency. In 1814, during the war with England, Monroe also took charge of the disorga-

nized Department of War, thus assuming a dual role in the Madison cabinet. As secretary of war, he performed well, and as the tide of war turned, Monroe became the most logical Republican to receive the presidential nomination in 1816. In the congressional nominating caucus, Monroe outdistanced his rivals. The faltering Federalists provided only token opposition, and Monroe won 183 electoral votes to 34 for Rufus King.

After his successful goodwill tour, Monroe and his wife settled into the White House, which had been partly restored after the British torching of 1814. Monroe had married Elizabeth Kortright of New York in 1786. As first lady she was quite a contrast to her spirited predecessor: Whereas Dolley Madison had skipped about Washington paying social calls, Mrs. Monroe stayed at home, and the capital's ladies came to her. Not that Elizabeth Monroe was antisocial—she was just formal. The spontaneity of Dolley's parties was replaced by the grandeur of Elizabeth's lavish dinners and balls, and she resumed the weekly levees, entertaining callers at the presidential residence on Wednesday evenings.

The Monroe cabinet was a gathering of quality and intellect. The president chose John Quincy Adams as his secretary of state, a judicious move that proved salutary at a time when American interests were jeopardized by European expansionists. Monroe kept William H. Crawford as a holdover secretary of the treasury, and made John C. Calhoun the secretary of war. William Wirt was appointed attorney general, and Return J. Meigs, Jr. took over the busy Post Office Department. In terms of sheer ability and acumen, it was probably one of the best cabinets any U.S. president ever assembled.

Expansion was the prevailing issue of the Monroe administration, and expansion, of course, inspired or brought to the surface of government a number of greater issues. A nation could not simply annex territory. A nation first had to discover which land was its own and which was not; borders had to be defined; the development of new areas had to be planned; policies regarding foreign rights to neighboring territory had to be established. And the nation had its own unique problem—slavery—to deal with: Which, if any, annexed territory should be slave, and which, if any, free?

In 1819, when Missouri applied for admission to the Union, there were eleven slave states and eleven free states in the country. This delicate balance in the Senate was threatened by the admission of Missouri, where slavery had long existed. Naturally, the North wanted Missouri admitted free, and the South wanted a state constitution recognizing slaveholders' rights. Northerners contended that in the future, slavery should be confined to territories below the 36°30' latitude of Missouri's southern border. Enraged Southerners claimed slavery ought to exist in any Western territory where the citizens desired it.

The ensuing debates were ferocious. "I have never known a question so menacing to the tranquillity and even the continuance of our Union as the present one," Monroe wrote. The acrimony on the floors of Congress upset the friends of the Union everywhere, perhaps nowhere more than at Monticello. Jefferson's notable letter to Congressman John Holmes of Maine alluded to the crisis as "a firebell in the night." Going further, Jefferson said "I considered it at once as the knell of the Union. It is hushed, indeed, for the moment. But this is a reprieve only, not a final sentence." A compromise had appeared as a temporary solution when Maine residents also asked for admission to the Union. Finally, bills passed to allow both Missouri and Maine to enter, but bad feelings abounded, particularly among Southern extremists.

Another not-quite-forgotten issue that expansion fostered was that of internal improvements. A growing United States needed post offices, an interstate highway system, canals, and conservation programs. Like Jefferson and Madison, Monroe was emphatically in favor of federal aid for internal improvements, but he was also certain that the Constitution gave the government no such legislative powers. During his northern trip in 1817, he thought he came up with a constitutional course to pursue: Acting as commander in chief, he ordered the Department of War to repair a number of damaged roads in New York, claiming that maintenance of the roads was essential to national defense. But there were other sticklers for proper usage of federal funds. Henry Clay of Kentucky, also an advocate of internal improvements, opposed congressional appropriation of the funds on the reasonable grounds that this was a roundabout method of handling a problem that required direct federal action. The president, however, having failed to convince Congress that a consti-

HENRY CLAY

Henry Clay was one of the most clever politicians ever to serve in the United States Congress—as a representative, Speaker of the House, and senator—but he never achieved the prize he sought the most: the presidency.

Born in Virginia in 1777, he was part of the moving force which invaded the back country that became the new state of Kentucky. In this rough-and-tumble atmosphere, his courtroom skills early on established Clay as a political "comer." He rose rapidly in party circles, committed to the Jeffersonian Republican party, and moved from the state legislature into the Washington arena. A "War Hawk" anxious to humiliate Great Britain, Clay as Speaker of the House helped whip up sentiment for the War of 1812. He then served on the peace commission which ended the fighting with the Treaty of Ghent in 1814.

Popular and ambitious, Clay pushed for his "American System" in Congress with its broad interpretation of constitutional powers. Clay wanted internal improvements, such as highways and canals, built with federal funds. He also favored a steep tariff and was friendly toward a national banking system—both ideas which placed him at odds in high party circles. Presidents Madison and Monroe frustrated his schemes and in time Clay left the Democrats to form the antiadministration Whig party.

Although he once said he would "rather be right than be president," Clay strived mightily to obtain the office. Last in a four-man field in 1824, he threw his support to the winning John Quincy Adams and gave rise to Andrew Jackson's charge of a "corrupt bargain" (Adams appointed Clay secretary of state). In 1832 he ran again as an anti-Jackson candidate and was soundly defeated. Then he sought the Whig nomination for president in 1840, 1844, and 1848. He won the nomination in 1844 but lost to James K. Polk.

In his declining years Clay came back to the Senate to forge the Compromise of 1850. This proved to be only a temporary respite from the brewing troubles over slavery, but at his death in 1852 Clay believed he had been a major force in preserving peace between the North and South.

tutional amendment should be passed, decided that he would have to veto bills for internal improvements.

And there was the problem of foreign policy. The United States was growing by leaps and bounds. How large it would ultimately get was becoming clearer: Americans were beginning to look to the wilderness between the Mississippi and the Pacific, but the definition of northern and southern borders was fuzzy. In 1817 Monroe dispatched a team of negotiators to London to settle the United States–Canada border, and the Convention of 1818 was arranged. The boundary was established along the forty-ninth parallel to the Rockies, beyond which lay the Oregon Territory, where Americans and Canadians would enjoy equal rights.

More troubling was the festering question of Spanish Florida, which American diplomats and freebooters had long coveted. The Spanish Empire was crumbling, but haughty Spanish officials were tough negotiators. In 1818 General Andrew Jackson and his men roamed at will through the Spanish possession in search of renegade Indians and runaway slaves. Madrid was slowly forced to the negotiating table. With the Spanish minister to Washington, Luis de Onís, Secretary of State John Quincy Adams worked out the details, and the Adams-Onís Treaty of 1819 added all of Florida to the United States. The bill for five million dollars in damage claims was assumed by the Americans, but a small price was paid to settle the Louisiana boundaries along the Sabine, Red, and Arkansas rivers up to the forty-second parallel. Spain's remaining claims to California, New Mexico, and Texas would soon be challenged by rebellious Mexicans.

At home, all the news was not good. A scandal in the Baltimore branch of the Bank of the United States caused a tightening of credit, which in turn triggered the Panic of 1819. Land prices fell sharply, bringing on an economic slump that lasted several years. Among those hardest hit by the panic were former presidents Jefferson and Madison. Jefferson was embarrassed by a co-signed twenty thousand dollar note that was in default, and in November 1819 he wrote John Adams a weary letter. "The paper bubble is then burst," Jefferson noted. No cash was to be found, and in Virginia lands "cannot now be sold for [what until recently was] a year's rent." Madison, also hard-pressed for cash, resorted to selling slaves, although he refused to break up black families in his distress. Coming as it did the year before an election, the Panic might have been a great threat to Monroe's desire for a second term, but it was not. The scapegoat in 1819–1820 was not the presidency, but the Bank of the United States. The "villainous" bank, which did not have to stand for public office, became the object of public fury, and calls for an end to its federal charter were renewed.

Thus circumstanced as an innocent bystander to the bank's scheming way, Monroe was not even opposed. The Federalists, still around but on their last legs, could not muster strength enough to put up a candidate. Except for one dissenting ballot cast (for John Quincy Adams, perhaps to ensure George Washington's place in history as the only president to win unanimously), Monroe received all the electoral college votes.

The issues of his first administration continued—in most cases were magnified—during the second. Two of the results were the Missouri Compromise, which postponed a decision on the expansion of slavery, and the Monroe Doctrine.

Like most momentous issues that refuse to be pigeonholed, the Missouri problem resurfaced. After the bill had been signed by the president, but before the date of official admission to the Union, the Missouri legislature itself revived the seemingly settled issue by passing a law excluding free blacks from the would-be state. Outraged, antislavery factions wanted to abrogate Missouri's admission. In his first triumph as "the Great Compromiser," Speaker of the House

Henry Clay came up with a solution: Until the Missouri legislature gave assurance that it would not deny rights to any American citizen, statehood would remain suspended. The compromise merely prohibited Missouri from passing any law contrary to the Constitution, and naturally Missouri agreed.

President Monroe did not fail to see the ambiguity of the wording of the Missouri Compromise; nor did he miss the fact that it had accomplished less than it had postponed. But he was genuinely puzzled by the constitutional questions that had been raised. First, the Constitution acknowledged slavery; it may not have favored it, but by declaring (for purposes of apportionment) each slave equal to three-fifths of a free man, it recognized the existence of the institution. Second, in Monroe's opinion, Congress did not have the right to restrict slavery in any state, as slavery was a local issue. But Congress did have the right to admit or deny admission to any territory. In short, the Constitution provided no clear answer. On the advice of his cabinet he signed the compromise, perhaps agreeing with John Quincy Adams, who, though he had advised the president to sign, said, "I take it for granted that the present question is a mere preamble—a titlepage to a great, tragic volume."

Monroe was similarly unable to settle the question of internal improvements. He sincerely believed that the government ought to provide for them, but when the House passed an internal improvements bill in 1822, he vetoed it because he thought Congress lacked the power to tap the federal treasury for local projects. (His successor, John Quincy Adams, would face the problem in reverse: Adams wanted the improvements made, claiming that the Constitution implied the necessary power to Congress, but by then Congress would not pass the improvements bill.) In time Congress approved a new bill, one carefully worded to take care of Monroe's complaints, and the president signed it. But some die-hard Democrats (such as Senator Martin Van Buren) still thought a

constitutional amendment was needed to use federal funds for state projects.

The question of European activity in the Americas first came up in the Monroe administration in 1821, when the czar announced that he was extending Russia's Alaska territory down the Pacific coast of North America to the fifty-first parallel, which was located well within the Oregon Territory. Monroe immediately took the issue to his cabinet and found Secretary of State Adams's words most agreeable. Adams said that "we should contest the right of Russia to *any* territorial establishment on this continent, and that we should assume distinctly the principle that the American continents are no longer subjects for *any* new

---

SECOND ADMINISTRATION

INAUGURATION: Mar. 5, 1821; House of Representatives, Washington, D.C.
VICE PRESIDENT: Daniel D. Tompkins
SECRETARY OF STATE: John Quincy Adams
SECRETARY OF THE TREASURY: William H. Crawford
SECRETARY OF WAR: John C. Calhoun
ATTORNEY GENERAL: William Wirt
POSTMASTER GENERAL: Return J. Meigs, Jr.;
   John McLean (from July 1, 1823)
SECRETARY OF THE NAVY: Smith Thompson;
   Samuel L. Southard (from Sept. 16, 1823)
SUPREME COURT APPOINTMENT: Smith Thompson (1823)
17TH CONGRESS (Dec. 3, 1821–Mar. 3, 1823):
   SENATE: 44 Democratic-Republicans; 4 Federalists
   HOUSE: 158 Democratic-Republicans; 25 Federalists
18TH CONGRESS (Dec. 1823–Mar. 3, 1825):
   SENATE: 21 Democratic-Republicans; 17 Federalists
   HOUSE: 187 Democratic-Republicans; 26 Federalists
STATE ADMITTED: Missouri (1821)

ELECTION OF 1820

CANDIDATES	ELECTORAL VOTE
James Monroe (Democratic-Republican)	231
John Quincy Adams (Independent-Republican)	1

For decades the Monroe Doctrine was almost a dead letter, but late in the nineteenth century President Cleveland threatened war with England over a Latin American quarrel, and Theodore Roosevelt bolstered the doctrine with his "big stick, soft speech" approach to give the doctrine real force, as expressed in this 1901 cartoon.

European colonial establishments." After the president ordered a protest lodged in St. Petersburg, the czar proved conciliatory and agreed to withdraw north of the territory, to the parallel of 54°40'.

Adams was also the chief architect of United States policy toward Latin America. Spain had bungled its attempts at colonization there and had lost, through revolutions, most of its American territories. In 1822 rumors were circulating that the Spanish, with French aid, were seriously considering the possibility of re-entering their former colonies, including Mexico. Great Britain, anxious as ever to slap French hands, suggested that England and the United States publish a joint statement in support of the Latin countries, but Adams objected. "It would be more candid," he

argued, "as well as more dignified, to avow our principles explicitly than to come in as a cockboat in the wake of the British man-of-war."

Thus the Monroe Doctrine, written by Adams but made United States policy by James Monroe: "The American continents, by the free and independent condition which they have assumed and maintain, are henceforth not to be considered as subjects for future colonization by any European powers." Monroe drew the words from one of Adams's state papers and included them in his State of the Union message to Congress on December 2, 1823. Although the principle of American intervention is couched in one sentence, by 1852 the so-called "Doctrine" was fixed U. S. policy. It has been employed as justification for a broad range of American actions, from the Spanish-American War to the Cuban Missile Crisis.

Monroe's foreign policy, in retrospect, seems among the president's greatest achievements. By contrast, he had many critics in his own party because of an evenhanded patronage policy. To such professional politicians as Senator Van Buren, Monroe's indifference to party affiliation in passing out jobs could be infuriating. Monroe's appointment of a rival to the lucrative Albany postmastership placed Van Buren and Monroe on a collision course. Van Buren denounced Monroe's lackadaisical attitude as a "fusion policy" where former Federalists received appointments coveted by Republicans. What was the point of winning an election, Van Buren reasoned, if the defeated men were offered the "crumbs of office?" To his cronies, Van Buren said that Monroe's patronage policy was a disaster which "was pulling the Republican party apart."

Party politics aside, the legal limits of power were determined in ways not foreseen by the Founding Fathers in 1787. During Monroe's two terms, the Supreme Court flexed its judicial muscles. In the panic year of 1819, with Chief Justice John Marshall still presiding, the high court ruled in the Dartmouth College case that valid contracts cannot be overturned by acts of state legislatures. The Bank of the United States won a momentous case when the Court decided, in *McCulloch v. Maryland*, that states cannot tax an agency of the federal government. In this latter case, Marshall laid down the dictum that "the power to tax . . . is the power to destroy."

Near the end of Monroe's tenure the aging Marquis de Lafayette, after 40 years' absence, returned for a visit to the United States. The reunion between the president and the French soldier who had become an American hero was moving, and the two men spent as much time as possible together during the next year. They said farewell on August 9, 1825, at a banquet given by the now ex-president.

Before Lafayette took his leave, however, there was much shuffling in Washington among the would-be presidential candidates. Jackson's whirlwind campaign gave him 99 electoral votes but not a majority. His followers cried "Foul!" when Clay threw his support behind Adams in the House of Representatives, where the vote was by states. Although Clay and Jackson were both Southerners and slaveholders, Clay believed Jackson would be a disaster in the White House. "I cannot believe that killing 2,500 Englishmen at New Orleans," Clay said, "qualifies [Jackson] for the various, difficult, and complicated duties of the Chief Magistracy." In the House balloting, Adams won with thirteen votes to seven for Jackson and four for Crawford. Adams was the standard bearer for the National Republicans, and his vice president would be John C. Calhoun, a Republican of dubious standing. Jackson's bandwagon started rolling at once, heading for the 1828 contest with more momentum than a runaway team of horses.

Monroe retired to Oak Hill, his home in Loudoun County designed by architect Thomas Jefferson. In 1829 he returned to public service, becoming presiding officer of the Virginia Constitutional Convention. He led a battle for fair apportionment of legislative representation, opposed enlargement of suffrage, and, once again, by and large avoided involvement with the slavery issue.

After his wife died in 1830, Monroe, ailing and in financial difficulty, sold his Virginia plantation and moved to New York to live with his daughter. He died there in 1831, on the Fourth of July.

—*DAVID JACOBS*
revised by ROBERT A. RUTLAND

JOHN QUINCY ADAMS

BORN TO LEAD

Few men have been as well trained for the presidency as John Quincy Adams. Born in the afterglow of the Stamp Act crisis, young Adams was to journey abroad, dine with Thomas Jefferson in Paris as a twelve-year-old boy, and serve as the American minister to the Netherlands while still in his twenties. Then he was elected to the United States Senate and was named President Monroe's secretary of state. What better credentials for a president?

And yet Adams was headed for a rocky four years in the White House, in part because President Monroe stepped aside and let factions within the Democratic-Republican party bloody each other in the presidential quest. In a four-way race between Senator Henry Clay, General Andrew Jackson, cabinet member William H. Crawford, and John Quincy Adams, none of these candidates had a majority. Jackson had more electoral and popular votes, but in the House of Representatives (where Clay was a powerful figure) the ultimate choice was Adams. Jackson's followers soon chanted that a "corrupt bargain" had been arranged so that Clay would be made secretary of state (and thus presidential timber for the 1828 race). Jackson's people vowed they would make a shambles of the Adams presidency—and they did.

Thus began a four-year struggle, with Adams unable to heal interparty wounds and constantly being thwarted by a rowdy Congress. Jefferson called the presidency a "splendid misery"; for Adams it was a misery with little splendor.

The second child and first son of John and Abigail Adams, he was born in Braintree (Quincy), Massachusetts, on July 11, 1767. When John Quincy was three, his father temporarily retired from politics; and as his reentrance was gradual, John Adams was home often enough to establish an extremely close if not a demonstrative relationship with his son. With the Revolution in the making, the precocious John

Quincy Adams was quite receptive to his father's anti-British sentiments and explanations of the issues. Before he was seven he had become a faithful reader of the patriot press, and when with his mother he witnessed the Battle of Bunker Hill in 1775, he saw testament to all he had read and heard and became a confirmed Anglophobe.

In 1778 and again the next year, John Quincy accompanied his father to Europe on diplomatic missions. The elder Adams would later recall the boy's fascination with Thomas Jefferson. Shortly before his son's inauguration as president, John Adams wrote Jefferson: "I call him our John, because when you were at the Cul de sac at Paris, he appeared to me to be almost as much your boy as mine." Educated at schools in Paris, Amsterdam, and Leyden, and by his father, the youth developed sophisticated interests, ranging from history to agriculture, from economics to gastronomy. These years abroad also marked the end of Adams's childhood.

In 1781 he served with the American minister to Russia. After two years he was about to settle down in the Netherlands with his books when his father appeared and sent him to Paris, where he could keep a closer eye on his son. There John Quincy watched the signing of the Treaty of Paris, ending the American Revolution, and held his own during dinner-table discussions with the American diplomats and their French friends.

In 1785 John Adams was sent to London as the minister to Great Britain, and John Quincy—once again on his own—decided he had better get on with his education, this time without distractions. He returned to the United States and enrolled at Harvard. After his experiences abroad he found college life dull, but he graduated in two years and entered the law offices of Theophilus Parsons in Newburyport, Massachusetts. Parsons was an arch-Federalist and a member of the Essex Junto—a band of upper-

Congressman John Quincy Adams posed for daguerreotypist Philip Haas, ca. 1843. After leaving the White House in 1829, Adams became one of the most respected members of the House of Representatives.

Adams was a thirty-year-old bachelor when he went to London on a diplomatic mission and was smitten by the lovely Louisa Catherine Johnson, daughter of the United States consul. They married in the Anglican parish of All Hallows Barking on July 26, 1797. Engraving by G. F. Storm, after a painting by C. R. Lewis.

tion in Federalist newspapers, and the president was impressed. In 1794 George Washington dismissed the Adamses' reservations and appointed John Quincy minister to the Netherlands. During his three years at The Hague, Adams was twice called to London to help negotiate Jay's Treaty, a pact that was lopsided in favor of Great Britain. In London he met and courted Louisa Catherine Johnson, daughter of the Maryland-born American consul. Louisa, born and raised in Europe, had never seen the United States. They were married in an English parish church in July 1797, a few months after Adams's father had been inaugurated as the second president of the United States.

Fearing complaints of favoritism, the sensitive president wanted to appoint John Quincy minister to Prussia, but he hesitated. Finally, with some trepidation, Adams named his son to the post, but not before securing a strong endorsement from George Washington. Writing from Mount Vernon, Washington insisted that the president had no right to deny the country the services of John Quincy Adams just because he was an Adams, and predicted that he "will prove himself to be the ablest of all our diplomatic corps." The difficulty of the assignment was made plain when the couple reached Berlin. As recorded in Adams's diary, he and Louisa arrived at the gates to the city and were detained "by a dapper lieutenant who did not know, until one of his private soldiers explained to him, who the United States of America were." Although many of his duties were routine, Adams did manage to conclude a treaty of commerce and friendship, no small feat at a time when the United States was considered by most Europeans to be a shaky, second-rate power. Otherwise his Prussian stay, if uneventful, was regarded at home as successful.

After losing to Thomas Jefferson in the 1800 presidential election, John Adams decided to recall his son. Perhaps the elder Adams wanted to dramatize the cleavage between himself and his successor, or

crust New England lawyers and bankers—that played a powerful role in state politics. Passing the bar in 1790, Adams set up practice in Boston, though he had no intention of spending his life as a lawyer. Since his father was by then vice president of the United States, John Quincy worried about charges of nepotism and was overcautious about entering governmental service.

For four years John Quincy Adams was one of the most prolific political writers in America. Young Adams stoutly defended the Washington administra-

perhaps he wanted to spare Jefferson the embarrassment of having an Adams in his service; his motive has never been clearly defined. Certainly the Adams-Jefferson friendship had chilled during Adams's presidency. In any event, the young Adams returned to America in the autumn of 1801 and soon reopened his Boston law office.

In truth, a private law practice still held little appeal for Adams. But being an Adams meant that John Quincy belonged in public service, with a destiny as a statesman, not a politician, and as such he followed a carefully delineated set of rules—all of his own devising—for statesmanly conduct. It meant that membership in a political party was a convenience—nothing more—and that his being a Federalist would make him no more predictable than his election by a Federalist constituency would make him blindly faithful to its interests. In April 1802, forty-eight hours after he took his seat in the upper chamber of the Massachusetts legislature, the Federalists who had elected him began to question the wisdom of their choice, for Adams voted in favor of giving the pro-French Democratic-Republican minority a proportionate voice in that chamber. He pursued his independent ways as a United States senator between 1803 and 1808, voting for the Louisiana Purchase, which his party opposed, and for Jefferson's Embargo Act of 1807, although its passage was regarded as disastrous to New England commerce. A storm of criticism arose, straining Adams's Federalist ties. Even though he often voted with the Democratic-Republicans, he was not one of them: He bore no affection for Jefferson and accused him of taking credit for being an economizer when in fact his economic measures were wasteful of "national safety, of national honour, of national glory. . . ."

Under persistent attack from all sides, Adams noted in his diary that when independence is besieged, "The qualities of mind most peculiarly called for are firmness, perseverance, patience, coolness, and forbearance." Adams did not have to acquire these traits; he had inherited them. Reserved, moral, able to labor twice beyond ordinary human exhaustion, vain one day and self-abusive the next, self-righteous, irritable, possessed with a firmness of purpose fluctuating between virtuous determination and stubborn inflexibility—this was the Adams character, fused in the father, solidified in the son. Moreover, to even a greater extent than his father, John Quincy Adams was practically paranoid about the family name. It

---

BIOGRAPHICAL FACTS

BIRTH: Quincy, Mass., July 11, 1767

ANCESTRY: English

FATHER: John Adams; b. Quincy, Mass.,Oct. 30, 1735; d. Quincy, Mass., July 4, 1826

FATHER'S OCCUPATIONS: Lawyer, statesman; U.S. vice president; U.S. president

MOTHER: Abigail Smith Adams; b. Weymouth, Mass., Nov. 22, 1744; d. Quincy, Mass., Oct. 28, 1818

BROTHERS: Charles (1770–1800); Thomas Boylston (1772–1832)

SISTERS: Abigail Amelia (1765–1813); Susanna (1768–1770)

MARRIAGE: London, England, July 26, 1797

WIFE: Louisa Catherine Johnson; b. London, England, Feb. 12, 1775; d. Washington, D.C., May 14, 1852

CHILDREN: George Washington (1801–1829); John (1803–1834); Charles Francis (1807–1886); Louisa Catherine (1811–1812)

RELIGIOUS AFFILIATION: Unitarian

EDUCATION: Studied in Paris, Amsterdam, Leyden, and The Hague; Harvard (B.A., 1787); studied law with Theophilus Parsons (1788–1790)

OCCUPATION BEFORE PRESIDENCY: Lawyer; professor

PREPRESIDENTIAL OFFICES: Minister to the Netherlands; minister to Prussia; member of Massachusetts Senate; U.S. senator; minister to Russia; minister to Great Britain; secretary of state

AGE AT INAUGURATION: 57

OCCUPATIONS AFTER PRESIDENCY: Congressman; writer

DEATH: Washington, D.C., Feb. 23, 1848

PLACE OF BURIAL: First Unitarian Church, Quincy, Mass.

was inconceivable to him that anyone might oppose him on rational grounds; his enemies were out to get the Adamses, of that he was certain. Fortunately, he restricted most of his personal rantings to his diary, which often reads like a drama cast with the damned and set in hell. (In 1835, for example, he listed thirteen men, including a former ally or two, whose entire faculties, he said, were devoted to "base and dirty tricks to thwart my progress in life.")

After three years the Federalist-dominated Massachusetts legislature soured on Adams. The lawmakers symbolically censured him by electing a successor to his seat nine months in advance of the March 1809 expiration date. Adams immediately resigned in a huff, thereby ending his affiliation with the Federalist party. He retired to Cambridge, where three years earlier, in 1805, he had been appointed Boylston Professor of Rhetoric and Oratory at Harvard. Although he still yearned for a political career, his star was dim indeed. His record had offended most New England politicians, and his anti-British bias was not then widely shared in the environs of blue-blooded Boston. Like his father, he found himself a man without a party and without a political base; but his shrewd father had waited until he was president before failing to tow the party line. At forty-one, Adams believed he was without a future.

In 1809 President Madison rescued John Quincy Adams's political career by appointing him minister to Russia. Surprised and delighted, Adams arrived in St. Petersburg in October and soon became a friend and confidant to Czar Alexander I. Two years later he received word that the president had appointed him to the Supreme Court. The Adams name carried its magic, for the Senate had unanimously confirmed the appointment; but the conscientious Adams regarded himself as unfit for the judiciary and declined. No evidence exists to suggest that Adams regretted turning down the offer. However, he was eager to return to the United States.

The War of 1812 was being fought at home, and perhaps Adams felt out of touch with the conflagration's big events. But then the czar changed the political atmosphere by offering his good offices for a peace conference between England and the United States. President Madison jumped at the chance to end the war, and though nothing came of Czar Alexander's efforts, Adams was now beckoned for higher duty. In 1814 Madison asked him to leave Russia for Ghent, Belgium, where he and four other American commissioners were to try to negotiate a peace treaty with England. A treaty was signed on Christmas Eve, 1814, but only after seven miserable months had passed, and not before Adams's dislike of the British had been confirmed, nor before Adams had indulged in a shouting match with fellow emissary Henry Clay.

Adams was now a seasoned diplomat, and President Madison offered Adams the minister's post at the Court of St. James. The wisdom of appointing an Anglophobic diplomat to represent the United States in London immediately after a British-American conflict may be questioned, but Adams went. He had no more success with the British than his father had had following the Revolution. In the afterglow of the Congress of Vienna, Great Britain was busy making the Atlantic into an English lake, so Adams's duties were again rather routine. On April 16, 1817, he received glorious news from Washington. He was ordered to sail home as soon as possible. President James Monroe had appointed him secretary of state.

Monroe's appointment of Adams was a brilliant stroke, as the overall record of his administration proves. Among Adams's triumphs was the Adams-Onís Treaty of 1819 that added Spanish Florida to the United States and laid out the western boundaries of the Louisiana Purchase. It was Adams who settled the Canada–United States border controversy in negotiations with England, and it was probably Adams's firmness that convinced the Russians to abandon their plans to penetrate the Pacific coast of North America. Most notably, when the president included in a State of the Union message the key phrase that became the Monroe Doctrine, it was Adams's policy, word for word. While there have been a number of presidents who have taken exclusive control of policy-making, employing their cabinet members merely as agents or pawns, Monroe was one who believed in delegating responsibility.

Monroe's skill was that of an able administrator; and as such he excelled in choosing, rejecting, and distilling various contributions in order to assemble his own, no less personal, policy. The prevailing issue of his two terms was national expansion, which shaped all the smaller issues, domestic and foreign, and which made the State Department what it had not been before: a hub around which auxilliary issues (such as statehood for territories) revolved. President Monroe was fortunate in having Adams as secretary of state, and he knew it. That Monroe chose to make Adams's policies his own indicates no lack of imagination but rather bespeaks his sound executive judgment.

While Adams had been a capable diplomat, his abruptness had prevented him from becoming a great one. Now, as a statesman, Adams channeled his articulateness, inexhaustible energy, and creative intellect to his new responsibilities, and thanks to the paternal Monroe, who discreetly edited the cantankerousness from Adams's papers, he became a superb, perhaps matchless, secretary of state. His day began at five in the morning and seldom ended before eleven at night, and the operations of his department went so smoothly that his labors were taken for granted. When Congress asked him to prepare a report on weights and measures, he agreed and produced a lengthy treatise (largely ignored in America, but applauded abroad) which is to this day widely regarded as one of the definitive expositions of the subject. Despite his feelings toward the British, his objectivity

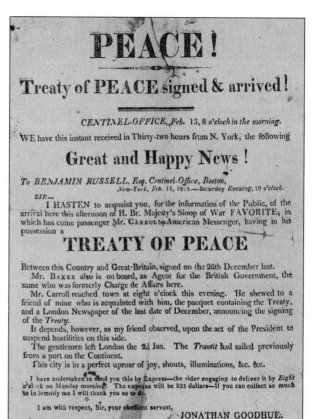

The end of the War of 1812 inspired shouts of joy from the people of Portsmouth, New Hampshire, among others, as reported in the broadside above. Adams's diplomatic skills helped the American delegation at Ghent negotiate a favorable treaty with Great Britain that ended the War of 1812 as a standoff, with no territory lost and national pride boosted.

took priority over his prejudice, and he forged a series of alliances with England that planted once and for all the seeds of lasting friendship.

Adams wanted to be president, and though he was the most distinguished member of the Monroe cabinet, his successes were somewhat neutralized by his lack of friends and inadequate organizational backing. (Martin Van Buren later blamed President Mon-

happy to see the Bank of the United States rechartered; but the bank was not beloved by the farmers and merchants who had to worry about interest rates and mortgage payments. Thus there was only one party in 1824—the Democratic-Republican—and a congressional caucus gave the presidential nomination to Secretary of the Treasury William H. Crawford of Georgia. This was not a popular choice in most states, and by Election Day there were three other candidates: Senator Henry Clay, General Andrew Jackson, and John Quincy Adams.

A combination of ex-Federalists and lukewarm Democratic-Republicans gave Adams his nomination from a New England that had long forgiven him and had come to view him as the man who would save the nation from the rabble-rousing "Old Hickory." Secretary of War John C. Calhoun, originally a presidential candidate, accepted the vice presidential nomination when Old Hickory's managers offered it to him, and he became a supporter of Jackson. Almost by default, Calhoun won his race for the second spot.

But none of the presidential candidates received a majority of electoral votes, so the election was placed in the hands of the House of Representatives. Because Jackson had led the balloting with 99 votes to Adams's 84, and had received over 40,000 more popular votes, his supporters claimed the House had no choice but to declare for the general. Clay, however, had been eliminated, finishing last with 37 votes. Crawford was out of the running, despite a smattering of votes, for his chances were ruined when he had suffered a paralytic stroke during the campaign. The election hinged on Clay's instructions to his small but devoted band of enthusiasts. After what must have been considerable soul-searching on Clay's part, he endorsed his old adversary, Adams, who soon emerged triumphant. The decision was not made official until three weeks before the inauguration.

When Adams announced that he had appointed

roe for not picking a successor, as Jefferson and Madison had done. Senator Van Buren thought that Monroe's "fusion policy" was tearing the old-time Jeffersonian political alliances into shreds. In short, Van Buren saw Monroe's politics as just shy of being Federalist in tone.)

The Federalists had bumbled their way into extinction by kowtowing to wealthy mercantile and banking interests. For example, the Federalists were

Henry Clay as his secretary of state, the Jackson-Calhoun forces cried foul. According to a Jacksonian newspaper, there had obviously been "a corrupt bargain." In Tennessee, Jackson's home state, the legislature passed a resolution of condemnation: "Mr. Adams desired the office of President; he went into the combination without it, and came out with it. Mr. Clay desired that of Secretary of State; he went into the combination without it, and came out with it." No evidence, then or since, has ever clarified the matter one way or the other; but even if there had been a deal, Clay had acted from conviction because he could have made the same arrangement with any candidate, and Adams, not one to rationalize, made it clear in his diary and personal correspondence that he thought Clay the best man for the job. Nevertheless, the charge of corruption echoed throughout the Adams administration, branding it.

What made the circumstances of Adams's presidency doubly unfortunate for American history was the potential for greatness that the man exhibited. His character, capacity for work, statesmanship, and intellect were well known; but in his first message to Congress, Adams revealed that he also had vision. Now that the vast expansion of the Monroe years had slowed and questionable border definitions were settled for the time being, Adams directed himself to the internal improvement of the country. His progressive program called for huge federal expenditures to establish an interstate network of roads and canals, a department of the interior to regulate use of natural resources, expeditions to map the country, a naval academy, a series of astronomical observatories, and government aid to education. Each provision, of course, did eventually become a reality, but not during the Adams administration.

The most vehement opposition came from the Jacksonians, who claimed that the president's plans placed too much power in the grip of the federal government. Yet, if passed, the program would actually have favored the common people to whom the Jacksonians expressed devotion. Development of the land and education of the people would have been expedited, thus providing "grassroots" Americans with the economic and intellectual strength to fight the Eastern, urban, big-money powers the Jacksonians so despised. Unfortunately, as the historian Samuel Eliot Morison points out, the Jacksonians, however significant their political accomplishments, did not always favor universal education. They sought support from

WILLIAM H. CRAWFORD

It is probable that only a series of paralyzing strokes in 1823 kept William Crawford from becoming the sixth president of the United States. The tall, handsome, engaging Southerner had served in the Senate since 1807 and had made many influential friends in Washington, yet he remained the maverick conservative he had been in the Georgia legislature. Basically a states' righter, he did advocate a moderate protective tariff and favored rechartering the Bank of the United States. He was minister to France from 1813 to 1815; later, during Madison's second term as chief executive, he was secretary of war and then of the treasury. Declining to run for president in 1816, he was Monroe's secretary of the treasury for eight years, working effectively for more roads and canals. His ambition and influence were strong, and he knew the power of patronage: "Crawford's Act" of 1820 limited the tenures of minor federal appointees to four years. In the free-for-all to succeed President Monroe, John Quincy Adams, Henry Clay, and Andrew Jackson all knew they had to beat Crawford, who had the support of Van Buren, Madison, and Jefferson. Then Crawford was stricken, and his nomination by a small congressional caucus was merely a gesture of respect and friendship. Winning only 41 electoral votes, he ran a distant third in the race. Crawford then faded from national prominence. He died in 1834.

Death of Capt. Ferrer, the Captain of the Amistad, July, 1839.

Don Jose Ruiz and Don Pedro Montez, of the Island of Cuba, having purchased fifty-three slaves at Havana, recently imported from Africa, put them on board the Amistad, Capt. Ferrer, in order to transport them to Principe, another port on the Island of Cuba. After being out from Havana about four days, the African captives on board, in order to obtain their freedom, and return to Africa, armed themselves with cane knives, and rose upon the Captain and crew of the vessel. Capt. Ferrer and the cook of the vessel were killed; two of the crew escaped; Ruiz and Montez were made prisoners.

John Warner's 1840 engraving captures the drama of the uprising on the slave transport *Amistad*. Adams, the only president to serve in the House of Repesentatives after his term as chief executive, became a spokesman for the antislavery movement in the House of Representatives and was involved in the legal battle following the mutiny that led to the capture of the infamous *Amistad*.

whatever sources were available, and it was always easier to appeal to the people's passions than to their minds. The rise of the Jacksonians coincided with the rise of bigotry in the United States.

On the other hand, the anti-Jacksonians, who were beginning to call themselves National Republicans, made no bones about their desire to limit suffrage to the moneyed and the educated. But, unlike the more aristocratic and now all-but-extinct Federalists, the National Republicans wanted that moneyed and educated class to eventually embrace all Americans. They opposed slavery and rallied behind President Adams's conscience-stricken appeal for justice for the American Indian. Denouncing the "crying sins for which we are answerable before a higher jurisdiction," Adams wanted to provide the Indians with territory in the West and guarantee their rights there. But the more popular attitude was reflected in Jackson's subsequent treatment of the Indians in Florida—a blend of eviction and extermination—and Congress defeated the Adams plea. On issue after issue, the National Republican and Jacksonian fac-

tions drifted further apart, and two-party politics returned to the nation.

Significantly, during Adams's first year in office the Erie Canal was completed. The canal linked the Great Lakes to the East Coast, funneling grain, whiskey, and other farm produce into the New York market. The canal's success touched off a wave of canal building. Instead of helping Adams, however, the canal became a political hot potato, because Senator Martin Van Buren and his friends insisted the venture proved that states did not need federal assistance to build roads or canals. Henry Clay, now secretary of state, had long advocated federal aid for a national highway linking Eastern markets with Western commerce. A strict constructionist, Van Buren had one more reason to oppose Adams: Van Buren wanted to rebuild the old two-party system, which he believed Monroe had almost destroyed.

Adams wanted no part of it. He did not like partisan politics; he would not stoop to patronage; he would not make appointments on the basis of party affiliation. But Van Buren and other professional politicians reasoned that the whole point of politics is power—and power meant jobs for friends. Then, when the partisan, highly regional issue of tariffs came up, Adams refused to take a stand, announcing that he would abide by the decision of Congress. Jackson's friends in Congress introduced a tariff bill (the Tariff of Abominations), the purpose of which is still disputed by scholars. To the surprise of many, including Van Buren, the bill narrowly passed and was placed on the president's desk. Adams had no alternative but to sign, thereby losing what support he had in the South. Still, every previous president but one had won reelection, and in 1828 Adams was a candidate once again. Jackson's friends were elated, seeing the tariff as Adams's albatross.

In Adams's favor were the progress made on the Chesapeake and Ohio Canal (one improvement for which Adams had been able to secure federal funds), a couple of commercial agreements with European countries, and the establishment of Pan-American rapport, as well as his character (if it could withstand the "corrupt bargain" charge). Against Adams were the corruption charges, his reputation for being anti-slavery and pro-Indian, a domestic program that was generally regarded as idiotic, a tariff that was indisputably idiotic, and an opponent who was the most popular military hero in America since George Washington—and who was backed by an efficient machine that had been campaigning for four years.

With Van Buren pulling the strings, the Democrats held the first presidential nominating convention in Baltimore and emerged with a Jackson-Calhoun ticket. The feeble National Republican ticket was labeled as a pseudo-Federalist ploy by the well-organized Democrats and their powerful allies in the press. Jackson won overwhelmingly in the popular vote and carried the day, 178 electoral votes to 83 for Adams. Hurt and disappointed, Adams sulked out of the White House on the day of inauguration without greeting the victorious general. Thus, without dignity or magnanimity, Adams retreated from the office that had been a bed of thorns almost from his own inaugural day.

Though sixty-one at the end of his term, Adams soon began his career anew as the only former president ever to run for and win a seat in the House of Representatives. For the last eighteen years of his life, Congressman Adams of Massachusetts fought the "gag rule" that shelved antislavery petitions and became known as "Old Man Eloquent." Always antislavery, Adams conducted a long, successful campaign to restore debate on abolition petitions. Moreover, on the grounds that statehood would extend slavery, he opposed annexation of Texas. He was one of the few public figures who dared to call the 1846 conflict with Mexico "a most unrighteous war." Instrumental in the establishment of the Smithsonian Institution, he also pressed for government provisions to make education available to all Americans. When the first observatory in the United States was finally established in 1843, the congressman was invited to lay the cornerstone on the hill site near Cincinnati that had been named Mount Adams.

In 1846 Adams suffered a paralytic stroke. Four months later he returned to the House, weak and with his speech impaired, and as he walked—with help—to his desk, the whole chamber rose and stood in homage. At that desk on February 21, 1848, he had another stroke. He was carried to the Speaker's Room, where he remained until he died two days later. He regained consciousness only once. "Thank the officers of the House," he said. "This is the last of earth. I am content."

—DAVID JACOBS, *revised by* ROBERT A. RUTLAND

ANDREW JACKSON

OLD HICKORY

Nothing like it had ever happened in Washington. Thousands descended on the nation's capital for days, filling every hotel and sleeping wherever there was a flat place—under a billiard table, or in hayracks at the livery stables. "I have never seen such a crowd before," said Daniel Webster. "Persons have come five hundred miles to see General Jackson, and they really seem to think that the country has been rescued from some dreadful danger."

The crowds had come to see "the People's President" inaugurated. Finally the great day arrived: March 4, 1829. After hiding behind clouds from early dawn, the sun broke through and warmed the people who clogged the streets and were packed onto every terrace, portico, and balcony along Pennsylvania Avenue.

At mid-morning the tall, sixty-one-year-old general departed from Gadsby's Tavern, where he had been staying. Lads perched on nearby window sills caught sight of him and called out excitedly; cannons boomed, and a cheer rose up and resounded down the avenue. As he advanced toward the Capitol, the ailing hero was slowed by the press of the crowd, but he did not seem to mind. Jackson paused to shake the hand of every well-wisher.

As the journalist Anne Royall notes, Andrew Jackson was the most plainly dressed man at the inaugural ceremonies. In deep mourning for his wife, who had died less than three months earlier, the president-elect was attired all in black. He was "thin and pale . . . his hair . . . almost white, and his countenance was melancholy." When he delivered his address, he spoke stiffly and softly, and the pages of the manuscript were seen to tremble in his hand as he turned them. Just as solemn was the Federalist chief justice, John Marshall, who must have regarded with extreme distaste the assignment of administering the presidential oath of office to Jackson, the unconvicted crack shot who had killed one man and wounded

a few others. But this was no time to dwell on the past—the American people had spoken.

As their new president rode horseback to the White House, the crowd followed, sweeping down the avenue, bursting past startled doormen into the executive mansion, fighting, scrambling, elbowing, scratching all the while. In the East Room, the mob hurled itself at the refreshments; to the sound of crystal breaking and china smashing, women fainted, fights erupted—noses were bloodied.

The riot was no surprise to Jackson's opponents. Throughout the decade preceding the election of 1828, as one state after another eliminated property-ownership qualifications for voting, the snowballing power of the common man had placed fear in the hearts of the American upper class. Beginning in 1824 Jackson and his supporters rallied the masses behind their cause, casting President John Quincy Adams and his administration in the role of aristocratic crooks. They captured the presidency with relative ease in 1828.

The rejected political establishment—the ousted National Republicans—went numb: Secretary of State Henry Clay spent most of the winter at home, lying on his couch under a black cape, as though in mourning. Outgoing President Adams waited until his last hours, then surrendered the White House without a word to his successor and stole away from Washington the night before the inauguration.

If any of Jackson's opponents considered the possibility that the people might be something more than a merciless mob, the tempestuous inaugural reception dispelled their doubts. "The country," said Congressman John Randolph, "is ruined past redemption."

The country was not ruined, of course, but the political scenery had changed. Under the leadership of four Virginia aristocrats and the two Adamses, American farmers, artisans, mechanics, and merchants had prospered and blended into an ever-growing middle class. By 1828 the nation was theirs, and they declared

A detail of the celebrated portrait of President Jackson painted by Ralph E. W. Earl in 1833.

BIRTH: The Waxhaws, S.C., Mar. 15, 1767
ANCESTRY: Scotch-Irish
FATHER: Andrew Jackson; b. Carrickfergus, Antrim,
    Ireland; d. The Waxhaws, S.C.; Mar. 1, 1767
FATHER'S OCCUPATIONS: Linen weaver; farmer
MOTHER: Elizabeth Hutchinson Jackson;
    b. Carrickfergus, Antrim, Ireland;
    d. Charleston, S.C., 1781.
BROTHERS: Hugh (1762–1780); Robert (1765–1780)
MARRIAGE: Natchez, Miss., Aug. 1, 1791;
    second ceremony: Nashville, Tenn., Jan. 17, 1794
WIFE: Rachel Donelson Robards; b. Halifax County, Va.,
    June 15, 1767; d. Nashville, Tenn., Dec. 22, 1828
CHILD: Andrew Jackson, Jr. (adopted) (1808–1865)
RELIGIOUS AFFILIATION: Presbyterian
EDUCATION: Attended public schools; studied law in
    Salisbury, N.C.
OCCUPATION BEFORE PRESIDENCY: Lawyer
MILITARY SERVICE: Judge adocate general of Davidson
    County militia (ca. 1791); maj. gen. of Tennessee
    militia (1802–1812); maj. gen. of U.S. Army
    (1814–1821)
PREPRESIDENTIAL OFFICES: Attorney general of Western
    District of North Carolina; delegate to Tennessee State
    Constitutional Convention; U.S. congressman; U.S.
    senator; Tennessee Supreme Court judge; governor of
    Florida Territory
AGE AT INAUGURATION: 61
OCCUPATION AFTER PRESIDENCY: Retired
DEATH: Nashville, Tenn., June 8, 1845
PLACE OF BURIAL: The Hermitage, Nashville, Tenn.

return to Jeffersonian principles, they now called themselves Democrats and welcomed citizens of all stripes to join their ranks.

Andrew Jackson won the people's support for a variety of reasons, but perhaps most significantly because he embodied what was then, and what would remain long after, the American dream. Born poor in the near-wilderness, he had forged success largely on his own, by his strength, his iron will, his exertions and convictions. The people placed him alongside George Washington in their affections—but there was a difference. While Washington was a gentleman-hero, venerated for his devotion to the common cause, Jackson was one of them, a self-made, unpretentious, and confident American citizen.

Jackson was born in the Waxhaws, a wooded frontier region on the North and South Carolina border, on March 15, 1767. He never knew his father; two weeks before the birth of his third son, the Irish immigrant lifted a heavy log, ruptured a vital organ, and died. Andrew's brothers, Hugh and Robert, and an uncle in South Carolina provided him with a degree of the companionship and guidance his father might have offered. The boy was no scholar, but by the age of five he had been responsive enough to his erratic education to know his ABCs, to read, and when eight, to write.

Jackson grew tall and agile, and as a blue-eyed, freckle-faced teenager with a thatch of hair as unruly as his hair-trigger temper, he would fight under the least provocation.

When the Revolution came to the Waxhaws in 1780, the Jackson boys joined up. Only Hugh was old enough to be a soldier, and he was killed in battle. Andrew, at thirteen, was a mounted orderly, a carrier of messages, but he did participate in an occasional skirmish. Following one encounter, he and Robert, who was sixteen, were taken prisoner. When Andrew refused a British officer's order to clean his boots, the officer slashed Jackson with a saber, cutting

their ownership official by electing Andrew Jackson to the presidency. In the spirit of the new America, Jackson changed the office, expanding its scope and power, and reinterpreting its responsibilities. Jackson and his supporters also drastically changed the course of American history by inventing the political convention as a way of nominating presidential candidates. They also finished off the last of the old-line Federalists, befuddled the discredited National Republicans, and christened their party anew. Avowing their plan to

his left arm to the bone and leaving a gash on his head. For good measure, he slashed Robert, too. During a subsequent forty-mile march to a military prison, the Jacksons' wounds were untended, and the boys contracted smallpox. Presently their mother, Elizabeth Jackson, appeared and persuaded the British commander to release her ailing sons into her custody. Drenched by rain throughout the long walk home, both boys became delirious. Robert died, but Andrew was saved by his incredible stamina.

Her one surviving son on the mend, Mrs. Jackson set out for Charleston Harbor, where two other Jackson relatives lay feverish and in need of nursing aboard a British prison ship. Before long, Andrew received a bundle containing his mother's clothes and a note informing him that she had been buried with other plague victims in an unmarked grave. "I felt utterly alone," Jackson later recalled.

To the people who remembered him, Andrew Jackson emerged from his loneliness "the most roaring, rollicking, game-cocking, horse-racing, card-playing, mischievous fellow . . . the head of rowdies hereabouts." But Jackson's wildness was not shiftlessness, for he was also extraordinarily ambitious. Shortly after his mother's death, he traveled to Salisbury, North Carolina, where he began reading legal treatises and serving as a law clerk. In 1788, after completing his studies, he accompanied his friend John McNairy to the Western District of North Carolina (now Tennessee). McNairy had been elected superior court judge for the district, and Jackson went along as public prosecutor.

The Western District was accessible only by an arduous trip through what had recently been Indian country. On the Cumberland River, 180 miles beyond the frontier line, was the settlement of Nashville, where for a time settlers lived in blockhouses to protect themselves from attacks by hostile Indians. It was a developing region, an ideal arena for a young, inexperienced, but eager attorney.

Jackson became the first president to have "woman troubles." In the frontier village, Andrew Jackson moved into the blockhouse of the Widow Donelson, whose daughter, Rachel Robards, was separated from her husband, Lewis. Rachel's beauty attracted the attentions of many men, and Lewis Robards was jealous. He left her, but later returned to attempt a reconciliation and was openly suspicious of Andrew Jackson. Jackson reacted by challenging Robards to a duel; the husband refused, and Jackson moved out of the blockhouse. Robards and Rachel eventually returned together to Kentucky, but in 1790 Mrs. Donelson informed Jackson that her daughter again wished to leave her husband. Jackson rode to Kentucky to pick up Rachel and escort her back to the Cumberland Valley. Alleging misconduct between his

Jackson's devotion to his beloved wife, Rachel, made him into a duelist and resulted in the death of one of her detractors. After the 1806 shoot-out, the future president carried a bullet in his chest for the rest of his life. Water color on ivory, ca. 1831, by Louisa Catherine Strobel.

wife and Jackson, Robards petitioned the Virginia legislature for a bill of divorce. (Kentucky was still a part of Virginia in 1790, so a divorce had to be approved by the Virginia General Assembly. It was rare that the legislature acted, unless a special case was made.) Although this was only the first step in a long legal process, Robards encouraged circulation of a rumor that the divorce was final. In August 1791 Jackson and Rachel Robards were married.

The divorce would not be final until two years later, but Jackson believed he was legally married and returned to Nashville with his bride. As a public prosecutor Jackson had been vigorous—in thirty days he had enforced seventy writs of execution—and conservative, generally siding with creditors against debtors. In his spare time, he speculated in land, slaves, and horses, and in that backwoods community he became a man of substance. He satisfied an interest in the military by becoming judge advocate of the county militia, and continued to nurse his hatred of the English and Indians. Jackson was, in sum, the epitome of a border man-on-the-make.

In December 1793 Jackson learned that his wife had been legally divorced for only three months. At first he refused to consider remarriage: His pride would not allow him to accept the obvious implication, but he was persuaded to reconsider. The second ceremony took place in January 1794. Nobody dared snicker or suggest that anything unusual had occurred.

In June of 1796 the territory became the state of Tennessee—a name Jackson reputedly gave it—and the rising young attorney was elected, unopposed, to the United States House of Representatives. Albert Gallatin saw him in the House chamber, and described him as "a tall, lanky, uncouth-looking personage [wearing his hair in a] queue down his back tied with an eel skin." In his one term, Jackson managed to acquire for the Tennessee militia almost twenty-three thousand dollars as payment for services in an Indian raid despite the probability that it violated the orders of the federal government. He also distinguished himself by stubbornly refusing to vote for the farewell tribute Congress wanted to tender George Washington. (Jackson disapproved of Jay's Treaty and thought Washington's liberal Indian policy was misguided.) Following his term in the House and a year in the Senate, he resigned his seat to return to Tennessee, for he had been appointed to the superior court of the state.

Although Jackson now had position and influence, he had not lost his "roaring, rollicking" tendencies. Back in Tennessee, where he was vulnerable to comments regarding his wife and marriage, he showed his contempt for gossip and innuendo. In 1806 Jackson challenged Nashville resident Charles Dickinson to a duel after he had twice alluded to Rachel's matrimonial record. Jackson took his enemy's shot in the chest, then straightened and aimed. Dickinson, confident of his own aim, staggered back in horror, thinking he had missed; and under the rules (Jackson had not yet fired) he had to return to the mark. Standing with his arms crossed, Dickinson took Jackson's .70-caliber ball in the groin and died a slow, agonizing death. So close was Dickinson's bullet to Jackson's heart that it could not be removed, and Jackson carried it, frequently in pain, for the rest of his life. Recalling the incident, Jackson said, "I should have hit him, if he had shot me through the brain." The story grew as it was repeated, and did nothing to harm Jackson's reputation.

Perhaps Jackson's most famous brawl was one with the Benton brothers, Jesse and Thomas Hart (later a political ally). Tom Benton had criticized Jackson's role as second for a friend in a duel. One day in 1813 Jackson arrived in Nashville, spotted Benton, and armed with a horsewhip, pursued him into a hotel to teach him a lesson. During the brawl that followed, Jackson was wounded. His shoulder was shattered by a bullet, but Jackson refused to have his arm amputated. Although a long time in healing, the arm was saved.

Jackson's set-to with the Bentons took place during

Even though the Battle of New Orleans was fought after the peace treaty had formally ended the War of 1812, Jackson's motley army gave the British troops a mauling that catapulted the victorious general into the national limelight. Jackson became the first "war hero" president, and for generations the anniversary of his January 8, 1815, victory was celebrated. Kurz and Allison lithograph, ca. 1890.

the War of 1812, in which the judge, despite his martial spirit and his credentials (he was then a major general in the United States Volunteers), had participated only briefly. In 1812 Jackson had organized a division and brought it down to Natchez, Mississippi, to fight the British, but as soon as he arrived, an order came from Washington to disband—eight hundred miles from home, without supplies or rations. Jackson flatly refused, grumbling about "the wicked machinations" of politicians, and resolved to take the two thousand men home at his own expense. During the difficult journey, one soldier remarked that Jackson was "tough as hickory." Soon the troops were referring to him as Old Hickory, and the name stuck.

In 1813 Old Hickory rose from his bed—still shaky from the wounds inflicted on him by Benton—to fight the Creek Indians. The campaign lasted into 1814 and proved to the leaders in Washington that Jackson had tactical skills that could not be ignored. After his victory, however, Jackson imposed on the Creeks a treaty so harsh that the federal government subsequently repudiated much of it. His hostility toward Indians was approved by his neigh-

bors but pained the Eastern establishment. When the major theater of war shifted south in 1814, the defense of New Orleans fell to him.

First—and without official authorization—Jackson led his men into Spanish Florida and drove the British from Pensacola, which he "liberated" because he felt it should be American (which it soon became). Then he headed for New Orleans, where he tried to block off the six major water routes through the Mississippi Delta. Hearing, however, that the British had already taken one, Lake Borgne, and were pressing inland within eight miles of the town, Jackson reportedly sprang up, slapped his hand down on a table, and cried, "By the Eternal, they shall not sleep on our soil!" His counterattack that night is credited by many military historians as being one of the most lopsided victories in history.

Twenty-four hundred British troops had halted their march to await the arrival of reinforcements, another 2,400 men. While they waited, Jackson sent the schooner *Carolina* downstream to shell the British; then he attacked. The following morning, with the enemy thrown off balance by the surprise assault, Jackson retired to defensive positions at the Rodriguez Canal. Then he assembled his men and increased his numbers in preparation for the assault he knew would soon come. To his unit of Kentucky and Tennessee frontiersmen he added regulars and irregulars—Creole dandies, free Negroes, a handful of Choctaw braves, and Jean Lafitte and his pirate crew.

On January 8, 1815, the British regulars—"the conquerors of the conquerors of Europe"—marched into a torrential cross fire. Unable to seize the artillery batteries, which they had planned to turn against the Americans, they found huge chunks blasted from their evenly spaced ranks. The battleground, a flat field overgrown with cane stubble, offered no place to hide. A withering fire broke the frontal attack, and men who had stood firm facing Napoleon now broke ranks and retreated in haste. After the battle, more than five hundred British troops rose from the heaped mounds of dead comrades to come forward as prisoners. "I never had so grand and awful an idea of the resurrection," said General Jackson. The American casualties were minimal: 71 killed, wounded, or missing; the British combined casualties numbered 2,037. The general's victory electrified the nation, even though it was fought after the Treaty of Ghent had been signed, two weeks earlier.

After the war, Andrew Jackson solidified his new national eminence by keeping active in the Florida area, where Americans saw opportunities to expand. The Spanish had had much difficulty controlling East Florida, a locale of considerable privateering in which many rebels claimed to represent an assortment of governments. Aided by unauthorized British soldiers, Seminole and Creek tribesmen raided along the Georgia border; fugitive slaves sought sanctuary there until American troops moved deeper into Florida. As the Indians retaliated, President Monroe ordered Jackson to lead troops against them but instructed him not to attack those who retreated into Spanish forts. Jackson interpreted his orders liberally; he

seized the town of St. Marks, burned a Seminole village, and executed two British subjects he claimed were aiding the Indians. In May 1818 he advanced on Pensacola and deposed the Spanish governor, installing in his place one of his own officers.

Amid Spanish protests, President Monroe denied ever giving Jackson permission to enter the Spanish colony. Eventually evidence came to light—a letter from Secretary of War Calhoun to the governor of Alabama—to support Jackson's claim that he had been "vested with full power to conduct the war as he may think best." In any case, despite the misgivings of some in Washington, Jackson's high-handed tactics were approved by most Americans in the South and West. After the contretemps was over, Monroe appointed Jackson governor of the Florida Territory, which had been officially ceded by Spain in 1819. Jackson served only four months and then returned to Nashville, where he was called on by a steady stream of politicians who saw in him a man of action capable of attracting voters. They wanted him to be president of the United States.

Jackson was not immediately amenable to the idea. "Do they think," he asked, "that I am such a damned fool as to think myself fit for President of the United States? No, sir; I know what I am fit for. I can command a body of men in a rough way; but I am not fit to be President."

There were at least two good reasons why Jackson balked. First, Rachel would have preferred that he did not run for president. Each of her husband's public services sent him away from his plantation and left her bereaved, anxiously awaiting his return. And second, Jackson's health was in a perilous state. "He is not a well man and never will be unless they allow him to rest," wrote Rachel to her niece. "In the thirty years of our wedded life . . . he has not spent one-fourth of his days under his own roof." But Jackson's ability to ignore the frailty of his body and to overcome his various infirmities was remarkable.

By 1822, despite his wife's misgivings, the general was reconciled to the role of undeclared candidate. Taking advice from Senator John Henry Eaton of Tennessee, he refused Monroe's offer of a ministerial appointment, but, against Jackson's wishes, he was elected senator. Jackson liked power, and he sniffed the scent of unlimited power, so he went to Washington and took his seat in the Senate.

The election year 1824 was a year of transition in the United States. Property qualifications for voting were eliminated in some states but retained in others; electors were chosen here by state legislators, there by districts, elsewhere by precincts or counties. All the candidates were Jeffersonian Republicans, or pretended to be. John Quincy Adams was expected to take the urban Northeast and share the old Federalist vote with William H. Crawford, who would be strong in the South. The new popular vote and the Western vote were sought by Henry Clay and Andrew Jackson. The situation was confused by President Monroe's unwillingness to choose a presidential successor from within his cabinet, thus breaking the tradition established by Jefferson and Madison.

After a bitter campaign marked by much switching and name-calling, the electoral college count gave Jackson 99 votes, Adams 84, Crawford 41, and Clay 37. In the absence of a majority, the election was thrown into the House, where members voted by states and thirteen constituted a majority. Clay distrusted Jackson and gave his support to Adams; when New York defected from Jackson, Adams won. Jackson resigned his Senate seat and immediately began the campaign to win in 1828.

Among the many politicians who had switched to Jackson was the New York senator, Martin Van Buren. For years Van Buren had smarted under the Monroe and Adams administrations, which he claimed had revoked Jeffersonian principles and had failed to understand that the point of politics is power. Power, to Van Buren and his friends, meant jobs for the party faithful, contracts for party contributors, and a multitude of favors for fellow Democratic-Republicans. When his friend William Crawford came in poorly in the 1824 race, Van Buren looked over the field and ultimately cast his lot with Jackson.

A clever politician, Van Buren moved Adams's critics toward a new conception of presidential politics. The congressional caucus he had once led was dropped in favor of party nominating conventions. The National Republican label, which President Adams and his cabinet bore, was traduced, and Jackson's men became "Democrats" without any hyphens. With Van Buren pulling the strings, Jackson's delegates met in Baltimore and picked a ticket that included John C. Calhoun as the holdover vice president.

As the 1828 campaign heated up, the rhetoric became ludicrous and excessively dirty. Colonel Charles Hammond, editor of the Cincinnati *Gazette* and a crony of Henry Clay, asked in a pamphlet, "Ought a convicted adulteress and her paramour husband to be placed in the highest offices of this free and christian land?" As a presidential candidate, Jackson could not demand a duel but he fervently vowed that "a day of retribution . . . [for] Mr. Clay and his tool Colonel Hammond must arrive. . . ." The Coffin Handbill was a widely circulated pamphlet detailing through words and pictures the deaths of John Woods (a mutineer Jackson had executed during the Creek War) and six Tennessee militiamen executed in Alabama. The handbill also showed Jackson sticking a sword into the neck of an innocent pedestrian.

Despite such scurrilous invectives, the Adams-Clay forces were on the defensive from the start. Jackson had newspaper allies, too, including the energetic Kentucky editor Amos Kendall, and they gave as good as they got. Months before the balloting ended, it was clear that the common man was in charge now, and he wanted Jackson. The general was headed for the White House with a solid victory in the electoral college of 178 votes to 83 for Adams. The torchlight

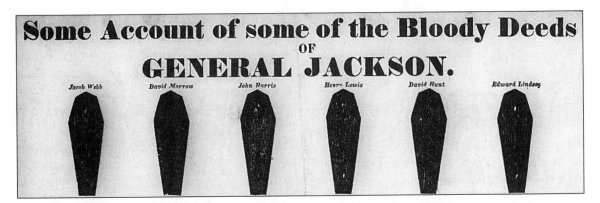

Some Account of some of the Bloody Deeds
OF
GENERAL JACKSON.

Jacob Webb   David Morrow   John Harris   Henry Lewis   David Hunt   Edward Lindsey

Republican editor John Binns created this 1828 handbill to publicize Jackson's record as a duelist and "blood-thirsty" commander. Not only had Jackson killed a man in a duel, he had ordered deserting soldiers in his militia command shot. Despite the candidate's scandalous reputation, the voters decided they wanted a bold man in the White House.

parades and the mudslinging were over. Now Old Hickory would be in charge.

However, the saddened widower could not forget his beloved Rachel, who had died three months earlier. The likely outcome of the election was fairly obvious when she became ill on December 17, 1828, and Mrs. Jackson had been far from thrilled at the prospect of becoming first lady. On the night of December 22 she told her maid that she would "rather be a door-keeper in the house of God than to live in that palace [the White House]." Twenty minutes later, General Jackson, in the adjoining room, heard her say, "I am fainting." He rushed to her, lifted her to the bed, and felt the convulsion of her muscles as her life ended. Jackson wept bitterly at the funeral. He spoke of "those vile wretches" who had destroyed his "dear saint." Out loud he cried, "May God Almighty forgive her murderers, as I know she forgave them. I never can."

So Andrew Jackson arrived in Washington, and the American republic was poised to absorb the Jacksonian brand of democracy. The nation's voters placed all their trust in an aging, ill, and mournful man who was, they thought, a symbol of themselves. To the factions he had defeated, Old Hickory was a radical; yet

in political service he had tended to be conservative. In truth, no one knew what sort of president Andrew Jackson would be. "My opinion is," wrote Daniel Webster, "that when he comes he will bring a breeze with him. Which way it will blow, I cannot tell."

Senator William Marcy of New York was not vague about his expectations. Marcy had once commented that the politicians of his state "see nothing wrong in the rule that to the victor belong the spoils," and he was not joking. The "loaves and fishes" of office, so dear to Marcy and Van Buren, were about to be distributed to loyal Jacksonians. Rotation in office was nothing new—Thomas Jefferson had removed 10 percent of the officials in John Adams's administration when he took office. Madison, Monroe, and Adams had not indulged in wholesale firings of Federalist officeholders. Still, the phrase "spoils system" had a negative ring to it. When during his first eighteen months in office Jackson had replaced about the same percentage of appointees as Jefferson, his opponents yelled that he had "introduced corruption into the central government."

Unashamedly, Jackson never denied employing far more Democrats than Whigs. Rotation in office, he explained, broke up an entrenched bureaucracy and prevented government from becoming a continuous "engine for the support of the few at the expense of the many."

Jackson's first major crisis in the White House, which occurred while he was president-elect, was not outwardly a political matter, although it did have great political repercussions. Margaret "Peggy" O'Neale, daughter of a tavern keeper who was a friend of Jackson and Senator John Eaton's, was a dark-haired vamp. While still in her teens, Peggy had reportedly caused one suicide, one duel, one nearly ruined military career, and one aborted elopement. Then she married landlocked Navy purser, John B. Timberlake. Eaton, infatuated with Peggy, had Timberlake sent to sea, and sought out the young bride to console her. The plan apparently worked, and Washington society watched in horror as the affair became notorious. In 1828 Timberlake died at sea from disease or drink, although proper Washingtonians preferred to believe that Timberlake had cut his throat because of his wife's unfaithfulness. Jackson wanted no woman's reputation sullied, so he told Eaton, whom he intended to name secretary of war, that he must marry Peggy Timberlake to "shut their mouths." The couple married on January 1, 1829.

Jackson's cabinet was divided down the middle by the affair. Vice President Calhoun, however, could not keep his wife in line. Floride Calhoun and most of the cabinet wives snubbed Mrs. Eaton. Van Buren, a widower, was loyal to his chief and sought to make Peggy Eaton welcome at official functions. Jackson blamed Calhoun for the teapot-tempest and never forgave his vice president. Political insiders knew that Calhoun's wife's conduct meant Secretary of State Van Buren was next in line for the vice presidency.

Perhaps Calhoun hoped that by embarrassing Eaton he would force him to resign, thus weakening the influence of Van Buren. But Eaton would not resign, nor would the president ask him to. Until April 1831, the Eaton affair continued to divide the administration and interfere with the business of government—although a "Kitchen Cabinet" of Jackson's cronies conducted business informally and became more entrenched as the president's inner circle. Then, suddenly and simply, Van Buren, the "Little Magician," produced a magic cure: He resigned. When Eaton took the hint and resigned, too, Jackson was able to ask the rest of the official cabinet—the

FIRST ADMINISTRATION

INAUGURATION: Mar. 4, 1829; the Capitol, Washington, D.C.

VICE PRESIDENT: John C. Calhoun (resigned Dec. 28, 1832)

SECRETARY OF STATE: Martin Van Buren; Edward Livingston (from May 24, 1831)

SECRETARY OF THE TREASURY: Samuel D. Ingham; Louis McLane (from Aug. 8, 1831)

SECRETARY OF WAR: John H. Eaton; Lewis Cass (from Aug. 8, 1831)

ATTORNEY GENERAL: John M. Berrien; Roger B. Taney (from July 20, 1831)

POSTMASTER GENERAL: John McLean; William T. Barry (from Apr. 6, 1829)

SECRETARY OF THE NAVY: John Branch; Levi Woodbury (from May 23, 1831)

SUPREME COURT APPOINTMENTS: John McLean (1829); Henry Baldwin (1830)

21ST CONGRESS (Dec. 7, 1829–Mar. 3, 1831):
SENATE: 25 Democrats; 23 National Republicans
HOUSE: 139 Democrats; 74 National Republicans

22ND CONGRESS (Dec. 5, 1831–Mar. 2, 1833):
SENATE: 24 Democrats; 22 National Republicans; 2 Others
HOUSE: 141 Democrats; 58 National Republicans; 14 Others

ELECTION OF 1828

CANDIDATES	ELECTORAL VOTE	POPULAR VOTE
Andrew Jackson (Democratic)	178	642,553
John Quincy Adams (National Republican)	83	500,897

JOHN CALDWELL CALHOUN

"If one drop of blood be shed [in South Carolina] in defiance of the laws of the United States," growled Andrew Jackson in 1832, "I will hang the first man of [the Nullifiers] I can get my hands on . . . ." Such drastic measures were never necessary, but Jackson always regretted not being able to hang John Caldwell Calhoun, the very voice of nullification.

In 1810, at the beginning of his congressional career, Calhoun was an ardent nationalist. Declaring that "our true system is to look to the country . . . to advance the general interest," he supported the War of 1812, internal improvements, a national bank, and protective tariffs. After seven years as President Monroe's secretary of state, he joined the 1824 presidential free-for-all and won the vice presidency under John Quincy Adams. Calhoun sensed the imminent swing to Jackson and, as Senate president, permitted antiadministration oratory from Adams's detractors. But Calhoun's animosity toward Peggy Eaton and his attempts to discredit Van Buren rankled Jackson, who was further infuriated when he discovered that Calhoun had criticized his conduct during the Florida campaign of 1818. Calhoun's espousal of nullification made the break with Jackson final.

The Nullification Crisis reached its boiling point in 1832, when South Carolina proclaimed federal tariffs not "binding upon this State." When President Jackson issued a proclamation stating that nullification could not be abided, Calhoun resigned the vice presidency, was appointed senator from South Carolina, and, amid saber rattling on both sides, led the fight in the Senate. A compromise tariff averted violence, but Calhoun's course was irrevocably plotted. In the Senate, as secretary of state under President Tyler, and in his writings, he feverishly deplored abolition and outlined his theory of "concurrent majorities." Rule by numerical majority, he held, was "but Government of the strongest interests," which, "when not efficiently checked, is the most tyrannical and oppressive that can be devised . . . ."

"If trampled upon," he warned in 1847, "it will be idle to expect that we will not resist." Frustration, failing health, and his own humorless intensity ground Calhoun down. He died in 1850, lamenting the fate of "the South, the poor South."

Calhoun wing—for their resignations. A great weight had fallen from the general's shoulders.

Jackson's cabinet was rebuilt, and with a recess appointment in his pocket, Van Buren sailed for London as minister to the Court of St. James. Meanwhile, Calhoun and the president fell further apart, a process accelerated by Jackson's discovery that the vice president had, contrary to his claims, spoken against the general's Florida adventure in 1818. Closer to home, Jackson was infuriated by Calhoun's success at convincing senators to deny confirmation of Van Buren's London appointment—as vice president, Calhoun broke a tie vote by rejecting the nomination. A gleeful Calhoun told Senator Thomas Hart Benton the rejection "will kill him, sir, kill him dead." Calhoun's strategy backfired, and Van Buren was nominated in 1832 for the vice presidency, as Hart had predicted.

Jackson was ready to flex his political clout, once he had cleansed his cabinet of pro-Calhoun men. Amos Kendall, who had once been pro-Clay, became fourth auditor of the treasury and chief adviser in Jackson's "Kitchen Cabinet." Now that he had his own men around him, and the administration's internal problems were behind him, Jackson was ready to enforce his program.

As a good Jeffersonian Democrat, Jackson thought that the chief executive was responsible for the protection of "the liberties and rights of the people and the integrity of the Constitution against the Senate, or the House of Representatives, or both together." And to make certain that the few never gained at the expense of the many—the measurement he generally used before taking a stand on an issue—he was prepared to use all the muscle at the disposal of the presidency. He had already indicated that he would not hesitate to employ a veto. In 1830 Jackson had vetoed the Maysville Road Bill, which committed government funds to the construction of roads entirely within the state of Kentucky, on the grounds that it benefited too small a percentage of those who would have to pay for it. Jackson thus came out against the internal improvements plank of Henry Clay's "American System." He would use the veto more frequently than any prior president, and Clay would deplore the "concentration of all power in the hands of one man."

Jackson also took aim at another keystone of Clay's "American System"—the Bank of the United States. In his first annual message to Congress, the president had voiced doubts about both the constitutionality and expediency of the bank. No action was then necessary, however, because the bank charter was not due to expire until 1836. But as early as 1831 Jackson told Charles Carroll, the last surviving signer of the Declaration of Independence, that he intended to stand for reelection with a vow to close the bank. His motto would be: "No bank and Jackson—or bank and no Jackson." His hostility reflected his suspicion of paper money and his conviction that the bank created an alliance between business and government that resulted in benefits to the few at a cost to many.

The issue became an emotional cocktail for the Democrats. The president of the bank, Nicholas Biddle, tried in 1830 and 1831 to woo Jackson, but when his efforts proved fruitless, he agreed to have Clay and Webster make the bank the major issue of the election of 1832. Biddle obviously believed he had the votes and could speed up the rechartering

process. Up to a point, he was right. In June the recharter bill passed the Senate, and in July it passed the House. That evening, while a night-long victory celebration rocked Biddle's lodgings, Jackson looked over the recharter bill with Van Buren, who had just returned from England to be Jackson's vice presidential candidate. "The bank, Mr. Van Buren," said the president, "is trying to kill me." Then he matter-of-factly added, "but I will kill it!"

A week later, on July 10, Jackson sent his veto message to Congress: "It is to be regretted that the rich and powerful too often bend the acts of government to their selfish purposes. . . . Distinctions in society will always exist under every just government . . . but when the laws undertake to add to these natural and just advantages artificial distinctions . . . to make the rich richer and the potent more powerful, the humble members of society—the farmers, mechanics, and laborers—who have neither the time nor the means of securing like favors to themselves, have a right to complain of the injustice of their Government." The veto was sustained, despite Biddle's cries of outrage.

Although the bank was not rechartered, it was not yet dead. But before issuing his final thrust, Jackson had other matters to deal with. South Carolina had been giving Jackson trouble since the start of his administration. The tariff of 1828, known as the "Tariff of Abominations," was the object of much animosity in the South because the protection of Northern manufacturers hurt Southern planters dependent on overseas trade. John Calhoun wrote the South Carolina Exposition, which included the "Protest Against the Tariff of 1828 and the principles of Nullification." When another, equally oppressive tariff was passed in 1832, the state legislature adopted the Ordinance of Nullification, which declared the tariff void, not "binding upon this State, its officers or citizens."

South Carolina's Ordinance of Nullification and threats of secession were a clear challenge to federal authority. Jackson acted swiftly. "No state or states has a right to secede . . ." he said. "Nullification therefore means insurrection and war; and other states have a right to put it down." Then, in his annual message, on December 4, 1832, he was more conciliatory, proposing a lowered tariff as a compromise. John Quincy Adams, who had returned to Washington as a congressman, believed this to be "a complete surrender to the nullifiers." But before the week was out, Jackson cleared the air. He issued a proclamation to the people of South Carolina, a statement strong enough even for Adams, Webster, and the other staunch Unionists: "Disunion by armed force is treason. Are you ready to incur its guilt?" Then he had a bill introduced in the Senate that would authorize the president to use force to sustain federal authority. Jackson was prepared to send an army to South Carolina, but his will proved stronger than the pride of the nullifiers. A token compromise tariff was passed, which enabled the state to rescind its ordinance.

The Union had been preserved, and Jackson's popularity was soaring. He and Van Buren overwhelmingly were chosen as the nominees of the Democratic convention, while the National Republicans made Clay their nominee at a Baltimore convention. The Anti-Masonic party came out of nowhere to nominate William Wirt. Jackson received 701,780 popular votes and 219 in the electoral ballot; Clay was far behind with 49 electoral votes. Wirt took only 7 electoral votes. Thus the two-party system was still viable, and the 1832 election vindicated Jackson's policies. He wanted to see the nation's people, so the following spring Jackson set out on a triumphal tour. He visited Baltimore, Philadelphia, New York, even parts of New England, where he had gained prestige through his vigorous defense of the Union and his new cordial relations with Daniel Webster. Wherever he waved to the crowds, the old general was received with tumultuous welcomes.

Because of his failing health and developments in his war against the Bank of the United States, Jackson cut his tour short and returned to the capital. The bank charter was about to expire, and the president's veto of the recharter had not been overridden. His more conservative advisers, Van Buren among them, suggested that Jackson had done enough; but the more radical Democrats, led by Kendall, thought that the government should remove its funds from the bank, for otherwise the unchartered bank would remain solvent. That being the case, a Congress fearful for the future of its deposits might well reconsider and vote for recharter after all. Of course, such a move would make Jackson look like a fool, for he had made rejection of the bank a key part of his overall policy.

Jackson understood the meaning of consistency, particularly when it came to being president. After first removing Secretary of the Treasury William J. Duane and replacing him with Roger B. Taney, who supported removal of public funds, Jackson dictated that after October 1, 1833, no federal deposits were to be made, and issued the first call for removal of funds from the bank. Nicholas Biddle fought back ferociously. "All the other Banks and all the merchants may break," he wrote to a friend, "but the Bank of the United States shall not break." Biddle had given the nation its strongest currency, and he was not about to see his accomplishments undone. Tightening credit, calling in loans, reducing discounts, he meant to demonstrate the power of the bank by creating a panic—and he succeeded. Some of those ruined were the bank's most vigorous supporters. Finally, in 1834, Biddle succumbed to the pressure and eased up on his restrictive policies, unwittingly proving that his ruinous measures had not been necessary in the first place. Ironically, the bank was enjoying a period of expansion when the charter expired in 1836. Rechartered as a state bank in Pennsylvania, it eventually failed, and countless depositors were devastated.

Indeed, Jackson's victory over the bank was a mixed blessing. The public deposits that had been transferred to state banks—Jackson's "pet banks," the opposition called them—and the loosening of credit led to an increased production of paper money. As a result of the inflation that followed, Jackson issued his Specie Circular of July 11, 1836, which stated that thenceforth the government would accept only hard cash, gold or silver, for public land payments. As a result, inflation was curbed, but a depression soon struck in 1837.

Meanwhile, Jackson's opponents finally moved back into the national scene. Led by Henry Clay, the former Federalists, National Republicans, and a few from the Anti-Masonic party (a New York phenomenon that had surprising strength) took the name "Whigs" to accentuate their differences with "King Andrew I." Their point was made by newspapers that claimed the Whigs in England had opposed royal misdeeds, as these Americans were fighting against Jackson's tyranny. Gone were the days when leading men decried parties as "baneful," for the two-party system was becoming entrenched, organized, and committed to carrying out the platforms forged at their conventions.

During his last days in the White House, Jackson was concerned with an international matter. Since the Mexican Revolution in 1821, American slave-owners had been migrating and settling in Texas. After Mexico won its independence, its government declared Texas a state but left it open for colonization and made generous land grants available to Americans who promised to be good law-abiding Mexican citizens. On April 8, 1830, however, the Mexican government passed a law forbidding slavery and the further colonization of Texas by Americans. Throughout the following five years, the American settlers took steps to separate from Mexico, and in 1835 General Santa Anna abolished all local rights in Texas and took an army of six thousand across the Rio

SECOND ADMINISTRATION

INAUGURATION: Mar. 4, 1833; House of Representatives, Washington, D.C.

VICE PRESIDENT: Martin Van Buren

SECRETARY OF STATE: Edward Livingston; Louis McLane (from May 29, 1833); John Forsyth (from July 1, 1834)

SECRETARY OF THE TREASURY: Louis McLane; William J. Duane (from June 1, 1833); Roger B. Taney (from Sept. 23, 1833); Levi Woodbury (from July 1, 1834)

SECRETARY OF WAR: Lewis Cass

ATTORNEY GENERAL: Roger B. Taney; Benjamin F. Butler (from Nov. 18, 1833.)

POSTMASTER GENERAL: William T. Barry; Amos Kendall (from May 1, 1835)

SECRETARY OF THE NAVY: Levi Woodbury; Mahlon Dickerson (from June 30, 1834)

SUPREME COURT APPOINTMENTS: James M. Wayne (1835); Roger B. Taney, chief justice (1836); Philip P. Barbour (1836)

23RD CONGRESS (Dec. 2, 1833–Mar. 3, 1835):
  SENATE: 26 Democrats; 20 National Republicans; 2 Others
  HOUSE: 147 Democrats; 53 Anti-Masons; 60 Others

24TH CONGRESS (Dec. 7, 1835–Mar. 3, 1837):
  SENATE: 26 Democrats; 24 Whigs; 2 Others
  HOUSE: 145 Democrats; 98 Whigs

STATES ADMITTED: Arkansas (1836); Michigan (1837)

ELECTION OF 1832

CANDIDATES	ELECTORAL VOTE	POPULAR VOTE
Andrew Jackson (Democratic)	219	701,780
Henry Clay (Whig)	49	484,205
John Floyd (Nullifier)	11	100,715
William Wirt (Anti-Masonic)	7	7,273

Grande to deal with the insurrectionists. While the dictator-soldier was defeating the American rebels at the Alamo, a convention declared Texan independence on March 2, 1836. Seven weeks later, Sam Houston reversed the trend and whipped the Mexi-

BORN TO COMMAND.

KING ANDREW THE FIRST.

President Jackson, standing on the torn Constitution, holds a "veto" in his left hand in a cartoon illustrating his 1832 veto of Congress' bill to recharter the Bank of the United States. Jackson's opponents left the Democratic party, branding Jackson "King Andrew I" and took for their new party the same name used by the British political faction that opposed the royal partisans in Parliament: the Whigs.

cans at San Jacinto. Mexico, however, refused to recognize the Texan Republic.

Congress passed resolutions calling for recognition of Texas early in July, but the president hesitated. The United States had recognized the Mexican republic, and Jackson felt obliged to honor that government's sovereignty in what was technically an internal struggle. Moreover, the Whigs opposed recognition on the grounds that it was a Southern trick to broaden slavery. Personally, Jackson owned slaves and saw nothing wrong with the institution, but 1836 was an election year; his hand-picked successor, Martin Van Buren, did not wish to hurt his chances in the North by allowing the slavery issue to creep into the campaign. On March 3, 1837, on the eve of Van Buren's inauguration, the president appointed an American representative to Houston's government, thereby giving de facto recognition to the new republic.

The next day Jackson left office. In eight tumultuous years he had thoroughly altered the course of American government. His mistakes had been many, his prejudices legion, his actions guided less by law than by ego and instinct; yet his impact on the office has been matched by few.

Jackson represented a complete break from his sophisticated, intellectual predecessors. While their paternalistic attitude toward the common man may have been outdated, their concern for the people was in many ways greater than Jackson's. Thomas Jefferson and John Quincy Adams had wanted all Americans to become educated voters who would elect the best candidates. Jackson was content to take advantage of the broad suffrage and was in no rush to educate the public. The first six presidents also had wanted slavery abolished, and most made at least token attempts to treat the Indians fairly. Jackson was all for equality as long as the men were white.

Jackson often referred to the law to justify his actions. His stated opposition to the Bank of the United States was spotted with references to constitutionality, yet an 1819 Supreme Court decision had declared the bank perfectly constitutional. The almost sanctified concept of the Union was enough to justify his firmness with regard to South

Carolina's Ordinance of Nullification; but because he had no liking for Indians, Jackson did nothing when Georgia nullified a federal treaty. On Georgia lands guaranteed by the United States, the Cherokee Indians were laboring to develop a civilized society based on their own folkways but updated to be compatible with American society. They had renounced war, had cooperated with whites, and were well on their way to establishing a system of self-government when Georgia, claiming the right to overrule federal law, ordered the Cherokees off the land. The Indians remained committed to the rule of law. Instead of raising arms they took their case to the Supreme Court—and won. The apocryphal story is that when Jackson heard of the court's action, he dismissed it with a wave of the hand. "The court has made their decision, now let them enforce it." Thus encouraged to defy the nation's highest court, Georgia proceeded to expel the Cherokees. This occurred in 1832, at the same time that Jackson was telling South Carolina that nullification was "treason."

Yet Jackson is considered by historians one of our greatest presidents. His firmness, his decisiveness, and his devotion to the principle that the Union was a permanent bond made him the people's hero. True to his Jeffersonian instincts, Jackson followed a frugal course, and during his administration the national debt was totally expunged. No other president has ever been able to fulfill so many promises.

As the first popularly elected chief executive, he pitted himself against the congressmen and senators who served some constituents, while he claimed to act for all. What Jackson grasped was not necessarily the essential fiber of an issue, but he understood how the public felt about it. Thus, his wisdom was the wisdom of the masses. As the historian Clinton Rossiter writes, "more than one such President a century

would be hard to take. Yet he was a giant in his influence on our system" and "he was second only to Washington in terms of influence on the Presidency."

Jackson was almost seventy when he retired to the Hermitage, his home in Tennessee. Unfortunately, the monumental inability of his adopted son, Andrew, Jr., to hold on to a dollar made the general's retirement less leisurely than he might have liked, and he had to spend much of his time trying to raise funds. He retained an interest and considerable power in his party—enough to boost the nomination of the dark horse James K. Polk for the presidency in 1844.

Hard-of-hearing, nearly blind in one eye, and suffering from the side effects of a tubercular hemorrhage, Andrew Jackson lived by his own words: "I have long found that complaining never eased the pain." An active interest in politics was the old chieftain's best tonic. He wrote to Polk on June 6, 1845, revealing that his mind was still vigorous; but according to the historian J. W. Ward, "his flesh from the waist down had literally to be wrapped to his body to keep it from falling away." On June 8 he fainted, and a spoonful of brandy was administered to revive him. Late in the afternoon Andrew, Jr., asked the general if he recognized him. Jackson said he did and asked for his spectacles. Shortly thereafter he died.

The Jacksonian Era continued, however. In the years between the election of Old Hickory and the election of Lincoln, the only way the opposition could loosen the Jacksonian hold on the presidency was by nominating two old soldiers who reminded the people of Jackson. Lincoln's election ended the Jacksonian Era. But even he would use the Jacksonian concept of the presidency to fashion his own power and preserve the Union.

—*SAUL BRAUN,*
revised by ROBERT A. RUTLAND

MARTIN VAN BUREN

THE RED FOX

In succeeding Andrew Jackson as president, Martin Van Buren became the second vice president to move into the White House. Van Buren moved up the presidential ladder after he had taken up the role as commander in chief of a reborn Democratic party. (He forged alliances with New York, Pennsylvania and Virginia Democrats, and kept Congress in line too.) Van Buren was the prime architect of the party structure that had helped to elect Jackson. He managed Old Hickory's campaign and delivered the support of New York's powerful political machine. After the election, he served Jackson as secretary of state, vice president, phrasemaker, and confidant. Their relationship was so close that a weary Jackson once considered resigning from the presidency during his second term, permitting Van Buren to replace him.

A bitter foe of John Quincy Adams, Van Buren had been critical of President Monroe as a "fusion" president rather than a party leader. In 1824 Van Buren tried desperately to arrange the nomination of William H. Crawford; that effort failed, but strengthened Van Buren's resolve to rejuvenate the old Jeffersonian Republicans. After some hemming and hawing, Van Buren decided the only way to save the party was to nominate Andrew Jackson as standard-bearer for the renamed Democratic party. As Arthur M. Schlesinger, Jr., writes, "Van Buren's understanding of the new functions of public opinion, as well as of Congress, furnished the practical mechanisms which transformed Jackson's extraordinary popularity into the instruments of power. . . . Without them, the gains of Jacksonian democracy would have been impossible." Van Buren lacked Washington's grandeur, had none of Jackson's dash, and lacked Jefferson's patrician intellect. But for all his rough edges and weaknesses of personality, he grasped intuitively three central political facts of his time: that Congress had declined in power and influence; that a stronger judiciary had emerged; and that executive power was to be gained by popular persuasion rather than by presidential pleading with Congress.

As state after state dropped ownership of property as a qualification for voting, the common man assumed control of the outcome of elections; and the masses needed guidance. Hence party newspapers, torchlight parades, mass meetings, and other devices became tools in the political process. The development of this election procedure, with its intense presidential electioneering during Jackson's two terms, sprang from the political acumen of Martin Van Buren. He was America's first political "boss."

Born on December 5, 1782, in the village of Kinderhook in New York's Columbia County, Martin was the son of Abraham and Maria Goes Hoes Van Alen Van Buren, both of Dutch ancestry. Although a more sophisticated Van Buren would suggest in post-presidential retirement that his ancestors might have been nobles, his father was, in fact, a tavern keeper who served in the Revolution, acted as the Kinderhook town clerk, and raised his son in the Dutch Reformed Church.

Traditionally, American presidents lisp republican principles from their trundle beds and seem destined at twelve to command ships of state. Not Van Buren. His education was limited to a few years at a provincial academy, and he openly confessed to a secondary intellect. Philosophical reflection was never his forte—action was. At some point, however, he acquired a penchant for law and polemics, and at fourteen entered the law firm of Francis Sylvester, a Federalist. He swept floors, served as scrivener, studied law, and, as a partisan Republican, talked himself out of a job. Van Buren then moved to New York City, where he campaigned for Jefferson in 1800—his political baptism—and pursued his law career under attorney William P. Van Ness, a disciple of Aaron Burr.

Little Van, so called because he was only five feet six inches tall, returned to Kinderhook, was admitted to

A photograph of Martin Van Buren taken ca. 1841.

the bar in 1803, and began a systematic ascent through the channels of local, state, and national politics. He kept a strict and circumspect counsel, avoiding controversial commitments and uniting antagonistic factions whenever possible. He married a distant relative, Hannah Hoes, on February 21, 1807 (she died twelve years later), and fathered four sons, one of whom, John, would share some of his father's distinction and promise as a leader in the Free-Soil movement. Another son, Abraham, was to serve as White House secretary during his father's presidency.

By 1808 the taverner's son was surrogate of Columbia County. In 1812 he was elected—on an anti–Bank of the United States platform—to the state senate. There he supported the War of 1812, the construction of the lucrative Erie Canal, and the revision of New York State's constitution. Van Buren also sponsored a bill to abolish imprisonment for debt—one of the first legislators in the United States to do so.

Van Buren slowly assumed command of New York's Republican "Bucktail" wing, which was formally committed to a strict adherence to Jeffersonian principles and opposed to Governor DeWitt Clinton's tolerance for Federalists. In securing control of the Bucktails, Van Buren glimpsed a truth that would serve him well as chief executive: the great advantage of a friendly press. His newspaper ally in Albany was the *Argus*, edited by handpicked Van Buren disciples. Without a paper managed by "a sound, practicable, and above all discreet republican," he stated with candor, "we may hang our harps on the willows."

Van Buren was elected to the United States Senate in 1821. Before leaving for Washington, however, he made certain that the New York sheep would not play while the Red Fox of Kinderhook (another of his many nicknames) was away: He sealed an already tightly capped party machine that became known as the Albany Regency. Its structural informality notwithstanding, the Regency governed political patronage, defined party policy, ran campaigns, and—

after freewheeling, secret party caucuses—assured its members a loyal, albeit strong-armed, public. Bucktail regulars were aware of the disciplinary penalty: prompt removal from office for any departure from the party line. Working in tandem with Tammany Hall in New York City, the Regency assured Martin Van Buren's hegemony in the state, which from 1830 to 1860 contained one-seventh of the population of the United States.

In 1824 Van Buren led William H. Crawford's unsuccessful presidential campaign against John Quincy Adams, Henry Clay, and—of all people—Andrew Jackson. But Van Buren swiftly learned the lessons from Adams's close victory and carefully moved to unify the supporters of Jackson, Calhoun, and Crawford into a viable political force. The objective for 1828: an appealing synthesis of Jackson's popularity and Jefferson's principles, packaged and sold by a newly named Democratic party. To sew up New York's pivotal vote for the general, Van Buren himself gave up his Senate seat to run for governor of New York, thus adding his own popular name to the ticket. Although his bitter enemy, DeWitt Clinton, preceded Van Buren into Jackson's camp, he lost no time once he had made up his mind. "Van Buren turned to Jackson," the historian Robert Remini notes, "because he could use the General to reform the party, eliminate Federalist principles from the national government, and oust Adams from office."

Van Buren's tactical coalition won. It was a nasty campaign, and his lieutenants abandoned their scruples in order to win. It was a contest, they said, between "John Quincy Adams, who can write" and "Andrew Jackson, who can fight." This unfair campaign technique would one day help to unseat Van Buren himself, but it worked for Old Hickory, even though the Adams forces campaigned in the mud too. At last the general was in the executive office.

Van Buren went back to Albany—but only for a short time. In two and a half months, he resigned as governor and was promptly named Jackson's secretary of state. He was easily the most powerful man in either Jackson's official cabinet or his "Kitchen Cabinet." As secretary of state, Van Buren's achievements were impressive. The world's chancelleries had been initially appalled by the mercurial and crotchety frontier president, and Van Buren—cordial, discreet, and immaculate—buffered them from Jackson's brusque manner. A French minister would praise Van Buren's "certain ease, which makes him superior, as a man of the world, to those of his compatriots I have seen until now." When Washington Irving was in the diplomatic corps, he noted that Van Buren was "one of the gentlest and most amiable men I have ever met with." Highly respected in London, Van Buren reached a settlement with the British on West Indian trade; he also negotiated American access to the Black Sea with Turkey, and even persuaded the French to pay American damage claims from the Napoleonic Wars.

For all his diplomatic skills, Van Buren's importance to Jackson remained primarily political. He and Jackson agreed that only with the support of a strong political party could the president exercise effective leadership. To build this base of power, the lessons learned in Albany were systematically applied to the national scene. There was no such thing as nonpartisanship: To the faithful belonged the jobs, and the key was patronage. Largely administered by Van Buren, the spoils system was dangled over the heads of the politically uncertain. "We give no reasons for our removals," said Van Buren, and the opposition seized on the patronage concept to paint a corrupt portrait of the administration. Actually, the number of dismissals of government employees was relatively modest—estimates range from one-eleventh to one-eighth, about the same proportion of people that Jefferson had removed.

Jobs, however, have long been the mother's milk of politics, and no president hoping for reelection could

BIOGRAPHICAL FACTS

BIRTH: Kinderhook, N.Y., Dec. 5, 1782

ANCESTRY: Dutch

FATHER: Abraham Van Buren; b. Albany, N.Y., Feb. 17, 1737; d. Kinderhook, N.Y., Apr. 8, 1817

FATHER'S OCCUPATION: Farmer; tavern keeper

MOTHER: Maria Goes Hoes Van Alen Van Buren; b. Claverack, N.Y., Jan. 16, 1747; d. Kinderhook, N.Y., Feb. 16, 1817

BROTHERS: Lawrence (1786–1868); Abraham (1788–1836)

SISTERS: Derike (1777–1865); Hannah (1780–?)

HALF BROTHERS: James Isaac Van Alen (1776–1870); two others, names unknown

MARRIAGE: Kinderhook, N.Y., Feb. 21, 1807

WIFE: Hannah Hoes; b. Kinderhook, N.Y., Mar. 8, 1783; d. Albany, N.Y., Feb. 5, 1819

CHILDREN: Abraham (1807–1873); John (1810–1866); Martin (1812–1855); Smith Thompson (1817–1876)

RELIGIOUS AFFILIATION: Dutch Reformed

EDUCATION: Local schools; studied law

OCCUPATION BEFORE PRESIDENCY: Lawyer

PREPRESIDENTIAL OFFICES: Surrogate of Columbia County, N.Y.; New York State senator; attorney general of New York; delegate to Third New York State Constitutional Convention; U.S. senator; governor of New York; secretary of state; U.S. vice president

AGE AT INAUGURATION: 54

OCCUPATION AFTER PRESIDENCY: Politician

DEATH: Kinderhook, N.Y., July 24, 1862

PLACE OF BURIAL: Kinderhook Cemetery, Kinderhook, N.Y.

ignore the cardinal principles of American politics. In the nineteenth century the pejorative term was "spoils system," in the twentieth century it was "government bureaucracy," but by any name the point was the same: jobs.

A man on a mission, Van Buren pressed hard in Congress for Jackson's legislation. He drafted the general's veto of the congressional bill authorizing federal investment in the sixty-mile Maysville Road in Kentucky. Such support, Van Buren argued, was an

Peggy Eaton is depicted as a ballerina whose dance mesmerizes the presidential cabinet in an 1836 cartoon by Albert Hoffay. The Eaton affair split Washington society down the middle, but President Jackson was disgusted by the social imbroglio and never forgot the loyalty displayed by some of his cabinet supporters, including Van Buren (far right).

unconstitutional federal intrusion in state affairs—even if the state wanted it. Most of the time, however, Martin Van Buren preferred to operate outside of the chambers of Congress. In the corridors, in drawing rooms, in his offices, he wheeled and dealt, playing faction against faction, molding consensus toward his own ends, earning another sobriquet: the Little Magician.

Among his impressive political feats was his disposal of Vice President Calhoun as a rival for succession to the presidency. Like most good tricks, it was simply executed. In 1830 Jackson and Calhoun had clashed over the principle of nullification, which the vice president had espoused. Van Buren dutifully reminded Old Hickory that Calhoun had also opposed Jackson's military intervention in Florida in 1818—and not without point, for Calhoun had assured General Jackson that he had supported the action.

In the famed Eaton affair, the political war escalat-

ed. Calhoun's wife and those of most cabinet members had ostracized Secretary of War Eaton and Mrs. Eaton, persuaded that the couple had been living together long before the death of Mrs. Eaton's first husband. No doubt because his own wife, Rachel, had suffered gravely at the hands of scandalmongers, Jackson vouched for Peggy Eaton's virtue and championed her cause. But Mrs. Calhoun and the cabinet wives remained adamant, despite the suspension of cabinet meetings by Jackson, who demanded that Mrs. Eaton be invited to their social events. In the ensuing stalemate the president found himself hog-tied. He could not provide the opposition with a critical issue by firing all the men in his cabinet who were loyal to Calhoun, but neither could he capitulate and accept Eaton's resignation. Van Buren, who had valued the Eatons' friendship, reached into his magic hat and pulled out his own resignation. Jackson was nonplussed until Old Kinderhook explained that his resignation as an apparent neutral in the imbroglio would force the entire cabinet to resign. Van Buren's strategy worked; Eaton withdrew, and Jackson ordered the rest of the cabinet to follow suit. The Eaton affair was thus cleverly resolved, and in the process Martin Van Buren earned himself the vice presidency in 1832.

The second part of the strategy was the appointment of Van Buren to serve as the American minister to Great Britain, where he could stay out of the political infighting until called to serve as vice president in Jackson's second term. As far as Jackson was concerned, Calhoun was a backbiter and disloyal to boot, and the president was eager to be rid of him. Van Buren had been picked for the post while Congress was in recess. But when the reconvened Senate was asked to confirm his appointment, Calhoun openly opposed it. The Senate's tie vote gave him his opportunity for revenge: As vice president he had the power to break the tie, and he gleefully voted "Nay." Triumphant, he sneered: "It will kill him, sir, kill him dead. He will never kick, sir, never kick." But Senator Thomas Hart Benton disagreed. To a Calhoun lieutenant sitting beside him, Benton predicted: "You have broken a minister, and elected a Vice President." Benton was right. An angry Jackson chose Van Buren as his running mate in 1832, and in 1835 named him his successor to the White House.

Only rarely have other presidents followed Monroe's impartiality, and certainly Jackson was determined to see Van Buren as his heir. The president's lieutenants carried out the orders at the Baltimore convention which met in May 1835, and in short order Van Buren was the Democratic nominee for the distant 1836 election. The Whigs held no convention but planned to once again throw the election into the House of Representatives, where a deal might be made to derail the Jackson strategy. To that end, the Whigs offered three favorite-son candidates—Senator Daniel Webster, General William Henry Harrison, and (from the Jackson-haters in Tennessee) Hugh

Lawson White. Harrison was also formally nominated by the Anti-Masonic party.

For his running mate, Van Buren picked Senator Richard Mentor Johnson of Kentucky. Few presidential tickets have combined so much practical political talent. In November 1836 Old Kinderhook, running on a Jacksonian platform of democracy versus aristocracy, was elected the eighth president of the United States. His 764,176 popular votes outdistanced the 739,358 votes cast for all his opponents put together.

The Little Magician had done it again—pulled off a remarkable campaign and licked the renowned Indian fighter William Henry Harrison in the bargain. During the campaign of 1836, the redoubtable William Seward called Van Buren "a crawling reptile, whose only claim was that he had inveigled the confidence of a credulous, blind, dotard, old man." To his detractors, Van Buren was the American Talleyrand: devious, hypocritical, professionally noncommittal. "The searching look of his keen eyes," observed one hostile contemporary, "showed that he believed, with Talleyrand, that language was given to conceal thought."

Yet despite all the invective, Martin Van Buren entered the White House with roseate good cheer. In his inaugural address in March 1837, he recalled that he was the first president born after the Revolution began; "whilst I contemplate with grateful reverence that memorable event," he said, "I feel that I belong to a later age. . . ." Then he addressed himself to the issues of the time, revealing that the inclinations of the New York politician would not be discarded by the new chief executive. To help unify the Democratic party, he dismissed Southern nullification of federal law as an embarrassment, a "partial and temporary evil," and blandly appealed for a healing of party wounds without rancor or revenge. On the eve of one of America's worst depressions, Van Buren assured the nation that prosperity was now "perfectly secured." Faced already with the angry rumblings of secessionists and antislavery lawmakers, he ignored dissension and hailed the Founding Fathers' respect for "distinct sovereignties" within the nation and for "institutions peculiar to the various portions" of the country. But he urged that the unrest of Southerners not be "exaggerated through sinister designs."

"I must go into the Presidential chair," Jackson's heir proclaimed, "the inflexible and uncompromising opponent of every attempt on the part of Congress to abolish slavery in the District of Columbia against the wishes of the slaveholding States, and also with a determination equally decided to resist the slightest interference with it in the States where it exists." Promising to veto any bill "conflicting with these views," Van Buren urged "forbearance" with "the delicacy of this subject [slavery]." He assured the nation that his beliefs were "in accordance with the spirit that actuated the venerated fathers of the Republic. . . ."

Van Buren had always been the backup man. Now in charge, he was not ready for the avalanche that was about to descend. Within days of his accession, President Van Buren faced a major national depression—the Panic of 1837—which was to plague his entire administration. Ironically, the panic was largely caused by the execution of and opposition to Jackson's Specie Circular. "In destroying the [Bank of the United States]," the historian Schlesinger observes, "Jackson had removed a valuable brake on credit expansion; and in sponsoring the system of [federal] deposit in state banks, he had accelerated the tendencies toward inflation."

The nation paid a price for wildcat banks. A speculative orgy and the disappearance of sound banking principles followed. The basic cause of the crash was the defiance by private business against Jackson's hard-money policy, which was deflationary. Overzealous bankers extended shaky loans to finance the boom in land speculation, manufacturing, transportation, and banking that had begun under John Quincy Adams. Hard money was withdrawn en masse from the banks to pay for inflated landholdings. The wheat crop of 1836 failed badly. The price of cotton fell by almost one-half. Food and fuel prices and rents soared, sometimes doubled. New Yorkers rioted over the cost of flour. Banks and businesses collapsed under pressure from England and Europe for repayment of short-term loans precisely when hard-

THE VAN BUREN ADMINISTRATION

INAUGURATION: Mar. 4, 1837; the Capitol, Washington, D.C.
VICE PRESIDENT: Richard M. Johnson
SECRETARY OF STATE: John Forsyth
SECRETARY OF THE TREASURY: Levi Woodbury
SECRETARY OF WAR: Joel R. Poinsett
ATTORNEY GENERAL: Benjamin F. Butler;
    Felix Grundy (from Sept. 1, 1838);
    Henry D. Gilpin (from Jan. 11, 1840)
POSTMASTER GENERAL: John M. Niles
SECRETARY OF THE NAVY: Mahlon Dickerson;
    James K. Paulding (from July 1, 1838)
SUPREME COURT APPOINTMENTS: John Catron (1837);
    John McKinley (1837); Peter V. Daniel (1841)
25TH CONGRESS (Sept. 4, 1837–Mar. 3, 1839):
    SENATE: 35 Democrats; 17 Whigs
    HOUSE: 108 Democrats; 107 Whigs; 24 Others
26TH CONGRESS (Dec. 2, 1839–Mar. 3, 1841):
    SENATE: 30 Democrats; 22 Whigs
    HOUSE: 124 Democrats; 118 Whigs

ELECTION OF 1836

CANDIDATES	ELECTORAL VOTE	POPULAR VOTE
Martin Van Buren (Democratic)	170	764,176
William H. Harrison (Whig)	73	550,816
Hugh L. White (Whig)	26	146,107
Daniel Webster (Whig)	14	41,201
Willie P. Mangum (Anti-Jacksonian)	11	1,234

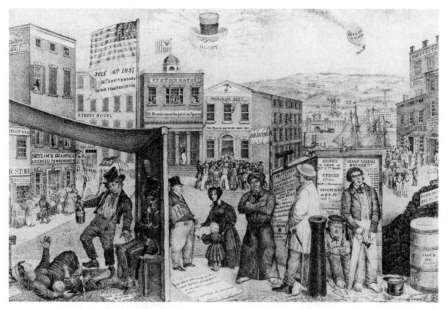

A bank sign reads, "No specie payments made here." Frantic customers mob the bank, as a well-to-do attorney boards a carriage at the far right (1837 print by Edward Clay). The first major depression in American history hit the country shortly after Van Buren's inauguration. Bank failures and widespread unemployment followed, leaving thousands of recent immigrants without jobs. The president's critics soon emphasized the seamy side of city life, including drunkenness and hunger.

money deposits were being depleted. Something new appeared in city life—breadlines for the unemployed. Jobs became scarce; poorhouses were crowded. The government alone lost nine million dollars in the failure of state banks. Nearly every bank in the country suspended specie payments.

By May 1837 President Van Buren could temporize no longer. He summoned Congress into special session to deal with the spreading depression. In Van Buren's mind, the remedy was simply a matter of controlling the flow of money. His own solutions: Stand fast for hard money; remove the federal deposits from all banks, state and national; establish an independent treasury that would wrest control of the government from the moneyed class. Van Buren sought the best advice from his Democratic friends but was thwarted by a predictable coalition of state banking interests, Whigs, and conservative Democrats who prevented passage of his Independent Treasury bill.

Democrats were not of one mind on the need for an Independent Treasury. The aim of the bill was to stabilize the banking system without favoring private interests. Instead of a hodgepodge of accounts, all federal funds would be deposited in the United States Treasury. Government funds would be kept in federal depositories, and all its business would be conducted in specie—not banknotes of uncertain value. Not until 1840, the last year of his administration, did Congress pass the bill. Van Buren would hail its passage as a "Second Declaration of Independence," and would delight in having won Jackson's battle with Nicholas Biddle, but his celebration was hasty. The Independent Treasury, in fact, would not be established on a permanent basis until 1846.

Van Buren's struggle for an Independent Treasury was by no means his main goal as president. Despite his repeated assertion that the federal government had no constitutional right to intervene in the economy, he issued in March 1840 an executive order limiting to a ten-hour day the work of all laborers on federal projects. In 1837 Canada seized in American waters the steamer *Caroline*, which was illegally carrying weapons to Canadian rebels. Van Buren defied both British bluster and American jingoist cries for vengeance by disarming the Yankee zealots involved. The British calmed down. Similarly, in 1840, when Maine citizens clashed with Canadians over the boundary of the Northeast United States, President Van Buren quietly ended the fuss through a diplomatic dialogue that led to the Webster-Ashburton Treaty of 1842.

Despite these displays of executive authority, the image of Van Buren as an evasive manipulator, unwilling to choose an unpopular course, remains. During his days in the Senate, Van Buren had sometimes avoided taking a stand on a controversial issue by ducking an important vote. Now he was in charge and could not avoid responsibility.

Van Buren's ambivalence was owing not only to political machinations but also to his limited view of the presidential and federal roles in the life of the nation. Generally, Van Buren was preoccupied by his interpretation of Jeffersonian guidelines. Too often he must have said to himself, "I must do now what Jefferson would have done in the same circumstances." This adulation of Jeffersonianism was Van Buren's excuse for using states'-rights doctrine as a screen for federal inaction. Van Buren's view of the Constitution was ambiguous. On the one hand, he anointed it as "a sacred instrument," while on the other he defied one of its fundamental principles by favoring an elective judiciary. He approved of the explicit right of Congress to collect taxes, but he felt that the Constitution gave Congress no authority to spend these taxes—even after all basic expenses of government had been met—on internal improvements such as public roads, schools, or canals. He also doubted that the federal government had a constitutional right to correct local inequities, resolve regional crises, or influence state affairs.

The fight for the Independent Treasury excepted, Van Buren's administration was the American apotheosis of laissez-faire government. In international affairs, he declared his opposition to foreign alliances. Precedents set by other presidents in our foreign relations, he explained, left "little to [his] discretion." What was good enough for Washington, Jefferson, and Jackson was good enough for him. Innovation did not appeal to Van Buren once he was president.

Historians agree that his appointments, even on the highest levels, were capricious and inept. His cabinet lacked distinction. A "little magician" in securing and sustaining power for others, Van Buren himself was weak in the exercise of it. He was blamed, as Hoover would be blamed, not only for the depression during his administration but for his failure to combat it head-on. He was regarded as proslavery in the North and antislavery in the South. And despite his victory over Biddle and the announcement of an Independent Treasury, he faced, in the campaign of 1840, a disappointed electorate. Whigs, desperate for a winner, nominated General William Henry Harrison, with John Tyler as the vice presidential candidate.

The tone of the campaign—one of the most emotional in American history—was sounded by Pennsylvania Congressman Charles Ogle in the House of Representatives on April 14, 1840. Commenting on a routine appropriation of $3,665 for maintenance and repairs of the White House, Ogle began an impassioned appeal for the election of William Henry Harrison, with an incredible assault on the person of the president. Van Buren, declared Ogle, wore the same perfume fancied by Queen Victoria and actually preferred Madeira to hard cider. Moreover, Ogle raged on, the president had purchased—in Europe, of all places—Brussels carpets, "dazzling foreign ornaments," French taborets for royal audiences, and other "womanish" contrivances! Van Buren, he insisted, actually slept in a Louis XV bed and used "gold-framed mirrors 'as big as a barn door' to behold his plain Republican self." The cost of three White House curtains alone, Ogle maintained, would build at least three goodly log cabins with money to spare to "treat the folks who came to the 'raisin' with as much HARD CIDER as they can stow away under the belts of their linsey-woolsey hunting shirts."

In contrast to Van Buren's alleged royal splendor, William Henry Harrison was hailed as a frontier messiah, and torchlight parades hailed "Tippecanoe and Tyler too" wherever individual votes counted (in some states, such as South Carolina, the legislature chose electors). Horace Greeley, who was an influence in national politics for the next forty years, cut his editorial teeth as the editor of the *Log Cabin*, a Whig campaign newspaper.

Harrison was elected in a landslide. Many conservative Democrats had defected to the Whigs, and the Harrison-Tyler ticket had won by a plurality of almost 150,000 in a smashing electoral victory of 234 votes to 60. Van Buren even lost his own state, New York.

Sad to say, at least half of the presidents have left the White House more mortified than proud. Van Buren, agreeing with Jefferson's sentiments, recalled of his predecessor's presidency that "the two happiest days of his life were those of his entrance upon the office and of his surrender of it." He returned to Kinderhook, moving into Lindenwald, a remodeled Italo-Gothic mansion. In 1844, after turning down President Tyler's politically motivated offer of a seat on the Supreme Court, Van Buren tried for the Democratic presidential nomination, failing because of his continued opposition to the annexation of Texas as a slave state.

The former president would not rest, and in his perception the slavery issue was becoming the dominant theme. In 1848 he was renominated by antislavery Democrats (the Barnburners) in coalition with Free-Soilers and liberal Whigs. The Democrats nominated Lewis Cass, while the Whigs again chose a war hero, Zachary Taylor. With the New York Democrats thus split, Taylor carried the state and won the election. In the course of the 1848 campaign, Van Buren finally concluded that slavery and freedom could not

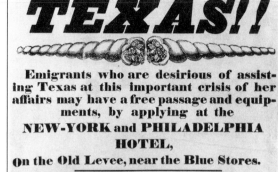

Southern sentiment for the annexation of Texas created a crisis in Van Buren's administration. The president leaned toward the antislavery position and decided to oppose statehood for the former Mexican territory.

coexist, and he wrote a moving appeal for adoption of a commitment that all future states would be admitted only when they banned slavery.

In retirement, besides playing patroon at Lindenwald, Van Buren traveled throughout Europe. He poked around ancestral Dutch towns and, without fear of political retribution, was able to indulge himself in the purchase of the European finery he enjoyed so much. During a sojourn in Italy the seventy-one-year-old former chief executive wrote his autobiography, which still interests scholars because of the author's inside knowledge and candor. Back in Kinderhook, Van Buren seethed over the policies of Presidents Pierce and Buchanan. In 1861, mourning the commencement of the Civil War, he expressed his confidence in Abraham Lincoln. Plagued by asthma for many months, Martin Van Buren died in the second year of the conflict, on July 24, 1862.

—*WILSON SULLIVAN,*
revised by ROBERT A. RUTLAND

WILLIAM HENRY HARRISON

Old Tippecanoe

The Whig party that coalesced during Andrew Jackson's second term owed Henry Clay a favor, but the Kentuckian was not a military hero. Looking over the field, party managers decided they had a winner in General William Henry Harrison—the hero of the Battle of Tippecanoe. "We could meet the Whigs on the field of argument and beat them without effort," claimed the Jacksonian New York *Evening Post*. "But when they lay down the weapons of argument and attack us with musical notes, what can we do?" When the election of 1840 ended, as politician Philip Hone put it, the aging general had been "sung into the Presidency."

The Whigs had deliberately conducted a campaign fat with songs, slogans, and chants but thin on real issues. Attempting to beat the Democratic incumbent, Martin Van Buren, at the Jacksonian game, they selected as their candidate a military hero, casting him in Andrew Jackson's image, assuming for themselves the role of the people's party, and depicting Van Buren as a fop with indulgent tastes.

> Old Tip he wears a homespun coat,
> He has no ruffled shirt-wirt-wirt.
> But Mat he has the golden plate,
> And he's a little squirt-wirt-wirt.

When a Democratic newspaper in Baltimore, alluding to Harrison's lack of intellectual depth, suggested that the candidate would be content with a log cabin and a barrel of hard cider, the joke backfired. Whigs immediately seized upon the idea and turned it to their advantage. For the first time in American politics, the possibility of a president born in a log cabin was too good to pass up. Horace Greeley called his New York newspaper the *Log Cabin* and in editorial after editorial contrasted the prissy president with the manly Harrison. A log-cabin-and-hard-cider presidential candidate was made to order. The vice presidential candidate, John Tyler of Virginia, was a pitch for the Old Dominion's electoral votes and little more.

The "log cabin" in which the candidate was born on February 9, 1773, was actually a three-story brick mansion at Berkeley, the Harrison family plantation in Charles City County, Virginia. His father, Benjamin, was a wealthy planter and a signer of the Declaration of Independence. Tutored privately at home until 1787, William Henry Harrison then entered Hampden-Sidney College where he studied for a brief time and then attended medical school. But in 1791 Harrison changed his mind about being a physician and enlisted in the United States Infantry.

"All this story about the log cabin . . . is a mean fraud," the Democrats protested. But the Whigs persisted on a technicality. Avoiding the facts regarding Old Tip's birthplace, they pictured him on their posters as the rough-hewn, hard-drinking, plow-pushing farmer of North Bend, Ohio, where, sure enough, Harrison did own a log cabin. In 1795 Lieutenant Harrison, stationed in Ohio, had become engaged to Anna Symmes, daughter of a prosperous North Bend farmer and judge. Before the wedding, he had bought a piece of land and built for his bride a five-room log cabin. Three years later he resigned from the Army and began to improve his property and take an active part in the affairs of the Northwest Territory. By 1840 the log cabin was only a corner of a much-annexed house—but it became the centerpiece of the Whig campaign.

Making the most of the symbol, the Whigs built a network of log cabin campaign headquarters, gave out log cabin songbooks, and dispensed log cabin cider. When the Jacksonians pointed out that Whiggery was a conglomeration of rich bankers, merchants, and planters, they failed to impress the voters.

William Henry Harrison, shown here in a daguerreotype taken shortly after his inauguration, was probably the first president to be photographed while in office. Just three weeks later he fell ill and died.

BIOGRAPHICAL FACTS

BIRTH: Charles City County, Va., Feb. 9, 1773

ANCESTRY: English

FATHER: Benjamin Harrison; b. Charles City County, Va., Apr. 5, 1726; d. Charles City County, Va., Apr. 24, 1791

FATHER'S OCCUPATIONS: Planter; politician

MOTHER: Elizabeth Bassett Harrison; b. Charles City County, Va., Dec. 13, 1730; d. Charles City County, Va., 1792

BROTHERS: Benjamin (1755–1799); Carter Bassett (?–1808)

SISTERS: Elizabeth (1751–?); Anna (1753–1821); Lucy (?–1809); Sarah (1770–1812)

MARRIAGE: North Bend, Ohio, Nov. 25, 1795

WIFE: Anna Tuthill Symmes; b. Flatbrook, N.J., July 25, 1775; d. North Bend, Ohio, Feb. 25, 1864

CHILDREN: Elizabeth Bassett (1796–1846); John Cleves Symmes (1798–1830); Lucy Singleton (1800–1826); William Henry (1802–1838); John Scott (1804–1878); Benjamin (1806–1840); Mary Symmes (1809–1842); Carter Bassett (1811–1839); Anna Tuthill (1813–1845); James Findlay (1814–1817)

RELIGIOUS AFFILIATION: Episcopalian

EDUCATION: Private tutoring; attended Hampden-Sidney College

OCCUPATION BEFORE PRESIDENCY: Soldier

MILITARY SERVICE: maj. gen. of Kentucky militia (1812); U.S. Army (1812–1814), rose from brig. gen. to maj. gen. in command of the Northwest

PREPRESIDENTIAL OFFICES: Secretary of Northwest Territory; U.S. congressman; governor of Indiana Territory and superintendent of Indian Affairs; Ohio State senator; U.S. senator; minister to Colombia

AGE AT INAUGURATION: 68

DEATH: Washington, D.C., Apr. 4, 1841

PLACE OF BURIAL: William Henry Harrison State Park, North Bend, Ohio

---

that their two votes would go to Harrison. Against such forces the Democrats found all their logic wasted, and by the time they came down to the Whig level, they found themselves in the path of a steamroller.

> What has caused the great commotion;
> motion, motion, Our country through?
> It is the ball a rolling on.
> For Tippecanoe and Tyler too—Tippecanoe
> and Tyler too.

Throughout the campaign, the Democrats called Harrison "Granny" (he was sixty-seven when he was nominated) and "General Mum" because of his reluctance to speak out on major issues. Nobody in the Harrison camp wanted to discuss the status of slavery in the western territories, or venture an opinion on the Texas Republic's yearning for statehood. A few Whigs did decry the Democrats' pet cause, the Independent Treasury, but why bother with issues? Even New York, Van Buren's home base, was on shaky ground. A New York newspaper did harp on Harrison's limitations by insisting that "all his ambitious efforts in legislative assemblies, as in the field, [were] unfortunate failures," and it asserted that the Whig candidate was notable only because of his "total want of qualifications."

While it was true that Harrison had suffered a number of political embarrassments and was at the time of his nomination nothing more than a county recorder in Ohio, he had had long experience in politics. In 1799, as the first representative to Congress from the Northwest Territory, he was instrumental in securing passage of a bill that divided the vast land into two smaller territories: Ohio and Indiana. In 1800 Harrison was appointed governor of the Indiana Territory.

Governor Harrison had his problems, as did most western governors, with slavery and with Indians. In

No matter who was behind the party, its campaigners, such as the Illinois Whig Abraham Lincoln, viewed Harrison with the vocabulary of the frontier. Even Chang and Eng, the famous Siamese twins, were coaxed from P. T. Barnum's museum to announce

1791 he had been a member of an abolition society, yet after 1802 he took the position that citizens of the territory should have the right to own slaves. Since the Northwest Ordinance of 1787 forbade slavery above the Ohio River, the point was moot east of the Mississippi. But the Missouri Compromise left the door open, as far as slavery advocates were concerned. They wondered, Were Harrison's convictions as changeable as a weathervane? Harrison biographer, Dorothy Goebel, suggests that he sided with the proslavery factions because most Indianians favored the institution.

On matters of criminal law, Harrison earned a reputation for being fair and compassionate. He deplored the prevailing practice of punishing Indians for crimes committed against whites while ignoring the crimes of whites against Indians. On issues of property, however, he was less magnanimous. President Jefferson had instructed him to secure as much Indian land for the United States as possible, and in 1802 Harrison was awarded full power to negotiate and conclude treaties. Since the Indians lacked a central, overarching organization, it was not difficult to purchase huge tracts of land from a needy tribe.

While Lewis and Clark were exploring the West, two Shawnee brothers, Tecumseh and Tenskwatawa (known as the Prophet), began to oppose the white man's expansion. The Prophet warned against whiskey and intertribal warfare as Tecumseh went from tribe to tribe, organizing a united front. So successful was the work of the Shawnee brothers that the United States was unable to arrange any significant land deals with the Indians of the Northwest Territory from 1806 until 1809. Then, on September 30, 1809, Harrison managed—through a careful combination of fair bargaining, whiskey distribution, and threats—to conclude the Treaty of Fort Wayne with the Miami tribe, which transferred 2.5 million acres of Indian land to the United States. Tecumseh refused to recognize the deal, claiming that the land was not the Miami's to sell. After a meeting with Tecumseh in 1810, Harrison reported to President Madison that he had explained to the Indian chief that the treaty was legal and that the United States now wished to survey the land. According to Harrison, Tecumseh replied: "When you speak to me of annuities I look at the land and pity the women and children. . . . Should you cross into Indian Territory I assure you it will be productive of bad consequences."

Until the 1840 presidential election, slogans and mottoes played little part in national elections. The Whig party nominated Harrison and portrayed the cultivated Virginian as a frontiersman born in a log cabin. The voters loved it.

TECUMSEH

After the Revolution, Americans viewed the Ohio River Valley as a prime area for national expansion. Aroused by the white man's encroachment, Tecumseh, a young Shawnee chief, conceived the idea of a vast Indian confederacy.

Most tribes claimed the right to dispose of their own hunting grounds, but Tecumseh claimed that land was held in common by all the tribes and no one tribe could sell its particular tract. "Sell a country!" he thundered. "Why not sell the air, the clouds, and the great sea. . . . Did not the Great Spirit make them all for the use of his children?"

Tecumseh was determined to hold the Ohio River as a dividing line. He visited tribes from Wisconsin to Florida, enlisting support for his movement. Often dispirited elders opposed him, but his proposals had an electrifying effect on young braves. After 1808 he and his brother, known as the Shawnee Prophet, began to gather a warrior band at Tippecanoe, their Indiana headquarters on the Wabash River.

On November 7, 1811, in Tecumseh's absence, the Prophet fought a pitched battle at Tippecanoe with Americans under General William Henry Harrison and was defeated. Frustrated as the Indi-

an movement degenerated into ineffective, isolated uprisings, Tecumseh joined the British in the War of 1812 and fell in battle on the Thames River on October 5, 1813, at the age of 45. With America's greatest Indian leader dead, the plan for a vast Indian nation remained an unrealized vision.

To Harrison, Tecumseh's threat was a "harangue"; moreover, Harrison insisted that the Shawnee leaders were nothing more than pawns of the British. Madison, however, was concerned with the possibilities of battle in West Florida and, wanting no military diver-

sion in the Northwest, instructed Harrison not to cross the boundary just yet.

On August 22, 1811, Harrison finally received permission to assemble forces. A month later, while Tecumseh was away, Harrison led a thousand troops across the old boundary and slowly advanced toward the Prophet's encampment located near the point where the Tippecanoe River empties into the Wabash. On October 1, the soldiers stopped to erect Fort Harrison, and they did not reach the vicinity of the Indian encampment until November 6. As they approached, Harrison's officers advised him to attack; the governor was inclined to agree, but the president's orders had been specific: No effort should be made to take the camp by force until the Prophet had been given the option to abandon it voluntarily. Thus an armistice was negotiated with the Prophet's messengers, and discussions were scheduled for the next day, November 7. The soldiers bivouacked for the night by the Tippecanoe River.

At 4 A.M. the Indians attacked. In a short and bloody battle, 188 Americans and a few dozen Indians were killed or wounded. After the initial rout, the outnumbered Indians retreated. On November 8 the Shawnee village, abandoned by the Indians, was taken by the Americans and burned.

The Battle of Tippecanoe accomplished little except to drive the Indians into the outstretched arms of the British. Harrison himself was both praised and criticized. He had indeed performed bravely and had erected a fort that would be valuable to the United States during the War of 1812; but there were many critics who thought that he should have attacked the Indians first, others who accused him of being careless about his selection of a campsite, and still others who claimed that he had no right being where he was in the first place.

Meanwhile, the War of 1812 started, in part because the western congressmen wanted the Indians thoroughly trounced and pushed beyond the Mississippi. Harrison, who had been commissioned a brigadier general of the Army, was appointed supreme commander in the Northwest in September 1812. His chief responsibility was to raise, feed, and clothe an army for defense against further British advances.

Early offensive moves against the Canadians and British (with their Indian allies) were repulsed. Only after Commodore Oliver Hazard Perry defeated the British fleet on Lake Erie on September 10, 1813, was there a chance to redeem American honor.

Harrison immediately led his troops toward Detroit, recapturing it on September 29. The British retreated into Canada, and Harrison pursued, overtaking them at a little town on the Thames River. There a bloody battle was fought, the British fled, and Tecumseh was killed. Indian participation in the War of 1812 ended. As the British never tried to retake the area, Harrison's duties as governor became routine; he resigned his commission and returned to his farm at North Bend.

In 1816 he was elected to the House of Representatives from Ohio; there he became a follower of Henry Clay. Harrison served as a state senator in 1819 but failed to win reelection—probably because of his ambiguous stand on slavery. Six years later, he

---

THE HARRISON ADMINISTRATION

INAUGURATION: Mar. 4, 1841; the Capitol, Washington, D.C.

VICE PRESIDENT: John Tyler

SECRETARY OF STATE: Daniel Webster

SECRETARY OF THE TREASURY: Thomas Ewing

SECRETARY OF WAR: John Bell

ATTORNEY GENERAL: John J. Crittenden

POSTMASTER GENERAL: Francis Granger

SECRETARY OF THE NAVY: George E. Badger

27TH CONGRESS (May 31, 1841–Mar. 3, 1843):
   SENATE: 29 Whigs; 22 Democrats
   HOUSE: 133 Whigs; 102 Democrats; 6 Others

ELECTION OF 1840

CANDIDATES	ELECTORAL VOTE	POPULAR VOTE
William Henry Harrison (Whig)	234	1,274,624
Martin Van Buren (Democratic)	60	1,127,781

IN MEMORY

OF

PRESIDENT

WM. H. HARRISON,

WHO DEPARTED
THIS LIFE,
APRIL 4, 1841,
AGED 68,

Deeply lamented
by 16 Millions of
people.

A shocked nation was saddened by Harrison's death in 1841. This mourning ribbon expressed a common sentiment when for the first time a sitting president died.

won a United States Senate seat representing Ohio and resumed his association with Clay, through whose influence he was appointed, in 1828, minister to Colombia. He failed to distinguish himself in any of these areas of civil service.

Harrison was a Whig for the same reason that Daniel Webster, Henry Clay, and John Quincy Adams became Whigs: He was opposed to Andrew Jackson. After the sweeping Democratic victory of 1828, abolitionists and slaveholders, anti-bank men and pro-bank men, Masons and Anti-Masons, neo-Federalists and states'-rights advocates, champions of the tariff and crusaders against it, found it convenient to blame the Jacksonians for whatever they did not like. Thus the Whig party was formed initially to thwart "King Andrew I," which became a nickname that stuck.

At the 1836 Whig convention, Harrison was one of three candidates nominated for president; he proved effective at pulling votes, but Van Buren was elected. Four years later, bypassing Clay and Webster, whose views were too well known to assure victory, the Whigs again nominated the popular, noncommittal, and heroic William Henry Harrison.

All the charges and doubts about the battles of Tippecanoe and the Thames were revived by the Democrats during the campaign. Accusing Harrison of having "cannon fever," the Democrats called him a *sham* hero." They pointed out that Harrison had resigned his commission from the Army before the end of the War of 1812, and thus let his country down "in the time of her utmost need." Moreover, the Jacksonians insisted that Vice President Richard M. Johnson, who served as a colonel under Harrison in the War of 1812, had in fact killed Tecumseh (hard to prove, since the Indian warrior's body was never found).

But, the Whigs countered, what had Van Buren accomplished in the Indian wars?

Why argue issues when a song would do?
When Martin was housed like a chattel,
Opposed to the war as you know,
Our hero was foremost in battle,
And conquered at Tippecanoe.

How did Harrison react to the utterly tasteless campaign? Quietly, for it was considered bad form for candidates to speak out. Horace Greeley would eventually change that, but for now Harrison kept his silence. As an individual he was a considerate, genial, and generous man, and his success, Dorothy Goebel suggests, was probably owing to his "fine personality." He was admired for his character rather than his political record, which was mediocre at best. He would promise anything to a friend, and if sincerity alone could keep promises, he would never have reneged on one.

Unfortunately, Harrison's memory was wanting. He promised cabinet posts two and three times over, and after his election, he was besieged at North Bend and in Washington by spoils seekers. As a British traveler wrote: "Whoever called to pay him a visit was sure to be asked to dinner; whoever called for a place in the government was sure to get a promise; whoever hinted at a want of money was sure to receive a draft; until it became the common talk that the President was overdrawing his account, overpromising his partisans, and overfeeding his friends."

He was an old man, and all the activity was taxing. The hustle and bustle of office and office seekers took its toll. Three weeks after his inauguration on March 4, 1841, he came down with pneumonia; he suffered a relapse on April 3, and around midnight said: "Sir—I wish you to understand the true principles of Government. I wish them carried out. I ask nothing more." The words were assumed to be addressed to the absent vice president, John Tyler. On April 4, exactly one month after becoming president, he became the first to die in office. As John Quincy Adams said, Harrison was "taken away thus providentially from the evil to come."

—DAVID JACOBS,
revised by ROBERT A. RUTLAND

At dawn on April 5, 1841, Daniel Webster's son, Fletcher, rode up to a large garden-edged home in Williamsburg, Virginia, dismounted wearily, and hammered on the front door. He had been on the road all night, bearing, in a letter from the cabinet addressed to "John Tyler, Vice President of the United States," the news of President William Henry Harrison's death.

The door was opened by Tyler himself—a tall, slender, sharp-featured man with a thin and prominent Roman nose. He had not even known that Harrison was ill. There is no record of his reaction to the news, but he must have been stunned. Like most vice presidents, he had deliberately suppressed any ideas of emergency succession. Unlike future vice presidents, he had no precedent to guide him in the immediate constitutional problem of his status in the government.

Tyler hurriedly packed and ate a quick breakfast. Two hours after Fletcher Webster's arrival they began the long trip to Washington, which waited abuzz with speculation. Was Tyler actually president, or only acting president? Would he follow Harrison's policies, such as they were? John Quincy Adams, former president and now a Whig representative from Massachusetts, was alarmed. He thought it highly unfortunate that John Tyler should be the agent of the first test of the Constitution's succession clause. Adams wrote in his diary, ". . . this is the first instance of a Vice-President's being called to act as President of the United States, and brings to the test that provision of the Constitution which places in the Executive chair a man never thought of for it by anybody." Tyler quickly dispelled any doubt as to his own status. He took the oath of office and made it authoritative. He was the president—with no "acting" or other stipulations restricting his way, just as he believed the Founding Fathers had intended.

The chickens of the 1840 nominating convention had come home to roost. Harrison's age—68 at his inauguration—made him an old man and the oldest up to that time to seek the presidency. Daniel Webster was not alone when he suggested that Harrison was perhaps not well. But in the rush to find a winner, the Whig matchmakers had not worried about Harrison's good health—or lack of it. Tyler was not a vague and bewildered old general like Harrison. He was not even a Whig—certainly not in the terms in which Adams, Webster, Henry Clay, and other leaders defined themselves. Like many Southerners, Tyler had walked backward into the Whig alliance in protest against Andrew Jackson's "dictatorship." A strict constructionist, he had consistently opposed protective tariffs, the national bank, and federally sponsored internal improvements—measures that were at the heart of the "American System," and which the Whig leaders had hoped to promote under Harrison. After several other prominent Whigs declined, the convention-manipulating Whigs had nominated Tyler as vice president simply to balance the ticket. They had played with fire, and they—and perhaps the whole country—had been burned.

What doubts the Washington crowd harbored were not bothersome to Tyler. He reached the capital before sunrise on April 6, 1841. The Constitution was vague about the matter of succession, declaring only that if the president were to die, resign, or become unable to discharge his duties, "the same shall devolve on the Vice President." Fair enough, Tyler said, and he must have known that Webster and other cabinet members believed he was now the chief executive. In all the confusion, Tyler's resolve proved exemplary. He deferred to Webster's opinion that a presidential oath-taking ceremony was in order. Some fifty-three hours after Harrison's death, Tyler was sworn in as the tenth (and, at 51, the youngest up to that time) president of the United States. The ceremony at the Indian Queen Hotel took less than five minutes.

Although some Whig congressmen claimed Tyler was usurping an office to which he had no right, his

During his second year in office, President Tyler sat for this painting by G. P. A. Healy.

bold interpretation of the Constitution had the support not only of most or all the members of the cabinet, but also of a majority in Congress. Feeble attempts were made in the legislature to reverse Tyler's precedent, but these efforts received only cursory attention and scant support.

The best argument against Tyler's accession was offered in the Senate by William Allen of Ohio, who pointed out its implications for the future: Whatever Tyler became now, a subsequent vice president would also become if he substituted for a president who was ill; and if the vice president became president and the man he replaced recovered, who would be president then? Allen foresaw a struggle. But Senator John C. Calhoun said "that as none of those circumstances existed which had been supposed [by Senator Allen], there could be no special occasion for discussion of this subject." The Senate then voted, as the House had already done, to name Tyler president.

Who was this Virginian, anyway? The public knew little, as did the Whigs, most of whom were still in a state of shock. Gradually the nation learned more about Tyler, the first "accidental president."

John Tyler was born March 29, 1790, on his family's plantation in Charles City County, Virginia. His father was Judge John Tyler, a friend of Thomas Jefferson and a leading member of Virginia's Revolutionary generation. His mother, Mary Armistead Tyler, bore the judge eight children before she died of a stroke the year young John was seven. Little else is known about Tyler's boyhood, but there are indications that his mother's death left him unusually dependent on his strong and active father, and that throughout his life he held himself up against standards he had not created and could not meet.

He graduated from the College of William and Mary in 1807. Four years later, at the age of twenty-one, he began practicing law and was elected to the Virginia House of Delegates for the first of several terms he was to serve there. He was elected to Congress in 1816, to the governorship of Virginia in 1825, and to the Senate in 1827. The root of his political philosophy was the Jeffersonian concept that the federal government derived its power from the initiative of the states, and that it should not be allowed to extend its power beyond that. In the Missouri Compromise debate, for example, Tyler fought against permitting Congress to concern itself with slavery in the territories—although as a slave-owner he wished the problem did not exist. In the South Carolina Nullification Crisis he never satisfied himself that nullification was proper, but he was more concerned with the federal reaction to the problem. He supported Jackson's lowering of the tariffs to levels acceptable to South Carolina, but he violently opposed the president's threat to move troops into that state. After helping to relieve the crisis by promoting the lower tariffs, Tyler voted against authorizing the president to use arms, if necessary, to enforce federal law in South Carolina. With most Southern members conveniently absent, the Senate approved the measure, 32 to 1. Tyler's lone negative vote was not based on the likelihood that the troops would actually be used, but on the principle that the federal government had no right to use troops against a state.

Tyler won the vice presidency despite an apparent disdain for the office. Late in 1835 a Democratic majority in the Virginia legislature began to prepare a resolution instructing the two Virginia Whig senators, Benjamin Leigh and John Tyler, to vote to expunge the 1833 censure of Andrew Jackson from the Senate Journal. Tyler was being asked to repudiate his earlier vote for the censure, and he felt that removing anything from the record was unconstitutional. But he also believed in the right of a state legislature to control the votes of the senators it appointed. Should he follow the instruction, or resign? Senator Leigh intended to ignore the order, and Whig leaders argued that the expunction would make a good campaign issue if both Virginia senators took the same course. The Whigs spoke pointedly of a vice presidential nomination for Tyler. But he refused to be swayed, and at the end of February 1836, he resigned. Still, he was nominated for vice president on two of the three regional Whig tickets that year—those headed by William Henry Harrison and Hugh L. White of Tennessee—and then ran third in a four-man race for the second office.

Less than two years later he was back in the Virginia House of Delegates, again being mentioned for the vice presidency. He decided to run for the Senate in 1839, and in the contest that followed he deadlocked with the incumbent, who had the support of "Clay Whigs," so-called at the time—loyalists who placed allegiance to Henry Clay ahead of any party loyalty. Tyler admired Clay, but he would not step aside, even when Clay promised the vice presidency as a reward. Tyler's stubbornness forced the state legislature to postpone the senatorial election; this upset the Whigs in Virginia, who refused to back him for the vice presidential nomination.

Thus renounced by his own state's Whig leadership, Tyler's status seemed precarious. He went on to support Clay for president, despite Clay's role in the senatorial contest and despite the fact that Clay's nomination would weaken his own chances for the vice presidency. When Clay lost the nomination to Harrison, the Whigs cast about among several possibilities for a running mate; they finally settled, without much enthusiasm, on John Tyler as a geographical, factional, and political counterweight to Harrison.

Whigs and Democrats alike admitted that Tyler was a kind, charming, generous man. Just as good breeding had given him this gracefulness, along with a rigid code of political behavior, it forbade his revealing details of his personal life to outsiders, or even appearing as if he had problems. He was almost always in financial difficulty; and Letitia Christian Tyler, to whom he had been happily married for

BIOGRAPHICAL FACTS

BIRTH: Charles City County, Va., Mar. 29, 1790
ANCESTRY: English
FATHER: John Tyler; b. James City County, Va., Feb. 28, 1747; d. Charles City County, Va., Jan. 6, 1813
FATHER'S OCCUPATIONS: Judge; governor of Virginia
MOTHER: Mary Marot Armistead Tyler; b. 1761; d. 1797
BROTHERS: Wat Henry (1788–1862); William (?–1856)
SISTERS: Anne Contesse (1778–1803); Elizabeth Armistead (1780–1824); Martha Jefferson (1782–1855); Maria Henry (1784–1843); Christianna Booth (1795–1842)
FIRST MARRIAGE: New Kent County, Va., Mar. 29, 1813
FIRST WIFE: Letitia Christian; b. New Kent County, Va., Nov. 12, 1790; d. Washington, D.C., Sept. 10, 1842
SECOND MARRIAGE: New York, N.Y., June 26, 1844
SECOND WIFE: Julia Gardiner: b. Gardiner's Island, N.Y., May 4, 1820; d. Richmond, Va., July 10, 1889
CHILDREN: (by first wife) Mary (1815–1848); Robert (1816–1877); John (1819–1896); Letitia (1821–1907); Elizabeth (1823–1850); Alice (1827–1854); Tazewell (1830–1874); (by second wife) David Gardiner (1846–1927); John Alexander (1848–1883); Julia (1849–1871); Lachlan (1851–1902); Lyon Gardiner (1853–1935); Robert Fitzwalter (1856–1927); Pearl (1860–1947)
RELIGIOUS AFFILIATION: Episcopalian
EDUCATION: Local Virginia schools; College of William and Mary (1807)
OCCUPATION BEFORE PRESIDENCY: Lawyer
MILITARY SERVICE: Capt. of volunteer company in Richmond, Va. (1813)
PREPRESIDENTIAL OFFICES: Member of Virginia House of Delegates; U.S. congressman; governor of Virginia; U.S. senator; U.S. vice president
AGE AT INAUGURATION: 51
OCCUPATION AFTER PRESIDENCY: Lawyer
DEATH: Richmond, Va., Jan. 18, 1862
PLACE OF BURIAL: Hollywood Cemetery, Richmond, Va.

twenty-seven years and who had borne him seven children, was by 1841—the year he succeeded Harrison—virtually an invalid, the result of a stroke. (She died in 1842.) But Tyler's private worries remained out of sight, behind the smile, the attentive gaze, the

After suffering a paralytic stroke in 1839, John Tyler's first wife, Letitia, became a recluse. In 1842 she made her only appearance at a presidential social function. That same year she died.

handsome compliment, the beautifully turned phrase of a Virginia gentleman.

Tyler would need to draw on all his Southern charm to win over Washington, for the stage was set for conflict. Within days of his arrival in the capital, Tyler was confronted by his first challenge from the party managers. Under Harrison, Webster said, executive decisions had been made in the cabinet, with the president having one vote. Would Tyler follow the same procedure? Certainly not, said Tyler. He wanted to keep the Harrison cabinet, but he alone would lead. If the cabinet members did not approve, they could resign. He would not only become president in name, but he would be president in fact.

The Whigs had a number of programs they wanted to enact into law, and they were led by men who interpreted the Constitution from a Northern and Western bias. In the executive chair sat Tyler, a man of opposite political prejudices, who declared his right to independent judgment and action.

And there was another, more crucial factor: Henry Clay wanted to be president. Harrison had promised to serve only one term. Clay had planned to use that time to promote his nationalist program in Congress and solidify his control over the Whig party so that he would win the 1844 nomination. Now the situation had changed. Tyler might be able to develop enough personal strength to block Clay's path to the executive office. Clay concluded that he had better grasp control while he could.

For the next two years the Clay-dominated Congress passed his pet bills (to revive the Bank of the United States, to repeal the Independent Treasury Act, and to distribute federal funds to states). Tyler declared in advance that he would not sign them and then, with politely stern explanations, vetoed most of them on constitutional grounds, to the accompaniment of loud and somewhat theatrical howls from the Clay Whigs. By September 14, 1841, five months after Tyler became president and five days after his second veto of a national bank bill, he had been burned in effigy in many cities, his entire cabinet, except Webster, had resigned in a body, and he had been solemnly expelled from the Whig party—for trespassing against principles that the Whigs had not dared to write into a platform for 1840.

To the Whig press, Tyler was now *persona non grata*, destined to be called Old Veto. There were charges of "executive dictation," assassination threats on the president's life, an effort to force Tyler's resignation, and even an abortive attempt to impeach him.

But Tyler stuck to his guns; he was isolated from partisan support, and the legislature refused to act on some of his routine requests, demonstrating petty vindictiveness by failing to appropriate funds for minor repairs to the White House.

In foreign affairs, however, Tyler's record was

impressive. The Webster-Ashburton Treaty, in which he played a dominant role, not only settled boundary disputes along the Canadian border, thus easing dangerous tension between Great Britain and the United States, but also made the United States a participant in policing the African coast to prevent illegal slave trading. Tyler enlarged the territory covered by the Monroe Doctrine to include the Hawaiian Islands, and a commercial treaty with China was signed in 1844. Indeed, Tyler was the first president to make gestures toward giving the United States a decided stake in the future of Pacific affairs.

Motivated by a long-standing continental image of the United States, Tyler also attempted to solve the boundary question in Oregon and to annex California. He was unsuccessful, but he provided the capstone for his administration, during its last days, by clearing the way for the annexation of Texas.

Tyler was concerned, practically from the beginning of his presidency, that he be remembered favorably. In October 1841 he wrote Webster about bringing Texas into the Union. "Could anything throw so bright a lustre around us?" he asked. As his term drew on, he thought of Texas annexation more and more as the means of assuring himself a respected place in history. Tyler saw in the status of Texas a method of creating a national political base that would serve as a springboard for the presidential campaign of 1844.

When, in the midterm elections, the Whig majority was swept from the House of Representatives and replaced by a sizable Democratic majority, Tyler interpreted the change as a public reproof to the Whigs for their opposition to the administration, and he decided that he could build out of the conservative Democrats and uncommitted Whigs an effective third force—a Tyler party. He probably would have accepted a second term as president in his own right, but it is unlikely that he believed in his chances of winning the election in 1844 without the backing of one of the two major parties; in midterm such backing seemed a faint hope. What he had in mind was the creation of "cells" in several important states in order to give himself political leverage and help him achieve something memorable as president. At the same time, he began to remove political enemies from federal offices.

The idea of Texas annexation had been under national consideration for about five years. The theory was that Texas would eventually be subdivided into perhaps four states, and consequently the central problem of annexation was slavery. Tyler argued that the slavery issue should be left alone; slavery would seek its economic and geographic limits and eventually its own

---

THE TYLER ADMINISTRATION

INAUGURATION: Apr. 6, 1841; Indian Queen Hotel, Washington, D.C.

SECRETARY OF STATE: Daniel Webster; Abel P. Upshur (from July 24, 1843); John C. Calhoun (from Apr. 1, 1844)

SECRETARY OF THE TREASURY: Thomas Ewing; Walter Forward (from Sept. 13, 1841); John C. Spencer (from Mar. 8, 1843); George M. Bibb (from July 4, 1844)

SECRETARY OF WAR: John Bell; John C. Spencer (from Oct. 12, 1841); James M. Porter (from Mar. 8, 1843); William Wilkins (from Feb. 20, 1844)

ATTORNEY GENERAL: John J. Crittenden; Hugh S. Legare (from Sept. 20, 1841); John Nelson (from July 1, 1843)

POSTMASTER GENERAL: Francis Granger; Charles A. Wickliffe (from Oct. 13, 1841)

SECRETARY OF THE NAVY: George E. Badger; Abel P. Upshur (from Oct. 11, 1841); David Henshaw (from July 24, 1843); Thomas W. Gilmer (from Feb. 19, 1844); John Y. Mason (from Mar. 26, 1844)

SUPREME COURT APPOINTMENT: Samuel Nelson (1845)

27TH CONGRESS (May 31, 1841–Mar. 3, 1843):
  SENATE: 29 Whigs; 22 Democrats
  HOUSE: 133 Whigs; 102 Democrats; 6 Others

28TH CONGRESS (Dec. 4, 1843–Mar. 3, 1845):
  SENATE: 29 Whigs; 23 Democrats
  HOUSE: 142 Democrats; 79 Whigs; 1 Other

STATE ADMITTED: Florida (1845)

His friends often referred to him as "the godlike Daniel." The expansive forehead underlined by heavy eyebrows; the wide, dark eyes; the deep, impressive actor's voice; and the brilliant grasp of oratorical effect made him one of the leading figures of the national capital for nearly forty years.

To John Tyler, Webster was, if not godlike, certainly a godsend. The secretary of state defined the vice president's role in the first succession crisis and supported Tyler's decision to become president. And it was Webster, alone among the members of the Harrison cabinet, who stuck by Tyler when Henry Clay, trying to isolate Tyler from the Whig party to aid his own drive toward the presidency, engineered a mass cabinet resignation on September 11, 1841. "Where am I to go, Mr. President?" asked Webster late on that unsettling day, knowing that if he did not quit, too, his party would make him suffer for it. "You must decide that for yourself . . ." said Tyler. "If you leave it to me, Mr. President," Webster replied, "I will stay where I am." Tyler shot to his feet and declared, "Give me your hand on that, and now I will say to you that Henry Clay is a doomed man." Diplomatically and politically Webster was of inestimable value to the president. Among their diplomatic successes was the Webster-Ashburton Treaty with Great Britain, setting the northern boundary of Maine and arranging United States participation in putting a stop to the African slave trade. When Webster at last felt forced to resign in 1843 because of the slavery implications of Texas annexation, there was no bitterness on either side, merely respect for each other's courage.

Webster was born January 18, 1782, the son of a New Hampshire farmer and small-time political leader. At fifteen he entered Dartmouth College, where he made his mark as a facile student and a budding orator. For a while after graduation he vacillated between the law and teaching, finally choosing the law, and by 1808 he was making his presence felt both in the courts and in politics. New Hampshire sent him to Congress in 1813, and from then until his death in 1852 he spent most of his life as a legislator and statesman. He was twice secretary of state. Throughout, he kept one eye on the presidency and sometimes trimmed his sails hoping to catch the breeze that might waft him closer to the White House. But he distinguished himself, nonetheless, by his nationalist vision and his grasp of issues. He rose to real greatness on occasion: the brave and patriotic support he gave Tyler; the thundering voice replying to Senator Robert Y. Hayne against nullification; the declaration of allegiance, not to Massachusetts (his home after 1816), nor to the North, but to Union and the Compromise of 1850. "You have manifested powers of intellect of the highest order," John Tyler told him in 1843, "and in all things a true American heart."

destruction. He urged, instead, concentration on the commercial advantages of having Texas in the Union—among other things, a virtual cotton monopoly for the United States—and its importance in terms of promoting a continental vision.

The argument did not, however, convince Webster. In May 1843 he resigned. With his antislavery Northeastern constituency to consider, Webster was unable to bring himself to work hard for Texas annexation. Tyler appointed Abel P. Upshur of Virginia to replace him as secretary of state. By October, Tyler and Upshur had begun secret negotiations with Texas, and before the end of the year it was apparent that annexation would have the necessary two-thirds support in the Senate. Tyler's playing down of the slavery question had succeeded, and his third-party drive had gained momentum. By mid-February 1844 the last important details of the treaty were worked out with the president of Texas, Sam Houston.

Meanwhile, Clay and John Calhoun hoped to win the 1844 nominations of their parties. To confuse matters, someone started a rumor that Tyler would soon announce he was not interested in being a candidate. But as the historian Norma Lois Peterson observes, "Tyler had not withdrawn." In fact, "he was stubbornly clinging to the frail hope that somehow the Democratic party might turn to him." And if that did not happen, perhaps he would be picked by "some nebulous third party."

Then, as Tyler stood within reach of his goal, tragedy struck: Upshur was killed in a freak accident, and Tylerite Henry A. Wise leaked information that Calhoun would be chosen to replace Upshur. Tyler had no such intention but was obliged to comply with the report to avoid the discord a denial would provoke in the South. So Calhoun, the South's leading intellectual, took over as chief negotiator of the Texas treaty, and the nationalist feeling that Tyler had worked so hard to create on the issue rapidly vanished. Instead of legitimate expansion of the Union, slavery became the central issue in the Texas question, and as the senators were forced to take sides, support for annexation dwindled away.

In the words of Robert Seager II, Tyler's most recent major biographer, "Tyler reluctantly reached for a political blackjack." The Democrats met in Baltimore on May 27 to nominate a candidate but were somewhat divided over the slavery question. The Tyler party also convened in the same city that day— as a reminder of the inroads the president had made in the conservative wing of the Democratic party— and nominated Tyler on the slogan "Tyler and Texas." The strategy worked. Van Buren, who opposed annexation, failed to get the Democratic nomination; the proannexation "dark horse," James K. Polk, was chosen as the candidate instead, and an annexation plank was included in the party's platform.

Exultant, Tyler now offered to withdraw from the race if the Texas treaty was ratified. But the damage done by the slavery issue could not be easily repaired. Annexation was defeated badly in the Senate on June 8, 1844. So in New York, New Jersey, and Pennsylvania, the Tyler organizations began to make plans to field candidates for every possible office in the fall elections, in competition with Democratic slates. This frightened Democratic party leaders, and in late July they capitulated, as Andrew Jackson communicated assurances about Texas and federal jobs for Tyler men. New York's Tammany Hall came to terms in August, and Tyler threw his support to Polk.

When Polk won in November, Tyler moved quickly to collect part of his debts. He declared that Polk's election represented a mandate concerning Texas. At Tyler's urging, Congress sidestepped the constitutional demand for a two-thirds Senate ratification of the treaty and approved a joint resolution calling for the admission of Texas as a state. On March 1, 1845, with less than three days left in his term, Tyler signed the bill.

With his new bride, Julia Gardiner Tyler, whom he had married in June of 1844, Tyler retired to a plantation in Virginia and raised wheat, corn, and a new family of seven. As a leading moderate he remained a possible presidential nominee every four years until 1860. In 1861 he presided over the Washington peace conference that attempted to avoid civil war. In mid-conference he became a secessionist, hoping he could help create a pacifying balance of military power between the two sections. When Richmond became the Confederate capital, Tyler accepted a seat in the Confederacy's Provisional Congress, and he won election to the Confederate House of Representatives in November 1861. But by now he was ill and tired. On January 12, 1862, he suffered a stroke; six days later he was dead. His body lay in state in the Confederate Congress and then was buried beside the grave of James Monroe.

—*Michael Harwood,*
revised by Robert A. Rutland

JAMES KNOX POLK

THE DARK HORSE

Although James Polk is often ranked in the second tier of American presidents, few occupants of the White House have worked as hard or taken their promises to the voters as seriously. Polk was also our first "dark horse" candidate—a nominee whose name was barely mentioned in the weeks before his selection—and yet he was by experience and connections destined to play a major role in the nation's history. If Manifest Destiny was the polestar of the nation in the 1840s and 1850s, Polk's efforts were the chief cause of real meaning behind the slogan.

Polk was in a sense the protégé of President Andrew Jackson. And it was Jackson who said in 1837 that the American people were chosen by Providence to be "the guardians of freedom to preserve it for the benefit of the human race." From Maine to Georgia, from Virginia to Missouri, the American people wholeheartedly agreed. Confident of their ability to read the mind of God, convinced of the superiority of their customs and institutions, they believed all their causes just and all their endeavors moral: What was good for them was good for everyone. Thus, in the 1840s, as the country reached across the wilderness toward the Pacific Ocean, Americans thought about and talked about expansion as though it were a great crusade.

It was this ambitious, cocksure, destiny-enraptured America that Polk was elected to lead. In the two decades preceding his election in 1844, missionaries, explorers, whalers, and traders in furs and hides had blazed new trails to the West. Then the pathfinders—the John C. Frémonts and Kit Carsons—cleared the way for settlers. Once seeming as remote as Mars, California and Oregon beckoned settlers who dreamed of a Utopia on the Pacific.

There were roadblocks, however. By 1844 Americans had reached and crossed the Western boundaries of their country. But California was Mexico's, and the Oregon Territory, in accordance with an 1818 treaty, was to be shared by the United States and Great Britain. The majority of the American people wanted these Pacific-facing lands for their own, and they elected Polk because he accepted the Manifest Destiny justification for national expansion.

First, Polk had to win the presidency by turning back the perennial Whig candidate, Henry Clay. The cagey Kentuckian was a formidable opponent, but Polk's determination attracted voters to his banner and he won in a three-way contest. James G. Birney, candidate of the antislavery Liberty party, was the spoiler as he received 62,103 popular votes. Polk edged out Clay by only 39,490 votes but won easily in the electoral college, 170 to 105. Clay was far from dead politically, but Polk was president.

Shortly after his inauguration in 1845, Polk confided to Secretary of the Navy George Bancroft that he had four goals for his administration. Slapping his thigh for emphasis, he enumerated them: "one, a reduction of the tariff; another, the independent treasury; a third, the settlement of the Oregon boundary question; and, lastly, the acquisition of California." These were not just Polk's goals; they were the nation's. Regarding his election as the people's mandate, he concentrated his energies on realizing their will. While accomplishing all four goals, he added more than a million square miles of territory to the United States and became one of the country's most effective presidents.

Polk was born in Mecklenburg County, North Carolina, on November 2, 1795, the first of ten children. His father, Samuel Polk, a prosperous farmer, was apparently indifferent to the pious Presbyterianism of his wife, Jane, whose great joy, a friend of Polk's reported, lay in "the Bible, the Confession of Faith, the Psalms and Watt's Hymns." On the occasion of his son's baptism, Samuel Polk engaged the minister in a bitter quarrel; the sacrament was not consummated, and Polk was not baptized until fifty-four years later as he lay on his deathbed.

A daguerreotype of James Knox Polk taken in Mathew Brady's studio on February 14, 1849.

President Polk's cabinet sat for John Plumbe, Jr., in 1845 for a daguerreotype which is believed to be the first ever taken in the White House. Postmaster General Cave Johnson stands in the rear (left) next to Secretary of the Navy George Bancroft. Seated are, from left, Attorney General John Y. Mason; Secretary of War William L. Marcy; President Polk; and Secretary of the Treasury Robert J. Walker.

Nevertheless, Polk's upbringing was religious, and he seems to have gained strength from his Calvinistic faith, which anchored Polk's feeling that destiny beckoned men and nations. Always frail and sickly, he was strong-willed enough to survive a gallstone operation performed in his seventeenth year, without anesthesia or antiseptics, on a bare wooden table in Danville, Kentucky. Polk was no coward, his neighbors reckoned, but was as tough as a hickory knot.

All the Polks were keenly interested in politics, and James Polk prepared himself for a political career. After graduating with honors from the University of

North Carolina in 1818, he traveled to Tennessee, where he studied law for two years and was admitted to the bar. He became a prominent lawyer in that rugged young state and renewed his acquaintance with his father's friend, General Andrew Jackson, who had become America's foremost national hero.

In 1824, following two years in the Tennessee legislature, Polk was a candidate for the House of Representatives, running as a Democratic-Republican on a ticket headed by Old Hickory. Jackson lost, but Polk did not. He journeyed on horseback and by stagecoach to Washington, where he attracted attention as an industrious Jacksonian Democrat who proved to be a thorn in the side of President John Quincy Adams. The chief executive found Polk to have "no wit, no literature . . . no elegance of language . . . no pathos, no felicitous impromptus; nothing that can constitute an orator but confidence, fluency, and labor."

In short, Polk was a Presbyterian workhorse who rarely made jokes but burned the midnight candles by the bundle. A political opponent, George McDuffie of South Carolina, was also both impressed and annoyed by Polk's performance in the House and credited the congressman "with a tact and skill and zeal worthy of a better cause."

Somber, stern, thin-lipped, James Knox Polk was physically undistinguished. He was slender and of medium height; he had cold, penetrating eyes, a large, broad forehead, and he wore his hair combed straight back. Carrying himself stiffly erect, he was formal, dignified, and fastidious. Although the historian Arthur Schlesinger, Jr., credits him with "an exceptionally winning smile," Polk apparently was stingy with it, and he was reluctant to express his personal feelings. One of his great political strengths was his excessive reserve, a tendency to be secretive, to hoard knowledge and say little. Polk made adroit use of his cool head in the tense House where he tried to be a fair but loyal Jacksonian.

During the administrations of Andrew Jackson and his hand-picked successor, Martin Van Buren, Polk's career flourished. In 1832 he achieved membership on the House Ways and Means Committee, where he loyally supported Jackson's opposition to the Bank of the United States. Three years later he became Speaker of the House, a position that exposed him to bitter attack. Called Young Hickory and accused of being the lackey of the president, Polk was also the convenient whipping boy for anti-Jacksonians who did not wish to incur public wrath by assaulting the heroic president himself.

BIOGRAPHICAL FACTS

BIRTH: Mecklenburg County, N.C., Nov. 2, 1795
ANCESTRY: Scotch-Irish
FATHER: Samuel Polk: b. Tryon, N.C., July 5, 1772;
  d. Maury County, Tenn., Nov. 5, 1827
FATHER'S OCCUPATION: Farmer
MOTHER: Jane Knox Polk; b. Iredell County, N.C.,
  Nov. 15, 1776; d. Maury County, Tenn., Jan 11, 1852
BROTHERS: Franklin Ezekiel (1802–1831); Marshall Tate
  (1805–1831); John Lee (1807–1831); William
  Hawkins (1815–1862); Samuel Wilson (1817–1839)
SISTERS: Jane Maria (1798–1876); Lydia Eliza
  (1800–1864); Naomi Tate (1809–1836); Ophelia
  Clarissa (1812–1851)
MARRIAGE: Murfreesboro, Tenn., Jan. 1, 1824
WIFE: Sarah Childress; b. Murfreesboro, Tenn.,
  Sept. 4, 1803; d. Nashville, Tenn., Aug. 14, 1891
CHILDREN: None
RELIGIOUS AFFILIATION: Presbyterian
EDUCATION: Private school; University of North Carolina
  (B.A., 1818); studied law
OCCUPATION BEFORE PRESIDENCY: Lawyer
PREPRESIDENTIAL OFFICES: Member of Tennessee
  Legislature; U.S. congressman; Speaker of the House of
  Representatives; governor of Tennessee
AGE AT INAUGURATION: 49
OCCUPATION AFTER PRESIDENCY: Retired
DEATH: Nashville, Tenn., June 15, 1849
PLACE OF BURIAL: State Capitol Grounds,
  Nashville, Tenn.

In 1839 the Democratic party of Tennessee drafted Polk as its candidate for governor. Although he would have preferred to remain in Washington, he accepted the draft and was elected. In his bid for reelection two years later, and in another try in 1843, he was defeated by a preference for the Whigs that had affected much of the nation. Van Buren, too, had lost his reelection bid for the presidency to William Henry Harrison; but John Tyler, Harrison's successor, soon alienated himself from the Whig leadership and was in turn rejected by his party. As the election of 1844 approached, Henry Clay, the oft-beaten, oft-thwarted

---

SAMUEL HOUSTON

"Gov. Houston," wrote Washington Irving of the hero of the Texas Revolution, was a "tall, large, well formed, fascinating man . . . given to grandiloquence." Friend and defender of the Cherokee Nation, Sam Houston led the rugged life of a frontier soldier and statesman. He fought in the Creek War with Andrew Jackson, became district attorney for Nashville, served two terms in Congress, and in 1827 was elected governor of Tennessee. Two years later, when his bride of three months left him, Houston resigned the governorship, went to live among the Cherokees in Indian Territory, and became an Indian trader on the Verdigris River. Establishing himself at Nacogdoches in 1835, he was soon enmeshed in the struggle for Texan independence. As commander of the Texas troops, he defeated Santa Anna's army at the San Jacinto in 1836 and was rewarded with the presidency of the new republic. Elected for a second term in 1841, Houston yielded to the popular cry of the expansionists and guided Texas into the Union. For thirteen years he served as a United States senator from Texas, and in 1859 he was elected governor. Opposed to secession and refusing to acknowledge the authority of the Confederate government, Houston resigned in 1861. Two years later the Texas patriot died at the age of seventy.

Whig aspirant, looked forward to a victorious race against Van Buren, who appeared to be the logical Democratic choice. And Polk, due to his long and faithful service to the Jacksonians, seemed to have earned the right to his party's vice presidential nomination.

There is a story, perhaps apocryphal, that Henry Clay was relaxing at his home when his son rushed in and asked him to guess who had won the Democratic nomination. "Why Matty of course," said Clay. His son shook his head. "Then Cass?" Again the younger Clay gestured negatively. "Then Buchanan?" No. "Then who in the hell is he?" Told that James Polk would oppose him, Clay reportedly groaned, "Beaten again, by God."

Clay's prophecy was fulfilled chiefly because he temporized on the Texas issue—the same issue that had cost Martin Van Buren his party's nomination. Immediately after the United States recognized the independence of Texas in 1836, the former Mexican region applied for admission to the Union; but since statehood would have destroyed the delicate balance between slave and free states that had existed since 1820, American politicians generally avoided the issue. In April 1844 President Tyler, hearing that Texas was negotiating a treaty with England, asked Congress to hedge no longer and approve annexation, but the legislators were unsure about the people's reactions and refused to vote for annexation in an election year. Both Clay and Van Buren announced that they intended to keep Texas out of the approaching campaign.

At the Hermitage, meanwhile, Andrew Jackson was disgusted with the political backing-and-filling. Jackson was confident that the people wanted Texas in the Union in no uncertain terms. Summoning several Democratic leaders, including Polk, to his Tennessee home, he told them that Van Buren's anti-Texas position was political suicide. Making "All of Oregon, All of Texas" a campaign pledge, he said,

U.S. Army Officer Henry Warre painted this view of Oregon City in 1846. During the 1844 presidential campaign there was much shouting about the disputed Oregon Territory–Canadian border, but once Polk was elected he dropped the warlike talk, and a settlement with England was negotiated.

would satisfy North and South and the people's desire to expand. Polk was from the region then considered the Southwest, Polk was for annexation, Polk could win. Following Old Hickory's advice, the Jacksonian leaders deadlocked the party convention in Baltimore for seven ballots (two-thirds of the delegate votes were required for nomination), then brought forth the previously unmentioned Polk, who won the nomination on the ninth ballot.

Despite the fact that Andrew Jackson had indeed measured the people's sentiments correctly, the odds seemed to be against a Polk victory. The people wanted all of Oregon and all of Texas, and they liked the Democratic slogan, "54°40' or Fight!" However,

Henry Clay was infinitely better known than Polk and had always been popular in the frontier states. Even in Polk's home state, the Tennessee Whigs insisted that Clay's turn had finally come to pass. Polk's service had been principally in party and legislative circles, but Clay was a national figure who had seldom strayed from the center of activity.

Indeed, the election was much closer than was expected in a nation so sure of its manifest destiny. Because of his hedging on the Texas question, Senator Clay lost votes in New York to the third candidate, abolitionist James Birney. As a result, Polk captured a small plurality of the New York vote, and its 36 electoral votes insured Polk's victory in the electoral college.

THE POLK ADMINISTRATION

INAUGURATION: Mar. 4, 1845; the Capitol,
   Washington, D.C.
VICE PRESIDENT: George M. Dallas
SECRETARY OF STATE: James Buchanan
SECRETARY OF THE TREASURY: Robert J. Walker
SECRETARY OF WAR: William L. Marcy
ATTORNEY GENERAL: John Y. Mason;
   Nathan Clifford (from Oct. 17, 1846);
   Isaac Toucey (from June 29, 1848)
POSTMASTER GENERAL: Cave Johnson
SECRETARY OF THE NAVY: George Bancroft;
   John Y. Mason (from Sept. 9, 1846)
SUPREME COURT APPOINTMENTS: Levi Woodbury (1845);
   Robert Cooper Grier (1846)
29TH CONGRESS (Dec. 1, 1845–Mar. 3, 1847):
   SENATE: 34 Democrats; 22 Whigs
   HOUSE: 143 Democrats; 77 Whigs; 6 Others
30TH CONGRESS (Dec. 6, 1847–Mar. 3, 1849):
   SENATE: 38 Democrats; 21 Whigs;
      1 Independent Democrat
   HOUSE: 115 Whigs; 108 Democrats; 4 Others
STATES ADMITTED: Texas (1845); Iowa (1846);
   Wisconsin (1848)

ELECTION OF 1844

CANDIDATES	ELECTORAL VOTE	POPULAR VOTE
James K. Polk (Democratic)	170	1,339,494
Henry Clay (Whig)	105	1,300,004
James G. Birney (Liberty)	—	62,103

Who, indeed, was this James K. Polk, whose significance was dismissed by many contemporaries and whose reputation has grown steadily and continues to grow in our own time? According to the historian Bernard De Voto, "Polk's mind was rigid, narrow, obstinate, far from first-rate. . . . But if his mind was narrow it was also powerful and he had guts. If he was orthodox, his integrity was absolute and he could not be scared, manipulated, or brought to heel. No one bluffed him, no one moved him with direct or oblique pressure." Like his mentor, Old Hickory, Polk "knew how to get things done, which is the first necessity of government, and he knew what he wanted done, which is the second." After a string of presidents who played second-fiddle to Congress, Polk "was to be the only 'strong' President between Jackson and Lincoln. He was to fix the mold of the future in America down to 1860, and therefore for a long time afterward. That is who James K. Polk was."

Polk was also indefatigable, and his tenacity served him well in the White House. Once, vexed with his secretary for taking an unscheduled pleasure trip, he accused the young man of not giving "that close and systematic attention to business which is necessary to give himself reputation." This was Polk's prescription, and he practiced what he preached. He worked so hard that he had "but little opportunity to read newspapers," and called himself "the hardest-working man in this country." Finding that too much time was lost daily to office seekers, favor seekers, curious businessmen, and visiting Indians, Polk resolved to see no visitors after the noon hour. He also inveighed against the spoils system, which so exhausted the nation's chief patronage dispenser. Polk was, in sum, a man who rose to fit the job, who worked as hard as was necessary to do whatever had to be done.

He brought to Washington a first lady much like his mother. He had married Sarah Childress in 1824, when she was a plain but vivacious twenty-year-old. A woman of unflinching Presbyterianism, she banned dancing in the White House, but she was considerably more popular in the capital than her husband. Henry Clay, no teetotaler himself, once gallantly informed her that there was "a general approbation expressed of her administration . . . [whereas] there was some difference of opinion about her husband's administration."

Polk first tackled the Oregon boundary question. Since 1818 the Oregon Territory had been held jointly by the United States and Great Britain, with both nations having the option to terminate the agreement on a year's notice. Although "54°40' or Fight!" had been the Democratic slogan during the election, Polk had instructed his secretary of state, James Buchanan, to suggest the forty-ninth parallel as a final border between the United States and Canada. When England refused, holding firm in its demands for all land north of the Columbia River, Polk decided to exercise the termination clause of the agreement. In his first annual message to Congress he said that "the extraordinary and wholly inadmissible demands of the British Government" could not be countenanced. A few days later he told a visiting congressman: "The only way to treat John Bull was to look him straight in the eye . . . if Congress faltered or hesitated in their course, John Bull would immediately become arrogant and more grasping in his demands." Congress was willing to gamble on war and authorized termination on April 23, 1846.

Meanwhile, owing to the pacific policies of British Foreign Minister Lord Aberdeen, public opinion in England inclined toward a settlement at the forty-ninth parallel. In June, Secretary of State Buchanan received almost the same offer that Britain had turned down the year before. A rejection of the new proposal would probably mean war; in view of the growing crisis with Mexico, Polk and most of his cabinet decided to avoid the risk by accepting the offer.

Buchanan, however, aspired to the presidency. He hesitated to endorse or reject the British settlement until he could determine where political capital could be made; after pursuing a soft line, he gradually turned truculent. The rest of the cabinet advised the president to lay the proposal before the Senate, but Buchanan, mumbling something about "caking out from 54°40'," sulkily refused to help Polk prepare the message. Polk was always stronger than his cabinet or any one member: The message he prepared was accepted, and the treaty was signed on June 15, 1846.

Repercussions came immediately from the Western war hawks. Senator William Allen of Ohio resigned the chairmanship of the Committee on Foreign Relations. Senators Edward Hannegan of Indiana, James Semple of Illinois, and David Atchison of Missouri "lashed themselves into a passion" over the loss of all of Oregon and immediately crossed the aisle

Polk's "House of Cards" was a Whig cartoon jibe at the dark-horse candidate in 1844. The resourceful president worked out solutions to the Oregon boundary dispute, the Mexico conflict, and the tariff issue, building a solid political structure around himself.

A lithograph shows General Winfield Scott leading the victorious U.S. Army into Mexico City in September 1847. Polk wanted to extend the United States to the Pacific Ocean, and he welcomed the war with Mexico that made such expansion possible. Within three years California was in the Union and Manifest Destiny was a reality.

to vote with the Whigs. Worse, as Polk noted, "they oppose, too, and embarrass the military bills for the prosecution of the war against Mexico."

Still, Polk preferred diplomacy to war and tried to buy out the Mexican opposition. In November the diplomat John Slidell was sent to Mexico to offer up to forty million dollars for Upper California, New Mexico, and the Rio Grande as a boundary for Texas, but the Mexican government refused to receive the American representative. Finally, in April 1846, the fighting began in a disputed area in Texas between the Nueces River and the Rio Grande. The presence of Americans in the disputed territory was regarded by Mexicans as proof that Mexico had been invaded; but the presence of Mexicans north of the Rio Grande meant to Americans that the United States had been invaded.

In all likelihood, Polk had planned to declare war anyway, but the battle provided the excuse. "American blood has been spilled on American soil," the war message claimed, and on May 13, 1846, Congress declared war.

Enraged Northern Whigs claimed Polk had started the war in connivance with the Southern states for the acquisition of more slave territory. Though Polk was a slaveholder with a Tennessee plantation, he sought to avoid the volatile issue insofar as his policy decisions were concerned. But Congress would not let him. Convinced that Mexico would not agree to peace terms unless it acquired enough money to at least pay its army, the president requested two million dollars be made available. Pennsylvania Congressman David Wilmot attached to the appropriations bill a proviso that slavery be excluded from any lands acquired from Mexico.

Not until a bloody civil war erupted would the issue disappear, and the next fifteen years saw a constant legislative turmoil revolving around the slavery question. The Wilmot Proviso did not pass, but neither did the appropriations bill. "What connection slavery had with making peace with Mexico it is difficult to conceive," wrote Polk. Deprived of working funds, he now decided to acquire territory solely by military means. As Polk soon learned, the military aspect of the war had become just as political as the congressional battlefield.

When "Old Rough-and-Ready," General Zachary Taylor, engaged and defeated the Mexicans with his underdog forces in southern Texas, he became a national hero and, in the eyes of Eastern Whig leaders, a potential presidential candidate. In Washington, Winfield Scott, another Whig presidential hopeful and commanding general of the Army, was anxious to follow up Taylor's victories with an immediate seaborne invasion of Mexico.

President Polk, however, had other ideas. In the first place, he was by no means anxious to assist either general into the White House, and in the second, he still had hopes of acquiring New Mexico and California by diplomacy. To increase his chances of diplomatic success, Polk agreed to enlist the services of the defeated former Mexican dictator Santa Anna, who was in exile in Cuba. A man of astonishing duplicity, Santa Anna was anxious to regain power in Mexico.

By Polk's order the Mexican general was to be afforded safe conduct through the American blockade and, having resecured his place in the Mexican government, was expected to cooperate with the United States in negotiating a settlement. In the meantime, he would supply the Americans with military advice. On August 16 Santa Anna arrived in Veracruz and, in a classic double-cross, immediately condemned any attempt to negotiate with the United States. Within a month he was back in uniform, and before the end of the year, he was elected president of Mexico and had pledged to drive the Americans back on all fronts.

As soon as Santa Anna revealed that he had no intention of working for the United States, President Polk no longer had reason to prevent an invasion of Mexico. After Taylor took Monterrey in September, nine thousand of his men were transferred to Scott's army. Despite his diminished forces, Taylor met Santa Anna at Buena Vista and won a bloody battle. In March 1847 Scott took Veracruz and proceeded inland through the spring and summer, reaching Mexico City by the middle of September. Santa Anna retreated to Guadalupe Hidalgo and renounced his presidency. Two months later the Mexican interim government named a commission to negotiate a treaty.

Representing the United States was Nicholas P. Trist, chief clerk of the State Department. Dispatched in April 1847, Trist had been empowered to offer fifteen million dollars (although he could go as high as twenty) for the Rio Grande as a boundary and the cession of New Mexico and Upper California. (California had actually been in American hands throughout much of the hostilities, and uprisings by local Mexicans were considered "insurrections.") The mission was supposed to be secret, but less than a week after Trist's departure from Washington, an item in the New York *Herald* gave all the details of the assignment. After that, Polk lost confidence in the mission.

When word reached him in October that the Mexicans had refused the terms offered by Trist, the president decided to recall his envoy and to pursue a program of total victory over Mexico. Even the possibility of annexing the entire country was considered. Trist ignored the notice of recall, however, and the president was furious, as the whole affair seemed out of his control. Yet, on February 19, 1848, when the Treaty of Guadalupe Hidalgo—signed seventeen days earlier by Trist and the Mexican commissioners—arrived in Washington, a grateful Polk submitted it to the Congress.

Why do otherwise? Trist's treaty contained provisions for everything he had wanted: The Rio Grande became the final border; New Mexico and California became American territory; and the Mexicans settled for fifteen million dollars in gold. As the New York Whig Philip Hone put it, the treaty, ratified March 10, was "negotiated by an unauthorized agent, with an unacknowledged government, [and] submitted by an accidental President to a dissatisfied Senate." But the Senate ratified the maligned document with a sigh of relief.

Observers in the capital and elsewhere realized that the treaty achieved the last of Polk's four goals. Most presidents want carte blanche when they take office, with no strings attached. Polk had made his promises—and kept them.

During the Jackson administration, Polk had labored long and hard against the Bank of the United States. Largely through Polk's efforts, Congress had agreed to withdraw public funds from the bank and allow its charter to expire. As Speaker during the Van Buren administration, Polk helped establish an Independent Treasury, but the Whig victory in 1840 led to its repeal a year later, and the management of public money was left to the secretary of the treasury, who had no legal guidelines to follow. Alongside his triumphs on the battlefield and diplomatic table, Polk restored the Independent Treasury Act in 1846—which remains in operation today.

After an arduous struggle, Polk also managed to enact the Walker Tariff of 1846, which greatly reduced the duties set on imports by the Whig Tariff of 1842. Northern industrialists denounced it bitterly, but it was one of the few issues on which the president had the full support of Senator John C. Calhoun. The significance of the tariff lay in the impetus it provided to free trade, a trend that lasted until the Civil War and helped avoid a repeated cycle of the depressions of the 1830s.

There was still one final triumph left for Polk, who

had announced he would not be a candidate for the presidential election. On December 5, 1848, as the lame-duck president gave his last annual message to Congress, he announced that gold had been discovered in California. The revelation gave impetus to westward movement, and within months the gold rush was on. Yet, despite the obvious potential of the West, a harshly divided Congress had failed to provide territorial governments for New Mexico and California in preparation for eventual statehood.

The troublesome slavery questions caused a stalemate in Congress. Polk did not want that issue to interfere with the future of the nation that now spanned the continent. He said, "In the eyes of the world and of posterity how trivial and insignificant will be all our internal divisions and struggles compared with the preservation of this Union of the States in all its vigor and with all its countless blessings! No patriot would foment and excite geographical and sectional divisions. No lover of his country would deliberately calculate the value of the Union." Southern Democrats and Northern Whigs ignored Polk's advice and left the territorial question unanswered when Congress adjourned in 1848.

Polk was eager to leave the White House. Predictably, the Whig hero General Zachary Taylor won the election of 1848, and at his inauguration in March 1849, Polk found his successor "exceedingly ignorant of public affairs, and . . . of very ordinary capacity." Then the ex-president retired to his home in Tennessee. The chronic diarrhea that had plagued him during his administration recurred, and it was soon evident that he had left his resiliency in the White House. He had been home less than four months when he died on June 15, 1849, and was buried in Nashville.

Like Andrew Jackson, Polk regarded himself as the servant and representative of the people. He opposed Clay's "American System" because he thought it unconstitutional in that it benefited few at the expense of many. He accepted the Manifest Destiny concept of American expansion because that is what the people wanted. He lowered the tariff because he felt the people—not the manufacturers—should choose their own goods from among the best available in an open market. He revived the Independent Treasury because he thought the people's money should be protected by law, not handled by the judgment of profit-minded bankers. He was able to carry out his program because he was a superb administrator, keeping his fingers in every crevice of government, and by his own tenacity setting an example he expected all to follow. A moderate in the midst of radicals and reactionaries, he had many enemies on both sides of the congressional aisles. Unlike the mediocrities who surrounded him, Polk kept his promises to the nation. For that achievement, he is still remembered as an outstanding leader and a promise-keeper.

—SAUL BRAUN,
revised by ROBERT A. RUTLAND

ZACHARY TAYLOR

OLD ROUGH-AND-READY

On the night of March 4, 1849, when "Old Rough-and-Ready" Zachary Taylor entered Washington for his inauguration as president, he was greeted by a crowd said to be the largest ever seen in the capital. A holiday mood prevailed as bonfires crackled, fireworks burst in the night sky, and cannons thudded salutes. All this clamor was simply the last act of a drama begun along the banks of the Rio Grande in 1846. As the historian Bernard De Voto writes, "It cost a lot of blood and treasure to make Zachary Taylor president of the United States for sixteen months."

When Taylor died, in July of 1850, the crowd was in a different mood. More than one hundred carriages and a procession nearly two miles long accompanied his flag-draped coffin to the grave, while thousands upon thousands of mourners lined the funeral route. To his contemporaries, Taylor was a war hero and a popular president.

Time, however, has eroded his stature. Taylor's modern-day obscurity is understandable, because in the tug of war that created and characterized the crisis of 1850, the president played only a passive role. All along, Whigs expected a dominant Congress to guide national policy on expansion and slavery; instead, its principal players shaped an ephemeral pacifier—the Compromise of 1850. A temporary solution was better than none, so the half-hearted measure became law only over Taylor's dead body.

Zachary Taylor was an offspring of Virginia's aristocratic revolutionary generation. His father, Richard Taylor, was descended from a line of wealthy planters and served in the 1st Virginia Regiment during the War for Independence, rising to lieutenant colonel. Richard's wife, Sarah Dabney Strother, was similarly wellborn and had been educated by private tutors. In 1784, after five years of marriage, Richard, his pregnant wife, and their two sons left their comfortable home near the Rapidan River to strike out for Kentucky and a new life. On November 24, in a rough-hewn outbuilding on a relative's estate that lay along the way, Sarah bore Richard a third son, whom they named Zachary. After a few months he was taken to a wilderness settlement on Beargrass Creek, near Louisville, where the family began to farm. "Here," wrote a visitor of Taylor's early childhood, "we were saluted every night with the howling of wolves." Here, also, Indians harassed the settlers. On the frontier Zachary received a rudimentary education—first from a wandering Connecticut schoolteacher, and then from an Irish scholar who set up a school in the neighborhood. Richard and Sarah passed on to their children the respect for culture and education inherent in Virginia society; but on the frontier, horsemanship and skill with a musket often counted for more.

At twenty-three, Zachary Taylor accepted a commission as a first lieutenant in the Army. During the next forty years, except for one brief hiatus after the War of 1812, he remained an Army officer. In 1810 he married Margaret Mackall Smith; they had six children, only four of whom—three daughters and a son—survived infancy. In addition to his roles as a husband, father, and career soldier, Taylor took on the ownership of a plantation and accumulated a small fortune in land and slaves in Louisiana and Mississippi. Acquaintances remarked how he preferred discussing crops, the weather, and farming methods to any other kind of talk. But he had to do most of his farming by mail, through plantation managers, as his Army service took him from Illinois to the Gulf of Mexico, from the District of Columbia to Minnesota.

Taylor showed courage and developed a flair for leadership when he fought the British and the Indians in the War of 1812; he gained a reputation for bravery and improvisational skills in battle and for fairness in administering Indian affairs. He built roads, bridges, and forts, and commanded numerous Army

Taylor's military heroics won him the presidency. This photograph was taken shortly before his death in 1850.

BIRTH: Orange County, Va., Nov. 24, 1784

ANCESTRY: English

FATHER: Richard Taylor; b. Orange County, Va., Apr. 3, 1744; d. near Louisville, Ky., Jan. 19, 1829

FATHER'S OCCUPATIONS: Soldier; landowner

MOTHER: Sarah Dabney Strother Taylor; b. Dec. 14, 1760; d. Dec. 13, 1822

BROTHERS: Hancock (1781–1841); William Dabney Strother (1782–1808); George (1790–1829); Joseph Pannill (1796–1864)

SISTERS: Elizabeth Lee (1792–1845); Sarah Bailey (1799–1851); Emily Richard (1801–1841)

MARRIAGE: Jefferson County, Ky., June 21, 1810

WIFE: Margaret Mackall Smith; b. Maryland, Sept. 21, 1788; d. Pascagoula, Miss., Aug. 18, 1852

CHILDREN: Anne Margaret Mackall (1811–1875); Sarah Knox (1814–1835); Octavia Pannill (1816–1820); Margaret Smith (1819–1820); Mary Elizabeth (1824–1909); Richard (1826–1879)

RELIGIOUS AFFILIATION: Episcopalian

EDUCATION: Limited tutorial education

OCCUPATIONS BEFORE PRESIDENCY: Soldier; farmer

MILITARY SERVICE: Volunteer in Kentucky militia (1803); rose from 1st lt. to maj. gen. in U.S. Army (1808–1849)

AGE AT INAUGURATION: 64

DEATH: Washington, D.C., July 9, 1850

PLACE OF BURIAL: Zachary Taylor National Cemetery, Louisville, Ky.

---

posts. Promotions came slowly; still, by 1844 he was a brevet brigadier general and commanding officer of the First Department, United States Army, at Fort Jesup, Louisiana.

"He looked like a man born to command," a fellow officer had written in 1832. Yet in many ways General Zachary Taylor's appearance was rather odd. His large head and torso did not seem to match his unusually short legs. A typical uniform for him consisted of baggy cotton pants, a plain coat bearing no insignia, and a farmer's wide-brimmed straw hat. He reviewed his troops or observed a battle's progress seated sideways on his war horse, "Old Whitey," with one leg thrown over the pommel of his saddle. From a distance he may have appeared merely eccentric. But in his seamed and craggy face could be read a remarkable depth of spirit. His gaze was direct—as was he. His officers respected Taylor's concern for his men and the thoroughness of his attention to details.

General Taylor's assignment in Louisiana in 1844 was a part of America's preparation for Texas annexation. While Congress argued over the delicate diplomacy involved, the Mexicans threatened war, convinced that Texas was still theirs despite a successful rebellion in 1836. When a Texas convention accepted annexation in July 1844, Taylor moved in with his forces and set up a base camp at Corpus Christi. There the growing army was drilled until early in 1846. By then Mexico seemed less decisive about opposing annexation, but a new dispute had surfaced: Texas claimed the Rio Grande as her southern boundary, and Mexico protested that the border should be farther north. Taylor began to head toward the Rio Grande.

The first skirmish of the war was fought on April 25, when an American scouting party was ambushed. Taylor hastened to inform his superiors that the shooting had started, and by the time war was formally declared by Congress—on May 13—two major battles had already been fought above the Rio Grande—at Palo Alto and the Resaca de la Palma. Taylor's army, although greatly outnumbered, had triumphed at both. The two battles, fought in the name of Manifest Destiny, soon made General Taylor a national hero.

Before a month was out, Taylor had also become a pawn in the game of national politics, for he made no bones about his party affiliation. He was a Whig. President Polk knew this and was not eager to push Taylor into the hero's role. Meanwhile, Thurlow Weed, a New York editor and the boss of the Eastern Whigs, predicted to the general's brother, Joseph, that

Taylor would be elected president. "Nonsense," said the general. The idea "seems to me too visionary to require a serious answer. . . . [It] never entered my head, nor is it likely to enter the head of any sane person." But fate had other plans. During the summer of 1846, while Taylor received a promotion to major general, organized his army for a southward sweep to Monterrey in Mexico, and tried to cope with the barely manageable flood of volunteers that increased his forces to 14,000 men, the presidential talk in Whig circles continued.

Support for Taylor came from all over the political spectrum; a union of Democrats, Whigs, and Native Americans (a precursor of the anti-Catholic, anti-immigration Know-Nothing party of the 1850s) seemed bent on nominating him for an election that was more than two years away. For Polk the crisis came when Old Rough-and-Ready's army stormed Monterrey and, after a bloody house-to-house battle, took it. When the fighting was over, Taylor held most of the town, but the Mexicans had holed up in a strong defensive position, and he would have been hard pressed to dislodge them: The conflict had already lasted three days, and American supplies were dwindling. Moreover, the general knew that Polk was offering to negotiate peace, and under the circumstances Taylor felt that "it would be judicious to act with magnanimity towards a prostrate foe. . . ." He let the surviving Mexicans leave Monterrey with their arms.

Polk, observing how the victory further enhanced Taylor's chances for the White House, was constrained to feel that the general—by letting the Mexicans go—had missed a chance in Monterrey to end the war. Whether or not the president had a point, politics demanded that he remove Taylor from the spotlight and diminish his command. Overall conduct of the war was handed to the Army chief of staff, General Winfield Scott. Taylor was told to stay at Monterrey (most of his best troops were transferred to Scott) and was ordered to conduct only defensive operations.

President Polk's plan almost backfired. General Scott's letter to Taylor about the transfer of troops fell into the hands of the Mexican commander, General Santa Anna. Taylor and his drastically reduced force looked like an easy conquest, and the Mexicans needed a victory. Twenty thousand Mexican troops

General Zachary Taylor was ordered to occupy territory in Texas, which Mexico claimed; the resulting 1845 army encampment near Corpus Christi, pictured here in an 1847 lithograph by Charles Parsons, served as a provocation and the dogs of war were soon let loose by the Rio Grande.

Nathaniel Currier's grim lithograph helped fuel anti-Whig sentiment in the 1848 presidential campaign. Democrats hooted at the war hero, Taylor, whose "one qualification" for the presidency was his record of bloody victories over Mexico.

standstill. Though the Americans had lost more than seven hundred men, they had suffered less than half the number of Mexican casualties. That night, Santa Anna retreated.

Coming at the end of a string of successes against all odds, Buena Vista virtually placed the old farmer-general in line to be the next president of the United States. Taylor helped his cause, once the presidential fever struck, by showing his own brand of political acumen. He avoided making deals and remained relatively noncommittal on the issues. He politely accepted nominations from local political groups of all stripes, and continued to assert, well into 1848, that he did not want to be a party candidate bound by party principles. Not until six weeks before the Whig National Convention were close friends able to persuade him to come out openly as a Whig.

Yes, Taylor confessed, he was a Whig. But what kind of Whig was he? Where did he stand on the tariff, slavery in the territories, and other controversial matters? Taylor sidestepped these political land mines. Instead, he maintained that he was no party "ultra," and promised the public that "if elected I would not be the mere president of a party—I would endeavor to act independent of party domination, & should feel bound to administer the Government untrammeled by party schemes. . . ."

The Democrats put forward the pro-expansionist Lewis Cass of Michigan. This caused Barnburners—the antislavery Free-Soil Democrats—to bolt the party in New York; they nominated Martin Van Buren for president. Early in August, a Free-Soil convention attended by abolitionists and Whigs of the Northeast, as well as Barnburners, seconded this nomination and thus ruined Cass's chances in crucial New York. In November he ran third in the state, behind Van Buren, who was second; Taylor won the state's 36 electoral votes with less than a popular majority. Pennsylvania's 26 votes also went to Taylor, helped by a Whig alliance with the Know-Nothings

marched toward Monterrey. Meanwhile, Taylor had grown bitter at being—as he saw it—victimized by the intrigues of Scott and Polk. Disobeying orders, he moved five thousand of his troops a few miles to the southwest of Monterrey. As Santa Anna advanced, the main body of Taylor's troops took up positions in a mountain valley, near a ranch called Buena Vista. There, on February 22 and 23, 1847, Taylor's outnumbered band hung on to the edge of annihilation; but at the end they had fought the Mexicans to a

in Philadelphia. Taylor beat Cass in the electoral college—163 to 127—and 1.3 million to 1.2 million in the popular vote.

Zachary Taylor himself probably did not vote in 1848, thus perpetuating a perfect record of never having cast a ballot in a presidential election. To some he seemed an utterly apolitical figure who would have to depend heavily on the guidance of experienced politicians. Still, he had opinions of his own, which he made known after his inauguration.

The central issues facing Taylor's administration were national expansion and slavery extension. The founding of the Free-Soil party exemplified the North's increasing political potency on the issue of slavery. A flurry of abolitionist writings rocked the North; the South feared the reaction antislavery propaganda would bring. When slaves escaped northward, their capture and return was difficult, and growing more so. Slave insurrections were a threat, as was, of course, abolition. Southerners felt that if the North won political control in Congress, abolition was a certainty. There were signs that the North would soon win that control: Its industries were attracting thousands of immigrants, swelling its voting population; the Missouri Compromise had shut out slavery from the Northern states; and the Oregon Territory had been created, in August 1848, with slavery excluded. For all these reasons many Southerners favored expansion of the United States to the south and west, enlarging the slave territory and maintaining the sectional equilibrium intended by the Missouri Compromise. Free-Soil activists naturally tried to block their efforts.

Civil government for the land wrested from Mexico was a responsibility assumed by the United States as soon as the war-ending Treaty of Guadalupe Hidalgo was signed in February 1848. Then, as the news began to fan out from the Sacramento Valley that gold had been discovered, territorial organization or statehood for California became crucial. The military govern-ment and the remnants of Mexican civil authority simply could not cope with the conditions that rapidly developed in California in 1848 and 1849.

New Mexico's predicament was different: Texas claimed land the New Mexicans believed was theirs, and full-blown armed hostility in the region between the Pecos River and the Rio Grande was a possibility.

Because of the slavery issue, Polk had been unable to push through Congress territorial bills for either area, and responsibility for solving the problem fell to Taylor. The president sent word to both California and New Mexico that applications for statehood would be welcome. Since congressional debate on territorial status would raise great bitterness between the sections, Taylor hoped by this method to present Congress with a fait accompli, with the slavery status of the two regions already settled by the inhabitants.

THE TAYLOR ADMINISTRATION

INAUGURATION: Mar. 5, 1849; the Capitol, Washington, D.C.
VICE PRESIDENT: Millard Fillmore
SECRETARY OF STATE: John M. Clayton
SECRETARY OF THE TREASURY: William M. Meredith
SECRETARY OF WAR: George W. Crawford
ATTORNEY GENERAL: Reverdy Johnson
POSTMASTER GENERAL: Jacob Collamer
SECRETARY OF THE NAVY: William B. Preston
SECRETARY OF THE INTERIOR: Thomas Ewing
31ST CONGRESS (Dec. 3, 1849–Mar. 3, 1851):
  SENATE: 35 Democrats; 25 Whigs; 2 Free-Soilers
  HOUSE: 112 Democrats; 109 Whigs; 9 Others

ELECTION OF 1848

CANDIDATES	ELECTORAL VOTE	POPULAR VOTE
Zachary Taylor (Whig)	163	1,361,393
Lewis Cass (Democratic)	127	1,223,460
Martin Van Buren (Free-Soil)	—	291,501

Both would probably apply for admission as free states, which he may have encouraged.

Taylor was a moderate, looking for a compromise. Here was a slaveholding president who wanted to stop congressional debate on slavery permanently; he and a good many other moderate Southerners felt that this could be accomplished by halting the extension of slavery but by guaranteeing a permanent status quo in the extant slave states.

In August 1849 Taylor let the country know what he had in mind. In a speech delivered at Mercer, Pennsylvania, he tried to calm the fears of moderate Northerners. "The people of the North need have no apprehension of the further extension of slavery," Taylor assured citizens. However, the South was growing alarmed. Slowly, Taylor's moderate Southern Whig backing began to dissolve and secessionist talk grew louder. Taylor's inexperience in party politics would start to tell. The truth was that he had few political friends, with no backlog of political debts to call in, and the only power that remained to promote his wishes was the prestige and force of the presidency. Inevitably, Taylor's stance of being above party politics had created an angry stalemate.

Now the Senate came to the rescue with the Compromise of 1850. Henry Clay, the Great Compromiser, moved into the leadership vacuum. He suggested the admission of California on its own terms, but the final deal also created territorial governments for New Mexico and the Mormon empire of Deseret (Utah). Under Clay's initiatives, Congress established a western boundary for Texas somewhat farther east than the Texans wanted, abolished slave trading in the District of Columbia, and enacted a tough fugitive-slave law. Congress also surrendered the power to legislate interstate slave trading. This was strong medicine, but it seemed that Doctor Clay was ordering the needed dosage.

Although Clay drew support from Daniel Webster, Stephen Douglas, and Lewis Cass, along with most of the congressional Democrats, and although talk of compromise put brakes on the secessionist movement in the South, he really only succeeded in intensifying the stalemate. Taylor refused to budge: California—which applied for free statehood in March 1850—had to come in by itself. If the Southern states tried to secede, Taylor swore he would personally lead the Army to put down the rebellion.

Taylor kept the pressure on. At his behest, New

Mexico requested admission (as a free state) in June. The president believed that once New Mexico was a state, the boundary dispute with Texas could be settled by the Supreme Court. Texas balked and prepared to raise troops to seize the disputed territory, then being protected by United States forces. For a while it appeared that the South might fasten on the Texas issue and make it a test case: What would be the federal reaction to a state rebellion?

Through the month of June 1850 the forces of Clay and Taylor, and of Texas and Taylor, remained deadlocked. Across the nation a vigorous debate raged on the merits of the Compromise—now wrapped up in a congressional omnibus bill—with Taylor giving every evidence of his readiness to veto the bill.

The president was also having other troubles. His cabinet appointments had not been popular, and now, in the spring of 1850, the secretaries of war and the treasury and the attorney general were revealed to have participated in a legal but shady scheme that had netted the secretary of war, George Crawford, a lot of money. The wrongness of their actions is debatable, but they certainly looked bad, and the cabinet scandal was soon tangled in the California-New Mexico debate.

One problem that rose from the California gold rush concerned a project to cut a canal across Central America. Because of British interests in that region, it seemed necessary to work out with Great Britain an agreement to neutralize the area before digging got under way. Secretary of State John Clayton began discussions with the English diplomat Sir Henry Lytton Bulwer in January 1850. Laced with maneuverings and misunderstandings that required President Taylor's personal attention, the negotiations dragged on until July 4, when the Clayton-Bulwer Treaty was finally signed, thus guaranteeing that any future canal route would be considered a neutral zone.

That hot and sunny Independence Day of 1850, President Taylor attended ceremonies at the unfinished Washington Monument. When he arrived back at the White House he took some refreshment—probably uncooked vegetables or fruit, and large amounts of cold milk or water. He soon came down with acute gastroenteritis, and died suddenly on the evening of July 9. A shocked nation heard the news in disbelief. Whigs realized that, once again, death had robbed them of their hold on the White House—twice in little more than a decade!

Where is Taylor to be ranked among U.S. presidents? It is common to think of him as a naive, good-hearted, tough old man, his nationalism conditioned by a lifetime of faithful Army service. His great weakness as chief executive was his lack of practical preparation for many aspects of his job. But as Holman Hamilton, Taylor's major biographer, points out, the president held the key to the passage or defeat of the Compromise, which surely would not have become law over his veto; Clay, Douglas, and Cass simply did not have the votes.

At the time, the alternative seemed to be a civil war in the Southwest, late in August 1850. This war might have been smaller and shorter than the one that would begin eleven years later, but would such a war have been a final solution? Idle speculation aside, the task of trying to keep the nation on a even course fell to a man who was ill-prepared for the presidency. And as the great senatorial giants died and the hotheads became louder in the halls of Congress, and in Charleston and Boston, the White House became the temporary home of another well-intentioned moderate who was baffled by the postponed crisis over the slavery question.

—*Michael Harwood,*
revised by Robert A. Rutland

MILLARD FILLMORE

FORGOTTEN LEADER

As a new century dawns, historians of the American presidency speculate on the future of the nation's highest office. Two presidents have been impeached, but neither was convicted. Four presidents have been assassinated; three presidents and one president-elect have been the targets of assassination attempts. None of these appalling facts were remotely anticipated when the Founding Fathers created the office, and one result of this oversight is that the vice presidency has never been sought by an outstanding leader. A high price has been paid for this neglect.

Congress has tried to make amends for the careless way the office was created, but thanks to John Tyler's assertiveness, the matter of succession was quickly settled in 1841. What was not settled in 1841, and is still a matter of concern, is the way the office has been politicized as a geographical trade-off. The Constitution prevents citizens of the same state from holding the presidency and vice presidency, but beyond that, anything goes. Politicians have always tried to convince voters that "geographical balance" is a good thing. Abilities? Background and training? These factors have been granted less importance, both in the state presidential primaries of today and in the smoke-filled rooms of yesteryear.

Millard Fillmore was the second victim of this flawed thinking. Fillmore's chief qualification as a Whig hopeful in 1848 was the story that, like William Henry Harrison, he had been born in a log cabin. However, Fillmore *was* born in a log cabin on January 7, 1800, in central New York State. His parents were poor but hard-working farmers. A bright child who was quick to learn when he could find the tools, he received little formal education. At eighteen he began to call on a local lawyer, a Quaker, who eventually hired him as a clerk and impressed him with the idea that the law could lead him to honor and distinction. By 1822 Fillmore was clerking in a

Buffalo law office, and within a year his knowledge and good judgment convinced Fillmore's associates that he was ready to be admitted to the bar.

As a young lawyer living in East Aurora, near Buffalo, Fillmore found it easy to make friends. He soon gained a reputation as an able and honest man, and before long he was considered a successful young bachelor. At twenty-six he married his sweetheart of seven years, Abigail Powers, a minister's daughter. Before he was thirty he realized that he had all the raw materials with which to build a career in politics: humble origin (almost a must in the early years of the Jacksonian era), friends, reputation, money, a wife, and a son. Tall and husky, good-natured and straightforward, Fillmore retained the rugged appearance of a backwoodsman. To this he added dignity. His voice was deep and masculine, but he spoke softly and carefully in short, unembellished sentences. He was logical, at times witty, and he projected himself not as a showman but as a good, sober citizen.

As the vehicle for his entrance into politics, Fillmore chose the Anti-Masonic party. The rise of the common man in the 1820s was marked by an instinctive dislike of clubs and fraternities with their policies of exclusiveness. Secret societies of all kinds were distrusted, including Freemasonry, which had counted among its members many of the nation's Founding Fathers. In 1826, after a bricklayer was allegedly kidnapped and murdered for betraying Masonic secrets, the Anti-Masonic party was born in Fillmore's backyard in upstate New York. The first wave of penniless immigrants hit American shores in this era and brought new features to urban life—unemployment, saloons, and petty crimes.

The time seemed ripe for a new national party. The old Federalist party was dead, the Democrats were arrogant, and the opponents of Andrew Jackson were in disarray. In this political atmosphere, there were opportunities for officeholders (and would-be

Upon hearing of Taylor's death, Fillmore responded, "I have no language to express the emotions of my heart." Photograph by Mathew Brady.

officeholders) who gravitated toward political parties such as the Anti-Masons, formed to rally for or against single issues; when the issue died, so did the party.

Fillmore never explained his reasons for joining the Anti-Masons. In 1828 he was elected on their ticket to the state assembly. During his three years in Albany, he distinguished himself by drafting a law

---

BIOGRAPHICAL FACTS

BIRTH: Locke, Cayuga County, N.Y., Jan. 7, 1800

ANCESTRY: English

FATHER: Nathaniel Fillmore; b. Bennington, Vt., Apr. 19, 1771; d. Mar. 28, 1863

FATHER'S OCCUPATION: Farmer

MOTHER: Phoebe Millard Fillmore; b. Pittsfield, Mass., 1780; d. May 2, 1831

BROTHERS: Cyrus (1801–?); Almon Hopkins (1806–1830); Calvin Turner (1810–?); Darius Ingraham (1814–1837); Charles DeWitt (1817–1854)

SISTERS: Olive Armstrong (1797–?); Julia (1812–?); Phoebe Maria (1819–1843)

FIRST MARRIAGE: Moravia, N.Y., Feb. 5, 1826

FIRST WIFE: Abigail Powers; b. Stillwater, N.Y., Mar. 13, 1798; d. Washington, D.C., Mar. 30, 1853

SECOND MARRIAGE: Albany, N.Y., Feb. 10, 1858

SECOND WIFE: Caroline Carmichael McIntosh; b. Morristown, N.J., Oct. 21, 1813; d. Buffalo, N.Y., Aug. 11, 1881

CHILDREN: (by first wife) Millard Powers (1828–1889); Mary Abigail (1832–1854)

RELIGIOUS AFFILIATION: Unitarian

EDUCATION: Attended public schools; studied law in Cayuga County and Buffalo, N.Y.

OCCUPATION BEFORE PRESIDENCY: Lawyer

PREPRESIDENTIAL OFFICES: Member of New York State Legislature; U.S. congressman; U.S. vice president

AGE AT INAUGURATION: 50

OCCUPATIONS AFTER PRESIDENCY: Politician; chancellor of the University of Buffalo

DEATH: Buffalo, N.Y., Mar. 8, 1874

PLACE OF BURIAL: Forest Lawn Cemetery, Buffalo, N.Y.

---

abolishing jail terms for debtors (but making fraudulent bankruptcy a punishable crime). He also established a close association with the Whig boss Thurlow Weed, who supported Fillmore's successful candidacy in 1831 for the United States House of Representatives. When Weed led the Anti-Masons into the new Whig party in 1834, Congressman Fillmore followed.

Throughout the 1830s the political fortunes of Millard Fillmore and Thurlow Weed advanced together. At the time the Whigs finally captured the presidency in 1840, Fillmore became chairman of the House Ways and Means Committee, and Weed, along with other party leaders, watched him closely. When Democrats had won landslide victories, Fillmore had won elections; in Whig years he had led the ticket. In any future national election, his ability to win in New York, with its large electoral vote, had to be considered.

As Ways and Means chairman, Fillmore played a significant role in the passage of a Whig relief plan to deal with the depression that had been lingering since 1837. Fillmore endeared himself to factory owners by supporting a protective tariff advantageous to American manufacturing. He also secured congressional appropriation to help Samuel Morse develop the telegraph. Yet, with his reputation never higher, Fillmore astonished the politicians by declining to stand for reelection in 1842. Fellow congressman John Quincy Adams, lamenting Fillmore's apparent return to his law practice in Buffalo, said, "I hope and trust he will soon return for whether to the nation or to the state, no service can be or ever will be rendered by a more able or a more faithful public servant."

Representative Adams need not have worried, for Fillmore had no intention of permanently retiring. Instead, he hoped to advance to the Senate, and he also knew that he had been mentioned as a possible vice presidential candidate for the 1844 election.

Weed urged him to try for the New York governorship instead. Reluctantly, Fillmore agreed.

Saddled again with the ego-driven Henry Clay as their presidential candidate, the Whigs suffered disastrously in the elections of 1844, in which Fillmore was defeated for the first time in his life. He lost the gubernatorial race to Democrat Silas Wright, one of the most popular men in the state and the bosom buddy of former president Martin Van Buren.

Although Polk pushed Manifest Destiny to the limit and saw the nation extended to the Pacific, the Democrats could not capitalize on his successes. Their lack of a military hero seemed to give Whigs an opening, for both Zachary Taylor and Winfield Scott were touted as Whigs with presidential ambitions. Despite this advantage, the Whigs found it difficult to regroup in advance of the 1848 elections, because the slavery issue seemed to hurt them as much as it hurt the Democrats. Both parties courted the Southern planters and the Northern industrialists and ignored appeals to the nation's largest voting bloc— the yeomen farmers in both regions who owned no slaves.

At their carefully orchestrated nominating convention, the Whigs settled on a military hero, General Taylor, a Louisiana slaveholder who was regarded as essentially pro-Union. To satisfy Northern Whigs, the Taylor camp suggested the nomination of the Massachusetts textile manufacturer Abbott Lawrence for vice president, but many Whigs wanted a Northern man with backing from the business community. Fillmore fit their bill.

Weed seems to have bowed to the pressure for a "balanced ticket" without great regret. For one thing, Fillmore and Weed had always had cordial relations, though Fillmore had never been a tool of the boss. Fillmore regarded Weed as essential to Whig fortunes, and he agreed to help Weed elect former New York Governor William H. Seward to the Senate. After Zachary Taylor's narrow Whig victory, Weed and

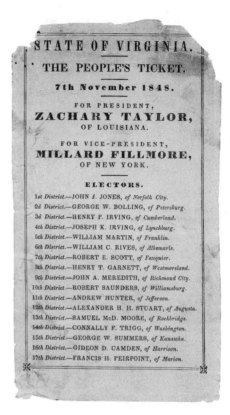

A Virginia campaign ticket for Zachary Taylor and Millard Fillmore. Whigs sought to balance their 1848 ticket by giving the slaveholder Taylor the top spot and making the New Yorker Fillmore the vice presidential candidate. Fellow congressmen thought Fillmore had real ability, but once he became president internecine political battles weakened his administration.

Seward immediately worked their way into President Taylor's confidence but in some devious way excluded Vice President Fillmore. Patronage was the key to power, as Weed knew, and he wanted Fillmore kept out of any discussions on dividing "the loaves and the fishes."

So far as patronage was concerned, Weed gloated, "We could put up a cow against a Fillmore nominee and defeat him." He was right: The vice president could not even have the man of his choice appointed port collector in his own city of Buffalo. Fillmore was sidetracked to a remote corner of the Capitol. As the Whig managers saw matters, Fillmore could only preside over the Senate and watch as North and South battled over the question of slavery in the territories won from Mexico.

In December 1849 President Taylor proposed that California be granted statehood and that a border dispute between Texas and New Mexico be settled by the Supreme Court. Slavery was not mentioned, the implication being that the states would themselves decide that question. The slave state of Texas, however, would fight rather than have its western border shaved by New Mexico, which, like California, was sure to enter the Union as a free state. Texas was

already in the Union and, by the terms of its annexation, might eventually be divided into four separate states. Tensions in the Senate were high; and Southern firebrands insisted that the matter of slavery in the former Mexican territory was far from settled by the long-standing Missouri Compromise.

Clay's Compromise of 1850 was designed to avert conflict, but Taylor did not approve all of it. In June a convention was called in Nashville, where representatives from the slave states met to solidify resistance to Clay's compromise and denounce federal interference. Texas was prepared to assemble an army of 2,500 men to meet the federal troops; and in the House of Representatives, Alexander Stephens of Georgia said, "The first federal gun [fired] against Texas will signal . . . freemen from the Delaware to the Rio Grande to rally to the rescue."

The guns seemed cocked for civil war when President Taylor suddenly fell ill and died. For Fillmore, who had learned of the gravity of Taylor's condition only a few hours before his death, this abrupt turn of events was overwhelming. Since January 1850 Fillmore had presided over a raucous Senate as the mellowed Daniel Webster, the dying John C. Calhoun, and the conciliatory Henry Clay sought a solution that would avert a breakup of the Union. Fillmore, aware that Taylor opposed a managed settlement, had threatened to veto any measures to that end. As vice president, Fillmore dreaded the likelihood that he might have the tie-breaking vote, and he was ready to approve the compromise despite Taylor's hostility. Then, as debate reopened, Taylor died.

Fillmore took the oath of office on the next day and sent a brief message to the seven members of the cabinet—men who had always ignored him or accorded him the barest civility. The new president then locked his door and spent a long, sleepless night in sober reflection.

After being sworn in before a joint session of Congress, Fillmore accepted the resignation of the cabinet but asked its members to remain for a month. They agreed to a week. Presently, Fillmore selected their replacements. Three, including Secretary of State Daniel Webster, were Northerners, two were Southerners, and two were from border states. Like Fillmore, all were pro-Union, and all favored compromise. Fillmore understood that California must enter the Union as a free state, but he had misgivings about the New Mexico and Utah territories as open to "popular sovereignty," despite protests from both the South and the North that Congress had no jurisdiction in the matter. A tough fugitive-slave law was advanced as a palliative to Southern demands for the return of slaves escaping to refuges above the Ohio River boundary.

Before signing the Fugitive Slave Law of the Compromise, Fillmore hesitated—for political as well as moral reasons. Although his attorney general, Ken-

A slave is depicted as arriving in the North after having been shipped from Richmond, Virginia, to Philadelphia in a packing box. During Fillmore's presidency Northern abolitionists sought to weaken slavery in the South through a secretive "Underground Railroad" that carried fugitive slaves to freedom.

Commodore Matthew Perry carried the Stars and Stripes to Japan in 1854 and negotiated a treaty of commerce. Japanese artist Sadahide Utagawa saw the first fruits of the agreement when cargo was carried aboard an American sailing vessel, and in 1861 he recorded the historic occasion with this woodcut.

further federal resistance to the expansion of slavery in the West.

While abolitionists vowed to "trample the law under our feet," and while Harriet Beecher Stowe's novel *Uncle Tom's Cabin* stirred a firestorm of resentment of the law, Fillmore threatened to send troops to the North to enforce the Fugitive Slave Law. "With what face," he asked, "could we require the South to comply with their constitutional obligations, while we in the North openly refuse to live up to ours?"

When the clamor subsided and a measure of tranquillity had been restored, Fillmore seized the opportunity to develop and encourage an expanding economy. The West, bursting with gold seekers, created an urgent need for a transcontinental railroad, and Fillmore cooperated with Illinois Senator Stephen Douglas to secure federal grants for heavily subsidized railroad construction. The infusion of capital caused by the gold discoveries, the expansion of the railroads, and prosperity on farms in the growing Midwest helped calm the troubled waters perhaps more than the Compromise of 1850. Moreover, Fillmore was fortunate that Congress was not rumbling and grumbling.

Always friendly to American commerce and manufacturing, the president sought to open new markets abroad. The principles of the Monroe Doctrine, strengthened by Polk, had not endeared the United States to the other nations of the hemisphere. Fillmore tried to better relations by formulating a good-neighbor policy, which also helped American businessmen. He began to restore diplomatic harmony with Mexico, and an American-built railroad was constructed across the Isthmus of Tehuantepec. Fillmore also favored plans to cut a canal through Nicaragua, and he resisted the efforts of American capitalists to seize Peruvian guano—much in demand as good fertilizer for American farms—and by so doing established with Peru an honorable agreement

tuckian John J. Crittenden, assured him that it was constitutional, Fillmore's wife warned him that signing it would be political suicide. But sign he did, convinced that he had no constitutional alternative. The president then sent troops to prevent a threatened insurrection in the South, where secessionists were certain that the Compromise was just a prelude to

that ultimately proved profitable to both nations. When Spanish troops executed a band of Americans who had attempted to overthrow the colonial government of Cuba, President Fillmore adamantly refused to retaliate.

Farther afield, American ships roamed the Pacific searching for profits in the whale-oil trade and markets in tea and silks. Trade with China had begun in 1843, but the Japanese were aloof and suspicious. Fillmore twice sent letters to the Japanese mikado urging trade. Although the letters revealed a complete lack of American understanding of Japanese ways or protocol, the emperor eventually sent a favorable response. (This occurred a year after the end of Fillmore's presidency, but it gave him satisfaction to know that it was during his administration that the Japanese barrier was lowered a bit.)

As the Oriental trade had ripened during the 1840s, Hawaii became an important Pacific supply depot. When French troops under Napoleon III seized Honolulu in 1849, the Americans protested, and although the French withdrew, the Yankees feared their return. In the United States a movement grew in favor of annexation, but Fillmore resisted it. Then, in 1851, the French presented the Hawaiian king with a list of demands that would essentially make the islands a French protectorate. Through Secretary of State Webster, Fillmore gave Napoleon a "hands off!" warning that extended to some degree the Monroe Doctrine to apply to that region. The basic issue was the independence of a backward nation, which Fillmore pledged to protect. The French got the message and withdrew. Fillmore's accomplishments in foreign affairs, however, were not matched by any real progress made on solving the smoldering domestic issue of slavery.

Indeed, President Fillmore's biographers have made a point of his apparent lack of personal ambition and his seeming indifference to the reelection fever that seizes most presidents at some time during their first term. Like Polk, Fillmore almost made himself a lame duck from the day he became president by announcing that he would not seek a second term. Fillmore somewhat reneged on that pledge when he allowed his name to be placed before the convention of 1852. But in fact he let his name go before delegates only after friends had convinced him that he was the only Whig with a chance of winning.

The Whigs were drifting. Senator Seward of New York, a man whose ego knew few bounds, was eager to enter the White House, and he had a loyal follow-

WILLIAM LLOYD GARRISON

William Lloyd Garrison of Massachusetts was the most uncompromising abolitionist of his day. "I hate slavery," he said, "as I hate nothing else in this world. It is not only a crime, but the sum of all criminality." In 1831 the twenty-five-year-old editor founded his famous weekly, the *Liberator*, with the promise, "I will be heard." For thirty-five years—from Van Buren's administration and on to the end of the Civil War— its pages rang out in a torrent of invective against the evils of slavery and oppression. In 1833 the young reformer helped to found the American Anti-Slavery Society and soon became its president and most vociferous defender. Inspiring an antipathy as broad and active as his following, he narrowly escaped with his life when, in 1835, an angry mob seized him and dragged him through the streets with a rope around his neck. Far from seeking conciliation with his adversaries of the South, Garrison publicly advocated disunion and denounced the Compromise of 1850 as a "hollow bargain for the North." At the end of the Civil War in 1865, the aging abolitionist turned his full energies to other reforms. In the remaining fourteen years of his life, Garrison fought vigorously for woman suffrage, the prohibition of liquor, the elimination of prostitution, and belated justice for the Indians of the United States. He died in 1879 at the age of 74.

Democratic cartoons tried to make Fillmore seem a bumbler who was unfit for the presidency. The Whigs were unhappy with Fillmore, too, and dumped him in favor of General Winfield Scott as their presidential candidate. Here *Young America* magazine depicted Fillmore as "The Champion of the Light Weights on His Guard."

more stepped aside and gave lip-service to the Scott candidacy.

As a military hero, Scott had good credentials, but as a presidential candidate, he fell on his face. Whig newspapers, and the New York *Tribune* in particular, tried to make Scott into a deserving warrior who could unite the country. But *Tribune* editor Horace Greeley's skills had a limited effect. Scott carried only four states, losing the election to Franklin Pierce, who captured 254 electoral votes. Pierce, himself a handsome former general, came from New Hampshire, which to many voters appeared to be the kind of neutral territory they wanted replicated in the western regions.

The day of Franklin Pierce's inauguration—March 4, 1853—was raw and snowy. Never in the best of health, Abigail Fillmore shivered in the cold. The next day she fell sick, and three weeks later she died. Grief-stricken and uncertain about his future, the ex-president turned instinctively to politics.

But a politician must have a party, and the Whigs had been reduced to a nonentity. Fillmore's dilemma was not unique. He was pro-Union and against slavery on principle, but he did not believe the federal government (that is, Congress) had the right to restrict slavery. On the shambles of the pitiful Know-Nothing movement and the embers of the Whig party, a new phenomenon was about to change the face of American politics. In 1854, after touring the South and West, Fillmore demonstrated that he had lost touch with the realities of American politics by deciding that the American, or Know-Nothing, party —not the rising Republicans—represented the wave of the future. Well-intentioned but naive, Fillmore hitched his wagon to the fading star of Know-Nothingism.

Soon Fillmore's White House tenure was only a vague memory and he became an invisible president. He was linked to the discredited American party, officially the Order of the Star-Spangled Banner. When

ing. Strangely, his main sponsor, Thurlow Weed, took an ill-timed trip to Europe, perhaps to avoid conflict with the Whig party because Seward had developed a jealous and implacable hostility toward Fillmore. Seward launched a divisive campaign that was destined to split the party and leave it fragmented beyond redemption. After 53 ballots, the party nominated General Winfield Scott. With no rancor, Fill-

queried by outsiders, members were instructed to reply, "I know nothing." What they did profess to believe, however, was that the Vatican wanted to control the United States and that foreigners, especially Irish and Germans, brought dangerous, un-American ideas with them to these shores. The party did well in the by-elections of 1854 and 1855, and nominated Fillmore for president in 1856, but when the presidential election was held most Americans realized that the time had passed for a party whose platform was based on hindsight. What little strength Fillmore had was in the border states; he ran a poor third, winning only 8 electoral votes to Democrat James Buchanan's 174 and Republican John C. Frémont's 114. The Know-Nothing party died a quick death, as the Republicans revived the two-party system with a bang.

Fillmore retired from politics for good. In 1858 he married a wealthy widow, Caroline McIntosh, and in their impressive mansion they entertained Abraham Lincoln as he traveled en route to the White House. When the Civil War came, Fillmore helped recruit volunteers for the Union Army. "Our Constitution is in danger," he said, "and we must defend it!" But in 1864 Fillmore decided that the Republican administration meant "national bankruptcy and military

despotism." "I have no faith," he wrote, "in that policy which proposes to exterminate the South, or hold it by military subjugation," and he announced his support of General McClellan for president. For these opinions he was accused of lack of patriotism and even treason.

Deeply hurt, Fillmore withdrew completely from public life. Only in April 1865 did he make an exception: when Lincoln's funeral train passed from Batavia, New York, to Buffalo, Fillmore headed the escort committee.

Fillmore died on March 8, 1874, shortly after suffering a stroke. Had he led his country a decade earlier or twenty years later, he might have been judged a good president, for he was a selfless public servant and a good administrator who accomplished much in a term of less than three years. But Millard Fillmore became president in 1850, and history in its judgment cannot divorce his achievements from the needs of the times. He is counted among the presidential mediocrities because of his lack of vision. He knew that slavery had to go, but he did nothing to hasten its end. So the nation continued to drift into an awful civil war.

—DAVID JACOBS,
revised by ROBERT A. RUTLAND

FRANKLIN PIERCE

OVERWHELMED BY EVENTS

History is never kind to losers. Victors not only divide the spoils, they grow in stature over time. Henry Clay might have said that he would "rather be right than be President," but he did not mean it. Clay and William Jennings Bryan, both perennial losers in presidential races, wanted the presidency and thought they deserved it—but the voters disagreed. And sometimes winners ultimately fail, and they, too, become part of the dustheap of history.

Franklin Pierce was such a president.

On paper, Pierce looked good; and in person he looked even better. A handsome man, Pierce was a sight to see in his sparkling uniform. Commissioned a brigadier general during the Mexican War, he was among the conquering Americans who followed Winfield Scott's trail from Veracruz to Mexico City in 1847. Although an accident prevented Pierce from being much more than a spectator, he shared in the glory.

Pierce's journey to the White House was almost preordained. His father, who had been a hero during the Revolutionary War, was twice elected governor of New Hampshire and wielded power in state politics for most of his life. His son graduated from Bowdoin College and was admitted to the state bar; before his twenty-fifth birthday young Pierce was elected to the New Hampshire legislature. Success came easily. He served as speaker of the state legislature, and at twenty-nine he was sent to the House of Representatives in Washington. Four years later New Hampshire lawmakers elected Pierce to the Senate. His political career was booming, but Pierce's home life was not. He had married Jane Means Appleton, the daughter of the Bowdoin College president, but she proved to be a neurotic woman whose religious fervor ran deep. Occasionally bedridden, she at all times seemed unhappy with the kind of life her husband had chosen. She loathed Washington, and her distaste for the capital's social whirl stood in contrast to the senator's enjoyment of society. Pierce finally gave up his Senate seat in 1842 and returned to Concord, where he became a leading member of the bar noted for his way with juries, his military bearing, and his good manners.

In his Senate days, Pierce had been friendly with his Southern colleagues and was impatient with the New England abolitionists whom he considered rabble-rousers. He was upset when the Democratic candidate for governor of New Hampshire apparently promised he would, if elected, ignore the Fugitive Slave Act. Pierce showed his political muscle by bringing a backer of the Compromise of 1850 to the ticket as a substitute. Impressed by his party loyalty and military service, many New England Democrats began to speak of Pierce as presidential timber.

At the 1852 Democratic nominating convention the front-runners had been Senator Lewis Cass, Senator Stephen Douglas, and James Buchanan. Ballot after ballot lead to more confusion, and another "dark horse" candidacy, like Polk's, appealed to the tired delegates. Finally, on the forty-ninth ballot, Pierce was chosen as their standard-bearer. When his wife heard the news, she fainted. Pierce's good friend, the novelist Nathaniel Hawthorne, reported that when Pierce himself heard of his nomination he showed "no thrill of joy, but sadness."

In the campaign that followed, Pierce maintained a dignified but reticent composure. His Democratic managers touted him as "Young Hickory," a former soldier in the mold of the great Andrew Jackson. Voters liked the image and gave him a victory over his old commander, Whig candidate Winfield Scott, with 254 electoral votes to Scott's 42. His popular vote margin was not as impressive, however; Pierce won by some 220,000 votes. Scott's defeat was the death knell of the Whig party.

Among those displeased by the outcome was Mrs. Pierce. While the campaign was in progress the couple's eleven-year-old son, Bennie, wrote his mother: "I

Franklin Pierce sat for this portrait sometime between 1855 and 1865.

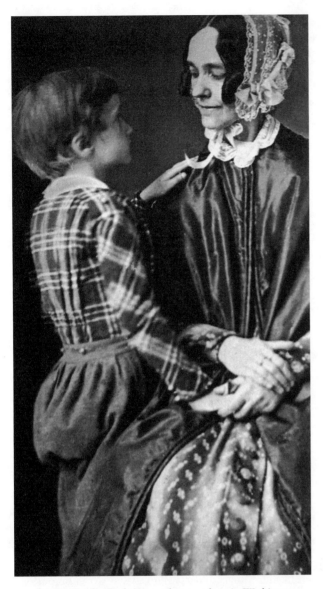

Jane Pierce loathed the social atmosphere in Washington and doted on her son, Bennie. The youngster was killed in a railway accident shortly before Pierce was inaugurated, and his wife never recovered from the tragedy.

But the voters had decreed otherwise, and they seemed content with the Democrat's campaign pledge to honor to the letter the Compromise of 1850. Hawthorne, an enthusiastic supporter, wrote that Pierce "has in him many of the chief elements of a great ruler. His talents are administrative, he has a subtle faculty of making affairs roll onward according to his will."

Then a horrible tragedy struck. In January 1853 the Pierces were on a train from Boston to Concord when their railroad car was derailed. Young Bennie was killed, while his parents were hardly scratched. But this was the third child they had lost, and the distraught, now-childless Mrs. Pierce made known her belief that the tragedy was a divine signal—all three of their children were dead so that Pierce could better serve as president. Thereafter, the first lady-to-be was a melancholy martyr residing in a place she detested.

Such events were bound to affect Pierce, but he carried on despite all the grief in his life. He traveled to Washington alone, headed straight to the Willard Hotel from the train station, and stayed out of the public eye until Inauguration Day. With much time on his hands, Pierce wrote his speech and memorized it, and was determined to tell the nation that he was ready to conduct the country's business. Since Pierce was still in mourning, no inaugural ball was held, but a lengthy reception took place at the White House.

After Mrs. Pierce arrived, the White House took on an air of somber Yankee piety as the first lady asked servants to attend church "for her sake" every Sunday. Her aunt, Mrs. Abby Kent Means, took over the social duties and became the official White House hostess. One disappointed visitor remarked that "everything in that mansion seems cold and cheerless" and concluded, "I have seen hundreds of log cabins which seemed to contain more happiness."

His personal life was cheerless, but Pierce was determined to be a firm president. His cabinet

hope he won't be elected for I should not like to be at Washington and I know you would not either." The boy expressed his mother's sentiments exactly.

appointments represented a broad spectrum within the Democratic Party, including Secretary of State William Marcy and Secretary of War Jefferson Davis. To the important post of minister to Great Britain, Pierce dispatched James Buchanan. Through these party leaders he hoped to make patronage less of a chore than usual, but that proved an unrealistic ideal as hundreds of office-seekers besieged the White House. Instead of settling sectional disputes, the Compromise of 1850 had exacerbated the pettiness that made politics so distasteful. President Pierce found he was trying to please everybody and was instead making enemies right and left.

There were troubling policy questions as well. In Congress most matters were considered as foils in the sectional game; even the pressure for a railroad to the Pacific coast was exerted by pro- and antislavery forces. Stephen Douglas and his allies appealed to Northerners for support of a rail line from Chicago westward, but Jefferson Davis and his friends wanted a southern route with the eastern terminal in New Orleans. In May 1853 Pierce authorized negotiations with Mexico for a small portion of the territory across which the southern route might pass. By December diplomat James Gadsden had signed a treaty with Mexico to purchase a 45,000 square-mile rectangle for ten million dollars, a sum later reduced but approved by the Senate.

An earlier attempt to organize the Nebraska Territory had failed because of Southern votes. Douglas now hoped to make new legislation more palatable by inserting a provision in the bill that the status of the region—slave or free—would be left to votes of the inhabitants. The Great Plains had been closed to slavery by the Missouri Compromise, and the effect of Douglas's plan would be to repeal that 1820 legislation. Southern members of Congress had long called for such a repeal, but in 1853 the outcry against admitting further slave states was heard throughout the North.

Pierce found himself trapped. The Southern bloc in the Senate would not back down, and antislavery senators were just as adamant. With deep misgivings, Pierce decided to support the Douglas amendment, hoping this would provide a way out of the slavery dilemma that was dividing the nation. The Fugitive Slave Law was being ignored in many Northern com-

---

BIOGRAPHICAL FACTS

BIRTH: Hillsboro, N.H., Nov. 23, 1804

ANCESTRY: English

FATHER: Benjamin Pierce; b. Chelmsford, Mass., Dec. 25, 1757; d. Apr. 1, 1839

FATHER'S OCCUPATIONS: Soldier; farmer; governor of New Hampshire

MOTHER: Anna Kendrick Pierce; b. 1768; d. 1838

BROTHERS: Benjamin Kendrick (1790–1850); John Sullivan (1796–1824); Charles Grandison (1803–1828); Henry Dearborn (1812–1880)

SISTERS: Nancy M. (1792–1837); Harriet B. (1800–1837); Charlotte (?–?)

HALF SISTER: Elizabeth Andrews (1788–1855)

MARRIAGE: Amherst, N.H., Nov. 19, 1834

WIFE: Jane Means Appleton; b. Hampton, N.H., Mar. 12, 1806; d. Andover, Mass., Dec. 2, 1863

CHILDREN: Franklin (b. and d. 1836); Frank Robert (1839–1843); Benjamin (1841–1853)

RELIGIOUS AFFILIATION: Episcopalian

EDUCATION: Attended public school and Hancock Academy; Bowdoin College (B.A., 1824)

OCCUPATIONS BEFORE PRESIDENCY: Lawyer; soldier

MILITARY SERVICE: Brig. gen. in U.S. Army (1847–1848)

PREPRESIDENTIAL OFFICES: Member and speaker of New Hampshire legislature; U.S. congressman; U.S. senator; president of New Hampshire Constitutional Convention

AGE AT INAUGURATION: 48

OCCUPATION AFTER PRESIDENCY: Retired

DEATH: Concord, N.H., Oct. 8, 1869

PLACE OF BURIAL: Old North Cemetery, Concord, N.H.

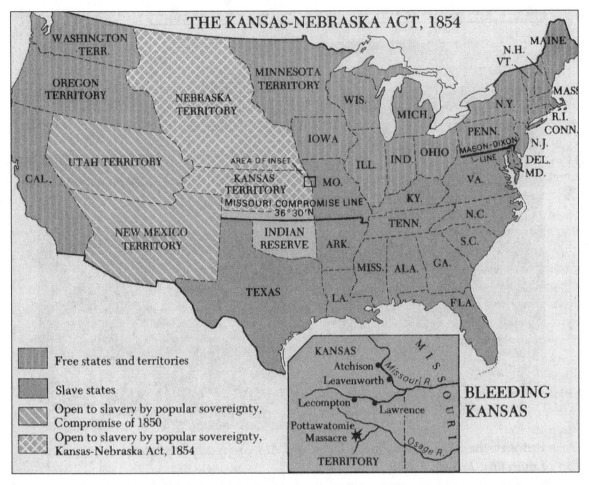

THE KANSAS-NEBRASKA ACT, 1854

Free states and territories

Slave states

Open to slavery by popular sovereignty, Compromise of 1850

Open to slavery by popular sovereignty, Kansas-Nebraska Act, 1854

BLEEDING KANSAS

As President Pierce signed the Kansas-Nebraska Act, he thought he was closing the chapter on the political bitterness growing out of the battle between Northern and Southern factions in Congress. Instead, the 1854 legislation proved to be a political bombshell that worsened sectional tension and hastened the outbreak of a civil war.

munities, and Pierce wanted desperately to pour oil on the troubled waters. The final version of the bill split the region into two territories—Kansas and Nebraska—and Southerners were confident that Missouri emigrants could take over the southernmost region of Kansas without difficulty. Knowing the president backed them, the majority in both houses of Congress supported the Kansas-Nebraska bill. When he signed the law, Pierce had good reason to

think he had found a way to reconcile the warring factions.

Instead, Kansas was turned into a battleground. The North sent rifles to the abolitionists, and the South pushed proslavery settlers into the disputed territory. A territorial capital was located at Lecompton, and efforts to hold a statehood convention were under way; antislavery partisans set up their capital at Topeka. Douglas thought the new law would surely make him the Democratic nominee for president in 1856, but Whigs like Abraham Lincoln saw the maneuvering as an effort to destroy the Missouri Compromise and open the West to slavery.

The Kansas-Nebraska Act thus became the tragic hallmark of Pierce's administration. With it he lost control of the Northern wing of the Democratic party and witnessed the rapid growth of the upstart Republican party which swallowed the Whigs, the Know-Nothings, and the Free-Soilers into one appealing and definitely antislavery political force. In the 1854 off year elections, the Democrats lost their hold of the House. The stage was now set for an end to the domination by the Democratic party that went back to Jefferson's day.

In all likelihood, Pierce did not realize what a wasp's nest the Kansas-Nebraska Act had stirred. He had problems elsewhere, anyway, for Southerners were making loud noises about acquiring Cuba. Indeed, President Polk had made unsuccessful overtures to Spain regarding the purchase of Cuba. Spain was also under pressure to emancipate slaves in the Caribbean, which was another reason the South was eager to make Cuba safe under the Stars and Stripes. Seizure of an American cargo ship in the port of Havana brought outcries from belligerent Americans, and for a time it seemed a Spanish-American war was a likely prospect.

Secretary of State Marcy sought a favorable solution through an international conference. The meeting in Ostend, Belgium, was supposedly secret but information leaked out that a manifesto would be issued favoring American possession of Cuba. James Buchanan, the American minister to Great Britain, hinted that if Spain would not accept an offer, force might be used to acquire one of Spain's few remaining American colonies. When the Democrats were overpowered in Congress, the idea of Cuban annexation became a dead issue.

Similarly, Pierce's hopes of annexing Hawaii were dashed as the halls of Congress became a sectional battlefield. The acquisition of Hawaii hinged on a rather blatant scheme involving bribes to the royal family that ruled the islands; but before the plan could be sent to Congress, the Hawaiian king died. So did the annexation scheme.

The foreign outlook was not all bad, however. Commodore Matthew C. Perry headed an American naval force that met with Japanese leaders and worked out a treaty in 1854 to end the Dutch monopoly on trade with Japan. A long-standing disagreement

---

THE PIERCE ADMINISTRATION

INAUGURATION: Mar. 4, 1853; the Capitol, Washington, D.C.

VICE PRESIDENT: William Rufus D. King (died Apr. 18, 1853)

SECRETARY OF STATE: William L. Marcy

SECRETARY OF THE TREASURY: James Guthrie

SECRETARY OF WAR: Jefferson Davis

ATTORNEY GENERAL: Caleb Cushing

POSTMASTER GENERAL: James Campbell

SECRETARY OF THE NAVY: James C. Dobbin

SECRETARY OF THE INTERIOR: Robert McClelland

SUPREME COURT APPOINTMENT: John A. Campbell (1853)

33RD CONGRESS (Dec. 5, 1853–Mar. 3, 1855):
    SENATE: 38 Democrats; 22 Whigs; 2 Others
    HOUSE: 159 Democrats; 71 Whigs; 4 Others

34TH CONGRESS (Dec. 3, 1855–Mar. 3, 1857):
    SENATE: 39 Democrats; 22 Republicans;
        1 American Party
    HOUSE: 108 Republicans; 83 Democrats; 43 Others

ELECTION OF 1852

CANDIDATES	ELECTORAL VOTE	POPULAR VOTE
Franklin Pierce (Democratic)	254	1,607,510
Winfield Scott (Whig)	42	1,386,942
John P. Hale (Free-Soil)	—	155,210

about fishing rights in waters off the American-Canadian border was finally settled in mid-1854. The Canadian Reciprocity Treaty defined the jurisdiction of both countries and also eliminated import duties on a variety of products traded between the United States and Canada.

The Kansas-Nebraska fiasco, meanwhile, grew into a full-blown headache for President Pierce. He made a stab at fairness by appointing a Southerner as governor of Nebraska and a Northern Democrat as the Kansas governor. The Kansas governor became involved in an illegal scheme infringing on Indian lands and had to be removed, along with two judges who were party to the swindle. The administration looked inept, and the Kansas border seethed. But things would get a lot worse before they got better.

In Kansas the shouting and sloganeering turned to

An abolitionist band mans an artillery weapon pointed toward Southern lines in Kansas. Border violence followed the enactment of the Kansas-Nebraska Act, and soon abolitionists urged Free-Soilers to emigrate into the territory west of slave-state Missouri. Southern sympathizers retaliated in force and made a farce of any authentic poll of Kansas settlers. Worse still, both sides began substituting bullets for ballots.

shooting. Blood was shed on both sides, and Pierce was forced to issue a proclamation ordering the Missouri proslavery freebooters to stay out. He also condemned the actions of free-state interlopers, and to give his words force, Pierce ordered federal troops to back his second appointee as governor.

These were not the acts of a weak president, but his own Democratic party was disenchanted with Pierce and ready to pick a candidate who wasn't tainted by the Kansas-Nebraska dispute. The pall of "Bleeding Kansas" hung over the Democrats as they assembled to pick their candidate. Pierce wanted the nomination, but it went instead to James Buchanan. Having spent four years in England, Buchanan was considered an experienced, conservative, and "safe" candidate who bore no scars from the Kansas-Nebraska imbroglio.

Once relieved of his office, Pierce took his wife on a long tour of Europe, then returned to Concord. He discounted all talk of running as the Democratic candidate in 1860. After the Civil War began, Pierce accused the Republicans of reckless conduct but thought no better of the secessionists in the South. Gradually Pierce became a harsh critic of Lincoln's conduct of the war. A crushing blow to his reputation came on July 4, 1863, when, speaking at a Democratic rally in Concord, he condemned the "fearful, fruitless, [and] fatal Civil War." As the meeting ended, news came of great Northern victory at Gettysburg.

Tragedy still plagued Pierce. His wife died late in 1863, and the next spring Pierce and his friend Hawthorne took off for a vacation in the White Mountains, in hopes of restoring the writer's deteriorating health. But Hawthorne was terminally ill, and he died one night as Pierce slept in an adjoining

WINFIELD SCOTT

Andrew Jackson had called him a "hectoring bully," and Polk termed him "visionary," but in the eyes of the nation General Winfield Scott was nothing less than a hero. Publicly acclaimed for his courage at Chippewa and Lundy's Lane in the War of 1812, he was brevetted a major general. He fought in the Black Hawk War, and when, in 1837, Jackson ordered an inquiry into General Scott's handling of the Creek and Seminole campaigns, the court praised the soldier's "energy, steadiness, and ability." His accomplishments as peacemaker in 1838 and 1839 were no less impressive. In little more than a year, he restored peace along the Canadian border; pacified some sixteen thousand dispossessed Cherokees; and averted a war with Great Britain in the Maine boundary dispute. As general in chief of the Army during the Mexican War, he led the victorious assault on the enemy capital and again won public applause. National sentiment was not strong enough, however, to make him president, and in the election of 1852 he was roundly defeated by Pierce. Resuming his military duties, Scott averted a serious conflict with Great Britain in 1859 over possession of San Juan Island off the Pacific coast. During the Civil War he remained loyal to the Union, serving briefly as general in chief. He retired in 1861 and died five years later, at eighty.

room. At Hawthorne's funeral, the former president was pointedly snubbed by the New England literati. Pierce returned to Concord, stayed out of the public limelight, and died a forgotten man on October 8, 1869.

—MARTIN LURAY,
revised by ROBERT A. RUTLAND

JAMES BUCHANAN

AN AMERICAN NERO

The long trail of compromises finally played out. Starting in 1820, presidents and political parties had tried to avoid a final settlement of the agonizing slavery problem that divided the American people into two sectional camps. When the slavery problem shifted from an economic policy to a moral imperative, there had to be a victim in the White House. James Buchanan was that victim.

President James Buchanan was the last in a string of temporizing politicians, the so-called "Northern men with Southern principles," who stood for compromise between two bitterly opposed groups of radicals. The Democrats chose the Pennsylvania bachelor because he was a party hack who was beloved by the compromisers. Pierce had been broken by the Compromise of 1850. Now it was Buchanan's turn.

When Buchanan assumed the presidency, this son of a small-town storekeeper had been in public life for more than forty years. Born April 23, 1791, in Cove Gap, Pennsylvania, he graduated from Dickinson College in 1809 and began to practice law three years later. He became a Federalist state legislator in Pennsylvania in 1814 and a member the U.S. House of Representatives in 1821.

Buchanan stood six feet tall and was a heavy man, but because his sight was uneven (one eye being nearsighted, the other farsighted), he cocked his head down and to one side when addressing or listening to someone, giving the impression of shyness and humility. Considered charming and good-looking, he nevertheless remained a bachelor all his life. He came closest to the altar when he was in his late twenties.

Perhaps this unhappy love affair gave Buchanan a streak of caution that would stay with him until he died. Caution certainly plagued him in the White House. Where Jackson trusted his instincts, Buchanan seemed to have none. Success came to him in politics because he played it like a game of chess—warily, step-by-step. He habitually kept his financial records

accurate to the penny and knew how every cent was spent; before long he had amassed a considerable fortune. With similar care he observed and took advantage of the constantly shifting schisms in politics and eased his way upward through the maze.

In 1832, after ten years' service in Congress, during which he left the moribund Federalists for the Jacksonian Democrats, Buchanan served as United States minister to Russia. He was elected to the Senate in 1834 and was reelected twice. Not a moving speaker as either a lawyer or a legislator, he was a conscientious committee member and was meticulously detailed when presenting a case. Contemporaries found his plodding manner irritating—but worthy of respect nonetheless.

By 1844 he had become a presidential possibility. Buchanan tossed his hat into the ring, but the convention was looking for a candidate who wanted to move the country toward the Pacific. Thus he lost the Democratic nomination to the forceful Polk, who told voters where he stood on expansion. Disappointed but loyal, Buchanan then worked hard to bring Pennsylvania into the Democratic column; as a result he was awarded the post of secretary of state. Although Buchanan and Polk respected each other, they battled constantly during the next four years. Polk had made all his cabinet members promise that they would not actively seek the presidential nomination of 1848, but Buchanan had taken the post for the prestige it would bring him, and he competed with Polk for leadership and laurels in foreign policy. "If I would yield up the government into his hands," wrote Polk, "and suffer him to be in effect President . . . I have no doubt he would be cheerful and satisfied."

Even though Buchanan showed no great talent as a diplomat, the nation expanded through the pipelines of diplomacy, often with Anglo-American cooperation. Like many presidents before and since, Polk was his own acting secretary of state, and

James Buchanan posed for Mathew Brady sometime between 1860 and 1865.

Buchanan functioned as his chief clerk. After three years in the State Department, Buchanan began to campaign quietly for votes at the Democratic convention, since Polk had announced he would not seek a second term. But at the 1848 convention he lost the Democratic presidential nomination to Lewis Cass of Michigan and retired to his farm, Wheatland, near Lancaster, Pennsylvania.

Cass lost the presidential election, and the political pot began to boil again. Buchanan, hoping that lightning would strike, watched in 1852 as the maneuvering for the presidential nomination intensified. Finally, the delegates decided another war hero would be their best bet, so Franklin Pierce won on the forty-ninth ballot.

Persistence is a great virtue in politics. In Democratic circles Buchanan was regarded as a deserving party loyalist. In the spring of 1853, President Pierce persuaded Buchanan to represent the United States in Great Britain. Three past presidents had served at the Court of St. James, so Buchanan probably thought London was a good place to hide while he nursed his own ambitions. Indeed, although his ministry was not a great success—he became involved in the controversial Ostend Manifesto—his absence from the United States during Pierce's administration proved fortunate: he was not a participant in the Kansas-Nebraska debate and, therefore, had no responsibility for "Bleeding Kansas."

Kansas and the larger question of slavery in the United States were to be the major issues of the 1856 campaign. Buchanan was known as a conservative, a compromise man. "I am not friendly to slavery in the abstract," he had said, "[but] the rights of the south, under our constitutional compact, are as much entitled to protection as those of any other portion of the Union." Consistently he had held to the view that the abolitionists should be quiet and that slaveholders should show forbearance. This straddling position was popular with the South and with Unionists in the North; Buchanan, a Northerner, thus fitted into the "safe" category from which the Democrats had been selecting their presidential nominees.

The country became embroiled in the question of whether the Kansas and Nebraska territories should be admitted to the Union as free or slave states. Both were north of latitude 36° 30', the line drawn in the Missouri Compromise, and therefore Northerners insisted the two had to be free states upon entering the Union. But Southern "fire-eaters" realized this decision would mean that all western lands would be henceforth closed to slavery, and they now insisted that the Missouri Compromise ought to be ignored. Senator Stephen Douglas of Illinois had engineered the Kansas-Nebraska Act through Congress and Pierce had signed it; but instead of calming the nation, it caused a wave of revulsion in the North.

Owing to the controversy at home, Buchanan's luck at the nominating conventions was about to change. After he returned from England, he began to emerge as the leading candidate because, unlike President Pierce and Senator Douglas, he had made no enemies over the Kansas-Nebraska Act which divided the Democrats. After twelve ballots at the convention, Pierce was out of the running. Douglas withdrew after four more, and Buchanan was nominated by acclamation.

In the wake of the turmoil caused by the Kansas-Nebraska Act, the old Whigs and various hangers-on came together to form a new political party. Senator William H. Seward and a host of congressmen from the Midwest helped rally all the opposition into a viable Republican party that was committed to holding the Missouri Compromise line as a final settlement. Horace Greeley's influential New York *Tribune* endorsed Republican nominee John C. Frémont, a popular explorer who was the son-in-law of Senator Thomas Hart Benton, a Jacksonian Democrat. Northern Democrats deserted their party and flocked to the Republican banner, but former president

Millard Fillmore hurt them by running as a Know-Nothing (a formidable third party, officially named the American party, that was crammed with xenophobic and anti-Catholic voters).

Portrayed by the Democrats as the candidate who "would not rock the boat," Buchanan won even though he polled less than half the popular vote. Buchanan led in the electoral college, 174 votes to 114 for Frémont and 8 for Fillmore. Ominously, though Buchanan won New Jersey, Pennsylvania, Indiana, Illinois, and California, the bulk of his strength lay in the South. The Republican party, in its first major test, had swept the Northeast.

Thus Buchanan came into the office of president as a contradiction: The Unionist was elected without the votes or strong support of the North. He was aware of the danger: "The great object of my administration," he wrote, "will be to arrest, if possible, the agitation of the slavery question at the North, and to destroy sectional parties." Had he accomplished this goal, he would be revered as one of our greatest leaders.

Fate decreed otherwise. The Kansas issue was the first crucial problem he had to meet, and for a while he did so with determination. Before he was inaugurated he suggested to friends on the Supreme Court that the Dred Scott case, then under consideration, be used as a platform for defining the role of Congress in the slavery question. Scott was a slave who had been taken from Missouri into the Wisconsin Territory and Illinois during the 1830s by his master, an Army doctor. Scott eventually sued in Missouri for his freedom on the grounds that his temporary removal to a free area had automatically made him legally free. Shortly after Buchanan entered office, the Court, announcing its decision, committed one of the greatest legal blunders in U.S. history. The Court held that Scott was a slave—not a citizen—and thus could not sue for anything. Further, since the Missouri Compromise had forbidden slavery north of the Mason-Dixon Line, it had deprived Southern slave

BIOGRAPHICAL FACTS

BIRTH: Cove Gap, Pa., Apr. 23, 1791
ANCESTRY: Scotch-Irish
FATHER: James Buchanan; b. County Donegal, Ireland, 1761; d. Mercersburg, Pa., June 11, 1821
FATHER'S OCCUPATIONS: Storekeeper; justice of the peace
MOTHER: Elizabeth Speer Buchanan; b. Lancaster County, Pa., 1767; d. Greensburg, Pa., 1833
BROTHERS: William Speer (1805–1826); George Washington (1808–1832); Edward Young (1811–1895)
SISTERS: Mary (1789–1791); Jane (1793–1839); Maria (1795–1849); Sarah (1798–1825); Elizabeth (1800–1801); Harriet (1802–1839)
RELIGIOUS AFFILIATION: Presbyterian
EDUCATION: Attended Old Stone Academy; Dickinson College (1809)
OCCUPATION BEFORE PRESIDENCY: Lawyer
PREPRESIDENTIAL OFFICES: Member of Pennsylvania legislature; U.S. congressman; minister to Russia; U.S. senator; secretary of state; minister to Great Britain
AGE AT INAUGURATION: 65
OCCUPATION AFTER PRESIDENCY: Retired
DEATH: Lancaster, Pa., June 1, 1868
PLACE OF BURIAL: Woodward Hill Cemetery, Lancaster, Pa.

owners of the right to take their property wherever they wished. In short, the long-honored Missouri Compromise was unconstitutional and void.

The implications were immense. Congress, the Court said, could not legislate slavery in a territory, and this implied (as a corollary) that slavery could not be excluded from any territory created by Congress. Thus, all territories were open to slavery and could exclude slavery only when they became states.

The South was jubilant, and the North was disgusted. Mass meetings in Northern communities denounced the decision. Longtime Democrats deserted their party and turned to the Republicans, who capitalized on the unpopularity of the decision

This 1860 political cartoon shows President Buchanan, Vice President Breckinridge, Republican presidential nominee Lincoln, and Senators Bell and Douglas, all dancing to Scott's makeshift tune. The Supreme Court is far from infallible, as the 1857 Dred Scott decision proved. The Court decided that Scott, a slave who had been moved to free territory and then back to Missouri, had not become a free man and had "no rights that a white man is bound to respect." The decision sparked a powder keg, and the blowup that followed rocked the nation.

in the forthcoming congressional elections. Instead of settling the slavery issue, the Scott decision tore open old wounds and hastened a sectional confrontation.

To cope with the immediate situation in Kansas, Buchanan selected Robert J. Walker of Mississippi to serve as territorial governor and to oversee the territory's progress toward statehood. Walker was a levelheaded, no-nonsense Unionist. But even he could not bring order out of the chaos.

Sooner or later, Kansas was going to become a free state. Senator Douglas had thought so; Pierce had agreed; and so did Buchanan. The odds were strongly against the proslavery faction; they were already outnumbered in the territory by about four to one. Any fair process of producing a state constitution would result in a prohibition of slavery. However, early in 1857 the proslavery group controlled Congress and managed all territorial appointments, hence it could manipulate the election of its delegates to a constitutional convention. The upshot

was a proslavery gathering at Lecompton, Kansas, which adopted a discredited constitution recognizing slavery. In the shambles that followed, Governor Walker lost his credibility, the Northerners vowed to ignore the convention's handiwork; and the Southerners decided to present only one question for popular vote: Should more slaves be allowed into Kansas?

For months Buchanan had vacillated between calling for a referendum limited to the slavery issue or for one dealing with the entire Lecompton constitution. He had recently promised Governor Walker support for the latter course, but when the results of the territorial election and the Lecompton convention arrived in Washington, the president's Southern advisers convinced him to change his mind again. He concluded that although the proslavery constitution would cause some trouble, the proceedings at Lecompton were legal. Hoping against hope, Buchanan said that establishing Kansas as a state—any kind of a state—would end the national quarrel over the territory. To the antislavery leaders, this represented a complete sellout by Buchanan to the Southern wing of his party.

Senator Douglas, who had bestowed assurances during the Kansas-Nebraska debate that Kansas would enter the Union as a free state as the result of a popular vote, saw the actions of the Lecompton body as a violation of the popular sovereignty principle. Moreover, he was up for reelection in Illinois, where the Lecompton plan was thoroughly disliked. Alarmed, Douglas hurried to the White House to talk to the president. At the end of an angry conference, he told Buchanan he would oppose the administration if it allowed the proslavery constitution to come to Congress without a vote on the entire document by the inhabitants of the territory. Buchanan, in turn, warned Douglas against fighting his administration. Douglas's hopes of becoming the Democratic nominee in 1860 were on the line.

In his annual message, delivered less than a week after Douglas broke with him, Buchanan told Congress he would deliver the Lecompton constitution following the "with-slavery, without-slavery" vote. Within two weeks, in a referendum held under the aegis of the Lecompton convention, pro-Southern residents voted 6,226 to 569 for the constitution with slavery. Then the new Free-Soil legislature in the territory called for another vote and offered a complete constitution, which was rejected, 10,226 votes to 162. Ignoring the antislavery legislators' actions, Buchanan sent the Lecompton constitution to Congress in February 1858, and advised that Kansas be admitted to the Union. After a bitter sectional debate on April 1, 1858, Douglas Democrats, Republicans, and Know-Nothings combined to reject the Lecompton constitution. For the moment, Kansas statehood was dead.

A disastrous step had been taken toward war. Buchanan had given way to pressure from the South. Certainly, anything he did at the time was bound to stir up bitterness. But the Southern extremists, who

were encouraged by their success with him and enraged by the defeat in Congress of the Lecompton constitution, grew more clamorous.

Other forces were at work to aid them. In August 1857 a business panic broke out in the North. To the South, aroused by religious revivalism and the

THE BUCHANAN ADMINISTRATION

INAUGURATION: Mar. 4, 1857; the Capitol, Washington, D.C.

VICE PRESIDENT: John C. Breckinridge

SECRETARY OF STATE: Lewis Cass; Jeremiah S. Black (from Dec. 17, 1860)

SECRETARY OF THE TREASURY: Howell Cobb; Philip F. Thomas (from Dec. 12, 1860); John A. Dix (from Jan. 15, 1861)

SECRETARY OF WAR: John B. Floyd; Joseph Holt (from Jan. 18, 1861)

ATTORNEY GENERAL: Jeremiah S. Black; Edwin M. Stanton (from Dec. 22, 1860)

POSTMASTER GENERAL: Aaron V. Brown; Joseph Holt (from Mar. 14, 1859); Horatio King (from Feb. 12, 1861)

SECRETARY OF THE NAVY: Isaac Toucey

SECRETARY OF THE INTERIOR: Jacob Thompson

SUPREME COURT APPOINTMENT: Nathan Clifford (1858)

35TH CONGRESS (Dec. 7, 1857–Mar. 3, 1859):
  SENATE: 39 Democrats; 20 Republicans; 5 Others
  HOUSE: 131 Democrats; 92 Republicans; 14 Others

36TH CONGRESS (Dec. 5, 1859–Mar. 3, 1861):
  SENATE: 38 Democrats; 26 Republicans; 2 Others
  HOUSE: 113 Republicans; 101 Democrats; 23 Others

STATES ADMITTED: Minnesota (1858); Oregon (1859); Kansas (1861)

ELECTION OF 1856

CANDIDATES	ELECTORAL VOTE	POPULAR VOTE
James Buchanan (Democratic)	174	1,836,072
John C. Frémont (Republican)	114	1,342,345
Millard Fillmore (Know-Nothing)	8	873,053

A 1939 mural by John Steuart Curry celebrates the militant abolitionist John Brown, whose depredations began in "Bloody Kansas" and came to a climax at Harpers Ferry, Virginia, with an abortive raid on the federal arsenal there. After a brief skirmish, Brown and his followers were captured by Colonel Robert E. Lee's forces. Brown was tried and hanged; Northern abolitionists made him into a folk hero, acclaimed by the song "John Brown's Body."

leading Southern cities, the idea was pushed that if the North did not conform to Southern wishes, the South would break the thread of the Union and flourish as an independent country.

More dramatic, and just as important, was an incident at a small town in Virginia in the fall of 1859. Commanding a handful of whites and blacks, an abolitionist named John Brown (an unstable Kansan who had led a massacre in Kansas in 1856) briefly seized the federal arsenal and a rifle factory at Harpers Ferry. He intended to start a black insurrection, which he thought would spread throughout the South like wildfire. The madcap scheme collapsed when federal troops captured Brown, who was tried and hanged. Brown soon became in both North and South a symbol of an impending storm. Even Southern moderates began to feel forced to choose between upholding the idea of Union or protecting a time-honored way of life.

Slavery was not the only issue of Buchanan's administration. Nor was Kansas the only territory that proved a problem for him. "Deseret," the Mormon promised land established by the Compromise of 1850 as the Territory of Utah, had been treated as an ill-favored stepchild by laymen and lawmakers for decades. Forced to flee from persecution in the settled states, the Mormons had settled in the unorganized territory beyond the Rocky Mountains, and they had prospered. Despite the population growth, all applications for statehood had been ignored, and in 1855 Pierce had made three federal judiciary appointments for the Utah Territory that were remarkable for their stupidity: All three men were enemies of the Mormon faith. The judges were unable to exercise much authority in the territory, mainly because the inhabitants ignored them; so in 1857 they came East to complain. Buchanan named a new governor, Alfred Cumming, to replace territorial magistrate Brigham Young and ordered a 2,500-man army to help sustain the law. The confused Mormons thought they were being invaded.

denominational schisms reflecting the slavery controversy, the financial ruin spreading in the North was interpreted as a godsend. The panic seemed a just retribution for the abolition movement and for the cluttered, seamy life of the cities. In the 1840s Ralph Waldo Emerson had written, "Cotton thread holds the Union together." But the South, almost totally dependent on a cotton-based economy, was barely troubled by the Panic of 1857, and the feeling grew that the mill owners in the North needed cotton far more than the mill owners in the South. Radicals insisted that Southern society was stable, while Northern society was corrupt and at the mercy of greedy financiers. At commercial conventions in

Thus, through bureaucratic incompetence and human misunderstanding, the so-called Mormon War began, highlighted by severe harassment of the approaching troops and a massacre of emigrants en route to California by Mormons and Indians. At last, Thomas L. Kane of Philadelphia, a friend of Buchanan and a Mormon sympathizer, suggested that he be sent to Salt Lake City to talk to Young. Buchanan agreed, and gradually the grievances were redressed. Cumming was finally accepted as governor.

Foreign policy turned out to be Buchanan's strong suit. Despite the restrictions imposed on him by the growing domestic crisis, his one limited success as president was in the diplomatic field. Relying on his contacts in Great Britain, he developed with the British an interpretation of the troublesome Clayton-Bulwer Treaty—an attempt to guarantee nonintervention in Central America by the United States and Great Britain—that was satisfactory to both sides. This strengthened the Monroe Doctrine as a fixture in the nation's foreign policy.

At the same time, the president labored to increase United States influence in Central and South America, partly as a step toward national expansion. While discouraging filibustering, Buchanan brought American power to bear on—among others—Nicaragua (winning the right to protect routes across the isthmus with American arms) and Mexico (which agreed to let the United States send troops into the country whenever uprisings threatened the Mexican government). The Senate refused to ratify these treaties; nonetheless, had Buchanan been president in a quieter time, he might today be remembered as an empire builder.

From the beginning of his term Buchanan had to deal with a chaotic situation in Congress. Though the reigning Democrats were a national party in form —and the only one then remaining in American politics—they were not national in substance. Rather, they were divided along sectional lines—North versus South. Washington was full of lobbyists for various enterprises, who had liquor to pour and money to spend. As sectionalism weakened party loyalty, and rising Republican strength foreshadowed an 1860 defeat, Democratic congressmen tended to look after their private and local power rather than national needs, and failed to provide the president with the national "consensus" he so ardently desired. What small chance there was for party unity vanished in the Lecompton fight; this left the Douglas Democrats and the Southern extremist Democrats antagonistic. After the 1858 midterm elections, Congress was controlled by men who were ready to do battle with the administration.

Buchanan's legislative program, an ambitious one which included the purchase of Cuba and an enlargement of the armed forces, was wrecked by sectionalist, bickering, and vindictive congressmen. Routine laws, needed to keep the government in operation, had trouble passing. Increasingly, Buchanan seemed disconnected from the realities surrounding him in Washington. After seeing the dismaying returns in the mid-term elections, he could still make the amazing statement that "the prospects are daily brightening. From present appearances the party will ere long be thoroughly united." Yet every day, the South drew further away from the ideal of the old Union. Frightened by the possibility of slave emancipation or insurrection, insulted and angered by William Lloyd Garrison, Harriet Beecher Stowe, and their kind, the South looked upon the North as an unfriendly foreign government. Party leaders, including Vice President John C. Breckinridge of Kentucky, saw Northern Democrats pulling out of line, as Douglas had done, and knew what this meant for 1860: the election of a Republican president endorsing an anti-slavery platform. Such an eventuality would, they reasoned, be sufficient cause for setting up a Southern confederacy.

Buchanan had decided before his inauguration not

to stand for reelection; he thought two terms were too long for any man to serve in the presidency. In the midst of rampant sectionalism, the Democrats were unable to unify behind one man. The Charleston convention finally chose Breckinridge, but the Douglas wing moved to Baltimore and nominated Stephen Douglas from Illinois. To complicate matters, the Constitutional Unionists met and picked Senator John Bell as their candidate. The united Republicans chose Abraham Lincoln over a host of aspirants; and he won despite being kept off Southern ballots entirely.

FREDERICK DOUGLASS

Without the verification of history, the story of Frederick Douglass would seem to be an improbable piece of fiction. The son of a slave and an unknown white man, Douglass was reared in bondage in Maryland. Despite laws forbidding the education of slaves, he learned to read and write, increasing his fierce desire to be free. In 1838, at the age of twenty-one, he succeeded: He fled first to New York, then to New Bedford, Massachusetts, where he worked as a laborer and lived with the realization that his "runaway" status might be discovered at any time. His impressive physique and commanding voice soon made Douglass a spokesman for the state's antislavery society; in 1845 he daringly sharpened the sword hanging over his head by publishing his life story, *Narrative of the Life of Frederick Douglass*. Two years later he arranged to buy his freedom and established a newspaper, the *North Star*, firmly setting his own policies despite conflicting advice from abolitionist friends. He lectured widely, advocated woman suffrage, and, during the war, recruited two black regiments, exhorting them, "Better even to die than to live as slaves. . . . The iron gate of our prison stands half open. One gallant rush . . . will fling it wide. . . ." During Reconstruction, he agitated for African-Americans' civil rights, and by the time of his death in 1895, Douglass had held a number of federal offices, including that of minister to Haiti.

In a country thus split by doctrine and geography, Lincoln won with much less than a popular majority. Led by the South Carolina legislature, which passed a secession ordinance in December 1861, the firestorm grew as the newly proclaimed Confederate States of America added dissenting states to their de facto government. Georgia, Alabama, Mississippi, Louisiana, and Florida were soon out of the Union. South Carolina, the old home of nullification, presented the most immediate danger to the Union. Because there was talk of the possible capture by the secessionists of the forts in Charleston Harbor, Colonel John L. Gardner, commanding the garrison there, decided to remove federal arms from the arsenal as a precaution. His plans were stymied by an outraged mob.

Buchanan wrung his hands but took no decisive action. He scolded Northerners for their abolition movement and pleaded with the South to be patient. In truth, Buchanan became more of a spectator than a leader in a time of grave crisis. The bold, forceful examples of Jackson and Polk were lost on this timorous president. While Buchanan prayed that the storm would not break until after Lincoln's inauguration, Southerners in his cabinet transferred critical military supplies to bases in the South where seizures of federal posts seemed likely.

The tension created by hotheads in Charleston vexed Buchanan. The resignation of many federal officers there provided the president with an excuse to do nothing. Thus the administration had reached the nadir of its futility. As a lame-duck president, Buchanan curtailed his already weak position with his nitpicking of legalisms when action was desperately needed. He denied himself powers that other presidents had grasped unhesitatingly in similar emergencies—notably Washington in the Whiskey Rebellion and Jackson in the Nullification Crisis.

While the chances of saving the Union slipped away, Buchanan stared out the White House windows, paralyzed by a lack of character. In the interim, the Southern rebels made vast strides. A provisional Confederate government had been organized by February 9, 1861. All over the South, federal forts and arsenals were captured. Hard to fathom is Buchanan's continuing insistence that by law he could take no action. Thus no federal troops were placed on emergency duty, no naval vessels ordered to stand by. Instead, the commander in chief held that he was powerless to act.

While a group of loyal Southerners planned a "peace convention" to be held in Virginia as a last-ditch effort to end the snowballing secessionist movement, Buchanan balked. He begged Congress to give the federal government new powers on the one hand and to provide a constitutional resolution to the crisis on the other. He believed that the best solution to the mounting turmoil lay in a clarifying amendment to the Constitution that would guarantee slavery in the states that wanted it. Congress refused to move. Buchanan apparently saw himself as standing firmly in the middle, giving in to no one, but pacifying both sides until a solution could be found. Those Northerners who support the South "are almost literally between two fires," he had once told John Calhoun. "I desire to come between the factions . . . with one hand on the head of each, counseling peace," he said now. He could not admit to—or recognize—his failure. After leaving office he told his niece, "I acted for some time as a breakwater between the North and the South, both surging with all their force against me."

When he retired to Wheatland that March, he left the nation in crisis, headed for a tragic conflagration. He was quickly made the scapegoat for the havoc that followed. Buchanan's failure to act at once to cut off secession was criticized—justly, if one assumes that a strong display of fortitude would have halted the secessionist movement. Buchanan used the Constitution as a device to shield his ineptness.

Out of office, Buchanan supported Lincoln and

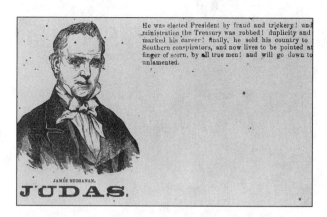

Buchanan's enemies printed derisive envelopes to carry bitter messages to their correspondents. The message here claimed that Buchanan had been elected "by fraud and trickery" and his career had been marked by "cowardice." In the 1860 presidential election, Buchanan was dumped for the more forthright Democrats, John C. Breckinridge and Stephen Douglas.

the war, saying that he would have done as Lincoln did, once Fort Sumter was fired on. Lincoln was not grateful; he needed someone to blame for the war and led off the attack on Buchanan's reputation. "It is one of those great national prosecutions," wrote Buchanan before he died in 1868, "necessary to vindicate the character of the Government." The world, he said, had "forgotten the circumstances" and blamed his "supineness."

In Buchanan's defense, it can be said that he reaped a political whirlwind that had been decades in the making. Perhaps the Civil War that soon enveloped the republic was an "irrepressible conflict"; still, Buchanan must bear the judgment of history. When a crisis threatened the very fabric of the Union, Buchanan let everybody down. The nation was to pay a terrible, bloody price to save the Union; and the political party that gave him so much would fall into near oblivion for more than a half-century.

—*Michael Harwood,*
revised by Robert A. Rutland

ABRAHAM LINCOLN
THE GREAT EMANCIPATOR

"It is a great folly," Lincoln once told a biographer, "to attempt to make anything out of me or my early life. It can all be condensed into a single sentence; and that sentence you will find in Gray's *Elegy*: 'The short and simple annals of the poor.'" Lincoln was born on February 12, 1809, in a one-room, dirt-floored log cabin in the backwoods of Kentucky. Thomas Lincoln, his father, was a Baptist, a Jacksonian, and a carpenter by trade. Able only to scrawl his name, he offered no inspiration to young Abe, whose bookish aversion to frontier chores Thomas grew to resent. Nancy Hanks Lincoln, the boy's mother, may have been an illegitimate child; Lincoln himself, according to William Herndon, said, "My mother was a bastard, was the daughter of a nobleman so called of Virginia." Whether or not Lincoln was right, he sometimes credited that unnamed aristocrat with any mental distinction he possessed. To the stoop-shouldered, religious Nancy he gave all his love. "God bless my mother; all that I am or even hope to be I owe to her," he said.

In 1811, when Abe was two, the family moved about ten miles northeast to Knob Creek, Kentucky. Five years later, because of an uncertain land title and, according to his son, "partly on account of slavery," Thomas moved again, this time to the free state of Indiana. He erected his new home at Pigeon Creek; Abe, age seven, helped to build it. When Lincoln was nine, his mother died. A year later Thomas married Sarah Bush Johnston, a widow. To the cabin in Indiana, Sarah brought her own three children and much love. According to Lincoln's friend Ward Hill Lamon, she cared for Abe and his sister, Sarah, as if they were her own, feeding, washing, and clothing them, making them look, in her own words, "a little more human." She took a fast shine to Abe: "His mind and mine—what little I had—seemed to run together." She encouraged his reading and apparently convinced Thomas Lincoln to let the boy be.

The years in Indiana, Lincoln later recalled, were "pretty pinching times." The family ate adequately, but they worked hard for any comfort they had. And young Abe pitched in, plowing, tending the fire, planting seed, picking berries. He became prodigious with an axe: Dennis Hanks, his cousin, recalled that if "you heard him fellin' trees in a clearin', you would say that there was three men at work by the way the trees fell."

To help his father financially, Abe hired himself out as a handyman. Some employers, such as John Romaine, were not pleased with him. "He worked for me," said Romaine, "but was always reading and thinking. I used to get mad at him for it. I say he was awful lazy. He would laugh and talk, crack jokes and tell stories all the time. . . . He said to me . . . that his father taught him to work but he never taught him to love it."

But for all his delight in people, talk, and sport, he was largely a loner, alone in the fields and forests of the frontier. "Silence," Carl Sandburg writes, "found him for her own. In the making of him, the element of silence was immense."

Lincoln possessed a quick and inquiring mind that cut to the marrow of facts and ideas and grasped their relationships with intuitive force. This mind must have been a birthright, for in Lincoln's words, in "unpolitical" Indiana "there was absolutely nothing to excite ambition for education." In the one-room schools of the day, formal education embraced nothing more than reading (*Dilworth's Spelling Book*), a little writing, and, as Lincoln later said, "cipherin' to the rule of three."

Despite this stifling environment, Lincoln sought to educate himself. Wherever he could find or make light, he read: *Aesop's Fables*, *Robinson Crusoe*, the Bible. Even at work in the field, when his horse rested, Lincoln's book would be out of his pocket. Books like Parson Weems's lyrical life of Washington affected him deeply. When he borrowed the Weems book and got it wet, he worked three days on a farm to pay for it and own it.

Abraham Lincoln, in an 1863 daguerreotype by Mathew Brady.

For all his introspection, Lincoln was a powerful young man—sturdy, muscular, a formidable foe in any bout. By nineteen, he was six feet four inches tall. Despite a relatively small chest and a slim waist, he had powerful shoulders and large limbs.

In February 1830 Thomas Lincoln pulled up stakes again, this time moving to Macon County in Illinois. The next year, Abe struck out on his own. Hired by Denton Offutt, he worked on a flatboat carrying goods to New Orleans. It was a decisive trip, for Offutt took a liking to him and offered him a job as a clerk in a general store and mill in New Salem, Illinois. And on this passage Lincoln first saw the horror of slavery: black men and women in chains, whipped and sold like cattle.

He arrived in New Salem in July 1831 and soon thereafter squared off in a wrestling match with the town bully, Jack Armstrong. Some say he beat Armstrong; others call it a draw. But unmistakably, Lincoln won his opponent's—and the townspeople's—respect. Affable behind the counter of Offutt's store, good to children, obliging to widows (for whom he chopped wood), Lincoln earned a reputation for kindness, reliability, and honesty. Also, clerking afforded him leisure for reading. Weems gave way to Voltaire and Thomas Paine, to Burns and Blackstone, to Indiana statutes and the Constitution, and to Shakespeare (*Macbeth* was his favorite work). Friends lent him books, the cooper opened his shop to him at night so that he could read by a fire of shavings, and schoolmaster Mentor Graham polished Lincoln's command of the English language.

In 1832 Lincoln served one brief term as a soldier in the field. When the Fox and Sauk, under Black Hawk, took to the warpath, the governor issued a call for volunteers, and Lincoln promptly signed up. Elected captain, he saw no battle, saved an Indian from being lynched, and served competently in two independent companies as a scout.

Returning to New Salem, the popular Lincoln campaigned for a seat in the Illinois general assembly as an anti-Jackson Whig. His approach was disarmingly to the point: "Fellow Citizens, I presume you all know who I am. I am humble Abraham Lincoln. . . . My politics are short and sweet like the old woman's dance. I am in favour of a national bank. I am in favour of the internal improvement system and a high protective tariff. . . . If elected, I shall be thankful; if not, it will be all the same." Predictably, Lincoln lost this first election in hard-nosed Jacksonian territory. But he won almost all the votes of his neighbors, Democrats or not.

He was soon back in the grocery business, in partnership with William F. Berry, who had served with him during the Black Hawk War. On credit and on Lincoln's high reputation in the town, the two veterans took over three stores. However, the enterprises foundered: Berry liked liquor too much, and Lincoln, the law, which he was studying in spare moments. It took him fifteen years of self-denial to pay off all his—and Berry's—creditors.

When the job of postmaster fell vacant in May 1833, Lincoln was named to the office. In charge of the mail, he could be less than efficient, keeping his postal receipts in an old blue sock and the mail in his hat; on his rounds, he was more than dutiful. He would walk miles to deliver a letter he knew was eagerly awaited. The postmaster's salary was based on receipts and ranged from $25 to $80 a year. So, probably through the influence of a Democratic friend, Lincoln was offered the more lucrative post of deputy county surveyor. He learned about surveying by poring over books late into the night.

Meanwhile, love found Lincoln, in the person of Ann Rutledge, the auburn-haired, blue-eyed, slender, and fair daughter of a taverner. Lincoln loved her, courted her, and became engaged to her. Ann's death, of typhoid, plunged him into a profound melancholy.

A seat in the Illinois assembly remained Lincoln's goal: When he sought election again in 1834, he won.

Through the first session of the legislature, he remained observant and silent in his new suit. But in succeeding sessions, he rose to the leadership of his party, becoming the Whigs' perennial candidate for Speaker of the House in the strongly Democratic assembly. He supported the removal of the state capital to Springfield, to which he himself moved in 1837. In the new capital, he boarded free with a tradesman named Joshua Speed, who took pity on his poverty and melancholy face and became his friend. These legislative years saw a maturing of Lincoln's moderate Whig philosophy and his development as an adroit partisan advocate and orator. Admitted to the bar in 1836, he fared well, not only as a capital attorney but also as a circuit lawyer.

Of primary interest in a review of his Springfield years is his position on slavery. The Illinois constitution of 1818 had granted the vote to all adult white male residents, without qualification. Consequently Lincoln's campaign appeal of 1836 that "all whites . . . who pay taxes or bear arms" be given the vote was radical only in his suggestion that taxpaying females be allowed to vote.

Yet Lincoln was always opposed to slavery. "I am naturally anti-slavery," he wrote in 1864. "If slavery is not wrong, nothing is wrong. I can not remember when I did not so think and feel." In response to the statewide rise of overt antislavery sentiment, the Illinois legislature in 1837 passed resolutions condemning abolitionism and denying the right of the federal government either to abridge slavery in the states or to abolish it without a vote in the District of Columbia. Lincoln and a friend, Dan Stone, were the only two legislators to submit a dissenting resolution which addressed not only abolitionism but the institution of slavery itself. Slavery, they said, was "founded on both injustice and bad policy. . . ." In a concession to the conservatives, they admitted that the abolition of slavery was also wrong because "the promulgation of abolition doctrines tends rather to increase than to

abate" the evils of slavery. As for the role of Washington, Lincoln and Stone agreed that the federal government could not constitutionally interfere with slavery in any state but that it could abolish it in the District of Columbia, though "that power ought not to be exercised unless" the people of the District so requested.

But all was not politics in Springfield. Lincoln was involved with a new woman. As a popular and respected legislator, he had access to the hub of Springfield's social life, the Ninian Edwards mansion, which was overseen by Mrs. Elizabeth Todd Edwards,

BIOGRAPHICAL FACTS

BIRTH: Hardin County, Ky., Feb. 12, 1809
ANCESTRY: English
FATHER: Thomas Lincoln; b. Rockingham County, Va., Jan. 6, 1778; d. Coles County, Ill., Jan. 17, 1851
FATHER'S OCCUPATIONS: Farmer; carpenter
MOTHER: Nancy Hanks Lincoln; b. Va., Feb. 5, 1784; d. Spencer County, Ind., Oct. 5, 1818
STEPMOTHER: Sarah Bush Johnston; b. Hardin County, Ky., Dec. 12, 1788; d. Charleston, Ill., Apr. 10, 1869
BROTHER: Thomas (1811–1813)
SISTER: Sarah (1807–1828)
MARRIAGE: Springfield, Ill., Nov. 4, 1842
WIFE: Mary Todd; b. Lexington, Ky., Dec. 13, 1818; d. Springfield, Ill., July 16, 1882
CHILDREN: Robert Todd (1843–1926); Edward Baker (1846–1850); William Wallace (1850–1862); Thomas "Tad" (1853–1871)
RELIGIOUS AFFILIATION: None
EDUCATION: Local tutors; self-educated
OCCUPATIONS BEFORE PRESIDENCY: Store clerk; store owner; ferry pilot; surveyor; postmaster; lawyer
MILITARY SERVICE: Served in volunteer company for three months during Black Hawk War (1832)
PREPRESIDENTIAL OFFICES: Member Illinois General Assembly; U.S. congressman
AGE AT INAUGURATION: 52
DEATH: Washington, D.C., April 15, 1865
PLACE OF BURIAL: Oak Ridge Cemetery, Springfield, Ill.

sister of Mary Todd of Lexington, Kentucky. Twenty-one-year-old Mary was well educated and charming, if high tempered. In its initial stage, her courtship with Lincoln lasted for about twelve months, and their wedding was set for January 1, 1841.

The event, however, did not take place on the appointed date. Possibly because he had fallen in love with another woman, Lincoln broke the engagement. Although the old story of his not showing up at the ceremony is untrue, he is said to have gone to Mary and told her that he could not go through with the marriage. It is certain that after he left Mary Todd, he experienced a profound emotional breakdown lasting almost a year and a half. Joshua Speed and Speed's mother nursed him back to mental health.

By mid-1842 Lincoln was moving toward stability, and Mary Todd was still willing. They reconciled and repledged their troth. On November 4, 1842, they were married in an Episcopal ceremony. A week later Lincoln concluded a business letter with an enigmatic remark: "Nothing new here except my marrying, which to me, is matter of profound wonder."

Lincoln's marriage to Mary was indisputably rocky. They fought hard and bitterly, often and audibly. Lincoln seems to have met Mary's assaults with a saddened forbearance, avoiding conflict when possible. A common love for their children bound them together: Robert, the eldest, who would go on to Exeter and Harvard and serve as secretary of war under Presidents Garfield and Arthur; Edward, who would die at three; William, who would die at eleven in the White House; and frail Thomas (Tad), who was afflicted with a speech defect.

In 1846 Lincoln was elected to the Thirtieth U.S. Congress by the largest majority in the history of his district. When he arrived in Washington, the United States was only several weeks short of victory in the Mexican War. In Congress, Lincoln joined the shrill Whig attack on the Democratic president, James K. Polk. On January 12, 1848, Congressman Lincoln explained his position. He rejected as the "sheerest deception" Polk's claim that the first American blood spilled by Mexicans was shed on American soil. Mexico was not the aggressor; the United States was. Back home in his Illinois district, the reaction to Lincoln's stand against the war was one of fury and shock. But the congressman stood his ground. "Allow the President to invade a neighboring nation whenever *he* shall deem it necessary to repel an invasion . . ." Lincoln wrote, "and you allow him to make war at pleasure. . . ."

In Congress, Lincoln consistently favored the exclusion of slavery in the territories ceded by Mexico, but he remained opposed to federal interference with slavery in the states where it already existed. A lame-duck congressman (by prearrangement with other party leaders in Illinois), he introduced, in January 1849, an amendment to a resolution instructing the Committee on the District of Columbia to report out a bill abolishing slavery in the District. Lincoln urged that children born of slaves in Washington after January 1, 1850, should be free, but should be apprenticed to their masters until they came of age. Masters wishing to free a slave would be compensated by the federal government. All fugitive slaves escaping into the District, under Lincoln's plan, were to be returned to their masters. The resolution did not become law.

In 1848 Lincoln took to the stump for the Whig presidential candidate, Zachary Taylor. He organized demonstrations and rallies and toured New England in a bid to unite Whigs and Free-Soilers behind the war hero. Taylor won, and after the inauguration the congressman looked for a patronage plum: the office of commissioner of the general land office. When he failed to get this position, a disillusioned Lincoln, now age forty, retired for five years from public political activity. Again he was a circuit lawyer, a natural politician who liked a good joke.

But the "irrepressible conflict" was approaching,

presaged even more formidably by the passage in 1854 of the Kansas-Nebraska Act. Sired by Illinois's Democratic senator, Stephen A. Douglas, the act, by repealing the Missouri Compromise prohibiting slavery in territories north of 36°30' and substituting popular sovereignty (the right of the settlers to decide the slavery question themselves), opened up, in effect, the entire area of the Louisiana Purchase to slavery. In the Northwest the reaction to the act was bitter and violent. On March 20, 1854, anger gave way to organized political rebellion when a coalition of Whigs, Free-Soilers, and antislavery Democrats met at Ripon, Wisconsin, and formed the Republican party.

Lincoln, outraged by Douglas's proslavery measure, attacked the Kansas-Nebraska Act in a forceful address at Peoria on October 16, 1854. Distinguishing between the institution's existence and its spread, he denounced the latter because of "the monstrous injustice of slavery itself." After first hesitating, he joined the new party in 1856 and campaigned hard for its first presidential candidate, John C. Frémont. By plumping for the party slate, he built his own reputation, county by county. According to Horace White, secretary of the Illinois Republican state committee, Lincoln was "one of the shrewdest politicians of the state. . . ." Nobody, White said, "knew better than he what was passing in the minds of the people. Nobody knew better how to turn things to advantage politically, and nobody was readier to take such advantage, provided it did not involve dishonorable means."

Two days after the inauguration of President Buchanan, in 1857, Chief Justice Roger B. Taney's heavily Southern Supreme Court handed down its decision in the Dred Scott case: It ruled that slaves were property, and declared the Missouri Compromise unconstitutional. In Springfield, Senator Douglas defended the Court's decision. "The Courts," Douglas said, "are tribunals prescribed by the Constitution. . . . Hence, whoever resists the final decision

Mary Todd, a few years after her marriage to Abraham Lincoln.

of the highest judicial tribunal aims a deadly blow at our whole republican system of government. . . ."

Lincoln, now emerging as the major advocate of Free-Soil Republicanism, spoke in Springfield on June 26, 1857. He derided Douglas's pious homily on the Court's preeminence, pointing out that Douglas himself had defied the Court's ruling on the Bank of the United States by applauding President Jackson's refusal to abide by its decision. Lincoln condemned the alliance of American business interests, educators, and theologians, who were, he said, joining forces to imprison blacks forever. Any man who justifies the enslavement of others, he added, justifies his own. If color is the excuse, and the lighter man has a right to enslave the darker, the lighter may himself be enslaved by a still lighter man. If intellectual superiority justifies slavery, all men are at the mercy of those more brilliant than they. If business interest justifies slavery, anyone with an interest in a man, white or black, may enslave him.

Lincoln's logic, now fired by political passion, was unassailable. To Douglas's statement that Lincoln's views were held only by people who wanted "to vote, and eat, and sleep, and marry with negroes," Lincoln replied that the fact that he did not want to have a Negro woman for a slave did not imply that he must have her for a wife. Could he not just leave her alone? "In some respects," he said, "she certainly is not my equal; but in her natural right to eat the bread she earns with her own hands without asking leave of any one else, she is my equal, and the equal of all others."

Lincoln's answer to Douglas initiated a verbal exchange that thrust him into national fame. On June 16, 1858, he was named by the Republicans to run for Douglas's senate seat. That same day he delivered his acceptance speech at the Illinois Republican state convention. Noting the rise of impassioned agitation against slavery, Lincoln told his party: "In *my* opinion, it *will* not cease, until a *crisis* shall have been reached, and passed." Then he turned to the language of the Bible: 'A house divided against itself cannot stand.' I believe this government cannot endure, permanently half *slave* and half *free*. I do not expect the Union to be *dissolved*—I do not expect the house to *fall*—but I *do* expect it will cease to be divided. It will become *all* one thing, or *all* the other. Either the *opponents* of slavery, will arrest the further spread of it, and place it where the public mind shall rest in the belief that it is in course of ultimate extinction; or its *advocates* will push it forward, till it shall become alike in *all* the States, *old* as well as *new*—North as well as South."

To a critic who complained that the speech was too strong, Lincoln rejoined: "If I had to draw a pen across my record, and erase my whole life from sight, and I had one poor gift or choice as to what I should save from the wreck, I should choose that speech and leave it to the world unerased."

Then he challenged Douglas to a series of debates which began at Ottawa, Illinois, on August 21, 1858, and ended at Alton on October 15, amid banners, brass bands, raucous crowds, and sweating reporters. At Freeport, on August 27, Douglas made a major ideological concession—his famed "Freeport Doctrine"—that would cost him Southern Democratic support and would nourish Democratic disunion. To Lincoln's question, "Can the people of a United States Territory, in any lawful way, against the wish of any citizen of the United States, exclude slavery from its limits prior to the formation of a State Constitution?" Douglas answered Yes. Further, he said, "it matters not what way the Supreme Court may hereafter decide as to . . . whether slavery may or may not go into a territory under the Constitution, the people have the lawful means to introduce it or exclude it as they please. . . ."

At the last debate, Douglas assailed Lincoln's "house divided" speech as a "slander upon the immortal framers of our Constitution," who, he said, had founded the country, both free and slave, under state sovereignties. He ridiculed Lincoln's egalitarian view of the Declaration of Independence, which was meant, Douglas said, for colonial and British whites only. And he condemned Lincoln's "crusade against the Supreme Court" following the Dred Scott decision.

Lincoln's retort: If Douglas affirmed the wisdom of the Founding Fathers, why did he defy their critical attitude on slavery by introducing his divisive Kansas-Nebraska Act? Lincoln envisioned new United States territories open to "free white people everywhere—the world over. . . ." He dismissed Douglas's charges that he sought a sectional war over slavery or favored "introducing a perfect social and political equality between the white and black races. . . ." The whole question, Lincoln said, was reduced to a choice between "the common right of humanity" or "the divine right of kings."

Because of the political pressure and widespread racism of the time, Lincoln conceded that he, too, was opposed to miscegenation. "Agreed for once—a thousand times agreed," he said in 1857. "There are white men enough to marry all the white women, and black men enough to marry all the black women; and so let them be married." Though avowing in July 1858 that he had "always hated slavery . . . as much as any Abolitionist," he insisted that he had never intended to do anything about it where it already existed. And finally he declared in Chicago, on July 10, 1858, that he wished that all talk of "inferior" people be discarded. Yet only two months later, in Charleston, Illinois, he contradicted himself:

"I will say then that I am not, nor ever have been in favor of bringing about in any way the social and political equality of the white and black races—that I am not nor ever have been in favor of making voters or jurors of negroes, nor of qualifying them to hold office, nor to intermarry with white people. . . . And inasmuch as they cannot so live, while they do remain together there must be the position of superior and inferior, and I as much as any other man am in favor of having the superior position assigned to the white race."

In the Senate election, held on November 2, 1858, Lincoln polled a popular majority of some four thousand votes over his opponent. But Douglas, through gerrymandered apportionment, won electoral control of the assembly, which reelected him to the Senate 54 to 46. Lincoln described his reaction to the defeat in words that would one day be echoed by another Illinoisan, Adlai E. Stevenson II. Likening himself to the little boy who stubbed his toe, he said, "It hurt too bad to laugh, and he was too big to cry." But friends assured a disappointed Lincoln that more and more influential people were eyeing him for the presidency. Replied Lincoln, "I . . . admit that I am ambitious, and would like to be President . . . but there is no such good luck in store for me. . . ."

Still, friends pressed the issue, urging Lincoln to make himself even better known. Calls for speeches poured in from Iowa, Pennsylvania, Missouri, and New York. On February 27, 1860, at Cooper Institute in Manhattan, he argued wholly on the basis of tradition, citing the personal attitudes and constitutional provisions of the Founding Fathers to support a policy of nonintervention with slavery in states where it existed and the exclusion of it from the territories. Lincoln denied that the Republican appeal for the restriction of slavery was sectional, urging the South to give it a chance at the polls. George Washington himself, he said, had heartily signed Congress' Northwest Ordinance barring the extension of slavery. Were Washington's motives sectional too?

Rejecting the extremism of both abolitionists and secessionists, Lincoln disproved Taney's claim that the Constitution "distinctly and expressly" affirmed the right of property in a slave. The Constitution, he said, certainly guaranteed property. But as for the slave, Lincoln explained, the Constitution cited him specifically as a "person," alluding to his master's claim over him solely in terms of "service or labor which may be due." To the South's claim that the election of a Republican president would destroy the Union, Lincoln replied: "That is cool. A highwayman holds a pistol to my ear, and mutters through his teeth, 'Stand and deliver, or I shall kill you, and then you will be a murderer!'" Slave-owners, he said, would apparently be appeased only if opponents of slavery would agree that slavery was morally proper and should be given "a full national recognition . . . as a legal right, and a social blessing." The South, he charged, was demanding that the righteous, not the unrighteous, be called to repentance. "Right," Lincoln concluded, "makes might. . . ." New York applauded.

Lincoln moved on to Providence, then to New Hampshire, where he was hailed by Governor Frederick Smith as "the next President of the United States." In May his political ship made for home port at the Illinois Republican state convention in Decatur. When John Hanks, a companion of Lincoln's from the old Mississippi flatboat, entered the convention hall bearing two rails allegedly split by Abe, the delegates erupted with joy.

The Republican National Convention of 1860, held in Chicago, ratified the decision made at Decatur. Senator William H. Seward, of New York, who had called the American conflict "irrepressible," entered the convention city a brassy and confident candidate. Others in the field were Salmon P. Chase, Edward Bates, and Simon Cameron.

A great roar went up for Seward when he was nominated, but there was an even greater cry for the candidate from Illinois. "The uproar" for Lincoln, a journalist reported, "was beyond description. Imagine all the hogs ever slaughtered in Cincinnati giving their death squeals together. . . ." Then the Republican party voted. Needed to win: 233 votes. First ballot: Seward, 173½ votes; Lincoln, 102; favorite-son votes for Bates, Cameron, Chase, and others. Second ballot: Seward, 184½; Lincoln, 181. "I've got him," cried Lincoln in Springfield when the news flashed to the capital. Third ballot: Lincoln, 231½. Ohio rose: four votes for Lincoln, Republican candidate for President of the United States.

In Springfield, Lincoln heard the news and went off to tell Mary. He seemed calm, Ward H. Lamon said, "but a close observer could detect in his countenance the indications of deep emotion."

The Republican platform of 1860 reaffirmed the equality principles of the Declaration of Independence, calling for the exclusion of slavery from the territories though pledging noninterference in slave states. It favored a homestead act to grant free land to settlers. In addition, the party advocated a mild pro-tectionist policy to succor burgeoning American industries, railroad subsidies to unite the country economically, improved mail and telegraph lines, and other measures that would aid the development of the American economy.

At the Democratic convention, meeting at Charleston, South Carolina, eight cotton states, indignant over the party's refusal to endorse a federal slave code for the territories, withdrew from the hall. Rump Democratic conventions in Baltimore nominated Douglas as the candidate espousing popular sovereignty, John C. Breckinridge of Kentucky as the candidate favoring a federal slave code, and Tennessee's John Bell as candidate of the new and moderate National Constitutional Union party. Lincoln directed a campaign strategy aimed at further deepening the critical schisms within the Democratic party. His running mate, Senator Hannibal Hamlin of Maine, was an ex-Democrat who had turned Republican.

It was a spirited campaign. Northern Democratic propagandists portrayed the politically sophisticated Lincoln as an ingenuous but patriotic plowman sacrificing farm and security to save his country; for the Republicans, free soil was the slogan of the day. Southerners declared that a Republican victory would mean the end of states' rights, of respect for private property, and of freedom itself.

Though his three opponents polled over 60 percent of the popular vote in the election of November 6, 1860, Lincoln won 180 out of 303 electoral votes, carrying every free state except New Jersey. But Republican joy was overshadowed by dark clouds of rebellion in the South, now thoroughly persuaded that Lincoln meant to destroy its economy and political foundations.

In Congress committees advanced compromise measures, among them the Crittenden proposal to sustain existent slavery and to divide the current and future territories between slavery and freedom at the old Missouri Compromise line. But while the presi-

The masthead of *The Pictorial Rail Splitter,* the Chicago edition of Lincoln's 1860 campaign newspaper.

dent-elect maintained public silence, he moved powerfully behind the scenes, instructing Republicans to vote against any measure that allowed the extension of slavery.

The Southern storm broke on December 20, 1860, in a slow roll of secessionist thunder. On that day South Carolina declared at Charleston that "the union now subsisting between South Carolina and other States under the name of the United States of America is hereby dissolved." On February 4, 1861, seven Southern states met at Montgomery to proclaim the Confederate States of America. The threat of decades had become a reality: The house was divided.

On February 11, Lincoln bade farewell to Springfield: "To this place, and the kindness of these people," he said, "I owe everything. . . . I now leave, not knowing when, or whether ever, I may return, with a task before me greater than that which rested upon Washington."

Lincoln's journey to the national capital was protracted to twelve days to permit speeches and receptions along the way. In Philadelphia, word reached the party of a plot to murder Lincoln in Baltimore, and plans were made to immediately curtail the president-elect's journey and to send him by private coach to Washington. While agreeing to bypass Baltimore, Lincoln insisted on proceeding with Washington's Birthday ceremonies at Independence Hall, which were highlighted by his raising of a 34-star flag, hailing the admission of Kansas to the Union as a free state.

Within hours Lincoln was hidden as an invalid in a Pullman berth, and he began his secret midnight journey to Washington. At six o'clock in the morning Saturday, February 23, 1861, a muffler around his neck, he slipped into the capital and quietly checked in at Willard's Hotel. There he received well-wishers, heard patronage requests, and organized his cabinet. Delegates to the celebrated "Peace Conference"—an attempt by representatives from twenty-one states to restore the Union—met with him, but Lincoln was firm before all insistence that in the interest of national unity he permit the extension of slavery: "My course," he said, "is as plain as a turnpike road. It is marked out by the Constitution."

On March 4, 1861, seated in an open carriage with Buchanan, protected at all points en route to the Capitol by cavalry and infantry and by riflemen perched in windows, Lincoln rode to his destiny. Speaking from the east portico of the Capitol, he offered massive reassurances and concessions to the South: "I have no purpose, directly or indirectly, to interfere with the institution of slavery in the States where it exists." He cited the Republicans' platform promise to maintain states' rights. He recalled the fact that the Republican platform had abjured an armed invasion of states by any domestic power as "the gravest of crimes" and upheld the Fugitive Slave Law's provision that runaway slaves must be returned to their masters. Then Lincoln turned to the crisis of secession. Even if the Constitution were merely a voluntary contract, he reasoned, one party to that contract could not declare it null and void. The Union was inviolable.

"I therefore consider that . . . the Union is unbro-

the States." In pursuit of this policy, he added, "there needs to be no bloodshed or violence; and there shall be none, unless it be forced upon the national authority." Then the president called the South back home: "In *your* hands, my dissatisfied fellow countrymen, and not in *mine*, is the momentous issue of civil war. The government will not assail *you*. You can have no conflict, without being yourselves the aggressors. . . ."

Then Chief Justice Taney arose. The author of the Dred Scott decision, his hands shaking, his face ashen, stepped forward to administer the oath of office: "I, Abraham Lincoln, do solemnly swear that I will faithfully execute the Office of President of the United States, and will to the best of my ability, preserve, protect and defend the Constitution of the United States." Lincoln was president.

But the South had made its decision; there was no going back. By the time Lincoln took his oath, the Confederates had seized all federal forts and Navy yards in the states under their control, except Fort Pickens in Pensacola, Florida, Fort Sumter at Charleston, South Carolina, and two minor ones in Florida.

Lincoln's cabinet was a formidable collection of Whigs, converted Democrats, and moderate and radical Republicans. His primary appointments were all men of extraordinary ability and integrity: William H. Seward, the antislavery senator from New York, as secretary of state; the abolitionist Republican Salmon P. Chase of Ohio as secretary of the treasury; Simon Cameron of Pennsylvania as secretary of war (he was replaced in January, 1862, by the articulate, unreconstructed, but efficient Democrat, Edwin M. Stanton); and Gideon Welles of Connecticut in the critical post of secretary of the Navy. It was a cabinet with massive potential for inner dispute, but it functioned well, largely through Lincoln's own personal ability to separate chaff from wheat.

Early in the administration, however, Lincoln's authority was challenged by Secretary Seward. The New Yorker clearly considered Lincoln his inferior in

ken," Lincoln declared, "and . . . I shall take care, as the Constitution itself expressly enjoins upon me, that the laws of the Union be faithfully executed in all

education, political experience, and judgment, and he moved swiftly to establish his position as de facto president. In an incredible memorandum to Lincoln on April 1, 1861, Seward lamented what he called the president's lack of firm policies, domestic or foreign, after one month in office. He urged Lincoln, among other things, to shift his emphasis from slavery to Unionism and to divert attention from American disunion by precipitating a war with Spain and France. Further, he said, if the president was unwilling to pursue these policies, he would do it himself. To this contemptuous and irresponsible letter, President Lincoln responded with quiet grandeur. Whatever had to be done by executive authority, he told Seward, he would do as president. "Still . . . I wish, and suppose I am entitled to have, the advice of all the cabinet."

War now seemed imminent as the South demanded the evacuation of Fort Sumter. On the day after his inauguration, Lincoln had received word from the fort's commander that he and his men had scant provisions in the face of still-silent Confederate shore batteries. A month later the president had still not decided whether to provision the fort or to arm it further to repel a threatened Confederate assault. Ultimately he decided to send food to the fort, making clear to the Confederates his decision against sending arms.

At 4:30 A.M. on April 12, 1861, the Confederate States of America fired upon Sumter, the first shots in a war that would kill 600,000 American men. Lincoln moved quickly to meet the assault. He called for 75,000 volunteers and ordered a blockade of the South. The capital city itself made new preparations for siege. Virginia, angered by what it considered Lincoln's despotic call for volunteers, left the Union, followed by Arkansas, North Carolina, and Tennessee.

On July 4 President Lincoln addressed a saddened special session of Congress. The Confederates, he stated, knew full well that he had sent bread and not bullets to Sumter and that the fort, hemmed in by Confederate guns, could scarcely have attacked them. Why, then, the assault? To destroy, Lincoln said, "the visible authority of the Federal Union, and thus force it to immediate dissolution. . . . This issue," declared the president, "embraces more than the fate of these United States. It presents to the whole family of man, the question, whether a constitutional republic, or a democracy . . . can, or cannot maintain its territorial integrity against its own domestic foes . . ."; whether, in fact, republics had an "inherent and fatal" flaw. The United States, Lincoln concluded, had no alternative: It must "resist force, employed for its destruction, by force, for its preservation."

On July 21 the North was decisively defeated at Bull Run (Manassas) in the first major encounter of the war. Lincoln replaced his field commander, General Irvin McDowell, with General George B. McClellan; he was confident that McClellan would press the war forward with dispatch. When, on November 1, General Winfield Scott, ill and cantankerous, though able, resigned his post as general in chief of the Union forces over policy differences, McClellan was named his successor. But although he was an efficient organizer, McClellan proved to be dilatory in executing his plans, tended to overestimate the strength of the forces opposed to him, and was smitten, besides, with an overweening egotism. He and Lincoln disagreed as to strategy; the president preferred a massive frontal assault at Manassas, while McClellan proposed a direct march from the rear on the Confederate capital at Richmond. In January 1862 McClellan had still not begun his offensive, and an impatient Lincoln ordered him to move by February 22.

In early February, however, Lincoln deferred to McClellan's plan to march on Richmond. On March 8, the president reorganized the Army in four corps, relieving McClellan of all duties except those of commander of the Army of the Potomac. McClellan moved by water to the mouth of the James River,

President Lincoln and General George B. McClellan confer in the general's tent at Antietam, October 1862.

then up the Virginia peninsula between the James and York rivers. In a series of bloody encounters he faced General Robert E. Lee, whose forces defended Richmond in the Seven Days' Battles, ending at Malvern Hill on July 1. When McClellan blamed Lincoln for not sending reinforcements, the president replied that he had sent as many as he could. Losses in the campaign were heavy, and Lincoln appealed for 300,000 more men.

The year 1862 was a bitter one for the president. In February his third son, eleven-year-old Willie, died after a bout of cold and fever. Lincoln was shattered. Mary, who wore mourning black for almost two years, collapsed in "paroxysms of grief." Even the president,

immured in his own anguish, warned her on one occasion that she would have to be committed to a mental hospital if she could not control herself.

Stricken with family sorrow, and with the hard news of mounting Union casualties in a war he had hoped would be brief, Lincoln was also harassed by a divided and personally ambitious cabinet; by abolitionists calling for total war on slavery and for the unconditional surrender of an occupied South; by the defeatism of those who demanded peace before Union; by uncooperative states; by the insubordinate and vacillating McClellan; by desertion from the Army; and by virulent abuse in the press.

"As a general rule," the president would say in his

last public address, "I abstain from reading the reports of attacks upon myself, wishing not to be provoked by that to which I can not properly offer an answer." But some attacks could not go unanswered. Among these was an assault by Horace Greeley, editor of the New York *Tribune,* in August 1862. In an open letter to the president, Greeley berated Lincoln for capitulating to the South by failing to issue immediately a decree emancipating the slaves.

It is true that Lincoln moved with great care on the slavery question. A political realist, he knew that basic institutions could not be changed by the stroke of a pen or a sword or by the dictates of personal idealism; he realized that even after the North won the war it would still have to face the issues of slavery and lingering disloyalty. He could not go forward, he believed, unless the people were with him, step by step.

He had, however, appealed to the border states to free slaves gradually and offered to compensate their owners with the assistance of the federal government. Congress had already passed legislation freeing the slaves of "disloyal" masters as well as those in the District of Columbia and in the territories. Then, in July 1862, the president summoned his cabinet and laid before it for discussion an emancipation proclamation which would free the slaves in areas still in rebellion. Seward agreed on principle but advised postponement. Current Union military reverses, he argued, might encourage some to consider the measure "the last shriek on our retreat." Lincoln concurred.

A month later, in his reply to Greeley, Lincoln placed the Union above all other considerations. "My paramount object in this struggle *is* to save the Union, and is *not* either to save or to destroy slavery. . . . What I do about slavery, and the colored race, I do because I believe it helps to save the Union; and what I forbear, I forbear because I do *not* believe it would help to save the Union. . . . I have here stated my purpose according to my view of official duty; and I intend no modification of my oft-expressed personal wish that all men every where could be free."

To restore the Union, Lincoln considered no measure ultimately too severe. "These rebels," he reasoned, "are violating the Constitution to destroy the Union; I

JEFFERSON DAVIS

As the president of the Southern Confederacy, Jefferson Davis was unable to achieve anything like Lincoln's renown. Born in Kentucky, he was a Mississippi plantation owner who had graduated from West Point, had distinguished himself in the war with Mexico, and served several terms in Congress as well as one of Franklin Pierce's capable secretary of war. His first wife, who was the daughter of his commanding officer, Zachary Taylor, died soon after the marriage. Ten years later, he married Varina Howell, a member of Mississippi's Whig aristocracy, who wrote, "Would you believe it, he is fine and cultivated and yet he is a Democrat." Although he would much have preferred military command to the presidency, because of his relatively moderate stance about secession he seemed to be the most available candidate, so that the Montgomery convention named him president in February 1861. Tall, slim, and elegant, he was unfortunately somewhat humorless and egotistical, injecting his personal likes and dislikes into the choice of generals and civilian appointees. As a Southern nationalist, he believed in some centralization, favored conscription, and suspended the habeas corpus, thus making many enemies, particularly among the advocates of states' rights. He adamantly refused to accept any peace terms other than Southern independence, and at the end of the war, notwithstanding Lincoln's hope that the Southern leaders escape "unbeknownst" to him, Davis was captured and imprisoned at Fort Monroe. In spite of widespread demands for his execution, he was released on bond in 1867. After spending the last years of his life in writing and business activities, he died in 1889.

will violate the Constitution, if necessary, to save the Union. . . ." Accordingly, President Lincoln unilaterally increased the size of the Army and Navy, imposed a blockade of the South, suspended the writ of habeas corpus where necessary, placed treason suspects in military custody, and forbade the use of the mail for "treasonable correspondence." In the actual military conduct of the war, Lincoln functioned literally as commander in chief, personally mapping strategy.

Despite such victories as the capture of Fort Donelson on the Cumberland River in Tennessee by General Ulysses S. Grant and the occupation of New Orleans by Flag Officer David Farragut, the North was being bled in battle after battle. Thirteen thousand Union troops became casualties at Shiloh in April. In August the Union suffered another crushing defeat at Bull Run. In September Stonewall Jackson captured twelve thousand Union troops at Harpers Ferry. Then Lee and Jackson met McClellan at Antietam on September 17, 1862, in a bloody but indecisive battle.

Now, on September 22, Lincoln issued the Preliminary Emancipation Proclamation, publishing the final version on January 1, 1863. "Things had gone from bad to worse," he confessed later, "until I felt we had reached the end of our rope on the plan of operations we had been pursuing; that we had about played our last card, and must change our tactics or lose the game."

The proclamation was issued, Lincoln said, as "an act of justice" as well as "a fit and necessary war measure." It freed slaves only in those areas of the Confederacy still in rebellion on January 1, 1863, not in Southern areas already occupied by the Union Army, such as parts of Louisiana and Virginia, nor in loyal slave states, such as Kentucky, Delaware, Missouri, West Virginia, and Maryland, as well as in Tennessee.

Secretary Seward was astonished: "We show our sympathy with slavery," he said, "by emancipating the slaves where we cannot reach them and holding them in bondage where we can set them free." And in fact the proclamation did not go nearly so far as the second Confiscation Act, which had provided freedom to slaves of disloyal owners, regardless of state of residence. Yet the proclamation freed all slaves in areas conquered as the Union armies advanced.

Documents notwithstanding, the war went on. An angry Lincoln fired McClellan on November 7, appointing General Ambrose Burnside to succeed him as commander of the Army of the Potomac. Burnside was defeated at Fredericksburg in December, and Lincoln was faced with a crisis affecting his cabinet. Members of Congress demanded that Seward resign; Chase had told them the cabinet did not meet regularly. The president met the challenge by asking his critics to return when the whole cabinet (save Seward, who had submitted his resignation) was present; confronted with various charges, Chase offered to resign too. Quickly accepting it, Lincoln then restored both the secretaries of state and of the treasury. "I can ride on now," he said; "I've got a pumpkin in each end of my bag."

In January 1863 Burnside was replaced by General Joseph Hooker, who would himself be succeeded by General George Meade in June.

In May 1863 Union forces suffered a crushing defeat at Chancellorsville. Then, as Grant was laying siege to Vicksburg in Mississippi, Lee led the entire Army of Northern Virginia through the Shenandoah Valley to southern Pennsylvania, where he met the Union Army in the greatest and most decisive battle of the war, at Gettysburg. After three days of battle with massive losses on both sides, Lee was forced to withdraw on July 4 to a position west of Sharpsburg, where the flooded Potomac blocked his passage to Virginia. Lincoln issued orders to pursue the foe and to destroy his army. But Meade hesitated; the Potomac subsided, and Lee escaped. Lincoln despaired, blaming Meade: "He was within your easy grasp, and to have closed upon him would . . . have ended the war. As it is the war will be prolonged indefinitely."

Over five thousand men, in both gray and blue, had been killed in the savage encounter at Gettysburg; their bodies had littered the field. On November 19, 1863, President Lincoln joined in the consecration of a new national cemetery at the site where the men had fallen. Edward Everett, a renowned orator, held forth for two hours in a verbal crescendo filled with classical allusions. Then Lincoln rose to offer ten sentences of splendid simplicity that told—and still tell—what the war was all about:

"Four score and seven years ago our fathers brought forth on this continent, a new nation, conceived in Liberty, and dedicated to the proposition that all men are created equal.

"Now we are engaged in a great civil war, testing whether that nation, or any nation so conceived and so dedicated, can long endure. We are met on a great battlefield of that war. We have come to dedicate a portion of that field, as a final resting place for those who here gave their lives that that nation might live. It is altogether fitting and proper that we should do this.

"But, in a larger sense, we can not dedicate—we can not consecrate—we can not hallow—this ground. The brave men, living and dead, who struggled here, have consecrated it, far above our poor power to add or detract. The world will little note, nor long remember what we say here, but it can never forget what they did here. It is for us the living, rather, to be dedicated here to the unfinished work which they who fought here have thus far so nobly advanced. It is rather for us to be here dedicated to the great task remaining before us—that from these honored dead we take increased devotion to that cause for which they gave the last full measure of devotion—that we here highly resolve that these dead shall not have died in vain—that this nation, under God, shall have a new birth of freedom—and that government of the people, by the people, for the people, shall not perish from the earth."

The immediate response to this timeless address was mixed. The Chicago *Times* asserted that the "cheek of every American must tingle with shame as he reads the silly, flat, and dish-watery utterances of

SECOND ADMINISTRATION

INAUGURATION: Mar. 4, 1865; the Capitol, Washington, D.C.

VICE PRESIDENT: Andrew Johnson

SECRETARY OF STATE: William H. Seward

SECRETARY OF THE TREASURY: Hugh McCulloch

SECRETARY OF WAR: Edwin M. Stanton

ATTORNEY GENERAL: James Speed

POSTMASTER GENERAL: William Dennison

SECRETARY OF THE NAVY: Gideon Welles

SECRETARY OF THE INTERIOR: John P. Usher

39TH CONGRESS (Dec. 4, 1865–Mar. 3, 1867):

  SENATE: 42 Unionists; 10 Democrats

  HOUSE: 145 Unionists; 46 Democrats

ELECTION OF 1864

(Because eleven Southern states had seceded from the Union and did not participate in the presidential election, eighty-one electoral votes were not cast.)

CANDIDATES	ELECTORAL VOTES	POPULAR VOTE
Abraham Lincoln (National Union)	212	2,218,388
George McClellan (Democratic)	21	1,812,807

the man who has to be pointed out to intelligent foreigners as the President of the United States." History, however, would agree with the Chicago *Tribune* that Abraham Lincoln's words would "live among the annals of man." And Edward Everett, the principal speaker at the ceremony, was wholly correct when he wrote to the president, "I should be glad if I could flatter myself that I came as near to the central idea of the occasion in two hours as you did in two minutes."

In late November the Union cause was buttressed by Grant's victory at Chattanooga, where Confederate soldiers were driven from Tennessee. Grant's services to the Union were rewarded on March 12, 1864, when the ruddy field soldier was named, at last, general in chief of the Union armies.

In May, at the Wilderness (the area south of the Rapidan River near Richmond, Virginia), at Spotsylvania, and at Cold Harbor, Grant's forces suffered over sixty thousand casualties. Then Grant shifted his troops, moving south toward Petersburg, hoping to cut Richmond off from the rebel states. Lee met him, and the siege of Petersburg began. For ten months Grant's forces were holed up in their trenches by a rugged Confederate defense.

On June 8 the Republican party nominated Lincoln at Baltimore for a second term. Andrew Johnson, a pro-Union Democrat who had been appointed military governor of Tennessee, was named for the vice presidency. A week earlier, Republican radicals had met in Cleveland to nominate John Frémont for president. In August the Democrats chose General McClellan to oppose Lincoln. Both the regular and rump Republican conventions affirmed support for a constitutional amendment to abolish all slavery forever, and Lincoln gave the proposed amendment his approval: "In the joint names of liberty and union," he said, "let us labor to give it legal form, and practical effect." (The president was to give the Thirteenth Amendment vital support in its consideration and adoption by Congress. Passed by the Senate in April 1864, after pressure by the president, it was finally approved by the House of Representatives in January 1865.)

It was a divisive political campaign. Lincoln was assailed in newspapers and campaign tracts. Horace Greeley pronounced the president "already beaten." Lincoln himself was doubtful about his chances of winning. "It seems exceedingly probable," he wrote confidentially, "that this Administration will not be re-elected."

But good news from the front—especially of the capture of Atlanta on September 2 by General William T. Sherman—aided Lincoln's cause. On September 22, after the conservative Montgomery Blair had quit the cabinet, Frémont withdrew. Even so, while Lincoln won the election on November 8 by an electoral victory of 212 to 21, his popular margin was merely 2.2 million to 1.8 million.

On March 4, 1865, the president, appearing markedly older, again took the oath of office. He could look with satisfaction on the success of the Union armies. At Nashville, Union forces had decimated John B. Hood's troops. Sherman had completed his march to the sea, had forced the evacuation of Savannah, and had then swung north to seize Columbia, South Carolina. In February, Union forces had occupied Charleston.

"Fondly do we hope—fervently do we pray—that this mighty scourge of war may speedily pass away," Lincoln said in his second inaugural address. "With malice toward none, with charity for all; with firmness in the right, as God gives us to see the right, let us strive on to finish the work we are in; to bind up the nation's wounds; to care for him who shall have borne the battle, and for his widow, and his orphan—to do all which may achieve and cherish a just, and a lasting peace, among ourselves, and with all nations."

On April 3 the time for making peace was upon the president: Richmond had fallen. At 4 P.M., April 9, 1865, General Lee, given generous terms by Lincoln through Grant, surrendered at Appomattox Court House.

Lincoln's plans for Reconstruction were only partially defined. In December 1863 he issued a Proclamation of Amnesty which allowed Southern states to reestablish state governments after 10 percent of the voters of 1860 had taken an oath of allegiance and accepted the Emancipation Proclamation. In July 1864 he had pocket-vetoed Congress' Wade-Davis Bill, which would have allowed the readmission of a state only after the majority of its electorate pledged past as well as present loyalty. At a preliminary conference with Confederate officials on board a ship off Hampton Roads, Virginia, on February 3, 1865, he had been conciliatory, excluding any punitive unconditional surrender by the South, promising pardons, urging only

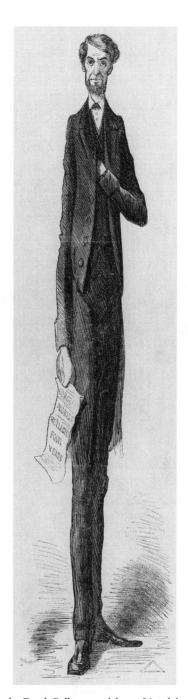

A drawing by Frank Bellew to celebrate Lincoln's reelection was published in the November 26, 1864, issue of *Harper's Weekly*.

Crowds surround Abraham Lincoln's residence in his hometown, Springfield, Illinois, which has been draped in black mourning on the occasion of his body's arrival by funeral train on May 3, 1865.

that Southern Americans once again embrace the Constitution. According to the former Confederacy's vice president, Alexander H. Stephens, he even suggested that the South might adopt the Thirteenth Amendment slowly, perhaps over a five-year period (certainly an erroneous recollection), and hinted at millions of dollars in federal compensation to former owners of freed slaves. On April 11, 1865, Lincoln spoke from a White House window to a delirious victory throng. He called for an end to debate over the "pernicious abstraction" as to whether the Southern states had ever truly left the Union. "Finding themselves safely at home," Lincoln said, "it would be utterly immaterial whether they had ever been abroad."

The president cited Louisiana as a model of Reconstruction. He conceded that a larger electorate would be desirable and that "very intelligent" blacks might properly be given the vote. But which was the wiser course, he asked: to take Louisiana as it was and improve it, or to discard its antislavery government and start again? Louisiana, he said, was well on its way to harmony with the Union, now that it had empowered its legislators to give blacks the vote, adopted a free constitution, and voted to ratify the Thirteenth Amendment. "We shall sooner have the fowl by hatching the egg than by smashing it," he said. Reconstruction, he warned, was a complex process to be pursued with realism and patience.

At 11 A.M., Good Friday, April 14, 1865, Lincoln met with his cabinet, mapping Reconstruction until 2 P.M. Then the president went for a carriage drive with his wife. They rejoiced that the bitter war years were over and looked forward to spending that evening at the theater. General and Mrs. Grant were unable to join them in the presidential box at Ford's Theatre, but Miss Clara Harris and Major Henry Rathbone—the daughter and stepson of Senator Ira Harris of New York—had accepted the Lincolns' invitation to see the comedy *Our American Cousin.*

The presidential party arrived late at Ford's. The actors stopped when they saw the president, and the band burst into "Hail to the Chief." Lincoln sat back, his hand in Mary's.

In a barroom near Ford's, a few minutes before 10 P.M., a twenty-six-year-old proslavery extremist and actor, John Wilkes Booth, finished his drink; he departed the tavern and entered the theater. His movements plotted step-by-step, Booth made his way to the door of the hallway leading to the president's box. Once inside, he bolted the outer door.

With a pistol in one hand and a dagger in the other, Booth opened the unguarded inner door of the box, aimed his pistol at Lincoln's head, and fired. Rathbone lunged at Booth, who stabbed him violently in the arm. Then the actor leaped from the box to the stage. Flashing his knife, Booth cried, "*Sic semper tyrannis!*" and escaped, though he had broken his leg.

Lincoln sat mute and immobile, his head fallen forward. He was, said a doctor, fatally wounded. Booth's bullet had torn through the president's brain and had lodged behind an eye. Carried across the street to a boardinghouse owned by a Mr. William Petersen, Lincoln was laid diagonally across a bed too small for his massive frame.

As the president lay dying, word spread that most of the cabinet had been murdered, too. In fact Seward, confined to bed by a bad fall, had been sav-agely bloodied by a Booth accomplice. But the rest of the cabinet was unharmed.

At the Petersen house, Mrs. Lincoln, convulsed by a new, insupportable grief, edged closer to mental derangement. Robert, his head on the shoulder of Senator Sumner, sobbed aloud as his father slowly slipped away. At about six o'clock in the morning, April 15, 1865, rain began falling. At 7:22 A.M., Abraham Lincoln died.

His body lay in state in the East Room of the White House on a black-draped catafalque. Thousands of the nation's stunned citizens came to see the dead president. Some had seen him before, others had merely heard of him: "Old Abe," "Honest Abe," the "Rail Splitter" of Illinois and Indiana, the savior of the Union, dressed now in his inaugural suit for a final ascent to greatness.

On April 19 Lincoln's body was borne from the White House to begin the long journey to Illinois. The cortege stopped for homage in many cities along the way. Finally, on May 4, the coffin of the "Great Emancipator" was closed, and Lincoln was buried at Oak Ridge Cemetery in Springfield.

"What is to be will be," Lincoln had said, "or rather, I have found all my life as Hamlet says: 'There is a divinity that shapes our ends, Rough-hew them how we will.'" Healing when others wounded, hoping when others despaired, assuring when others feared, he grew in the presidency taller than himself. He remains a symbol of liberty, his memory nourished by his own great words and deeds.

"Now," said a sorrowing Edward M. Stanton for the nation, "he belongs to the ages."

—*Wilson Sullivan,*
revised by Hans L. Trefousse

ANDREW JOHNSON

BETWEEN NORTH AND SOUTH

The Senate chamber was filled to overflowing. The chief justice, Salmon P. Chase, presided. "Mr. Senator Anthony, how say you," he intoned. "Is the respondent, Andrew Johnson, president of the United States, guilty or not guilty of a high misdemeanor as charged in this article?" "Guilty," said the senator, and the vote on the conviction of Andrew Johnson, seventeenth president of the United States, on charges of having violated the Constitution and his oath of office by removing Secretary of War Edwin M. Stanton in violation of the Tenure of Office Act, having denied the legitimacy of Congress, and having failed to carry out the Reconstruction Acts, was under way.

It was really the last of these charges that mattered. As Thaddeus Stevens, the radical leader of the House of Representatives, said in January 1867, "it was impossible to reconstruct the South with Andrew Johnson as President. As long as he remained there, the laws of Congress would be inoperative." And he was right. Unlike Abraham Lincoln, Johnson, a Southerner, was a bitter racist. "The black race of Africa," he explained in Congress in 1847, was "inferior to the white man in point of intellect—better calculated in physical structure to undergo drudgery and hardship—standing, as they do, many degrees lower in the scale of gradation that expressed the relative relation between God and all that he had created than the white man." The impeachment, indeed, though technically largely about the violation of the Tenure of Office Act, was in reality a question of the differences between Congress and the president on the issue of Reconstruction, and particularly the rights of the freed men and women in the South. The majority of the Republicans in Congress wanted to secure at least a modicum of civil rights to the blacks, while Johnson was merely interested in restoring the seceded states as quickly as possible without worrying too much about the former slaves. The Republicans' motives were partially idealistic and partially practical, for without the blacks, Southern restoration would result in a Democratic Congress and the undoing of the gains of the Civil War.

It was not surprising that Johnson stood in the way. The only senator from a seceding state to remain loyal, Johnson was nevertheless a Southern Democrat with all the prejudices of his region. To be sure, East Tennessee, his home, was a region of few slaves and a Unionist majority, but its ideas were otherwise similar to those held in other parts of Dixie.

Johnson was born poor white in Raleigh, North Carolina, on December 29, 1808. Losing his father at an early age, he was apprenticed to a tailor shortly after his tenth birthday, a position that was not too different from that of a slave. At fifteen he took flight and his master offered a $10 reward for his recapture. "Ran away from the Subscriber," read a notice in the Raleigh *Star* in 1824, "on the night of the 15th instant, two apprentice boys, legally bound, named WILLIAM AND ANDREW JOHNSON. . . . I will pay the above Reward to any person who will deliver said apprentices to me in Raleigh, or I will give the above reward for Andrew Johnson alone. All persons are cautioned against harboring or employing said apprentices. . . . JAMES J. SELBY, Tailor." After trying in vain to come to an understanding with his employer, Johnson walked to Tennessee, finally settling in Greeneville, where he opened a tailor shop. He married Eliza McCardle, who helped him improve his reading and writing, which, though he had never been to school, he had learned while he worked and by listening to an itinerant teacher. He joined two debating societies and soon began attracting attention as a public speaker. Presently his tailor shop became a gathering place for the townspeople who, during the course of discussions, decided that they should have a voice in the local government. The man they chose to represent them was Andrew Johnson; he was elected alderman at the age of twenty, then mayor for two years, and state legislator after that. All the while he was developing his skills as a stump speaker; and in 1843 he was elected as a Democrat to the United States House of Representatives.

Andrew Johnson was a good congressman, industrious and sincerely dedicated to the needs of the working people. He pressed for economy in government, opposed high tariffs that would raise the cost of living, and advocated a homestead act that would issue land to settlers. He practiced his elocution and, with his rich and mellow voice, held his own in an age of brilliant orators. A *New York Times* reporter wrote that in his speeches Johnson "cut and slashed right and left, tore big wounds and left something behind to fester and remember. His phraseology may be uncouth, but his views are easily understood and he talks strong thoughts and carefully culled facts in quick succession."

Johnson lived simply, in a boardinghouse, and he dressed simply, always in black. Sturdily built, of medium height, he had black hair and piercing eyes set in a face that the visiting Charles Dickens called "remarkable . . . indicating courage, watchfulness, and certainly strength of purpose."

An admirer of Jefferson and Jackson, Johnson was a Democrat but by no means a faithful party man. The needs of the people came first: He spoke for religious liberty, freedom of speech, and adherence to popular will. Once, foreshadowing a position he would take later on, he defended the presidential veto, calling it "a breakwater . . . to arrest or suspend for the time being hasty and improvident legislation until the people . . . have time and opportunity to consider of its propriety." His independent posture frequently irritated Democrats as well as Whigs, and he was often the victim of bipartisan attack. Vexed by the congressman's opposition to increased appropriations for West Point, Jefferson Davis sneered on the floor of the House: "Can a blacksmith or tailor construct . . . bastioned field-works . . . ?" But Johnson was proud of having made his way "by the sweat of his brow," and

he resented any slur on any workingman. "Sir," he responded to one such insult, "I do not forget that I am a mechanic. I am proud to own it. Neither do I forget that Adam was a tailor and sewed fig leaves, or that our Saviour was the son of a carpenter."

While he antagonized his Southern colleagues, he continued to please his constituency, which reelected him four times. In 1852, unable to defeat him at the polls, the Tennessee Whigs gerrymandered his district out of existence. Their shrewdness promptly backfired: The ex-congressman returned home and was elected governor of the state. Once installed, Johnson drove his victory home, favoring Tennessee's public school system and placing the needs of the working people over those of the slaveholding aristocracy, for whom he never hesitated to express contempt. The Whigs attacked him savagely, calling him "an apostate son of the South," a "leveler," "low, despicable and dirty." In responding, Johnson only solidified his position with the common man. "Whose hands built your Capitol?" he once asked. "Whose toil, whose labor built your railroads and your ships? . . . I say let the mechanic and the laborer make our laws, rather than the idle and vicious aristocrat." In 1855, during a bitter campaign against Whigs and Know-Nothings, he was advised to tone down his attacks on the opposition and his defense of Catholics and foreigners. "I will make that same speech tomorrow," he responded, "if it blows the Democratic party to hell." He won the election, and in 1857 the state legislature named him to the United States Senate. "I have," he said, "reached the summit of my ambition."

Back in Washington, Johnson resumed his fight for passage of his homestead act, which would give 160 acres of land to the head of any family that would settle on it for five years. Congress, however, was preoccupied with slavery, and while the North embraced the bill—viewing it as a remedy for the evil of slavery—the Southerners opposed it, seeing in it eventual loss of their congressional power. Johnson's reaction: "Why lug slavery into the matter?" A slaveholder himself, he did not oppose the institution, which he believed to be a local matter peculiar to the states and beyond the province of Congress, nor did he consider it the most important issue facing the nation.

In 1860 the Tennessee delegation to the Democratic National Convention gave Johnson its favorite-son votes for the vice presidency, but what little chance he might have had was nullified when the Southern states withdrew over the slavery issue and nominated John C. Breckinridge to oppose the regular Democrats' choice, Stephen Douglas. Johnson campaigned for Breckinridge only because he was pro-Union. Asked what he would do if the South used the election of Lincoln as a pretext to secede, Johnson answered: "When the crisis comes I will be found standing by the Union."

Between Lincoln's election and inauguration, Andrew Johnson, alone among senators from a seceding state, called on Congress to act to prevent secession; and he pledged himself—"my blood, my existence"—to save the Union. In the North his words were acclaimed; in the South he was hanged in effigy. After the inauguration, he hurried back to Tennessee, disregarding threats on his life and narrowly escaping a lynch mob, to try to keep his state from seceding. His mountain and valley people voted overwhelmingly to remain in the Union, but the richer and more populous western districts were too strong; Tennessee joined the Confederacy. Branded a traitor, Johnson was obliged to flee to Kentucky.

In Washington, Senator Johnson pressed for the military deliverance of East Tennessee, whose people were suffering for their Union sympathies. Like many Unionists, Johnson's wife and youngest son were turned out of their home. (His two older sons were in the Union Army, and his son-in-law was engaged in guerrilla fighting in the Tennessee mountains.) Then, early in 1862, General Ulysses S. Grant took Nash-

Andrew Johnson opened this tailor shop shortly after moving to Greeneville, Tennessee, in 1826. When he became mayor, the shop also served as the town hall. The front room contained the tools of his trade, while the back room housed his living quarters.

ville and part of West Tennessee, and President Lincoln appointed Johnson military governor of the state, ordering him "to provide . . . peace and security to the loyal inhabitants of that state until they shall be able to establish a civil government" to conform with the Constitution. Johnson accepted the mission, but not until late in 1863, when most of Tennessee had been cleared of Confederate troops, could he begin to establish a civilian government.

Two years later the Republican convention (meeting under the name of National Union party) acknowledged Johnson's remarkable services to the nation by nominating him for the vice presidency. After the victorious election, Johnson returned to Tennessee to continue Reconstruction. By the end of February 1865 the job had been done; all that remained was the election of a civil governor, and that was set for March 4, which was also the date of Johnson's inauguration.

Ill, anxious, and exhausted, Johnson asked to take his oath of office in Nashville. Lincoln, however, felt that the inauguration of a Southerner would symbolize the national unity he hoped to restore. At the president's request, Johnson returned to Washington, arriving a day or two before the inauguration, still ill and further exhausted by the trip. As he sat waiting for the ceremonies to begin, he said he did not feel well and asked for a stimulant. Some brandy was sent for; he had a sizable drink, then two more. Then, when he was called upon to speak, he slurred his words uncharacteristically and spoke extemporane-

ously and irrationally as a condemning assembly and a compassionate Lincoln looked on. "I have known Andy Johnson for many years," he said afterward; "he made a bad slip the other day, but you need not be scared, Andy ain't a drunkard."

Forty-one days after the inauguration, less than a week after Appomattox, Andrew Johnson—tailor, reputed drunkard, Southerner, Democrat, and staunch Unionist—became president of the United States. He took the oath on the morning of April 15, 1865, in the parlor of his hotel. Secretary of the Treasury Hugh McCulloch wrote that Johnson was "grief stricken like the rest, and he seemed to be oppressed by the suddenness of the call upon him to become President . . . but he was nevertheless calm and self-possessed."

On the day of Lincoln's death the radical Republicans met in caucus and, remembering Johnson's consistent opposition to Southern aristocratic leadership, agreed that his accession to the presidency "would prove a godsend to the country." They proposed a peace in which the gains of the Civil War—emancipation and a modicum of civil rights for the blacks— would be safeguarded, some asking for the confiscation of insurgents' lands, disfranchisement of leading Confederates, and black suffrage. But it took the radicals only one month to discover that Johnson meant to continue Lincoln's magnanimous policy, albeit without regard for freed peoples' rights. Firmly convinced that the Southern states were still in the Union, he called for a policy of restoration, not Reconstruction. Consequently, to all former insurgents except for fourteen classes of high Confederate officers and the owners of property of more than $20,000, he offered amnesty and asked that they reconstitute their governments. Hoping that they would ratify the Thirteenth Amendment, repudiate the Confederate debt, and nullify the secession ordinances, he did not even insist on these mild conditions.

The result of these moves was the reconstitution of all insurgent governments but that of Texas, the election of leading ex-Confederates (including the vice president of the defunct regime) to Congress, and the passage of harsh Black Codes virtually remaining the freed people to a condition very much akin to slavery.

At first the people of the North agreed with President Johnson: With the exception of Maine, Massachusetts, and Pennsylvania, the summer and autumn conventions of state Republicans enthusiastically endorsed the president's program. Moreover, the leading Union generals—among them Sherman, Meade, and Grant—supported Johnson, and by December every Confederate state but Texas had met the Reconstruction qualifications and had elected local officials, congressmen, and senators. The excesses of the newly restored states and the election of unpardoned rebels, however, changed this attitude. Outraged by the particularly harsh Black Code of Mississippi, the *Chicago Tribune* wrote, "We tell the white men of Mississippi, that the men of the North will convert the state of Mississippi into a frog pond before they will allow such laws to disgrace one foot of the soil in which the bones of our soldiers sleep and over which the flag of freedom waves."

Johnson's scheme was soon met with a setback. When Congress convened in December of 1865, none of the Southern representatives were seated, and the radicals established a joint Committee on Reconstruction to which all matters pertaining to the subject were to be referred.

In view of the fact that the Republican party was divided into radical, moderate, and conservative factions, and that the radicals never had a majority, Johnson might easily have come to terms with the moderates, had he merely softened his stand somewhat. But the moderates, too, insisted on some safeguards for black rights, and Johnson was unwilling to compromise. When a bill that extended the powers of the Freedmen's Bureau was drawn up by the mod-

erate leader Lyman Trumbull and was passed by Congress, Johnson vetoed it, partially because he objected to government largess to support a portion of the population, partially because he felt military rule was uncalled for, and especially because the measure affecting the South had been passed while the Southern states were unrepresented. His veto was overridden. When he vetoed a second one of Trumbull's measures, the Civil Rights Bill for the protection of the rights of all persons, including the freedmen, again on states' rights as well as other grounds, he was unable to muster the necessary votes to override. His actions had so alienated the moderates who now collaborated with the radicals that from that time on, he was unable to overcome the hostile two-thirds majority in Congress.

In the meantime, the Reconstruction committee

THE JOHNSON ADMINISTRATION

INAUGURATION: Apr. 15, 1865; Kirkwood House, Washington, D.C.

SECRETARY OF STATE: William H. Seward

SECRETARY OF THE TREASURY: Hugh McCulloch

SECRETARY OF WAR: Edwin M. Stanton ; Ulysses S. Grant (from Aug. 12, 1867); Edwin Stanton (from Jan. 13, 1868); John M. Schofield (from June 1, 1868)

ATTORNEY GENERAL: James Speed; Henry Stanbery (from July 23, 1866); Orville H. Browning (from Mar. 13, 1868): William M. Evarts (from July 20, 1868)

POSTMASTER GENERAL: William Dennison; Alexander W. Randall (from July 25, 1866)

SECRETARY OF THE NAVY: Gideon Welles

SECRETARY OF THE INTERIOR: John P. Usher; James Harlan (from May 15, 1865); Orville H. Browning (from Sept. 1, 1866)

39TH CONGRESS (Dec. 4, 1865–Mar. 3, 1867):
   SENATE: 42 Republicans; 10 Democrats
   HOUSE: 145 Republicans; 46 Democrats

40TH CONGRESS (Mar. 4, 1867–March 3, 1869):
   SENATE: 42 Republicans; 11 Democrats;
   HOUSE: 143 Republicans; 49 Democrats

STATE ADMITTED: Nebraska (1867)

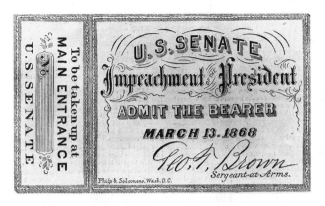

Impeachment tickets were difficult to obtain and most spectators preserved them carefully among their papers. They were the mementos of a trial that was also a major social event.

held hearings about conditions in the South and eventually perfected the Fourteenth Amendment. It provided that all persons born or naturalized in the United States were citizens of the United States and of the state in which they resided; it prohibited the states from depriving any person of life, liberty, or property without due process of law; nor could a state deny to any person the equal protection of the laws. Disfranchising merely those high-ranking Confederates who had previously sworn allegiance to the Constitution, it was not a harsh measure. Yet, while Johnson could not veto it, he nevertheless opposed it with all his might. A new Freedmen's Bureau Bill was easily passed over his veto, and when Tennessee ratified the amendment, the state was readmitted to the Union.

The president now attempted to form a new political party consisting of conservative Republicans and Democrats. In order to do so, he called a Union convention to meet at Philadelphia in August, where the delegates from South Carolina and Massachusetts entered arm in arm and all present fully endorsed his program. But the majority of Republicans rejected his bid, and the midterm elections of 1866, clearly a contest between Johnson and his opponents, resulted in

his complete defeat. He contributed to it by his so-called "swing-around-the-circle," a speaking tour to Chicago and St. Louis in which he repeatedly delivered ill-received orations that were interrupted by hecklers, particularly at St. Louis, where he was trying to blame the recent riots in New Orleans, in which white and black radicals were killed, on Congress. His opponents replied in kind, calling him a traitor to the party that elected him, accusing him of plotting with Southern enemies against Northern power, while Thaddeus Stevens referred to him as "an alien enemy, a citizen of a foreign state . . . and therefore not now legally President."

When the election results were in, it became evident that Johnson had been repudiated. He might now have compromised, but again he refused. The result was that Congress passed several measures to restrict him—a law calling the Fortieth Congress into session immediately after the expiration of its predecessor, an act requiring him to issue orders to the Army only through the general in chief, a Tenure of Office Act providing for the dismissal of officers appointed by and with the consent of the Senate only with the consent of that body, and the Reconstruction Acts that remanded the Southern states once more to military rule and required them to adopt the amendment as well as black suffrage before they could be readmitted. Moreover, Representative James M. Ashley of Ohio introduced a motion calling for the impeachment of the president, and the Judiciary Committee initiated hearings about the subject. For his part, Johnson saw himself as the tribune of the people, the defender of the Constitution against congressional despotism. "I intend to assert the power which the people have placed in me," he said firmly. And he was contemptuous of the effort to displace him. "Let them impeach and be damned," he commented.

Because of Johnson's opposition to congressional Reconstruction, several members of his cabinet had already resigned. The secretary of war, Edwin M. Stanton, however, who collaborated with Congress, had refused to do so, and in August 1866 the president finally suspended him and appointed General U. S. Grant secretary ad interim. At the same time, Johnson began to remove some of the more radical commanding generals in the South. These actions naturally infuriated his opponents. In July the Judiciary Committee, which had renewed the impeachment investigation in the Fortieth Congress, had not found any real evidence of high crimes and misdemeanors. However, when Congress reassembled in December, one of its members had changed his mind, and the committee submitted a resolution of impeachment. Because of the weakness of the charges, the House voted it down. But then Johnson committed the blunder of quarreling with Grant, who had resigned after the Senate, in accordance with the Tenure of Office Act, refused to concur in the dismissal of Stanton. The unseemly quarrel led to a further effort to impeach the president, Thaddeus Stevens claiming that Reconstruction could not proceed as long as Johnson was in office, but that effort also failed. Only when the president, determined not to permit Stanton to remain in the cabinet, again dismissed him, and appointed Adjutant General Lorenzo Thomas secretary ad interim while the Senate was in session, did the impeachment finally succeed. "Didn't I tell you so?" exclaimed Thaddeus Stevens. "If you don't kill the beast, it will kill you."

The House closed in quickly. The joint Committee on Reconstruction resolved to impeach the president. There were two days of sensational debates. On February 24, 1868, by a vote of 126 to 47, Andrew Johnson became the first U.S. president to be impeached. The word *impeachment*, which is sometimes erroneously used to mean removal from office, is actually the parliamentary equivalent of the legal term *indictment*. Under the Constitution, "the sole power of Impeachment" belongs to the House of Representatives, which functions as a grand jury. The Senate has the sole responsibility for conducting a trial; conviction requires a two-thirds majority vote of the senators and may result in the president's removal.

Stanton, whom Sumner had sent a one-word telegram, "Stick," refused to leave the war department and swore out a warrant for General Thomas's arrest. Released on bail, the latter went to see the president. "Very well," Johnson said, "That is the place I want it. In the courts." Then Thomas attempted to take over his new office, but Stanton told him to go back to his own. After some further controversy, Thomas left, and when Stanton followed him, he said, "The next time you have me arrested please don't do it before I get something to eat." Stanton, putting his arm around him, then ordered some whiskey, which the two drank together. But the secretary steadily refused to leave the war office.

After the impeachment vote, the House appointed two committees, one to notify the Senate, which it did, and another to draw up specific articles of impeachment. Of the committee's eleven articles, the first eight accused Johnson of disregarding the Constitution by removing Stanton in violation of the Tenure of Office Act, the ninth dealt with the command of the Army provisions, and the tenth charged him with attempts to disgrace Congress by delivering "with a loud voice" certain intemperate, inflammatory, and scandalous harangues against it. The eleventh was a catchall, reiterating the first ten and accusing the president of plotting to violate the Reconstruction Acts. While Johnson's supporters, like Gideon Welles, considered most of the charges "a mountain of words, but not even a mouse of impeachment material," it was quite obvious that what was really involved was Johnson's opposition to congressional Reconstruction.

At one o'clock on March 5, Chief Justice Salmon P. Chase, impressive in his black robe, took his seat on the Senate rostrum. In the front and to the right

"Not only the slave states," declared Thaddeus Stevens in his first congressional speech, "but the general government, recognizing and aiding slavery as it does, is a despotism." Articulate, uncompromising, and grim, "Old Thad" was a dominant figure in the House of Representatives for nearly fifteen years, waging a relentless war on slavery. A Pennsylvania lawyer and businessman who had risen from dire poverty, Stevens was known to defend fugitive slaves without fee. After four years in the state legislature, he entered Congress as a Whig in 1849 and served until 1853. Reelected as a Republican in 1858, he served as chairman of the House Ways and Means Committee during the Civil War and urged harsher measures in dealing with the "Rebels" of the South. After Johnson's inauguration he was made House chairman of a joint committee on Reconstruction and launched an open battle against the moderate policies of the president. As the most influential member of the Republican-dominated House of Representatives and leader of the radicals, he succeeded in overriding presidential vetoes and imposing military Reconstruction on the South. Yet the moderates toned down several of his measures, and he was unable to effect the confiscation of Southern lands. As one of the men chosen to conduct the impeachment case against Johnson, he was deeply disappointed at the failure of the effort to convict the president. He died shortly after the trial.

Benjamin F. Butler, who had decided to try the case as if it were a "horse case," delivered the opening speech. After making some lengthy, dry arguments denying Johnson's right to test the constitutionality of a law, he exclaimed: "By murder most foul did he succeed to the Presidency and is the elect of an assassin to that high office, and not the people."

The trial proceeded, although no particularly new facts were brought forth. The managers, as the prosecution was called, tried to show that Johnson had indeed violated his oath of office. But Johnson had excellent lawyers, among them former Supreme Court Justice Benjamin Robbins Curtis, who based their defense on two points: that the President had appointed General Thomas as secretary of war in order to test the constitutionality of the Tenure of Office Act; and that, constitutional or not, the act could not apply in this case because Stanton was Lincoln's appointee. The prosecution consistently objected to testimony regarding Johnson's intent—seventeen times the Senate overruled the chief justice's decisions regarding the admission of evidence. Nor did it permit members of the cabinet to testify for the president.

There were fifty-three senators at the time. Thirty-six votes were needed for conviction; Johnson was sure of twelve. If seven Republicans deserted their party to support him, the Senate would lack the necessary two-thirds for conviction. That meant the radicals had to swing the support of just one of the remaining seven. The pressure on those seven, and on Johnson, mounted as the trial drew near its conclusion. Thaddeus Stevens, too ill to deliver his final closing plea for conviction, had it read for him: By his actions the president had clearly violated the Constitution, he wrote, "and now this offspring of assassination turns upon the Senate who have . . . rebuked him in a constitutional manner and bids them defiance. How can he escape the just vengeance of the law?" Those who voted for acquittal could expect to be eter-

of the rostrum sat the president's counsel (but not the president; although he wanted to attend, his advisers had insisted that he stay away). To the left sat the seven managers of impeachment for the House. The senators occupied the first two rows of seats; behind them were the accusers, the members of the House of Representatives. With great pomp Chase swore in the senators, and the trial began. It would last for three months.

The opening took place on March 30. General

nally "tortured on the gibbet of everlasting obloquy." On May 7 the trial ended, and the Senate adjourned until May 11. During the recess, as before, the pressure from the newspapers, from constituents, from colleagues, party leaders, preachers, Army officers, and lobbyists closed in on the seven doubtfuls: Convict!

But Johnson had not been inactive. Although refusing to compromise before, he now made deals to save himself. Meeting with Senator James W. Grimes of Iowa, he promised not to interfere further with Reconstruction and he consented to appointing General John M. Schofield as secretary of war. He also agreed to Senator Edmund G. Ross's demand that he transmit the new constitutions of Arkansas and South Carolina without delay.

When the Senate reconvened, four of the undeclared—William Pitt Fessenden of Maine, Grimes's close collaborator, Lyman Trumbull of Illinois, Grimes, and Joseph S. Fowler of Tennessee—revealed that they would vote to acquit. This upset the impeachers; they managed to have the vote, originally scheduled for the twelfth, postponed until the sixteenth. That same afternoon Senator Grimes buck-

A *Harper's Weekly* cartoon from the May 30, 1868, issue is titled "Effect of the Vote on the Eleventh Article of Impeachment." The left panel, "Elevation—At The White House," depicts "King Andrew's" joy at the Senate's failure to convict him, but also mocks him for his alleged drinking problem and humble beginnings as a tailor. The right panel, "Depression—At The *Tribune* Office," shows editor Horace Greeley's disappointment, which was shared by other radicals.

led under the pressure and had a stroke that left him partially paralyzed. The sad news was coupled, however, with a hopeful word for Johnson: Peter G. Van Winkle of West Virginia could be depended on, and John B. Henderson of Missouri would probably vote for acquittal. That left one senator: Edmund G. Ross of Kansas, a freshman Republican, devoted to his party but silent throughout the trial. As for Grimes— whether or not he would be able to make it to the Senate chamber was a matter of doubt.

On May 16th, the chamber was again closely packed. Senator Fessenden rose to ask a half hour's delay to await the arrival of the stricken Grimes. The radicals had no time to object, for as Fessenden spoke, Senator Grimes was helped to his seat by friends. The chief justice requested the clerk to call the roll concerning the eleventh article and asked each senator for his vote. Senator after senator rose, and when Ross of Kansas was reached, he voted "not guilty." In view of the tally of senators' votes of Senators following the letter *R*, it became obvious that Johnson would be acquitted, although if Ross had voted to convict, others later on would have changed their vote. The result was Johnson's acquittal by one vote, 35–19. Thaddeus Stevens, upset about the verdict, exclaimed, "The country is going to the devil."

There were two more articles to be voted on, and although the managers obtained a ten-day postponement, they could not retrieve even one of those seven precious votes. The final result was again a vote of 35–19, one short of the necessary two-thirds to convict. The court adjourned *sine die.*

What were the reasons for the Republicans' failure to convict the president? First, a number of the senators felt that to convict for what were essentially political rather than substantial reasons would undermine the tripartite system of executive, legislative, and judicial government. Second, the case was weak—whether the Tenure of Office Act applied to Stanton was not clear. Third, the president *pro tem* of the Senate, Benjamin F. Wade of Ohio, who would have succeeded Johnson in the absence of a vice president, was too radical for any number of senators; he advocated not only rights for the freed people but also a new deal for labor and votes for women. And finally, Johnson's term had only nine more months to run. The president's acquittal showed that it was not possible to convict a chief executive for mere political reasons, and when it was attempted again in 1998–99, the outcome was the same, thus reaffirming this result.

Understandably, Johnson had no love for the exec-

WILLIAM HENRY SEWARD

William Henry Seward's influence on the course of American politics spanned almost half a century, from the election of John Quincy Adams through the administration of Andrew Johnson. As a young lawyer in Auburn, New York, Seward boldly opposed the presidential candidate of the Albany Regency and spoke out for "John Quincy Adams—and better government." His independent spirit never wavered. As governor of New York for four years and United States senator from 1848 to 1860, he took a firm stand against slavery. Opposing the Compromise of 1850, he argued the inherent freedom of the territories on the basis of "a higher law than the Constitution" and saw in the whole slavery issue "an irrepressible conflict" between North and South. A masterful secretary of state under Lincoln and Johnson, he skillfully averted European intervention in the Civil War and later secured France's promise of withdrawal from Mexico. An expansionist, he purchased Alaska in 1867. Favoring a moderate Reconstruction policy, he staunchly supported President Johnson during the impeachment proceedings; efforts to entice him into the radical camp were met with an emphatic rejoinder: "I will see you damned first." Retiring from public service in 1869, Seward died three years later in Auburn.

utive office, but he thought the 1868 Democratic nomination for the presidency would mean "a vindication such as no man had ever received." While the party was loud in its praise, it nonetheless nominated Horatio Seymour, who lost to Grant, the Republican nominee.

In December 1868, with Grant safely elected and the Republicans anxious to get their administration under way, Johnson appeared before Congress to give his last annual message. His racism was still in evidence: "The attempt to place the white population under the domination of persons of color in the South . . . has prevented that cooperation between the two races so essential to the success of industrial enterprise. . . ." Already the Ku Klux Klan was riding and the seeds of lasting hatred were sown. He had sought to keep the South a "white man's country," and he had succeeded in so undermining congressional Reconstruction that it could not last in the long run.

The Johnson administration, for all its battles, agonies, and turmoil, demonstrated an essential truth of American history—that the government goes on. That it did under Johnson is largely to the credit of most of the cabinet members, especially Gideon Welles and William H. Seward.

Seward, once a leading presidential aspirant, supported the president consistently and wrote many of Johnson's veto messages; he was also one of the most active secretaries of state since John Quincy Adams. During the Civil War, Napoleon III of France had sent troops to Mexico and had placed Austrian Archduke Maximilian on the Mexican throne. Early in 1866, with Johnson's approval, Seward decided to reassert the Monroe Doctrine and ordered the French to withdraw; for emphasis he sent General Sheridan and fifty thousand troops to the Mexican border.

Napoleon III acquiesced in the spring of 1867, but Maximilian, ambushed by a band of Mexican partisans, was executed. Later that year, the Midway Islands were claimed by the American fleet. In October, Seward negotiated the purchase of the Danish West Indies (the Virgin Islands), but the Senate killed the purchase bill.

Seward's most famous achievement was the purchase of Alaska from Russia for $7.2 million. He submitted this bill to the Senate in March 1867 after just three weeks' negotiation, and managed to have it passed by convincing Senator Sumner to support it. It was at first an unpopular purchase, and Alaska became known as "Seward's Folly" and "Johnson's polar bear garden."

So, thanks to Seward and others, Johnson's presidency had not been entirely devoid of accomplishments. But the ex-president still sought vindication. Back in Tennessee, he again grew active in state affairs, and in 1874–75 he ran once more for the United States Senate. He was elected, a considerable feat in view of the opposition of former Confederates as well as radicals. In March he returned to Washington to attend a special session of Congress. Nervously he entered the chamber: From the galleries came a great burst of applause; he found his desk covered with flowers. When the senators—even those who had judged him guilty seven years before—pressed forward to shake his hand, he shook with them all. He had achieved his vindication.

Andrew Johnson was only briefly a senator. He suffered a stroke at his daughter's Tennessee home and died on July 31, 1875. He was buried on a hilltop outside Greeneville, his winding sheet the flag, his pillow the Constitution.

—DAVID JACOBS
revised by HANS L. TREFOUSSE

ULYSSES SIMPSON GRANT

THE HERO AS POLITICIAN

"Nothing," said Ulysses S. Grant of presidential hopeful General Winfield Scott in 1846, "so popularizes a candidate for high civil positions as military victories." Scott did not win the presidency, but Grant, the supreme Union hero of the Civil War, proved his own point. When Lincoln issued a call for federal volunteers in April 1861, thirty-eight-year-old "Sam" Grant was imprisoned by poverty and despondency: He was a West Point graduate with no prospects, performing menial odd jobs and haunted by the memory of forced resignation from the Army for excessive drinking. Three years later he would be general in chief of the Union armies. Seven years later he would be elected president.

Grant was born on April 27, 1822, in a two-room frame house overlooking the Ohio River at Point Pleasant, Ohio. After a solemn family assembly to vote the future hero a name, the child was christened Hiram Ulysses Grant; later the boy himself changed it to Ulysses Hiram Grant, to avoid initials that spelled "HUG." It was the beginning of Grant's continuing battle to secure his name against ridicule.

Grant's father, Jesse, was an enterprising tanner. He was a Whig (he supported Jackson, however), a Methodist, and a Mason. He loved to talk politics, forging a second career out of letters to the local editor. Grant's mother, Hannah Simpson, was a farmer's daughter, quietly strong and direct, of whom her son said, "I never saw my mother cry."

In 1823 the Grants moved to Georgetown, Ohio, where Ulysses was to spend his boyhood. The family—Ulysses was one of six children—was free of both hardship and luxury. "Useless" Grant, as wags liked to call him, farmed, hauled wood, helped his father at the tannery, ran his own wagon-taxi to Cincinnati when he was ten, and earned a formidable reputation for breaking difficult horses. He attended school regularly until he was seventeen.

Grant was a diffident, quiet boy—blue-eyed, russet-haired, pink-cheeked, and fair-skinned. A muscular five feet one inch at seventeen (he was to grow seven more inches at West Point), he had unusually small hands and feet. And though sometimes prankish, young Grant was essentially a pleasant, retiring boy who wanted to be called Hiram and be let alone.

In 1839 Jesse Grant received word that the West Point appointment he had sought for his son appeared certain. "But I won't go," Grant informed his father. He thought I would go, Grant remembered; and so he did.

Still, Grant was a reluctant soldier. He relished the initial trip to West Point chiefly as an opportunity to travel to Philadelphia and New York. "When these places were visited," he confessed, he "would have been glad to have had a steamboat or railroad collision, or any other accident happen" to make him unable to enroll at the Point.

"A military life," he was to say candidly, "had no charms for me, and I had not the faintest idea of staying in the army even if I should be graduated, which I did not expect." But for good or ill, he was now Cadet Ulysses Simpson Grant, his name incorrectly registered by his congressman. From the first, he was to his classmates "Uncle Sam" or "Sam" Grant, as fellow students hailed "U. S. Grant" on the roster.

Cadet Grant detested Academy discipline and was an indifferent scholar. He flavored the rigid curriculum with large doses of Sir Walter Scott and Frederick Marryat and was elected to preside over the cadet literary society, The Dialectic. He also found diversion from the regimen in perfecting his horsemanship; his equestrian high-jump record would remain unbeaten at the Point for twenty-five years.

As a cadet, Grant received numerous demerits for slovenly dress, unsoldierly bearing, and tardiness. Not a man for dancing or social etiquette, he preferred

Lieutenant General Grant at City Point. Taken during the 1864-1865 siege of Petersburg, this portrait reveals his pensive mood during the costly Virginia campaign.

sauntering off to a local pub for off-limits drinking. Promoted to sergeant in his third year, he confessed that the higher rank was "too much" for him, and he willingly served his senior year as a private.

Despite these setbacks, Grant learned to admire the Academy as "the most beautiful place I have ever seen" as well as for the future security it promised. "I would not go away on any account," he wrote to a cousin. "If a man graduates here, he is safe for life, let him go where he will."

Grant graduated from West Point in 1843, academically 21st in a graduating class of 39, and 156th in conduct among the Academy's 223 cadets. The Academy's best horseman requested, but was denied, a coveted cavalry commission. He was named a brevet second lieutenant in the 4th U.S. Infantry at $779 per year and was assigned to Jefferson Barracks near St. Louis.

While at Jefferson Barracks, Grant made the acquaintance of comely and pert Miss Julia Boggs Dent, sister of his fourth-year roommate at the Point. Julia was the amiable, sensible daughter of a well-to-do colonel, Frederick Dent, who owned a plantation near the barracks. A distinguished horsewoman, Julia caught Ulysses's romantic eye at first sight. They married on August 22, 1848, and enjoyed a stable and happy relationship throughout almost thirty-seven years of marriage. The Grants would have four children: Frederick Dent, Ulysses Simpson, Nellie Wrenshall, and Jesse Root.

Grant was stationed for two years in Missouri and Louisiana before joining Zachary Taylor's army at Corpus Christi, Texas, prior to the Mexican War. From July 1846 he was a regimental quartermaster, fighting under both Taylor and Winfield Scott. Active in all major battles except Buena Vista, Sam Grant distinguished himself for bravery in hand-to-hand combat, once making a heroic dash through enemy-held territory to secure ammunition for his troops. He later marched with Scott from Veracruz to Mexico

City, and he emerged from the war as a first lieutenant and brevet captain.

Like Lincoln, who introduced resolutions demanding the president to point out the exact spot where American blood had been spilled on American soil by Mexicans, Lieutenant Grant was thoroughly opposed to the Mexican War, which was being waged, he said, as "a war of conquest." But despite his convictions, Grant obeyed the command to fight the Mexicans. "Experience proves that the man who obstructs a war in which his nation is engaged, no matter whether right or wrong, occupies no enviable place in life or history," he explained.

In Mexico, Grant felt the injustice of the war, his heart going out to the ragged and starving Mexicans. It was a side of Grant not often remembered during his later military victories or during the corruption of his presidency. It was the Grant who, despite being given the vicious Civil War title of "the Butcher," was horrified by the cruelty of hunting and found bullfights "sickening." It was the Grant, too, who preferred to sit out in the cold, drenching rain at Shiloh rather than in a warm tent where he might see the blood of his soldiers in surgery. "I never went into a battle willingly or with enthusiasm," he would confess in later years.

When the Mexican War ended, Grant was stationed at Sackets Harbor, New York. But whatever domestic pleasure he and Julia might have shared was roughly curtailed in 1852 when the captain was assigned to bleak frontier posts on the Pacific Coast. Julia, already a mother, did not accompany him. After a treacherous crossing of the Isthmus of Panama, in which cholera killed one-third of his companions, he arrived in San Francisco, moving north to Fort Vancouver (near today's Portland, Oregon) in late September.

It was at Fort Vancouver that the great shadow that would sully Grant's name first began to descend: compulsive, excessive drinking. The thirty-year-old soldier missed his young wife, longed for a first look at his second son, Ulysses, Jr., and bitterly regretted the fact that he could not afford to bring them West. His excesses were noted by General George B. McClellan, among others. "It was not that Grant drank much," a friend recalled. "The trouble was that a very little would . . . thicken his never glib or lively tongue. On far less liquor than many a comrade carried without a sign, Grant would appear half-stupefied."

Grant's tippling became a critical issue when he was summoned to Fort Humboldt at Humboldt Bay, California, in the summer of 1853. His mission: to take command of a company under Colonel Robert C. Buchanan, a fastidious officer with whom Grant had already exchanged angry words at Jefferson Barracks. Despondent and depressed because of Julia's absence, Grant found sedation in drinking—heavily, often, and straight.

In April 1854 Sam Grant, then a commissioned captain, was discovered drunk in public by Buchanan, who promptly demanded that Grant either resign or stand trial. Fearing a scandal and the heartbreak a trial would bring to Julia, Grant chose to resign. He was relieved of his command on May 1, his resignation having been accepted as tendered by Secretary of War Jefferson Davis. "If you ever hear from me again," Sam told his comrades, "it will probably be as a well-to-do farmer."

Grant now faced eight ineffably bitter years of squalor and failure. He, Julia, and the family moved at first to a sixty-acre tract, twelve miles from St. Louis, that had been given to Julia by her father. Grant cleared the land, squared logs, and built a house. By the spring of 1855 he was plowing and planting, hauling cordwood for sale to St. Louis, and hoping to be free and clear within three years. But Grant lacked the capital to make the farm a paying enterprise, and crop prices collapsed in the Panic of 1857. Grant leased the property and took over the old Dent farm, until "fever and ague" put him to bed. Subsequent efforts to earn

BIOGRAPHICAL FACTS

BIRTH: Point Pleasant, Ohio, Apr. 27, 1822
ANCESTRY: English-Scotch
FATHER: Jesse Root Grant; b. Westmoreland County, Pa., Jan. 23, 1794; d. Covington, Ky., June 29, 1873
FATHER'S OCCUPATION: Leather tanner
MOTHER: Hannah Simpson Grant; b. Montgomery County, Pa., Nov. 23, 1798; d. Jersey City, N.J., May 11, 1883
BROTHERS: Samuel Simpson (1825–1861); Orvil Lynch (1835–1881)
SISTERS: Clara Rachel (1828–1865); Virginia Paine (1832–1881); Mary Frances (1839–1898)
MARRIAGE: St. Louis, Mo., Aug. 22, 1848
WIFE: Julia Boggs Dent; b. St. Louis, Mo., Jan. 26, 1826; d. Washington, D.C., Dec. 14, 1902
CHILDREN: Frederick Dent (1850–1912); Ulysses Simpson (1852–1929); Nellie Wrenshall (1855–1922); Jesse Root (1858–1934)
RELIGIOUS AFFILIATION: Methodist
EDUCATION: Local schools; U.S. Military Academy, West Point, N.Y. (1843)
OCCUPATIONS BEFORE PRESIDENCY: Soldier; farmer; real estate agent; leather store clerk
MILITARY SERVICE: 2d lt. in 4th U.S. Infantry (1843); capt. (1853); brig. gen. (1861); gen. in chief of Union Army (1864)
AGE AT INAUGURATION: 46
OCCUPATIONS AFTER PRESIDENCY: Businessman; writer
DEATH: Mount McGregor, N.Y., July 23, 1885
PLACE OF BURIAL: Grant's Tomb, New York, N.Y.

money as a real estate agent and collector of overdue accounts also failed.

In desperation, Grant appealed to his father, who offered him only an $800-per-year post as a clerk in his Galena, Illinois, leather shop under the patronizing direction of two younger brothers. There Grant lifted heavy stock, unloaded wagons, and kept books. Spiritually he was at rock bottom.

When President Lincoln issued his call for seventy-five thousand Union volunteers on April 15, 1861, Captain Sam Grant, forgetting his former disappoint-

The New York *Herald* April 16, 1861, reports on Lincoln's call for troops. The headlines reflect the arousal of patriotism in the North after the attack on Fort Sumter.

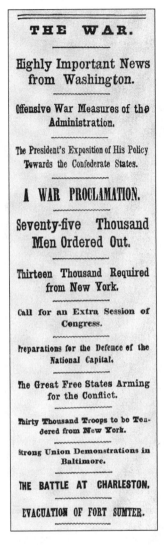

THE WAR.

Highly Important News from Washington.

Offensive War Measures of the Administration.

The President's Exposition of His Policy Towards the Confederate States.

A WAR PROCLAMATION.

Seventy-five Thousand Men Ordered Out.

Thirteen Thousand Required from New York.

Call for an Extra Session of Congress.

Preparations for the Defence of the National Capital.

The Great Free States Arming for the Conflict.

Thirty Thousand Troops to be Tendered from New York.

Strong Union Demonstrations in Baltimore.

THE BATTLE AT CHARLESTON.

EVACUATION OF FORT SUMTER.

charge of troops in southern Illinois and southeastern Missouri.

Early in 1862 Grant's military star began its incredible national rise. He captured Confederate-held Fort Henry on the Tennessee River, then Fort Donelson on the Cumberland, where he demanded the enemy's "unconditional surrender" and pushed the Confederates back to Tennessee. The North was jubilant; Grant was named a major general. The Battle of Shiloh, in which Grant defeated the Confederates despite initial misjudgments, took place in April 1862; when Lincoln was advised to dismiss him, the president said, "I can't spare this man; he fights." Memphis fell to the Union forces by June 6, establishing federal control of the Mississippi as far as Vicksburg. By July 4, 1863, Vicksburg itself had fallen; five days later Nathaniel P. Banks took Port Hudson, Louisiana, securing Union control of the entire Mississippi. In late November, in the Battle of Chattanooga, General Grant—then commander of the Union armies of the West—drove the Confederate forces out of Tennessee and opened the road to Georgia.

On March 9, 1864, a grateful Lincoln named Grant a lieutenant general and three days later placed him in charge of the entire Union Army. There were still rumors of his drinking, but Lincoln was said to have suggested that if he could know Grant's type of whiskey, "he would send every general in the field a barrel of it." In June, Grant began his historic siege of Petersburg, Virginia. Almost a year later, the Confederate Army was caught between his forces in the North and Sherman's troops in the South. When Richmond surrendered on April 3, Grant pursued and surrounded Lee's men.

On Palm Sunday, April 9, 1865, General Lee surrendered to Grant in the Virginia village of Appomattox Court House. On this historic occasion, the Union's chief general appeared wearing a borrowed private's uniform (decorated only by his lieutenant

ments in the Army, came to life, promptly offering to drill a company of Galena volunteers. He served next as a clerk in the state adjutant general's office. He appealed to the U.S. adjutant general in Washington to give him a regiment and let him fight, but his request went unanswered. General McClellan, soon to command all the Union armies, refused to see him. Undeterred, Grant persevered and in June 1861 was appointed a colonel to lead the 21st Illinois Volunteers. In August he was named a brigadier general in

general's shoulder straps) and muddy boots. As he looked at Lee in defeat, Grant could feel only compassion. He had considered the Confederate cause "one of the worst for which a people ever fought," but now he felt profoundly sad.

After chatting about old Army days in Mexico, Grant informed Lee of the magnanimous terms of surrender on which he and Lincoln had agreed. There would be no reprisals, no prisons, no hangings. The Confederate officers would be allowed to keep their side arms; to deprive them of these, Grant felt, would be an "unnecessary humiliation." The Confederate troops were only to sign paroles and were "not to be disturbed by the United States authority so long as they observe[d] their paroles and the laws in force where they reside[d]." Informed that Lee's men were hungry, Grant ordered Union rations shared with them immediately. As news of the surrender reached the troops, Union artillery burst in celebration, but Grant ordered it stopped. "We did not," Grant said later, "want to exult over their downfall."

But the victorious North did exult, and Grant's name shone second only to Lincoln's. Even the fallen South hailed Grant for his manly consideration and kind terms at Appomattox. Wherever the general went, he was mobbed by crowds. In Washington, Lincoln received him with deep emotion, inviting the Grants to join him and Mrs. Lincoln at Ford's Theatre. Grant promptly accepted the invitation, but Julia decided that they should not go, offering the excuse that she wanted to get back to her children. It was a fateful decision, for Grant's name, too, was on the assassins' list. En route to New Jersey, Grant heard the shocking report of Lincoln's murder and returned to the capital. "It would be impossible for me," he wrote, "to describe the feeling that overcame me at the news. . . ."

Grant's position under President Andrew Johnson was extremely awkward. On the one hand, the new president was his constitutional commander in chief.

On the other hand, both he and the president knew that Grant now stood first in the eyes of the nation, enjoying unprecedented esteem. Johnson also realized that Grant was a possible Republican presidential candidate for 1868.

Johnson tried to exploit Grant's popularity by

ROBERT E. LEE

"He became a God figure for Virginians," wrote Thomas L. Connelly of Robert E. Lee, a characterization expressing the judgment of the entire white South. An exemplary member of the class of 1819 at West Point, where he later served as superintendent, Lee won praise for his bravery in the Mexican War and in 1861 was offered the command of the Union Army. Although he could not "see the good of secession," he said his first allegiance was to his native state, Virginia, which he vowed to follow "with my sword, and if need be, with my life."

When he took command of the Army of Northern Virginia, Lee, though generally outnumbered, frustrated General McClellan's effort to take Richmond in the Seven Days' Battles. He routed General John Pope at the second Bull Run and, in spite of a setback at Antietam, achieved crushing victories at Fredericksburg and Chancellorsville. He then invaded Pennsylvania but was defeated at Gettysburg. In 1864 he conducted a splendid defense of Virginia against General Grant. In the end, after a ten-month siege at Petersburg, he surrendered to Grant at Appomattox Court House. He bade his men to go home peaceably and soon thereafter wrote of the "duty of every one to unite in the restoration of the country and the establishment of peace and harmony. . . ."

Inspiring in victory, he was a source of consolation in defeat. He became president of Washington (now Washington and Lee) College in Lexington, and when he died in 1870, he was mourned throughout the South as the apotheosis of the Christian gentleman-warrior.

sending him on a tour of the South in 1865, but he and the general were men of different mind and mettle. And any doubt of their basic disparity and popular standing was dispelled when the president, contrary to Grant's handwritten terms at Appomattox, sought to have General Lee arrested for treason. Grant was enraged that Johnson would even contemplate breaking the nation's—and his own—solemn word at the surrender table. When Lee appealed to him, Grant intervened on his behalf, threatening to take his case to the people if the president did not desist. Johnson backed down.

For the most part, Grant maintained a studied public neutrality on divisive political issues. Even when Johnson tried to fire Edwin M. Stanton as secretary of war, Grant—who had been named interim secretary—maintained neutrality. But his neutrality ended when, after Congress refused to permit Stanton's dismissal, he resigned, quarreled with the president about the surrender of the war office, and became the nominee of the Republican party.

Grant was nominated for the presidency by acclamation on the first ballot at the Republican convention of 1868 in Chicago. Speaker of the House Schuyler Colfax of Indiana was named his running mate. Only four words of Grant's reaction to the news of his nomination remain to posterity: "Let us have peace."

But if Grant wanted peace, there was no peace. Atrocities in the South against the freed people caused many moderates to side with the radicals, and Grant followed suit. VOTE AS YOU SHOT, Republican posters proclaimed. Grant was lionized as the almost superhuman savior of the Union, the hero of Vicksburg, now trampling the Confederate flag in the dust. Grant's Democratic opponent, Horatio Seymour, wartime governor of New York, who had addressed antiwar rioters as "my friends," could be pilloried as a Copperhead—a Northerner with Southern sympathies—and a tool of Tammany Hall. For all his popularity, however, Grant won the presidency by a surprisingly small margin of only three hundred thousand popular votes.

"The office," said Grant in his inaugural address, "has come to me unsought; I commence its duties untrammeled." He hinted at what his relationship with Congress would be as chief executive: He would be a prime minister, a first among equals. "I shall on all subjects have a policy to recommend," he explained, "but none to enforce against the will of the people." As for the critical issues of Reconstruction, Grant now urged that they "be approached calmly, without prejudice, hate, or sectional pride. . . ."

The new president advocated prompt payments on the nation's staggering war debt of $400 million; a return, when possible, to specie currency; and a sounder national credit. Soon to witness the nation's profit from mining stocks, Grant saluted Providence's gift of "a strong box in the precious metals of the West, which we are now forging the key to unlock." Assuring industry and commerce encouragement, President Grant also urged fairer treatment of the Indians. He concluded by asking for passage of the Fifteenth Amendment, which would give black Americans the constitutional right to vote. (On March 30, 1870, the amendment was ratified.)

General Grant presided over the United States at the beginning of an era of fabulous growth and optimism, creativity and invention, glory and shame. It was the era of Mark Twain and New York's notorious Boss Tweed, of Susan B. Anthony, Horatio Alger, and J. P. Morgan. Two months after Grant's inauguration the Union Pacific and Central Pacific railroads were linked in Utah. The thrust of Western settlement, spurred by the Homestead Act (passed under Lincoln), continued to carve farms out of prairies. From New York to the Mississippi, commerce hummed, quickened by industrial steam and the refrigerated railroad car.

It was a brash, heady era—the "Gilded Age"—in

which no one wanted the federal government meddling in his affairs, unless that intervention took the form of railroad subsidies, grants of free public land, a protective tariff to stem foreign competition and keep prices up for consumers, or defense against the Indians as settlers moved West. In Ulysses S. Grant the movers of American society had precisely the man they wanted to preside over their expansion and pursuit of wealth. They desired a "chairman of the board" who would defer to their sound judgments in arcane matters of finance and legislation. And that is what Grant wanted too. A president, he believed, should follow the will of the people and administer the laws passed by their elected representatives.

Grant's was a narrow interpretation of executive power, one calculated to please congressional bosses such as Roscoe Conkling, Simon Cameron, and James G. Blaine, who virtually governed the nation through control of patronage and federal disbursements. Grant's attitude was epitomized in his first annual message. "The appropriations estimated for river and harbor improvements and for fortifications are submitted . . ." he declared. "Whatever amount Congress may deem proper to appropriate for these purposes will be expended."

If hope lingered that the Grant administration would provide an inspired, reforming government, it died when the general announced his cabinet appointments, most of which were made on the basis of personal friendship. An undistinguished congressman, Elihu B. Washburne, who had favored Grant's career, was elevated to secretary of state. He was replaced two weeks later, however, by New York's highly competent Hamilton Fish, who would serve under Grant in lone distinction. As secretary of war, Grant appointed General John Schofield, who, having enjoyed this honor for one week, stepped aside for Grant's Civil War confidant, General John A. Rawlins. A Philadelphia businessman, Adolph E. Borie (whose principal distinction seems to have been his

affluence), was named secretary of the Navy. Impressed with wealth, Grant appointed Alexander T. Stewart, a rich New York merchant, as secretary of the Treasury, but an old law specifically forbidding anyone with a financial interest in business to head the Treasury Department, stood in the way. Unimpressed, Grant urged the Senate to make Stewart an exception. But the president was rebuffed, and the Treasury post went to George S. Boutwell of Massa-

FIRST ADMINISTRATION

INAUGURATION: Mar. 4, 1869; the Capitol, Washington, D.C.

VICE PRESIDENT: Schuyler Colfax

SECRETARY OF STATE: Elihu B. Washburne; Hamilton Fish (from Mar. 17, 1869)

SECRETARY OF THE TREASURY: George S. Boutwell

SECRETARY OF WAR: John A. Rawlins; William T. Sherman (from Sept. 11, 1869); William W. Belknap (from Nov. 1, 1869)

ATTORNEY GENERAL: Ebenezer R. Hoar; Amos T. Akerman (from July 8, 1870); George H. Williams (from Jan.10, 1872)

POSTMASTER GENERAL: John A. J. Creswell

SECRETARY OF THE NAVY: Adolph E. Borie; George M. Robeson (from June 25, 1869)

SECRETARY OF THE INTERIOR: Jacob D. Cox; Columbus Delano (from Nov. 1, 1870)

SUPREME COURT APPOINTMENTS: William Strong (1870); Joseph P. Bradley (1870); Ward Hunt (1872)

41ST CONGRESS (Mar. 4, 1869–Mar. 3, 1871):
 SENATE: 61 Republicans; 11 Democrats
 HOUSE: 170 Republicans; 73 Democrats

42ND CONGRESS (Mar. 4, 1871–Mar. 3, 1873):
 SENATE: 57 Republicans; 17 Democrats
 HOUSE: 139 Republicans; 104 Democrats

ELECTION OF 1868

CANDIDATES	ELECTORAL VOTE	POPULAR VOTE
Ulysses S. Grant (Republican)	214	3,013,650
Horatio Seymour (Democratic)	80	2,708,744

chusetts, a leader in the impeachment of Andrew Johnson.

It was a triumph of cronyism and idolization of the rich. "A great soldier," snapped Henry Adams, "might be a baby politician." When it became known that Stewart had sent costly gifts to Grant and that Borie had entertained him lavishly, the American people began to share Adams's indignation. Nor were minds relieved when the general nominated as minister to Belgium a friend who was a livery-stable supervisor.

HORACE GREELEY

Horace Greeley was more a social reformer than a politician when he ran for president in 1872. Founder and editor of the New York *Tribune*, Greeley had issued his first edition in 1841, pledging that his paper would stand "removed alike from servile partisanship" and "mincing neutrality." He succeeded in both objectives, shaping public opinion through the high moral tone of his editorials. Espousing the Fourier social reform movement, homestead legislation, labor unions, and women's rights, he attacked all forms of social and economic tyranny. He supported the free-soil movement; and while he advocated preservation of the Union, he was willing to see it dissolved rather than allow the extension of slavery. A founder of the Republican party, he supported Lincoln in 1860 but attacked his cautious emancipation policy. Hailing Grant's election, he later denounced the administration as corrupt and illiberal toward the South. When the Liberal Republicans split from the regular party in 1872, Greeley became their candidate and was also endorsed by the Democrats in an effort to block Grant. Urging a conciliatory attitude toward the South, Greeley failed to carry a single Northern state. The vituperation of his opponents hurt him deeply. Crushed by the magnitude of his defeat, the death of his wife, and the loss of his editorship, Greeley died, tragically insane, soon after the 1872 election.

President Grant functioned under major personal limitations: an unwillingness to consult with informed counselors who might have taken his chestnuts out of the fire or roasted them more palatably, and a consuming awe of the world's rich and influential. His mistakes were titanic. He permitted himself, for example, to be entertained publicly by the infamous speculators James Fisk and Jay Gould, allowing them to wine and dine him aboard their yacht and to urge upon him their conviction that the government should stay out of the gold market, which Fisk and Gould were conspiring to corner. They did so, after making allies of Abel Corbin, the president's brother-in-law.

Informed by Horace Greeley and others, the public became aware of the intended swindle. Hoping against hope for a cordial way out, Grant ultimately ordered the Treasury to release federal gold. The price of gold fell, and the conspiracy was foiled. But the administration, almost directly involved in the scandal, never escaped its taint.

In 1870 another scandal ripped through the administration, this time in connection with the Dominican Republic in the Caribbean. The dictator of that nation, Buenaventura Báez, surrounded and buttressed by financial speculators, informed the United States of his desire to sell the country at a profit to himself. Bypassing Secretary of State Fish, Grant sent his personal aide, Colonel Orville E. Babcock, to work out a deal with Báez. To Fish's dismay, Babcock returned with a treaty to which Grant promptly pledged full support. The president also dispatched warships to the island to protect Báez against threats to his life.

When he learned of these events, Secretary Fish threatened to resign. But Grant, in an almost unique display of executive will, remained adamant in support of the treaty. When Senate opposition to the deal flared, Grant personally visited the Capitol and lobbied in the Senate corridors. Still, the Senate refused to ratify the treaty. If only his plan had been adopted, Grant said, the recently freed blacks might have been settled in a rich new country of their own.

Grant's first administration was also rocked by a scandal at the New York Customs House, whose collector, Thomas Murphy, had been a personal appointee and intimate racetrack associate of the president. Murphy inherited and sustained a system of graft under which a Colonel Leet used presidential influence to secure a monopoly on the storage of imports. Leet charged an entire month's rent for one day's storage in the Port of New York, reaping huge profits. Faced with a presidential election in 1872 and a congressional investigation of the scandal, the administration reluctantly sacked Murphy. Grant, however, paid tribute to his "honesty."

In the realm of Reconstruction, the administration pursued a policy of attempting to sustain congressional efforts to remake Southern states. As president, Grant upheld radical governments in the South, regimes dominated by carpetbaggers (Northerners who had moved to the section), scalawags (the Southerners who collaborated with them), and freedmen who supported them. Southern whites bristled under the black militia and the stifling taxes made necessary by the establishment of welfare institutions following emancipation. The white South responded with the Ku Klux Klan and other vengeful secret societies.

Spurred by the radicals, the Union League, and other wavers of the "bloody shirt," Grant lent strong support in 1871 to the passage of three Enforcement Acts, including the so-called Ku Klux Act, which authorized direct federal intervention in the legal structure of the South. The president was given the power to declare martial law and suspend the writ of habeas corpus at will anywhere in the South. Those accused of crimes were to be turned over directly to federal authorities, bypassing Southern courts and juries.

Incensed Southern whites were close to rebellion.

A photograph of two members of the Ku Klux Klan—"ghouls" as they called themselves—shows one of the disguises worn by Klansmen in 1868. Dedicated to keeping black men from voting, the Klan functioned as the terrorist arm of the Democratic party, murdering and terrorizing freed men. The Ku Klux Klan was outlawed in 1871, but its members continued their reign of terror under other names.

In South Carolina, Grant used his new power to declare martial law in nine counties and suspend habeas corpus. Mass arrests and trials before packed juries followed. Under the act some 7,400 were indicted, but there were few convictions, and this attempt at protection for the blacks wrote a new legacy of bitterness in the South.

Grant's first term, however, was not totally without achievement. The government moved closer to responsibility in paying the national debt and in creating a stable currency and a more reliable national credit. Internationally, the country was beginning to emerge from insularity. Under Secretary of State Fish—who graced the Grant cabinet, as Richard Hofstadter writes, "like a jewel in the head of a toad"— America negotiated with Great Britain an arbitrated settlement whereby Britain agreed to pay the United States $15.5 million for damages inflicted on the Union by the vessel *Alabama*, which the British had sold to the Confederates. Washington and London also agreed on the location of the southern Canadian border and on fishing rights in adjoining waters.

But not even Fish's unimpeachable integrity and distinction could compensate for the appalling presidential retinue of grafters, scheming speculators, and calculating merchants and industrialists or for the disproportionate influence of the military. And rumors of the president's inordinate drinking persisted, despite the insistence of friends that he had given up liquor immediately upon arrival at the White House.

Nor was the criticism of Grant limited to the Democrats. While Grant was easily renominated by the regular Republicans at the convention of 1872, dissident Republicans and other foes of his policies chose the editor Horace Greeley as the presidential candidate put forth by a newly organized Liberal Republican party. The Liberals called for civil service reforms, less stringent Reconstruction policies, a general amnesty for the South, and impartial suffrage. In response the Grant forces pursued the same poster tactics used in 1868: Grant in his tanner's apron and military boots, holding the Union shield. The president won reelection, 286 electoral votes to 63. Greeley, who had been endorsed by the Democrats, took only six states.

"I have been the subject of abuse and slander," Grant said at the end of his second inaugural address, "scarcely ever equalled in political history, which today I feel that I can afford to disregard in view of your verdict, which I gratefully accept as my vindication." He again expressed regret that the nation had failed to annex the Dominican Republic, urged the reform of the civil service, and asked for clemency toward the Indians. And in a statement that would please both radicals and Southern white supremacists, he concluded: "Social equality is not a subject to be legislated upon, nor shall I ask that anything be done to advance the social status of the colored man, except to give him a fair chance to develop what there is good in him, give him access to the schools, and when he travels let him feel assured that his conduct will regulate the treatment and fare he will receive." The pattern of Reconstruction was now clear: It would simply be left to die. The South would be allowed to establish the status quo antebellum, substituting second-class citizenship for bondage for the former slaves. When the Democrats gained control of the House in 1874, in a clear repudiation of congressional Reconstruction, the days of the radicals were numbered.

If General Grant and his entourage hoped for a term less tempestuous than the first, they were to face major disappointments. A month before he was re-elected, another national scandal began breaking wide open and led to a congressional investigation ending in February 1873. Even before Grant's first election to the presidency, promoters of the Union Pacific Railroad had organized a camouflage company, Crédit Mobilier, to divert profits from railroad construction and to control charges levied by the railroad, itself heavily subsidized by the government.

One of the corporation's prime movers, Congressman Oakes Ames, realizing that Congress might one day investigate the fraud, had distributed blocks of the valuable stock among members of Congress, in whose hands, Ames reasoned, it would be most beneficial. Vice President Schuyler Colfax, dumped in the 1872 campaign because he dared presidential ambitions, was also given some of the stock, as were his successor, Henry Wilson, a number of Republican senators, and a congressman named James A. Garfield. It was a sorry spectacle of official corruption. And although the swindle had its genesis before Grant became president, the fact that it involved many of his associates and was exposed during his presidency further tarnished his name.

Nor did the Panic of 1873, precipitated by uncontrolled credit, inflation, wild speculation, and overexpansion, enhance Grant's now-dwindling public stature. With the collapse of Wall Street's powerful Jay Cooke and Company and the subsequent stock market decline, pressure mounted for a new greenback bill to inflate the currency. Grant's veto of the popular greenback law passed by Congress further inflamed resentment toward his administration. In the wake of the Panic, unemployment soared and businesses failed. Then, incredibly, new scandals broke.

The notorious "Whiskey Ring" was uncovered in 1875. Headed by General James McDonald, supervisor of the U.S. Internal Revenue Bureau in St. Louis, the ring worked in cooperation with a network of revenue officers and distillers who had highly-placed allies in the federal Treasury itself. Their system: abating taxes paid on whiskey and diverting the unreported revenue to their own pockets or to Republican campaign coffers.

Previous complaints made directly to the president, urging that the ring be exposed and broken, elicited no response. Eventually an agent was sent to St. Louis to investigate, but he was silenced when he returned to Washington. Later, Grant and his personal secretary, General Orville E. Babcock, were guests of McDonald in St. Louis, and Grant accepted as a

The dying General Grant finishing his memoirs is captured in an 1885 photograph. Suffering from cancer of the throat, the general completed his manuscript just before he died. Its publication enabled Grant's family to meet its expenses.

rior departments, and the payrolls of Navy yards were padded just before the elections by the secretary of the Navy. But the crowning scandal of the Grant administration erupted when it was learned that the secretary of war, General William W. Belknap, had received kickbacks from the sale of trading posts in the West. Again, Grant rose to the defense of a man openly guilty of corruption, but his attempt to shield Belknap from impeachment was of no avail. Although Belknap resigned, an angry House voted impeachment proceedings. Administration efforts to bring the House investigating committee itself into court to discredit its case against Belknap were defied. But the trial in the Senate bordered on farce, the defense counsel ridiculing the accusers and anointing Belknap, who was acquitted, a loyal son of the Union.

The Belknap verdict was par for the course in an era in which Congress could increase its own pay, retroactive for two years, on the final day of its session in 1873. And although Congress also decreed equal pay for equal work for women in federal agencies and passed Grant's Resumption Act providing for specie payment by 1879, the prevailing tone on Capitol Hill was one of cynicism and chicanery.

Still, Grant's popularity was only slightly diminished, and there was some clamor for him to run again. But the House, in a 234–18 vote, declared that a third term would be "unwise, unpatriotic and fraught with peril to our free institutions." The general did not appear disappointed. "I never wanted to get out of a place as much as I did to get out of the Presidency," he would say. And he was quick to use his new leisure to realize an old boyhood dream: a trip around the world.

If Grant left the presidency under a cloud, the world beyond the United States did not seem to know it. For the entire period of their travel abroad, the Grants were received everywhere as royalty. They dined with Queen Victoria at Windsor Castle and chatted with Disraeli and Bismarck. Mont Blanc and

gift from the Whiskey Ring a costly team of horses.

With the advent of a new secretary of the Treasury, Benjamin H. Bristow, the ring's days were numbered. Bristow uncovered the fact that Babcock had received from the ring a direct bribe to remain silent and to have the investigation called off. McDonald was indicted and jailed. Although the president stated, "Let no guilty man escape," Babcock, while indicted, retained Grant's undiminished support and was declared not guilty.

Corruption also engulfed the Post Office and Inte-

the Parthenon were illuminated in their honor. They sailed the Nile on the khedive's own vessel, and they met Pope Leo XIII at the Vatican, Richard Wagner at Heidelberg, and the czar in St. Petersburg. The Japanese emperor gave his own sitting-room furniture to the Grants because Julia admired its lacquer finish.

Stateside, popular acclaim was again demonstrated by a series of receptions across the country when Grant returned home in 1879. The scandals and cronies were forgotten, and the image of the plain soldier doing his job, sometimes let down by his friends but unblemished himself, emerged once more. The move by some Republican party leaders was predictable: Why not run Grant for president again in 1880? Grant himself appeared open to a draft, and his name was placed in nomination. But the old soldier lost to Garfield.

The Grants now turned their backs on politics. A fund of $100,000, raised by twenty friends, including A. J. Drexel and J. P. Morgan, enabled them to buy a mansion in New York City. In 1882 another friend, William H. Vanderbilt, lent Grant $150,000 to found a brokerage firm, Grant and Ward. Grant thus gave prestige and money to the fiscal operations of Ferdinand Ward and James D. Fish. In mid-1884 the firm suddenly failed, and Grant was left penniless and humiliated. Although Vanderbilt would gladly have written off the debt, the proud Grants turned all their property over to him.

Again Grant faced financial hardship. He would be somewhat relieved when Congress restored him to the rank and full pay of a general, but more money was needed to finance his household. To provide this, Grant accepted a generous offer by Mark Twain to publish his memoirs.

A few months earlier, Grant had felt the first stabbing pain of cancer in his throat. He had demanded, and received, the truth from his doctor: He was dying. It became difficult for the general to eat enough to live; the malignancy had spread to his tongue. But the old soldier had one final, personal battle to win, and despite the incessant pain and numbing sedation, he meant to win it. He would finish his memoirs.

Gradually, General Sam lost even the shy, quiet voice he had. When he could no longer bear the pain of whispering dictation, he himself wrote. Eventually he had to scribble his most elementary needs and wishes. As the memoirs neared conclusion, he laboriously penned a confession to his doctor: "I am ready now to go at any time. I know there is nothing but suffering for me while I do live."

In June 1885 Grant was moved to a cottage at Mount McGregor in the Adirondack foothills. There he was served tenderly and selflessly by Julia. On July 16, 1885, he completed his 295,000-word *Personal Memoir*, which would earn $450,000 for Julia and his family within two years.

On July 24 the General, who had been forced to remain propped up in an armchair to avoid choking to death, asked to be put to bed. The next day he died.

Grant was buried on New York City's Riverside Drive, in a funeral that rivaled Lincoln's in massive tribute. Four words are engraved on Grant's tomb: "Let us have peace." As Lincoln's favorite general, Grant had won peace for the nation. Now he had earned it for himself.

—*WILSON SULLIVAN*
revised by HANS L. TREFOUSSE

RUTHERFORD BIRCHARD HAYES

STRIVING FOR A FRESH START

utherford Birchard Hayes became president at a moment when the American people had lost faith in their political leaders in the wake of Andrew Johnson's impeachment trial and the gross corruption of some of Grant's aides and cabinet secretaries. Hayes was faced with the task of restoring dignity and popular confidence to the American presidency.

The United States was in transition when Hayes took office in 1877. America had celebrated its centennial in 1876. Its population had risen from approximately 2.5 million in 1776 to 46 million. Three times as many Americans lived in rural areas as in cities and towns. But the urban sector was growing faster than the rural. Most Americans—men, women, and children—worked hard. Farmers toiled from sunup to sundown, and factory workers put in ten- to twelve-hour days, six days a week. Although pay was low, it was better than in Europe. The right to vote was far from universal. In Philadelphia, the center of the centennial celebration, nearly a thousand women marched to protest their lack of the right to vote. Black men were losing that right, conferred by the Fifteenth Amendment to the Constitution, through intimidation and fraud, especially in states where they made up nearly a majority of the electorate.

Rutherford Hayes, who was destined to lead this nation, was born in Delaware, Ohio, on October 4, 1822, to Sophia Birchard and the late Rutherford Hayes. His parents, both of New England stock, had migrated to Ohio from Dummerston, Vermont, where the future president's father had owned a store. Rutherford's father was struck down by a fever and died two and a half months before his son was born. Sophia's younger bachelor brother, Sardis Birchard, became a surrogate father to the boy.

Although as president, Hayes was a steadfast advocate of public education, he never attended public schools. His mother taught him to read, write, and spell. In 1838 he entered Kenyon College in Gambier, Ohio, from which he graduated at the head of his class. He went on to Harvard Law School, winning his degree in 1845.

Hayes began his law practice in what is now Fremont, Ohio, the hometown of his Uncle Sardis. Restless and driven by patriotic zeal, Hayes planned to enlist in the war with Mexico, but Sardis nudged doctors into convincing Hayes that his health, somewhat frail, could not stand the severe Southern climate. Instead, Hayes found new challenges by moving to a large city—Cincinnati—in 1849 to practice law. He quickly ranked at the forefront of the city's younger lawyers, and married Lucy Webb, a graduate of Wesleyan Female College in Cincinnati. Eventually, she would become the earliest first lady to hold a college degree.

A devout Methodist, Lucy was a dedicated reformer, already committed to temperance and abortion rights. Her new husband identified largely with traditional values and the reasoning processes of the legal profession. An admirer of Ralph Waldo Emerson, Hayes was not by inclination a religious man. He never joined a church, but he dutifully accompanied Lucy on her faithful church attendance and willingly noted that "where the habit does not Christianize, it generally civilizes."

Lucy is credited with steering Hayes toward enlarging his reformist tolerance. Soon after their marriage he defended a runaway slave, and he joined the Republican party to help thwart slavery's dominance in the western territories, then awaiting transformation into states.

Hayes's first sortie into public officeholding occurred when he was elected as Cincinnati's solicitor. The nation was on the brink of a civil war. When Fort Sumter was attacked and captured, Hayes was enraged, seeing the nation's survival at stake. With Lucy's encouragement, he joined Ohio's 23d volunteer company as a major in 1861, leaving his post in the Cincinnati Solicitor's Office. Gallant in action,

A daguerreotype of Rutherford B. Hayes, taken in 1852, shortly before he married Lucy Webb.

RUTHERFORD B. HAYES DURING THE WAR.

The man who would leave the Battle Field to stump a State for Congress. while his Country is in danger. ought to be Scalped.

While serving with the Union Army in 1864, Hayes decided to run for the U.S. House of Representatives. He continued his army duties and declined to campaign, a choice that alarmed some of his Republican supporters. The engraving explains why Hayes did not campaign. He won the election, and did not take his seat until December 1865.

Hayes was wounded six times and rose to major general.

In 1865 he returned to Ohio politics and was elected to the House of Representatives. He consistently supported the stern Reconstruction measures of the radical wing of the Republican party, and despised the softer policies of Andrew Johnson. As a freshman legislator, Hayes had no claim to a major committee assignment. His most important work occurred as chairman of a joint House-Senate committee to create a structure—the future Library of Congress—to house the already sizeable accumulation of books scattered in places hither and yon. But he chafed under the slow congressional pace and the modesty of legislative achievements, and he yielded to Republican pressures that he run for governor of Ohio.

He was an astute strategist in defining his opposition and himself. Democrats were the party of slavery, rebellion, repression, and corruption. He presented himself as a sound money man—guardian of the gold standard and foe of those who would dilute it with less valuable currency. He urged "honest payment" of the national debt, only in gold and never in depreciated currency. He spoke of equal civil and political rights for all persons. Saving the Union, he cried, must make "the people one nation." Hayes, who expected defeat, was elected governor of Ohio by a margin of less than 3,000 votes.

Hayes quickly won national attention as a courageous governor who sought economy in government, upheld a civil service based on merit rather than political influence, and advocated an unpopular black suffrage amendment to the state constitution. He was reelected, and after completing his second term, he returned to Fremont and resumed his law practice. In 1875, pressed by Ohio Republicans, he ran and won a third term as governor. Hayes's proven vote-getting ability, assisted by his status as a war hero, prompted murmurings that he must run for president. He was appropriately demure, saying, "How weird, nobody is out of reach of that mania."

But Ohio newspapers continued the chant for a Hayes presidency. Early in 1876 the Ohio Republican convention unanimously declared Hayes their candidate for president. He continued to play the game of reluctant candidate but took pains behind the scenes to assure the Ohio delegation's unanimity for his candidacy when a delegate thought briefly of supporting James G. Blaine.

At the national convention in Cincinnati, after a push to nominate Grant for a third term quickly wilted, Blaine became the front-runner for the Republican presidential nomination. As Speaker of the House of Representatives, Blaine was a popular national figure. But he had weaknesses. He had made an enemy of the New York Republican leader, Roscoe Conkling, a man of enormous vanity, by describing Conkling's lapses into posturing as a "turkeygobbler strut." Blaine suffered from accusations that he was paid $64,000 by the Union Pacific Railroad for favors rendered while he was Speaker of the House. He denied the charge and declared that his accusers were suppressing evidence that would vindicate him.

Lesser candidates, who also had weaknesses, shifted their votes to Hayes. The race remained tight when Hayes won the nomination on the seventh ballot by only thirty-three votes. The vice presidential nominee was William A. Wheeler of New York. A slate that combined a Midwesterner and an Easterner honored the tradition of a geographically balanced ticket. As the convention closed, Hayes reported to his elder son Birchard, "My hand is sore with shaking hands."

The Democratic presidential nominee was Governor Samuel J. Tilden of New York. Thomas A. Hendricks of Indiana, a key swing state, was the vice presidential nominee. Hayes and Tilden both observed the custom that presidential nominees did not campaign publicly. Each issued the usual letter of acceptance of the nomination. Hayes's statement was notable for including a pledge not to seek a second term. Why he chose this self-inflicted constraint is unclear. Possibly he meant to reassure voters that he was no Grant, who competed for the 1876 nomination and a third term.

In his letter of acceptance, Hayes also condemned the spoils system, supported "sound money"—the gold standard—and pledged his best efforts toward "a

civil policy which will wipe out forever the distinction between North and South in our common country." His plea that a civil service merit system be established clinched the support of the reform Republicans.

Hayes's single major public appearance in the campaign was his trip to the Centennial Exhibition at Philadelphia in October 1876. The crowds that flocked to see him must have been somewhat disappointed. Hayes was one of the most ordinary

---

BIOGRAPHICAL FACTS

BIRTH: Delaware, Ohio, Oct. 4, 1822

ANCESTRY: English

FATHER: Rutherford Hayes; b. Brattleboro, Vt., Jan. 4, 1787; d. Delaware, Ohio, July 20, 1822

FATHER'S OCCUPATION: Store owner

MOTHER: Sophia Birchard Hayes; b. Wilmington, Vt., Apr. 15, 1792; d. Columbus, Ohio, Oct. 30, 1866

BROTHER: Lorenzo (1815–1825)

SISTERS: Sarah Sophia (1817–1821); Fanny Arabella (1820–1856)

MARRIAGE: Cincinnati, Ohio, Dec. 30, 1852

WIFE: Lucy Webb; b. Chillicothe, Ohio, Aug. 28, 1831; d. Fremont, Ohio, June 25, 1889

CHILDREN: Birchard Austin (1853–1926); Webb Cook (1856–1934); Rutherford Platt (1858–1927); Joseph (1861–1863); George Crook (1864–1866); Fanny (1867–1950); Scott (1871–1923); Manning (1873–1874)

RELIGIOUS AFFILIATION: None

EDUCATION: Kenyon College (B.A., 1842); Harvard Law School (LL.B., 1845)

OCCUPATION BEFORE PRESIDENCY: Lawyer

MILITARY SERVICE: Maj. in 23d Ohio Volunteers (1861); resigned as maj. gen. in June, 1865

PREPRESIDENTIAL OFFICES: Solicitor of Cincinnati; U.S. congressman; governor of Ohio

AGE AT INAUGURATION: 54

OCCUPATIONS AFTER PRESIDENCY: Philanthropist; president of the Slater Fund

DEATH: Fremont, Ohio, Jan. 17, 1893

PLACE OF BURIAL: Spiegel Grove State Park, Fremont, Ohio

---

looking men ever to run for president. He was short, rumpled in dress, and had a rat's-nest beard. The *New York Times* noted that he wore "a dreadfully shabby coat and a shockingly bad hat, all brushed up the wrong way."

On election night, Hayes went to bed believing that he had lost. Tilden had a substantial lead in the popular vote and seemed certain to win a majority of the electoral votes (the winner needed 185). But Republican despair diminished as speculation began among party leaders of possible combinations of states for a Hayes victory. Perhaps, it was thought, several Southern states with local Republican administrations could be saved. From Republican headquarters in the Fifth Avenue Hotel in New York City, telegrams went out to Republican leaders in South Carolina, Florida, and Louisiana, and also to Oregon, whose count had not yet been completed: "With your state sure for Hayes, he is elected. Hold your State." John C. Reid, a Republican zealot and editor of the *New York Times*, refused to concede the election to Tilden in his newspaper and declared the early results inconclusive.

The task ahead required the shifting of 19 electoral votes in South Carolina, Louisiana, and Florida to tip the election to Hayes. Thereupon his electoral vote total would be 185 and Tilden's 184. Several days would elapse before the election boards in each state officially reported the popular vote and linked it to the electoral vote. Hayes's managers concentrated on election boards controlled by Republicans and therefore could determine the outcome. The boards counted the popular votes and were empowered by law to disqualify fraudulent ballots. Leading Republicans and Democrats sped South to join the struggle. The preliminary count in the states underwent intense scrutiny. The popular votes, as they stood, were close. Hayes seemed to carry South Carolina by 600 to 1,000 votes and Florida by 43 votes if the Baker County election board disqualified the vote of two

precincts, where fraud was thought to be widespread. But if those votes were counted, Tilden would carry Florida by 94 votes.

Evidence abounded that fraud and intimidation were rampant against black voters in the disputed states, to the point of making it hard to determine who had won the election. Stuffed ballot boxes, repeaters, imported voters, ballots that Democrats printed with Republican symbols to trick illiterate voters—all were used. Hayes's campaign manager, William E. Chandler, accompanied by justice, Treasury, and post office officials, led the effort to insure that the Florida election board would include their state in Hayes's count. Louisiana required more flagrant Republican measures. There was little provable intimidation, and Tilden appeared to have carried the state by more than 1,300 votes. But undaunted Republicans rushed to Louisiana, led by two of Ohio's most expert politicians, Congressmen James A. Garfield and John Sherman, who oversaw the collection of "evidence of intimidation and violence." Their agile efforts eliminated enough votes for the Hayes forces to claim Louisiana. Hayes agreed with his surrogates that in a fair election he would have won 40 Southern electoral votes. "But, he cautioned, "we are not to allow our friends to defeat one outrage and fraud by another. There must be nothing crooked on our part."

On December 6, 1876, under existing law, the electors cast their ballots. But in the contested states, both Republican and Democratic electors balloted and sent two sets of electoral votes to Washington. On the basis of uncontested electoral votes, Tilden had 184 votes and Hayes 165. Twenty votes remained in dispute.

The Constitution specified the next steps. The electoral votes, it reads, shall be "directed to the President of the Senate"—the vice president—who "shall, in the presence of the Senate and the House of Representatives, open all the Certificates and the

Votes shall be counted." But the Constitution was distressingly silent on whether the presiding officer of the Senate or a combined House and Senate vote was to decide what to count when conflicting sets of ballots were sent to Washington. The vice president, Henry Wilson, had died, and the president of the Senate in 1876 was Thomas W. Ferry, a Michigan Republican. The Republican solution to the dilemma was to let Ferry decide. The Democrats urged a combined House-Senate vote, which would give them a comfortable majority. But as debate proceeded, significant numbers of Democrats and Republicans became disaffected, leaving matters even more uncertain. Murmurs were heard of resorting to the Supreme Court, or of establishing a special commission to rule on the issues.

Early in 1877 Congress began clearing a way out of the impasse by creating an "electoral commission" of Democrats and Republicans—seven from each party. David Davis, a Supreme Court justice and political independent, was expected to cast the deciding vote. But Davis escaped the onerous task by being elected to the Senate. He was replaced by a Republican Supreme Court justice, Joseph P. Bradley, who voted with his party and awarded the disputed states to Hayes in a series of 8 to 7 votes. The final electoral vote tally was 185 votes for Hayes and 184 for Tilden. The Hayeses were en route to Washington when they got the good news during a stop at Marysville, Pennsylvania. The next day Hayes called on President Grant. Both were jubilant.

On March 5, 1877, Hayes was inaugurated at the East Portico of the Capitol, with an estimated thirty thousand people watching. Hayes wore formal attire, and Lucy, the press reported, "wore a black hat, trimmed with white lace, and a scarf of lace about her neck. Beneath her coat, she was dressed in rich black silk, almost entirely unadorned." Hayes's address largely repeated his acceptance letter.

Civil service reform was high on his agenda. It

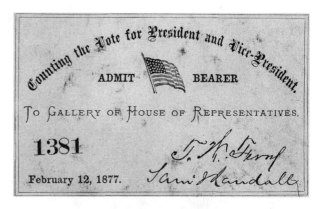

This ticket admitted one person to the House of Representatives' gallery to attend the debate on who had won the 1876 presidential election—Hayes or Tilden. Eventually Hayes was declared the winner.

must, he said, "be thorough, radical, and complete." The nation's currency must remain "sound." Greenbacks—the paper money issued in the Civil War and not backed by gold—were, according to Hayes, "one of the greatest obstacles to the return to prosperous times." With a bow to foreign policy, Hayes pledged "non-interference" in other nations' affairs.

Various auguries for the new presidency were not good. Many Americans believed he had robbed Tilden of the presidency. Some detractors, even in his own party, renamed him "Rutherfraud Hayes." On Capitol Hill the Democrats, then in control of the House of Representatives, approached the coming midterm elections of 1878 with good hopes of capturing the Senate. A crippling economic depression rolled on, inherited from the Grant administration.

But there were also several favorable elements in Hayes's situation. His early political home had been the Whig party, but as president he rejected the Whig ideal of a weak chief executive, obeisant to Congress and deferential to his cabinet. Emancipating himself from these Whig principles was an essential first step toward reversing the decline of the presidency under Johnson and Grant.

appointments "would have been to invite the intrigues and obstructive acts, personal animosities." But by ignoring powerful party leaders, Hayes risked igniting their hostility.

Hayes recruited a cabinet that had at least several strong, talented personalities. At their forefront was William M. Evarts as secretary of state, often described as the nation's foremost lawyer of the day. Carl Schurz, secretary of the interior, was a champion of civil service reform and ethical public administration. John Sherman, secretary of the Treasury, was highly informed about the economics and politics of public finance. The remaining cabinet secretaries were all able men, and the cabinet's membership proved exceptionally stable, with only several departures. Hayes made good use of his cabinet. When complex or critical issues arose, the cabinet would meet daily. Usually, though, it met on Tuesdays and Thursdays, from 12 to 2 P.M. All business, from minor departmental appointments and correspondence to major decisions, was discussed. Normally, harmony prevailed, although Hayes sometimes imposed his will on his advisers.

High on Hayes's agenda was the question of policies toward the South. The era of radical Republicanism, which treated the Confederate states as conquered provinces and imposed military rule, was over. Only two Republican governments, in South Carolina and Louisiana, remained with federal troops. Hayes was well aware that prospects for genuine black suffrage were shaky in the Southern states without the deployment of federal troops. He expected that the Democratic-controlled House of Representatives would not provide additional funds for the federal military presence, especially in a poor economy, and that public opinion, preoccupied with the depression, would not rally behind a hard-line policy. Hayes was also lured by prospects of support from Southern Whigs whose earlier ties with Northern Whigs might be restored if federal troops were

More problematic was Hayes's strategy in forming his cabinet. He shunned the common practice of offering cabinet appointments to competitors for the nomination, such as James G. Blaine. Presumably a lesser prize might soften any lingering disappointments and secure support from the rejected leaders. Hayes later explained his fear that granting such

President-elect Washington's triumphant entry to the temporary capital in New York was met with a huge welcome. He was ferried across the Hudson in a decorated barge powered by thirteen oarsmen, as depicted in L. M. Cooke's 1901 painting. "The decorations of the ships, the roar of cannons and the loud acclamations of the people . . . filled my mind with sensations as painful . . . as they were pleasing," Washington noted in his diary.

Jefferson's election in the 1800 presidential race was an inspiration for an unknown partisan who painted a commemorative banner on linen. The enthusiastic artist expressed his opinion on the election results by adding, "John Adams is no more."

The Whig opposition to President Van Buren tried to portray the Democratic incumbent in 1840 as a champagne-sipping dandy—and the Whig candidate as a man of humble origins whose tastes ran to hard cider, the drink of the common people. This campaign flyer, printed on cardboard, reflects the Whig strategy—avoid issues and stress personalities.

A BEAUTIFUL GOBLET OF WHITE-HOUSE CHAMPAGNE

AN UGLY MUG OF LOG-CABIN HARD CIDER

The 1840 presidential race was more about sloganeering than issues, and William Henry Harrison's Whig partisans insisted their hero was born in a log cabin, even though he had been born in a brick mansion in Virginia. Here are two representations of Harrison's log cabin, ca. 1840. Both include a second important symbol: the cider barrel close to the front door. In early America, cider barrels near ballot boxes were part of every presidential campaign.

An 1844 campaign flag portrays James K. Polk and his running mate, George M. Dallas, as candidates who favor the annexation of Texas, symbolized by the lone star outside the field of twenty-six state stars surrounding Polk's portrait. Democrats were appealing to voters who wanted the United States to expand its borders westward.

A multicolored 1848 campaign poster, designed for Whig parades and torchlight rallies, shows the party's nominee, General Zachary Taylor, mounted on a white charger and surrounded by the names of the popular general's Mexican War victories, with the words "Justice" and "Peace" printed above the emblazoned "Union."

A detail of a painting by artist George Caleb Bingham depicts a county election place in 1852. Voters stood in line as candidates begged for their support offering liberal quantities of hard liquor and cider as enticements.

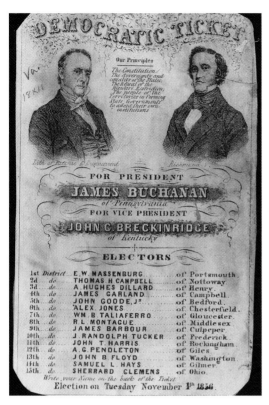

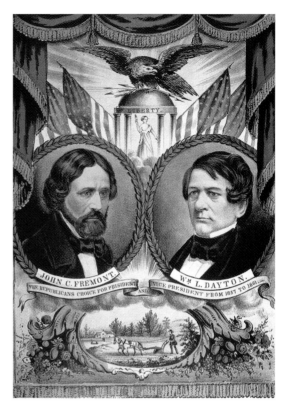

A Democratic ticket, available at the Virginia polls in 1856, lists the presidential and vice-presidential candidates, James Buchanan and John C. Breckinridge, and their fifteen supporters in the electoral college. Voting was a public exercise: Voters picked up a printed ticket, like this one, readily passed out by partisans, and placed it in the ballot box.

Nathaniel Currier created a poster to promote John C. Frémont and his running mate from New Jersey, William L. Dayton, in 1856. Frémont had been nominated for president by the newly formed Republican party, made up of former Whigs, disgusted Democrats, and other voters appalled by the Kansas-Nebraska Act.

This 1864 campaign item is a "ball-shot" game. Deliberately appealing to the military interests of wartime voters, President Lincoln's portrait is surrounded by various Union generals. Among those pictured are not only the most successful, such as General U. S. Grant, but also the controversial Benjamin F. Butler, who had been in charge of occupied New Orleans.

The widespread corruption during President Grant's regime presented an easy target for cartoonists. This *Puck* cartoon by Joseph Keppler captures the public's disgust with the corruption rampant in Grant's administration. Grant, suspended by the whiskey and Navy rings, in turn supports such dubious cabinet members and associates as George M. Robeson, William W. Belknap, and Orville E. Babcock.

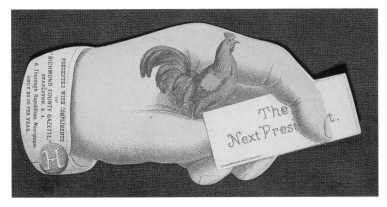

A hand and a cock became campaign symbols for the Democratic presidential nominee in 1880, General Winfield Scott Hancock. A corps commander and hero at Gettysburg, and a moderate administrator of Louisiana and Texas during Reconstruction, Hancock was expected to have wide voter appeal. He lost the election when James A. Garfield triumphed in New York.

A Republican banner proclaims the party's presidential ticket for 1876, Rutherford B. Hayes and his running mate William A. Wheeler of New York. A five-term congressman widely respected for upholding his principles, Wheeler opposed the infamous salary grab of 1873, which legislated a salary increase for members of Congress, and refused to accept the disputed pay raise that followed.

Republican bosses tried to control the presidential nomination in 1880, as illustrated by J. A. Wales for *Puck*. James G. Blaine, the powerful senator from Maine, wanted the nomination. His longtime enemy and rival boss, Roscoe Conkling of New York, blocked his nomination. James A. Garfield, the eventual nominee, was independent of both Blaine and Conkling.

In the election of 1888, the Republican party, eager to oust the incumbent Democratic president, Grover Cleveland, put forward a large number of candidates. Here, in a cartoon from *Puck*, their sponsors vie to pin their names to the donkey as the eventual nominee. The front-runner, an ailing James G. Blaine, withdrew from the race and declared that "the one man remaining who in my judgment can make the best run is Benjamin Harrison." Nonetheless, the field remained crowded, and on the national convention's first ballot Harrison ran fifth among the candidates. Widely seen as "everybody's second choice," Harrison won most of New York's huge bloc of 72 votes when Chauncey M. Depew dropped out. Harrison finally won the nomination on the eighth ballot.

In Joseph Klir's 1893 illustration, "The Lost Bet," President Cleveland pulls a cart carrying Vice President Adlai Stevenson. Klir conveys the enthusiasm Americans had for Cleveland. The banner aloft has portraits of Cleveland, Stevenson, and the Democratic governor of Illinois, John Peter Altgeld.

Campaign trinkets were widely popular in the early 1900s. The pin made in the shape of Theodore Roosevelt's trademark pince-nez, with images of himself and his running mate, Charles W. Fairbanks, is from Roosevelt's 1904 reelection bid. The button on the right shows a winning hand of cards with the injunction "Stand Pat!"—stick with his tried-and-true presidency. The other button pictures TR on horseback in uniform, the words "San Juan" refer to his heroic leadership of the Rough Riders in taking San Juan Hill in Cuba during the Spanish-American War.

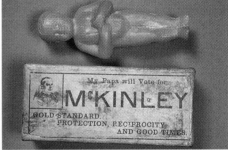

From 1896, a "soap baby" inside a box with William McKinley's campaign slogans on the cover. His opponents used the same device with their slogans on the cover. This reminded many people of a baby in a coffin, and soap babies were never used again in election campaigns.

Gold as the backing of money—which William McKinley supported and William Jennings Bryan was against—was the biggest issue in the 1896 campaign. In his speech to the Democratic National Convention Bryan declared, "You shall not press down upon the brow of labor this crown of thorns. You shall not crucify mankind upon a cross of gold." In the cartoon Bryan brandishes both a crown and a cross.

Theodore Roosevelt was a tough act to follow in the White House. Many people came to regard his successor, William Howard Taft, as not up to the job. Joseph Keppler's 1910 cartoon for *Puck*, "Good Gracious! I Must Have Been Dozing!" depicts Taft as an old woman tangled up in balls of knitting yarn while an indignant Roosevelt looks on. All those images spoke to the troubles that impelled Roosevelt to split the Republican party by running against Taft in 1912.

Theodore Roosevelt loved all kinds of combat, especially in politics. A 1912 photograph shows him grinning after he was nominated again for president, this time by his new Progressive or "Bull Moose" party.

AMERICA FIRST

Wilson, That's All!

A poster from Woodrow Wilson's reelection campaign in 1916. The slogan "America First" refers to his policies toward World War I that spawned the campaign cry, "He Kept Us Out of War!" The caption, "Wilson, That's All!" was taken from advertisements of a popular brand of whiskey that used the same slogan.

Eugene V. Debs ran for president on the Socialist ticket in 1920 while serving a sentence in a federal penitentiary for violating World War I laws that limited free speech. A campaign button shows Debs in his prison uniform and prominently lists his convict number.

In 1928 the Hoover campaign used an asbestos pot holder to urge voters to safeguard their hands just as the Republican candidate would watch over their homes. Hoover's appeal as an advocate of what would later be called "family values" proved effective against Al Smith and the Democrats. No one knew then of the environmental dangers of asbestos.

The 1920 campaign was one of the last times when a presidential candidate was formally "notified" of his nomination several weeks after the convention. This medal was given to members of the committee that journeyed to Warren G. Harding's home in Marion, Ohio, to inform him of his nomination by the Republican party.

The Democrats in 1932 made ending Prohibition an important part of their platform as depicted in a campaign license plate. Legalizing the sale of beer was seen as a key step in the return of legal alcohol.

The issue of a third term for FDR was important in his 1940 contest against Wendell L. Willkie. Republicans sought to capitalize on this subject with Democrats for Willkie clubs and posters like this one expressing disdain for Roosevelt's break with tradition of the president serving only two terms.

The 1948 election pitted Harry S. Truman, the folksy president from Missouri (renowned for his piano playing), against the urbane, crime-fighting Governor Thomas E. Dewey of New York. The contrast provided cartoonists with ample inspiration. Truman's down-home style proved more appealing to the voters than did Dewey's stuffiness. Dewey was the last presidential candidate to sport a moustache.

A brown derby became identified with Al Smith, the governor of New York, who came from Manhattan's Lower East Side. Smith's Catholicism was a major political obstacle for rural Protestant voters in the South and West. Smith's running mate, Joseph T. Robinson of Arkansas, was on the ticket to reassure those Democrats.

During the 1952 campaign, a tobacco company put out "Stevenson for President" cigarettes. While such a campaigning device would be unthinkable today when few Democrats would want to be associated with the tobacco industry, in the 1950s when many more adults smoked, it was seen as a clever marketing tactic. It didn't help Adlai Stevenson win, however.

Adlai Stevenson was a divorced man, and the Republicans emphasized his marital status with a button that showed the wives of their two candidates, Pat Nixon and Mamie Eisenhower. The first divorced president would be Ronald Reagan, nearly three decades later.

"I Like Ike" became a catchy slogan in 1952, especially because it reflected the Republican candidate's popularity as a hero of World War II. Enthusiastic and large crowds consistently turned out to see Eisenhower, and his election was never really in doubt.

In the race for the 1960 Democratic nomination, John F. Kennedy took some strong criticism from former President Harry S. Truman for his youth and inexperience as a candidate. Once Kennedy was the nominee, Truman supported him strongly, but anti-Kennedy cartoonists pointed out the contrast between Truman's charges and his later backing of Kennedy.

In his 1964 campaign, Lyndon B. Johnson emphasized his links with his martyred predecessor. Johnson's first speech to Congress after John F. Kennedy's death took as its theme "Let Us Continue," as depicted on this button.

The Democratic ticket in 1960, John F. Kennedy and Lyndon B. Johnson, was a winning one, but their public smiles in this photograph conceal tensions that lay beneath the surface. Johnson and Robert F. Kennedy, the candidate's brother (on the right in the background) cordially detested each other.

Hubert Humphrey, the Democratic candidate in 1968, was never at a loss for words. The joke was that he spoke a hundred words a minute, with gusts up to two hundred. Here he addresses a Democratic rally with typical earnestness.

Richard Nixon's political comeback in 1968 led all the way to the White House. His campaign attracted large, enthusiastic crowds. Here his wife, Pat, also waves to the throng.

Jimmy Carter's smile and background as a peanut farmer were both selling points in 1976, as the toothy Carter mask from that election attests. His image fared less well when he ran for reelection against Ronald Reagan.

In 1984 Jesse Jackson became the first serious African-American candidate for the presidency. His Rainbow Coalition, encompassing all shades of the political spectrum, did not prove to be strong enough to gain the Democratic nomination against former Vice President Walter Mondale. In his uphill race with Ronald Reagan in 1984, Mondale tried a daring strategy of selecting Geraldine Ferraro as the first female nominee of a major party.

The Democratic team of President Bill Clinton and Vice President Albert Gore did not face much of a challenge from Bob Dole and Jack Kemp, the Republican nominees, in the 1996 election. The third-party challenge of Ross Perot also fizzled. Fund-raising scandals, however, held down the margin of the Clinton-Gore victory.

Running on his own after eight years as Ronald Reagan's vice president, George Bush was happy to be identified with some of the heroic figures of the Republican past—Abraham Lincoln, Theodore Roosevelt, Dwight D. Eisenhower, and Ronald Reagan.

The race for the White House in 2000 proved to be exciting in its early stages. Vice President Albert Gore and former Senator Bill Bradley vied for the Democratic nomination, while Republicans Governor George W. Bush of Texas and Arizona Senator John McCain competed for their party's bid. By mid-March, Gore and Bush had locked up the nomination.

removed from South Carolina and Louisiana. (The Whigs, a conservative party of the 1800s, split into factions over the issue of slavery, had disappeared by 1860, when Southern Whigs returned to the Democratic party and Northern Whigs embraced the Republicans.) The president's moderate policies, such as the withdrawal of federal troops, outraged former abolitionists who decried them as a faint-hearted compromise. Nonetheless, numerous Northern Republicans supported Hayes.

The midterm elections of 1878, which swept Democrats into control of both congressional houses, battered Hayes's hopes that the South would respect blacks' civil rights. A congressman from South Carolina, whose opinion Hayes valued, reported that "whites are resorting to intimidation and violence to prevent colored people from organizing for the elections."

After the elections, Hayes declared that "violence of the most atrocious character had prevented Negroes from voting." In further public statements he urged that those who won dubious elections with substantial violence should not be seated in Congress. Basic to Hayes's thinking about the future for African-Americans was his belief in the indispensability of education. Democracy could be served only if blacks had adequate access to education so that they could use effectively their recently won right to vote.

Hayes not only provided substantial policy initiatives as a restoration of presidential prestige and power; he also reinvigorated the president's constitutional and legal powers. He took a giant step in this direction by his use of the veto. A confrontation began when the Democratic-controlled House of Representatives, looking ahead to the coming elections of 1880, moved to repeal federal election laws, known as the Force or Enforcement Acts, adopted during the Reconstruction period. The Acts authorized the use of federal troops to keep peace at the polls and the federal courts to appoint supervisors of federal elections who would halt or prevent election abuses. Legislation providing for repeal was incorporated as a rider in a key appropriations bill.

Democratic strategists foresaw that if the laws could be terminated, with elections thereby passed into local control, then by dexterous manipulation in the South and in Northern boss-run cities, their party could defeat the Republicans. Hayes vetoed the legislation, declaring the right of every citizen to have his ballot counted honestly. He attacked the legislation as "radical, dangerous, and unconstitutional." He explained that if the measure prevailed, the House could force the Senate and the president to accept any rider attached to an appropriations bill. Such action, Hayes contended, would give the House despotic power, shattering the balance between the branches.

The Senate concurred with the House, but an attempted override of the veto failed. Congress then passed a law barring the use of federal troops to oversee elections. Again, Hayes vetoed, asserting that the legislation created an unconstitutional premise of state supremacy over federal authority. And again, the president's veto prevailed. Presidential power, diminished in the Johnson and Grant eras, was effectively defended with the veto.

But Hayes also had a positive agenda. A principal policy initiative of the Hayes administration was civil service reform, promised in the inaugural address and promoted by upper-class intellectuals such as George William Curtis. Curtis headed the short-lived Civil Service Commission in the Grant administration. The commission died when Grant rejected the reforms Curtis proposed and Congress withheld appropriations. During the Hayes administration, reformers contended that appointees under the spoils system were more likely to become drones and time-servers. The public was left to suffer from the bumblings of an incompetent bureaucracy. Defenders of the spoils system claimed that it better assured a bureaucracy loyal and responsive to the chief executive. Spoils rewarded party workers, making it a kind of glue that held a party together. The spoils system was also a principal source of party financing for elections, through assessments of workers' pay, usually 2 to 7 percent of their annual salaries.

Although Carl Schurz was the only cabinet member who advocated civil service reform, Hayes issued an executive order in 1877 instructing federal employees not "to take part in the management of political organizations, caucuses, contributions, or election campaigns." Hayes's order prohibited political assessments of federal officeholders. Reformers were jubilant and many politicians disgruntled.

A prime target of reformers were the customshouses in the nation's principal ports. A study by a special investigating commission, the Jay Commission, found gross overstaffing in the New York Customs House, and recommended that 20 percent of its twelve hundred employees be let go. The commission cited abuses such as employees reporting for work an hour late and taking long lunch breaks. Shoddy bookkeeping, the commission said, deprived the government of one-fourth of its rightful revenues.

Despite the severity of the commission report, the Hayes administration was initially conciliatory, preferring not to antagonize the powerful New York political machine. The Republican boss Roscoe Conkling and the New York Customs House chief administrator, Chester Arthur—who would soon become president of the United States—were angry and defiant. Hayes soon learned from his own informants that the staff cuts were proceeding with "outrageous partiality and knavery." Even worse, the second-in-command at the New York Customs House, a naval officer, Alonzo B. Cornell, refused to resign from his post on the Republican national committee, a flagrant violation of the president's order prohibiting political activity by federal employees. An angry Hayes cracked down by announcing that Arthur and Cornell would be replaced. Undeterred by Conkling's

cries of outrage, Hayes installed new leadership at the New York Customs House. Conkling became the president's lifelong enemy. In defeating Senator Conkling, Hayes also overrode a sacred political tradition: the practice of senatorial courtesy. Its underlying idea is that senators are entitled to review federal appointments in their states; if these senators object, the president will extend the "courtesy" of dropping the nomination. The practice can sharply curtail presidential authority, but presidents seldom resist it. Hayes is one who did.

Hayes took another major step toward reviving the presidency by handling with a sufficient degree of success a domestic mounting calamity, novel in his office's experience. In July 1877, a crisis arose in the dispute between railroad workers and managers. As the economic depression lingered on the railroads cut wages by 18 percent but increased capital stock and bonded indebtedness by 16 percent. To reduce operating costs, railroad managers pooled westbound freight in New York and laid off workers they no longer needed. Wage cuts continued, and strikebreakers were brought in to keep the railroads running. Given the essentiality of railroads to the economy, a national emergency seemed in the offing. Both management and workers could muster powerful economic arguments and evidence for their cause, while the strikes spread. In the railroad town of Martinsburg, West Virginia, where stalled freight cars were accumulating, violence erupted, and more was threatened. An alarmed governor requested that the president send federal troops to disperse the strikers and avoid further violence.

Hayes set his course, influenced by several strands of feelings and judgment. He believed that the strikes should be dealt with on a state level. Therefore, governors and mayors who found the crisis on their doorsteps held the primary responsibility of resolving it. He also believed that strikers had no right to keep nonstrikers from working. As a lawyer he advocated law and negotiation as the best means of resolving disputes, rather than threats and violence. He was opposed to strike leaders, usually outsiders, who incited local workers to riot. But Hayes also sympathized with individual workers, desperate in the economic depression, and he distrusted the magnates often found among railroad owners and executives. He also believed that vast wealth, barely restrained by regulation and taxation, constituted a threat to good government and liberty. In short, his villains were strike agitators and ruthless railroad moguls.

Federal troops, if dispatched, Hayes determined, would have the primary task of protecting federal property, such as arsenals and sub-Treasury buildings, and would by their presence encourage public peace. Troops could prevent violence, but they were not to operate the railroads. The president did not intervene to break the strikers' cause.

Typically, as the strike spread and violence seemed imminent, federal troops were used in establishing a calm atmosphere. Hayes's measured, nonviolent response contrasted with the exaggerated stories of local conflict reported by the press. The most decisive interveners were antilabor federal judges who ruled that the strikers had disregarded court rulings in cases involving bankrupt railroads and in the functioning of court-appointed receivers. The Hayes administration accepted the courts' reasoning. The public approved of his moderate course, the economy improved, railroad leaders halted their heavy-handedness, and strikers returned to work.

Hayes then faced another crisis. The economic depression, inherited from the Grant administration, prompted business and financial leaders to demand a "sound money system" based on the gold standard; this, they hoped, would help forestall inflation generated by a watered-down currency. Critics of the money system, who abounded in the West and South, contended that there was too little currency in circulation, a circumstance that spurred higher interest rates, to the disadvantage of farmers who borrowed for the next year's crops or acquired more acreage. Simultaneously, the ongoing depression lowered prices for farm products.

Hayes firmly supported the gold standard, or "hard money," as it was called. He opposed inflation in any form, even as the depression continued. Secretary of the Treasury John Sherman built up the Treasury's gold reserve to meet the demand to reduce the national debt. While not opposed to coining silver, whose production was increasing, Hayes meant to keep silver from driving gold from circulation by

---

CARL SCHURZ

In 1848 Carl Schurz was a cloak-and-dagger agent during a democratic uprising in his native Germany; thirteen years later he was fighting against a rebellion to destroy the union of his adopted country, the United States. Twenty-three years old when he emigrated in 1852, Schurz settled in Wisconsin, where he became a prominent opponent of slavery and a supporter of Lincoln. After serving briefly as minister to Spain, he returned in 1862 to urge immediate emancipation; in June he was appointed a Union general. His military career was marred by wrangles with field superiors and by unsupported charges that his German-American troops were cowardly under fire. Schurz made a postwar survey of the South and held a number of newspaper jobs before his election to the Senate in 1868. A civil service reformer, he was bitterly attacked by the pro-Grant press. Schurz helped to found the Liberal Republican party in the early seventies, but in 1876 he supported Hayes, who made him secretary of the interior. Schurz's dealings with the Indians were commendably fair; his establishment of an interdepartmental merit system for promotion was a landmark of reform. After 1881 he again turned to editorial writing and was a strong anti-imperialist. He wrote a biography of Henry Clay and his own *Reminiscences*.

In a cover for *Puck* by Joseph Keppler, President Hayes vetoes the anti-Chinese bill, which prohibited further Chinese laborers from entering the country; in the background, labor leader Dennis Kearney threatens San Francisco's secession from the United States. The prolonged depression of the 1870s inflamed white workers' resentment of Chinese workers in to the United States.

maintaining a ratio between gold and silver that reflected their commercial value.

But Congress passed the Bland-Allison Act, limiting silver's coinage to $2–$4 million a month and calling for the creation of a supportive international bimetallic convention. Hayes vetoed the act, contending that it impaired contractual obligations—for example, paying off government bonds with money that was cheaper, or worthless, than when the bonds were purchased—and injured the public credit. Congress overrode the veto. Hayes minimized the law's impact by coining only $2 million, the statute's minimum requirement, and he kept silver dollars equal in value to gold dollars. Fortunately, the economy began to rally again near the end of his administration. His policies restored financial confidence, and business improved. Inventors and commercial enterprises became more confident, capital expanded, industries hummed, and foreign trade rose.

But problems were stirring in international affairs. The French entrepreneur, Ferdinand-Marie de Lesseps, began preparing to build a canal in Central America. President Hayes believed the United States had a special interest in any project to connect the Caribbean Sea with the Pacific Ocean. He quickly opposed de Lesseps's venture as a French imperialist threat to the Western Hemisphere.

De Lesseps, defying Hayes, organized a syndicate to build a canal in possible locations in Panama, Mexico, and Nicaragua. In a message to Congress, Hayes declared that a canal anywhere in Central America must be under the protective auspices of the United States. In 1880 Hayes dispatched two naval vessels to the Caribbean and requested congressional support for establishing coaling stations in the area. Congress did nothing, and Hayes did not press his request. The meagerness of American arms undercut presidential assertion in international affairs. Congress authorized an army of 30,000 men but financed one of 25,000. The Navy was small and grossly outdated. Later presidents would also be troubled by the canal problem, until Theodore Roosevelt led the United States into building its own canal.

Hayes fared poorly in his relations with China, which became tense over the question of the immigration of Chinese workers and their families to California. Their numbers had sharply increased in the earlier years of the Gold Rush and surged again when Chinese immigrants contributed inestimably to the construction of railroads, factories, and homes. But in the depression of the 1870s, with rising unemployment, white workers became hostile to Chinese workers. In 1876 both the Democratic and Republican parties adopted anti-Chinese planks in their platforms, notwithstanding the Burlingame Treaty of 1868 which guaranteed unrestricted immigration of the Chinese to the United States. When Congress enacted legislation restricting Chinese immigration and repealing provisions of the Burlingame Treaty, Hayes vetoed it. Supported by civil service reformer George William Curtis, and by clergy led by Henry Ward Beecher, the veto prevailed. Although Hayes sympathized with white workers in California, he wrote that he must "stand for the sacred observance of treaties." The Hayes administration subsequently negotiated an agreement with China to restrict immigration to the United States.

Hayes's grappling with affairs of state were lightened by the happy, informal spirit of life in the White House. Lucy led Sunday night "sings" in the upstairs library, with Secretary of the Interior Carl Schurz at the piano. Family entertainment took place in the Red Room. Visitors approached the president in a steady flow: Clara Barton with plans for America to take part in a proposed International Red Cross; Marie Salika, "the celebrated colored prima donna"; and Thomas Edison with his newly invented phonograph, then delighting the nation. Clergy were pleased when the Hayeses declined to serve alcoholic beverages at state functions. Grumbling was inevitable, as was ridicule of "Lemonade Lucy," but the quality of food and service and sprightly conversation did not diminish.

Hayes was equally consistent in observing his pledge to serve only one term as president. Among the field of Republican aspirants to be his successor, he favored James A. Garfield. After the presidential term ended, the Hayeses returned to their comfortable, sylvan home at Spiegel Grove, Ohio. Hayes pursued his real estate interests and extensive correspondence. True to his faith in education as a solvent for social issues, he became a diligent trustee of the Peabody Fund, which helped educate blacks and whites in the South, and he served as the first president of the Slater Fund to promote the education of African-Americans.

Lucy, who wholeheartedly supported the former president in his reform and philanthropic activities, suffered a stroke and died in June 1889. On January 8, 1893, after visiting Lucy's grave, he wrote in his diary: "My feeling was one of longing to be quietly resting in a grave by her side." Nine days later, he joined her.

In rating the presidents, Hayes's place is securely established among those who served well. He restored the presidency to a firm footing after the troubled tenures of Johnson and Grant. He guided the nation through one of its worst economic depressions, and, after the failures of the initial Reconstruction efforts, he advanced North-South reconciliation. He acquitted himself well of the presidency's first serious encounter with labor-management conflict in the railroad strike. Hayes profited from his unflagging self-confidence in facing the adversities of public affairs. Moderation was his guiding principle. Bold initiatives were not for him or his time. As he wrote in his diary, "We are in a period when old questions are settled, and the new are not yet brought forward."

—*Louis W. Koenig*

JAMES ABRAM GARFIELD

THE PREACHER

James Abram Garfield is one of the few American presidents who genuinely fulfill the log cabin myth that graces the office. He rose from humble beginnings to the nation's highest post, performing hard physical labor along the way. Lincoln the rail-splitter and Garfield the canal boy are the best examples of reality coinciding with the mythic ideal. Garfield is also remarkable for the brevity of his tenure: at less than six months, it is the second shortest in U.S. history.

Unlike Rutherford Hayes, who struggled with an almost endless economic depression, Garfield, on becoming president in 1881, was favored with a booming economy. The Industrial Revolution was in full flower; the factory system was spreading rapidly, employing masses of workers, skilled and unskilled. Politics provided popular entertainment in an age without movies, the automobile, or professional sports. Picnics, bonfires, and torchlight parades delighted people and lifted their spirits. Great crowds sat through lengthy speeches on complex problems like the currency, the tariff, and civil service reform. Voters flocked to the polls.

The man who reached the presidency in these politically-aware times, James A. Garfield, was born on November 19, 1831, in a farm hut near Orange, Ohio, in the heart of the Western Reserve. When James was two years old, his father battled a nearby forest fire. In an exhausting struggle, he dug ditches and helped to extinguish the fire, then struggled home where he fell ill and died.

James's parents, Abram and Eliza Ballou, were from New England. They migrated to Otsego County in western New York, and eventually moved to Cuyahoga County, Ohio, where Abram farmed. Life was hard, and it was even harder after Abram died. A courageous woman, Eliza carried on the farm chores, including cutting wood and plowing the fields. Sens-

ing that James was gifted, Eliza encouraged him to pursue an education. At a nearby district school he displayed a keen mind and fertile memory. Later in life he said he had always felt a "hunger and thirst for knowledge." Before entering college James found work on an Ohio canal vessel, where his chief responsibility was to drive a team of horses along the canal's towpath. He fell into the water repeatedly, he recalled, and made "miraculous escapes from drowning."

Eliza also steered James toward religion. At eighteen he was baptized into the Disciples of Christ, a Protestant evangelical church. Previously indifferent to religion, James attended the Disciples of Christ's new Western Reserve Eclectic Institute, which later became Hiram College, in Hiram, Ohio. He came to see himself as an instrument "of God's destiny." He completed his studies at Williams College in Williamstown, Massachusetts, entering as a junior in 1854. After graduating, Garfield moved to West Troy (now Watervliet), New York, where he taught penmanship, then a skill in high demand. His future running mate, Chester Arthur, was also on the faculty of the district school.

Garfield's interest in teaching led to his return to Hiram College as a professor of ancient languages, and he became the college's president before he was thirty years old. He extended his association with the Disciples of Christ by becoming an ordained minister. As a circuit preacher, he traveled throughout Ohio during the summer months, delivering sermons. While advancing his career, Garfield married Lucretia Rudolph, whom he had known since childhood. Their marriage was graced by seven children.

Garfield's career of public service began with his election to the Ohio senate in 1859. His candidacy seemed a natural consequence of his rising popularity as a debater. But his immediate drive to a leadership position in the state senate was halted by the onset of

Although Garfield is best known for the brevity of his presidential tenure, he had a substantial earlier public career, serving nine terms in the House of Representatives. This photograph was taken sometime between 1870 and 1881.

the Civil War in 1861. He resigned from his seat to recruit the 42d Ohio Volunteer Infantry, and was commissioned the regiment's colonel. Garfield served for two years in the Army of the Cumberland. The high point of his service was the battle of Chickamauga, which led to his promotion to major general.

Despite his military success, he was eager to resign his commission and run for Congress. He feared that as Union generals sought office at the war's end, he might fade into obscurity. His efforts were rewarded by election to the House of Representatives by Ohio's solidly Republican Nineteenth District. Just thirty-two years old when he took his seat in the House, he served there for seventeen years until his nomination for president in 1880.

In his political beliefs and policy views, Garfield offered impeccable conservative credentials. He opposed labor unions and agitators for the eight-hour workday as an undue interference with the rights of workers to negotiate the terms of their employment. In 1874 he favored property qualifications for voters and strongly opposed woman's suffrage as "atheistic, and destructive of marriage and family."

Upon entering the House of Representatives, Garfield was immediately placed on the Committee on Military Affairs; later he joined the committees on Appropriations and on Ways and Means. He quickly orated his way to prominence in the House, advocating stern Reconstruction and conservative financial policies.

After nine terms of oratorical prowess in the House of Representatives, Garfield faced the question of what he would do next as a successful career politician. Three possible roles beckoned: senator, Speaker of the House, or president of the United States. Of the three, friends reckoned, he would prefer to become Speaker, which, with its central congressional function, seemed the most powerful office.

However, election to the Senate was more viable. Senators at this time were chosen by state legislatures. With his lengthy history of party service and flawless record of winning elections, Garfield was elected to the Senate by Ohio's grateful Republican state legislature. By a twist of fate, he never took his Senate seat; instead he became president of the United States.

In 1880, with the presidential election approaching, two main Republican factions were fighting each other in many states: the Stalwarts and the Half-Breeds. Despite the often ferocious warfare between them, their differences were not stark or

---

BIOGRAPHICAL FACTS

BIRTH: Orange, Ohio, Nov. 19, 1831

ANCESTRY: English and French

FATHER: Abram Garfield; b. Worcester, N.Y., 1799; d. Orange, Ohio, 1833

FATHER'S OCCUPATION: Farmer

MOTHER: Eliza Ballou Garfield; b. Richmond, N.H., 1801; d. Mentor, Ohio, 1888

BROTHERS: Thomas (1822–1881); James Ballou (1826–1829)

SISTERS: Mehitabel (1821–1909); Mary (1824–1884)

MARRIAGE: Hiram, Ohio, Nov. 11, 1858

WIFE: Lucretia Rudolph; b. Hiram, Ohio, Apr. 19, 1832; d. Pasadena, Calif., Mar. 14, 1918

CHILDREN: Eliza Arabella (1860–1863); Harry Augustus (1863–1942); James Rudolph (1865–1950); Mary (1867–1947); Irvin McDowell (1870–1951); Abram (1872–1958); Edward (1874–1876)

RELIGIOUS AFFILIATION: Disciples of Christ

EDUCATION: Attended Western Reserve Eclectic Institute (Hiram College); Williams College (1856)

OCCUPATIONS BEFORE PRESIDENCY: Schoolteacher; college professor; preacher; canal worker; soldier; president of Hiram College

MILITARY SERVICE: Lt. col. of 42d Ohio Volunteers (1861); brig. gen. of Volunteers (1862); maj. gen. of Volunteers (1863)

PREPRESIDENTIAL OFFICES: Member of Ohio Senate; U.S. congressman; chairman of House Committee on Appropriations; minority leader in U.S. House of Representatives

AGE AT INAUGURATION: 49

DEATH: Elberon, N.J., Sept. 19, 1881

PLACE OF BURIAL: Lake View Cemetery, Cleveland, Ohio

neatly definable. The Stalwarts presented themselves as conservative, and the Half-Breeds, as moderates. The two groups clashed over personal differences and the distribution of government jobs rather than over domestic and foreign policies. Garfield stood between the two factions and kept some of the confidence of both. As the election of 1880 neared, the Stalwarts, led by Senator Roscoe Conkling of New York, promoted the nomination of the former two-term president and foremost national hero, Ulysses S. Grant. The Half-Breeds championed the candidacy of their leader, Senator James G. Blaine.

The boss of most consequence to Garfield both before and after the election was Roscoe Conkling. Tall, vain, imperious, given to dandy-like dress, Conkling was, in Garfield's words, "a great man, inspired more by his hates than his loves." Conkling's candidate, Grant, had just returned from a triumphal world tour. Grant's most powerful competitor for the nomination at this point was Blaine, who brimmed with charm and ambition. Blaine vigorously sought the presidency in 1876, but in 1880 a Stalwarts–Half-Breed standoff opened the way for Garfield as a compromise candidate. Blaine began to move for the nomination again. "When I want something," he once said, "I want it dearly."

John Sherman also entered the race. A former secretary of the treasury in the Hayes administration and a senator from Ohio, Sherman had meager oratorical talents; instead, he excelled at political maneuvering and in political judgment. He was held in high esteem by President Hayes and other Republican politicians.

Sherman's manager and principal spokesman at the nominating convention in Chicago was James Garfield. The assignment gave Garfield a valuable opportunity for self-advertisement. Best of all was his address to the convention. It was vintage Garfield. After placing Sherman in nomination, he did not elaborate on his candidate's virtues but instead launched into an eloquent appeal for party unity. Time and

A photograph taken ca. 1864 of General James A. Garfield (seated, center) and his staff. Garfield studied accounts of historic battles, especially the tactics of Napoleon and Wellington. He plotted his battle strategy by using wooden blocks for men.

again, the audience yelled and stomped their approval. Conkling snidely congratulated Garfield on being "Ohio's real candidate and dark horse."

The convention's first ballot for the nomination disclosed the deep split in the Republican party. Grant led with 304 votes, Blaine followed with 284, and Sherman trailed with 93. This pattern persisted on a number of ballots. Tensions soared. Several delegates urged Garfield to offer himself as a compromise candidate. He refused, restating his commitment to remain loyal to Sherman.

On ballot after ballot, the impasse continued. Finally a break came when Wisconsin threw 16 votes to Garfield. After a moment of stunned silence, great cheers swelled across the floor. On the thirty-fifth ballot, the Indiana delegates, led by Benjamin Harrison, a future president, committed 27 votes to Garfield. On the thirty-sixth ballot, the dam broke: Connecticut, Illinois, Iowa, and Maine switched to Garfield,

An 1880 campaign poster features "Farmer Garfield" clearing his way to the White House through weeds and snakes of fraud and corruption. Garfield prevails by wielding his scythe of "Honesty, ability, and patriotism."

and with further switches, he soon clinched the nomination. Then Conkling sprang up and moved to make the nomination unanimous. While the convention carried on a roll call of states, Garfield sat somber and pale as ten thousand voices sang "Rally Round the Flag."

The vice presidential nominee was Chester Alan Arthur, whom President Hayes had ousted for his inadequate performance as collector of customs at the port of New York. Arthur was said to be crushed by the nomination, believing it to be an act of sympathy. Another interpretation suggested that the naming of Arthur "was a sop thrown to Conkling." Clearly, New York had to be courted—the election was unlikely to be won without New York's 35 electoral votes.

The Republican platform of 1880 was mostly similar to the party platform of 1876. It advocated a tariff policy that would "discriminate as favoring American labor." It spoke approvingly of veterans' pensions and federal improvements. It favored limits to Chinese immigration and further land grants awarded to railroads and corporations. The platform straddled the important issues of civil service reform—whether some jobs should be filled based on the merit of the candidate rather than through the existing system of patronage and spoils.

The Democratic nominee was General Winfield Scott Hancock of Pennsylvania, a corps commander at the battle of Gettysburg. The Democrats hoped that Hancock's distinguished military background would draw strong support from Union veterans and that, as a moderate administrator of Louisiana and Texas in the Reconstruction years, he might appeal to Southerners.

In the campaign's early stages, Garfield followed the usual decorum of presidential nominees and remained at his home in Mentor, Ohio, twenty miles northeast of Cleveland. He made brief speeches and issued a bland letter accepting the nomination. The purpose of the letter was primarily to keep peace in the Republican party. He initiated a letter-writing campaign designed to enhance the confidence of party conservatives and various Stalwart and Half-Breed leaders.

Garfield's efforts did not calm top party leaders like Blaine and Conkling, whose pessimism persisted. In perhaps the most important move of his campaign, Garfield decided to depart from his Ohio home and journey to New York to meet with leaders of all his party's factions at the Fifth Avenue Hotel, the Republican headquarters. Blaine, a Half-Breed leader, was there, but Conkling was not.

Garfield needed Conkling's support in order to win New York, and that support carried a high political price tag. The New Yorkers confronted Garfield with the demand that he make Levi P. Morton secretary of the treasury, with the prospect that Morton's department, with its numerous revenue collectors, would be a rich source of patronage for Conkling's New York and fellow Stalwarts. The appointment and its implications would distress the rival Half-Breeds beyond measure. Morton, a wealthy, highly influential New York banker and financier who had already collected large sums for the Garfield campaign, met privately with Garfield during his New York visit. Conkling would be pleased and inspired with Morton at the Treasury. The nature of the agreement—if any—reached in New York remains in dispute. The "Treaty of Fifth Avenue," as it became known, was strictly a verbal arrangement. Conkling approved the meeting's outcome and later visited Garfield in Ohio, and campaigned in New York for his election.

Garfield's response to the Fifth Avenue Hotel event was that, while he shared Morton's views on "sound money"—the gold standard—financial power was already heavily concentrated in New York, and the appointment of a Treasury secretary from the New York financial world "would create jealousy in the West," the stronghold of the silverites. Garfield returned to Mentor and recorded in his diary, "No trades, shackles, and as well-fitted for defeat or victory as ever."

It is difficult to explain how Garfield emerged from the Fifth Avenue Hotel meeting without having made some deal with Conkling's machine. Possibly he felt that he had agreed only to "consult" with the Stalwarts on patronage. Or perhaps he was reluctant to acknowledge that he had caved in. And perhaps each side got half a loaf, sufficient to claim victory.

The election of 1880 was the closest ever in American history. Nearly 80 percent of the electorate voted, a percentage never equaled, before or since. Garfield's popular vote exceeded Hancock's by one-twentieth of 1 percent, with 9.2 million popular votes cast. The electoral vote, as it sometimes does, exaggerated the division between the candidates' popular vote margins. Garfield won 214 electoral votes, Hancock, 155. The vote of New York State was pivotal;

had Hancock won New York, he would have won the election.

Another outcome of the election was its solidification of the South's embrace of the Democratic party. The Republicans regained control of the House of Representatives by 152 to 130. The Senate was evenly divided between the major parties. The Republicans successfully countered the Democrats' strength in the South by carrying every other state except New Jersey, California, and Nevada—a feat that underscored the nation's abiding polarization after the Civil War and Reconstruction.

Doubtless those circumstances prompted the comment made by Carl Schurz, secretary of the interior in the Hayes administration, in a letter to Garfield: "Your real troubles will now begin." The selection of

THE GARFIELD ADMINISTRATION

INAUGURATION: Mar. 4, 1881; the Capitol, Washington, D.C.

VICE PRESIDENT: Chester A. Arthur

SECRETARY OF STATE: James G. Blaine

SECRETARY OF THE TREASURY: William Windom

SECRETARY OF WAR: Robert T. Lincoln

ATTORNEY GENERAL: Wayne MacVeagh

POSTMASTER GENERAL: Thomas L. James

SECRETARY OF THE NAVY: William H. Hunt

SECRETARY OF THE INTERIOR: Samuel J. Kirkwood

SUPREME COURT APPOINTMENT: Stanley Matthews (1881)

47TH CONGRESS (Dec. 5, 1881–Mar. 3, 1883):
  SENATE: 37 Republicans; 37 Democrats; 2 Others
  HOUSE: 147 Republicans; 135 Democrats; 11 Others

ELECTION OF 1880

CANDIDATES	ELECTORAL VOTE	POPULAR VOTE
James A. Garfield (Republican)	214	4,446,158
Winfield S. Hancock (Democratic)	155	4,444,260
James B. Weaver (Greenback)	—	305,997

the cabinet brought more trouble. It was payoff time for Republican factional leaders.

The imperious Roscoe Conkling was among the most aggressive spoilsmen. He journeyed to see "this man Garfield." An eight-hour visit intended to clarify the all-important question of cabinet membership, ended, like the earlier meeting in New York: Participants walked away with contradictory recollections. Again, Garfield interpreted the meeting as one with "no promises." Conkling's gaze remained fixed on the Treasury, a paradise of spoils. Conkling's first choice for secretary of the Treasury had been Levi Morton, but Garfield had appointed Morton minister to France. For secretary, Conkling's man was now Charles J. Folger, the respected chief justice of the New York Supreme Court. Conkling thought Garfield would appoint Folger to the Treasury, but the president-elect wanted Folger as attorney general. President Hayes, John Sherman, and James Blaine had all warned Garfield not to hand over the Treasury Department to the Stalwarts. Blaine argued that Conkling, controlling Treasury jobs, would be like a "strychnine upon your administration—first, bring contortions and then followed by death."

Slowly, the cabinet appointments fell into place. Blaine became secretary of state; Senator William Windom from Minnesota was named secretary of the Treasury; Wayne MacVeagh, a Philadelphia lawyer, was attorney general; Thomas L. James, a competent postmaster of New York City who was not in Conkling's pocket, was named postmaster general. In sum, Conkling and the Stalwarts were blocked from controlling the patronage.

In political circles, not surprisingly, opinions differed over Garfield's management of cabinet appointments. Some saw the selections as producing a "balanced cabinet," one that excluded the influence of no important party faction. But critics felt that Garfield was splitting the party further. Once again, they said, Garfield had broken his word and hurt party leaders where it hurt most, largely blocking them from assurance of a fair share of patronage. Conkling saw Vice President Arthur as the only reliable contact in the administration. Blaine felt lonely as the only Half-Breed in the cabinet. Stalwarts felt cheated since they were not awarded the Treasury.

Garfield's other prepresidential activity was the preparation of his inaugural address. Nearly one-third of the address was devoted to the American blacks and the South. Mindful of the role education had played in his own rise from poverty, Garfield proclaimed that black-white equality must come through "the extension of the suffrage." He admonished the South that "there can be no permanent disenfranchised peasantry in the United States." Only education promised a lasting solution to black-white relations.

Garfield knew that the drive to provide blacks with education as the key to a better life would face an uphill struggle. During his administration, 70 percent of Southern blacks were illiterate, and Northern states spent three times as much on education as the South.

Following his inauguration, Garfield settled easily into an efficient routine. Rising at seven, he read the newspapers and after breakfast tackled the ever-rising tide of correspondence. By ten o'clock he opened his doors to visitors—members of Congress, political leaders and office-seekers. Garfield was assisted by a team of six clerks, headed by twenty-four-year-old Joseph Stanley Brown, who oversaw the process of clipping newspapers with articles of particular interest to the president, organizing correspondence, and mapping out the president's schedule, with careful attention to the priority of selected visitors and the time allowed to each caller. But the greater part of Garfield's day was spent with office-seekers.

Lucretia performed her duties as first lady with dignity and grace. Handsome and somewhat reserved, she took command of the White House social duties, undeterred by occasional pinpricks of petty criticism. At high social functions, following

John Sherman's advice, the Garfields offered their guests liquor but did not drink themselves.

Policy-making during Garfield's brief tenure was almost minimal. The House of Representatives was in session for only a short time during his presidency, and therefore he was spared from vetoing or approving new legislation. His chief policy initiative was a refunding of the national debt. He instructed Secretary of the Treasury Windom to call in outstanding bonds, issued during the Civil War at 6 percent, and give bondholders the option of cashing them in at 6 percent or continuing to hold them at 3½ percent, which was more in accordance with prevailing interest rates. Most bondholders continued to hold them at the lower rate, and a savings of $10 million was effected—a substantial sum, since federal expenditures in 1881 were less than $261 million.

Garfield's most demanding activity was the dispensing of jobs in the executive branch. Unfortunately, the task of presiding over the endless parade of job seekers and determining who among the many petitioners for a particular post should be selected, was unappealing to the president. "I like to deal with doctrines and events," he said. "The conflicts of men about men I greatly dislike."

At the State Department, Blaine moved to make the United States a more active force in Western Hemisphere diplomacy. He intervened in disputes between Chile and Peru and between Mexico and Guatemala. When Great Britain moved to assert her interest in an isthmian canal, he reminded her of the Monroe Doctrine. He proposed a Pan-American conference under United States leadership and pushed for the opening of markets for the United States in Europe, Asia, and Africa.

Although Garfield was a forceful and controlling administrator, he was by disposition and inclination more a legislator than an executive. He deemed it improper for the president to "use the power of his great office to force upon Congress his own peculiar views of legislation." Rather than a leader, Garfield was a conciliator. He shunned a fight if it could be avoided. Critics of this rule, ordinarily one of good sense, found him "lacking sand."

Despite his political and policy initiatives, Garfield is best remembered for the tragedy of his assassination. It occurred just as he was preparing a plan that included an education program to enable African-Americans to escape poverty, as he himself had, for a better life.

Garfield was discussing his initiative with Blaine, as they entered the Baltimore and Potomac railroad station in Washington on July 2, 1881. The president was on his way to pick up an honorary degree at Williams College. Suddenly, the crackling sound of two fired bullets broke the station's muffled calm. Garfield clutched his back, crying out, "My God! What is this?" A policeman grabbed the assassin, a disappointed office-seeker and religious fanatic named Charles J. Guiteau.

President Garfield clung to life for several months. As his strength continued to wane, he was transported by train to Elberon, New Jersey, where it was hoped that cool breezes from the Atlantic Ocean would strengthen him. But the effort failed, and Garfield died there on September 19, 1881. Subsequently, Guiteau was hanged for his crime.

Garfield's election and brief tenure illustrate the high value of a president who is a skilled mediator and conciliator. Rejecting the legacy of conflict and ill will lingering from the Civil War and Reconstruction, Garfield emphasized economic and social issues. His support of bimetallism diminished the clashes between the gold and silver camps. He envisioned the Republican party as the party of prosperity, through high protective tariffs and "sound money." Republican presidents who followed, especially William McKinley, built upon that foundation and the Republicans became a majority party for forty years.

—LOUIS W. KOENIG

CHESTER ALAN ARTHUR

THE SELF-REFORMER

Chester Alan Arthur miraculously transformed himself from a master spoilsman, handing out jobs to fellow Republicans to an advocate of civil service reform. For several decades, dedicated reformers had sought to replace loyalty to the party as the chief qualification for employment with proof of merit through civil service examinations.

But it was the murder of President Garfield by a rejected office-seeker that gave urgency to enacting reform. President Arthur's promotion of change in pleas before Congress and his steadfast execution of the new law were also essential. Those who agonized over the prospect of Arthur as president, fearing that his New York boss, Roscoe Conkling, would be "the power behind the throne," were pleasantly surprised by the new chief executive's actions. Republican governor Charles Foster of Ohio had it right when he said, "The people and the politicians will find that Vice President Arthur and President Arthur are different men."

Chester Arthur was born on October 5, 1829, in Fairfield, Vermont, to parents who were always on the move. His mother, Malvina Stone, hailed from Vermont; his father, William, born in Ireland, was a Baptist minister whose unspectacular sermons kept the family relocating from one tiny parish to another. By one count, William Arthur served in eleven different parishes in northern Vermont and central and northern New York.

Chester first attended school in Union Village, New York, and spent a year in the Lyceum before entering Union College in Schenectady, New York. There, in 1845, he studied a classical curriculum and lived by a well-ordered daily program. He followed breakfast and prayers with a study session and a series of recitations; the day closed with more study at 7 P.M. He joined a social fraternity and became president of

the debating society. His excellence as a student was rewarded with election to Phi Beta Kappa.

Upon graduating in 1848, Arthur took on teaching posts in Vermont and New York. Seeking a more lucrative career, he enrolled in law school. In 1852, having been named principal of the academy at Cohoes, he drew upon his monthly salary of $55 to journey to New York City to serve in the law office of E. D. Culver and prepare for admission to the bar. Two years later he was made a partner in the law firm of Culver, Parker, and Arthur.

The newly minted lawyer was a good-looking man, fashionably dressed and of polished manners, who had the air of being well educated. He wore his hair long and sported a light beard. Topping six feet, he was described by a colleague to be "as slender as a maypole." Arthur displayed a special gift for forging strong emotional bonds that would serve him well in his political career. There were already signs that his future lay in politics. In the 1850s he attended meetings of the Free-Soilers party, which opposed the admission of any new slave states. Arthur became a party worker, signing on as an inspector of elections in New York City in 1856. He became a member of the eighteenth ward Young Men's Fremont Vigilance Committee. Thurlow Weed, the New York State leader of the Whig party (which soon would split and die over the issue of slavery) known to both his admirers and enemies as "the dictator," was at the peak of his power. Weed was impressed with his new, diligent party worker and took him under his wing. Arthur absorbed early lessons from the New Yorker on how to run a flourishing spoils system.

Weed had close ties with wealthy businessmen, who loosened their wallets when reminded of past favors and future promises. The Whig leader introduced Arthur to this politico-economic world, peopled with wealthy supporters such as New York

President Arthur, photographed during a fishing trip at Alexandria Bay, New York, sometime between 1881 and 1885. He was one of the nation's finest fishermen, adept at catching magnificent trout, salmon, and striped bass.

merchant, Edwin D. Morgan, whom Weed hand-picked to run for governor of New York in 1858. Morgan was elected and then reelected in 1860.

Governor Morgan, like other powerful men, was struck by Arthur's talents and promise. He selected the young man for the post of engineer in chief of New York State. In this post Arthur headed a large, unpaid social corps who often appeared with the governor at state ceremonies. Outfitted with his colleagues in gaudy, military-like uniforms, Arthur became the adjutant of Governor Morgan, who was also a powerful leader of the New York State Republican party.

Appropriately, at this high point of his fortunes, Arthur married Ellen Lewis Herndon, an Episcopalian from Virginia, and moved into her New York City home. Then the Civil War erupted: Fort Sumter was fired upon, and flags were draped everywhere in New York City as thousands of young men marched off to war to the tune of "Yankee Doodle." As engineer-in-chief, Arthur was commissioned a brigadier general and entrusted with the task of feeding and housing federal recruits passing through New York City to the battlefields.

When Morgan was defeated for reelection in 1862, Arthur returned to civilian life. Perhaps influenced by his wife, some of whose family fought in Confederate ranks, Arthur opposed the growing sentiment that the war was an antislavery crusade. He also shared with his wife, Nell, as she was called, a love of the high life of the finest foods and wines, servants, and a place in New York society. All this required a lot of money, and again Arthur measured up: He returned to practicing law. For years his specialty was war claims, and his law firm gained a fine reputation for its drafting of legislative bills in Albany and Washington to better compensate claimants.

Arthur's adroit socializing aided his ascent in the New York State Republican party. His influence soon ranked just below that of Weed, Morgan, William H. Seward (Lincoln's secretary of state), and Henry L. Raymond (editor of the *New York Times*). Arthur's interest lay not in taking stands on public policy issues but in continuing to ingratiate himself to party leaders as a faithful, efficient subaltern who could be counted on to perform his share of party work. His forte was helping others to gain office. A skilled raconteur, drawing easy laughter over the cigars and whiskey he provided, Arthur excelled at entertaining leaders, and they in turn enjoyed his company.

Arthur's ingratiation faced new tests with the onset of fresh leadership of the New York State Republican party. The most spectacular of these rising stars was Roscoe Conkling. He was handsome and refined on the outside, but on the inside he seethed with hostility. His fires of hatred burned most intensely for a leading national politician of the day, James G. Blaine, a Republican senator from Maine. But Arthur seemed never to stumble in his relation with Conkling. Best of all, with Conkling's support, President Ulysses S. Grant awarded Arthur the richest plum on the patronage tree, the appointment as collector of the New York Customs House.

The New York Customs House, whose jurisdiction extended over the waters of New York State and over both Hudson and Bergen counties in New Jersey, collected 75 percent of United States customs receipts. In 1877, the receipts it took in totaled $108 million. The New York Customs House was a rich source of revenue and steady income for the Republican party. Assessments on the salaries of federal employees produced increasing yields as payrolls rose. By 1872 the annual payroll at the New York Customs House had reached $1,800,000. At the assessment rate of 2 percent, the party could count on a contribution of $36,000 a year. When Arthur took over the New York Customs House, it was the largest federal office in the United States, exceeding the rosters of every office in Washington. Politicians throughout the country sought jobs there for their constituents. The collector's own compensation was a politician's dream: With salary and additional monies and fees, Arthur's gross income easily matched the president's pay of $50,000.

The building in which Arthur performed as collector was the former Merchants' Exchange Building, an enormous structure of solid granite, with huge blue-gray columns set on gray blocks. It commanded a frontage of two hundred feet on Wall Street. The building's immensity was reinforced on the inside, where a huge dome looked down on a rotunda that housed a large, four-faced clock. Encircling the clock were the desks at which deputy collectors and their clerks toiled. The usual scene was busy and noisy, as throngs of merchants and brokers pushed their way to officials. Wealthy businessmen appreciated the ready attention and facilitation they received. They respected Arthur's knowledge of the laws of commercial transactions. Businessmen and politicians liked his Whig views on the necessity of fiscal orthodoxy, a protective tariff, and limited government. Arthur also diligently served the political machine. He was reliable, kept his word, and steadily cared for his upper-class constituency.

Arthur was a model of loyalty and service to his political boss, Roscoe Conkling. Each year, Arthur led a large delegation of fellow Conkling loyalists to the state Republican convention in Utica, Conkling's hometown and political base. Delegates canvased in Arthur's suite of hotel rooms and partook freely of his drinks and cigars.

At the 1876 Republican national convention, Arthur supported Conkling for the Republican presidential nomination. When Rutherford B. Hayes became the nominee, Arthur applied his full-powered diligence to raising assessments from the New York Customs House workers for the campaign.

Nonetheless, Hayes was not deterred from ordering an investigation of corruption in the major customs houses. The investigator's report in 1878 called for Arthur's suspension as collector. Undaunted by

BIOGRAPHICAL FACTS

BIRTH: Fairfield, Vt., Oct. 5, 1829

ANCESTRY: Scotch-Irish and English

FATHER: William Arthur; b. County Antrim, Ireland, 1796; d. Newtonville, N.Y., Oct. 27, 1875

FATHER'S OCCUPATION: Baptist minister

MOTHER: Malvina Stone Arthur; b. Berkshire, Vt., Apr. 24, 1802; d. Newtonville, N.Y., Jan. 16, 1869

BROTHERS: William (1834–1915); George (1836–1838)

SISTERS: Regina (1822–1910); Jane (1824–1842); Almeda (1826–1899); Ann Eliza (1828–1915); Malvina (1832–1920); Mary (1841–1917)

MARRIAGE: New York, N.Y., Oct. 25, 1859

WIFE: Ellen Lewis Herndon; b. Fredericksburg, Va., Aug. 30, 1837; d. New York, N.Y., Jan. 12, 1880

CHILDREN: William Lewis Herndon (1860–1863); Chester Alan (1864–1937); Ellen (1871–1915)

RELIGIOUS AFFILIATION: Episcopalian

EDUCATION: Union College (1848)

OCCUPATIONS BEFORE PRESIDENCY: Teacher; school principal; lawyer

MILITARY SERVICE: Brig. gen. in New York State militia (1862)

PREPRESIDENTIAL OFFICES: Quartermaster general of New York State; collector of New York Customs House; U.S. vice president

AGE AT INAUGURATION: 50

OCCUPATION AFTER PRESIDENCY: Lawyer

DEATH: New York, N.Y., Nov. 17, 1886

PLACE OF BURIAL: Rural Cemetery, Albany, N.Y.

the disgrace that loomed, he continued toiling for the New York Republican party, chiefly by collecting assessments. Upon surrendering the collectorship, he returned to his law practice. Life dealt Arthur another hard blow when his wife died in January 1880. He sank into deep depression, with bouts of self-blame for his preoccupation with his political career to the neglect of his wife and marriage.

In 1880, as in 1876, it was clear that the vice presidential candidate would be from New York, given the state's pivotal role in the outcome of presidential elections. At the Republican National Convention,

Ellen Lewis Herndon, daughter of a naval officer, married Chester Arthur in 1859. She died in 1880. Arthur's election to the vice presidency was bittersweet without her there to share his triumphant moment.

Arthur, as Conkling's chief lieutenant, helped lead the effort to nominate Grant for a third term. But when the nomination went to Garfield, his messengers sounded out Arthur for the vice presidential post. Arthur accepted it, despite Conkling's angry objections. Doubtless, the New York boss dreaded losing his most reliable and talented lieutenant.

Arthur had only a modest role in the 1880 campaign. His efforts were concentrated in New York, where he helped coordinate party efforts by arranging meetings and rallies throughout the state, recruiting speakers, levying and distributing assessments, and prodding local campaigns.

The Republican victory in the close election of 1880 did not lift up Arthur into sudden exuberance. He still despaired over the loss of Nell and the disgrace of his ouster from the collectorship. But once again he came within the glow of good fortune, as the seventh New Yorker to attain the vice presidency. The office would provide him with national recognition and influence and a stage for his cherished social prominence. In addition, he no longer had to toil exclusively for the party machine.

At the inauguration, Arthur was at his sartorial best, attired in a blue Prince Albert coat, light trousers, a colored scarf, and white gloves. The next day, as he nervously performed his constitutional duty of calling the Senate to order, his hands trembled.

That Arthur would have no meaningful role in the real business of the Garfield administration became shockingly clear when he received the initial list of the president's nominations for federal offices. His eyes were riveted on the nomination of William H. Robertson for collector of New York Customs House. Robertson was Conkling's relentless reform antagonist. Arthur folded Garfield's list and sent it to Conkling. Conkling raged that Blaine, head of the rival Half-Breed faction, was behind the mischief—the president was his puppet. Conkling chaired the Senate committee through which Robertson's nomination would pass. The Half-Breeds appealed to Garfield to hold firm. John Hay, serving as the temporary editor of the New York *Tribune*, warned the president that "the least wavering would be fatal." Garfield assured the alarmists that with respect to Robertson, "They may take him out of the Senate head first or feet first—I will never withdraw him."

Arthur rushed to his New York home to meet with the Stalwart leaders and to map strategy. Half-Breed critics assailed him for disloyalty to Garfield. Actually, in this moment of excruciating torment, Arthur was torn between the president and the source of his own political strength: Conkling and the New York

Stalwart machine. He chose the machine and his long-standing friends.

In private conversation, Arthur tried to dissuade the president from sticking with the Robertson nomination, but Garfield was adamant. When Conkling's Senate committee recommended withdrawal of Robertson's name, Garfield refused—and ultimately prevailed. Robertson was approved by vote of the entire Senate.

The president had little time to rejoice in his victory. Scarcely four months in office, Garfield was shot by Charles J. Guiteau. During the desperate interval as Garfield lay dying, Arthur largely remained in his New York home, chiefly to avoid the appearance of acting prematurely as "president." Notified of Garfield's death, he left at once for Elberon, New Jersey, where the president's body lay. At Elberon, Arthur called on Mrs. Garfield, lunched with the cabinet, and boarded the funeral train bearing the late president to Washington.

Arthur took over the presidential reins at a time when the office was held in high esteem. The public approved of his careful conduct and dignified reserve following Garfield's death. Arthur himself felt no exultation on reaching the pinnacle of a political career—the presidency of the United States—for he was to enter the White House alone, without Nell.

As a widower, he needed help with White House social functions and other duties that ordinarily would be assumed by a first lady. Fortunately, his youngest sister, Mary Arthur McElroy, agreed to take four months of leave from her family each year to assist her brother. Mary, a graduate of the Emma Willard Seminary, handled her new role with charm and grace.

Arthur quickly lifted the presidency to new heights of sartorial refinement. His clothes were made by a leading New York tailor. For his afternoon attire he favored a sack coat, derby, and scarf. For business wear he preferred cheviot, a choice wool made from a specific breed of sheep. He wore a tuxedo and black tie for dinner. Arthur was said to have once tried on some twenty trousers before selecting a single pair.

The new president's social life was concentrated in the White House. He seldom went to the theater or the opera, and attended receptions given by only high-ranking politicians. Almost invariably, he was the most noticed figure at these occasions. Tom Platt, the New York senator and party leader, described President Arthur's visage: "his head of silken wavy hair, and a heavy, carefully controlled Burnside-type whiskers, trimmed to a perfect point, blue kindly eyes, straight nose, ruddy cheeks, polished manners, a Chesterfield." When entertaining, he was a stickler for details and insisted on quality. A servant said, "He

THE ARTHUR ADMINISTRATION

INAUGURATION: Sept. 20, 1881; New York, N.Y.

SECRETARY OF STATE: James G. Blaine; Frederick T. Frelinghuysen (from Dec. 19, 1881)

SECRETARY OF THE TREASURY: William Windom; Charles J. Folger (from Nov. 14, 1881); Walter Q. Gresham (from Sept. 24, 1884); Hugh McCulloch (from Oct. 31, 1884)

SECRETARY OF WAR: Robert T. Lincoln

ATTORNEY GENERAL: Wayne MacVeagh; Benjamin H. Brewster (from Jan. 3, 1882)

POSTMASTER GENERAL: Thomas L. James; Timothy O. Howe (from Jan. 5, 1882); Walter Q. Gresham (from Apr. 11, 1883); Frank Hatton (from Oct. 14, 1884)

SECRETARY OF THE NAVY: William H. Hunt; William E. Chandler (from Apr. 17, 1882)

SECRETARY OF THE INTERIOR: Samuel J. Kirkwood; Henry M. Teller (from Apr. 17, 1882)

SUPREME COURT APPOINTMENTS: Horace Gray (1881); Samuel Blatchford (1882)

47TH CONGRESS (Dec. 5, 1881–Mar. 3, 1883):
  SENATE: 37 Republicans; 37 Democrats; 2 Others
  HOUSE: 152 Republicans; 130 Democrats; 11 Others

48TH CONGRESS (Dec. 3, 1883–Mar. 3, 1885):
  SENATE: 40 Republicans; 36 Democrats
  HOUSE: 200 Democrats; 119 Republicans; 6 Others

wanted the best of everything in wines and food, and wanted it served in the best manner."

Arthur's first annual message urged tightening of the currency by early retirement of silver certificates and abandonment of coinage of a fixed amount of silver. With the Treasury enjoying a surplus of $130 million in revenues, he recommended a repeal of all revenue taxes except those on tobacco and liquor, and a revision "with caution" of the tariff laws. He supported the war department's advice that the army be increased to its full strength of thirty-thousand men, chiefly to protect settlers and their property in the West against Indian attacks. But he also called for legislation to prevent encroachments on lands set aside for the Indians and for measures to help them become citizens of the United States. On Capitol Hill, the message was largely ignored. However, President Arthur was more successful in using the veto power as an instrument for positive presidential leadership. He used it most tellingly against the legislation championed by John F. Miller, a Republican of California, that excluded Chinese labor from migrating to the United States and denied citizenship to the Chinese already in residence. Arthur's veto message declared that while the livelihoods of some Americans might be threatened, the unrestricted prohibition of Chinese labor for twenty years, or "nearly a generation," was "unreasonable." Finding the registration provisions set forth by Miller "undemocratic and hostile to the spirit of our institutions," he recalled the Chinese laborers' important contributions to the construction of the transcontinental railroad. Above all, the proposed legislation violated an outstanding treaty with China—the Burlingame Treaty—that guaranteed free immigration. The veto was successful and showed that the new president was more than a lavish entertainer and master spoilsman.

Arthur's most politically daring veto was fired at one of Congress's sacred laws, a pork barrel bill known more formally as a rivers and harbors bill. Legislators rely on those bills to jog up their local economies and please their constituents. The Rivers and Harbors Bill of 1881, containing appropriations of $11,451,300 worth of local public works projects, was described by the *New York Times* as "a monstrous swindle." Arthur's sweeping veto objected to the many provisions of the legislation which were "not for the common defense" and therefore lay beyond the powers given by the Constitution to Congress and the president. With explosive bipartisan wrath, Congress overrode the veto, and the bill became law.

One of the hotter political potatoes on Arthur's plate was the star route frauds. These rural mail-delivery routes were contracted out to private individuals and companies who often inflated their costs and successfully petitioned Congress to provide more funds. Arthur instructed Attorney General Benjamin Harris Brewster to initiate prosecutions "earnestly and thoroughly" against the frauds that had transpired during previous administrations.

Brewster and the Justice Department pressed their cases against such defendants as Stephen Dorsey, secretary of the Republican National Committee, a major contributor to the 1880 election victory. The prosecutions of star route frauds were enormously complex, spanning six months and accumulating 4,481 pages of testimony. Only two minor convictions resulted. To Arthur's credit, the frauds were stopped, saving the government some $2 million from being drained off annually in star route deceit.

The most remarkable shift by President Arthur from his earlier career was his enlistment in the cause of civil service reform. Arthur, a stellar practitioner of the spoils system, put his past aside to promote change in the acquisition of government posts. In his first annual message as president, he sounded the cry for reform, contending that the civil service should be conducted like a private business, with eligibility based on "fitness" for the position occupied, and with the offer of stable tenure and prompt investigation of

On a cover of *The Judge*, cartoonist J. A. Wales discounts President Arthur's first annual message as largely repetitious of his two predecessors' messages. However, the American public was impressed by the new president's ample agenda and the call for civil service reform by the onetime master spoilsman.

abuses. He proposed that a central examining board be formed to suggest nominations.

The resulting Pendleton Act, named after its chief congressional promoter, provided for a five-member bipartisan commission, empowered to conduct examinations for positions on the classified list. By no means was this a death knell for the federal spoils system; the new law applied to only a limited number of

positions in Washington and did not extend to any employees outside the capital. Only 12 percent of federal employees were covered, but the president was empowered to extend this number.

In addition to civil service reform, Arthur in his domestic policy was attentive to several of the nation's principal minorities. For the Indians, he proposed, in his first annual message, reforms aimed at inducing nomadic tribes to settle into "the pursuit of civilized life." Based on the notion of "the assurance of permanent title to the soil which they might toil," the Arthur administration frequently restricted white settlement in areas designated as Indian Territory, a formidable undertaking since each year thousands of American squatters rushed into Indian lands. He also stressed education for Indians, especially vocational instruction, and wished to provide them with livestock and farm equipment.

Toward African-Americans, however, Arthur's record was mixed. He preferred such personal and friendly acts as contributing from his own funds to a black church, and awarding diplomas at a black high school in Washington, D.C. However, he was much criticized when he told a delegation of white Georgia Republicans that he found white party officers more helpful to the party than Southern black officers, who, he said, chiefly excelled at "office begging."

Most important was Arthur's response to a Supreme Court decision striking down the Civil Rights Act of 1875, which provided that all persons, regardless of race, were entitled to the full and equal enjoyment of the accommodations, advantages, facilities, inns, public conveyances, theaters, and other places of public entertainment. He promised to support any "right, privilege, and immunity of citizenship" that Congress might enact, noting that the purpose of the Fourteenth Amendment was to insure "to members of the colored race the full enjoyment of civil and political rights." Arthur also proposed federal aid for education to combat illiteracy among African-Americans. But Frederick Douglass, the black leader and distinguished scholar, declared, in an overview of Arthur's performance, "There is nothing in his career as President of the U.S. that proves him to have had any sympathy with the oppressed colored peoples in the South."

On the home front, Arthur rescued the White House from the tattered, crumbling state into which it had fallen. At long last, after years of neglect, Congress provided money for substantial improvements. For the first three months of his presidency, Arthur lived on the second floor of the residence of Senator John P. Jones of Nevada while extensive, if not lavish, renovations were made to the White House. Louis Comfort Tiffany, the renowned New York jeweler and decorator, dispatched designers to oversee the planning and workmanship. Arthur took close interest in the vast enterprise and nearly every evening strolled to the White House to review its progress and make suggestions.

Arthur's cabinet also underwent a degree of reconstruction. William Windom resigned as secretary of the Treasury for understandable reasons: Windom had supported Arthur's removal from the collectorship. As his replacement, Arthur chose Charles J. Folger, chief justice of the New York Supreme Court, a Conkling supporter. At last the Stalwarts had the key to the Treasury's rich patronage. James G. Blaine served as secretary of state for about the first half of Arthur's presidency but then resigned to pursue the Republican presidential nomination. Blaine had used his post as secretary of state to regain national attention. A strong nationalist and anglophobe intent on shifting from America's usual preoccupation with Europe to a closer relationship with Latin America, the secretary sailed into rough waters when he initiated mediation in the war between Chile and Peru. Chile coveted territory in southern Peru, imposed a blockade, waged a naval war, and occupied Lima, Peru's capital. Blaine favored Peru and offered to mediate in the dispute. Chile remained recalcitrant, and Blaine soon left the administration to pursue his presidential ambitions.

His successor as secretary of state, Frederick T. Frelinghuysen, abandoned Blaine's mediation project and returned to European affairs by seeking Britain's approval of a total abrogation of the Clayton-Bulwer Treaty that gave Britain rights to construct a canal in any part of Central America. The British rejected this effort to settle the stressful issue of European construction of an isthmian canal.

Possibly Arthur's chief contribution to an enlarged American presence in foreign affairs was his move to strengthen the Navy, long neglected since the Civil War. The Arthur administration induced Congress to increase the number of the Navy's fighting ships and to underwrite several important institutional initiatives: the establishment of the Naval War College, at Newport, Rhode Island, and the Office of Naval Intelligence.

Despite these innovations, Arthur is in no danger of ranking among the hardest working presidents. After long evenings of socializing, he usually reached his desk the following morning at 10 o'clock. He received legislators until noon. After lunch, he saw further visitors by appointment until 4 or 5 P.M. From then until 7:30, he was devoted to reading, resting, and horseback riding. The cabinet normally met twice a week at noon. Arthur was a champion procrastinator. His staff had to nudge him to attend to matters requiring action.

A second term for Arthur? No clamor for that notion was heard anywhere. In the latter part of his term, he had become a president without a party. The Stalwarts, his chief base of support, were outraged by what they considered his meager dispensations of patronage. The Half-Breeds, while supportive of his civil service reforms, felt underappreciated. Arthur evidently tried to be evenhanded in addressing his presidency to the quarreling factions. Carl Schurz, secretary of the interior during the Hayes administration, analyzed Arthur's political shortfall: "He literally sat down between two chairs."

At the Republican nominating convention in 1884, Blaine easily prevailed. President Arthur, humiliated once again, pledged his "earnest and cordial support." But in the campaign that followed, Arthur and his cabinet did almost nothing for Blaine. His former machine boss, Conkling, when asked to campaign for Blaine, said, "I do not engage in criminal practice." For the remainder of his administration, failing health further restricted Arthur's activities. He suffered from Bright's disease, an affliction of the kidneys.

After leaving the presidency in 1885, Arthur returned to New York City and became counsel to his old law firm. He died of a cerebral hemorrhage on November 17, 1886.

—LOUIS W. KOENIG

THE TWENTY-SECOND PRESIDENT ★ 1885–1889
THE TWENTY-FOURTH PRESIDENT ★ 1893–1897

GROVER CLEVELAND

THE LAW MAN

G rover Cleveland brought a sense of moral order to the presidency. With a rare strength of character, he closely adhered to a set of principles of virtuous conduct, and was unafraid to make ethical judgments that sometimes were politically costly. His two terms as president provided a kind of road map of the benefits and liabilities of moral leadership in public office. Cleveland's efforts were targeted toward routing out corruption and upholding observance of the law. The American people, he believed, deserved efficient government, free of waste and incompetence.

Cleveland's morality, however, did not include a commitment to governmental regulations or welfare expenditures to aid needy communities and individuals, although he personally contributed to private charities. Even in one of the most severe economic depressions the nation has known, he clung to his convictions. It remained for future presidents—Theodore Roosevelt, Woodrow Wilson, Franklin Roosevelt, and others who followed—to commit the government and the public to aiding Americans in need.

Ethical leadership was an antidote to the abuses of power rife at a time when industrialists and financiers dominated society, with few holds barred. These were years when Tammany Hall pushed corruption ever onward, when the crusading journalist Henry Demarest Lloyd declared that Standard Oil Company "has done everything with the Pennsylvania legislature except refine it."

Amid the rampant moral decay, Cleveland, it was said, remained "ugly honest." During his first presidential election campaign, when he underwent embarrassing attacks for having fathered an illegitimate child, Cleveland gave his nervous aides a directive of absolute integrity: "Tell the truth."

Grover Cleveland was born in Caldwell, New Jersey, on March 18, 1837. Several years later the Clevelands moved to Fayetteville in western New York. His father, Richard Falley Cleveland, was a Yale-educated Presbyterian minister, whose droning style in the pulpit confined his career to village parishes. Grover's boyhood home life included daily prayers and the disciplined environment of a preacher's household. Moral principles, pertinent to one's conduct in life's journey, were thoroughly memorized. There were recitations of the catechism, Bible study, and family worship every evening. A code of behavior reflecting these sources was strictly enforced.

Grover was sixteen when his father died; with no hope for a college education, he headed West to seek a better life. En route to Ohio he stopped in Buffalo, where his uncle, Lewis F. Allen, was a leading citizen and a master at accumulating wealth from real estate, banking, and insurance. Buffalo was a model of the nation's surging industrial development, bursting with factories, incoming floods of immigrant workers, and the thriving commerce of the Great Lakes. Cleveland joined the Allen family on their farm outside the city. Allen placed Cleveland in a leading Buffalo firm to read law. He subsequently joined the bar. For the next twenty-seven years, from 1855 to 1882, Cleveland's life was centered on Buffalo. He seldom ventured beyond its borders.

The lawyer launched a second career in politics as a ward worker, whose chief responsibility was to get out the vote. Politicians valued his hard work and dependability. He was drawn to the Democratic party because several of his law partners were Democrats, and he disliked the flamboyant style of John C. Frémont, the Republican presidential nominee in 1856.

Cleveland was elected a ward supervisor in 1862 at the age of 25. He avoided service in the Civil War by recruiting and paying a substitute; a common practice of the day, it deprived him of a puff for self-enhancement enjoyed by other politicians who had served in the war and tirelessly cited their military records. Instead, he served briefly as an assistant district attor-

President Grover Cleveland dressed in formal attire for a portrait taken in 1888.

ney during the Civil War, followed by a three-year term as sheriff in the 1870s. The latter post, not normally sought by a lawyer, suggests his growing interest in holding political office. After his term as sheriff, he joined a top local law firm. He rarely appeared in court and was reputed to request only modest fees, because he didn't believe in charging clients large fees. He took few vacations, lived in rooming houses, and saved his money. His chief extravagance was ownership of the best bird dog in his hunting circle.

With Cleveland's hulking physique—his weight neared 250 pounds—and hearty manner, he was a forceful figure, with broad shoulders and a muscular build. He projected an air of determination and candor and was not afraid to speak his mind. Lawyer by day and carouser by night, he knew few wants. The hazards and hurts afflicting most Americans—fear of unemployment, long working hours, low pay—were beyond his ken.

If the 1880s were years of "robber barons" and burgeoning trusts, of railroad empires and fights for the regulation of railroads, of rampant discontent among farmers, of industrial warfare and the birth of unions, they were at least in equal measure years of the dirtiest government America had ever seen. In New York City, Tammany Hall—a Democratic political machine that controlled the city and exerted great power in New York state politics—and the New York Customs House strove to exceed one another in corrupt activities. Buffalo was afflicted by a graft-ridden aldermanic ring. A "ring" was once defined by a New York politico of the day as an alliance between the two major parties to mutually plunder the body politic without fear of exposure to censure by either party.

But reform soon had its day. In 1881 a Buffalo reform group decided to try for City Hall. They approached a number of honest men with political experience, but none wanted the thankless job of mayor of Buffalo. A reluctant Grover Cleveland, with his clean record as sheriff, became their candidate. He campaigned and won without spending a penny or making a single political deal. Within a year of taking office, Cleveland saved the city one million dollars simply by vetoing fraudulent sewage and street-cleaning contracts. He was given to pointing out, with indignant anger, those portions of bills that were nakedly graft-grabbing.

When the Buffalo *Sunday Times* declared that Cleveland would make an excellent governor, supporters flocked to him. He was nominated to oppose the Republican Charles J. Folger, a good man who had the bad luck to appear a mere puppet of both Chester Arthur, collector of the New York Customs House, and the stellar financial manipulator, Jay Gould. Cleveland captured thousands of Republican votes. Having incurred no political debts of significance, he was elected as the "unowned candidate."

Cleveland told a caller, after his election as governor: "I have only one thing to do, and that is to do right, and that is easy." He added, later in their conversation, "Let me rise or fall. I am going to work for the interests of the people of the State, regardless of party or anything else."

In fulfilling his vow, Cleveland managed to thwart moves by Tammany Hall to appoint incompetent party workers to public office. He alienated John Kelly, Tammany's leader. Kelly was a dangerous enemy. Without New York State, a Democratic presidential candidate stood little chance of winning the election, and without Tammany, it was generally agreed, New York could not be carried. Yet it was Cleveland's stubborn opposition to Tammany that captured the imagination of the voters and made him a national figure.

In June of 1884 the Republicans convened in Chicago to nominate their candidate for president. A small but distinguished group of influential reformers was present, headed by Carl Schurz, a former secretary of the interior, and the New York legislator

Theodore Roosevelt. The machine Republicans treated them with contempt—noting that they "had their hair parted in the middle" and were "neither male nor female" but some aberration. "Mugwump," an Indian word meaning "chief," was used sarcastically to describe the reformers. The delegates nominated James G. Blaine, who as Speaker of the House had allegedly sold railroad stocks and bonds under the shadiest of circumstances. The reformers distrusted Blaine as an enemy of honest government and bolted their party to support Cleveland. Exulted when the Democratic nominee Cleveland was chosen on the second ballot, General E. S. Bragg said in his nomination speech, "We love him for the enemies he has made." Former Indiana governor Thomas A. Hendricks, a talented campaigner, was nominated for vice president.

Tammany Hall fought hard against Cleveland's nomination at the Chicago convention. In bars and hotel rooms its minions whispered that Cleveland was a drunkard, anti-Catholic, and antilabor, and could not possibly win the election. Leading journalists opposed Cleveland's nomination, perhaps because of his rapid rise in politics; Henry Watterson of the Louisville *Courier Journal* called Cleveland unqualified because of his inexperience, with unknown positions on national issues. Charles Dana of the New York *Sun* was put off by Cleveland's "plodding mind, limited knowledge, and narrow capabilities." But journals such as the *New York Times*, *Harper's Magazine*, and the Springfield *Republican* endorsed Cleveland.

Cleveland followed the long-established protocol of the presidential candidate's restrained campaign. He stayed at his desk in Albany, wrote the standard acceptance letter, and made only a few short speeches, including one announcing his nomination. The *Nation* called his remarks a "collection of platitudes drawn out to the utmost limits of verbosity." He endorsed his party's platform, which called for new

BIOGRAPHICAL FACTS

BIRTH: Caldwell, N.J., Mar. 18, 1837
ANCESTRY: Irish-English
FATHER: Richard Falley Cleveland; b. Norwich, Conn., June 19, 1804; d. Holland Patent, N.Y., Oct. 1, 1853
FATHER'S OCCUPATION: Minister
MOTHER: Ann Neal Cleveland; b. Baltimore. Md., Feb. 4, 1806; d. Holland Patent, N.Y., July 19, 1882
BROTHERS: William Neal (1832–1907); Richard Cecil (1835–1872); Lewis Frederick (1841–1872)
SISTERS: Anna Neal (1830–1909); Mary Allen (1833–1914); Margaret Louise (1838–1932); Susan Sophia (1843–1938); Rose (1846–1918)
MARRIAGE: Washington, D.C., June 2, 1886
WIFE: Frances Folsom; b. Buffalo, N.Y., July 21, 1864; d. Oct, 29, 1947
CHILDREN: Ruth (1891–1904); Esther (1893–1980): Marion (1895–1995); Richard Folsom (1897–1974); Francis Grover (1903–1977)
RELIGIOUS AFFILIATION: Presbyterian
EDUCATION: Public schools
OCCUPATION BEFORE PRESIDENCY: Lawyer
PREPRESIDENTIAL OFFICES: Erie County assistant district attorney; sheriff of Erie County; mayor of Buffalo; governor of New York
AGE AT FIRST INAUGURATION: 47
OCCUPATION AFTER PRESIDENCY: Lawyer
DEATH: Princeton, N.J., June 24, 1908
PLACE OF BURIAL: Princeton, N.J.

progress for civil service reform, laws to help the workingman, opposition to prohibition, and advocacy of a constitutional amendment limiting the president to one term.

There followed one of the most memorable mud-slinging campaigns in American politics. Blaine's correspondence with the Boston firm that had handled his stock transactions was published in a local newspaper by the Mugwumps. On the back of one note, written in 1876, Blaine had scrawled, "Burn this letter!" And so the Democrats had their campaign song:

Blaine, Blaine, James G. Blaine,
The continental liar from the State of Maine,
Burn this letter!

In Cleveland's past, the Republicans discovered a Mrs. Maria Halpin, who claimed that the candidate was the father of her illegitimate son. It was not certain who the boy's father was, but Cleveland could have been, and he accepted the responsibility. The Republicans then sang:

Ma! Ma! Where's my pa?
Gone to the White House.
Ha! Ha! Ha!

Blaine, who ran a more active campaign than Cleveland, made two crucial blunders. He was present at a speech by the Reverend Dr. Samuel Burchard in New York at which Burchard said: "We are Republicans and don't propose to leave our party and iden-tify ourselves with the party whose antecedents have been rum, Romanism and rebellion." Blaine, tired from campaigning, missed the slur against Catholics and did not dissociate himself from Burchard. Overnight he doubtless lost the loyalty of innumer-able Irish voters in the all-important state of New York, not to mention Catholics in the rest of the nation. On the very same day—six days before the election—he was present at a dinner in his honor, offered by Jay Gould and Russell Sage, at Delmoni-co's in New York. The next day Joseph Pulitzer's news-paper, the New York *World*, reported in banner headlines: "The royal feast of Belshazzar Blaine and the money kings . . . an occasion for the collection of a republican corruption fund."

Like other presidential elections of that era, the Cleveland-Blaine race was close. For several days, the election results were in doubt. Cleveland won New York State by a plurality of 1,149 votes. He won every Southern state, and the pivotal states of Indiana, New

In a cartoon titled "Another Voice for Cleveland," from the Republican weekly *The Judge*, the future president is assailed by the tearful mother and child who scandalized his campaign and by Republican taunts of "Grover the Good."

Jersey, and Connecticut. Ultimately, his popular-vote majority was less than 25,000 out of the more than 10 million votes cast. Cleveland won 219 electoral votes and Blaine 182.

The new Cleveland administration provided more of a change in moral spirit than a change in policy. The inaugural address contained no arresting initiatives or ringing calls to arms. Strong on platitudes, it was delivered without a manuscript; the new president excelled at memorization. The cabinet was composed chiefly of Easterners, who were successful, often wealthy, worldly conservatives who could have easily been Republicans. Most were lawyers and businessmen, with ties to the railroads and the financial world. They favored a low tariff, distrusted government regulation, and disapproved of subsidies, except to railroads.

Early on, Cleveland launched an assault on graft and corruption in the Department of the Interior by exposing mining and timber-cutting abuses in Indian territories. Cattle overlords, lumber companies, and crooked surveyors were favorite targets. Railroads, historic snatchers of public and Indian lands, felt the reforming hand of Secretary Lucius Lamar. Cleveland fully supported the initiative of his secretary of the Navy, William C. Whitney, to rebuild the long-neglected naval fleet.

Cleveland conducted his presidential duties with the same moral imperative he had brought to the offices of mayor and governor. He ordered his cabinet secretaries to eliminate "abuses and extravagances" in their departments. "The presidency," Cleveland said, "is essentially executive in nature." He did not take kindly to Washington's political world, viewing its inhabitants as a breed apart and, at their worst, violators of the public trust. Great policy-making visions did not appeal to him, nor did the deals, compromises, manipulations—all common currencies of politics. Beguiling rhetoric was not a weapon in his political arsenal.

JAMES G. BLAINE

In James G. Blaine, the magnetic and eloquent "Plumed Knight" of the Republican party, Grover Cleveland had a formidable opponent for the presidency. Born in Pennsylvania in 1830, Blaine settled in Augusta, Maine, entered the state legislature, and became the acknowledged leader of the Maine Republicans. Elected to Congress in 1862, he served for almost two decades as representative, Speaker of the House, and senator. As leader of the liberal element of the party, Blaine was an attractive presidential prospect. But charges of graft in his dealings with the railroads cost him the nomination in 1876, and he was thwarted again in 1880. In 1884 he finally became the Republican candidate; but the railroad scandal continued to hurt him, and a supporter's reference to the opposition as the party of "rum, Romanism and rebellion" alienated the Irish Catholics in the key state of New York. Defeated by Cleveland, Blaine returned to foreign affairs. In 1881 he had been secretary of state under Garfield. Supporting Harrison in 1888, he accepted the post again and resumed his fight for a more constructive Latin American policy. A statesman of vision, he was instrumental in organizing the first Pan-American Conference, in formulating policy for a United States–controlled isthmian canal, and in increasing trade with Latin America. Blaine died in Washington in January 1893.

Neither did Cleveland relish his most arduous and time-consuming duty as president: meeting with the endless streams of office-seekers and their congressional sponsors. His natural brusqueness was sharpened by the daily ordeal. It was after tortuous hours of dealing with a large number of beseeching spoilsmen that Cleveland exclaimed to a friend: "My God, what is there about this office that anyone should ever want to get into it?"

Cleveland was also battered by the money issue, rooted in the demands of the South and West to

that investors and businessmen might become alarmed and a depression might follow. The president was haunted by the Bland-Allison Act, which required the secretary of the Treasury to purchase sizeable amounts of silver each month. Cleveland, to diminish the pressure, asked Congress to suspend the purchases under the act, but the House rejected the request by 170 votes to 118. A mere 52 Democrats sided with the president.

At first Cleveland mustered only a modest interest in tariff reform. He shared the prevailing Democratic view that favored a low tariff. Mugwumps attacked the tariff as "shameful" in light of the federal "surplus." Henry Ward Beecher, the eminent preacher and Mugwump reformer, protested that protection was the "jugglery of the devil." For a time Cleveland remained cautious, fearful of the political dangers of relaxing the tariff, which had been adopted during the Civil War to protect established commerce as well as "infant industries." He believed that the tariff law raised the prices of protected goods and encouraged the growth of monopolies. He was also concerned that serious tariff revision would crack Democratic unity in the approaching congressional elections of 1886. Dissension was rising between the bankers and industrialists of the East and the farmers of the South and West. Industrialists wanted a high tariff to protect high prices. Farmers wanted low tariffs so they would not have to pay high prices for imported manufactured goods. Cleveland's annual message to Congress called for only modest tariff reform. The tariff was at the forefront of the 1886 midterm elections. But the outcome was indecisive for an issue that would continue to torment Congress and the president.

However engrossed by affairs of state, Cleveland also turned to matters of the heart. On June 2, 1886, the 49-year-old Grover Cleveland married Frances Folsom, the tall, handsome, 21-year-old daughter of one of his Buffalo law partners. Cleveland had con-

expand the currency. The quantity of money in circulation, the critics said, was not keeping up with the nation's expanding wealth and population. They cited the widespread hardship of high interest rates levied on farmer's mortgages for land and machinery. Simultaneously, the price of agricultural produce was falling. Cleveland, faithful guardian of sound money—the gold standard—did not respond, fearing

sidered himself her virtual guardian from the time of her father's death in 1875, and he entertained her and her mother at the White House for ten days in 1885. He proposed to her shortly after her graduation from Wells College. They were married in the executive mansion to the strains of the wedding march played by John Philip Sousa. Mrs. Cleveland brightened Washington society and her husband's life. With her arrival, the president became far more sociable, took more vacations, was generally less irritable, and launched bolder legislative initiatives.

Following his marriage, Cleveland gravitated to a broader, more positive vision of moral leadership. His evolution was most fully expressed in the last annual message to Congress near the close of his presidential term. He decried cities where "wealth and luxury" existed callously beside "poverty and wretchedness and unremunerative toil." "The gulf between employers and the employed," he said, "is constantly widening, and classes are rapidly forming. . . ." "Corporations," he warned, were "fast becoming the people's masters" while the farmers were struggling against "impoverishment." Nonetheless, Cleveland's leadership was not broad enough nor responsive enough to assure his reelection in 1888. Although he won the popular vote, he lost the electoral vote to the Republican nominee, Benjamin Harrison, 233 electoral votes to 168. The 1888 election stands as the most clear-cut example of the lack of synchronization between the popular and the electoral votes in American presidential elections. The election demonstrates that a sizeable plurality, such as Cleveland's, is vulnerable to the accidents of its distribution. Cleveland lost major electoral votes by small margins of popular votes. For example, he lost New York by 14,373, Indiana by 2,376, and Ohio by 20,598. A slight shift in Cleveland's popular majority could have made him victorious with the electoral vote.

When the Clevelands departed from the White House, Mrs. Cleveland said to Jerry Smith, a caretak-er: "Now, Jerry, I want you to take good care of all the furniture and ornaments in the house, for I want to find everything just as it is now when we come back again. . . ." To Smith's astonishment, she added, "We are coming back just four years from today." Mrs. Cleveland's prediction came true.

In 1893, at the start of Cleveland's second term, the country was far more restless than it had been in several decades. The Populist candidate for president, James B. Weaver, had received more than a million votes in the 1892 election. Eugene V. Debs had just organized the American Railway Union, which, by 1893, had 150,000 members. The General Managers' Association—which employed 221,000 workers—was formed to combat the unions. Beneath the glitter of the new skyscrapers, conflict and turmoil were brewing. Ten days before Cleveland took office, the Philadelphia and Reading Railroad, with debts of over $125 million, went bankrupt. Immediately after his inauguration the great National Cordage Company collapsed, setting off a panic on Wall Street. The Treasury gold reserve dropped below the $100 million mark—considered the minimum necessary to guarantee "sound money." The stock market sank. Some five hundred banks failed before the end of 1893. Mortgages were foreclosed. Within a year, an estimated two to three million American workers were unemployed.

In an attempt to restore confidence in the American dollar, President Cleveland called for the repeal of the Sherman Silver Purchase Act of 1890, which was devouring the Treasury's gold reserve. Westerners and Southerners clamored for silver coinage, believing that if more money were put in circulation, the plight of the farmers and laborers would be alleviated. Cleveland firmly believed in Gresham's Law—that bad money drives out good—and insisted on maintaining the gold standard.

As chief executive, Cleveland called for a special session of Congress to repeal the Sherman Silver Pur-

An 1893 issue of *Puck* hails the repeal of the Sherman Silver Purchase Act, which President Cleveland believed would restore confidence in the dollar and end the financial panic that devastated the economy in his second term. On the cover, Uncle Sam rescues a woman (business interests) from the silver flood, using a rope (public opinion) fastened to a rock representing the action by the Fifty-third Congress.

chase Act. Then, in the very midst of preparation for the battle, Cleveland noticed a rough spot on the roof of his mouth. His doctor advised immediate removal of the cancerous growth, and in order to avoid plunging the country into further panic, Cleveland boarded a yacht in New York bound for Buzzards Bay, off the coast of Massachusetts, and had the whole of his upper left jaw removed on the way. After debarking he set to work immediately on his message for the special session.

Back in Washington, Cleveland presented his case to Congress. When legislators, after long deliberation, brought the president a compromise plan, Cleveland reportedly exploded in anger, banged his fist on the table, and declared he would not yield. He lashed his followers into stronger efforts. Ten days later, on October 30, 1893, the Sherman Silver Purchase Act was repealed.

While Cleveland struggled to regain his health, the country began to undergo a magical transformation wrought by Thomas Edison's mastery of electricity and its debut in American society. But there was another force thrusting across the land. The Panic of 1893 was worsening—and fastening its grip on Cleveland's second term. A business depression settled in, first in Eastern states, then rolling westward. Its hand fell most brutally on the nation's primary industry, agriculture. Farmers, deep in mortgage debt, suffered severe collapses of prices for their products while struggling with 10 percent mortgages.

Farmers lived in dread that their local sheriff would appear unannounced and post a foreclosure notice on their homes. The force of these miseries produced new political leaders who declaimed for a fairer distribution of wealth and a curbing of the trusts—the giant combinations of corporations that dominated the sugar and oil industries, among others, and were mercilessly eliminating competitors and bleeding consumers with high prices. Meanwhile, a rash of new leaders were appearing in the West and the South: populist orators, including the youthful William Jennings Bryan.

After the repeal of the Sherman Act, Secretary of the Treasury John Carlisle, in an effort to shore up the federal gold reserve, twice issued fifty million dollars worth of bonds in 1894. When the public responded feebly to second offering, he was compelled to issue the bonds to Wall Street bankers, who simply cashed in their old notes at the New York sub-Treasury to obtain the gold to buy the new bonds. Nothing was gained, and by January 1895 the Treasury was losing gold at a rate of three million dollars a day. Then J. P. Morgan offered to raise sixty-two million dollars in gold for the government—half of it to come from abroad—and to ensure that it would not be immediately withdrawn. At 3.75 percent the interest rate was high, but the main provision was that the government not make a public bond issue again and deal with Morgan alone.

The terms seemed too stiff to Cleveland, and he made preparations for another public issue. A bill was introduced in Congress, where it was defeated on February 7, 1895. At the very moment when Congress was voting, Morgan was on the train from New York. He was greeted in Washington by a Cleveland aide and told that the president could not see him that evening. Furious, Morgan said he would return to New York and let the country go bankrupt. He was persuaded to stay, however, and sat up all night in his hotel room playing solitaire.

The next morning Morgan and Cleveland met at the White House; neither would yield. Then the phone rang; a Treasury official informed the president that there was less than nine million dollars in gold at the New York sub-Treasury. Morgan knew of an outstanding note for twelve million dollars. "Mr. President," he said, ". . . if that [note] is presented today; it is all over." The stubborn, independent Cleveland, the man who responded to coercion with contrariness, gave in.

In saving the gold standard, Cleveland lost the Democratic party to the Populists. The gold crisis ended with a fourth and final bond issue in 1896. In that year, the silver forces captured the Democratic presidential nominating conventions and put forth their foremost orator, William Jennings Bryan.

Despite the president's declining political fortunes, he enjoyed two striking achievements in foreign policy. During Harrison's tenure a treaty to annex Hawaii had been negotiated and sent to the Senate for ratification. Five days after taking office, Cleveland recalled the treaty and quashed it. Some Hawaiians, to be sure, wanted to join America, but most did not.

A drawn-out dispute with Great Britain, dating from 1887, finally exhausted Cleveland's patience in

SECOND ADMINISTRATION

INAUGURATION: Mar. 4, 1893; the Capitol, Washington, D.C.
VICE PRESIDENT: Adlai E. Stevenson
SECRETARY OF STATE: Walter Q. Gresham; Richard Olney (from June 10, 1895)
SECRETARY OF THE TREASURY: John G. Carlisle
SECRETARY OF WAR: Daniel S. Lamont
ATTORNEY GENERAL: Richard Olney; Judson Harmon (from June 11, 1895)
POSTMASTER GENERAL: Wilson S. Bissell; William L. Wilson (from Apr. 4, 1895)
SECRETARY OF THE NAVY: Hilary A. Herbert
SECRETARY OF THE INTERIOR: Hoke Smith; David R. Francis (from Sept. 4, 1896)
SECRETARY OF AGRICULTURE: Julius Sterling Morton
SUPREME COURT APPOINTMENTS: Edward D. White (1894); Rufus W. Peckham (1895)
53RD CONGRESS (Aug. 7, 1893–Mar. 3, 1895):
  SENATE: 44 Democrats; 38 Republicans; 3 Others
  HOUSE: 220 Democrats; 126 Republicans; 10 Others
54TH CONGRESS (Dec. 2, 1895–Mar. 3, 1897):
  SENATE: 44 Republicans; 39 Democrats; 5 Others
  HOUSE: 246 Republicans; 104 Democrats; 7 Others
STATE ADMITTED: Utah (1896)

ELECTION OF 1892

CANDIDATES	ELECTORAL VOTE	POPULAR VOTE
Grover Cleveland (Democratic)	277	5,551,883
Benjamin Harrison (Republican)	145	5,179,244
James B. Weaver (Populist)	22	1,029,846
John Bidwell (Prohibition)	—	264,133

1895. The crux of the disagreement was over the boundary between British Guiana and Venezuela. Cleveland, invoking the Monroe Doctrine, maintained that Britain was attempting to expand its interests in the Americas. He has been criticized for the vehemence with which he finally attacked Great Britain over the matter. Yet, however bellicose his words, he labored to stem any jingoism that might have followed his message, and he brought the issue to arbitration quickly. The historian Allan Nevins notes

---

EUGENE V. DEBS

In 1912 Eugene V. Debs was the presidential candidate of the Socialist party for the fourth consecutive time. Long before his conversion to socialism in 1895, Debs had been an important force in the labor-union movement. A fireman on the Terre Haute and Indianapolis Railway, in 1875 he helped to organize the Brotherhood of Locomotive Firemen, becoming a national officer five years later. As president of the American Railway Union, which he helped to found in 1893, he led its members in a sympathy strike against the Chicago Pullman Company in 1894. Arrested and sentenced to six months in prison, Debs became acquainted with the writings of Karl Marx and emerged from jail a socialist. In 1897 he founded the Social Democratic Party of America, which three years later became the Socialist Party of America. After Debs had urged opposition to the war with Germany and had publicly denounced the sedition policies of the government, he was convicted of breaking the wartime Espionage Act and sentenced to ten years imprisonment in 1918. In spite of his confinement he headed the Socialist ticket for the fifth time in 1920 and polled more than 900,000 votes. Pardoned by President Harding in 1921, Debs spent his last five years in the service of his party. He was an editor of two Socialist journals, *Appeal to Reason* and *American Appeal,* and author of a book on prison conditions, *Walls and Bars,* published posthumously in 1927.

---

that Cleveland's move had an important side effect in "clearing the atmosphere between Great Britain and the United States." The president initiated "a virtual entente that within a generation was to prove of the profoundest importance in world history."

Unfortunately, the domestic scene continued to deteriorate. Increasingly, mills, factories, and mines shut down. Samuel Gompers, leader of the young American Federation of Labor, estimated that three million workers were unemployed, and the numbers kept growing. Mounting desperation was vented in a march on Washington by many of the unemployed to demand an issuance of $500 million in irredeemable paper money to jog up the economy. "Coxey's Army," led by the wealthy quarry owner Jacob Coxey, set out from Massillon, Ohio, and headed for Washington to awaken an unresponsive Cleveland. The army sustained many dropouts in the long march and numbered about three hundred on reaching Washington. Many of the remaining bedraggled men were arrested for carrying a banner on Capitol grounds and trampling the grass.

President Cleveland was more severely tested in the strike of railroad workers against the Pullman Palace Car Company in Chicago in July 1894. Some four thousand workers protested against a 25 percent pay cut. Other railroad workers joined the strike, led by Eugene Debs. Freight traffic in and out of Chicago stopped. The post office reported obstruction of the mails. Cleveland faced hard questions: How much right did government have to interfere in the strike? What is "lawless obstruction?" Absorbed in efforts for legislation to reduce the tariff, Cleveland relied on Richard Olney, the attorney general and a former railroad lawyer. Olney obtained a federal court injunction forbidding the strikers to interfere with movement of the mail. The president dispatched United States troops against the strikers, declaring, "if it takes the army and navy of the United States to deliver a postcard in Chicago, that card will be delivered." When

"Coxey's Army" leaves Brightwood Camp in Ohio in 1894 for the march on Washington to petition for relief from mass unemployment.

Illinois governor John Peter Altgeld objected that the president should have consulted him before sending in troops, Cleveland replied, "I have neither transcended my authority nor duty. . . . In this hour of danger and public distress, discussion may well give way to active efforts on the part of all in authority to restore obedience to the law and to protect life and property." After two days of rioting and pillage in Chicago, order was restored, and the strike was effectively broken. Cleveland's actions won wide public support, although he alienated Altgeld and labor leaders, thus further splitting the Democratic party.

Evaluations of Cleveland were strongly divided upon completion of his presidency. Senator Allison of Iowa declared: "It was God's mercy to this country that Grover Cleveland, and not Harrison, was elected President." But Governor Altgeld said: "to laud Cleveland on Jefferson's birthday, is to sing a Te Deum in honor of Judas Iscariot on Christmas morning." Among historians, his reputation has fluctuated with changing times and tastes. In the 1920s and 30s, he was widely rated among the near-great presidents. But after the Great Depression and World War II, his standing fell because his strong commitments to limited government and maintaining the gold standard seemed retrospectively out of step with the needs of his day. His usual rating in the numerous polls is above average to average.

After completing his presidency, Cleveland practiced law with a leading New York firm headed by Francis Stetson, the lawyer for J. P. Morgan. Cleveland became the first president to argue a case before the United States Supreme Court. He died on June 24, 1908, in Princeton, New Jersey, where he had lived and enjoyed close ties to the university.

—*Louis W. Koenig*

Benjamin Harrison, twenty-third president of the United States, fits the pattern of one-term presidents during the post–Civil War period. Hayes, Garfield, and Arthur each served one term, while Cleveland lost his bid for reelection but, after a four-year wait, won a second term. The reasons for this trend are as varied as the individuals themselves. In Harrison's case, the president failed to court the Republican bosses. In addition, party leaders were put off by his icy demeanor and air of superior intelligence.

In 1890 Attorney General—and future president—William Howard Taft took note of Harrison's genius for offending party leaders and members of Congress. "The President is not popular with the members of either house," he stated. "His manner of treating them was not at all fortunate, and when they have an interview, they generally come away mad . . . I think this is exceedingly unfortunate because I am sure we have never had a man in the White House who was more conscientiously seeking to do his duty."

Yet, despite his handicap, President Harrison is credited with compiling a record worthy of emulation by other presidents. During his term, two prime historic statutes were adopted: the Sherman Antitrust Act and the McKinley Tariff Act. Some historians have contended that the first two years of his presidency are the equal of Lincoln's first two years. Although Harrison, like other Republican presidents of the Gilded Age, was enamored of the Whig doctrine of congressional supremacy, he worked with astute diligence to secure legislation, such as the Sherman Antitrust Act, which would be politically viable. He abhorred public policy shipwrecked on the shoals of impracticality.

Benjamin Harrison, the president of unrelenting confidence, was born on August 20, 1833, on his grandfather's farm in North Bend, Ohio, the second of nine children. His grandfather, William Henry Harrison, had served briefly as president of the United States in 1841, and his father, John Scott Harrison, had been a member of the House of Representatives. Both scholarly and athletic, Benjamin Harrison had a private tutor and also attended public school. His father's principal occupation was farming, so he sent his son to Farmers' College in Cincinnati. After three years, Benjamin transferred to Miami University, in Oxford, Ohio. Benjamin graduated with distinction in 1852. There he met and married Caroline Lavinia Scott, daughter of the president of the Western College for Women in Oxford.

The Harrisons moved to Cincinnati, where Benjamin read law and was admitted to the bar in 1854. Later that year they moved to Indianapolis, and Benjamin opened up his own law firm. He later recalled his struggle to build his practice. "They were times," he said, "when a five-dollar bill was an event."

Benjamin Harrison was eager for a political career, but his father, although a dedicated and hardworking Whig congressman, had little good to say about the political profession, admonishing his son to stay away from its "temptations" and declaring that none but knaves would enter the political arena. Nevertheless, Benjamin Harrison was attracted to politics. To the distress of his father, Benjamin joined the newly formed Republican party in 1856. The following year he ran successfully for the office of Indianapolis city attorney, and in 1860 he was elected state supreme court reporter.

In July 1862, with the Civil War in full progress, Governor Oliver Perry Morton asked Harrison to recruit men for the 70th Indiana Volunteers. Harrison did so and was made colonel of the regiment, which was dispatched to Kentucky to guard the Louisville and Nashville Railroad. He soon realized that his men were soldiers in name only and began to equip and drill them for battle. There are men who can apply discipline sternly and retain the respect

Candidate Benjamin Harrison giving a speech in Peru, Indiana, in 1888.

BIRTH: North Bend, Ohio, Aug. 20, 1833

ANCESTRY: English-Scotch

FATHER: John Scott Harrison; b. Vincennes, Ind.,
Oct. 4, 1804; d. North Bend, Ohio, May 25, 1878

FATHER'S OCCUPATIONS: Farmer; U.S. congressman

MOTHER: Elizabeth Irwin Harrison; b. Mercersburg, Pa.,
July 18, 1810; d. Aug. 15, 1850

BROTHERS: Archibald Irwin (1832–1870); Carter Bassett
(1840–1905); John Scott, Jr. (1844–1926);
James Friedlay (1847–1848); James Irwin (1849–1850)

HALF BROTHER: William Henry Harrison (1827–1829)

SISTERS: Mary Jane Irwin (1835–1867); Anna Symmes
(1837–1838); Anna Symmes (1842–1926)

HALF SISTERS: Elizabeth Short (1825–1904);
Sarah Lucretia (1829–?)

FIRST MARRIAGE: Oxford, Ohio, Oct. 20, 1853

FIRST WIFE: Caroline Lavinia Scott; b. Oxford, Ohio,
Oct. 1, 1832; d. Washington, D.C., Oct. 25, 1892

SECOND MARRIAGE: New York, N.Y., Apr. 6, 1896

SECOND WIFE: Mary Scott Lord Dimmick; b. Honesdale,
Pa., Apr. 30, 1858; d. New York, N.Y., Jan. 5, 1948

CHILDREN: Russell Benjamin (1854–1936);
Mary Scott (1858–1930); Elizabeth (1897–1955)

RELIGIOUS AFFILIATION: Presbyterian

EDUCATION: Private tutoring; attended Farmers' College;
Miami University (B.A., 1852)

OCCUPATIONS BEFORE PRESIDENCY: Lawyer;
notary public; soldier

MILITARY SERVICE: Col. in 70th Indiana Volunteers
(1862); resigned as bvt. brig. gen. in 1865

PREPRESIDENTIAL OFFICES: Commissioner for the Court
of Claims; city attorney; secretary of Indiana
Republican Central Committee; state supreme court
reporter; U.S. senator

AGE AT INAUGURATION: 55

OCCUPATION AFTER PRESIDENCY: Lawyer

DEATH: Indianapolis, Ind., Mar. 13, 1901

PLACE OF BURIAL: Crown Hill Cemetery,
Indianapolis, Indiana

After the war, Harrison continued his political ascent. His proven ability to win elections and his reputation as an ethical lawyer and devout churchman created a politically invaluable impression of decency in an age of rascality and corruption. The eloquent reformer Ignatius Donnelly declared, "Corruption dominates the ballot box, the legislatures, the Congress, and touches even the ermine of the bench." By the early 1870s Republicans urged Harrison to run for governor, but he turned down their requests as well as others that he be a candidate for Congress. In 1876, when the Republican gubernatorial nominee withdrew during the campaign because of his alleged involvement in corrupt activities, the state committee selected Harrison to run in his place. But Harrison did not enter the race until late in the campaign and lost the election by about 5,000 votes. Despite the loss, his political prestige was much enhanced by his strong showing.

President Rutherford B. Hayes considered Harrison for a cabinet post but appointed him instead to the Mississippi Power Commission, which gave Harrison national exposure. However, it was the death of Senator Morton in 1877 that left a void in the Indiana Republican machine and allowed Harrison to rise to power. Harrison quickly assumed leadership of the party.

Harrison also took initiatives to extend his quest. He chaired the Indiana delegation to the Republican National Convention in 1880. Harrison cast 27 votes for James Garfield's nomination on the thirty-fifth ballot, a key step that influenced other states to join the rising tide for Garfield's nomination. President Garfield wanted Harrison in his cabinet, but Harrison declined, preferring to serve in the United States Senate, to which he was elected by the Indiana legislature in 1881.

In the 1880s various friends of Harrison laid the groundwork for a possible presidential campaign. An overseer of the promotional strategy was his longtime

and even the affection of their men; Harrison was not one of them. His aloof and brusque manner made him one of the least popular brigade commanders.

friend and chairman of the Indiana Republican State Committee, Louis Michener. Like previous Republican presidential candidates of this era, Harrison faced a formidable obstacle, James G. Blaine.

Speaker of the House of Representatives at 39, Blaine was a leading politician and a perennial presidential candidate. After losing out to Hayes in 1876, Blaine was elected to the Senate in 1877. In the 1880s he dominated Republican politics despite his fragile health, which included a recurring case of gout. During the 1880 nominating convention, Blaine's battle with Garfield for the nomination struggled on for 36 ballots. Blaine finally won the nomination in 1884, but he lost the election to the Democratic candidate Grover Cleveland. Even in the face of these setbacks, Blaine never gave up on his desire to become president.

Harrison's plan to become president included a failed dark horse strategy in 1884. (A dark-horse candidate has scanty support in early balloting, but might become the delegates' choice if the the convention is deadlocked over major candidates.) In 1888 Harrison's fortunes rose when Indiana delegates endorsed his nomination. Fortune smiled again when Blaine, plagued by health problems, bowed out of the race. But Harrison faced another problem: No less than nineteen candidates sought the nomination.

Louis Michener cultivated the second-choice votes of delegates in anticipation that their first-choice candidate would eventually abandon the race. Second choices might become first choices in further balloting. Harrison was offered a deal by the Pennsylvania boss Matt Quay: the support of the Pennsylvania delegation in exchange for a blanket promise of any cabinet post. Despite the intense urgings of his aides to accept the deal, Harrison refused it. Tired of the entreating and wailing, Harrison reminded his aides of his preconvention instruction that "purchasing capacity" must not displace "moral practicality" in competing for the nomination. Harrison's break-

through came when Blaine, then traveling in Scotland, let it be known that he wanted Harrison to be the nominee. The nomination occurred on the third ballot. The vice presidential nominee was Levi P. Morton, a New York financier who had been minister to France during Garfield's administration.

In an era of close presidential elections, Harrison faced an arduous struggle against the Democratic nominee, the incumbent president, Grover Cleveland. To win, Harrison had to succeed in the swing states of New York, New Jersey, Connecticut, and Indiana. Recent presidential elections had been determined by the outcome in those states. Other pivotal states included Illinois and Ohio. Cleveland could count on great success in the South, owing to bitter memories of the Republican-led Civil War and Reconstruction, and could challenge Harrison strongly in the pivotal states. Cleveland chose not to campaign actively,

A cotton campaign banner, from 1888, depicts Harrison and his running mate, Levi Morton, with their pledge to aid domestic industry through tariffs.

believing that course was beneath the dignity of the presidency.

Harrison's chief money-raiser was John Wanamaker, the merchant prince of Philadelphia. Wanamaker was given a broad mandate to solicit business contributors. An unprecedented fund was quickly collected. Wanamaker underwrote a campaign featuring salaried speakers, and tons of material extolling the protective tariff. His enterprise was attacked as a ploy to soften up the public to accept a coming shower of favors from a future Harrison administration on business contributors.

Wanamaker's inspired money-raising was a by-product of civil service reform. The Pendleton Act, adopted during the Arthur administration, prohibited the long-standing practice of political assessments. Assessments were levied on a set percentage of a worker's salary as a contribution to the party. The money collected underwrote election expenses. With assessments prohibited, Wanamaker felt driven to solicit funds from business.

On Election Day, Harrison was all confidence. He predicted that "if we can secure an appropriately fair election, I think we are safe." Harrison predicted right, but the outcome had a strange twist. He won a majority of the electoral vote—which gave him the victory—while Cleveland won a majority of the popular vote.

How to explain this difference in outcomes? Harrison carried large states by narrow margins of popular votes. For example, he won New York by 14,000 popular votes, which gained him 36 electoral votes. He won by similar small margins in Indiana, Illinois, Michigan, Ohio, and Pennsylvania. Cleveland's victory over Harrison in the popular vote margin was due to rising Democratic majorities in Southern states.

In the days between the November election and the inauguration the following March, Harrison laid the foundation of his coming administration. His principal task, and the one most fraught with political danger, was selecting his cabinet. Party leaders and groups journeyed to his home in Indianapolis to plead for a place in the cabinet for favored candidates. And seldom did a day pass that did not bring letters from possible appointees.

However, Harrison's biggest headache was the question of what to do about James Blaine, whose support had been pivotal to his nomination. And there were signs that Blaine wanted to be, once again, secretary of state, just as he had been in the Garfield-Arthur administration.

Harrison believed that the offer of a cabinet post to Blaine should be delayed as long as possible: that an early offer might renew the image of Blaine having undue influence, as had been the case in the Garfield-Arthur administration. Harrison waited for three months before inviting Blaine into his administration. The delay and the suspense kept Blaine's supporters under a measure of control for fear that Blaine might ultimately lose out if they pressed too hard.

Harrison's letter to Blaine, offering him the appointment as secretary of state, was a masterpiece of plain talk: "I have another great purpose and duty with which I am sure you will cooperate . . . that is preserving the harmony in the party. Each member of my official family will have my full confidence and I'll expect his." Blaine's reply, accepting his selection as secretary of state, well accommodated Harrison's strategy: "I have no motive, near or far, inconsistent with the greatest strength and highest interest of the administration and yourself as official and personal head." This candid exchange seemed to assure a dignified and effective beginning of the new administration.

Harrison's other cabinet appointments were, if anything, an exercise in creating disappointment and future enmity. The president-elect seemed bent on assembling a cabinet of politically obscure appointees. Party leaders who hoped or expected to have a cabinet place were offended and distressed. The single most important criterion was that the appointee be a

Presbyterian. Harrison also required his secretaries to have a background similar to his. His appointees were lawyers, Civil War generals, or Ohio natives. Harrison's own conduct in choosing his cabinet seemed intended to maximize hurt feelings. He apparently mistrusted anyone from New York, the state most crucial to his election victory. Thomas C. Platt, the New York boss, believed that since he had delivered the New York delegates' support for Harrison's nomination, he should become secretary of the treasury, a department rich in patronage appointments. But Harrison, like earlier presidents, blanched at the thought of handing the Treasury and its patronage over to the New York boss, or to any New Yorker with ties, present or future, to Platt or his New York rival, Warner Miller. Harrison ultimately chose William Windom for the Treasury, a longtime Midwesterner who happened to be living in New York. Benjamin Tracy, a native New Yorker, was selected as secretary of the Navy, a department that had been neglected for decades.

Matt Quay, the Pennsylvania boss, who was also spurned, joined Platt in open warfare against Harrison. Quay, who felt threatened by John Wanamaker, visited Harrison to offer names for the cabinet. Harrison rejected them all.

The inaugural was almost as cheerless as the cabinet-making process. The ceremony took place on March 4, 1889, during a relentless rainstorm. Harrison's audience peered at the proceedings from beneath a mass of umbrellas. Outgoing President Cleveland held an umbrella over his successor's head while Chief Justice Melville Fuller delivered the oath. The fifty-five-year-old Harrison made no concessions to the weather. A slim five feet five inches in height, he stood only slightly taller than James Madison who, at five feet four inches, had been the shortest president. Harrison was immaculately dressed in a Prince Albert coat—his collar turned down—and a high silk hat. He defied the storm, omitting nothing from his

Cartoonists ridiculed Harrison's small stature, exaggerating it by enlarging his head. This typical portrayal, by Joseph Keppler, titled "The Raven," appeared in *Puck*.

four-thousand-word address, which he read in a soft, high-pitched voice. The address covered a substantial list of public problems. Among other things, he urged further civil service reform and the development of America's military and economic power.

Like other presidents of his era, Harrison was besieged by office-seekers. During his first eighteen months in office, he spent four to six hours a day

fingers on his desk, or opened his watch and said, "In five minutes I'm going fishing."

Those who had expected Harrison to use his patronage to placate Republican factional leaders and bosses were disappointed. Quay, Platt, and other party potentates continued to voice their displeasure with Harrison's hiring policies. Civil service reformers were encouraged by Harrison's good words for reform during the campaign and in the inaugural address. They applauded even louder when he ordered department heads to observe civil service law in their hiring practices—especially its call for competitive examinations. But the Republican party, having suffered a loss of federal jobs to the Democrats during Cleveland's presidency, now wanted to turn the tables and bring Republicans in to the federal bureaucracy. (Since civil service law covered only a fraction of federal positions, Harrison could accommodate their demands.) For the first two years of the new administration, Republican appointees widely replaced Democratic incumbents in the federal bureaucracy. Reformers, who had believed the president was more committed to their cause, were disappointed. The New York *Tribune* assailed Harrison in an editorial for carrying on "an orgy of decapitation."

But in the second half of Harrison's term, reformers were pleased with his appointments to the Civil Service Commission. Of the new members, Theodore Roosevelt was especially notable. Flamboyant and aggressive, the youthful Roosevelt was soon complaining that Harrison regularly ignored his recommendations. Roosevelt was particularly troubled by Postmaster General John Wanamaker's effort to bring economy and efficiency to his department, including a system of promotion based on merit. Roosevelt contended that such personnel matters should be handled by the Civil Service Commission. Doubtless, Roosevelt wanted the spotlight of reform to shine only on himself.

At almost every turn of the Roosevelt-Wanamaker

on the task and made nearly seventeen hundred appointments. Harrison did not shrink from hurrying the process along. Those who got into his office to state their case were hustled through it. They remained standing while the president drummed his

dispute, Harrison supported Wanamaker. Roosevelt, although remaining loyal to the administration, was said to have complained that "the little grey man in the White House" treated him "with cold and unhesitating disapproval." In another judgmental moment, Roosevelt was reported to have said, "Harrison had never given the Commission one ounce of backing." Harrison's valued friend and adviser Louis Michener wrote, concerning Roosevelt, "It seems to me that he should be given to understand that it would be well for him to have less to say to the newspapers."

The commissioner of pensions, Corporal James R. Tanner, who lost both legs in the war, had declared, on taking over his pensions post, his resolve "to be more liberal to our boys." In a stormy tenure of six months, he advocated benefits for veterans well beyond the abundant improvements the administration was contemplating. Tanner became a favorite target of the opposition press, and a thorn in the administration's side. Harrison soon rid himself of Tanner by inducing a friend of the corporal to visit his home one midnight with word that his resignation was requested.

The Tanner episode was costly to Republicans in close races in the 1890 midterm congressional elections. Veterans comprised 15 percent of all voters. They were impressed more by Tanner's complaints than by Harrison's approval of a new pension law that increased soldiers' benefits and provided benefits to their widows, minors, dependents, and parents. Pension outlays in the Harrison administration rose from $1 million to $135 million. It was the most generous pension, up to that point, in American history.

An even more contentious issue was the tariff. What became the McKinley Tariff Act of 1890 sparked a struggle that was sharpened by the close division between Republicans and Democrats in Congress. In 1889 the Republican margin over the Democrats in the Senate was two votes, and in the House seven votes. The parties were sharply divided in their views of the tariff, with the Republicans committed to high tariffs to protect domestic industries, while the Democrats saw such tariffs as burdens on consumers and a principal contributor to the growing surplus in the Treasury. The excessive revenue collections pulled money from circulation and depressed the economy.

What emerged was the McKinley Tariff Act of 1890, many of whose provisions were framed by a diversity of business leaders. Their lobbyists and supportive congressmen then wrote their version of protection into the new tariff law. Tariffs rose by an average of 49.5 percent. Harrison participated actively with congressional leaders in the act's development. Consumers promptly experienced rising prices for many staples of everyday living, generated by higher tariff rates. Fortunately, the McKinley Tariff Act provided for reciprocity agreements, enabling the president to lower tariffs if a nation with which the United States traded made similar concessions. Harrison and Blaine brokered this provision with congressional leaders. More than a dozen agreements were negotiated with other countries.

Another major accomplishment of the Harrison administration was the passage of the Sherman Antitrust Act. Trusts are combinations of businesses, formed to control ever larger shares of the market, to reduce competition, set higher prices, and reap greater profits. They were growing rapidly in industries such as sugar, shoes, oil, and gas.

Both Republicans and Democrats adopted antitrust planks in the 1888 elections. Harrison, in approving the Sherman Act, had redeemed a campaign pledge. He advocated competition and opposed monopolies, the ideal of the trusts. When given a large Siberian bloodhound, he noted that "the dog looks very much like an overfed monopolist." With the midterm congressional elections approaching, Harrison hoped that the Sherman Antitrust Act would offset the McKinley Tariff Act, by bringing lower prices and freer competition. However, he could do little to enforce the Sherman Act. He was blocked by congressional failure to appropriate the funds to investigate the trusts and to bring legal actions against them. The Senate, which passed the Sherman Act by one vote, was the trusts' ultimate fortress against the government.

Unlike trusts, the debate about silver and the currency was not prominent in the 1888 election. But soon after the inauguration, the issue gathered force. The matter cut across party lines, although both parties were antisilver. Generally, the West and South were strongholds of silver advocates, while the East and to a lesser degree the Midwest supported the gold standard. Harrison seemed friendly to silver, but he dodged commitment to free coinage of silver at a set ratio to gold—such as the often prevailing market rate of sixteen ounces of silver to one ounce of gold. Many delegates to the 1888 Republican nominating convention from Western silver mining states voted for Harrison, expecting that he would be supportive of silver. They were encouraged by the presence of Secretary of the Treasury William Windom, who in the past had supported the silver cause. The Sherman Silver Purchase Act of 1890, which Harrison signed, required the government to purchase 4.5 million ounces of silver each month at the prevailing market price, through issuance of treasury notes redeemable in gold or silver. It was feared that the greater outpouring of paper money would seriously strain the Treasury's reserves of gold.

Harrison was not enamored of the gold standard. A common complaint against reliance on gold was that it unduly restricted the amount of money in circulation, raising interest rates paid by borrowers, and bringing particular hardship to farmers. But, as president Harrison announced his opposition to expanding the currency further. The silver faction was outraged. Harrison had put another nail in the coffin of his chances for reelection.

The dejected silverites and Eastern Republicans upset over patronage joined in common cause against Harrison. In 1891 he tried to make amends by declaring that he "believed in bimetallism and the fullest use of silver with our currency compatible with parity between gold and silver dollars in our commercial use." But these cautiously qualified words were not enough to rescue the president from the damage done.

In another major initiative, Harrison strove to enhance the effectiveness of voting rights for blacks in the South. He was alert to the necessity of strengthening Republican voting performance in that region where his own campaign had done poorly. In Congress, legislation emerged, which sought to protect black suffrage by putting Southern elections under federal control. Harrison actively supported the legislation. He called congressional opponents and fence-sitters to the White House and worked at inducing them to support the legislation. But Republican legislators were divided, and the legislation failed. Big city bosses feared the application of the bill to their tightly controlled and abused domains. Harrison also supported the Blair education bill as a potential boon to black interests, calling for federal aid to combat illiteracy. Harrison felt that education was the most promising antidote to black repression. But Congress was again divided, and the Blair bill failed. A *Nation* editorial warned that the bill opened the gates to "complete federal control of education."

Like earlier Republican presidents of his era, Harrison continued the practice of awarding patronage appointments to accomplished blacks, preferring the young to the old. The distinguished black leader Frederick Douglass was named minister to Haiti. Harrison tried, not always successfully, to appoint blacks to postmasterships in larger Southern cities. On balance, Harrison's efforts improved his standing with black leaders and the black press.

The second half of the Harrison presidency centered more on foreign affairs than on domestic policy. Various influences contributed to the shift. The 1890 elections changed drastically the party composition of Congress. Where in the first half of Harrison's presidency the major parties were largely in balance, the 1890 elections were a rich harvest for the Democrats, and drained prospects for the president's initiatives. Foreign affairs, in contrast, allowed the president more freedom from legislators and party leaders, many of whom Harrison had alienated. The international canvas permitted greater play for a president supremely confident of his own capabilities and reluctant to delegate power and decision to others of lesser talent.

Harrison's role in foreign affairs was also enlarged by the faltering health of Secretary of State James G. Blaine, whose ailments kept him in bed for weeks at a time. The president worked easily with the second in command at the State Department, John W. Foster. The foreign policy of Harrison and the department were influenced by Alfred Thayer Mahan's classic study, *The Influence of Sea Power Upon History, 1660–1783*. Harrison, reflecting on Mahan's analysis, saw the military importance of an isthmian canal in Central America, a Navy of sufficient strength to protect it, the securing of naval coaling stations in the Caribbean, and the annexation of Hawaii. Hawaii plus an improved Navy could enhance defense of the American west coast.

Mindful of Mahan, Harrison rescued a Navy whose fortunes in past decades had been erratic. Following the Civil War, Congressional appropriations declined, as did the Navy's manpower. In the 1880s congressional support of naval expansion wavered, with shifts in the party balance in Congress. Harrison pressed for, and won, increased congressional support. When the United States entered the Spanish-American War in 1898, seven of the Navy's ten modern ships had been authorized during the Harrison administration.

This military capacity was aided by the swift progress of the industrial revolution. The Civil War had commenced an expansion of manufacturing and

Frederick Douglass, the eminent black leader who criticized Harrison's efforts on behalf of black Americans, posed for this portrait ca. 1879. Douglass served in the Harrison administration as minister to Haiti.

banking that rolled swiftly onward in the decades that
followed. Science and invention, led by Thomas Edison, exploited new resources of iron and power. Harrison and Blaine agreed that the nation's fast-growing
industrial production required expanded foreign markets. Blaine proposed increased trade with Latin
America and asked the president to convene a conference of Latin American countries to consider a broad
agenda.

Seventeen Latin American countries sent delegates
to Washington. Blaine skillfully presided over the
conference, and Harrison watched its proceedings
closely. But one item after another of the United
States agenda was voted down. The delegates were
suspicious that the United States was set on a course
of dominance and exploitation. The conference's
principal achievement was the establishment of the
Pan-American Union, a clearinghouse for disseminat-
ing information and for facilitating cooperation
among the member countries. The conference also
included a forty-two-day, 6,000-mile tour of the
United States to impress the visitors with the country's size, wealth, and manufacturing capabilities. In
reviewing the conference's lack of policy-making,
Harrison and Blaine agreed that future endeavors
might be more successful if they negotiated commercial reciprocal trade agreements and treaties.

Otherwise, in his Latin American initiatives, Harrison advocated construction of a Central American
isthmian canal. The United States also came close to
war with Chile. Trouble erupted when American
sailors on leave in Valparaiso, Chile, were caught up
in a saloon brawl, in which two American sailors were
killed, seventeen injured, and others chased by rioters.
When Chile failed to express any regret, Harrison
sent a sharp note, complaining of the delay of an
apology. As Chile continued to move slowly, Harrison
in his annual message to Congress on December 9,
1891, declared that if the United States did not
receive an appropriate response, he would bring the
matter before Congress "for such action as may be
necessary." The dispute rolled on, and Harrison
ordered the Navy to prepare for action.

The Democratic press accused Harrison of maneuvering to create a war, while seeking reelection
with a wartime slogan: "Don't swap horses in mid-
stream." Ultimately Blaine's preference for patience
and peace prevailed, and Chile responded with an
apology and indemnity.

Harrison's expansionist interests extended to the
Pacific with his goal of annexing the Hawaiian Islands
to the United States. Late in his term, Queen Liliuo-

kalani was overthrown. Harrison immediately dispatched troops to Hawaii to protect American lives and property. He placed a treaty before the Senate on February 16, 1893, urging an "annexation full and complete." It was essential, the president said, that no other foreign power acquire Hawaii, since "such possession would not consist with our safety, and with the peace of the world." But the Senate, controlled by the Democrats, declined to act before Harrison's tenure expired. His successor, a firm antiannexationist, Grover Cleveland, withdrew the treaty.

With the Republican nominating convention scheduled for June 1892, Blaine suddenly resigned as secretary of state for reasons not altogether clear—whether because of his continued illness or a desire to run again for president. His statement soon followed, declaring that his name would not be introduced at the convention, but it said nothing about Harrison, his presidential record, or his renomination.

At the convention in Minneapolis, Platt, Quay, and other bosses, looking for a candidate other than Harrison, supported Blaine. On the first ballot, Harrison received 535 votes, Blaine 182, and Ohio Governor William McKinley, also 182. The Democrats nominated Grover Cleveland, and for the first time in American history two presidents were competing with each other for the right to serve a second term. Both candidates ran dignified but largely uninspired campaigns. The Republican party was badly divided, with party bosses resentful of Harrison's handling of patronage, and the Mugwump reformers disdainful toward him for having done little for civil service reform. Harrison was dejected by the death of his wife from tuberculosis only weeks before the election. Cleveland won with 277 electoral votes, to Harrison's 145; the Populist candidate, James B. Weaver, received 22.

Upon leaving the presidency, Harrison returned to his law practice. He delivered a series of lectures at Stanford University in 1894. He toured the Northwest and vacationed in upstate New York. He died of pneumonia on March 13, 1901.

History has been kind to Benjamin Harrison. Emphasizing his ability in extracting legislation from Congress—with its centerpiece, the Sherman Antitrust Act—and his leadership in laying the groundwork for an expanded United States presence in international affairs, some historians hail the Harrison presidency as the most achieving in the half-century between Lincoln and the progressive era of Theodore Roosevelt and Woodrow Wilson.

—LOUIS W. KOENIG

WILLIAM McKINLEY

Silent crowds watched the coffin pass through the streets of Buffalo, New York, of Washington, D.C., and of Canton, Ohio, in September 1901. The more reflective mourners may have noted that the casket contained the remains of the last Civil War veteran to be elected to the White House. William McKinley had led the nation through a different war, and his victory had planted the American flag halfway around the world. At home McKinley had bequeathed to his successor a restless people whose progress could now be measured by smoking steel mills, rising cities, and the growth of giant trusts.

Under McKinley the United States had plunged ahead but had not yet learned to read the signposts pointing to its future. The day before he was shot, the president told visitors at the Pan-American Exposition in Buffalo: "Isolation is no longer possible or desirable. . . . The period of exclusiveness is past." And yet, despite his vision of international affairs, McKinley was caught between the 1800s and the turbulent new century of which he lived to see so little.

William McKinley, Jr., the seventh of nine children of William and Nancy Allison McKinley, was born on January 29, 1843, in Niles, Ohio. As a child, he liked school and developed into a religious, intelligent, and diligent young man. At seventeen he entered Allegheny College but withdrew after one term because of illness. A downturn in family finances prevented his return to college, and he taught school and clerked in a post office until the outbreak of the Civil War.

Stirred by his family's abolitionist sympathies and attracted by the adventure that war seemed to offer, McKinley enlisted in the 23d Ohio Volunteer Infantry Regiment. He fought courageously in some of the bloodiest battles of the war, rising to the rank of major. His commanding officer, Rutherford B. Hayes, called him "one of the bravest and finest officers in the army."

After the war McKinley read law, was admitted to the Ohio bar, and started a practice in Canton, a county seat. Friendly, handsome, self-assured, and modest, McKinley moved confidently in Canton's social and professional circles. As a Republican and a friend of gubernatorial candidate Hayes, he established a reputation for himself as an effective speaker and vigorous campaigner. In 1869 he was elected prosecuting attorney of Stark County.

Clearly an impressive figure in Canton, McKinley remained an eligible bachelor until he met the socially prominent Ida Saxton, a fragile but attractive young woman who returned his love. They were married in January 1871, and their first child, Katherine, was born on Christmas Day of that year. The young family seemed to have a bright future. But just before their second child was born in the spring of 1873, Ida's mother died, and the new infant, another girl, lived only a few months. Ida sank into a mental and physical depression and began to have epileptic seizures. Then in 1875 their four-year-old daughter Katherine died. After that, Ida's mind and body steadily declined. She clung possessively to her husband and insisted that he cater to her every whim. For the rest of his life McKinley bore this burden privately.

Politics provided some relief. Elected to Congress in 1876, McKinley moved with his wife to a Washington hotel and struggled to pay her doctors and the bills run up by her expensive tastes. Hayes was now president, and the new congressman enjoyed this masculine political world, where his cordial, graceful manner endeared him to his colleagues.

Representative McKinley established himself as a dependable and thoughtful party regular, who was also attentive to the interests of the workingman. His consuming interest was the tariff. McKinley set out to master its many intricacies. He championed protection for industrial products because he was convinced that barriers to cheap foreign goods would buttress both the wages of the American laborer and the profits of up-and-coming businesses. By 1888, he had

President McKinley radiates confidence and success as he rides through the streets of Buffalo, New York, in September 1901.

had a mixed record. In 1878 he voted for the inflationary Bland-Allison Act that provided for free coinage of silver; then he voted to pass the act over Hayes's veto. During the 1880s McKinley followed most Ohio Republicans in falling back on a compromise bimetallist position that would allow for some silver money but not full-fledged inflation through free coinage. In 1890 he supported the Sherman Silver Purchase Act, a further attempt to compromise the issues, authored by another of his Ohio mentors, Senator John Sherman, the brother of General William T. Sherman. The Sherman Act backfired, offending both silverite inflationists and anti-inflationist "goldbugs." McKinley later became a strong champion of the gold standard.

The McKinley Tariff Act of 1890 made its author a well-known figure across the country. At the 1892 Republican convention, where he supported Senator Sherman's presidential candidacy, McKinley refused to allow his name to be placed on the ballot as a compromise candidate. But it was at this convention that Marcus A. "Mark" Hanna resolved that someday McKinley would become president. Hanna, a shrewd millionaire industrialist from Cleveland—who would later be called a kingmaker—always played a supporting role behind McKinley. Hanna supplied the money and organized the campaign while McKinley stood out front as the wise statesman.

In 1890 a slump in Republican fortunes, together with a Democratic gerrymander in his homestate, cost McKinley his seat in Congress. The next year, however, aided by Hanna, he easily won the Ohio governorship.

As governor, McKinley reformed the state tax structure to lighten the burden on homeowners. He dealt with a violent coal miners' strike in 1894 by calling out the National Guard to restore order, but for the most part he remained sympathetic to the workers. He set up a board to arbitrate labor disputes, and raised funds and collected food for strikers.

risen within the House Republican ranks to become chairman of the Ways and Means Committee, a stature which allowed him to write a tariff act of his own. He regarded this task as his greatest achievement in Congress. The high rates placed by the McKinley Tariff Act on agricultural products and manufactured goods reflected the protectionist view, but the act also included a reciprocity arrangement that permitted the president to lower certain duties if he found that other nations were willing to lower duties on American goods.

On the other big economic issue of the time, monetary inflation through coinage of silver, McKinley

His landslide reelection to the governorship in 1893 made McKinley the front-runner for the Republican presidential nomination in 1896. Early that year, he and Mark Hanna began to prepare for the presidential quest. A severe economic depression during the current Democratic administration made Republican chances seem bright. Still, the monetary issue disrupted the political scene, and McKinley tried to avoid taking a firm stand on either side. Hanna, meanwhile, awed Republican leaders with such an expensive, well-organized campaign that McKinley had the nomination in the bag before the delegates met.

The main interest at the convention centered on what stand the party—and McKinley—would take on the money issue. Western Republicans wanted free silver and threatened to bolt the party if they did not get it. Nevertheless, McKinley and Hanna decided to declare for gold. Their platform stated that the party was "opposed to the free coinage of silver" and that "the existing gold standard must be maintained." McKinley defied the bolting Westerners because he believed that the gold plank would clinch the Northeast and give him a good chance in the Midwest, where industrial workers could be told that a shift to silver would jeopardize their wages and their jobs. Garret A. Hobart, a New Jersey lawyer, was chosen to be McKinley's running mate.

Silverites dominated the Democratic gathering in July. That convention reached its climax when former Congressman William Jennings Bryan of Nebraska spoke. This masterful young orator thundered defiance: "Having behind us the producing masses of this nation and the world, supported by the commercial interests, the laboring interests and the toilers everywhere, we will answer their demand for a gold standard by saying to them: You shall not press down upon the brow of labor this crown of thorns. You shall not crucify mankind upon a cross of gold." The Democrats chose Bryan as their nominee, as did the

agrarian radical Populist party and the silver Republican rebels.

Bryan barnstormed around the country giving speeches, but he had little money for the campaign. McKinley stayed at home on his front porch in Canton, where he received carefully screened delegations and targeted his appeals to their concerns. This was a businesslike campaign, both in its use of market research and sales techniques and in its lavish but selective spending. Hanna raised millions of dollars; he spent the money mainly on pamphlets and press releases that broadcast McKinley's views to targeted

A political cartoon from the 1896 campaign shows McKinley, his opponent William Jennings Bryan, and their running mates as interchangeable cut-out paper dolls.

the presidency in November, with the first popular majority in six elections and an electoral vote margin of 271 to 176.

One of President McKinley's first orders of business was, predictably, the tariff. Calling for higher tariffs in his inaugural address, McKinley approved the Dingley Bill of 1897, which raised rates to new heights, but once more empowered the president to negotiate tariff concessions with other nations.

The tariff and other domestic issues in McKinley's presidency were soon overshadowed by the Spanish-American War. Earlier in the 1890s the Cubans had revolted against their Spanish overlords. The rebel leaders mounted a violent guerrilla war against both the Spanish authorities and civilian property. The Spanish governor, Valeriano Weyler, retaliated by herding Cubans into *reconcentrados*—or concentration camps. The violence in Cuba also affected Americans. By the end of 1897, loss of American property there amounted to sixteen million dollars.

In his inaugural address, McKinley had said that he wanted "no wars of conquest; we must avoid the temptation of territorial aggression." And although he was horrified by events in Cuba, he assured Carl Schurz, the venerable German-American editor and politician, that there would be "no jingo nonsense under my administration."

Those pledges were easier to make than to keep. The Cuban rebels organized a shrewd publicity campaign that appealed to Americans' anticolonial sentiments and exaggerated Spanish barbarities while downplaying their own. The atrocity stories found a ready outlet in the American press, particularly in the new mass-circulation city newspapers which purveyed "yellow journalism." In New York City the rival press barons Joseph Pulitzer and William Randolph Hearst were fighting a circulation war that used the Cuban revolt as the main weapon. Both publishers sent celebrity correspondents, including the novelist Stephen Crane and the artist Frederic Remington, to

groups. Hanna also gave many state delegations train fare to come and see McKinley in Canton. The railroads cooperated by offering reduced rates so that citizens from many states could journey to the home of the Republican candidate. On one day alone, McKinley spoke to some thirty thousand visitors. He won

Cuba. Hearst told Remington, "You furnish the pictures and I'll furnish the war."

For more than a year McKinley sought a diplomatic solution. Spain refused his offers to mediate, but then the Spanish moderated their policies and promised a degree of autonomy for Cuba. The Spanish ambassador in Washington, however, lost his influence in February 1898, when Hearst's New York *Journal* secured and published a copy of a letter in which he described McKinley as "weak and a bidder for the admiration of the crowd, besides being a would-be politician who tries to leave a door open behind himself while keeping on good terms with the jingoes of his party."

Meanwhile, disaster struck in Havana Harbor. In late January the battleship *Maine* had made a courtesy call there. On February 15 an explosion ripped open the hull and sank the ship, killing some 260 men. To this day, no one knows what caused the explosion. The Hearst papers thundered, "The *Maine* was destroyed by treachery."

In March the president secured a fifty million dollar defense appropriation to use at his discretion. He told Spain that the United States wanted peace brought to Cuba immediately; implicit was a demand that the island be freed. Although Spanish leaders knew Cuba was lost, they regarded defeat in war as more honorable than surrender without a fight.

The president now believed that he had no more time to negotiate; it seemed likely that Congress might declare war without waiting for him to request it. He therefore sent a war message to Congress. McKinley deeply regretted this final step, but he believed that he had made every reasonable effort to avert war. Congress declared war on April 25, 1898. The New York *Sun* proclaimed, "We are all jingoes now; and the head jingo is the Hon. William McKinley."

The Navy was prepared for war, thanks to gradual modernization under previous presidents. In the fall of 1897 McKinley had approved Navy Department plans to station Commodore George Dewey's Pacific fleet in Hong Kong, a location from which it could strike at the Spanish-held Philippine Islands. With the declaration of war, Dewey attacked on May 1 and sent most of the Spanish fleet to the bottom of Manila Bay. Before the battle few Americans knew anything about the Philippines; indeed, McKinley himself had to hunt for the islands on the White House globe. But the nation went wild at the news of victory.

The main theater of war was in Cuba, where the

JOHN M. HAY

John M. Hay's record as a statesman was, President McKinley said, "one of the most important and interesting pages of our diplomatic history." Trained as a lawyer, Hay left Springfield, Illinois, in his early twenties to act as assistant private secretary to President-elect Abraham Lincoln, whom he served until 1865. After traveling abroad as a diplomat, he returned to the United States in 1870 and wrote for the New York *Tribune*. Hay served as assistant secretary of state from 1879 to 1881, and in 1897 he was appointed ambassador to Great Britain by McKinley. Named secretary of state after the outbreak of the Spanish-American War in 1898, he pushed President McKinley's policy of American rule in the Philippines. In 1899 he formulated the Open Door policy in China and helped preserve China's territorial integrity during the Boxer Rebellion of 1900. Retaining his post under Theodore Roosevelt, Hay settled the Alaskan boundary dispute in 1903 and concluded the Hay-Pauncefote Treaty with Britain, which cleared the way for construction of the Panama Canal. Hay was a poet, novelist, and historian as well as a diplomat. Among his published works are *Pike County Ballads*, *Castilian Days*, *The Bread-Winners*, and the ten-volume *Abraham Lincoln: A History*, which he wrote with John Nicolay in 1890.

weeks later the city surrendered. On July 25 American forces also landed on Puerto Rico.

Late that month Spain sued for peace. McKinley stated his terms: independence for Cuba; transfer of Puerto Rico to the United States as a war indemnity; and the fate of the Philippines would be decided at a peace conference. Spain accepted these terms on August 10.

Other contemporaneous events of lasting importance occurred in the Pacific. In 1897 McKinley had failed to win approval by two-thirds of the Senate of a treaty annexing the Hawaiian Islands. A year later he accomplished this goal by a joint resolution of Congress, which required only simple majorities; Hawaii was formally annexed on August 12, 1898. That same summer, American forces bound for the Philippines occupied Wake Island and the Spanish island of Guam, which were later ceded to the United States.

The future of the Philippines was the major question at the peace conference held in Paris during the fall of 1898. The decision was up to McKinley, who later said, "I walked the floor of the White House night after night until midnight, and . . . I went down on my knees and prayed to Almighty God for light and guidance more than one night. And one night late it came to me . . . that there was nothing left for us to do but to take them all, and to educate the Filipinos, and uplift them and civilize and Christianize them. . . ."

Spain yielded the islands in exchange for a payment of twenty million dollars, but approval of the treaty by the United States Senate was not so easy. The main issue was whether a nation that had gained its own independence through revolution against a colonial power should now become a colonial power itself.

Not only Democrats but also a number of Republicans like Carl Schurz and independents like Mark Twain denounced this as "imperialism" and an imitation of European despotisms. Southern Democrats

Army and Navy carried out a joint assault. The Army was not prepared for war. Wheezing, potbellied senior officers faltered in the tropical heat. Ill-trained volunteers were rushed into action because the standing Army was too small. Troops massing at Tampa, Florida, suffered from shortages of food, water, and medicine while sweltering in winter uniforms. The Army finally landed east of Santiago de Cuba in late June, and after a series of small battles, they pushed the Spanish back toward the city. Meanwhile, Rear Admiral William T. Sampson trapped a Spanish fleet in Santiago Bay. When the fleet attempted to escape on July 3, it was destroyed by American ships. Two

balked at the prospect of bringing additional non-white "inferiors" under the American flag. McKinley invoked party discipline, appealed to national pride, and dispensed patronage that bordered on bribery. He also benefited from a major tactical blunder by William Jennings Bryan, who urged Democratic senators to vote for the Treaty of Paris so that their party could make the Philippines an issue in the next election. Finally, by the time the senators voted, the Filipinos were in rebellion against their American "liberators." Their action probably changed the votes of a few previously antitreaty senators who were outraged by the insurrection. On February 6 the Senate consented to the treaty by just one vote more than the two-thirds required.

One aspect of the decision to annex Hawaii and take the Philippines that got little attention at the time was its revolutionary impact on American foreign policy. The nation that had prided itself on "isolation" from the Old World and avoidance of "entangling alliances" was now reaching out thousands of miles to accept security commitments in distant parts of the world. The Asian side of the Pacific was a cockpit of rivalry among the European imperial powers, and one of McKinley's reasons for acquiring the Philippines was fear that some other nation would get them. That area was also the seat of commercial competition for the potentially vast trade of China, and advocates of taking the Philippines were interested in the islands chiefly as a foothold and staging place for future involvement in China. Few moves in American history have proved more momentous than McKinley's dimly conceived decision to take the Philippines.

A White House office does temporary duty in 1898 as a command post where McKinley and his aides follow the progress of the Spanish-American War.

WILLIAM JENNINGS BRYAN

The election of 1900 was a rematch for William Jennings Bryan as he campaigned for a second time against McKinley. He continued to call for free coinage of silver as a cure-all for the ills of the masses. Bryan saw the campaign as more than a contest of politics and economics. "Every political . . . [and] economic question," he asserted, "is in reality a great moral question." To Bryan it was a contest between good and evil; a struggle on behalf of the "toiling masses."

Born in Salem, Illinois, in 1860, Bryan was raised to believe in Protestant morality and government by majority rule. With these ideals the young lawyer moved to Nebraska, where he was elected to Congress in 1890. Already known as a silver-tongued orator, he spoke against the protective tariff and the repeal of the silver-purchase law. But he was not invincible as the Democratic nominee for president. He lost not only in 1896 and 1900 but also again in 1908 to William Howard Taft. Continuing as a leader in the Democratic party, he kept his ideas before the people through lecture tours and editorials in his weekly newspaper, the *Commoner*. In 1913 Woodrow Wilson appointed him secretary of state. Unable to reconcile his antiwar convictions with the risks of American involvement in World War I, Bryan resigned in 1915.

Bryan continued to be active in Democratic politics and in religious and moral causes for the rest of his life. Shortly before his death, in 1925, he became involved in the prosecution of John T. Scopes, an instructor who was indicted for teaching the theory of evolution, then banned by law from the Tennessee public schools. Bryan, a fundamentalist who had helped to draft such legislation, was subjected to a stinging cross-examination by Clarence Darrow that held his religious beliefs up to ridicule. It was a sad end to the career of "the Great Commoner." To the "plain people" of America he was, as one Nebraskan put it, "the brightest and purest advocate of our cause. . . ."

The Philippine "insurrection" lasted three years. The United States committed 120,000 men, 1,000 of whom were killed. The insurgents, losing battle after battle, reverted to a brutal form of guerrilla warfare in 1900, which in turn provoked counteratrocities by American forces. Not until 1902 was the last rebel leader captured and the acquisitions "pacified."

McKinley named William Howard Taft to head a commission to establish civil government in the Philippines, and Taft set up a stable, relatively benign colonial regime. Likewise, in Puerto Rico a civil government was established, while Major General Leonard Wood, appointed military governor of Cuba, guided that island toward self-government.

Meanwhile, at home, the monetary debate was settled once and for all in 1900 with the adoption of the Gold Standard Act, supported by McKinley. The act declared the gold dollar the sole standard of currency. This domestic accomplishment and the victory in war supplied the main issues on which McKinley stood for reelection in 1900. Theodore Roosevelt became his running mate, replacing Vice President Hobart, who had died in 1899. Bryan ran again as the Democratic nominee, speaking out for free silver and against imperialism, but McKinley owned the only thing that counted—prosperity.

The prosperity continued into his second term, and social and economic problems seemed hidden by the glossy facade of wealth. McKinley's popularity grew even greater after his reelection, but he continued to study public opinion and to guide it when he could.

Mrs. McKinley's health remained the president's gravest personal problem. Although she was having fewer and fewer "good days," Ida McKinley would not be shunted aside as White House hostess. Her frequent seizures startled guests at receptions and state dinners. Her stubborn "courage" added immeasurably to her husband's burdens.

On September 5, 1901, McKinley spoke at the

Pan-American Exposition in Buffalo. The following day he held a public reception in the Temple of Music on the exhibition grounds. Among those who attended was an anarchist, Leon Czolgosz, who carried a gun wrapped in a bandaged hand. He stepped in front of McKinley and shot him twice in the abdomen. The president was rushed to an emergency hospital on the exposition grounds, but the doctors failed to locate the second bullet, which had ripped the stomach walls. The lighting in the operating room was inadequate, and the wound was sewn up, without proper drainage, with only the aid of the setting sun and a reflecting mirror. McKinley rallied briefly, and on September 7 a medical bulletin assured the worried public that "no serious symptoms have developed." Within a few days, however, a gangrenous infection set in. On the evening of September 14, the physician attending William McKinley announced to the nation: "The president is dead." His last words to Ida had been those of a favorite hymn, "Nearer, my God to Thee, Nearer to Thee."

Those last words captured the mixed quality of McKinley as man and president. He retained the beliefs that he had learned in his small-town Ohio childhood, and yet he had presided over some of the biggest changes in American life. At home, he had aided the growth of big business and industry, which were already obliterating the world in which he had grown up. Abroad, he helped to thrust America onto the world stage and set a course that would lead to great events in the next century. McKinley was a wise,

The terrifying face of anarchist Leon Czolgosz stares from behind bars in the first photograph of the killer, published on the cover of *Leslie's Weekly* on September 9, 1901. He was convicted of murder and executed in a newly installed electric chair.

thoughtful man. He remains a divided figure, both the last president of the nineteenth century and, barely, the first president of the twentieth.

—DONALD YOUNG,
revised by JOHN MILTON COOPER, JR.

THEODORE ROOSEVELT

THE GIANT IN THE BULLY PULPIT

Theodore Roosevelt could not have been more unlike his predecessor in the White House. Roosevelt epitomized a brash new breed of political activists. "Get action, do things," Roosevelt once declared, ". . . take a place wherever you are and be somebody. . . ." Hunter and scholar, rancher and soldier, black-tie patrician and controversial reformer, he was a man of volcanic energy. Impatient with precedent, sensitive to the new needs and conflicts of a nation expanding industrially and asserting its place in the world, he was a prime mover in shaping the modern presidency as we know it today.

Roosevelt is the only native of New York City to have become president. "Teedie" was born on October 27, 1858, at 28 East 20th Street. His grandfather, Cornelius Van Schaack Roosevelt, had been a tycoon who ranked with Cornelius Vanderbilt and William B. Astor among New York's titans. Teedie's father, Theodore, Sr.—whom his son considered "the best man I ever knew"—was a glass importer with substantial banking interests and an active Republican. "Take care of your morals first, your health next," he advised Teedie, "and finally your studies." Teedie's mother was Martha Bulloch, an aristocratic Georgian who, despite her husband's friendship with Lincoln, remained loyal to the South during the Civil War. It was a lively family, including three children besides Theodore.

"Nothing in this world is worth having or worth doing," an older TR declared, "unless it means effort, pain, difficulty. . . ." Roosevelt's childhood, despite wealth and status, gave the future president great pain indeed. As a young boy, Teedie was frail, nearsighted, and wracked by asthma. Educated at home by tutors, Teedie read widely and voraciously, and cultivated an abiding interest in natural science, turning his bedroom into a museum of stuffed birds and animals.

He entered Harvard at seventeen, his original aim to become a naturalist like Audubon. But his father's death from cancer during his junior year plunged him into grief, and he went through an identity crisis that drove him away from his early affinity for science and left him determined to enter politics. Still a serious scholar, he graduated twenty-first in a class of 177 and was elected to Phi Beta Kappa. In addition to his studies, he also boxed in the college gym and rode horseback and hiked outdoors in all weather. Likewise, he hobnobbed with Boston's aristocracy, from whose ranks he picked a bride, Alice Hathaway Lee. Married in 1880, the year of TR's graduation, they moved in with his widowed mother.

At Columbia Law School TR sought diversion by joining the National Guard, riding horseback in Central Park, and attending big parties. Also, in 1881 he joined New York City's Twenty-first District Republican Club. A year later the twenty-three-year-old Roosevelt won the Twenty-first District's seat in the New York assembly. His upper-class accent was promptly heard in the chambers of Albany as the fledgling assemblyman accused financier Jay Gould of attempting to corrupt New York State politics, denouncing him as "part of that most dangerous of all dangerous classes, the wealthy criminal class." Roosevelt was soon contemptuously christened a Harvard "goo-goo," or one committed to good government.

Actually, TR's political reform record in Albany was spotty. He was something of a maverick whom his party's leaders could not manage, but he was also a fiercely partisan Republican. The most important consequence of these early years in the New York legislature was his relationship with the press. He made good copy, and New York newspapers gave him lots of coverage. He, in turn, learned how to cultivate reporters to his advantage.

Tragedy hit the Roosevelt family again in February 1884. On the same day, TR's mother died of typhoid fever and his young wife died of Bright's disease, two

Theodore Roosevelt used every chance he got to preach to the American people about the "strenuous life." This photograph was taken in Hannibal, Missouri, in 1903.

President Roosevelt's rambunctious family gathers in an uncharacteristically subdued pose. Left to right, Quentin, the president, Theodore, Archibald, Alice, Kermit, Mrs. Roosevelt, and Ethel.

days after giving birth to a daughter whom he named Alice. These fresh tragedies plunged Roosevelt into another crisis of grief and soul-searching. After completing his work in Albany and briefly taking part in national Republican politics, he gave up his seat in the state legislature and left his infant daughter in the care of his older sister. He headed west to the newly settled Dakota Territory, where he sought to conquer sorrow through "the strenuous life . . . of labor and strife."

This Western interlude completed the self-transformation that Roosevelt had begun as a teenager. Later, politically, this experience also gave him a reputation for being a man of the people who could hold his own in a rough environment. TR gained strength and confidence from branding steers and breaking stampedes at a ranch in the Badlands. There is no

doubt that he won the respect of his ranch hands, despite their initial derision of him as a "four-eyed tenderfoot." Although given to patrician commands, such as "Hasten forward quickly," he could ride herd with the best of them.

His daughter Alice and affairs of the heart called him home, as he renewed a childhood affection for Edith Kermit Carow, a strong, independent woman. They were married in December 1886, and Edith Roosevelt became a major, though quiet force in her husband's life. They had five children, four sons and a daughter, who formed a rambunctious family. As a stepmother, however, Edith never established a warm relationship with Alice, who became a difficult, rebellious young woman.

A small political reward fell to Roosevelt in 1889 when President Benjamin Harrison appointed him to the United States Civil Service Commission. The position had few powers and involved investigating abuses of the civil service law. Nevertheless, TR gained national attention by vowing to uphold the law and "let the chips fall where they will." He spotted blackmail in the New York Customs House and fought campaign assessments of federal workers. He helped to remove thousands of federal jobs from political patronage before he left the post in 1895.

In 1895 TR was appointed New York City police commissioner by reform Mayor William L. Strong. Again TR courted headlines by fighting both Democrats and Republicans to establish a merit system of police appointment and promotion. He helped condemn tenements, fought graft, supported social work, and pounded the precincts until dawn to keep officers on their toes. TR's two years as police commissioner added to his public image as a swashbuckling character. Cartoonists delighted in caricaturing him with his glasses, walrus moustache, big teeth, and broad-brimmed Western hat.

In 1897 President McKinley appointed Roosevelt assistant secretary of the Navy. TR seized every chance to thrust himself forward. An overt imperialist and a disciple of Alfred Thayer Mahan's theory of naval supremacy as a key to world power, he hailed territorial conquest as a hallmark of racial superiority over the "weak and craven." He thought a direct assault upon Spanish-held Cuba would be "a bully war."

On February 25, 1898, TR cabled Commodore Dewey in the Pacific, ordering the fleet to Hong Kong. "In the event of declaration of war [against] Spain," he ordered, "your duty will be to see that the Spanish squadron does not leave the Asiatic coast, and then offensive operations in Philippine Islands." TR always portrayed this action as a bold stroke that helped assure American victory in Manila Bay. Actually, it was a routine order approved earlier by President McKinley. After war was declared, Roosevelt resigned from the Navy Department to raise a caval-

ry regiment. He rounded up an improbable band of uppercrust sportsmen and ranch hands, whom he whipped into shape as the renowned "Rough Riders." Charging up San Juan Hill, in Cuba, Roosevelt dis-

BIOGRAPHICAL FACTS

BIRTH: New York, N.Y., Oct. 27, 1858

ANCESTRY: Dutch, Scotch, English, and Huguenot

FATHER: Theodore Roosevelt; b. New York, N.Y., Sept. 22, 1831; d. New York, N.Y., Feb. 9, 1878

FATHER'S OCCUPATIONS: Glass importer; merchant; banker

MOTHER: Martha Bulloch Roosevelt; b. Roswell, Ga., July 8, 1834; d. New York, N.Y., Feb. 14, 1884

BROTHER: Elliott (1860–1894)

SISTERS: Anna (1855–1931); Corinne (1861–1933)

FIRST MARRIAGE: Brookline, Mass., Oct. 27, 1880

FIRST WIFE: Alice Hathaway Lee; b. Chestnut Hill, Mass., July 29,1861; d. New York, N.Y., Feb. 14, 1884

SECOND MARRIAGE: London, England, Dec. 2, 1886

SECOND WIFE: Edith Kermit Carow; b. Norwich, Conn., Aug. 6, 1861; d. Oyster Bay, N.Y., Sept. 30, 1948

CHILDREN: Alice Lee (1884–1980); Theodore (1887–1944); Kermit (1889–1943); Ethel Carow (1891–1977); Archibald Bulloch (1894–1979); Quentin (1897–1918)

RELIGIOUS AFFILIATION: Dutch Reformed Church

EDUCATION: Private tutoring; Harvard (B.A., 1880); attended Columbia Law School

OCCUPATIONS BEFORE PRESIDENCY: Writer; historian

MILITARY SERVICE: Lt. col.; col., 1st U.S. Volunteer Cavalry Regiment (Rough Riders), 1898

PREPRESIDENTIAL OFFICES: New York State assemblyman; U.S. Civil Service commissioner; New York City police commissioner; assistant secretary of the Navy; governor of New York; U.S. vice president

AGE AT INAUGURATION: 42

OCCUPATIONS AFTER PRESIDENCY: Writer; politician

DEATH: Oyster Bay, N.Y., Jan. 6, 1919

PLACE OF BURIAL: Young's Memorial Cemetery, Oyster Bay, N.Y.

played conspicuous personal courage in leading his men into the teeth of Spanish fire. The press covered him and the Rough Riders extensively, and he emerged from the war as its biggest hero.

New York's Republican bosses, who badly needed a winning candidate for governor, recognized Roosevelt's great political potential. Senator Thomas Platt, main boss of the party and friend of big business, did not like Roosevelt, branding him an "altruist," using the word, said TR, "as a term of reproach, as if it was Communistic. . . ." But Platt could not ignore the man's popularity, and he believed that TR could be controlled. The senator engineered Roosevelt's nomination for governor. In a strenuous whistle-stop tour of the state, with a Rough Rider escort noisily at his elbow, Roosevelt won the governorship for the GOP by just 18,000 votes. He was now "Teddy" to the public—a name he disliked—and one of the most talked-about politicians in the United States.

Taking office in January 1899, Governor Roosevelt quickly declared his independence. Avoiding an open break with Platt, he nevertheless asserted that he would make his own appointments and pursue reform policies. He took as his motto a West African proverb: "Speak softly and carry a big stick; you will go far."

TR's voice, however, was heard all over New York State. He tightened laws regulating sweatshops, pushed for closer supervision of utilities and insurance companies, sponsored regulations of the workday for women and children, and secured passage of a state tax on corporation franchises.

TR's Albany victory came at the cost of infuriating Platt. "I want to get rid of the bastard," the boss thundered. "I don't want him raising hell in my state any longer." He hatched a scheme to bury the troublemaker in the vice presidency. Roosevelt bristled at the suggestion: "I will not accept under any circumstances and that is all there is about it." Platt, however, brought off a draft to nominate the rough-riding

colonel for the second spot. Senator Marcus A. "Mark" Hanna, the GOP national chairman, erupted: "Don't any of you realize there's only one life between this madman and the White House?" TR swallowed his medicine and waged a colorful campaign for the McKinley ticket in 1900.

The vice presidency, with its built-in aura of "second best," did not dampen Roosevelt's spirits for long. On September 13, 1901, while he was on a climbing vacation in the Adirondacks, he received word that McKinley, who had been shot by a fanatic a week earlier in Buffalo, lay close to death. After a hair-raising nighttime descent down tortuous, pitch-black mountain roads, Roosevelt arrived in Buffalo just after McKinley died. On September 14, 1901, he took the oath of office as the twenty-sixth president of the United States. He was the youngest person ever to assume the office and the first president who had been too young to serve in the Civil War.

"Now look," Hanna fumed privately, "that damned cowboy is president of the United States!" But Roosevelt assured Hanna and other Republican conservatives that he would "continue, absolutely unbroken" the policies of McKinley. To a friend Roosevelt wrote: "It is a dreadful thing to come into the Presidency this way; but it would be a far worse thing to be morbid about it. Here is the task, and I have got to do it to the best of my ability. . . ."

Roosevelt came to presidential power at a moment of unprecedented social and economic ferment in the nation. Already reform movements had arisen to demand an end to the abuses of industrial capitalism, if not to capitalism itself. Democrats under William Jennings Bryan, as well as socialists were crying against domination by plutocracy and swollen trusts. The oppressed also found eloquent literary champions in such writers as Upton Sinclair, Ida Tarbell, Frank Norris, Lincoln Steffens, and Brand Whitlock. By 1900 even some Republicans, such as Wisconsin's new "progressive" governor, Robert M. La Follette, were joining in the outcry for economic reform: an eight-hour work day, a graduated income tax, public ownership of utilities, and varying degrees of government supervision of industry.

The new president moved warily. An assassin's bullet, not his own election, had put him in the White House, and he headed an overwhelmingly conservative and business-friendly party. Roosevelt's own views also put him at odds with Bryanite Democrats and insurgent Republicans like La Follette.

Despite his caution, Roosevelt did stage two important confrontations with big business in his first term. Barely six months after his accession to the presidency, he pushed legal action against the trusts—the combinations of big corporations, organized to stifle competition and to control prices and rates through collusion. Acting under the loosely drafted Sherman Antitrust Act of 1890, Roosevelt agreed to press suit against the powerful Northern Securities Company, a holding company organized by J. Pierpont Morgan to monopolize transportation in the Northwest. When Morgan suggested compromise, the president replied, "There can be no compromise in the enforcement of the law." The government won the suit, and in 1904 the Supreme Court upheld a decree by the United States circuit court at St. Paul dissolving Northern Securities Company. In his remaining years in office Roosevelt oversaw other antitrust actions in the beef, coal, and sugar industries.

In May 1902 TR faced a fresh challenge when the United Mine Workers called a strike of 140,000 men for better wages and working conditions. The mine owners, led by George F. Baer, president of the Philadelphia and Reading Railroad, refused to compromise. Said Baer: "The rights and interests of the laboring man will be protected and cared for—not by the labor agitators, but by the Christian men to whom God in his infinite wisdom has given the control of the property interests of this country." Concerned about the danger of a coal famine as fall

THE FIRST ADMINISTRATION

INAUGURATION: Sept. 14, 1901; Buffalo, N.Y.
SECRETARY OF STATE: John M. Hay
SECRETARY OF THE TREASURY: Lyman J. Gage;
    Leslie M. Shaw (from Feb. 1, 1902)
SECRETARY OF WAR: Elihu Root;
    William H. Taft (from Feb. 1, 1904)
ATTORNEY GENERAL: Philander C. Knox;
    William H. Moody (from July 1, 1904)
POSTMASTER GENERAL: Charles E. Smith;
    Henry C. Payne (from Jan. 9, 1902);
    Robert J. Wynne (from Oct. 10, 1904)
SECRETARY OF THE NAVY: John D. Long;
    William H. Moody (from May 1, 1902);
    Paul Morton (from July 1, 1904)
SECRETARY OF THE INTERIOR: Ethan A. Hitchcock
SECRETARY OF AGRICULTURE: James Wilson
SECRETARY OF COMMERCE AND LABOR: George B.
    Cortelyou; Victor H. Metcalf (from July 1, 1904)
SUPREME COURT APPOINTMENTS: Oliver Wendell Holmes
    (1902); William R. Day (1903)
57TH CONGRESS (Dec. 2, 1901–Mar. 3, 1903):
    SENATE: 56 Republicans; 29 Democrats; 3 Others
    HOUSE: 198 Republicans; 153 Democrats; 5 Others
58TH CONGRESS (Nov. 9, 1903–Mar. 3, 1905):
    SENATE: 58 Republicans; 32 Democrats
    HOUSE: 207 Republicans; 178 Democrats

approached, Roosevelt stepped in to urge arbitration of the strike. The mine workers agreed but management refused, charging the president with illegal interference in the affairs of business.

Despite a public outcry against them, the managers remained adamant. At a White House conference on October 3, they refused to accept arbitration and declined to offer terms of their own. An enraged Roosevelt again warned of the revolutionary potential of a coal famine, predicting "the most terrible riots that this country has ever seen." Then the president acted on his own. He made plans, he later revealed, to instruct the Army to seize and operate the coal mines. "I did not intend," he said later, "to sit supinely when

President Roosevelt and Gifford Pinchot, whom he appointed as the first head of the Forest Service, were the dynamic duo of the conservation movement.

such a state of things was impending." Pressured, ironically, by J. P. Morgan, the coal operators agreed to support an impartial commission's investigation of the dispute. The workers returned to the mines pending the inquiry. "The whole country breathed freer," said the president, "and felt as if a nightmare had been lifted. . . ."

It was a landmark in presidential initiative and leadership, casting Roosevelt irrevocably in the image of a popular crusader. TR never doubted that he had acted correctly. ". . . [t]he Buchanan principle of striving to find some constitutional reason for inaction" was not for him, he declared. Nor did he care for "the little, feeble, snarling men who yell about executive usurpation" whenever a president acts with strength. "My business," he wrote in 1903, "is to see fair play among all men, capitalists or wage workers," and to face great national crises with "immediate and vigorous executive action." All he wanted, he said, was "to see to it that every man has a square deal, no more and no less."

In 1903 TR made a few more moves in the direction of reform. He oversaw the establishment of the Department of Commerce and Labor, with the Bureau of Corporations acting as a watchdog over big business. The Expedition Act gave the United States power to obtain speedier trials for those being prosecuted under antitrust laws. The Elkins Act strengthened the Interstate Commerce Commission by forbidding railroads to deviate from published rate schedules. And Roosevelt personally urged states to prohibit the employment of women or children in industries with unsafe or unsanitary conditions.

By far, Roosevelt's boldest domestic actions during his first term came in the field of conservation. Beginning with the Reclamation Act of 1902 and the enlargement of the Bureau of Forestry, he moved to redeem and irrigate neglected land in the West. TR considered conservation second only to trust-busting as "the most vital internal question of the United States." Roosevelt's devotion to conservation went well beyond rhetoric. In 1905 he established the Forest Service, naming his friend and fellow conservation zealot Gifford Pinchot chief forester. Roosevelt set aside some 150,000,000 acres of timberland for national use, established fifty game preserves, doubled the number of national parks, and founded sixteen national monuments.

In foreign policy, too, Roosevelt demonstrated

extraordinary executive vigor. He was committed to policies of increased naval power, greater assertiveness in the Pacific, and domination of the Western Hemisphere. America, he said, was no longer insulated by protective oceans; sea power and modern technology were dissolving old barriers. "We have no choice as to whether or not we shall play a great part in the world," he declared. ". . . All that we can decide is whether we shall play it well or ill."

On December 16, 1901, Roosevelt secured Senate consent to the second Hay-Pauncefote Treaty. In that treaty Britain acknowledged the exclusive right of the United States to construct and fortify a Central American canal. On June 28, 1902, Congress authorized TR to build a canal across Panama (then a part of Colombia) on the condition that the president could acquire from Colombia permanent control of the canal zone and buy rights from the New Panama Canal Company, a French group that had failed in an earlier attempt to build a canal.

The Hay-Herran Convention, signed with Colombia on January 22, 1903, met the terms set by the United States. In less than two months the U.S. Senate approved the treaty, but Colombia's legislature rejected it in August, demanding more money and objecting to what it considered an assault on Colombia's sovereignty. Roosevelt exploded, vowing to "warn these cat-rabbits that great though our patience has been, it can be exhausted." Conveniently, Panama declared its independence on November 3, 1903, after an uprising spearheaded by Philippe Bunau-Varilla, former chief engineer of the French canal company, and an American attorney named William Cromwell, both of whom stood to gain financially from the sale of rights to the United States. Troops dispatched by Colombia to quell the revolt were bribed either to join it or to ignore it while the United States Navy stood by at the Isthmus of Panama. Within three days, the United States had recognized the infant republic and on November 18

negotiated—with Bunau-Varilla—a treaty, whereby the United States acquired a canal zone ten miles wide and paid forty million dollars directly to the French canal company. Panama received ten million dollars and a two-hundred-and-fifty-thousand-dollar annuity. The United States guaranteed the neutrality of the Canal in return for the right to fortify it.

As chief executive, TR also sustained the United States dominance over Central and South America. When Great Britain, Germany, and Italy blockaded

ELIHU ROOT

"Thank the President for me," Elihu Root remarked when he was offered the job of secretary of war in 1899, "but say that it is quite absurd. I know nothing about war. . . ." McKinley responded that he was looking for "a lawyer to direct the government of these Spanish islands," and Root, a New York corporate lawyer, agreed to accept the cabinet post. Taking office in 1899, he formulated policies for the administration of Cuba, the Philippines, and other new colonial possessions. Stressing economic rehabilitation, the guarantee of individual liberties, development of local institutions, and protection of United States interests, he laid the foundations of American colonial rule. Before he resigned in 1904, he also reorganized the Army and created the Army War College. Later, as secretary of state under Theodore Roosevelt from 1905 to 1909, Root worked to develop friendly relations with Latin America and Japan; his efforts won him the Nobel Peace Prize in 1912. From 1909 to 1915 he served in the United States Senate. Critical of American neutrality at the beginning of World War I, he favored—with reservations—United States membership in the League of Nations. He also helped found and advocated American membership in the Permanent Court of International Peace. President of the Carnegie Endowment for International Peace, Root remained a respected elder statesman until his death at ninety-one in 1937.

Venezuelan ports in 1902, insisting that Venezuela pay its debts, Roosevelt dispatched an American fleet to Caribbean waters and warned Kaiser Wilhelm II that invasion would be met with naval force. The dispute was submitted to arbitration, and the blockade was lifted in 1903. Similarly, when European powers sought to compel the Dominican Republic to pay its debts in 1904, TR proclaimed the celebrated Roosevelt Corollary to the Monroe Doctrine. Threats of foreign intervention or wrongdoing in the Western Hemisphere, Roosevelt warned, might force the United States, "however reluctantly . . . to the exercise of

an international police power" to maintain order. TR did not content himself with preaching. He forced the Dominican Republic to establish a financial receivership and dispatched an American comptroller to the Caribbean nation. "I put the agreement into effect . . ." Roosevelt declared, "and I would have continued it until the end of my term, if necessary, without any action by Congress."

Roosevelt's concept of the presidency was no less explicit in words than in deeds. "I believe," he wrote in 1908, "that the efficiency of this Government depends upon its possessing a strong central executive, and wherever I could establish a precedent for strength in the executive . . . I have felt . . . [that] I was establishing a precedent of value." The president's power, he argued, is "limited only by specific restrictions and prohibitions appearing in the Constitution or imposed by the Congress under its Constitutional powers."

The White House during the Roosevelt years rang with excitement, laughter, and fun. But it was TR himself, contagiously energetic, who hogged the spotlight. "I enjoy being President," he said in 1903, and America shared his joy as he made the presidency come alive. He "belonged" to the people, representing at once what they were and what they wanted. The man on the street could identify with him: pillow fighting with his children, sparring with the boxing champion John L. Sullivan in the White House gym, getting away from it all to hunt panthers in Colorado. After one of those hunts, reporters ran a story about his sparing the life of a mother bear with cubs. A Brooklyn toy maker promptly christened his small stuffed product the "teddy bear." As much as he hated that nickname, Roosevelt profited from it politically. The toy also captured the juvenile side of his public image. Quipped one observer: "You must always remember that the President is about six."

A hero to American youth, Roosevelt arose at 6 A.M. for push-ups. He boxed daily, championed the

ORVILLE AND WILBUR WRIGHT

"For some years I have been afflicted with the belief that flight is possible to man," wrote Wilbur Wright to a fellow aviation pioneer in 1900. Only the year before, Wilbur and his younger brother, Orville, partners in a bicycle-manufacturing firm in Dayton, Ohio, had constructed a kite-like biplane. In 1900 they built their first free-flying glider and conducted the first of their famous experiments at Kitty Hawk, North Carolina. With the pilot lying flat to reduce air resistance, the plane could be made to glide more than three hundred feet. After testing another glider with the help of a wind tunnel, the Wrights built their first powered plane, a four-cylinder machine of 750 pounds, which they launched at Kitty Hawk in 1903. The first powered flight in history lasted only twelve seconds, but it was the beginning of modern aviation. The brothers perfected their machine and two years later made a twenty-four-mile circuit flight over Huffman Field in Dayton. In 1909 the Wright brothers' patented machine was adopted by the U. S. Army, and in the same year the American Wright Company was organized to manufacture airplanes commercially. After Wilbur's death at forty-five in 1912, Orville Wright became president of their company; he lived until 1948.

Theodore Roosevelt must have felt on top of the world on November 16, 1906, when he took control of a gigantic steam shovel that was digging the Panama Canal, his proudest accomplishment as president.

fifty-mile hike, rode to hounds, and played football on the White House lawn. When he was not exercising or running the government, he read voraciously in four languages.

Roosevelt was also a president of "firsts." He was the first president to leave the shores of the United States while in office—in a 1906 visit to the Panama Canal site. He was the first Republican president from the Northeast and the first vice president who succeeded to the presidency who was then elected to the office in his own right. He was the first president to fly in an airplane, though not until after he had left office. (The government's purchase of a twenty-five-thousand-dollar plane from the Wright brothers during his presidency gave birth to the U.S. Army Air Forces.) He established a White House press room, added two office wings to the mansion to ensure greater family privacy, and coined such classic American expressions as "mollycoddle," "muckraking," "lunatic fringe," and "my hat is in the ring."

As his first term ended, Roosevelt fretted about securing the Republican nomination in 1904. His worries proved groundless. Although Republican conservatives and some big businessmen grumbled about him, he still mustered the support of a number of the nation's biggest money men. Aware of his immense popularity, J. P. Morgan, E. H. Harriman, John D. Rockefeller, and Henry Clay Frick cheerfully backed him. Running against perhaps the most forgettable opponent of the twentieth century, the Democratic nominee Alton B. Parker, Roosevelt galloped to victory, 7,626,593 votes to 5,082,898.

Escorted to the Capitol steps by cowboys, Indians, and Rough Riders on March 4, 1905, he gave an inaugural address notable for its brevity and for its consciousness of America's new role in the world. "We have become a great nation, forced by the fact of its greatness into relations with the other nations of the earth, and we must behave as beseems a people with such responsibilities. . . ." The development of corporate capitalism, TR also declared, had brought "marvelous material well-being" but had imposed "the care and anxiety inseparable from the accumulation of great wealth in industrial centers." This situation, Roosevelt warned, must be faced squarely and solved: "If we fail, the cause of free self-government throughout the world will rock to its foundations. . . ."

Now president in his own right, Theodore Roosevelt stepped up his battle against the abuses of big business. In 1905 and 1906 he used considerable force and skill to get Congress to enact two major pieces of reform legislation. One was the Pure Food and Drug Act, which prohibited the manufacture, sale, or interstate transportation of adulterated food, drugs, medicine, or liquor, and which required honest labeling of ingredients. A separate act ordered the regular inspection of stockyards and packinghouses by the Department of Agriculture. Helping these measures along to passage was the public outrage generated by Upton Sinclair's novel *The Jungle*, which described in stomach-turning detail the unsanitary working conditions in a Chicago meatpacking plant. The other major reform legislation was the Hepburn Act, which gave the Interstate Commerce Commission the right to set the rates of railroads, express companies, and terminal facilities. Republican conservatives and their business backers fiercely resisted all of these laws as the opening wedge of government intervention in the economy. Taken together, the Roosevelt-initiated reforms took the United States a long way down the road of government regulation of private enterprise.

Roosevelt has been accused of using reform largely as an instrument of his own political power. He was unquestionably a practical politician, a realist unwilling to risk personal position for pie in the sky. He worked with his party as closely as possible. "One must learn . . ." he said, "not to jeopardize one's power for doing the good that is possible by efforts to correct evils over which one has no control. . . ." He also detested the "lunatic fringe," where he lumped some Republican reformers, Bryanite Democrats, Socialists, and anybody he considered dangerous. Politically, socially, and morally, Roosevelt was conservative, but he espoused a kind of conservatism that has been unusual in America. He did not worship moneymaking or business, instead considering them little more than necessary evils. He approved of government power more enthusiastically and less critically than any other American president.

Roosevelt became more, not less, of a reformer as his presidency drew to a close. During his last two years in office, he proposed income and inheritance taxes, more economic regulation, federal aid to workers, and expanded conservation actions—all of which met a stone wall of resistance on Capitol Hill. When

HENRY FORD

Even as a young boy Henry Ford had a passion for machinery. Abandoning the Michigan farm on which he was born, Ford moved to Detroit as a machine-shop apprentice at the age of sixteen, began experimenting with various types of engines, and in 1887 became chief engineer at the Edison power company. His most exciting work, however, was being done in a woodshed behind his house, where, in 1896, he completed his first motor vehicle, a crude contraption of two cylinders mounted on bicycle wheels. Five years later his more sophisticated "999" racing car broke all speed records and made him an international figure. In 1903 he organized the Ford Motor Company, and six years later the first "Model T" rolled off the assembly line. Ford had realized a lifelong dream. By perfecting the art of mass production he had revolutionized industry, bringing luxury items within reach of the average citizen. In 1914 he made headlines by instituting an unprecedented eight-hour workday, by more than doubling the minimum daily wage to five dollars, and by organizing an employee profit-sharing plan. A dedicated pacifist, Ford sent a "Peace Ship" to Europe in 1915 in a valiant, if naive, attempt to mediate World War I. Three years later he ran unsuccessfully for the Senate. With his son, Edsel, he established the philanthropic Ford Foundation in 1936. He died in 1947.

word got out that Roosevelt was going to hunt lions in Africa after he left the White House, conservative Republican senators toasted, "Health to the lions!"

Another factor that soured relations between TR and conservatives was the Panic of 1907, when a stock market plunge on Wall Street threatened to precipitate a depression. Conservatives readily blamed the market panic on Roosevelt's attacks on "malefactors of great wealth" and regulatory programs. Actually, Roosevelt responded to the economic crisis by working hand in glove with J. P. Morgan. Acting as an unofficial central banker, Morgan con-

THE LATEST ARRIVAL AT THE POLITICAL ZOO

DRAWN BY E. W. KEMBLE

Edward W. Kemble's 1912 cartoon from *Harper's Weekly* depicts Roosevelt's new Progressive party mascot—a bull moose—hovering near a barrel, which represents Roosevelt's controversial stand on regulating rather than busting the trusts.

tained the collapse with strategically placed loans and investments. Roosevelt aided Morgan by promising not to bring antitrust suits against him for his moves to save weak companies by adding them to his holdings. In the meantime, TR got all the blame from conservatives for allegedly causing the panic and none of the credit for helping to keep it from turning into a depression.

In foreign affairs TR's second term was equally dramatic. Alarmed by Japan's victory in the Russo-Japanese War, he personally prevailed on both sides in 1905 to accept international arbitration. Roosevelt's suggested terms of settlement were largely incorporated in the Treaty of Portsmouth (New Hampshire), signed on September 5. For this effort Roosevelt won the Nobel Peace Prize.

TR sustained his close vigil in Latin American affairs. When an anarchic Cuba requested U.S. aid in restoring order in 1906, he intervened directly, dispatching Secretary of War William Howard Taft to head an occupation administration until an election could be held. Again TR had acted without consulting Congress. "I should not dream of asking the permission of Congress. . . . You know as well as I do that it is for the enormous interest of this government to strengthen and give independence to the executive in dealing with foreign powers," he told Taft.

Easily the most decisive of Roosevelt's foreign policy moves in his second term was his dispatching of the Battle Fleet of the United States Navy—sixteen battleships and twelve thousand men—on a world cruise from late 1907 to February of 1909. The first ports of call were in Japan. Alarmed by reports of a Japanese military buildup aimed at the United States, TR saw the fleet off on a "courtesy" cruise, which, he insisted, would have a "pacific effect." Japan greeted this first visit of a Western battle fleet to its home waters with enthusiasm and interest. As for Roosevelt, he hailed the cruise as "the most important service that I rendered to peace." In sending the fleet he had acted, as with Cuba, without consenting Congress.

The critics scoffed at his actions. He waged an evangelical war of words on "the timid good," the pacifists, the effete. The White House, he decided, was a "bully pulpit" from which to preach "the fundamental fight for morality." "Keep your eyes on the stars, but . . . your feet on the ground." Be like the soldier and hunter; help restore "the fighting edge" to American life.

TR's last full year in the White House was 1908. Four years earlier, on the night of his election victory in 1904, he had renounced a third term. So, having nominated and helped to elect Taft as his handpicked successor, he stepped down on March 4, 1909.

Nineteen days after leaving the White House, Roosevelt was off on a Smithsonian-sponsored hunting expedition to Africa, where he bagged more than five hundred animals and birds. He emerged from the jungle to tour Europe, where he reviewed the kaiser's troops, lectured at Oxford and the Sorbonne, represented the United States at the funeral of England's King Edward VII, and delivered a speech when he accepted the Nobel Peace Prize awarded to him in 1905. "I felt that if I met another king I should bite him," Teddy said. His political retirement was short-lived. Angered at what he regarded as Taft's betrayal of his policies, TR decided to run again for president in 1912. "My hat is in the ring," the colonel declared, "the fight is on, and I am stripped to the buff." He raised his banner: "We stand at Armageddon, and we battle for the Lord." But the Republican convention of 1912 renominated Taft, and TR bolted the party. Pronouncing himself fit as a bull moose, he accepted the presidential nomination of the newly formed Progressive party. Shot by a would-be assassin in Milwaukee on October 14, 1912, Roosevelt was saved only by a metal spectacle case and a folded speech in a breast pocket that covered his heart. Despite the pain and loss of blood, he delivered a fifty-minute address. It was a noble moment in an inspiring campaign. Roosevelt outpolled Taft by 632,874 votes, but in the process he split the Republican vote and helped give the presidency to Woodrow Wilson.

Energetic and restless as always, TR went on a crisis-filled expedition in 1914 to an unknown tributary of the Amazon River. He returned home with an injured thigh, gravely weakened by jungle fever. When World War I broke out later that year, Roosevelt found a new political cause. He became a passionate champion of the Allies—Britain and France—and foe of Germany, despite his acquaintance with the kaiser. He denounced Wilson for failing to arm the United States properly and for his "spineless neutrality" toward Germany.

After the United States entered the war in 1917, Roosevelt stumped vigorously in Liberty Bond drives to finance the war and campaigned tirelessly for Republicans. But his spirit, darkened by his son Quentin's death behind German lines in July 1918, started to sink. On Armistice Day, November 11, 1918, the colonel, just past sixty, entered the hospital with inflammatory rheumatism. On January 6, 1919, while Republicans were hatching plans to run him again for president in 1920, he died of a coronary embolism.

Roosevelt remains one of the brightest lights in the history of the American presidency. He brought great and unusual gifts to the White House. He was its first occupant to exploit the public dimensions of the office, and none of his successors has ever outdone him in making the president the center of political debate. Perhaps the greatest tribute to his abilities came after he stepped down, when he became the most politically significant former president in American history. He was the only third-party candidate ever to outpoll a major party nominee, and he staged a comeback in which only death could keep him from another term in the White House. Not just chronologically but in nearly every way, the twentieth-century presidency began with and took its shape from Theodore Roosevelt.

—*WILSON SULLIVAN,*
revised by JOHN MILTON COOPER, JR.

WILLIAM HOWARD TAFT

RELUCTANT LEADER

William Howard Taft felt relieved when he knew for certain that he would leave the White House at the end of a single term. During those four years he had lost his closest friend; many of his programs and policies had failed; his wife's health had declined; and he found himself locked in political struggles for which he had neither the taste nor the temperament. He had few illusions about himself as president. "I have proven," he told a friend, "to be a burdensome leader and not one that aroused the multitude. . . . I am entirely content to serve in the ranks." But "Big Bill" Taft underestimated himself. He was a better president than he gave himself credit for being.

Taft came from a political dynasty founded by his father, Alphonso, who had been secretary of war and attorney general under President Ulysses S. Grant and minister to Austria-Hungary and then to Russia under President Chester A. Arthur. Determined, practical, single-minded, Alphonso Taft had settled in Cincinnati, Ohio, to build his career and found his dynasty. From his sons he demanded "self-denial and enthusiastic hard work," first rank in class, careers in the law, and preeminence wherever they went. "I am not superstitious," Will Taft said as he attended his dying father in 1891, ". . . but I have a kind of presentiment that Father has been a kind of guardian angel to me in that his wishes for my success have been so strong and intense as to bring it success . . ."

At the time of his father's death, the younger Taft was solicitor general of the United States, the first in a series of offices that led eventually to the presidency and, finally, the office he had wanted most, the chief justice of the United States in 1921.

The future president was born on September 15, 1857. As a young boy he was called Willie, Will, and Big Lub, because of his weight. Taft went to Woodward High, where he ranked second in his graduating class. (When he had ranked fifth after one school

marking period, his father had commented, "Mediocrity will not do for Will.") In 1874 he entered Yale, where he became, according to a classmate, "the most admired and respected man not only in my class but in all Yale." Once again he was second in his class.

The summer after graduation he began reading law in his father's office and that fall entered Cincinnati Law School. Even before he passed the state bar examination, he got into Republican politics, participating in his father's unsuccessful campaign in 1880 for governor of Ohio. Later that year he was appointed assistant prosecutor. His first federal job came in 1882 when he was named district collector of internal revenue by President Arthur.

An unsettling disagreement with Arthur over patronage impelled Taft to resign and reenter private law practice. He remained active in politics, and in 1887 he was named to a seat on the state of Ohio superior court.

In 1890 Taft went to Washington, D.C., at the behest of President Benjamin Harrison, to assume the office of solicitor general—the federal government's attorney before the Supreme Court. By then he had married Helen Herron, a graduate of Mount Holyoke in South Hadley, Massachusetts, whose ambition for Taft matched that of Taft's father. Before Alphonso Taft died, he had begun to believe his son could be president and had told him so. Helen—"Nellie"—took up where Alphonso left off.

In 1891 Taft secured an appointment to a new appeals court judgeship on the sixth circuit—Ohio, Kentucky, Michigan, and Tennessee. This meant leaving Washington, and Nellie tried unsuccessfully to talk him out of it. It would, she warned, "put an end to all the opportunities . . . of being thrown with the bigwigs." Still, when the appointment was offered, he took it. On the court, Taft found the relative quiet he craved. ("I love judges," he had once said, "and I love courts. They are my ideals, that typify on earth what we shall meet hereafter in heaven under a just God.")

On November 10, 1911, President Taft gave a dramatic speech at Manassas Court House in Virginia.

By his peers he was considered a good judge, even an outstanding one, and soon he seemed to be in line for a Supreme Court seat.

In January 1900 Taft's life took an unexpected turn. President William McKinley asked him to head a commission being formed to govern the recently annexed Philippine Islands. McKinley knew Taft's record as a judge and had come to know and admire him earlier in Washington when he was solicitor general. Although Taft had initially disapproved of the annexation, he now shared McKinley's view that the Filipinos would have to be taught self-government before independence could be granted.

He hesitated to take the assignment because he hated to leave the bench. But when McKinley promised him an eventual appointment to the Supreme Court, Taft accepted. In mid-April 1900, accompanied by Nellie and their three children, he sailed for the Philippines. He expected to be away less than a year. As it turned out he became the first American civil governor of the islands in July 1901 and remained in that post until the beginning of 1904. Sympathetic toward Filipinos, he brought them quickly into the government. He built up educational facilities, reformed the corrupt courts, and improved roads and harbors.

Taft worked hard despite illness and despite the heat—which he hated. The new president, Theodore Roosevelt, twice offered Taft an appointment to the Supreme Court. But Taft felt responsible for the Filipinos' welfare. Roosevelt got him back to Washington at last only by making him secretary of war, a post that allowed Taft to continue to oversee the Philippines.

His friendship with Roosevelt, which had also begun during Taft's tenure as solicitor general, blossomed into an extraordinary relationship. Roosevelt was intense, energetic, and always conscious of himself as "the Leader." Taft was judicious, an orderly administrator, and a loyal lieutenant. The two men complemented each other. Taft quickly found that his role far exceeded that of his cabinet post: He also was an intimate adviser and a roving ambassador, even sometimes a presidential stand-in. Once Roosevelt went off on vacation, telling the press the government was in good hands. Taft was in Washington, he said, "sitting on the lid."

Roosevelt had once described the qualities needed in a governor of the Philippines as being the ones that would make a good president and chief justice. Taft, he had said then, was the only American who filled the bill. Now, as the president looked ahead to 1908, he offered Taft a remarkable choice: To be president or chief justice. They talked about it a good deal, and one night in the White House library Roosevelt broached the subject to the Tafts again. Sitting in a chair with his eyes shut, Roosevelt intoned: "I am the seventh son of a seventh daughter and I have clairvoyant powers. I see a man weighing three hundred and fifty pounds. There is something hanging over his head. I cannot make out what it is. . . . At one time it looks like the presidency, then again it looks like the chief justiceship." "Make it the presidency," said Nellie. "Make it the chief justiceship," said Taft.

Taft knew his strengths and his shortcomings. Although he began to be considered for the presidential nomination by the summer of 1905, he did not really want it. "If the chief justice would retire," he said, "how simple everything would become." But Chief Justice Melville Fuller did not retire, and there were strong forces pushing Taft toward the White House. Roosevelt encouraged him. So did Nellie and the rest of the Taft clan—except his mother, who thought he would be unhappy as president. When Roosevelt, unsure of what Taft wanted, offered to appoint him to a vacant associate justice seat in 1906 and promised to raise him to the chief's spot if the opportunity arose, the family fought successfully to keep the secretary of war on the political merry-go-round.

Roosevelt, by controlling the 1908 convention, dictated the nomination for his handpicked successor, and by advising and intervening he helped win the election for Taft. When Taft defeated William Jennings Bryan by more than a million votes, Roosevelt expressed his delight to a British friend: "Taft will carry on the work substantially as I have. . . . I have the profound satisfaction of knowing that he will do all in his power to further . . . the great causes for which I have fought. . . ."

But Taft could not be Roosevelt. Clearly his term would be slower paced, more legalistic, and less exciting than his predecessor's. It would be disappointing to a public used to a show in Washington and disappointing, ultimately, to Roosevelt. Taft foresaw this. As TR left for his post-presidential hunting trip in Africa, Taft composed a fond farewell message in which he told Roosevelt that whenever he was addressed as Mr. President he instinctively looked around to see where the president—Roosevelt—was. "I have no doubt that when you return, " Taft wrote, "you will find me very much under suspicion by our friends in the West [the progressive Republicans]. . . .

Joseph Keppler's King Teddy and his "little prince" Taft appeared on the cover of *Puck* in August 1906. Taft, who had never run for office before, got the party's nomination for president and won the election of 1908 solely because Theodore Roosevelt chose him to be his successor.

reforms to meet the challenges posed by the industrial revolution. Big business was tremendously powerful and barely regulated. The exploitation of land and natural resources posed grave danger to the nation's supply of water, timber, minerals, and farmland. A growing population and huge European immigration to the industrialized cities were creating a new urban America, with attendant problems. Government, too, was growing—and needed reorganizing.

For the record, Taft did not do badly. He moved quickly to fulfill a campaign promise for a lower tariff schedule—a reform favored particularly by farmers and consumers alarmed at the rising cost of living. Business did not want tariff rates lowered, and the president had to struggle to get even a nominally reduced tariff through Congress. The Taft administration also stepped up enforcement of the Sherman Antitrust Act. The Roosevelt years had seen forty antitrust suits brought against allegedly monopolistic corporations in nearly eight years. Taft's attorney general, George W. Wickersham, with the president's enthusiastic support, instituted seventy-five such suits in his four years in office. The biggest of those suits was against United States Steel and cited its acquisition of the Tennessee Coal, Iron and Railroad Company in 1907 as a major violation. Roosevelt had personally approved that acquisition and saw the suit as a betrayal.

Taft also initiated a bill that became the Mann-Elkins Act of 1910, giving the Interstate Commerce Commission jurisdiction over the communications industry and making it easier for the I.C.C. to regulate transportation rates. Another act, one of the last that Taft signed, further enhanced the I.C.C.'s powers by allowing it to base its judgments concerning increases in railroad rates on an investigation of the physical value of a railroad and its cost of operation. Taft, later labeled a conservative, was thus invading the "private sector."

In the area of conservation, Taft was again less an

I have not the prestige which you had. . . . I am not attempting quite as much as you did. . . . I have not the facility for educating the public as you had through talks with correspondents. . . ."

Taft sought to continue Roosevelt's domestic

innovator and more a consolidator and legalizer than Roosevelt. Whereas TR had used executive authority to make millions of acres of public land off-limits to private development, Taft doubted that the president had this right and, instead, got Congress to enact a law specifically giving him such power. Taft's governmental reforms were likewise impressive. He set up the Commission on Economy and Efficiency to report on the financial operations of the federal government, while the Taft-sponsored Publicity Act opened to public scrutiny the lists of campaign contributions made in races for the House of Representatives. A constitutional amendment providing for the direct election of United States senators was sent to the states for ratification, along with another amendment that authorized federal income taxes.

All told, it was a productive administration domestically. But there were failures that proved politically fatal to the president. There was a schism within the Republican ranks, in which Taft felt forced to depend upon the conservatives in his party. This move laid Taft open to attack by the progressives, who wanted to dump the old leadership. When the Payne-Aldrich Tariff was passed with conservative help, the progressives rebelled; some of them claimed that the law actually increased the tariff rates. This was not true, but clearly the new tariff was only a small start at reform.

Conservation got Taft into even more hot water with the progressives. Before six months of his administration had elapsed, he was locked in combat with Roosevelt's close friend Gifford Pinchot, whom Taft had retained as head of the Forest Service. In what soon came to be called the Ballinger-Pinchot Affair, Taft showed the defect of his virtues. An Interior Department investigator was digging into earlier dealings by the department's secretary, Richard A. Ballinger, who had briefly served as head of the Land Office under Roosevelt. Ballinger, the investigator charged, had corruptly allowed private interests to acquire coal mining leases on public lands in Alaska.

Ballinger appealed to the president to judge the facts of the case. Taft decided that Ballinger had done nothing wrong and ordered everyone involved to drop the matter. Pinchot, who resented Ballinger as a less committed conservationist and a rival for power over natural resources, continued to leak damaging rumors to the press. In January 1910 Pinchot wrote a letter to a Republican senator in which he attacked Ballinger as corrupt. For this insubordination the president fired Pinchot—reluctantly, knowing it might damage his

OLIVER WENDELL HOLMES, JR.

"The life of the law . . ." wrote Oliver Wendell Holmes, Jr., "has been experience. The felt necessities . . . have had a good deal more to do than the syllogism in determining the rules by which men should be governed." A Boston Brahmin and a veteran of the Civil War, Holmes became an attorney and a legal editor whose skepticism and refusal to accept all legal precedents and principles as automatically valid characterized his opinions during fifty years on the Massachusetts and United States supreme courts. He played no favorites; with a singularly detached intelligence firmly grounded in legal philosophy and psychology, he was neither liberal nor conservative and often dissented from Court opinions. He shocked Roosevelt, who appointed him to the Supreme Court in 1902, by voting to reject the government's antitrust suit in the Northern Securities case, but later introduced the "stream of commerce" concept that greatly tightened federal control over interstate trade. He established "clear and present danger" as the sole basis for limiting freedom of speech (but then saw the Court disavow his dictum). Holmes hated verbosity: "The 'point of contact' is the formula, the place where the boy got his finger pinched; the rest of the machinery doesn't matter." Justice Holmes retired in 1932 at the age of ninety after having served thirty years on the Supreme Court, and he died three years later.

friendship with Roosevelt. To Taft's dismay, Pinchot scurried off to Europe to meet Roosevelt when the ex-president emerged from his hunting safari in Africa in order to get his side of the story in first.

After that, the old friendship between the two presidents was never the same. A congressional investigation eventually exonerated Ballinger, but the Pinchot side was so ably presented by the liberal lawyer Louis Brandeis that the press wound up blaming Taft. Republican progressives in Congress also sided with Pinchot. A few months later Ballinger quietly resigned, and Taft appointed as his successor a noted conservationist, Walter Fisher, who carried on constructive though unspectacular work to protect natural resources.

There were also clouds over Taft's record in foreign affairs. He and his secretary of state, Philander C. Knox, pursued "Dollar Diplomacy" in Asia and Latin America. Dollar Diplomacy was a two-edged sword. It did openly what McKinley and Roosevelt had done more quietly, namely to use diplomacy to promote American business interests abroad. It also enlisted American capital in support of diplomacy, as in the effort to offset Japanese influence in China by proposing that American bankers finance railway construction there. Like Taft himself, Dollar Diplomacy was too frank for its own good, earning the enmity of Democrats and progressive Republicans at home as a sellout to big business and the suspicion of nationalists abroad as a tool of Yankee imperialism.

Taft did have some small diplomatic successes, but he suffered a big disappointment when the Senate mauled one measure that he had hoped would be a bright achievement in foreign policy. Taft favored the creation of a system by which nations could adjudicate disagreements that might lead to war. In 1910 he began sounding out other countries on the subject, and the next year treaties were signed with Great Britain and France. The United States and each "partner" nation agreed to submit disputes to an authori-ty, such as The Hague Court of Arbitration. These treaties included, as potentially subject to arbitration, questions of national honor—in Taft's words, "the questions which . . . are likely to lead to war." In the Senate, senior members of Taft's own party loaded the instrument of ratification down with reservations that gave the Senate a veto over whether the president could present a dispute for arbitration. "To play the game of 'Heads I win, tails you lose,' " Taft said, "is to accomplish nothing . . . toward Christian civilization." He refused to ratify the treaties, and they never went into effect.

One of Taft's major opponents in the arbitration-treaty argument had been Roosevelt. Home from his African safari and back in the political arena, the ex-president sided with the progressives against his old friend. Roosevelt also blamed him personally for the antitrust suit brought against U.S. Steel. Taft, puzzled and sorrowful, refused for many months to respond publicly to Roosevelt's attacks. But when Roosevelt took radical, "socialistic" positions and ran against him for renomination, Taft decided to seek reelection. Even after this open split he hesitated to fight back. After finally answering Roosevelt's charges, a reporter found him sitting alone, head in hands. "Roosevelt was my closest friend," he said, and then he burst into tears.

Taft was doomed politically. He won the Republican nomination, but Roosevelt and his supporters bolted the party and ran TR as the nominee of the newly formed Progressive party. "The only question now," quipped Chauncey M. Depew "is which corpse gets the most flowers." Roosevelt won 600,000 more popular votes than Taft, but Woodrow Wilson, the Democratic candidate, easily won the election.

"The nearer I get to the inauguration of my successor the greater the relief I feel," wrote Taft a month after the election. In March 1913, at the age of fifty-five, he happily returned to private life. His alma

In the last decade of his life, Taft found political fulfillment as chief justice of the United States. He and Mrs. Taft found the happiness that had eluded them in the White House.

mater, Yale, offered him the Kent Chair of Constitutional Law. (He replied that he could not accept a chair but that a sofa of law would be fine.) Taft enjoyed teaching; he also lectured widely and wrote a syndicated newspaper column. He lost weight, and his wife, Nellie, who had suffered a stroke soon after they went to live in the White House, recovered her health.

But Taft did not remain a private citizen for long. During World War I, President Wilson named him cochairman of the National War Labor Board. He also worked for the creation of a world peace organization and strongly supported Wilson's effort to take the United States into the League of Nations. In 1921 Harding appointed Taft to the post he had wanted for decades, the chief justice of the United States. "The truth is that in my present life I don't remember that I ever was president," he wrote in 1925. Taft found the happiness and fulfillment on the Court that had eluded him in the White House. Besides instituting administrative changes in the judicial system, he was a major political and intellectual force on the Court. He melded together divergent personalities and philosophies among the justices and often subtly bent them to his side. He gave the Court a clear direction in constitutional interpretation. Taft's direction could be called conservative, inasmuch as he upheld property rights, gave greater latitude to private businesses, and restricted some congressional and state regulatory and taxing powers. But he still remained the advocate of strong central government, both by upholding other regulatory actions and by promoting the activism and intervention of his own and lower federal courts. He continued as chief justice until a heart ailment forced him to retire from the Supreme Court in February 1930. He died a month later.

—MICHAEL HARWOOD,
revised by JOHN MILTON COOPER, JR.

WOODROW WILSON

PROPHET WITHOUT HONOR

Early in the evening of September 15, 1910, a lean man with iron-gray hair and slate-blue eyes behind rimless glasses was making his way through the crowd at the Taylor Opera House in Trenton, New Jersey. "God! look at that jaw!" exclaimed an onlooker. It was his first glimpse of Woodrow Wilson, the president of Princeton University, whom the Democrats of New Jersey had just nominated as their candidate for governor.

Some of the Democrats assembled there awaited his acceptance speech with sullen suspicion. Wilson had been the candidate of the political bosses, but the party progressives were soon pleasantly surprised. "I did not seek this nomination," Wilson declared. "It has come to me absolutely unsolicited." If elected, he promised, he would be free to serve uncommitted by any prior pledges. This personal declaration of independence elated the progressives. "Thank God, at last a leader has come!" one of them shouted.

Thomas Woodrow Wilson had followed a curious path to the 1910 New Jersey gubernatorial nomination. He had been born on December 28, 1856, in Staunton, Virginia. His father, Joseph Ruggles Wilson, a native Ohioan of Scotch-Irish stock, had been a printer and a teacher before becoming minister of Staunton's First Presbyterian Church. Jessie Woodrow, his mother, was the daughter of a Presbyterian minister and had been born in England. Less than a year after the birth of their first son, the Wilsons moved to Augusta, Georgia, and later to Columbia, South Carolina.

In September 1875 Wilson entered the College of New Jersey, at Princeton. A serious, independent-minded, friendly student, he excelled at debate and oratory during his undergraduate years. Daydreaming of the political career to which these talents might lead, he sometimes wrote out on cards: "Thomas Woodrow Wilson, Senator from Virginia."

Upon his graduation from Princeton in 1879,

Wilson entered the University of Virginia Law School. But health problems and a dislike of his studies cut short his attendance, and he completed his law studies at home. In 1882, he started to practice law in Atlanta and was admitted to the Georgia bar.

Practicing law was no more to the young Wilson's taste than studying law had been. Still fascinated with politics and aspiring to a literary career, he entered graduate school at Baltimore's Johns Hopkins University in 1883. Two years later his first book of political analysis, *Congressional Government*, was published to enthusiastic reviews. Carefully scrutinizing the constitutional provisions of checks and balances, Wilson found the system sorely lacking. Not only was Congress completely dominant, wrote Wilson, but power there was diffuse, hidden, and unaccountable. The United States would be better served, he argued, if Congress modeled itself after the British Parliament. The book established Wilson's reputation as a political scientist and launched him on his academic career. His first teaching post was at the newly opened women's college near Philadelphia, Bryn Mawr.

The year 1885 also brought him a bride. Two years earlier, twenty-six-year-old Woodrow, who had dropped the name Thomas after graduation from Princeton, had fallen head over heels in love with Ellen Axson, a Presbyterian minister's daughter from Rome, Georgia. Within six months they were engaged to be married, and over the next year and a half he poured out his heart to her in letters that told "how passionate love grew rapidly upon me; how all my thoughts used to center in plans to win you. . . ." Just before their wedding, Woodrow avowed, "I would have you catch a glimpse of my purpose for the future and of the joy which that future contains for me, of the gratitude I feel for your priceless gift of love, and of the infinite love and tenderness which is the gift of my whole heart to you. . . ."

In 1886 Wilson was awarded a Ph.D. from Johns Hopkins, thereby making him the first and only

On July 9, 1919, President Wilson, returning from the Versailles Peace Conference in France, greets Americans in New York's harbor.

WOODROW WILSON ☆ 337

holder of a doctorate to become president. His academic star rose rapidly. After two years at Bryn Mawr, he moved to Wesleyan University in Middletown, Connecticut, where he taught for three years. Then, in 1890, he accepted a professorship at his alma mater, Princeton. He steadily built a towering reputation in academic circles. In addition to teaching at Princeton, he lectured regularly at Johns Hopkins and by 1902 had published a host of books and articles, not only in scholarly journals but also in such respected magazines as *Harper's Magazine* and the *Atlantic*

Before becoming president, Wilson had been a college professor and president of Princeton University. Here he is escorting the multimillionaire philanthropist Andrew Carnegie at the university's 1906 commencement.

Monthly. Several times during his tenure at Princeton, he was offered university presidencies, including that at the University of Virginia, but each time his wealthy friends among the Princeton trustees succeeded in keeping him. It came as no surprise, therefore, when those trustees unanimously elected him president of Princeton in 1902.

That presidency got off to a spectacular start. Wilson wooed faculty stars away from other universities and raised lots of money to construct new classrooms, dormitories, and laboratory buildings. Like other college presidents, he cultivated big donors, particularly Andrew Carnegie, from whom he hoped to get funds for a new library. Instead, Carnegie foisted one of his pet schemes on Princeton, which was to promote rowing as a less violent alternative to football. "We wanted a library," Wilson groused privately, "and he gave us a lake!"

Wilson first ran into trouble in 1907 when he tried to create a system of quadrangles, after the model of Oxford and Cambridge colleges, in which students would live and eat as well as study together with resident faculty members. The main stumbling block to this plan arose from Princeton's exclusive, fraternity-like eating clubs, which Wilson proposed to supplant with the "quads," promoting intellectual rather than social values. At first the trustees approved Wilson's plan. But when the clubs' alumni violently objected, the trustees backed down, and he tried to go over their heads. Traveling around the country, he explained his plan, hoping to rouse support among the various alumni clubs. The trustees refused to budge, and the next year the quadrangle plan was dropped.

During the last two years of his presidency at Princeton, a struggle developed over the location and control of a Graduate College, a residential facility for graduate students. The issue—a largely separate graduate school located off campus versus one on campus—seemed trivial to some at the time, but to Wilson the location was critical. He wanted to mix the older, intellectually serious graduate students with the undergraduates as a means of providing further role models for them. His antagonists lined up conservative trustees and wealthy donors on their side. An increasingly bitter fight raged on for two years and ended anticlimactically in June 1910. A bequest for several million dollars rested on the establishment of an independent graduate school, off campus. Wilson, swallowing his pride, accepted the money, and the battle was over.

Wilson did not wallow in defeat. Thanks to his prominence as Princeton's president, he had begun to be sought out for his political views, and just after he lost the Graduate College fight he was given the Democratic nomination for governor of New Jersey. Wilson quickly warmed up to campaigning and became an increasingly hard-hitting advocate of reform measures largely modeled on those enacted earlier in Wisconsin by Robert M. La Follette and his Republican progressives. On November 8, 1910, Wilson won 34,000 more votes than the combined total of his Republican opponent and several minor candidates.

Wilson's governorship was a spectacular success. No other career in American history better vindicated the study of politics as preparation for the practice of politics. As an academic, Wilson had examined and reflected on how power really worked and how to make political institutions more efficient and responsive. The critical instrument to make democracy work, in his view, was the political party. A leader must enlist and organize support from his own party, which must be ridded of bossism, cronyism, and corruption.

Even before his gubernatorial inauguration on January 17, 1911, Wilson moved to put his ideas to work by declaring his independence from the bosses who had nominated him. Then, the new governor immediately drafted a program of reform on which he intended to base his entire administration and lined up his party's caucus behind him. The program con-

sisted of four measures: direct primaries and election reform, legislation against corrupt practices, a workmen's compensation law, and regulation of public utilities. By April, bills pertaining to all four issues had been passed by the legislature, despite opposition from the bosses.

This record of accomplishment and the widespread desire for a fresh, new face at once made him a leading contender for the 1912 Democratic presidential nomination. A nucleus of backers soon gathered among men like Wilson, Southerners who had moved North to further their careers. Two of these Southern expatriates would play large roles in his presidency. One was William Gibbs McAdoo, a Georgian who had made a fortune in New York construction and who proved to be the most effective organizer and strategist of the Wilson-for-President movement. McAdoo later became Wilson's secretary of the Treasury. The other expatriate Southerner was "Colonel" Edward M. House, a wealthy Texan who had developed an irrepressible yen to be a president-maker. House later became Wilson's most influential adviser and his most trusted diplomatic emissary. In the pre-nomination campaign, however, House hedged his bets.

Despite Wilson's energetic pursuit of the endorsement in speaking tours that crisscrossed the continent in late 1911 and early 1912, the nomination was by no means his for the asking. James Beauchamp "Champ" Clark, the Speaker of the House, won a series of primaries. Representative Oscar W. Underwood of Alabama, chairman of the House Ways and Means Committee, took delegates away from Wilson in the South.

When the Democratic convention opened at Baltimore on June 25, 1912, Champ Clark was the leading contender, with some 435 votes. A two-thirds majority—726 of the 1,088 delegates—was needed for the nomination. When the balloting began, Clark led but an anti-Clark alliance between the Wilson and Underwood delegates stood fast. A seemingly interminable round of balloting followed. Behind the scenes McAdoo tirelessly courted delegates and made deals. On the thirtieth ballot Wilson passed Clark, and on the forty-sixth ballot Underwood released his delegates, thereby giving Wilson the two-thirds needed for the nomination.

Two weeks earlier the Republicans had renominated President William Howard Taft, but Theodore Roosevelt's delegates had bolted and organized a third party, the Progressive or Bull Moose party, which

nominated him in August. It would be the first real three-way contest for the presidency since 1860. Yet, by mid-August, it was generally agreed that the contest was between Wilson and Roosevelt; Taft was on the sidelines.

Between them, the dynamic, colorful Roosevelt and the poised, articulate Wilson staged the finest presidential campaign in American history. Both of them ran as progressives and cast aspersions on the other's reform credentials, but they also expounded political philosophies. With his New Nationalism, Roosevelt urged that big government control but not break up big business. Wilson, with timely tactical advice from the progressive lawyer Louis D. Brandeis, countered with his New Freedom, under which he urged vigorous antitrust policies. "What the Democratic party proposes to do is to go into power and do the things that the Republican party has been talking about doing for sixteen years," Wilson declared at the end of the campaign.

On November 5 Thomas Woodrow Wilson was elected the twenty-eighth president of the United States. The final tally was: Wilson, 6,293,152; Roosevelt, 4,119,207; Taft, 3,486,333. (Socialist Eugene V. Debs received nearly a million votes.) Taft won only 8 electoral votes, Roosevelt 88, and Wilson took the remaining 435.

As he had done earlier in New Jersey, Wilson applied his ideas about leadership to his presidency. Right after the election, he drew up a legislative program, which was also called the New Freedom, and worked to line up Democratic congressional leaders behind his measures. A valuable liaison with those leaders was William Jennings Bryan, whom he appointed secretary of state. Just a month after his inauguration on March 4, 1913, he made a bold departure by appearing in person to address a joint session—the first president since John Adams to do so. The purpose of Wilson's appearance on Capitol Hill, he said in the address of April 8, was to demonstrate that the president "is a person, not a mere department of the Government hailing Congress from some isolated island of jealous power. . . ."

The preliminary order of business was a downward revision of the tariff, the first major overhaul of the American protective system in sixty-five years. Democrats had made an issue of this government-sponsored protection of industry since the 1880s, deriding it as a subsidy to business, paid out of the pocket of the consumer. In just a month the House passed the Wilson-supported Underwood Tariff Bill, and the measure went to the Senate, where a long and often heated debate went on until September. Wilson's persistent lobbying paid off, as the Senate's version lowered the tariff still further. It also included a progressive income tax.

While the battle for tariff revision was still raging, Wilson introduced his second major New Freedom measure. "It is absolutely imperative," he announced to another joint session of Congress on June 23, 1913, "that we should give the businessmen of this country a banking and currency system by means of which they can make use of the freedom of enterprise and of individual initiative which we are about to bestow upon them by tariff reform."

By 1913, banking reform was unquestionably an idea whose time had come. The country's seven thousand banks operated without any real coordination among themselves. Even worse, there was no uniform currency but rather a miscellaneous collection of gold and silver coins, certificates, and greenbacks. The world's largest industrial economy had long since outgrown such an antiquated, fragmented banking and currency system. The Federal Reserve Act of 1913 created a system of regional banks run by the government but with private bankers on their boards. Overseeing and controlling those banks would be a board of governors appointed by the president, with power to control interest rates and the money supply and act as a central bank. It took six months of

intrepid debating and lobbying by Wilson and Bryan to get the Federal Reserve Act passed. Though changed by later reforms, it is Wilson's largest single legislative monument.

The third and final big New Freedom measure

FIRST ADMINISTRATION

INAUGURATION: Mar. 4, 1913; the Capitol, Washington, D.C.
VICE PRESIDENT: Thomas R. Marshall
SECRETARY OF STATE: William Jennings Bryan: Robert Lansing (from June 23, 1915)
SECRETARY OF THE TREASURY: William G. McAdoo
SECRETARY OF WAR: Lindley M. Garrison; Newton D. Baker (from Mar. 9, 1916)
ATTORNEY GENERAL: James C. McReynolds; Thomas W. Gregory (from Sept. 3, 1914)
POSTMASTER GENERAL: Albert S. Burleson
SECRETARY OF THE NAVY: Josephus Daniels
SECRETARY OF THE INTERIOR: Franklin K. Lane
SECRETARY OF AGRICULTURE: David F. Houston
SECRETARY OF COMMERCE: William C. Redfield
SECRETARY OF LABOR: William B. Wilson
SUPREME COURT APPOINTMENTS: James C. McReynolds (1914); Louis D. Brandeis (1916); John H. Clarke (1916)
63RD CONGRESS (Apr. 7, 1913–Mar. 3, 1915):
  SENATE: 51 Democrats; 44 Republicans; 1 Progressive
  HOUSE: 290 Democrats; 127 Republicans; 18 Others
64TH CONGRESS (Dec. 6, 1915–Mar. 3, 1917):
  SENATE: 56 Democrats; 39 Republicans; 1 Other
  HOUSE: 231 Democrats; 193 Republicans; 8 Others

ELECTION OF 1912

CANDIDATES	ELECTORAL VOTE	POPULAR VOTE
Woodrow Wilson (Democratic)	435	6,293,152
Theodore Roosevelt (Progressive)	88	4,119,207
William H. Taft (Republican)	8	3,486,333
Eugene V. Debs (Socialist)	—	900,369

addressed the antitrust problem. Despite the revival of the Sherman Antitrust Act under Roosevelt and Taft, progressives in both parties believed that stronger legislation was needed to control big business and combat monopolistic practices. One idea was to enact a more detailed, sharply focused antitrust law that spelled out prohibited practices. Another idea was to set up a regulatory agency to oversee business practices and formulate changing antitrust policies. The Clayton Antitrust Act of 1914 was a comprehensive statute that remains the basic federal law in this field. Also, in one section this act granted partial exemption to labor unions, which had been subjected, unfairly in their own view, to the Sherman Antitrust Act. Samuel Gompers, head of the American Federation of Labor, called this section of the Clayton Act "labor's Magna Carta." A separate act established the Federal Trade Commission, which functioned as an oversight agency.

In all, this was a tremendously important achievement. Wilson had kept Congress in session continuously for eighteen months—the longest stretch up to that time, even during the Civil War. He had disappointed some progressives by declining to push for more measures, such as a law forbidding child labor, but he believed that he had gotten all he could out of this Congress. Wilson also disappointed woman suffragists, including two of his daughters, by failing to back a constitutional amendment to guarantee suffrage. He likewise outraged African-Americans by allowing some of his Southern cabinet members to try to introduce racial segregation into federal offices. He reversed this course in the face of protests by the newly founded National Association for the Advancement of Colored People.

Wilson made up for those shortcomings partially by mounting a second wave of New Freedom reforms in 1916. Measures that he pushed through Congress then included a child labor law, financial aid to farmers, more sharply graduated income and inheritance taxes, shipping regulation, and an eight-hour law for railroad workers. Also, overruling his more cautious advisers, he nominated Brandeis to sit on the Supreme Court, its first Jew, who prevailed in a hard-fought confirmation battle. Wilson also came out for woman suffrage and later played a strong part in securing passage of the Nineteenth Amendment. In all, Wilson's domestic record ranks him along with Franklin Roosevelt and Lyndon Johnson as one of the three greatest legislative leaders among twentieth-century presidents.

Privately, the Wilsons and their three daughters made the White House a happy home. Two of the Wilson girls were married during their father's presidency: Jessie on November 25, 1913, to Francis B. Sayre of Williams College; and Eleanor on May 7, 1914, to William G. McAdoo, Wilson's secretary of the Treasury. Sadly, Eleanor's wedding turned out to be one of the last public appearances the first lady was to make. Shortly afterward she was diagnosed with Bright's disease, and on August 6—five days after World War I had erupted in Europe—she died. Gently releasing his wife's hand, which he had been holding in a bedside vigil, Wilson went to a window, stared out, and cried, "Oh my God, what am I to do?"

The man most deeply concerned by Wilson's seemingly incurable depression following Ellen's death was the White House physician, Dr. Cary T. Grayson, who urged the president to take up golf and was his frequent companion in the White House. In October 1914 Dr. Grayson introduced an attractive Washington widow, Edith Bolling Galt, to the president's cousin, Helen Woodrow Bones, who was serving as White House hostess. In March 1915 Miss Bones invited Mrs. Galt, by then a close friend, to tea at the White House. Wilson arrived unexpectedly with Grayson, and the two men joined the ladies for tea. A few days later Wilson invited Mrs. Galt to dinner, and shortly thereafter he began taking long drives

President Wilson and his second wife, Edith Bolling Galt, whom he married after being widowed in 1914, attend an opening-day major league baseball game.

with her. In May he proposed marriage, and in September she accepted his proposal. "She seemed to come into our life here like a special gift from Heaven," Wilson wrote to a friend, "and I have won a sweet companion who will soon make me forget the intolerable loneliness and isolation of the weary months since this terrible war began." On December 18, 1915, the two were married quietly at Mrs. Galt's home in Washington, D.C.

By the time of their wedding, the greatest challenges facing Wilson lay in foreign policy. "It would be the irony of fate if my administration had to deal chiefly with foreign affairs," he had told a friend just after his election to the presidency. Yet Wilson was to be faced with more immediate and far-reaching international problems than any of his predecessors. Almost from his inauguration in March 1913 until his retirement eight years later in March 1921, he was to be confronted with an unending series of foreign crises for which there were no precedents nor easy solutions.

In selecting his cabinet, Wilson had named Bryan secretary of state because he was their party's long-time leader. The two men got along quite well for a while. Wilson and Bryan had chiefly their own inexperience to blame for a long and ultimately unsuccessful imbroglio with Mexico. Although the administration did meddle in the Mexican Revolution, some of the meddling was in response to the arrest of U.S. soldiers at Tampico in 1914, and Pancho Villa's murder of 17 Americans in Columbus, New Mexico, in 1916. By the end of his first term, when the troops were finally withdrawn, Wilson had succeeded in doing little more than embittering United States–Mexican relations. The best that can be said about Wilson's involvement in Mexico is that he learned from it how complex foreign situations, especially revolutions, could be, and he later exercised greater restraint.

It was the outbreak of World War I in August 1914 that led to Wilson's most agonizing trials and his supreme accomplishments. Like nearly everyone else in 1914, he assumed that America would remain neutral, but maintaining neutrality was to test all his powers of leadership and perseverance. At first, the United States was probably as neutral as possible.

Early on in the war, there were a number of clashes with Britain but none that would have led to war. Germany's introduction of unrestricted submarine warfare early in 1915 was what most sorely tested, and eventually overcame, Wilson's efforts to keep the United States on the sidelines.

The first major crisis erupted on May 7, 1915, when a German U-boat sank the British Cunard liner *Lusitania*. Among the 1,198 passengers who went down with the ship were 128 Americans. The sinking of the *Lusitania* plunged Wilson into a year-long duel with the Germans over submarine warfare. Despite Bryan's resignation in protest over Wilson's risking war, and despite attacks by Roosevelt and Republicans for being too soft, Wilson adroitly managed both the diplomatic contest and the political conflict at home. In April 1916 he got the Germans to back down in their submarine warfare, thereby giving the United States a respite from the threat of being dragged into the war. He also established his undisputed leadership of the Democrats and brought the party together on a platform of progressivism and peace in time for the 1916 presidential campaign.

It was a strenuous election. The Republicans appeared to be reunited, because Roosevelt had smothered his Progressive party and rejoined the fold. They had an attractive candidate in former New York Governor and, until his nomination, Associate Justice Charles Evans Hughes. They also enjoyed a hold on the most populous regions of the country that had allowed them to win the presidency in four straight elections before their defeat in 1912. But Hughes and the Republicans had trouble getting their campaign to function smoothly, while Wilson and the Democrats moved flawlessly and trumpeted their outstanding record of accomplishment. In the end, the Republicans' edge almost carried the day. If California, where the outcome was close and in doubt for several days, had gone to Hughes, he would have prevailed by one vote in the electoral college. Instead, Wilson won and carried an almost 600,000-vote popular plurality. He was the first Democrat since Andrew Jackson to win a second consecutive term and the first to keep the Republicans out of the White House for longer than four years.

Despite its narrowness, Wilson interpreted his reelection as a mandate from the people to act as an international peacemaker. He started by asking the opponents to state their war aims. Both the Germans and the Allies replied evasively. Wilson then escalated his peace offensive before the Senate on January 22, 1917, to deliver a call for a "peace without victory." Unknown to the president, Germany was already taking steps that would make America's involvement in the war unavoidable.

On January 31, 1917, the German ambassador informed the State Department that his country would resume unrestricted submarine warfare the following day. All the concessions President Wilson had wrung from Germany the previous year vanished. He severed diplomatic relations with Germany but held back from war. As an interim measure, he asked Congress for permission to arm United States merchant ships against submarine attack. By a lopsided vote of 403 to 13, the House passed the Armed Ships Bill on March 1. In the Senate, however, eleven members, led by La Follette of Wisconsin and George Norris of Nebraska, filibustered until the session's end on March 4. Wilson immediately got a ruling from the State Department that he had authority to arm merchant ships entering the war zone; congressional approval was not required.

The same day the House was voting, the State Department published an intercepted telegram from German Minister of Foreign Affairs Alfred Zimmermann to the German ambassador in Mexico. The message had been decoded by experts in London. In the event of war between Germany and the United States, Zimmermann had signaled, Mexico was to be offered an alliance and promised to regain "lost provinces" in New Mexico, Texas, and Arizona. As sensational as the Zimmermann telegram was, it did not convince many Americans that intervention was necessary, especially not President Wilson. Only after a month of agonized soul-searching did he finally choose to go to war.

On the evening of April 2 Wilson went before Congress to ask for a declaration of war against Germany. The president reviewed his efforts to maintain neutrality and commented bitterly on Germany's increasing disregard for that stance. Now he vowed "to fight thus for the ultimate peace of the world and for the liberation of its peoples, the German peoples included: for the rights of nations great and small and the privilege of men everywhere to choose their way of life and of obedience. The world must be made safe for democracy." The Senate, by a vote of 82 to 6 on April 4, and two days later the House, by 373 to 50, approved the declaration of war.

Wilson proved to be a surprisingly effective war leader. He recognized his own ignorance of military affairs and delegated the conduct of the war to the professionals. His willingness to delegate also extended to the domestic war effort. Introducing centralized government controls on an unprecedented scale, he appointed such able men as Herbert Hoover to oversee food production and deliveries to the Allies; Bernard Baruch to manage industrial production and coordination; and McAdoo to run the railroads. Less prudently, he permitted the Justice Department and the Post Office to suppress free speech in an effort to stamp out dissent, which included the conviction and imprisonment of the socialist leader Eugene V. Debs. Those actions helped inflame broader wartime hysteria.

Despite the 1916 defense increases, America was sadly unprepared for the vast undertaking of a foreign war, and more than a year passed before United States troops entered the fighting in division strength. Meanwhile, in the spring of 1918, Germany launched a series of initially successful offensives that nearly

CHARLES EVANS HUGHES

Charles Evans Hughes was one of the few Republicans who seemed capable of wooing the Progressives back into the Republican fold in 1916. An associate justice of the Supreme Court and a former governor of New York, he was remembered by Progressives for reforming state government, whereas Republicans liked his removal from the fratricidal politics of the 1912 split when he was on the Court. A graduate of Brown University, Hughes received his law degree from Columbia in 1884. Practicing in New York City, he distinguished himself as a prosecutor in well-publicized cases involving abuses by public utilities and life insurance companies. He served as New York's reform governor from 1906 until 1910, when President Taft appointed him to the Supreme Court. Nominated by the Republicans in 1916, he was supported by many leading Progressives after Theodore Roosevelt refused their nomination; Roosevelt endorsed the bewhiskered Hughes, whom he privately dubbed the "bearded lady," because he was bent on defeating Wilson. Narrowly beaten in the election, Hughes returned to his law practice. He served as secretary of state from 1921 to 1926, became a member of the Permanent Court of Arbitration in 1926, and in 1930 was appointed a judge on the Permanent Court of International Justice. That same year he was named Chief Justice of the United States, and he served in that post until 1941. He died in 1948.

defeated the Allies. At Château-Thierry and Belleau Wood in June, however, the "doughboys" helped stop the Germans, and that summer Americans contributed substantially to the Allied counteroffensives that turned the tide. Germany collapsed quickly and sued for peace, which resulted in the Armistice on November 11, 1918.

Wilson was prepared for peace. In a memorable address before Congress on January 8, 1918, he had outlined the major points that would serve as the basis for peace. Eight of the famous Fourteen Points

U.S. Army troops stand in the trenches in France in 1917. A reluctant and belligerent Wilson took the nation into World War I in 1917, and by the time the war ended on November 11, 1918, two million "doughboys" were serving on the Western Front.

had pertained to territorial adjustments after the war. Others had called for open negotiations and treaties, freedom of the seas, removal of economic barriers and equality of trade, reduction of armaments, and impartial adjustment of colonial claims. The fourteenth and, to the president, most important point had called for a league of nations.

A week after the Armistice, Wilson revealed how determined he was to shape the outcome of the war. He announced that he would lead the United States delegation to the peace conference in Europe, and on December 4 President and Mrs. Wilson sailed from New York on the liner *George Washington.* In France, in Britain, and in Italy, Wilson received tumultuous

receptions from war-weary peoples; they served to reinforce his growing conviction that he must strive to bring a just, lasting peace.

It did not take Wilson long after the formal opening of the peace conference in Paris on January 18, 1919, however, to realize that he would have to fight for that vision. Most of the work was conducted by the "Big Four"—Wilson, Prime Minister Lloyd George of Britain, Premiere Georges Clemenceau of France, and Premiere Vittorio Orlando of Italy. The other three leaders were quietly contemptuous of the president: many of Wilson's points directly contradicted their secret arrangements to divide Europe and Germany's colonies, and they were unwilling to surrender the territorial concessions contained in those agreements.

In the subsequent months of negotiations, Wilson often conceded on matters of substance, although he yielded far less than disappointed idealists thought at the time. One thing mattered to him above all: a league of nations as part of the peace treaty. Even before the negotiations began, Wilson gathered a small committee that worked intensely for a month to produce the Draft Covenant of the League of Nations. This was the charter of an international organization that would be empowered to keep the peace and prevent aggression and war. Wilson unveiled the Draft Covenant to the peace conference and the world on February 14, 1919.

Immediately afterward, he returned to America to sign important measures before the adjournment of Congress. On that visit he tried but failed to convince Republican congressional leaders to accept the Draft Covenant. This was a critical failure because in the November 1918 elections the Republicans had won control of both houses. Senator Henry Cabot Lodge, a white-bearded patrician from Massachusetts, would become the chairman of the Foreign Relations Committee and Senate majority leader in the next Congress. On March 2 Lodge headed the list of thirty-nine Republican senators—more than the one-third needed to block Senate approval of the treaty—who signed a "round-robin" resolution opposing the Draft Covenant and demanding that the League not be incorporated in the treaty.

Initially, Wilson reacted defiantly to the "round-robin," but back in Paris he made revisions in the League to try to meet Republican objections. In April he suffered an attack of influenza, which many later believed was symptomatic of a steady decline in his mental and physical health.

Meanwhile, the political wrangling at the conference grew worse, the meetings often verging on brawls. Wilson himself once threatened to leave the conference, and Orlando actually did withdraw temporarily after the American president appealed over his head to the Italian people.

On June 28, 1919, the Germans signed the peace

SECOND ADMINISTRATION

INAUGURATION: Mar. 5, 1917; the Capitol, Washington, D.C.

VICE PRESIDENT: Thomas R. Marshall

SECRETARY OF STATE: Robert Lansing; Bainbridge Colby (from Mar. 23, 1920)

SECRETARY OF THE TREASURY: William G. McAdoo; Carter Glass (from Dec. 16, 1918); David F. Houston (from Feb. 12, 1920)

SECRETARY OF WAR: Newton D. Baker

ATTORNEY GENERAL: Thomas W. Gregory; A. Mitchell Palmer (from Mar. 5, 1919)

POSTMASTER GENERAL: Albert S. Burleson

SECRETARY OF THE NAVY: Josephus Daniels

SECRETARY OF THE INTERIOR: Franklin K. Lane; John B. Payne (from Mar. 13, 1920)

SECRETARY OF AGRICULTURE: David F. Houston; Edwin T. Meredith (from Feb. 2, 1920)

SECRETARY OF COMMERCE: William C. Redfield; Joshua W. Alexander (from Dec. 16, 1919)

SECRETARY OF LABOR: William B. Wilson

65TH CONGRESS (Apr. 2, 1917–Mar. 3, 1919):
  SENATE: 53 Democrats; 42 Republicans; 1 Other
  HOUSE: 216 Republicans; 210 Democrats; 9 Others

66TH CONGRESS (May 19, 1919–Mar. 3, 1921):
  SENATE: 48 Republicans; 47 Democrats; 1 Other
  HOUSE: 237 Republicans; 191 Democrats; 7 Others

ELECTION OF 1916

CANDIDATES	ELECTORAL VOTE	POPULAR VOTE
Woodrow Wilson (Democratic)	277	9,126,300
Charles E. Hughes (Republican)	254	8,546,789
A. L. Benson (Socialist)	—	589,924
J. Frank Hanly (Prohibition)	—	221,030

As portrayed in a 1919 cartoon from *Punch*, Wilson tried and failed to bring the United States into the League of Nations. The league's mission was to maintain peace and prevent war.

treaty in the glittering Hall of Mirrors of the Palace of Versailles. Wilson sailed for home immediately and laid the Treaty of Versailles before the Senate for its advice and consent. "The stage is set, the destiny disclosed . . ." he told the senators. "We can only go forward, with lifted eyes and freshened spirit, to follow the vision. . . . The light streams upon the path ahead, and nowhere else."

Nearly all of the members of the Democratic minority in the Senate supported the treaty and the League of Nations, and they would follow faithfully Wilson's leadership in the subsequent fight. The Republican opponents, however, were divided into three factions according to how they wanted to han-

dle League membership. A small group of "mild reservationists" wished to limit American obligations under the League only slightly. The largest group, the "strong reservationists" led by Lodge, were bent on restricting commitments to uphold peace and security so severely that some believed League membership would become meaningless. Finally, a small group of "irreconcilables," which included La Follette, Idaho's William E. Borah, and California's Hiram Johnson, rejected the League totally and attacked other provisions of the treaty as imperialistic.

In September 1919 Wilson—realizing he lacked the votes in the Senate—appealed directly to the people. Traveling nearly ten thousand miles throughout the Midwest and West, he delivered some 40 speeches in thirty cities between September 4 and 24. At Pueblo, Colorado, he stumbled while stepping up to the speaker's platform, but he went on to deliver an emotional oration that brought tears to many eyes.

That night Wilson suffered what probably was a slight stroke. The months and years of his wartime presidency, the six-month-long ordeal in Paris, the frustrations upon his return to Washington, the grueling tour—all had taken their toll. The remainder of the trip was canceled, and the presidential train rushed back to Washington. There, on October 2, Wilson had a massive stroke that left him partially paralyzed.

For the next five months the president was almost a recluse in the White House, cut off from most contacts with the outside world and attended principally by Dr. Grayson and Mrs. Wilson.

Much has been written—mostly unfavorable—about Edith Wilson's role during the president's illness, and she has even been called the nation's first female president. In her memoirs she maintained that she had acted, at the doctors' advice, as a shield for her husband, judging who should be brought into the sickroom. In fact, she did act as something of a surrogate president by controlling the access of people and information to her husband. No one should have been playing such a role. This was the worst crisis of presidential disability in American history, and it was handled miserably. A senatorial "smelling committee" was sent to ascertain Wilson's incapacity but came away deceptively reassured by an elaborate charade staged by the president and Dr. Grayson. Vice President Thomas R. Marshall refused to hear any talk about taking over and maintained a low profile.

During Wilson's convalescence, the Senate had decided on the fate of the Treaty of Versailles and the League of Nations. On November 6 Lodge announced that he was for ratification with—ironically—fourteen reservations. In a letter from the sickroom on November 18, Wilson directed his supporters to reject Lodge's reservations. Unquestionably, his defiance and refusal to compromise sprang at least in part from the way that the stroke had warped his perception and judgment. Another attempt to approve the treaty on March 19, 1920, also failed, although a number of Democrats defied Wilson and voted to consent with the Lodge reservations.

Wilson talked about making the 1920 presidential election "a great and solemn referendum" on the League. Ill as he was, he even wanted a third-term nomination. But as the enfeebled chief executive sat on the sidelines, the Democratic nominee, Governor James M. Cox of Ohio, tirelessly thumped for the League—and went down to a landslide defeat at the hands of Warren G. Harding.

On March 4, 1921—Harding's Inauguration Day—police screened off photographers as Wilson was all but bodily lifted into the car that would take him and the president-elect to the Capitol. There, in the president's office, as the clock ticked away the last minutes of his term, he signed a few final bills. At last a committee from both houses of Congress arrived to ask permission to adjourn; its chairman was Henry Cabot Lodge. The two bitter opponents addressed one another in frigid, formal phrases.

Former President and Mrs. Wilson did not stay for the inauguration; they left the Capitol by a side door and went immediately to the house on S Street in Washington's Northwest section that they had purchased for their retirement. Woodrow Wilson lived out the remaining three years of his life in semi-seclusion. Early in 1924 word leaked out of the quiet house that Wilson was dying. Crowds once more gathered as famous people came to leave their cards. At 11:15 A.M. on February 3, Wilson died; his last word had been "Edith."

Calvin Coolidge—president since Harding's death the preceding summer—attended the small private funeral at the S Street house, but Senator Lodge, named to a committee to represent Congress, was excluded at Mrs. Wilson's request. Presbyterian though he was, Wilson was interred in a tomb in the Episcopal National Cathedral—the only president to be buried in Washington.

Wilson's reputation suffered badly after his death in the moods of postwar disillusionment of the 1920s and 1930s. During World War II, however, he enjoyed a posthumous apotheosis as a prophet whose message should have been heeded. Much of the enthusiasm behind the founding of the United Nations and a rejection of postwar retreat into isolationism sprang from desires to honor Wilson's memory. Later, Cold War "realists" tended to scorn him as a naive idealist, but gradually Wilson has come to be honored as one of the twentieth century's greatest leaders, both as an effective champion of reform at home and as the architect of an approach to world order and peace that continues to resonate through the decades.

—JOSEPH L. GARDNER,
revised by JOHN MILTON COOPER, JR.

THE TWENTY-NINTH PRESIDENT ★ 1921–1923

WARREN GAMALIEL HARDING

A BABBITT IN THE WHITE HOUSE

Will Rogers called it the "great morality panic of 1924." Stirred by rumors of corruption in the Harding administration, and further stirred by the approaching presidential election, the Senate had decided to do some investigating. The rumors were well founded. First there was former Secretary of the Interior Albert B. Fall, who had leased two government oil deposits—the Teapot Dome reserve in Wyoming and the Elk Hills fields in California—to private developers under questionable terms and had received at least $400,000 in personal "loans." Then there were Harding's Veterans Bureau chief and alien property custodian, who were denounced for defrauding the government by giving contracts to whoever gave them the largest kickback. Worst of all, there was Attorney General Harry M. Daugherty, who, it was discovered, had known about corruption in the Justice Department but had not prosecuted the corrupt nor even tried to stop them. Because all had been political appointees, their deeds cast a pall over the administration of the president who put them in office: Warren Gamaliel Harding.

The Teapot Dome scandal seemed the most lurid, although it involved less money and influence peddling than the others. Secretary of the Interior Fall suggested that the oil reserves for which Navy Secretary Edwin Denby was responsible be transferred to the Department of the Interior. Denby had no objection; and the president approved the transfer, and Fall leased the oil reserves. Everything was properly signed and filed. Even after the scandal broke, it took the government three years to cancel the Teapot Dome and Elk Hills leases.

Mercifully for him, President Harding did not have to endure the disgrace of his misplaced trust. He had died on August 2, 1923, a year before the scandals were made public. "Few deaths are unmingled tragedies," writes his biographer Samuel Hopkins

Adams. "Harding's was not. He died in time." If he had lived, he would have been brokenhearted, but he probably would have stood by his friends; for Warren Harding, by agreement of most historians a poor president, was a very good friend.

Harding, the oldest of eight children, was born on November 2, 1865, in Blooming Grove, Ohio. His father, George Harding, was a farmer and horse trader who later took a quick medical course and became a physician. In 1879 his family sent Warren to Ohio Central College, where he enjoyed playing the horn in the band, debating, and editing the yearbook.

After his graduation in 1882, the young Harding tried teaching school for a few months and then joined his family in Marion, where his father had moved to set up a medical practice. He studied law briefly, sold insurance, and managed the finances of the local baseball team and of the Citizens' Cornet Band. Harding's big chance came in 1884 when he bought the *Star*, a town newspaper that was failing. As Marion grew, the *Star* held its own and survived.

Change came to the *Star* in the person of Florence Kling De Wolfe, the daughter of a rich Marion real estate and banking magnate. Harding was twenty-six years old; "Flossie," a widow with a son, was thirty-one. He was handsome, amicable, and pleasant; she was plain, lacking in charm, and aggressive. Harding does not seem to have loved Flossie, but she loved him and pursued him. They were married in 1891. Shortly afterward, Mrs. Harding appeared at the *Star* office; she recalled "intending to help out for a few days and remained fourteen years." She organized things. She hired and trained a force of delivery boys. "It was her energy and business sense which made the *Star*," according to one of her newsboys.

In the 1890s Harding began to take an active part in Republican politics. The party was glad to have him: He was a prospering editor; an influential citizen active in church, civic, and business ventures; a good speaker; and a willing campaigner. By 1898 Harding

Senator Warren G. Harding relaxes at the Elks' National Home, in Bedford, Virginia, in 1920.

was taking politics seriously and was elected state senator. His genuine charm, friendliness, and enthusiasm made him an ideal conciliator for the faction-ridden Ohio Republican party.

He also attracted the attention of Harry Daugherty, a skillful, shrewd machine politician and lobbyist. Daugherty, who had first seen Harding at a Republican rally, later said that he had thought, "Gee, what a President he'd make!" Daugherty soon began applying his political skills to advance the career of his new friend. In 1904 he helped Harding win the lieutenant governorship. In 1910 Harding ran for governor and lost. Harding was chosen to renominate Taft for president at the Republican National Convention.

That same year Harding lost a second bid for the Ohio governorship and was prepared to abandon politics, but his wife and Harry Daugherty pressed him into running for the United States Senate in 1914. Harding won and went to Washington.

As a senator, Harding was a reliable Republican conservative. He voted for whatever the party deemed best and opposed most government regulation of industry, even during World War I. He initially voted against the prohibition amendment, but when he saw that it was going to pass, he switched his vote. And although he admitted that he thought the law unenforceable, he voted to override Wilson's veto of the Volstead Act. In foreign affairs, he generally supported Wilson's conduct of the war, though not always his aims. Harding was, in sum, a run-of-the-mill senator endowed with extraordinary personal charm that made him one of the best-liked men in Washington.

These were the happiest years of Harding's life. He liked poker games; he had many good friends; his matronly wife had even emerged as something of a socialite. The Hardings traveled a good deal together, and the senator took occasional trips alone, as he had done earlier in Ohio. Some of those trips were for extramarital affairs. In 1915 he began an affair with twenty-year-old Nan Britton, a Marion girl who claimed to have had a crush on him since she was a child. According to her later story, Harding found her a job in New York, where he visited her frequently and fathered her daughter, who was born in 1919. There are strong reasons to doubt the veracity of Nan Britton's account, particularly because Harding had never conceived a child with either his wife, who had a son by her previous marriage, or with his lover Carrie Phillips, and because evidence does not support the times and places of their supposed assignations. In the end, however, nothing except the scandals of his administration would do greater damage to Harding's reputation than Nan Britton's story.

Harding's biggest political break came at the end

of World War I. America was a frustrated country. Its economy was suffering through a staggering postwar inflation (which would shortly slide into a recession); senators were divided over the controversial League of Nations. Harding, who was now being touted as a possible nominee for president, began to speak out, and his words voiced the sentiments of the frustrated nation. Harding defined the patriot's duty: "To safeguard America first. To stabilize America first. To prosper America first. To think of America first. To exalt America first. To live for and revere America first." America's need was, he said, "not revolution but restoration, not surgery but serenity, not nostrums but normalcy." Those utterances began to make Harding look good to a few leading Republicans as a presidential possibility.

On a summer day in 1919 one of the most powerful party leaders, Senator Boies Penrose, sent for his colleague. "Harding," he said, "how would you like to be President?" Harding protested that he was not fit for the job. "Am I a big enough man for the race?" Harding later asked his Ohio mentor. "Don't make me laugh," answered Daugherty. And it was he who convinced Mrs. Harding, who was at first unreceptive to the idea, that her husband should run.

There was no Harding bandwagon. The candidate did poorly in the few primaries that he entered. But this did not worry Daugherty. Early in 1920, he told reporters, "I don't expect Senator Harding to be nominated on the first, second, or third ballots, but I think we can afford to take chances that, about eleven minutes after two, Friday morning of the convention, when ten or twenty weary men are sitting around a table, someone will say, 'Who will we nominate?' At that decisive time the friends of Harding will suggest him and can well afford to abide by the result."

At the Chicago convention those men did talk about Harding and asked if there was anything in his past that might embarrass the party if he were to be its presidential candidate. Neither Carrie Phillips's nor Nan Britton's stories had come out yet, so Harding's managers answered, No, nothing.

Contrary to later legend, this "smoke-filled room" conclave did not control the convention and make Harding president. The leading contenders for the nomination were General Leonard Wood, Theodore Roosevelt's friend and a commander in the Rough Riders; Governor Frank Lowden of Illinois, a folksy, self-made man; and Senator Hiram Johnson of California, a fiery progressive and total opponent of the League of Nations. In their slashing pre-nomination campaigns, these men had so thoroughly antagonized each other and their supporters that the usual compromises among front-runners had become impossible. In that situation, Harding emerged as a natural second choice, based upon his affability and his being from the vital swing state of Ohio. Few party leaders had any illusions about his qualifications to be president. "There ain't any first-raters this year," snarled one of his fellow senators, ". . . we got a lot of second-raters and Warren Harding is the best of the second-raters."

Ironically, the Republicans' well-financed, superbly orchestrated campaign in 1920 was largely superfluous. The levels of frustration and discontent were so high among the voters that no one doubted that the Republicans would win easily. The Democrats were correspondingly divided and dispirited and also picked a compromise candidate, James M. Cox, largely on the basis of his having had nothing to do with the Wilson administration and his being governor of Ohio. Cox and his running mate, Assistant Secretary of the Navy Franklin D. Roosevelt, barnstormed around the country giving speeches, but they were always inadequately funded underdogs.

Harding's victory in November was so big that the Republicans carried New York City and Boston, and reduced their opponents' congressional delegations to rumps. Harding got 60 percent of the popular vote, defeating Cox by more than seven million votes. The socialist candidate Eugene V. Debs polled nearly a million votes despite his being a prisoner in a federal penitentiary.

"Well, Warren Harding," his wife said, "I have got you the Presidency; what are you going to do with it?" Daugherty thought himself responsible for Harding's

---

THE HARDING ADMINISTRATION

INAUGURATION: Mar. 4, 1921; the Capitol, Washington, D.C.
VICE PRESIDENT: Calvin Coolidge
SECRETARY OF STATE: Charles Evans Hughes
SECRETARY OF THE TREASURY: Andrew W. Mellon
SECRETARY OF WAR: John W. Weeks
ATTORNEY GENERAL: Harry M. Daugherty
POSTMASTER GENERAL: Will H. Hays;
   Hubert Work (from Mar. 4, 1922);
   Harry S. New (from Mar. 5, 1923)
SECRETARY OF THE NAVY: Edwin Denby
SECRETARY OF THE INTERIOR: Albert B. Fall;
   Hubert Work (from Mar. 5, 1923)
SECRETARY OF AGRICULTURE: Henry C. Wallace
SECRETARY OF COMMERCE: Herbert C. Hoover
SECRETARY OF LABOR: James J. Davis
SUPREME COURT APPOINTMENTS: William H. Taft, chief justice (1921); George Sutherland (1922); Pierce Butler (1922); Edward T. Sanford (1923)
67TH CONGRESS (Apr. 11, 1921–Mar. 3, 1923):
   SENATE: 59 Republicans; 37 Democrats
   HOUSE: 300 Republicans; 132 Democrats; 1 Other
68TH CONGRESS (Dec. 3, 1923–Mar. 3, 1925):
   SENATE: 51 Republicans; 43 Democrats; 2 Others
   HOUSE: 225 Republicans; 207 Democrats; 3 Others

ELECTION OF 1920

CANDIDATES	ELECTORAL VOTE	POPULAR VOTE
Warren G. Harding (Republican)	404	16,153,115
James M. Cox (Democratic)	127	9,133,092
Eugene V. Debs (Socialist)	—	915,490
Parley P. Christensen (Farmer-Labor)	—	265,229

---

election, and their Ohio cronies demanded plenty of spoils; fellow senators, such as Fall of New Mexico, also wanted their due. Harding was not totally naive. He knew that his mentors were not the most talented men in government, but he brought them into his administration. "God," he said, "I can't be an ingrate!"

Harding did make three outstanding appointments to his cabinet: Charles Evans Hughes, secretary of state; Andrew W. Mellon, secretary of the Treasury; and Herbert C. Hoover, secretary of commerce. When Mellon's budget-reform program was passed in June 1921, Harding appointed the able Charles G. Dawes director of the Budget Bureau. And he named former President Taft as chief justice of the United States.

Harding displayed mixed attitudes toward the presidency. Sometimes he felt firmly in command. He decided that the United States should not join the League of Nations but should make a separate peace with Germany. He gave Hughes the green light to pursue a creative foreign policy that included naval disarmament and large-scale foreign lending to break the war debt reparations tangle in Europe. He likewise backed Mellon's and Hoover's pro-business domestic policies. At other times, however, he seemed baffled by the job. "I listen to one side and they seem right," he commented on one issue, "and then— God!—I talk to the other side and they seem just as right, and here I am where I started. I know somewhere there is a book that will give me the truth, but hell! I couldn't read the book."

The president also struggled with the recession he had inherited. Although the deflation was checked somewhat during Harding's administration, the American farmer got no relief. Harding tried unsuccessfully to produce solutions to the labor problems of 1921 and 1922, especially in the coal and railroad industries. Otherwise, he seldom showed much initiative, in part because he believed in all but unquestioning executive cooperation with Congress.

"My God, what a hell of a job," Harding said as his awareness of his responsibility increased. Occasionally he made a grand gesture. In his first year in office President Harding ignored the advice of his friends and pardoned the imprisoned Eugene Debs. "I was persuaded in my own mind that it was the right thing to do," Harding explained, adding that he was "growing less a partisan than I once was."

Meanwhile, the first scandals broke. Late in 1922 talk began to circulate about Charles Forbes and the Veterans Bureau. Early the next year, the rumors were strong enough—and true enough—to cause two tragedies: First, Charles Cramer, Forbes's sidekick in the Veterans Bureau frauds, shot himself to death, leaving a suicide note addressed to the president. (Harding refused to open it.) Then Daugherty's Ohio crony of many years, Jesse Smith, also committed suicide. Smith had been a fixer in arranging protection from raids by prohibition agents and for selling permits for the manufacture of alcohol. The president began to feel the pressure, and several people thought that he was worried and depressed when he started on a cross-country trip in the summer of 1923. "I have no trouble with my enemies. . . ," he admitted as he left, "But my damn friends, they're the ones that keep me walking the floor nights."

Harding never returned to Washington. He died in San Francisco on August 2, 1923. A heart attack was almost certainly the cause. Mrs. Harding refused, however, to allow an autopsy. Soon gossip started to percolate: he had killed himself; Daugherty had killed him; Mrs. Harding had killed him. No evidence ever supported any of those speculations.

Harding was first mourned and then disgraced. Teapot Dome and related scandals lasted until 1927. Then, just as the investigations got wrapped up, Nan Britton published *The President's Daughter*, which included a plea for some of Harding's estate for their child. (She received nothing.)

Harding's reputation has never recovered from

A cartoon published in the Memphis newspaper *The Commercial Appeal* depicts a teapot with the face of a sad GOP elephant. The best-known of several financial scandals in Harding's administration was called Teapot Dome, after the oil-bearing geological formation in Wyoming, site of oil reserves leased by the U.S. government.

both the scandals of his administration and the revelations about his personal life. Later, he became something of a national joke. Cynics claimed that his presidency proved how an uncaring, irresponsible people had gotten the leader they deserved. That was unfair. Harding was a man of some ability and great political gifts. His administration also included a record of accomplishment. Perhaps the best assessment of Harding came in a eulogy by Herbert Hoover: "Here was a man whose soul was seared by a great disillusionment. . . . Warren Harding had a dim realization that he had been betrayed by a few of the men whom he had believed were his devoted friends. That was the tragedy of . . . [his] life. . . ."

—*DAVID JACOBS,*
revised by JOHN MILTON COOPER, JR.

When Calvin Coolidge was nominated for vice president by the Republican party in Chicago in 1920, one newspaperman covering the proceedings offered "to bet all comers that Harding, if elected, would be assassinated before he had served half his term. Someone in the crowd remonstrated gently, saying that any talk of assassination was unwise and might be misunderstood. . . . But the Bostonian refused to shut down. 'I don't give a damn what you say,' he bawled. 'I am simply telling you what I know. I know Cal Coolidge inside and out. He is the luckiest _____ in the whole world!' "

Luck and political skill carried Calvin Coolidge from Massachusetts to the White House within a single decade, and during his lifetime "Silent Cal," as he was known, seemed to have a magic touch with the voters. After he left office in 1929, however, his historical reputation experienced a precipitous slide. In recent years, admirers such as Ronald Reagan and a number of historians have sought, with some success, to rehabilitate Coolidge and his standing in history. Because of doubts about his performance in the years preceding the Great Depression, though, he has remained in the second tier of twentieth-century presidents.

Coolidge governed during a turbulent decade. The nation grappled with urban-rural tensions, expressed in the rise and fall of such controversial organizations as the Ku Klux Klan, the social experiment of Prohibition, and the change to a consumer-oriented society. Coolidge represented older American values during this time of upheaval, and his link to the rural past was a key part of his appeal. Coolidge's response to the social uneasiness of the 1920s was largely to ignore its symptoms while promoting, by personal example, such virtues as law and order, calmness, and civic responsibility. But after the Great Depression bit in the fall of 1929, Coolidge's conservatism seemed an inadequate answer to the challenges of the decade.

He was born in Plymouth Notch, in southern Vermont, on July 4, 1872. Then as now, the mountainous region retained some of the character of the frontier; the rocky soil resisted cultivation, and the wilderness tenaciously encroached on the farms. Plymouth's inhabitants honored old Puritan values—hard labor, self-sufficiency, and community responsibility. Emotion was seldom shown. Wit was dry and understated.

The future president was originally named after his father, John Calvin Coolidge, a farmer, storekeeper, and holder of local and state offices. Calvin—the first name was soon dropped—lived a farm boy's life: There was firewood to be split, corn to be planted, maple sap to be collected. Coolidge went to the local school, where he showed no remarkable aptitude. Nevertheless, at the age of thirteen he passed an examination that qualified him to teach school. He then went on to study at Black River Academy, a private school in Ludlow, twelve miles from home.

Coolidge planned to enter college in the fall of 1890, but he caught a bad cold on his way to Massachusetts for the Amherst College entrance examinations and failed them. He spent the following spring term at St. Johnsbury Academy in upstate Vermont and then was admitted to Amherst on the recommendation of the principal. At college he was an "Ouden," or nonfraternity man, for the first three years; he played no sports and was only a fair student. But by his senior year diligence in study and an ability to make people laugh had given him some status in his class and confidence in himself. This confidence was enhanced immeasurably by his exposure to Charles E. Garman, a professor of philosophy, who taught that Christianity, in particular Congregationalist Christianity, was superior to all other philosophical systems in the world. Garman thus rationalized for a grateful Coolidge all the things the student had been raised to believe in: hard work; consecration to the welfare of one's neighbor; the performance of

President Calvin Coolidge throws out the first ball of the 1924 World Series.

good deeds, all of which serve God's plan. Coolidge made a fraternity his senior year; in the spring he graduated cum laude.

That fall he was back in the vicinity—at Northampton, only a few miles from the college—to begin studying law in the office of John C. Hammond and Henry P. Field. Almost immediately he entered politics. Henry Field was the Republican candidate for mayor of Northampton in the fall of 1895, and Coolidge served as one of his campaign workers. Field won, and in the same election John Hammond was elected district attorney. Coolidge, without taking undue advantage of these fortunate connections,

---

---

entered the Republican organization at the bottom. By 1897 he was a party committeeman in his ward. That year he was admitted to the bar and shortly thereafter opened an office.

Coolidge's social life consisted mostly of visits to people who made him feel at home—those who ran or frequented the barbershop, the cobbler's, the druggist's. Otherwise he kept to himself, reading and thinking. He was looked upon as an "odd stick," tight with his words, his confidences, and his money, but he was also earning a reputation as an honest worker and a faithful friend.

Then, unexpectedly, he fell in love with Grace Goodhue, "a creature of spirit, fire, and dew," wrote Alfred Pearce Dennis, "given to blithe spontaneous laughter . . . as natural and unaffected as sun light. . . ." She was a graduate of the University of Vermont and taught at a school for the deaf in Northampton. Recognizing the contrast between Coolidge and Grace, a friend remarked that "having taught the deaf to hear, Miss Goodhue might perhaps cause the mute to speak." For Grace herself, her goal was to help to teach Coolidge to enjoy life. Grace did assist him with the social side of politics, providing a buffer for his sharp edges and relief from the moodiness he often displayed in public. They were married in October 1905. Their first son, John, was born the following fall and the second, Calvin, in 1908.

By then Coolidge had moved through the posts of county court clerk, city councilman, and city solicitor and had served two terms in the Massachusetts state house of representatives. He continued to rise rapidly: after two terms as mayor of Northampton, he was elected in 1911 to the state senate, where, three years later, he was made presiding officer. Elected lieutenant governor in 1915, he was chosen governor in 1918.

Coolidge claimed in later years that each step upward, until he became president of the Massachusetts state senate, was taken because it would serve the public and make him a more successful lawyer, not because he wanted a career in politics; he also liked to please his father. His ambition was tempered by his shyness. "It's a hard thing for me to play this game," he told his friend Frank Stearns. "In politics, one must meet people. . . . When I was a little fellow . . . I would go into a panic if I heard strange voices in the kitchen . . . and the hardest thing in the world was to have to go through the kitchen door and give them a greeting. I'm all right with old friends, but every time I meet a stranger, I've got to go through the old kitchen door, back home, and it's not easy."

Still, having been chosen president of the senate, he decided to try for the governorship. And, having won that post, he served well, successfully encouraging the enactment of laws prohibiting unfair practices by landlords, raising workmen's compensation allowances, and limiting the work week for women and children to forty-eight hours. He mediated labor-management arguments fairly. And he urged increases in pay for factory workers, teachers, and the Boston police force, as well as better working conditions for the police.

Had he been successful in this last effort he might never have become president. But the city government, administered by a Democratic mayor, did little to improve the policemen's lot, and by the summer of 1919 Boston's police had decided to join the American Federation of Labor. "A police officer," said Police Commissioner Edwin U. Curtis, "cannot consistently belong to a union and perform his sworn duty." Curtis suspended nineteen members of the policemen's union. Coolidge might then have moved in to mediate the potentially dangerous situation. But jurisdictions were unclear: The police commissioner was appointed by the governor (Coolidge's predecessor had named Curtis) and was more or less a law unto himself, responsible to no one. This was not just a labor-management quarrel; Coolidge would have had to mediate between government agencies, and he refused to do it. Publicly he took the position that the

The Boston Police Strike of 1919 made Coolidge a national figure. Here, striking policemen leave a meeting in August after casting their votes to walk out. Coolidge responded that there was "no right to strike against the public safety by anybody, anywhere, anytime."

demands of the police were reasonable, but that they should not unionize or go out on strike—which they did on September 9, the day after the suspensions. Coolidge still preferred to leave the initiative in the hands of the local officials, but they let the situation get out of control. The night of the walkout there was looting and rioting in Boston. By the time the mayor asked Coolidge to call out part of the state guard to restore order, a general strike—one that might spread beyond Boston—seemed possible. By not acting as commander in chief of the commonwealth, Coolidge was jeopardizing the peace and risking the

Republican hold on the governorship, since he was up for reelection that fall. Party leaders put pressure on him, and after a tense day and a second violent night he finally took charge, calling up the rest of the guard. Curtis had been virtually replaced by an act of the mayor; Coolidge restored his power. Then, in a proclamation, Coolidge asked for the support of the public and the police. As the situation quieted, Coolidge emerged a national hero. He was a defender of the faith against "the Reds." All that was needed to cap the event was a battle cry, and soon he supplied it: "There is no right to strike against the public safety by anybody, anywhere, anytime." The spark had been struck that would make him president, and he was reelected governor by a landslide.

Frank Stearns, a Boston merchant and Amherst friend, had been promoting the fortunes of Calvin Coolidge since 1915. He steered a collection of Coolidge's speeches (*Have Faith in Massachusetts*) to publication and in 1920—while Coolidge was blocking all formal attempts to make him an active presidential candidate—Stearns sent a copy of the book to every

delegate chosen to attend the Republican National Convention. At the convention a second collection of Coolidge's speeches was distributed. The senators who controlled the convention dictated the presidential candidate, however, and Coolidge did not have a chance. But then the delegates rebelled: Instead of choosing the anointed candidate, Senator Irvine Lenroot, of Wisconsin, as Harding's running mate, they backed Coolidge. The news reached Coolidge by telephone. Grace Coolidge, knowing how disappointed he had been at the end of his presidential hopes, said: "You're not going to take it, are you?" "I suppose I'll have to," Governor Coolidge answered.

When the presidential election was over, Warren Harding set a precedent by asking Coolidge to sit as an official member of the cabinet. But Coolidge did not stand out as vice president. His contributions to cabinet meetings were few. Once, when asked to use his power of recognition as the Senate's presiding officer to favor the administration, thus displeasing an important senator, he avoided the duty. At the critical moment he handed the gavel to a proadministration senator, left the chamber, and returned when the deed was done. His office required him to attend social functions, and he had other opportunities to cultivate high-level politicians. But for the most part he kept to himself, even in company. "Silent Cal," the Yankee loner, was still put off by the strangers in the kitchen. When reporters asked why the vice president and Mrs. Coolidge dined out every night, Coolidge replied: "Gotta eat somewhere."

There were indications that the party might not renominate him in 1924, but "Coolidge luck" intervened. On August 2, 1923, when the vice president was on vacation in Plymouth Notch, Harding died in San Francisco. Calvin Coolidge was sworn in as the thirtieth president by his father, a notary public, in the lamplit sitting room of the Coolidge home in Vermont.

Coolidge, a throwback to old American attitudes,

was the ideal man to carry on Harding's promotion of "normalcy." His mode of action was thoroughly conservative. "If you see ten troubles coming down the road," he would say, "you can be sure that nine will run into the ditch before they reach you and you have to battle with only one of them." He also gained a reputation as a deft humorist. Coolidge, said Will Rogers, never told jokes but "had more subtle humor than almost any public man I ever met." When a woman at dinner told the president she had bet her friends she could get him to say more than three words, Coolidge replied: "You lose." Alice Roosevelt Longworth repeated the remark of a friend's dentist, who said that he wished the president didn't always look as if he had been "weaned on a pickle."

Though his administration exuded calm, Coolidge attacked his job with characteristic thoroughness and organization. Through his office in the first few months passed experts in many fields: the members of the Harding cabinet, liberals and conservatives, enemies and friends. All had their opinions sought. Most of the ordinary problems of administration he delegated to his staff and his department heads. It is said, for example, that he once refused to read a batch of papers sent to him by Secretary of Labor James J. Davis, who wanted the president's approval of a decision he had made. "You tell ol' man Davis I hired him as Secretary of Labor," he said, "and if he can't do the job I'll get a new Secretary of Labor." He handled his first major domestic crisis the same way. When a coal strike was threatened in Pennsylvania for September 1, 1923, he talked to Secretary of Commerce Herbert C. Hoover, the members of the U.S. Coal Commission, the head of the Interstate Commerce Commission, and Pennsylvania Governor Gifford Pinchot and dumped the responsibility in their laps. It was Pinchot who worked out the settlement.

Similarly, when the Harding scandals over the Teapot Dome oil fields in Wyoming began to break in January 1924, Coolidge let events more or less take

Miguel Covarrubias's 1932 cartoon paired the former president with the actress Greta Garbo in an "impossible interview." Both were known for saying as little as possible, although Coolidge was talkative in private.

their own course in Congress, although he did appoint special counsel to investigate the questionable oil leases. When the Senate demanded that Secretary of the Navy Edwin Denby be asked to resign, Coolidge declared, at the insistence of two leading senators, that he would not dismiss Denby without proof of guilt—but he accepted the secretary's resignation when Denby offered it. Pressed by Senator William E. Borah and others to fire Attorney General Harry M. Daugherty, Coolidge called in Borah and confronted him with Daugherty. In a painful scene the two antagonists fought the matter out while Coolidge watched silently. After Daugherty had left the room in a rage, Coolidge told Borah, "I reckon you are right." But Daugherty did not resign, and Coolidge did not act, even though a Senate investigation was casting dark shadows on the attorney general's reputation. Only when Daugherty refused to allow the Senate investigators into his department's files did Coolidge ask for his resignation.

The president's policy of watchful waiting, his delegation of responsibility, his caution, and his tolerance for people who disagreed with him sometimes led to conflicts of purpose within the administration. These habits were also responsible for his failure to act decisively when he saw that the stock market was getting out of hand at the end of the decade. But they helped to win him a nomination for president in his own right. One of his first acts in the White House had been to appoint a skilled Southern Republican politician, C. Bascom Slemp, as White House secretary. Slemp was a former congressman, a veteran dispenser of patronage and raiser of funds, and his job—which he performed successfully—was to get Coolidge a four-year term. As the Harding scandals unfolded in Congress the Democrats tried to implicate Coolidge, but he actually benefited from their charges. He handled the situation with restraint, while the Democrats, attacking a man who was obviously the epitome of honorable government, appeared vindictive. The Republicans drew together in self-defense behind Coolidge; nomination of Harding's successor began to seem the best way of demonstrating to the electorate that the corruption of individuals, not of the whole Republican party, was responsible for the disgraceful oil leases. Herbert Hoover was dispatched to California to conduct the Coolidge campaign in the state primary, in which his most formidable competitor for the nomination, Senator Hiram Johnson, was also entered. After a victory there, Coolidge won the nomination easily. Charles G. Dawes was chosen as his running mate. The slogan for the Republican campaign was "Keep Cool With Coolidge."

Elected by a plurality of some two and a half million popular votes over the combined total of his opponents Democrat John W. Davis and Progressive Robert M. La Follette, Coolidge could now turn his attention to the enactment of his legislative program—such as it was. He believed that the most important product of government was good community behavior on the part of the people it served. Peace and prosperity would foster good behavior. Prosperity was undeniably linked to business, which, as he said in one of the most famous of his pithy epigrams, was America's chief business. So he maintained high tariffs to protect American industries. Regulation of business was relaxed. Federal gift taxes were eliminated, and other taxes were lowered, while the national budget and debt were sharply reduced. The result was "Coolidge Prosperity."

Unfortunately, the prosperity stood on unsteady legs—the hyperactive stock market. And when those legs trembled, Coolidge and his secretary of the Treasury, Andrew Mellon, steadied them by public reassurances, and stock sales continued to increase. Coolidge was warned by a number of experts of the sickness of the market, and there are indications that he believed the warnings. But as he saw it, regulation of the New York Stock Exchange was the responsibility of New York State, not of the federal government.

Much of the speculation depended on brokers' loans to investors. At the beginning of 1928 when those loans stood at about four billion dollars, there was considerable uneasiness in the economic community over the high figure.

Nevertheless, in January 1928 Coolidge issued a statement saying the loans were not too great: Bank deposits were on the rise, too, as were the number of securities offered for sale. Almost immediately afterward, in conversation with H. Parker Willis, an important business editor, he remarked, "If I were to give my own personal opinion about it, I should say that any loan made for gambling in stocks was an 'excessive loan.'" Willis was astonished. "I wish very much, Mr. President," he said, "that you had been willing to say that instead of making the public statement you did." Coolidge explained that he regarded himself "as the representative of the government and not as an individual" and indicated that he had simply repeated what his economic advisers had said. However, he did allow the Federal Reserve Board to try to tighten money in mid-1928, but in general he felt he could only sustain public confidence and hope the proper people would act to cure the sickness.

Save for greasing the wheels of business, Coolidge's administration produced little effective legislation. Farmers were suffering from overproduction and poor prices, and the president vetoed two versions of the McNary-Haugen bill, which would have made the government responsible for fixing prices and selling surplus crops. Farmers, he thought, should work out their own problems.

If he was laissez-faire in domestic matters, he was an active diplomat—notwithstanding former Secretary of State Elihu Root's remark that "he did not have an international hair in his head." Coolidge had the guidance of two excellent secretaries of state, Charles Evans Hughes and Frank B. Kellogg. In addition he had good instincts of his own. A month after he came to office, an earthquake and typhoon devastated Japan. The night he got the news, he ordered the Pacific fleet to Yokohama to help the Japanese. The good effects of this action were undone, however, by the disastrous Immigration Act of 1924, which, against Coolidge's strongly expressed wishes, included a provision banning Japanese from entry.

American relations south of the border were improved largely through Coolidge's appointment of excellent emissaries. He set a precedent when, at the invitation of the president of Cuba, he went to Havana in January 1928 to address the Sixth Inter-American Conference.

Aside from the ban on Japanese immigration, the American foreign policy that provoked the greatest repercussions involved Europe and the attempts to secure a permanent peace. Germany owed a repara-

CHARLES G. DAWES

President Coolidge's colorful, outspoken vice president, Charles G. "Hell and Maria" Dawes was one of the ablest statesmen of his time. Born in Ohio in 1865, he practiced law in Lincoln, Nebraska, and moved to Evanston, Illinois, in 1894, where he became a leading businessman, banker, and financier. Entering politics in 1896, he managed William McKinley's campaign in Illinois and was subsequently appointed comptroller of the currency. Chief procurement officer and a brigadier general during World War I, he was called upon by a postwar congressional committee to testify on military spending. Enraged at the petty nature of the investigation, he exploded in one of his famous outbursts: "Hell and Maria, we weren't trying to keep a set of books, we were trying to win the war!" In 1921 Dawes became the country's first director of the Bureau of the Budget. In 1924, while he served as chairman of a commission to settle the complex problems of German reparations, his Dawes Plan won him the Nobel Peace Prize. That year he was elected vice president on the Republican ticket. Clashing head-on with the Senate on the matter of rules, he gradually tempered his aggressive approach and won the respect of that body. Declining to run for reelection, he served as ambassador to Great Britain and head of the Reconstruction Finance Corporation under President Herbert Hoover. He died in 1951.

tions debt to the Allies, who, in turn, owed debts to the United States. Partly due to the high tariff, Europe did not have a large surplus of dollars with which to meet its commitments to America, and Germany was unable to keep up her payments to the Allies. Although Coolidge was unwilling to either lower tariffs or cancel the Allies' debts, American financing did maintain the status quo for a while. As Coolidge's most perceptive biographer, Donald R. McCoy, put it, the two and a half billion dollars lent to Germany under the Coolidge administration's

Dawes Plan for supporting the German economy "corresponded to the amounts that that country paid in reparations, which in turn corresponded to the war debt payments that the United States . . . received from its wartime allies."

Like Harding, Coolidge had to face the questions of participation in the League of Nations and improvement of the diplomatic machinery for keeping the world out of war. American membership in the League was still politically impossible, but under Coolidge the country took part in numerous League-sponsored conferences. Entry of the United States into the Permanent Court of International Justice, which President Coolidge endorsed, was prevented by crippling "reservations" or amendments such as those that had blocked American entry into the League of Nations. In 1927 Coolidge asked for a conference of the great naval powers, hoping to limit the growth of navies; the result was a failure. A treaty to outlaw war, worked out by Kellogg and Aristide Briand of France in 1928, was signed by sixty-two nations, but it included no provisions for enforcement.

"Coolidge's chief feat," writes H. L. Mencken, with typical exaggeration, "was to sleep more than any other President. . . . The itch to run things did not afflict him; he was content to let them run themselves." At his regular press conferences, Coolidge provided the press with informed answers that belied his reputation as a man of few words. Mencken summed him up in sympathetic tones: "His failings are forgotten; the country remembers only . . . that he let it alone. Well, there are worse epitaphs for a statesman."

The country owed something else to Coolidge: At a moment when the presidency was in danger of losing a great deal of prestige due to the Harding scandals, he reaffirmed its dignity by the honesty of his public actions. Mrs. Coolidge's glamour and style also restored some of the allure to the personal side of the presidency. She had artists perform for the First Family, including the Irish-American tenor John McCormack and the pianist-composer Sergei Rachmaninoff. The White House, said Alice Roosevelt Longworth after her first post-Harding visit, had changed. "The atmosphere was as different as a New England front parlor is from a back room in a speakeasy."

The office was exhausting to him. His health and stamina were poor. And just after he had gained the signal triumph of nomination for his own term, his

---

SECOND ADMINISTRATION

INAUGURATION: Mar. 4, 1925; the Capitol, Washington, D.C.
VICE PRESIDENT: Charles G. Dawes
SECRETARY OF STATE: Frank B. Kellogg
SECRETARY OF THE TREASURY: Andrew W. Mellon
SECRETARY OF WAR: John W. Weeks; Dwight F. Davis (from Oct. 14, 1925)
ATTORNEY GENERAL: John G. Sargent
POSTMASTER GENERAL: Harry S. New
SECRETARY OF THE NAVY: Curtis D. Wilbur
SECRETARY OF THE INTERIOR: Hubert Work; Roy O. West (from Jan. 21, 1929)
SECRETARY OF AGRICULTURE: William M. Jardine
SECRETARY OF COMMERCE: Herbert C. Hoover; William F. Whiting (from Dec. 11, 1928)
SECRETARY OF LABOR: James J. Davis
SUPREME COURT APPOINTMENT: Harlan Fiske Stone (1925)
69TH CONGRESS (Dec. 7, 1925–Mar. 3, 1927):
    SENATE: 54 Republicans; 40 Democrats; 1 Other
    HOUSE: 247 Republicans; 183 Democrats; 5 Others
70TH CONGRESS (Dec. 5, 1927–Mar. 3, 1929):
    SENATE: 48 Republicans; 47 Democrats; 1 Other
    HOUSE: 237 Republicans; 195 Democrats; 3 Others

ELECTION OF 1924

CANDIDATES	ELECTORAL VOTE	POPULAR VOTE
Calvin Coolidge (Republican)	382	15,719,921
John W. Davis (Democratic)	136	8,386,704
Robert M. La Follette (Progressive)	13	4,832,532

After the presidency, the Coolidges returned to their home in Northampton, Massachusetts, where the former president posed for photographers as Mrs. Coolidge worked on her knitting.

younger son, Calvin, died of blood poisoning. "When he went the power and the glory of the Presidency went with him," wrote Coolidge. Shortly afterward the president told his father he would never again stand for public office. On August 2, 1927, the fourth anniversary of his succession, he announced, "I do not choose to run for President in 1928." Ten years, he told Senator Arthur Capper, "is longer than any other man has had it—too long!" There were other reasons too. Mrs. Coolidge was not well, and then there was the economy. "Poppa says there's a depression coming," remarked Grace Coolidge, speaking of her husband. Coolidge himself said that he thought the time was near for government to become more aggressive and constructive. "I do not want to undertake it," he said.

And so he retired to Northampton and the two-family house. But his privacy was continually invaded there, and in 1930 he and Grace moved to a twelve-room home on nine acres, where he could sit in a rocker on the porch without attracting the curious. Coolidge wrote a newspaper column for a year and an autobiography. And he watched, with increasing bewilderment, the Crash and the Depression. He died on January 5, 1933, of a coronary thrombosis.

Coolidge was an effective, popular president for his time, but the long shadow of the Depression and the efforts of early critical biographers created a historical image of insensitive conservatism that has dogged him ever since. Periodic efforts to rehabilitate him or to reappraise his record have not been successful in changing the perception that Coolidge was a disappointment as president.

—*Michael Harwood*
revised by Lewis L. Gould

HERBERT CLARK HOOVER

THE GREAT ENGINEER

When Herbert Hoover campaigned for the presidency in 1928, he told the nation that he foresaw the end of poverty in the United States— provided, of course, that he was elected. He did win the presidency, but the prediction of a poverty-free nation proved illusory. Instead of well-fed Americans driving to good jobs in new cars, by the end of Hoover's term they stood in breadlines or sold apples on street corners. Instead of purchasing gleaming consumer goods from stores, the unemployed improvised to simply stay alive. The makeshift products, however, did have brand names. Newspapers wrapped around the body for warmth were "Hoover blankets." Cars that had broken down and had to be pulled by mule teams were "Hoover wagons." The ubiquitous empty pocket turned inside out was a "Hoover flag," and unappetizing jackrabbits were called "Hoover hogs." Spotting the nation from coast to coast were compounds of ramshackle shanties, made of packing crates, scrap tin, and tar paper, built by destitute Americans with nowhere to go. These little towns were called Hoovervilles.

The Great Depression tested Hoover and the beliefs he had acquired as a youth. One of the great ironies of Hoover's career was that he first made his reputation as someone who brought relief to those who were hungry and starving in Belgium and Russia during and after World War I. Yet when he faced a similar situation in his presidency, he was incapable of adapting his convictions about individual responsibility and self-reliance to the needs of a national crisis. Hoover did more to fight a depression than any president before him had tried to do, but it was not enough to spare him rejection by his fellow citizens in 1932.

Herbert Clark Hoover, the second son of Jesse Clark and Hulda Minthorn Hoover, was born in West Branch, Iowa, on August 10, 1874. His father, a blacksmith by trade, died from typhoid at the age of thirty-four. Two years later, when Herbert was only eight, his mother died of pneumonia.

The uncles and aunts who raised him were, like his parents, devout Quakers. Hoover's reserved and impersonal manner was often attributed to his ascetic upbringing, which also encouraged his boundless energy and industry and nurtured the concept of service that was an animating force throughout his life.

In the fall of 1891 Hoover enrolled at the new free university founded by Senator Leland Stanford in California. There, according to fellow undergraduate Will Irwin, Hoover won a sort of eminence, if not affection. "'Popularity' is not exactly the word for his reaction and influence on his fellows," wrote Irwin. "A better word probably would be 'standing.'" Hoover supported himself while at college, and there met his future wife, Lou Henry, the daughter of a Monterey banker. Hoover was not a brilliant student, and he was never quite able to get the hang of writing English without using stuffy phrases and occasionally impenetrable sentences. His major was geology, which led him to mining and then engineering. His devotion to engineering was unstinting, romantic, and idealistic. "To feel great works grow under one's feet and to have more men constantly getting good jobs is to be the master of contentment," he wrote later.

Following his graduation in 1895, Hoover went to the gold-mining district of Nevada City and there got a menial job "pushing a car in the lower levels of the Reward mine for $2 a day, on a ten-hour night shift and a seven-day week." Tall, sturdy, and energetic, with broad shoulders, hazel eyes, a round face, and straight grayish-brown hair, Hoover was optimistic and confident that he would prosper. But after only a few months the work slackened and Hoover found himself out of a job. "I then learned what the bottom levels of real human despair are paved with," he recalled. "That is the ceaseless tramping and ceaseless refusal at the employment office day by day."

Herbert Hoover aboard a ship on January 11, 1917.

Grant Wood's study for the painting of Hoover's birthplace in West Branch, Iowa, evoked the rural world from which the president emerged. The ability to unite the farm and the new world of technology was a key element in Hoover's appeal as a presidential candidate in 1928.

Despite these humble beginnings and early hard times, by 1914 Hoover was to accumulate a personal estate that was estimated to be worth four million dollars. Starting with an engineering job in Australia, followed by another in China and then by a partnership in the London firm of Bewick, Moreing and Company, Hoover rose to preeminence in his field. A leading international engineer and businessman, he traveled the globe many times over.

He and his wife lived in London with their two sons, Herbert and Allan. Lou Hoover, an accomplished linguist, collaborated on translating a Latin mining text with her husband. Later she would become active in the Girl Scouts and be a proponent of women's athletics. The president was always to look back nostalgically on this pre-World War I period as a good time when "the Government offered but small interference with the economic life of the citizen."

With the advent of the Great War, Hoover became involved in humanitarian work on a vast scale as the head of an organization that developed into the Commission for Relief in Belgium. This charitable work enraged some American isolationists, notably Senator Henry Cabot Lodge of Massachusetts, who wanted Hoover prosecuted for dealing independently with a foreign government. During the war years, the commission spent nearly $1.5 billion and fed as many as ten million persons.

With the entry of the United States into the war, Hoover returned home to serve as food administrator, another challenging assignment that he handled with great skill. To "Hooverize," in those days, meant to save food. At the war's end, he returned to Europe to help alleviate starvation in Austria and Germany and, later, in Russia. Said John Maynard Keynes of Hoover's relief activities, "Never was a nobler work of disinterested good will carried through with more tenacity and sincerity and skill. . . ."

Hoover's entrance into politics in the twenties was inevitable, since, as Keynes pointed out, "Mr. Hoover was the only man who emerged from the ordeal of the Paris peace conference with an enhanced reputation." Franklin Delano Roosevelt, who was at that time assistant secretary of the Navy, said of him, "He is certainly a wonder, and I wish we could make him president of the United States." Hoover's nonpartisanship jelled into a moderate Republicanism, and according to the historian Frederick Lewis Allen, he "was conducting a highly amateur campaign for the nomination; the politicians dismissed him with a sour laugh." The 1920 Republican presidential nomination went instead to Warren G. Harding, and Hoover was later named secretary of commerce.

The extent to which he revitalized a moribund Department of Commerce was remarkable. A predecessor had told him that he would have to work only two hours a day, "putting the fish to bed at night and turning on the lights around the coast. . . ." Instead, Hoover made the department as important as any in the big-business–oriented administrations of Harding and Coolidge. Hoover, who believed passionately in thrift, hard work, and self-reliance, encouraged those values both in his department and across the nation. He saved a great deal of money for the country by eliminating bureaucratic inefficiencies. In his attacks on waste, he instituted an impressive—some said endless—sequence of meetings and conferences. (His own tally was more than three thousand.) Hoover also insured that the public knew about his work through an extensive press operation.

On the issue of who should control hydroelectric power—government or industry—Hoover said, "It is my own view that Federal Government should not go into the business of either generating or distributing electrical power." This pronouncement by the secretary of commerce was printed in pamphlets that were widely distributed by the privately owned public-utility interests.

When Calvin Coolidge announced that he did not choose to run for reelection in 1928, Hoover nevertheless asked the president if he meant to file in the Ohio primary. "No," said Coolidge. Would he mind if Hoover filed? "Why not?" replied Coolidge. Some

months later, when Hoover offered him his four hundred convention delegates, Coolidge replied, "If you have four hundred delegates, you better keep them." Coolidge was not an admirer of Hoover, styling him in a pejorative phrase of the day, "the Boy Wonder."

The campaign of 1928 pitted Hoover against Governor Alfred E. Smith of New York, a Catholic, a "wet" in regard to prohibition, and a big-city politi-

---

BIOGRAPHICAL FACTS

BIRTH: West Branch, Iowa, Aug. 10, 1874
ANCESTRY: Swiss-German
FATHER: Jesse Clark Hoover; b. Miami County, Ohio, Sept. 2, 1846; d. West Branch, Iowa, Dec. 14, 1880
FATHER'S OCCUPATION: Blacksmith
MOTHER: Hulda Randall Minthorn Hoover; b. Norwich, Oxford County, Canada, May 4, 1849; d. West Branch, Iowa, Feb. 22, 1883
BROTHER: Theodore Jesse Hoover (1871–1955)
SISTER: Mary "May" Hoover (1876–1950)
MARRIAGE: Monterey, Calif., Feb. 10, 1899
WIFE: Lou Henry; b. Waterloo, Iowa, Mar. 29, 1875; d. New York, N.Y., Jan. 7, 1944
CHILDREN: Herbert Clark (1903–1969); Allan Henry (1907–1993)
RELIGIOUS AFFILIATION: Quaker
EDUCATION: Local schools; Newberg Academy; Stanford University (B.A., 1895)
OCCUPATIONS BEFORE PRESIDENCY: Miner; engineer
PREPRESIDENTIAL OFFICES: Chairman of Commission for Relief in Belgium; U.S. food administrator; chairman of Supreme Economic Council; secretary of commerce
AGE AT INAUGURATION: 54
OCCUPATIONS AFTER PRESIDENCY: Chairman of the Commission for Polish Relief; chairman of Finnish Relief Fund; coordinator of European food program; chairman of Commission on Organization of the Executive Branch of the government (Hoover Commission); writer
DEATH: New York, N.Y., Oct. 20, 1964
PLACE OF BURIAL: Hoover Presidential Library, West Branch, Iowa

cian with ties to Tammany Hall. Hoover later noted that he was sure he would win "if we made no mistakes. General Prosperity was on my side." Except for farmers, everybody was doing just fine: Wages and profits were high, and the stock market was soaring. "We in America today," said Herbert Hoover on August 11, 1928, "are nearer to the final triumph over poverty than ever before in the history of any land. The poorhouse is vanishing from among us. We have not yet reached the goal, but given a chance to go forward with the policies of the last eight years, we shall soon with the help of God be in sight of the day when poverty will be banished from this nation." It was a noble and apparently attainable vision to which the electorate responded warmly. Hoover received 444 electoral votes to Smith's 87.

Hoover's inauguration took place on a cold and rainy day, but all the portents were otherwise auspicious. "We have reached a higher degree of comfort and security than ever existed before in the history of the world," he said. From Coolidge, Hoover received the following advice on how to deal with White House visitors: "Nine-tenths of them want something they ought not to have. If you keep dead still they will run down in three or four minutes. If you even cough or smile they will start up all over again."

As president, Hoover was energetic and hardworking. Up by seven each morning, he was soon out on the lawn tossing a medicine ball with old friends, cabinet members, and White House regulars. Then he went in to begin work. He would end the day by dining with Mrs. Hoover in formal dress—a presidential ritual that would end with his administration.

Just seven months after Hoover's inauguration, the bottom fell out of Republican prosperity. The security turned out to be illusory and the comfort transient. The first awful Wall Street lurch occurred on Thursday, October 24, otherwise known as Black Thursday. On that day, writes John Kenneth Galbraith,

"12,894,650 shares changed hands, many of them at prices which shattered the dreams and the hopes of those who had owned them." The next day, following a dramatic noontime meeting of several important bankers, at which millions of dollars reputedly were pledged to support the market, Wall Street rallied. That weekend President Hoover was quoted as having said that "the fundamental business of the country, that is production and distribution of commodities, is on a sound and prosperous basis." But the following Tuesday, October 29, was, according to Galbraith, "the most devastating day in the history of the New York stock market, and it may have been the most devastating day in the history of markets."

In the White House the president acted swiftly by announcing a tax cut meant to increase purchasing power and expand business investment. But taxes were already low and Hoover's cut accomplished little. The president held conferences with business leaders, asking them to maintain wages and production levels. These sessions were often followed by confident forecasts of the future. John Galbraith called them "no-business meetings," from which "no positive action resulted. At the same time they gave a sense of truly impressive action. . . . Some device for simulating action, when action is impossible, is indispensable in a sound and functioning democracy. Mr. Hoover in 1929 was a pioneer in this field of public administration." By March of 1930, Hoover looked for the worst of the crisis to be over within sixty days. Before the Chamber of Commerce in May, Hoover said, "I am convinced that we have now passed the worst and with continued unity of effort we shall rapidly recover."

At first Hoover tried to encourage expansion of public and private construction—the "greatest tool which our economic system affords for the establishment of stability." He urged larger expenditures by industry and state governments; Washington, he said, would do its best "within its own province." But private industry was feeling the pinch, and state and federal building projects were too modest to prevent a sizable decline in total construction.

Ultimately the use of public works as an aid to recovery was doomed because of the president's preoccupation with a balanced budget. Hoover loathed the idea of deficits; "the primary duty of the Government," he said, was ". . . to hold expenditures within our income." In December 1930 he denied that public works were the answer: "Prosperity cannot be restored," he said, "by raids upon the public Treasury." Instead the president and the first lady emphasized volunteerism as an answer to the economic downturn. In one of these initiatives, Mrs. Hoover sought to enlist the Girl Scouts in a series of self-help measures designed to create work and opportunity. She made similar appeals to 4-H clubs and women in the engineering profession.

In the summer of 1930 the Republican Congress had passed, with Hoover's approval, the Hawley-Smoot Tariff, which served to aggravate conditions. Its high tariff wall outraged many nations with which the United States traded, and resulted in a drastically reduced foreign market. It was, writes Richard Hofstadter, "a virtual declaration of economic war on the rest of the world."

The rest of the world was not doing so well either. The collapse of the Kreditanstalt, Austria's largest bank, caused the same sort of depression in Western Europe in 1931 that the stock market crash had caused in the United States. On June 20, realizing that the payment of war debts and reparations was not possible, Hoover advocated a one-year moratorium on all international debt payments. French opposition delayed acceptance of the moratorium, with the result that all German banks failed. The proposal was passed on July 6, but the German collapse had already started a chain reaction that deepened the depression in Europe.

In the Far East, a crisis erupted in Manchuria in

ALFRED E. SMITH

"He has," said Franklin Roosevelt of Alfred Emanuel Smith, "a marvelous faculty for cutting the Gordian knots of argument . . . with the sharp sword of common sense." Unhappily for "the Happy Warrior," his common sense, combined with a flair for politics and a long record of useful public service in New York State, was not enough to win him the presidency, for Smith was a Catholic. Born in 1873 on New York City's Lower East Side, he was a newsboy and a fish-market employee in his teens. He entered politics as a Tammany Hall supporter and was sent to Albany as an assemblyman in 1904, beginning a career that led to the governorship in 1919. Except for one two-year interval, he remained in that office through 1928. He was honest and progressive, a plain talker who knew his business and kept his promises. Three times an aspirant to the Democratic presidential nomination, he won it once, in 1928. He called for repeal of prohibition, which took courage. But each time he lost a battle in national politics, whether at a convention or against Hoover, the basic reason was that capsuled by H. L. Mencken: "Those who fear the Pope outnumber those who are tired of the Anti-Saloon League." Smith, who became a bitter maverick, died in New York in 1944.

September 1931 when an alleged act of Chinese sabotage induced Japan to seize Mukden and eventually to overrun all of Manchuria and turn it into the puppet state Manchukuo. Secretary of State Henry L. Stimson suggested that the United States respond with force or threat of force and possibly (in conjunction with the League of Nations) with economic sanctions. But Hoover rejected any posture that would disturb the nation's isolationist position. He would employ moral condemnation and no more. American public opinion would not have tolerated a larger commitment.

Hoover's diplomatic high-mindedness was presaged by an earlier moral response to the question of recognition of the Soviet government in Russia: "I often likened the problem to having a wicked and disgraceful neighbor. We did not attack him, but we did not give him a certificate of character by inviting him into our homes."

But if not invited into American homes during the thirties. Communism and its rash of spokesmen could hardly help but find some sympathetic ears in the United States. Factories were shutting down, businesses failing, banks closing; unemployment hit twelve million in 1932, and that year nearly two million hoboes were roaming the countryside. Farm Belt towns were deserted; in New York City public school leaders said that about twenty thousand children were malnourished; formerly self-reliant men stood in breadlines waiting for soup. Yet in the Depression's third winter (1931–32) there was little sign of organized revolt; the country was numb and dispirited and was waiting for something to be done.

In the fall of 1931 Hoover had stated with disarming candor that "the sole function of government is to bring about a condition of affairs favorable to the beneficial development of private enterprise." At another time he had said, "I am opposed to any direct or indirect government dole" for the unemployed. He had therefore vetoed the Norris bill, which Congress had passed on March 3, 1931. Once before, Senator Norris of Nebraska had won passage of a bill for a government-operated Tennessee Valley project at Muscle Shoals, Alabama, only to see it suffer a presidential veto (by Calvin Coolidge). The project would not have been a "government dole." It would have provided work for thousands of Americans. But President Hoover declared, "I am firmly opposed to the Government entering into any business the major purpose of which is competition with our citizens."

The dole—direct federal relief to individuals—was anathema to Hoover for several reasons. He felt the Constitution did not permit it. He thought that a dole could only serve to feed the panic he continued to minimize. Relief was a matter of state and local responsibility; to tamper with that principle would "have struck at the roots of self-government." And the dole ran counter to his thesis of "rugged individualism"; a dole would have "injured the spiritual responses of the American people." Federal aid was the last bastion, the final alternative to starvation, and Hoover said he had "faith in the American people that such a day shall not come."

But the resources of public and state relief organizations dwindled as the demands upon them rose (some state constitutions prohibited the use of funds for direct aid). The president set up the Organization on Unemployment Relief to coordinate local efforts; its primary achievement was an advertising campaign exhorting Americans to support private charity. Mrs. Hoover endorsed this organization through her projects with the Girl Scouts and her radio broadcasts asking Americans to share their resources with their neighbors.

Although there was some response to the emergency (in many areas bartering organizations sprang up; tradesmen and artisans swapped their wares for staples), local efforts fell far short of what was needed. A New York man caught the mood in 1930: "I am neither an anarchist, socialist, or communist—but, by God, at times I feel as if I should associate myself with the radicals." By this time jokes about Hoover were becoming commonplace. It was said that if you put a rose in his hand it would wilt. Another jest had the president asking Secretary of the Treasury Mellon for a nickel (the price of a phone call in 1932) "to call a friend." To which Mellon was said to have responded: "Here's a dime, Mr. President; call all your friends."

Hoover had no fear of injuring the spiritual responses of America's financial and industrial leaders, for whom he created the Reconstruction Finance Corporation with a credit pool of five hundred million dollars. Hoover felt that the RFC was salutary because it required firm collateral—it was businesslike; it lent, it did not give away. The theory behind it, noted the popular humorist Will Rogers, was that "the money was all appropriated for the top in the hopes it would trickle down to the needy." But

The desolation and human despair that the Great Depression brought to the United States produced a derisive label for the places nationwide where the homeless and unemployed clustered: Hoovervilles.

it did not trickle down. There was favoritism in loan disbursement (two RFC board members authorized sizable loans to banks of which they were directors), which, combined with the publicized tax abatements extended to some giants of industry, reinforced the public's view that the federal government was interested only in helping big business.

Through it all, Hoover's dedication to principle remained firm; as the historian Arthur Schlesinger, Jr., said, circumstance "helped confirm his intellectual rigidities." Experimentation was out of the question; his conservative theory of government left no room for it. He called for voluntary cooperation: He asked farmers not to "deliberately over-plant" and told business that self-regulation was "the truest form of self-government." He continued to veto bills that he believed would constitute raids on the Treasury.

In the summer of 1932 Hoover dealt a further blow to his chances of reelection. A Bonus Expeditionary Force, known popularly as the Bonus Army, came to Washington to seek early payment of the World War I bonus that they were scheduled to receive in 1945. The marchers camped out on the banks of the Anacostia River and waited for Congress to act. When the lawmakers failed to do so in July 1932, the Hoover administration urged the marchers to leave Washington. Some in the White House wanted a confrontation with the Bonus Army to underline the president's commitment to law and order. After police failed to disperse the marchers, the Army was sent in under General Douglas MacArthur. The action was captured by news photographers, and the administration suffered a political disaster. "If the Army must be called out to make war on unarmed citizens," said one newspaper, "this is no longer America." The bonus marchers put the same sentiment into verse:

—Mellon pulled the whistle,
Hoover rang the bell,
Wall Street gave the signal
—And the country went to Hell!

The president was not ignorant of the suffering going on about him. As his political philosophy and humanitarian instincts clashed, he grew gloomy and grumpy; his press relations worsened; one cabinet member said a session with the president was "like sitting in a bath of ink."

Hoover believed that his reelection in 1932 was crucially important to the nation because his emphasis on individual responsibility was preferable to the more activist government that the Democratic nominee Franklin Roosevelt proposed. He campaigned furiously against Roosevelt, who, he said, advanced "changes and so-called new deals which would destroy the very foundations of our American system." Hoover was convinced that he had done everything in the government's power "to save community values and protect every family and fireside, so far as it was humanly possible, from deterioration. . . ." He stood squarely on his record. At Madison Square Garden on October 31 he said, "This thirty years of incomparable improvement in the scale of living . . . did not arise without right principles animating the American system which produced them. Shall that system be discarded because vote-seeking men appeal to distress and say that the machinery is all wrong and that it must be abandoned or tampered with?" He thought not, but the voters disagreed. Roosevelt received 472 electoral votes to Hoover's 59.

The transition from Hoover to Roosevelt was an awkward one for both men. They did not trust each other, especially when Hoover sought to have Roosevelt commit himself to some of the president's anti-Depression proposals before March 4, 1933. Their automobile ride on Inauguration Day was difficult. Hoover stared stiffly at the crowds, while Roosevelt smiled and waved. In the years after the New Deal, Hoover maintained that Roosevelt's programs were a failure, insisting that only World War II restored prosperity. He also blamed Roosevelt for doubling the national debt.

Hoover was the first chief executive, said Arthur Krock, a columnist for the *New York Times*, "for whose nomination, election and repudiation after one term the American people, not the party leaders, were wholly responsible." He was, Krock thought, plagued by "his inability to convey to the people the humanitarian qualities and understanding of their plight which were essential in the desperate circumstances." It is certainly true that few presidents, if any, left the White House under a darker cloud. Only after he reemerged as an international humanitarian in 1946 was there a substantial mellowing of the popular dislike of Hoover.

In the postpresidential years, Hoover resided in Palo Alto, California, where he and Mrs. Hoover occupied themselves with the activities of the Hoover

Institute on War, Revolution, and Peace at Stanford University. Hoover opposed American entry into World War II. "To align American ideals alongside Stalin will be as great a violation of everything American as to align ourselves with Hitler," he said in June 1941.

Following the death of Mrs. Hoover in 1944, the former president thrice returned to public service. After the war in Europe ended, President Truman asked him to help organize the food-distribution programs for Europe's thousands of displaced persons. In 1947 Truman authorized a Hoover Commission to consider reorganization of the executive branch of the government. The commission functioned as a sort of efficiency expert, making recommendations intended to eliminate administrative waste. President Eisenhower authorized another Hoover Commission in 1953.

Between Coolidge's death and Truman's departure from office, Hoover was the only living ex-president and, until Eisenhower's term ended, the only living Republican ex-president. As such he became a much-exalted permanent fixture at Republican conventions, where he was invariably welcomed with "spontaneous" demonstrations as, time after time, he gave what was billed as his "farewell address." The convention of 1964 was the first one he missed, being too ill to attend.

Active to the end of his days—he employed six secretaries to handle his correspondence—Hoover died at the age of ninety on October 20, 1964. Only one other president, John Adams, had lived as long.

Hoover had been brilliantly successful as an engineer and as a humanitarian, but historians have not been kind in their appraisals of his one-term presidency. As Arthur Schlesinger, Jr., writes, Herbert Hoover's tragedy was that "of a man of high ideals whose intelligence froze into inflexibility and whose dedication was smitten by self-righteousness."

At the same time, scholars now recognize that

Peter Arno's cover for the March 4, 1933, issue of *The New Yorker* never ran. The magazine's editors pulled the cover following Giuseppe Zangara's failed attempt to assassinate Franklin Roosevelt on February 15. Arno contrasts the smiling, confident Roosevelt with the dour, defeated Hoover. In reality, the ride to the Capitol was just as awkward as the cartoon suggests.

Hoover did more to fight the Depression than was recognized at the time. He used the power of the government to deal with the economic problems, but he lacked the capacity to address the issue of relief with the same vigor he had shown in feeding the hungry in Belgium and Russia. As a result, his reputation has never escaped the repudiation that the American people delivered to him in 1932.

—SAUL BRAUN,
revised by LEWIS L. GOULD

FRANKLIN DELANO ROOSEVELT

NEW DEALER AND GLOBAL WARRIOR

During the twelve years and forty days of his presidency, Franklin D. Roosevelt aroused both a loyalty and an opposition unequaled in American history. Since his death in 1945, however, Roosevelt has become revered as the architect of the New Deal, the man who rescued the nation from the Great Depression, and the victor in World War II. Even in the party that once opposed him, Republicans such as Ronald Reagan identified with Roosevelt after enough time had passed.

Franklin Delano Roosevelt was born on January 30, 1882, in New York's Dutchess County, the only son of James and Sara Delano Roosevelt. He grew up in an atmosphere of social privilege and wealth. His parents were Democrats, unlike the Oyster Bay side of the family that produced Theodore Roosevelt. Sara, half the age of her husband and independently wealthy, was the dominant influence on young Franklin. "He was brought up," said an aunt, "in a beautiful frame." The young Franklin traveled abroad, learned French and German, and acquired a lifelong love of the sea.

When he was fourteen his mother allowed him to attend the Groton School in Massachusetts. Young Franklin craved social acceptance but did not achieve it. "He was nice," said a classmate, "but colorless." In 1900 Roosevelt moved on to Harvard, where his rooms were chosen and decorated by the ubiquitous Sara. He did not gain entrance to the top social club (Porcellian), but he graduated in three years and was president of the undergraduate newspaper, *The Crimson*. During his college years, he also fell in love with his distant cousin, Eleanor Roosevelt, the niece of President Theodore Roosevelt. Despite the opposition of Franklin's mother to the union, the couple were married on March 17, 1905. Theodore Roosevelt, then president, gave the bride away.

The Roosevelts had six children, five of whom reached adulthood. Through her financial control of Franklin, Sara literally assumed command of Eleanor's household and built adjoining town houses for herself and Franklin's ménage on New York's fashionable 65th Street. After attending Columbia Law School and passing the bar exam, Roosevelt ran successfully for the New York State Senate in 1910. In Albany he became friends with a newspaperman named Louis Howe who served as his closest adviser for the next two decades.

"His seat in the Senate wasn't warm before he became a bolter," said a veteran politician. Roosevelt led the fight against Tammany Hall's handpicked candidate for the U.S. Senate and succeeded. Already his personal charm was becoming noticed. As the *New York Times* put it, "With his handsome face and his form of supple strength, he could make a fortune on the stage and set the matinee girl's heart throbbing with subtle and happy emotion."

Roosevelt won reelection to the state senate in 1912, and also began dabbling in presidential politics. At the Democratic nominating convention in Baltimore in 1912, the dashing young Roosevelt helped swing the New York delegation to Woodrow Wilson. Once Wilson was elected, Roosevelt moved on to Washington as assistant secretary of the Navy under Josephus Daniels. For the next eight years, Roosevelt received an invaluable education in the ways of Washington.

During World War I, Franklin began a relationship with the social secretary of his household, Lucy Mercer. Eleanor discovered the liaison in 1918 and confronted her husband with the possibility of divorce. Mercer, a Roman Catholic, would not marry a divorced man, and the breakup of his marriage would have ruined Franklin politically. The Roosevelts stayed together, but their relationship never regained its earlier intimacy.

In 1920 FDR was nominated for vice president with James M. Cox, the Democratic presidential nominee. His famous name and presumed strength in

Franklin D. Roosevelt, with his wife, Eleanor, and son Elliott, waves to a crowd of campaign supporters in 1932.

New York were behind the selection. Roosevelt said: "I got to know the country as only a candidate for national office can get to know it." Despite the vice presidential candidate's hard work, Cox lost to Warren G. Harding in a landslide.

In the year after his vice presidential race, Roosevelt's life changed forever. While vacationing at the family home on Campobello Island, New Brunswick, in 1921, Roosevelt contracted infantile paralysis. He was paralyzed from the waist down and never walked again without assistance. Rather than leave public life, as his mother had wanted him to do, Roosevelt decided to regain his strength and resume his career. Through faithful exercise with special equipment, he built up his chest, neck, and arm muscles to prodigious strength. Friends believed that the illness deepened his character. "If you have spent two years in bed trying to wiggle your big toe," he once said, "everything else seems easy."

By 1924 Roosevelt was ready to return to politics. He gave the nominating address for Governor Alfred E. Smith at the Democratic National Convention in New York City, though John W. Davis was nominated. He took ten painful steps on crutches to the rostrum, where he called Smith "the Happy Warrior" of American politics. Four years later, as the candidate of the Democrats, Smith persuaded Roosevelt to run for governor of New York. To Republican protestations that Roosevelt's crippled legs disqualified him for the office, Smith retorted: "We do not elect [a governor] for his ability to do a double back flip or handspring." Roosevelt traveled the state to show he was not an

Franklin and Eleanor Roosevelt share a relaxed, intimate moment at their family retreat on Campobello Island, New Brunswick, Canada. Their marriage experienced strains that would make such occasions very rare.

invalid, and he squeaked out a narrow victory by some 25,000 votes while Smith was losing his office in New York State and the 1928 election to Herbert Hoover.

Roosevelt proved a creative and innovative state executive, and he was reelected in a landslide in 1930. As governor, FDR sponsored legislation for improvement of labor conditions, old-age pensions, farm relief, unemployment relief, and public works to help the hungry and poor. He said, "The duty of the State toward the citizens is the duty of the servant to its master." With the Great Depression destroying the prospects of Hoover and the Republicans, Roosevelt became the front-runner for the Democratic nomination in 1932. He faced stiff opposition from Smith, still bitter about his defeat in 1928, and conservatives within the party such as John Nance Garner of Texas and the publisher William Randolph Hearst. Roosevelt came to the convention in Chicago with a majority of the delegates but was still short of the two-thirds needed for the nomination.

A series of deals made Garner the vice presidential nominee and put Roosevelt over the top on the fourth ballot. Roosevelt broke precedent and flew to Chicago to accept the nomination in person. "I pledge you, I pledge myself," he declared, "to a new deal for the American people. This is more than a political campaign; it is a call to arms. Give me your help, not to win votes alone, but to win in this crusade to restore America to its own people." In the campaign FDR crisscrossed the nation to once again demonstrate his vitality. He attacked Hoover's deficit spending but also promised to use government funds to aid the needy. The outcome of the contest was never really in doubt. Roosevelt received almost 23 million popular votes to Hoover's nearly 16 million, and the Democratic candidate carried all but six states in the electoral college.

Between November 1932 and March 1933, sharp declines in the economy and danger for the banking

system produced a crisis. During this difficult period, the president-elect survived an assassination attempt on February 15, 1933, when an unemployed bricklayer named Giuseppe Zangara fired at Roosevelt. Five people near the candidate were wounded, Mayor Anton Cermak of Chicago fatally. FDR's calm during the ordeal aroused admiration for this new demonstration of his courage.

The sun shone on Inauguration Day, March 4, 1933. On the Capitol steps Franklin Delano Roosevelt took the oath of office as the thirty-second president of the United States. Then he addressed the stricken nation.

"This is preeminently the time," President Roo-

four days and gave the American people a breathing spell before summoning the Seventy-third Congress into special session on March 9.

The bloodless revolution called the New Deal that followed Roosevelt's inspiring inaugural address was a complex series of governmental programs improvised to fight the Depression, reform the nation's economic and political system, and provide relief to fourteen million unemployed Americans. The first phase, the Hundred Days, saw the president and Congress enact a wide variety of measures aimed at dealing with the economic crisis. The leading issue was the banking system, which had nearly collapsed. The Emergency Banking Relief Act, passed and signed within eight hours on March 9, 1933, gave the president and the Treasury Department sweeping powers to control transactions in credit, currency, and foreign exchange; empowered the Treasury to call in gold and gold certificates and to issue more currency; and authorized the comptroller of the currency to administer insolvent banks. By March 13 the banks, no longer afraid, reopened their doors.

Other measures included legalizing beer and wine, starting the Civilian Conservation Corps (CCC) to put young men to work in forests and fields, and taking the United States off the gold standard. The Federal Emergency Relief Act, passed on May 12, provided direct relief to states and municipalities. The Agricultural Adjustment Administration, also created on May 12, subsidized farmers by paying them to curtail their crops in an effort to reduce price-deflating overproduction.

An innovative New Deal measure was the Tennessee Valley Authority Act, passed on May 18, 1933. This historic law called for the rehabilitation of the entire forty-thousand-square-mile Tennessee Valley basin through the institution of public power, cheap electricity, soil conservation, and other improvements. The Truth-in-Securities Act of May 27, 1933, addressed abuses in the stock market, and the creation

sevelt declared, "to speak the truth, the whole truth, frankly and boldly. . . . This great Nation will endure as it has endured, will revive and prosper. So, first of all, let me assert my firm belief that the only thing we have to fear is fear itself . . . nameless, unreasoning, unjustified terror which paralyzes needed efforts to convert retreat into advance." He promised the country "action, and action now." In the wake of his address, the new president closed all the banks for

of the Home Owners Loan Corporation on June 13 made more credit available for prospective home buyers and helped refinance mortgages for existing homeowners. One of the most important of the changes in the first Hundred Days was the creation of federal deposit insurance under the Glass-Steagall Banking Act, which established the Federal Deposit Insurance Corporation. This measure introduced a needed degree of stability and confidence into the American banking system.

The centerpiece of the early New Deal, however, was the National Industrial Recovery Act, which created the National Recovery Administration (NRA). Looking back to the ideas of Theodore Roosevelt's New Nationalism and the experience of business-government cooperation during World War I, the law sought to devise codes for fair competition and fair practices for industry and to guarantee labor's right to organize and bargain collectively. The act also set up the Public Works Administration to make jobs in construction projects for the unemployed.

The end of the Hundred Days brought a moment to assess what the New Deal had accomplished. Right-wingers condemned "the New Dole." An enraged judge complained that "King Franklin" was "playing tiddley winks with the entire universe." FDR approached the New Deal in a pragmatic, nonideological way. "It is common sense," he said, "to take a method and try it. If it fails, admit it frankly and try another." The New Deal was less a carefully formulated stage-by-stage plan than a makeshift series of experiments, some brilliantly effective, some impractical, some discriminatory and punitive if noble in vision, but all aimed directly at real problems. Despite the claims of his conservative critics, Roosevelt was no radical. He believed in the gold standard and a balanced budget, but he also thought that these principles should yield when imperative economic necessity demanded government action. He did not, however, adopt during the first term the ideas of the British economist John Maynard Keynes for government spending to help alleviate a depression.

The American people also responded to the activist approach of the new first lady. Eleanor Roo-

A woman displays the Blue Eagle of the National Recovery Administration during the early phase of the program, which encouraged Americans to rally to fight the Great Depression. The NRA was a key part of the recovery strategy of Roosevelt's New Deal.

ELEANOR ROOSEVELT

The young GI could scarcely believe it. It was true, though. There, indeed, was Eleanor Roosevelt, right on Guadalcanal in the middle of a war. Everyone knew that she was apt to appear anywhere; but it still took some getting used to—the first lady doling out soup on a Depression breadline, or visiting a WPA project, or lunching with the union of railroad porters, or reading to kids in the desolate Dust Bowl, or tending the sick in city slums. She had been taught, like all young ladies of breeding, that she, as one of the privileged, was obliged to do something for the less fortunate; but the lesson took far more strongly than her teachers had intended. She got the idea that the elevation of the human condition was more than an afternoon-a-week affair: It was a reason for being. She had gone to the right schools without mastering the right "style." Her engagement to her fifth cousin, Franklin, was regarded as incredible: he was handsome and playful, a prince with a future in politics. She was plain (or so she thought) and, at the time, a volunteer inspector of women's lavatories in garment factories. But they did get married, and they lived how and mostly where his mother, Sara, told them to. Eleanor had to fight Sara in 1921 when Franklin came down with paralytic polio. His mother wanted him to retire to Hyde Park, but Eleanor won, and by 1924 FDR had a future in politics again. He became governor of New York, and she worked in the slums. He was a presidential candidate, and she ate with the Bonus Army marchers. He was president, and she went everywhere. When he died, reporters who asked her plans were told, "The story is over." It was not. She wrote columns for newspapers, was a delegate to the United Nations, worked with emotionally disturbed children, supported reform Democrats in New York, and met the world's statesmen, including Nikita Khrushchev of the U.S.S.R. She had made the institution of the first lady into a vital part of the American presidency.

sevelt held press conferences with female reporters, visited the unemployed around the country, and spoke on the radio about social problems. She became an advocate for women, African–Americans, and the less fortunate. So prominent did her travels become that a famous cartoon showed two miners in an underground pit, one observing: "For gosh sakes, here comes Mrs. Roosevelt!"

During the next two years more laws were added to the record of Roosevelt's presidency. The Securities and Exchange Act of June 6, 1934, set up the Securities and Exchange Commission to regulate the operation of the stock market. Other laws led to the Federal Communications Commission and the adoption of the Federal Housing Act.

While active in domestic policy, the Roosevelt administration also faced a world in which the inter-national Depression and the rise of dictators in Europe were creating dangerous conditions for the United States. At first Roosevelt went his own way as far as Europe was concerned. He did not support the efforts of the London International Monetary and Economic Conference of 1933 to stabilize international exchange and set a currency standard. Instead, Roosevelt adopted a unilateral policy of nationally managed currency and exchange, thus assuring American fiscal independence and freedom from arbitrary limitations imposed by European banks.

Roosevelt approached other problems with less obvious nationalism, such as granting diplomatic recognition to the Soviet Union's sixteen-year-old government. At the Seventh International Conference of the American States, at Montevideo, Uruguay, in December 1933, Secretary of State Cordell Hull made an unprecedented U.S. pledge of nonintervention in South American affairs. Roosevelt called his approach toward Latin America the "Good Neighbor Policy." The president supported independence for the Philippines in 1946 through the Tydings-McDuffie Act of 1934 and negotiated a treaty with Cuba that repealed the Platt Amendment, which had permitted United States intervention in Cuban affairs.

FDR's success in the presidency arose from his mastery of the art of politics. He met the press, usually twice a week, in a give-and-take that put his achievements and his plans in the headlines. More important, he addressed the American people periodically by radio in his famed "fireside chats," explaining his programs and purposes with elegant simplicity.

Roosevelt was first and last a Democrat. He loved his party and lifted it from the disorder and bickering that had made it a minority party since Woodrow Wilson's second term. He created the New Deal coalition that dominated American politics for more than three decades. In Roosevelt's White House, citizens of previously unrepresented races and origins found a political home, as did grateful farmers, laborers, progressives, intellectuals, women, small-business operators, and the needy and dispossessed.

As administrator of a diverse and gifted cabinet, Roosevelt pursued a policy of pitting one of his trusted lieutenants against another, thus assuring himself of ultimate control in addition to more objective counsel and data. The cabinet included such striking personalities as Harold L. Ickes as secretary of the interior, Henry A. Wallace as secretary of agriculture, and as secretary of labor, Frances Perkins, the first woman to serve in a presidential cabinet.

Roosevelt believed that his office represented the entire electorate and that the chief executive should defend the interests of all groups. His general approach to the presidency, Roosevelt said, combined "Wilson's appeal to the fundamental" and Theodore Roosevelt's success "in stirring people to enthusiasm

over specific individual events." As for the burdens of his office, FDR remarked, "It's a terrible job. But somebody has to do it."

Though utterly dependent on his braces and wheelchair, Roosevelt only once—when he appeared before Congress after the Yalta Conference in 1945—projected the image of a disabled person. By agreement among themselves, photographers did not show the president in his wheelchair. So adroit was Roosevelt in moving about, Secret Service man Michael Reilly said, that "literally thousands who had seen him at ball games, rallies, and inaugurations

FRANCES PERKINS

Secretary of Labor Frances Perkins was the first woman to hold a cabinet post. When a reporter asked her if being a woman was a handicap, she replied in her cultured Bostonian accent, "Only in climbing trees." She was, writes Arthur Schlesinger, Jr., "brisk and articulate . . . a Brahmin reformer . . . [with] a compulsion to instruct. . . ." Born in 1882 and educated at Mount Holyoke College, the University of Pennsylvania, and Columbia University (where she earned a master's degree in 1910), she was a young social worker when she witnessed the Triangle Shirtwaist Factory fire in New York in 1911. She was employed by the state's Factory Investigating Commission, which was established because of the fire, and later became executive secretary of the New York Committee on Safety. Subsequently she held several important state posts concerned with industry and labor. She had been Governor Roosevelt's industrial commissioner for four years when he, newly elected to the presidency, appointed her to his cabinet. Persuasive, energetic, a New Dealer to the core, she helped bring about numerous reforms and innovations, including Social Security. After leaving office in 1945, Madame Perkins—as she was called—remained active in public affairs. She gave many lectures, the last one just two weeks before she died in 1965.

never suspected his condition." The quiet conspiracy between press and White House could only have occurred before the age of television and round-the-clock news coverage.

Politically, the New Deal confirmed the president's popularity and carried the Democratic party to new victories. In the congressional elections of 1934 the party in power actually gained seats, a rare occurrence in the nation's history. During the months that followed that accomplishment, the administration saw a number of important measures clear Congress. Indeed, 1935 proved to be the culmination of the first Roosevelt term.

The key enactments included the Works Progress Administration that was authorized to grant loans for nonfederal projects, placing five billion dollars in the president's hands to stimulate the economy. On July 5, the Wagner Act committed the government, once again, to support the right of labor to organize and to bargain collectively. The Wheeler-Rayburn Act of August 26 provided for regulation of electric power holding companies engaged in interstate commerce. The Wealth Tax Act increased surcharges on individual incomes of fifty thousand dollars or more and on estates valued at more than forty thousand dollars.

The main accomplishment of this phase of the New Deal, and the legislation of Roosevelt's presidency that reshaped American life, was the Social Security Act of August 14, 1935. This law provided for a system of old-age retirement payments, financed through a payroll tax on employers and employees, and for financial compensation to the unemployed during fixed periods. The act also provided aid to the needy, aged, and blind, and to dependent mothers and neglected children. It proved to be Roosevelt's most enduring domestic legacy.

Renominated by acclamation in 1936, Roosevelt faced the amiable Alfred M. Landon of Kansas, in what became the greatest presidential victory in American history up to that time. Roosevelt took every state except Maine and Vermont, rolled up a popular vote of 27,757,333 to Landon's 16,684,231, and carried into power Democratic majorities of 333 to 89 in the House and 75 to 17 in the Senate.

Then Roosevelt blundered. After his inauguration on January 20, 1937, the first chief executive to be sworn in under the Twentieth Amendment, Roosevelt turned to the United States Supreme Court. During 1935 the justices had declared much of the New Deal unconstitutional. On May 27, 1935, the Court voted unanimously to strike down the National Industrial Recovery Act on the grounds that Congress had allowed government intervention into intrastate affairs. The Court also ruled that the Agricultural Adjustment Act, the Railroad Act, and other laws were invalid. Roosevelt believed that the "nine old men" of the Court were acting as a super-legislature to thwart the will of the American people.

In February 1937 Roosevelt proposed what became known as his "Court-packing" plan. He had devised the plan in secret without consulting Democratic leaders in Congress. Aimed at unseating Supreme Court justices who had ruled against the New Deal and thus enabling Roosevelt to create a New Deal majority, this plan would have given the president the right to appoint one new justice (up to a total of fifteen) for each justice who refused to retire six months after reaching the age of seventy.

Roosevelt's plan was a political disaster. Democrats in Congress were divided on the scheme, and the Republicans let their opponents struggle among themselves. After five months of heated debate, the Court-packing plan failed. FDR had lost the initiative with both Congress and the country. Ironically, the Supreme Court changed its position and approved the Wagner Act and the Social Security Acts by 5–4 margins. Roosevelt soon got his Supreme Court majority anyway, thanks to retirements of conservative justices, but the episode ended his dominance of Congress.

The remainder of the second administration was a difficult one for Roosevelt and the Democrats. The White House did succeed in having Congress pass the second Agricultural Adjustment Act in February 1938 and the Fair Labor Standards Act on June 25, 1938. The latter measure mandated maximum work

An unemployed man lying on a New York City pier, photographed in 1935 by Lewis W. Hine, attests to the persistence of the Great Depression despite the efforts put forth by President Roosevelt in the New Deal.

hours and minimum wages and banned child labor in the production of goods shipped in interstate commerce. A sharp recession in 1937–1938 made Roosevelt more sympathetic to Keynesian ideas about government spending.

THE THIRD ADMINISTRATION

INAUGURATION: Jan. 20, 1941; the Capitol, Washington, D.C.
VICE PRESIDENT: Henry A. Wallace
SECRETARY OF STATE: Cordell Hull;
  Edward R. Stettinius (from Dec. 1, 1944)
SECRETARY OF THE TREASURY: Henry Morgenthau, Jr.
SECRETARY OF WAR: Henry L. Stimson
ATTORNEY GENERAL: Robert H. Jackson;
  Francis Biddle (from Sept. 5, 1941)
POSTMASTER GENERAL: Frank C. Walker
SECRETARY OF THE NAVY: Frank Knox;
  James V. Forrestal (from May 19, 1944)
SECRETARY OF THE INTERIOR: Harold L. Ickes
SECRETARY OF AGRICULTURE: Claude R. Wickard
SECRETARY OF COMMERCE: Jesse H. Jones
SECRETARY OF LABOR: Frances Perkins
SUPREME COURT APPOINTMENTS: Harlan Fiske Stone,
  chief justice (1941); James F. Byrnes (1941);
  Robert H. Jackson (1941); Wiley B. Rutledge (1943)
77TH CONGRESS (Jan. 3, 1941–Dec. 16, 1942):
  SENATE: 66 Democrats; 28 Republicans; 2 Others
  HOUSE: 267 Democrats; 162 Republicans; 6 Others
78TH CONGRESS (Jan. 6, 1943–Dec. 19, 1944):
  SENATE: 57 Democrats; 38 Republicans; 1 Other
  HOUSE: 222 Democrats; 209 Republicans; 4 Others

ELECTION OF 1940

CANDIDATES	ELECTORAL VOTE	POPULAR VOTE
Franklin D. Roosevelt (Democratic)	449	27,313,041
Wendell L. Willkie (Republican)	82	22,348,480
Norman M. Thomas (Socialist)	—	116,410
Roger W. Babson (Prohibition)	—	58,708

The Republicans rebounded in the congressional elections of 1938 as they gained seventy-five seats in the House and seven in the Senate. The president's effort to purge the Democratic party of its more conservative members also fizzled. By 1938 several presidential hopefuls such as Vice President John Nance Garner were already lining up support in the expectation that Roosevelt would observe tradition and not run for a third term. The Democratic party was increasingly divided into liberal and conservative blocs.

The New Deal faced not only a resurgent conservatism but also a troubled world. While Germany and Japan advanced in Europe and Asia, Roosevelt warned in October 1937: "Let no one imagine that America will escape" the impending confrontation. As the world moved closer to war in 1938 and 1939, FDR took what steps he could to prepare the nation for an external threat, but he faced the opposition of a Congress in which isolationist sentiment ran strong. Even as Hitler signed a nonaggression pact with the Soviet Union before launching an attack on Poland, Roosevelt sought in vain the repeal of the arms embargo provision of the Neutrality Act of 1937 to permit the sale of arms to the Allies. In September 1939 Congress refused, and polls suggested in early 1940 that a majority of Americans would oppose U.S. involvement in the war even if Britain and France were under assault.

After the German offensive in the spring of 1940 that left much of France occupied and Britain isolated, American sentiment changed. A break in the official United States neutrality took place on September 3, 1940, when the president authorized the exchange of fifty overage United States destroyers for ninety-nine-year leases on air and naval bases in the British West Indies. On September 16, 1940, the first peacetime draft was authorized

As war approached, FDR faced another presidential election. Although some Democrats questioned

In a 1944 caricature, Roosevelt, Churchill, and Stalin appear very confident of winning their game of dominoes against the disconsolate Axis triumvirate—Hirohito, Hitler, and Mussolini.

whether he should seek an unprecedented third elective term, the party nominated Roosevelt with Secretary of Agriculture Henry A. Wallace as his running mate. The Republicans selected an outsider, former electric utility executive Wendell L. Willkie. The Republican made a strong race. Roosevelt's popular vote margin was smaller than in 1932 and 1936, but his margin in the electoral college was 449 to 82. Days before the election, he said in Boston that "your boys are not going to be sent into any foreign wars."

With his reelection accomplished, Roosevelt asked Congress for money through what became known as the Lend-Lease program to support Britain and, after Hitler's attack on the U.S.S.R. in June 1941, the Soviet Union. The United States must become, he said, "the arsenal of democracy." During the remainder of 1941, the United States moved closer to a shooting war with Nazi Germany in the North Atlantic as the United States became involved in convoying merchant vessels across the ocean. When a United States freighter was sunk by a Nazi submarine, Roosevelt declared a national emergency, closed German consulates, and froze Axis credits in the United States. The United States was headed for war with Germany in the Atlantic and moving toward a confrontation with Japan in the Pacific.

On August 14, 1941, in a meeting that removed all doubt of American intentions, Roosevelt conferred with British Prime Minister Winston Churchill aboard a ship off Newfoundland to announce what became known as the Atlantic Charter. The document looked toward the establishment of the United Nations.

While war loomed in the Atlantic, events in the Pacific put the United States and Japan into conflict. In July 1941 the Japanese government announced a protectorate over French Indochina and were already advancing toward the Dutch East Indies and Malaya.

Code breakers in the United States could read the Japanese diplomatic ciphers and knew that a war was in the offing. Meanwhile, Roosevelt played for time to build up American armed strength. Later charges that he knew in advance of the Japanese assault on Pearl Harbor are false. The United States experienced an intelligence failure, not a presidential betrayal.

On Sunday morning, December 7, 1941, Japanese carrier-based bombers struck without warning at the American naval base at Pearl Harbor in the Hawaiian Islands. The surprise attack occurred while Japanese envoys were in Washington, ostensibly seeking a peaceful resolution of the dispute between the two countries. The night before, Japan had bombed the Philippines, Hong Kong, Wake Island, Guam, and Midway. The day after the bombing of Pearl Harbor, Roosevelt told Congress in an emergency session that December 7, 1941, was "a date that will live in infamy." He asked the lawmakers to declare that a state of war existed with the empire of Japan. Congress agreed with only one dissenting vote, and soon the nation was also at war with Germany and Italy.

Roosevelt played a major role in shaping the overall war strategy of the United States. He insisted on a Germany-first approach to victory, he mobilized the American military and industrial war machine, and he conducted the coalition diplomacy with Britain and the Soviet Union that was so essential to Allied success over Germany and Japan.

Roosevelt's performance as a war leader came into sharp focus at three conferences that developed Allied strategy. At Casablanca in January 1943, he and Churchill formulated an Anglo-American invasion strategy and the president announced the Allied commitment to "unconditional surrender" as the peace terms with Germany. In November 1943 at the Tehran Conference, FDR and Churchill met with Joseph Stalin for the first time and the Western leaders promised the Russian dictator that there would be a second front in Europe in exchange for Soviet promises to attack Japan once Germany had been defeated. Most controversial of all was the Yalta Conference of February 1945. At this meeting the time of Russia's entry into the war against Japan was fixed and an agreement reached on the postwar occupation of enemy territory. Eastern Poland was placed under Stalin's protection when the dictator promised to include democratic officials in its government. While there were legitimate disagreements about Roosevelt's performance, for the most part he made the best he could of the Allied military situation in the winter of

1945. The Allies needed, or thought they needed, the Soviet Union to complete the defeat of Japan. In Eastern Europe the presence of Soviet troops on the ground limited Roosevelt's options. FDR and Churchill believed that they still had to have Stalin's help, and they extracted as much benefit from the deliberations as they could.

Aside from the unfortunate concordance at Yalta, the conference represented a major victory for world order and for the realization of Roosevelt's dream—the establishment of the United Nations as a going concern in 1944–1945. In that way Roosevelt accomplished what Woodrow Wilson had failed to achieve with the League of Nations. The Yalta meeting established that a conference of the United Nations would "meet at San Francisco . . . on April 25, 1945." The United Nations would be "a general international organization to maintain peace and security."

American domestic politics had continued even during the war, and in 1944 Roosevelt faced a bitter campaign in his bid for a fourth term in the White House. Led by New York's governor, Thomas E. Dewey, Republicans waged a highly personal campaign against Roosevelt. The president made one last effort to demonstrate his skill as a campaigner and to quiet fears about his health. The result was a victory for Roosevelt and his running mate, Harry S. Truman, by a popular vote of 25,612,610 to 22,017,617 and an electoral count of 432 to 99. Roosevelt's fourth inauguration took place on January 20, 1945.

When he returned from the Yalta Conference, Roosevelt addressed Congress, for the first time, from a sitting position and referred to the weight of his braces and to the arduous trip he had just completed. His health was failing, and insiders knew that FDR might not live much longer. In late March, following a medical checkup and an order to rest, President Roosevelt left Washington for Warm Springs, Georgia, where he had often spent time since his polio attack.

On April 12, 1945, Roosevelt donned his Harvard crimson tie and black Navy cape to sit for a portrait by artist Elizabeth Shoumatoff in his Warm Springs cottage. Also present was his old love Lucy Mercer Rutherfurd whom he had been seeing, unknown to Eleanor, for some time. At 1:15 P.M. he put his hand to his head, complained of a violent headache, and slumped back in his chair. Carried to his bed, he lay in a coma and cold sweat until, at 3:35 P.M., he died at age sixty-three of a massive cerebral hemorrhage.

Millions, to whom Roosevelt had embodied the presidency, mourned the fallen commander in chief as if they had lost their own father. Stalin, clearly moved by grief, permitted Moscow's newspapers to print FDR's picture and news of his death on the front page (foreign news was usually published on the back page). Churchill said that he felt as though he had been "struck a physical blow." Across the world when people said that the president had died, nobody asked which president, or president of what, because to all of them Franklin Delano Roosevelt had been The President. As Roosevelt's cortege moved from Warm Springs slowly northward by train, the nation wept.

Roosevelt was buried at Hyde Park, New York. After her death in 1962, Eleanor Roosevelt was laid to rest beside him. President Roosevelt died as the nation was on the verge of victory in World War II. He had created a record against which future presidents would measure themselves and, in turn, be measured by history. Angry Republicans adopted a constitutional amendment to insure that no subsequent president could serve more than two terms. In ways large and small, Franklin D. Roosevelt and the New Deal had put an indelible mark on American history as no other president had done since the trials and tragedy of Abraham Lincoln.

—*Wilson Sullivan, revised by Lewis L. Gould*

Vice President Harry S. Truman had spent a quiet afternoon presiding over the United States Senate on April 12, 1945, when he received a message that he should come to the White House and go immediately to see Mrs. Eleanor Roosevelt. She told him that President Franklin D. Roosevelt had died in Warm Springs, Georgia, a few hours earlier. Truman was now the thirty-third president of the United States. "Boys," Truman said to the White House reporters, "if you ever pray, pray for me now." After they began to address him as Mr. President, he said, "I wish you didn't have to call me that." Conversing with reporters on April 13, Truman said, "When they told me yesterday what had happened, I felt like the moon, the stars, and all the planets had fallen on me."

At the time he left office, almost eight years later, Harry Truman seemed unlikely to ever be ranked among the great American presidents. Because of the unpopular Korean War, minor scandals within his administration, and the Republican victory in 1952, Truman appeared to be a discredited heir to Franklin D. Roosevelt. In the years since, however, Truman's reputation has rebounded, and he now stands among the most respected and admired of all the modern presidents. His forthrightness and determination, his plain speech and candid manner have endeared him to succeeding generations. As the feisty Truman himself might well have said, "that's all there was to it."

Born on May 8, 1884, in Lamar, Missouri, Truman was afflicted from boyhood with poor eyesight and had to wear thick glasses. Nonetheless, according to legend, by the age of thirteen or fourteen he had read every book in the public library at Independence, Missouri, where his family had moved. His favorite subject was history, a topic he continued to relish for the rest of his life. Again and again his debt to history was mentioned in his writings and was reflected in his presidential decisions. For example, through his reading, he learned that "a leader is a man who has the ability to get other people to do what they don't want to do, and like it." He could not have imagined how valuable that lesson would become.

His father's financial difficulties around the turn of the century made it impossible for Truman to enter college, and his poor eyesight prevented his admission to West Point. Before the outbreak of World War I, he worked first at a series of clerical jobs—most of them in Kansas City—and then on his parents' farm, outside Independence. In August 1917 the National Guard unit to which he belonged was mobilized, and he served in France as an artillery officer. He demonstrated leadership abilities under fire, and was discharged as a captain in May 1919.

Seven weeks later he married the wellborn Elizabeth "Bess" Wallace. He had been smitten with Bess ever since they had met as fifth-grade classmates. With no definite future, Truman had been reluctant to marry, although the couple had an "understanding." When he returned from the war, he was thirty-five years old and Bess was a year younger. Future or no future, they married. Their one child, Margaret, was born in 1924.

After the war, Truman tried the haberdashery business, but the venture failed in 1922. That same year, Mike Pendergast, the father of an Army buddy of Truman's and the brother of Kansas City political boss Tom Pendergast, talked Truman into running for district judge (in Missouri an administrative, not a judicial, position). He won and served honestly for two years but suffered his only political defeat in 1924, when he lost his bid for reelection. In 1926, however, "Big Tom" himself guided Truman to victory in a race for chief judge of Jackson County. He proved to be a dedicated official who kept his distance from the Pendergast organization.

A United States Senate seat was open in 1934. After several faithful Pendergast men refused to run, the boss turned to Truman. In a Democratic year, the judge won the race. The new senator voted consis-

President Truman relaxes during a fishing trip in Key West, Florida, in 1946.

tently for New Deal measures that the Pendergast machine opposed. Nevertheless, Truman was regarded in Washington as "the senator from Pendergast." He found it difficult to establish a rapport with the administration. Having trouble making ends meet in Washington, Truman considered not standing for reelection in 1940. But then Missouri Governor Lloyd Stark decided to run for Truman's Senate seat. President Roosevelt preferred Stark and offered Truman an appointment to the Interstate Commerce Commission. Truman's proud mind was made up for him: He had to make the race. He drove around the state in his own car and met the people where they lived or worked. Labor began to support the candidate, and contributions started to trickle in. He narrowly defeated Stark in the primary and won a comfortable plurality in the election.

During the campaign Truman had been struck by the waste and inefficiency at some of the munitions plants and Army bases he had visited; afterward, he quietly drove through twelve Southern states to see how widespread the problem was. In the next session of Congress the Senate established the Special Committee to Investigate the National Defense Program, with Truman as chairman. By 1944, without seeking headlines, the committee had saved the taxpayers approximately fifteen billion dollars by Truman's own estimation. As the Democratic National Convention of 1944 approached, President Roosevelt's candidacy for a fourth term was a foregone conclusion. But many party leaders supported a powerful drive to drop from the ticket Vice President Henry Wallace, whom they viewed as too dreamy and too liberal. The chairman of the Democratic National Committee, Robert Hannegan, preferred either Justice William O. Douglas or Truman for the second spot on the ticket.

On the eve of the vice presidential balloting, Hannegan summoned Truman to his suite. The chairman picked up the phone and held it away from his ear.

"Bob," boomed the big, unmistakable voice of Franklin Roosevelt, which was clearly audible to Truman, "have you got that fellow lined up yet?" "No," said Hannegan. "He is the contrariest Missouri mule I've ever dealt with." "Well, you tell him," said the president, "that if he wants to break up the Democratic party in the middle of a war, that's his responsibility." Without waiting for a reply, Roosevelt hung up.

"Why the hell didn't he tell me in the first place?" said Truman, who was nominated on the second ballot. Roosevelt won his fourth term, and Truman moved from his desk in the Senate to the podium of the chamber. Then came April 12, 1945. Truman assumed the presidency under trying circumstances. He settled in quickly and approached the presidency in an organized manner. He gave his subordinates room to perform their duties but did not flinch from the responsibilities of his office, as was succinctly conveyed by the famous sign on his desk: THE BUCK STOPS HERE. He governed with a small, effective staff in an era before the presidency grew to its modern size. A hardworking president, Truman sometimes overdid it, becoming tart and petulant when he was tired. His relations with the press varied from comfortable to awkward, depending on his mood and the attitude of reporters. He was an adept politician, a strong campaigner, and a tough fighter when crossed.

The first problems that Truman faced arose from the imminent end of World War II. The wartime partnership between the United States and the Soviet Union eroded as Joseph Stalin pressed on with his intention to surround his country with a buffer zone of satellite states. Truman could understand Soviet preeminence in a country such as Poland, but neither he nor his administration could accept the total dominance that Stalin imposed on other countries in Central Europe.

In San Francisco, during the spring of 1945, the countries of the world met to create the framework of the United Nations, an international organization that Truman passionately fought for. Negotiations with the Soviets over the status of Poland resulted in a few exiled Poles being placed in the Communist government, and the seating of Poland in the new world body. The United Nations Charter was signed on June 26. Secretary of State Edward R. Stettinius was appointed U.S. ambassador to the United Nations, and James F. Byrnes replaced him as secretary of state.

Meanwhile, on May 8, the war in Europe ended; and in July President Truman traveled to Potsdam, Germany, to meet with Churchill and Stalin. The principal achievements of this conference were the establishment of territorial lines in Europe and the renewal of the Yalta agreement that the Soviet Union would enter the war against Japan. On such matters as the reconstruction of Poland, the rights of the Western powers to their pre-war property in Romania and Bulgaria, and the presence of American troops in the Mediterranean and the Near East, there was no decision. From such issues sprang the Cold War.

At Potsdam, President Truman was informed that the premier test of an actual atomic bomb had been successful; it was up to him to formalize the unofficial decision to employ it. Truman had learned about the atomic bomb for the first time after becoming president, and he had promptly established a committee of distinguished citizens to study the military and moral issues that the emergence of atomic power would raise.

As the war in the Pacific raged on, Truman's decision to drop the bomb occurred in the context of fierce Japanese resistance on Okinawa, where Americans suffered forty-five thousand casualties, and the continuing threat of kamikaze attacks. Available information indicated that although the Allies were closing in on the Japanese islands, the invasion itself would probably take as long as a year at a possible cost of hundreds of thousands of Allied casualties. Under these circumstances, the decision was made to use the

bomb. Hiroshima was all but obliterated on August 6; Nagasaki, three days later. The Japanese agreed to surrender on August 14. During the half-century since the bombings, scholars have continued debating whether these weapons were necessary to end the war. (Most believe they were.) Truman never doubted that he had done the right thing. Though it was popular at the time—especially with military personnel—his fateful decision became the most controversial act of his presidency.

BIOGRAPHICAL FACTS

BIRTH: Lamar, Mo., May 8, 1884

ANCESTRY: Scotch-English

FATHER: John Anderson Truman: b. Jackson County, Mo., Dec. 5, 1851; d. Grandview, Mo., Nov. 3, 1914

FATHER'S OCCUPATION: Farmer

MOTHER: Martha Ellen Young Truman; b. Jackson County, Mo., Nov. 25, 1852; d. Grandview, Mo., July 26, 1947

BROTHER: John Vivian (1886–1965)

SISTER: Mary Jane (1889–1978)

MARRIAGE: Independence, Mo., June 28, 1919

WIFE: Elizabeth "Bess" Virginia Wallace; b. Independence, Mo., Feb. 13, 1885; d. Independence, Mo., Oct. 18, 1982

CHILD: Margaret (1924–)

RELIGIOUS AFFILIATION: Baptist

EDUCATION: Public high school; attended Kansas City School of Law

OCCUPATIONS BEFORE PRESIDENCY: Timekeeper for a railroad construction company; bank clerk; farmer; haberdasher

MILITARY SERVICE: Missouri National Guard; capt. in 129th Field Artillery (1917–1919)

PREPRESIDENTIAL OFFICES: County judge for Eastern District of Jackson County, Missouri; presiding judge, County Court, Jackson County, Missouri; U.S. senator; U.S. vice president

AGE AT INAUGURATION: 60

OCCUPATION AFTER PRESIDENCY: Writer

DEATH: Kansas City, Mo., Dec. 26, 1972

PLACE OF BURIAL: Independence, Mo.

First Administration

INAUGURATION: Apr. 12, 1945; the White House, Washington, D.C.

SECRETARY OF STATE: Edward R. Stettinius; James F. Byrnes (from July 3, 1945); George C. Marshall (from Jan. 21, 1947)

SECRETARY OF THE TREASURY: Henry Morgenthau, Jr.; Fred M. Vinson (from July 23, 1945); John W. Snyder (from June 25, 1946)

SECRETARY OF DEFENSE (department created in September 1947): James V. Forrestal

SECRETARY OF WAR: Henry L. Stimson; Robert P. Patterson (from Sept. 26, 1945); Kenneth C. Royall (from July 25, 1947; department disbanded in September 1947)

ATTORNEY GENERAL: Francis Biddle; Thomas C. Clark (from July 1, 1945)

POSTMASTER GENERAL: Frank C. Walker; Robert E. Hannegan (from July 1, 1945); Jesse M. Donaldson (from Dec. 16, 1947)

SECRETARY OF THE NAVY: James V. Forrestal (department disbanded in Sept., 1947)

SECRETARY OF THE INTERIOR: Harold L. Ickes; Julius A. Krug (from Mar. 18, 1946)

SECRETARY OF AGRICULTURE: Claude R. Wickard; Clinton P. Anderson (from June 30, 1945); Charles F. Brannan (from June 2, 1948)

SECRETARY OF COMMERCE: Henry A. Wallace; W. Averell Harriman (from Jan. 28, 1947); Charles Sawyer (from May 6, 1948)

SECRETARY OF LABOR: Frances Perkins; Lewis B. Schwellenbach (from July 1, 1945); Maurice J. Tobin (from Aug. 13, 1948)

SUPREME COURT APPOINTMENTS: Harold H. Burton (1945); Fred M. Vinson, chief justice (1946)

79TH CONGRESS (Jan. 3, 1945–Aug. 2, 1946):
SENATE: 57 Democrats; 38 Republicans; 1 Other
HOUSE: 243 Democrats; 190 Republicans; 2 Others

80TH CONGRESS (Jan. 3, 1947–Dec. 31, 1948):
SENATE: 51 Republicans; 45 Democrats
HOUSE: 246 Republicans; 188 Democrats; 1 Other

The atomic bomb did not prove to be the decisive foreign policy weapon that had been initially anticipated. Early on, the Soviets realized that the United States would employ the bomb only to win an all-out war. Since its use was restricted to an ultimate situation, the Soviets understood its limits as a threat, and the United States had to put forward a plan for international control of the new weapon. The U.S. proposal called for an international authority over atomic weapons, but the Soviets were disturbed by the idea of foreign inspectors visiting at will. The Soviet Union turned down the plan and rushed development of its own nuclear weapons. By 1946 Truman decided that the possibility of meaningful negotiations with Moscow had diminished. He noted in a personal memorandum "I'm tired of babying the Soviets." The initial phase of the Cold War had begun.

At home, Truman faced an array of tricky problems as he sought to manage conversion from a wartime to a peacetime economy. The president wanted to avoid a much-feared repetition of the Great Depression and to forestall a resurgence in inflation. To achieve these goals, the administration upheld the price controls on consumer goods that had been imposed during the war. As black markets flourished and prices for many products rose, Truman became the focus of much of the resulting political discontent.

The higher cost of living required higher wages. No longer hampered by the no-strike laws of wartime, and anxious to test the strong right-to-strike legislation passed in the 1930s, organized labor emerged from the war with muscles flexing. By the end of 1945 nine hundred thousand workers were on strike from several industries, and early in 1946 another million joined them.

The most serious threats came from the United Mine Workers and the various railroad unions. John L. Lewis, the UMW president, had closed the soft-coal mines in March 1946, and with factories inoperative and the lights of cities dimming because of fuel shortages, the nation could not endure with a shutdown of transportation, too. On May 21 Truman seized the coal mines and sent Secretary of the Interior Julius A. Krug to negotiate with Lewis. The settlement infuriated the mine operators, but they had no choice in the matter, and the miners went back to work.

The railroad strike, meanwhile, was scheduled to begin on May 25. The day before, the president told his cabinet that he intended to draft the striking employees into the Army and thus compel them to run the trains. On the afternoon of the twenty-fifth, Truman addressed a special session of Congress to ask for the induction bill. Just as he approached that part of the speech, a note was handed to him: "Agreement signed, strike over." Truman asked for the antistrike legislation anyway, but the Senate defeated the measure.

In October, the UMW rose up again. Engaged in a power struggle with other union leaders, Lewis aimed to demonstrate his strength in a battle with the government. Using a minor point in the contract as an excuse, he demanded that negotiations be reopened. When Secretary Krug refused, Lewis announced that the mine workers would consider the contract void as of November 20. Bristling with anger, the president asked for an injunction, and on November 18 the court ordered the miners not to strike. They struck anyway, and on December 3 the union was fined $3.5 million, and Lewis personally, $10,000. Still, the strike went on, and the president announced that he would make a radio appeal to the miners. Perhaps fearing that his men were no longer with him, Lewis ordered the miners back to work.

The elections of 1946, which produced the first Republican-controlled Congress since 1930, were a serious repudiation of Truman's administration. Republicans campaigned on the slogan, "Had enough?" A telling quip of the day went, "To err is Truman." Senator J. William Fulbright, then a freshman Democrat, suggested that Truman ought to resign, since the people were obviously against the president. There were many reasons for his unpopu-

larity: Labor did not like his toughness on strikes, and business did not like the intrusion into the marketplace that price controls represented; the South had no use for his civil rights proposals, and the North did not like his folksy Missouri style.

The public had so soured on organized labor throughout 1946 that Truman's firm hand might have stopped or reversed the fast decline in his popularity; but he neutralized his victory by vetoing the antilabor Case Bill of 1946. The Eightieth Congress, which was seated in 1947, was, however, a much more conservative legislature and was able to override Truman's veto of the somewhat milder labor-restricting Taft-Hartley Act.

Meanwhile, relations with the Soviet Union were worsening, and the Cold War continued to define the East-West situation into 1947. In Asia as in Europe,

John L. Lewis was central to the labor troubles that dogged President Truman in 1946. Cartoons depicted the leader of the United Mine Workers as "the man at the switch," but Truman was able to use the courts and large fines to compel Lewis to abandon the strikes.

GEORGE CATLETT MARSHALL

"I have no feelings," George C. Marshall told Dean Acheson in 1947, "except a few which I reserve for Mrs. Marshall." Joseph McCarthy agreed. Charging in 1951 that the general was a Communist-dominated traitor, the senator from Wisconsin asserted that Marshall "would sell his grandmother for any advantage." The charge, of course, was ridiculous. Despite his poor health, Marshall had been quietly serving his country for years.

McCarthy's "man steeped in falsehood" had been promoted over 34 senior officers to the post of Army chief of staff by President Franklin D. Roosevelt, and he had been the principal military strategist for all Allied operations in Europe and the Pacific during World War II. The man who McCarthy said was party to "a conspiracy so immense and an infamy so black as to dwarf any previous venture in the history of man" was, after the war, immediately pressed into service by President Truman, who asked him to tackle the frustrating and hopeless job of trying to make peace between the warring Nationalist and Communist forces in China. The hardworking soldier turned statesman—whose activities as Truman's secretary of state from 1947 to 1949, McCarthy held, were "invariably serving the world policy of the Kremlin"—helped the president to formulate the containment policy that halted Russian expansion and the Marshall Plan that revitalized Europe. As the secretary of defense in 1950 and 1951, Marshall rebuilt the armed forces, equipping them to deal with Communist aggression during the Korean conflict.

Actually, both Marshall and McCarthy had equivocated. While secretary of state, Marshall told Acheson, his major associate, that he had no feelings so that Acheson would not hesitate to criticize the State Department. McCarthy lied, the political commentator Richard H. Rovere writes, to demonstrate that not even the most "unassailable" American was immune to his inquisition. He succeeded in muddying the chaste reputation of the man Truman considered "the greatest living American."

Born in Uniontown, Pennsylvania, in 1880, Marshall began his Army career in 1901, after graduating from the Virginia Military Institute. Serving in the Philippines from 1913 to 1916, he was called by his commanding officer "the greatest military genius since Stonewall Jackson." During World War I he was instrumental in plotting the successful strategy of the St. Mihiel and Meuse-Argonne offensives. His administrative skills were bolstered by an extraordinary ability to recognize talent—one of the reasons why Roosevelt elevated him to the number-one military position during World War II. It was General Marshall who recommended that Dwight D. Eisenhower be appointed—over 366 senior officers—to command the United States forces in Europe.

In 1952, however, when Ike was running for the presidency, he delivered what was probably Marshall's harshest blow: Eisenhower refused to condemn McCarthy's assault on his old mentor. The retirement that Marshall had so long sought was finally his after Eisenhower's election. But both Eisenhower and the American people who had allowed the vilification of one of their greatest men were reminded of Marshall's achievements when he was awarded the Nobel Peace Prize in 1953, five years before his death.

the Axis had roiled with uncomfortable alliances of potential antagonists. After the war had ended, the old lines had been redrawn. General George C. Marshall, anxious to pledge American dollars to a peaceful China, was unable to effect a coalition between Chiang Kai-shek's Nationalists and the Communists. One by one the Eastern European nations that the Soviet Union had overrun as they pushed back the Nazis became little more than satellites of Moscow. In Iran, where the Allies had maintained several bases, the Russians refused to honor an agreement to evacuate. In Greece the opposing forces—one Communist, one royalist—were at each other's throats as soon as the British withdrew.

A decisive moment came in early 1947 when Truman asked Congress for huge sums for aid to Greece and Turkey. In his request he enunciated what became known as the Truman Doctrine. Its ideological premise was to contain Soviet expansion and gain time for Western Europe to defend itself. Truman told the Soviet Union that it could expand no farther. It was a strong statement, and it set what became known as "containment" as the keystone of American foreign policy.

The Truman Doctrine was not universally applicable. In many places, including Italy, France, the Low Countries, and Scandinavia, the Communists had formed well-organized parties that operated legally. So long as these nations remained impoverished and devastated from the war, the possibility of Communist dominance was great.

On June 5, 1947, Secretary of State Marshall proclaimed in a speech at Harvard University that the United States would offer funds to nations that wanted to reconstruct their economies. Marshall's speech attracted worldwide attention, and out of it came a program of economic reconstruction that became known as "the Marshall Plan." By implication, this American economic aid would also be made available to the countries of Eastern Europe; but Russia denounced the Marshall Plan as an "imperial" plot to enslave Europe. In so doing, the Soviets forfeited a historic opportunity and allowed the West to rebuild its strength and cohesion. The Marshall Plan distributed more than twelve billion American dollars to the people of Europe for reconstruction.

Truman's efforts to avoid war were challenged in June 1948. As part of the wartime agreements, Germany had been divided into occupation zones held by the four major powers: Great Britain, France, the United States, and the Soviet Union. The city of Berlin had been similarly divided. The West held the industrial part of Germany; the Soviets had the more agricultural sectors. In June the Russians closed off the autobahn through the Soviet occupation zone in Germany, blocking Allied access to Berlin. Truman quickly turned the dare around: He began sending airplanes—carrying supplies—over the Soviet zone and into West Berlin. This put it to the Soviets to fire the first shot, and they did not. The Berlin Airlift, which lasted for nearly a year, kept the city going and dealt the Soviets a major foreign policy blow.

In April 1949 the North Atlantic Treaty Organization (NATO) had been established by the United States and its European allies. NATO banded together a loose coalition of nations to forestall a Soviet threat in Western Europe. The treaty declared that an attack on one country would be considered an attack on all, and integrated the European defenses of all members. The two Cold War blocs faced off on the European continent while, behind the protection of NATO and with the aid of the Marshall Plan, Western Europe recaptured its economic vitality and prosperity. By 1949 the structure of the American response to the Soviet Union had been put in place.

With all his success and imaginativeness in foreign policy, Truman was still not getting along with the Eightieth Congress, which against Truman's wishes had cut the budget and passed tax cuts. Despite this disjunction, Truman had decided to seek a four-year term of his own, and the idea prompted a variety of responses. Radicals were appalled, reactionaries shocked, regular Democrats gloomy, and regular Republicans joyful. Democrats on the left, led by

Henry Wallace, vice president in the third Roosevelt administration, organized a third party to fight for the presidency. Democrats from the South, dismayed by Truman's strong civil rights proposals, defected and ran South Carolina's governor Strom Thurmond as the Dixiecrat (States' Rights) candidate, creating a rare fourth ballot line in the presidential race. Seeing no further need to conciliate the Southern defectors, Truman issued an executive order mandating integration of the armed forces, a move which increased his popularity among black voters. Despite his bleak election prospects, the Democrats had no choice but to accept Truman and what seemed to be his inevitable defeat. The Republicans nominated Thomas E. Dewey, governor of New York, who seemed a sure winner.

The president appeared before his battered party to accept its nomination. No one had mentioned the word "win" with any conviction, and Truman's incumbency made him the underdog rather than the favorite in a race against Dewey and the Republicans. But Harry Truman said, "Senator [Alben] Barkley and I will win this election and make these Republicans like it—don't you forget that."

Next Truman announced his strategy: "On the 26th day of July, which out in Missouri we call 'Turnip Day,' I am going to call Congress back and ask them to pass laws to halt rising prices, to meet the housing crisis—which they are saying they are for in their platform. . . . Now my friends, if there is any reality behind that Republican platform, we ought to get some action from a short session of the Eightieth Congress." If the legislators passed his proposals, he explained, they would increase the president's strength; if they ignored his recommendations, they would remain the "do-nothing Eightieth Congress." They chose to do nothing, and Truman made the Congress itself a principal election issue.

After the July "turnip session," Truman assumed an optimism shared by almost no one. To reach as

---

SECOND ADMINISTRATION

INAUGURATION: Jan. 20, 1949; the Capitol, Washington, D.C.

VICE PRESIDENT: Alben W. Barkley

SECRETARY OF STATE: Dean G. Acheson

SECRETARY OF THE TREASURY: John W. Snyder

SECRETARY OF DEFENSE: James V. Forrestal; Louis A. Johnson (from Mar. 28, 1949); George C. Marshall (from Sept. 21, 1950); Robert A. Lovett (from Sept. 17, 1951)

ATTORNEY GENERAL: Thomas C. Clark; J. Howard McGrath (from Aug. 24, 1949); James P. McGranery (from May 27, 1952)

POSTMASTER GENERAL: Jesse M. Donaldson

SECRETARY OF THE INTERIOR: Julius A. Krug; Oscar L. Chapman (from Jan. 19, 1950)

SECRETARY OF AGRICULTURE: Charles F. Brannan

SECRETARY OF COMMERCE: Charles Sawyer

SECRETARY OF LABOR: Maurice J. Tobin

SUPREME COURT APPOINTMENTS: Thomas C. Clark (1949); Sherman Minton (1949)

81ST CONGRESS (Jan. 3, 1949–Jan. 2, 1951):
  SENATE: 54 Democrats; 42 Republicans
  HOUSE: 263 Democrats; 171 Republicans; 1 Other

82ND CONGRESS (Jan. 3, 1951–July 7, 1952):
  SENATE: 48 Democrats; 47 Republicans; 1 Other
  HOUSE: 234 Democrats; 199 Republicans; 2 Others

ELECTION OF 1948

CANDIDATES	ELECTORAL VOTE	POPULAR VOTE
Harry S. Truman (Democratic)	303	24,179,345
Thomas E. Dewey (Republican)	189	21,991,291
Strom Thurmond (States' Rights)	39	1,176,125
Henry Wallace (Progressive)	—	1,157,326

Residents of Berlin watch the arrival of an Air Force plane laden with food and supplies for their beleaguered city. The Berlin Airlift was one of the foreign policy triumphs of the Truman years.

many people as he could, as cheaply as possible, the president set out on a number of whistle-stop train trips, stopping wherever the public had gathered to hear him. While Tom Dewey was eloquently stating idealistic abstractions, Truman campaigned against the Eightieth Congress. In Albuquerque, New Mexico, he later recalled, he was making a speech attacking the Republicans when "some big voice way up in the corner of that 7,000-people auditorium said, 'Give 'em hell, Harry!' Well, I never gave anybody hell—I just told the truth on these fellows and they thought it was hell!" But the polls still forecast a landslide for Dewey.

Of election night, Truman later said, "At six o'clock I was defeated. At ten o'clock I was defeated. Twelve o'clock I was defeated. Four o'clock I had won the election. And the next morning . . . in St. Louis, I was handed this paper [the *Chicago Tribune*] which said DEWEY DEFEATS TRUMAN! Of course, he wished he had, but he didn't and that's all there was to it!" Truman had pulled the New Deal coalition together one last time. Ironically, the presence of Strom Thurmond on his right and Henry Wallace on his left convinced many voters that Truman was a moderate candidate. Dewey's weaknesses as a campaigner—overconfidence and an inability to connect with the people—gave Truman his upset.

Following the election, the president announced a

A young naval officer and his wife in San Diego, California, stare at the aircraft carrier on which he will serve. The Korean War dislocated many lives.

sweeping program on domestic issues for the new Democratic Congress. He named it the Fair Deal as a continuation of Roosevelt's New Deal program, and it called for civil rights legislation, national health insurance, repeal of the Taft-Hartley Act, and other liberal legislation. Yet little enthusiasm greeted his ambitious program. The problem was that while the country did not want to see the New Deal threatened, there was scant support for expanding liberalism. A newer issue was grabbing the public's attention: internal security.

While Truman and his administration had been successful in creating the structure of the Cold War, they had not been able to avoid foreign policy setbacks. Among these were the fall of China to the Communists in the summer of 1949 and the explosion of the first Russian nuclear weapon a few weeks later. In the wake of these events, the administration decided in a document called NSC-68 to have the nation rearm. Another decision called for the creation of a thermonuclear weapon to counter a similar threat from the Soviets.

For many Americans the Communist triumph in China and the news of a Russian atomic bomb—so soon after America's absolute victory in World War II—suggested a more sinister explanation. The role of Soviet agents and the possibility of subversion came to the fore in the case of Alger Hiss, who had worked in the State Department and had been convicted of perjury when he denied spying for the Russians. The arrest and conviction of Julius and Ethel Rosenberg as spies for the Soviets who had passed nuclear secrets to Moscow worked against the administration. Republicans charged that the Democrats were too trusting of the Russians or, in the phrase of the day, that Truman and his secretary of state, Dean G. Acheson, were "soft on Communism." This increasingly suspicious atmosphere gave ammunition to the Republicans who assembled the House Un-American Activities Committee to root out Communists, which Truman once described as the most "un-American activity in the whole government."

The embodiment of this sentiment became Senator Joseph R. McCarthy of Wisconsin who charged in early 1950 that there were 57, 81, 205, or "a lot" of Communists in the State Department. Facing a difficult reelection campaign, the senator seized upon the Communist issue as a way of gaining votes and improving his image at home. The Truman administration tried to discredit McCarthy, but the government also tightened security procedures and sought to find alleged subversives on its own. For many scholars on this period, the zeal of the Truman administration inflamed the climate of hysteria in which McCarthy thrived.

When the army of North Korea invaded South Korea in 1950, the threat of war further stoked anti-Communist feelings. After World War II the United States and Russia, according to the agreements made at Potsdam, had jointly liberated and occupied Japanese-held Korea. The dividing line was the thirty-eighth parallel. South Korea had had its elections;

North Korea had not. When the North Koreans crossed the border into the South, Truman's containment doctrine was put to the test in the Far East.

Truman sent American planes and ships to Korea on June 25, just hours after the invasion had taken place. That day the Security Council of the United Nations examined the events and declared that the invasion constituted an act of armed aggression. The council was in a position to convert Truman's unilateral decision into a United Nations action because the Soviet Union (which could have vetoed the resolution) was at the time boycotting its sessions.

General Douglas MacArthur, the ranking officer in the Far East and military governor of Japan, was placed in command of the Korean operation, and from early in the conflict he disagreed with the United Nations strategy of containment, rather than destruction of the aggressor.

The containment policy had worked well in Europe, but in Korea the problem was more complicated. The Russians were not directly involved; neither were the Chinese. But the chance of their intervention was great, and this possibility influenced the United Nations strategy.

MacArthur insisted that the Chinese were not going to intervene and that thus there was no reason to limit Allied military action to the South. But in late 1950, as the United Nations forces neared the Yalu River, which separated North Korea from Manchuria, China did intervene; its troops poured across the border and pushed the Allies south of the thirty-eighth parallel.

United Nations orders maintained that all fighting was to be done in or over Korea; the war was not to be introduced into Chinese Manchuria. This presented MacArthur with the frustration of having planes from Chinese bases assault United Nations depots, supply lines, and troops and then retreat to their sanctuary north of the Yalu. By openly criticizing this state of affairs, MacArthur was not only publicly rebuking the commander in chief, the joint chiefs of staff, and the United Nations, he was also informing the enemy of what was not going to be done.

On March 20, 1951, the United Nations drafted a proposal for a negotiated settlement of the war, and a copy was sent to MacArthur. In an extraordinary ges-

DEAN G. ACHESON

In 1945 Undersecretary of State Dean G. Acheson said he had "no objective reason to suppose" that the vital interests of the United States and Russia would ever conflict. By 1949, just after he became head of the State Department, he (along with millions of other Americans) had changed his stance. He then saw Communism as "economically fatal to free society and to human rights and fundamental freedoms." Over the next four years Acheson confirmed his commitment to this stiffer view. He helped create NATO and engineered the 1951 peace treaty with Japan; he supported the European Defense Community and implemented President Truman's policies in Korea. Acheson, who had attended Groton, Yale, and Harvard Law School, had been appointed undersecretary of the Treasury in 1933; opposed to FDR's gold-purchase plan, he was back at his law practice inside of a year. In 1941, however, he became assistant secretary of state. He soon helped secure congressional passage of the Lend-Lease Act and, later, of the Bretton Woods Monetary Agreement. In 1946 he headed the committee that produced the Acheson-Lilienthal report, on which Bernard Baruch, the U.S. representative to the United Nations Atomic Energy Committee, based his proposal for international control of atomic energy. Acheson returned to private practice in 1953; during the fifties he wrote a number of books on statecraft. He was one of the "Wise Men" that Lyndon B. Johnson consulted after the Tet Offensive in Vietnam in 1968. Acheson's memoir *Present at the Creation: My Years in the State Department* was published in 1969, two years before his death.

ture, the general made a public statement in which he offered to negotiate. His plan completely disregarded the official statement made by the president and the United Nations.

Truman considered firing MacArthur then, but hesitated. A few days later, however, on April 5, House Minority Leader Joe Martin read a letter to the House from MacArthur, in which the commander again attacked the official policy of the United Nations. MacArthur had been ordered by the joint chiefs not to make any policy statements without

---

SAM RAYBURN

"They don't make them like that any more," was John F. Kennedy's apt remark as he left the bedside of Sam Rayburn shortly before the death of the Speaker of the House in the fall of 1961. "Mr. Sam" was elected to the first of a record twenty-five consecutive congressional terms in 1912; he was Speaker of the House for seventeen years, more than doubling Henry Clay's tenure. Tennessee-born and Texas-raised, Rayburn knew poverty firsthand. His father told him, "Character is all I have to give you. Be a man." Rayburn worked his way through college and prepared for service on Capitol Hill with six years in the state legislature. Though a staunch Democrat, he was justly noted for his skill at persuasion and constructive compromise. In 1941 Congress was ready to kill the draft; Rayburn marshaled all his resources and saved it—by one vote—four months before Pearl Harbor. He led the postwar fight against isolationism, which could only "break the hearts of the world." Permanent chairman of three Democratic National Conventions, he was one of the most powerful men in government (and did some of his best politicking at informal "Rayburn Board of Education" sessions in his office). Once he was asked how he could remember all the promises he had made—or had refused to make. "If you tell the truth the first time," answered the Speaker of the House, "you don't have to remember."

---

clearance. Twice within ten days he had disobeyed that order. On April 10 Truman ordered him to come home.

MacArthur had challenged the constitutional premise that in the United States military power is subject to civilian rule. Despite the hero's welcome that he received, MacArthur was not exonerated in the eyes of the public. The calls for impeachment of the president died out when Senate hearings revealed that Truman had been on firm constitutional grounds. MacArthur did not receive the presidential nomination he probably wanted, and Truman preserved the principle of civilian leadership of the nation.

In addition to all the political rigors of the Cold War period, the first family had to endure renovation of the aging and creaking White House throughout most of the president's second term, during which the Trumans lived across the street in Blair House. There, in 1950, two Puerto Rican nationalists attempted to kill the president. Truman was unhurt, but one Secret Service man and one would-be assassin were killed.

When the White House was ready for occupancy again, Margaret Truman was around less; she had begun a career as a concert singer. After Truman was widely criticized for writing a blunt, bitter letter to Paul Hume, the *Washington Post* music critic who had reviewed one of his daughter's performances harshly, the president wrote in his diary: "I'm accused of putting my baby who is the apple of my eye in a bad position. I don't think that is so. She doesn't either— thank the Almighty."

By late 1951 the Truman presidency was running down. Minor scandals among aides close to the president contributed to an impression of seediness and low morality in the White House. At the end of March 1952 Truman announced that he wouldn't be a candidate for the third term he could have pursued. His popularity ratings hovered around 30 percent in the polls. He backed Adlai Stevenson in the 1952 election, but Dwight D. Eisenhower became president. By this time, Truman and Eisenhower had attacked each other in the 1952 campaign and were no longer friendly. Eisenhower treated Truman rudely at the inauguration in 1953. Truman went home to Independence to start a library of his papers and to refight all his battles in his memoirs. He spent time at the library reading history as he always had and regaling visiting historians, schoolchildren, and the public with tales of his presidency. Truman died on December 26, 1972.

Longtime Speaker of the House Sam Rayburn once said that as president, his friend Harry Truman had been "right on all the big things, wrong on all the little ones." Frankly corny and at times crude, Truman conducted one of the most liberal administration in the nation's history, but he allowed into his circle political hacks who were corrupt and inept, and he stood by them when they were denounced. One day he might play ballads on the piano for foreign dignitaries; the next he might propose legislation so visionary that it would not be enacted until the 1960's (for example, the Civil Rights Act of 1964 and Medicare of 1965).

In the final year of the Truman administration, Winston Churchill visited the United States. He had an admission for Truman: "The last time you and I sat across a conference table was at Potsdam. I must confess, sir, I held you in very low regard. I loathed your taking the place of Franklin Roosevelt. I misjudged you badly. Since that time, you more than any other man, saved Western civilization."

As time passed and the passions of the 1950s cooled, historians' assessments of Truman improved. His candor and frankness seemed especially refreshing in the wake of what the public believed was presidential deception during the Johnson and Nixon administrations. The 1948 presidential election became a classic in American politics, invoked by

An enthusiastic piano player, Harry S. Truman performs at the Truman Library on September 3, 1959, with the comedian Jack Benny, renowned for his humorous ineptitude with his fiddle.

every trailing candidate in the national races that followed. "Give 'em hell, Harry" was indelibly associated with the feisty president from Independence.

On a 1964 television program about his presidency, Truman recalled: "The day I left Washington, I wrote my daughter Margaret a letter. . . . And it said this: 'There is an epitaph in Boot Hill cemetery in Arizona which reads, "Here lies Jack Williams. He done his damnedest! What more can a person do?"' Well, that's all I could do. I did my damnedest, and that's all there was to it."

—DAVID JACOBS, *revised by* LEWIS L. GOULD

Dwight David Eisenhower

"I Like Ike"

During the four decades since he left office in 1961, the evaluation of Dwight D. Eisenhower's performance as president has risen steadily. Dismissed at first as a passive executive dominated by others, he is now seen as a master of the "hidden-hand" executive style that allowed him to use subordinates and intermediaries to accomplish his goals. Eisenhower's skillful avoidance of the foreign policy dangers of the 1950s also attracts high marks. His performance on the race issue was more spotty, but on balance Eisenhower's reputation stands at a higher level than would have seemed possible when he gave way to John F. Kennedy in January 1961.

Dwight David Eisenhower was born in Denison, Texas, on October 14, 1890, one of the six sons of David and Ida Eisenhower. He grew up in Abilene, Kansas, where his father worked as a mechanic in a creamery. A talented athlete, Eisenhower was a good football player. He gained an appointment to West Point, where he played on the line and then switched to left halfback. During a game with Tufts, he wrenched a knee and a week later broke the knee in a horseback riding accident. He never played football again. Eisenhower plunged into a two-year funk over the end of his football career. He found, however, that he had a natural aptitude for the military.

After Eisenhower graduated from West Point in the middle of his class, he was assigned to Fort Sam Houston in San Antonio, Texas. There he met and courted Mamie Doud, a strikingly pretty brunette socialite from Denver. Four months later they became engaged, and on July 1, 1916, they were married. Their first son, Doud Dwight "Icky," born in 1917, died in 1921, a loss both Eisenhowers mourned until the end of their lives. A second boy, John Sheldon, was born in 1922.

During World War I, Eisenhower commanded a tank-training school at Camp Colt, near Gettysburg, Pennsylvania. By the time he turned twenty-seven,

some six thousand men had passed under his command and his administrative ability had been noted.

From 1922 to 1924 he served in the Panama Canal Zone as an executive officer for Brigadier General Fox Conner, who had compared Eisenhower favorably with a young major named George C. Marshall and had inspired Ike to continue studying strategy and the history of warfare.

In 1925 Eisenhower entered the Command and General Staff School. Although he had previously been an average student, he graduated first in a class of 275, having been able to cope with the competitive pressures that drove other Command students to exhaustion, retirement, and even nervous breakdowns and suicide. In 1927 Ike was assigned to write a guide to the European battlefields of World War I. It remains one of the best works on the war. From 1929 to 1932 he served as an assistant executive to the assistant secretary of war, and was then assigned to the staff of General Douglas MacArthur, the Army chief of staff, in Washington, D.C. From 1935 until Hitler attacked Poland in 1939, he was General MacArthur's assistant in the Philippines. He later said that he had studied dramatics under MacArthur.

In September 1941, in order to test the new U.S. Army then in training for the impending war, a mock battle was staged in Louisiana. Eisenhower was named chief of staff for the 3d Army, which fought and won two battles against the 2d Army. He had learned about tanks during World War I, he had learned to fly a plane in the Philippines, and he had always believed that mastery of these two weapons would determine the victor in any future war. It was the precise coordination between tanks and planes that won the battles in Louisiana. Two days after the victory, Eisenhower was promoted to the temporary rank of brigadier general.

Shortly after the attack on Pearl Harbor, Eisenhower was called to Washington to serve as an assis-

General Eisenhower returns home to Abilene, Kansas, June 21, 1945.

tant chief of staff to Chief of Staff George Marshall. He helped draft a global strategy for the war, followed this up with an outline for a cross-Channel invasion of the Continent, designed the European Theater of Operations command that would carry out the strategies, and then boarded the plane to London.

Eisenhower led the invasions of North Africa, Sicily, and the Italian mainland, the cross-Channel invasion of France, and the defeat of the German armies beyond the Rhine in 1945. He demonstrated a talent for coalition warfare, and welded together the British and Americans into an effective fighting force. His rapport with the troops under his command was excellent. He seemed approachable and friendly, and the respect of his men laid the basis for his political popularity.

The focus of Eisenhower's years in Europe was the cross-Channel invasion that was given the code-name "Operation Overlord." He spent months on the detailed planning for the attack, which both sides recognized would mark a turning point in the conflict. Eisenhower's most dramatic moment came on the eve of D-day when he made the lonely decision to launch the invasion of Europe after learning that a brief break in the bad weather would make the landing possible. He managed the Allied coalition across Europe until it achieved its mission, the defeat of Germany, on May 7, 1945. After the war, he served as chief of staff, overseeing the demobilization of the American forces.

In 1948 Eisenhower's war memoir, *Crusade in Europe,* was published, and it added to his fame and popularity. He served for two years as president of Columbia University in New York City, and was recalled to the Army in 1950 by President Truman to head the creation of military forces for the North Atlantic Treaty Organization, a job he completed with dispatch.

By 1951 moderate Republicans began to court Eisenhower to run for the presidency during the following year. If he did not do so, they warned, Senator Robert A. Taft of Ohio would receive the nomination and take the party on an isolationist course. Eisenhower believed in the containment policies of the

On July 12, 1952, at the Republican National Convention in Chicago, Illinois, Senator Richard M. Nixon raises the hand of Republican presidential candidate Dwight D. Eisenhower. Pat Nixon and Mamie Eisenhower stand beside their husbands.

Truman administration, and he was convinced that the Republicans should not turn their back on international affairs.

After a primary battle, Eisenhower defeated Taft on the second ballot at the Republican National Convention. The nominee chose Senator Richard M. Nixon of California as his running mate. The campaign got off to a slow start against the Democratic nominee, Adlai E. Stevenson of Illinois. One Republican newspaper complained that Eisenhower was "running like a dry creek." The theme of the Republican campaign was expressed in the formula K1, C2, or "Korea, Communism, and Corruption."

An early crisis involving Nixon occurred when a newspaper revealed that he had been the beneficiary of money raised for his expenses by wealthy donors. Faced with pressure to remove Nixon from the ticket, Eisenhower watched on television as the vice presidential candidate delivered the "Checkers" speech, in which Nixon refuted the charges and said his daughters would not return the dog named Checkers that they had been given. The speech was a popular hit, and Eisenhower greeted Nixon at the airport with the words "You're my boy." Nonetheless, the episode introduced an element of distance in Eisenhower's relations with Nixon that lasted throughout his presidency.

On the issue of the Communist-hunting senator, Joseph R. McCarthy of Wisconsin, Eisenhower was outraged by McCarthy's charge that Eisenhower's mentor, George C. Marshall, had been a Communist pawn. But when Eisenhower removed a passage praising Marshall from a speech for delivery in McCarthy's presence, and when he publicly embraced Senator William Jenner of Indiana, who had called Marshall "a living lie," he was severely criticized. He chose to wait, he told his friends, until McCarthy destroyed himself, insisting that it was McCarthyism, not McCarthy, that needed destroying—and that only McCarthy himself could destroy McCarthyism. The statement foreshad-

owed Eisenhower's presidential technique to defuse McCarthy.

Eisenhower's most successful campaign maneuver was his promise to go to Korea and end the war there if elected. The promise clinched what was probably already a certain victory. He carried all but nine states, trouncing Stevenson with a plurality of more than six million votes.

BIOGRAPHICAL FACTS

BIRTH: Denison, Texas, Oct. 14, 1890

ANCESTRY: Swiss-German

FATHER: David Jacob Eisenhower; b. Elizabethville, Pa., Sept. 23, 1863; d. Abilene, Kan., Mar. 10, 1942

FATHER'S OCCUPATION: Mechanic

MOTHER: Ida Elizabeth Stover Eisenhower; b. Mount Sidney, Va., May 1, 1862; d. Abilene, Kan., Sept. 11, 1946

BROTHERS: Arthur (1886–1958); Edgar (1889–1971); Roy (1892–1942); Earl (1898–1968); Milton (1899–1985)

MARRIAGE: Denver, Colo., July 1, 1916

WIFE: Marie "Mamie" Geneva Doud; b. Boone, Iowa, Nov. 14, 1896; d. Washington, D.C., Nov. 1, 1979

CHILDREN: Doud Dwight "Icky" (1917–1921); John Sheldon (1922–)

RELIGIOUS AFFILIATION: Presbyterian

EDUCATION: Public schools; U.S. Military Academy, West Point, N.Y. (1915); Command and General Staff School (1926)

OCCUPATIONS BEFORE PRESIDENCY: Soldier; president of Columbia University

MILITARY SERVICE: 2d lt. in U.S. Army (1915); various posts in United States, Panama, and Philippines (1915–1942); comdr. of European Theater of Operations (1942); supreme comdr. of Allied Expeditionary Force in Western Europe (1943); gen. of the Army (1944); Army chief of staff (1945); supreme comdr. of Allied powers in Europe (1951)

AGE AT INAUGURATION: 62

OCCUPATIONS AFTER PRESIDENCY: Writer; political adviser

DEATH: Washington, D.C., Mar. 28, 1969

PLACE OF BURIAL: Eisenhower Museum, Abilene, Kan.

ADLAI E. STEVENSON

"A funny thing happened to me on the way to the White House!" said Adlai Stevenson after the presidential election of 1952. "I was happy to hear that I had even placed second."

Stevenson had not even wanted the Democratic nomination. He had hoped to be reelected governor of Illinois; he had been uncertain of his ability to serve as president; he had been reluctant to oppose the probable Republican candidate, General Dwight Eisenhower, the popular war hero who was, according to Stevenson, as familiar as "the ketchup bottle on the kitchen table." Despite his reluctance, Stevenson had been drafted by the Democrats and, as expected, had been badly beaten.

But curiously, when President Eisenhower, more popular than ever, stood for reelection four years later, Stevenson actively sought his party's nomination, won it, and leaped into a campaign that offered him virtually no chance of victory. The former Chicago lawyer and diplomat aimed his attacks not only at the administration in general but at the popular Ike in particular; and he raised the important but avoidable issue of nuclear fallout. Eisenhower called Stevenson's request for an end to atmospheric testing of nuclear bombs a "moratorium on common sense." (Two years later, the president would make the same proposal.) Typical of the odds against which Stevenson was running was a series of crises in the Middle East—just two weeks before Election Day—which, although largely the result of administration blunders, served to further solidify the American people behind President Eisenhower. Stevenson carried only seven states in the November election.

Theodore H. White once suggested that Stevenson placed "the virus of morality in the bloodstream of both parties." Condemning the use of "soft soap, slogans, gimmicks, bandwagons and all the other infernal machines of modern high-pressure politics" as "contempt for people's intelligence, common sense and dignity," he introduced a wit, an eloquence, and a moral tone to campaigning that had not before been present.

In 1961 Stevenson wanted to be secretary of state, but President Kennedy appointed him ambassador to the United Nations. During the Cuban Missile Crisis the next year, when Soviet Ambassador Valerian Zorin hedged on Stevenson's query regarding the presence of Russian missiles in Cuba, the American ambassador cried, "I am prepared to wait for my answer until hell freezes over!" But as his role in policy-making declined even more under President Johnson, the United Nations job increasingly frustrated and exhausted Stevenson. In 1965 in London, a few days before his fatal heart attack, he privately announced his intention to resign soon. "Ah, well," Stevenson sighed, "for a while, I'd really just like to sit in the shade with a glass of wine in my hand and watch the people dance."

The new president and first lady adapted easily to life in the White House. He wrote in his diary after the first complete day of his presidency that "today just seems like a continuation of all I've been doing since July '41." Mamie Eisenhower ran the social side of the White House with a strong hand. She proved an excellent hostess and otherwise kept the family quarters as a refuge for her busy husband.

Eisenhower approached the presidency in the orderly manner of organization he had learned in the military. He made his political liaison, former New Hampshire Governor Sherman Adams, his assistant and gave him cabinet rank. Eisenhower's critics have maintained that he surrendered too much of his power to Adams; Eisenhower, however, clearly felt that domestic politics required a cabinet official in the same way that foreign affairs required a secretary of state.

For the position of secretary of state, Eisenhower chose John Foster Dulles, the leading Republican expert on foreign affairs. Dulles became famous for his tough talk and strongly anti-Communist views. "Foster has been studying to be secretary of state since he was five years old," the president once remarked.

Dulles became associated with most of the foreign policy successes and failures of the Eisenhower years. Instead of seeing Dulles as the framer of foreign policy and Eisenhower as his passive pupil, scholars now give the president more credit for shaping the direction and execution of American diplomacy during the 1950s and view Eisenhower as the man in charge. As the president said of Dulles, "There's only one man I know who has seen more of the world and talked with more people and knows more than he does, and that's me."

In July 1953, a few months after Eisenhower took office, the Korean War was ended by armistice. The stalemate in negotiations between the United States on one side and the Chinese Communists and the North Koreans on the other over the fate of prisoners of war was broken when Eisenhower signaled that atomic weapons might be used if talks remained stalled. The Communists and the United Nations forces agreed on voluntary repatriation of prisoners of war—the greatest stumbling block in negotiations to that point—and began to discuss a cease-fire line. The armistice was signed on July 27, 1953; it created a buffer zone between North and South Korea which still exists.

The Eisenhower years also saw an expansion of the American commitment in Southeast Asia. The French were fighting Communist guerrillas there with American financial support. By 1954 the French were losing the war. To achieve an elusive victory, the French sent forces to a fortress called Dien Bien Phu. The French faced imminent defeat if American military power was not deployed. Eisenhower announced what became known as the domino theory regarding

Vietnam: "You have a row of dominoes set up and you knock over the first one, and what would happen to the last one was certainly that it would go over quickly." Lacking support from Congress and American allies, the United States had no alternative but to let Dien Bien Phu fall. In the wake of the French

FIRST ADMINISTRATION

INAUGURATION: Jan. 20, 1953; the Capitol, Washington, D.C.
VICE PRESIDENT: Richard M. Nixon
SECRETARY OF STATE: John Foster Dulles
SECRETARY OF THE TREASURY: George M. Humphrey
SECRETARY OF DEFENSE: Charles E. Wilson
ATTORNEY GENERAL: Herbert Brownell, Jr.
POSTMASTER GENERAL: Arthur E. Summerfield
SECRETARY OF THE INTERIOR: Douglas McKay; Frederick A. Seaton (from June 8, 1956)
SECRETARY OF AGRICULTURE: Ezra Taft Benson
SECRETARY OF COMMERCE: Sinclair Weeks
SECRETARY OF LABOR: Martin Durkin; James P. Mitchell (from Jan. 19, 1954)
SECRETARY OF HEALTH, EDUCATION, AND WELFARE (department created Apr. 1, 1953): Oveta Culp Hobby; Marion B. Folsom (from Aug. 1, 1955)
SUPREME COURT APPOINTMENTS: Earl Warren, chief justice (1953); John M. Harlan (1955); William J. Brennan, Jr. (1956)
83RD CONGRESS (Jan. 3, 1953–Dec. 2, 1954):
  SENATE: 48 Republicans; 46 Democrats; 2 Others
  HOUSE: 221 Republicans; 213 Democrats; 1 Other
84TH CONGRESS (Jan. 5, 1955–July 27, 1956):
  SENATE: 48 Democrats; 47 Republicans; 1 Other
  HOUSE: 232 Democrats; 203 Republicans

ELECTION OF 1952

CANDIDATES	ELECTORAL VOTE	POPULAR VOTE
Dwight D. Eisenhower (Republican)	442	33,936,234
Adlai E. Stevenson (Democratic)	89	27,314,992
Vincent Hallinan (Progressive)	—	140,023

withdrawal and the creation of the nation of South Vietnam, the United States helped establish the Southeast Asia Treaty Organization (SEATO) to block Communist expansion in the region and began supplying weapons and advisers to South Vietnam. Out of these steps would come the commitment to Vietnam that John F. Kennedy and Lyndon B. Johnson would extend and broaden in the 1960s.

The containment policy soon adapted itself to other parts of the world. The United States sponsored a coup to overthrow a pro-Communist government in Iran in 1953 and achieved a similar result in Guatemala a year later. Throughout the Eisenhower years the Central Intelligence Agency pursued covert actions against other third-world nations that were perceived to be unfriendly to the United States. These covert actions set a precedent for other such ventures during the remainder of the Cold War.

During the first term, the issue of Senator McCarthy continued to plague the Eisenhower administration. The president tried to ignore the demagogic senator, saying that he was not going to get "into the gutter" with the Wisconsin Republican.

While undermining McCarthy in private where he could, Eisenhower did a great deal to appease him in public by firing those accused of being security risks and by allowing McCarthy's influence in the State Department. Eventually McCarthy overreached himself by attacking alleged Communist influence within the United States Army in 1954. The televised hearings undercut McCarthy's prestige, and censure by the United States Senate ended his era of power. He died three years later of the effects of alcoholism. Eisenhower believed that his strategy had worked. Other critics gave more weight to the impact of the hearings, McCarthy's own mistakes, and the Senate opposition to McCarthy's use of the technique of character assassination and unsupported charges against members of that body.

On May 17, 1954, the Supreme Court handed down its epochal decision that racial segregation in public schools was unconstitutional. But Eisenhower privately objected to the Court's decision and refused to endorse it in public. His skepticism that America could be integrated by force of law and his certainty that the process could not be speedy led him to adopt a passive course on civil rights. Not until Governor Orval Faubus of Arkansas called out National Guard troops to prevent African-American students from entering Central High School in Little Rock in September 1957 did Eisenhower act firmly—and only because as president, he felt he must uphold the orders of the Court. On just thirteen previous occasions had a president dispatched federal troops into a state to enforce federal law. But after rioting broke out in Little Rock, Eisenhower sent in one thousand paratroopers and federalized more than ten thousand National Guardsmen. The episode underlined for Southerners that they could not use their state military forces to block integration. A week after Governor Faubus called out the National Guard, the first civil rights bill to pass Congress since 1875 had been approved, with President Eisenhower's blessing, authorizing a Civil Rights Commission. With this bill, the nation's most painful domestic problem was brought into the open.

Although much of his foreign policy during his initial four years solidified the hostility between America and Russia, Eisenhower nonetheless worked at reducing the tension. In one of his first speeches as president (to the American Society of Newspaper Editors on April 16, 1953), Eisenhower had said: "Every gun that is made, every warship launched, every rocket fired signifies, in the final sense, a theft from those who hunger and are not fed, those who are cold and are not clothed. . . . The cost of one modern heavy bomber is this: a modern brick school in more than thirty cities. . . . We pay for a single fighter plane with a half-million bushels of wheat. We pay for a single destroyer with new homes that could have housed more than eight thousand people." Humanity, he had said, hung from a "cross of iron." He proposed universal disarmament.

During the presidential campaign, the candidate had pledged "peace and prosperity." In spite of Eisenhower's often-stated dislike for the welfare state, New Deal policies were solidified. Ten million people were added to the Social Security rolls during his two terms; student loans were made available through the National Defense Education Act of 1958; and the Department of Health, Education, and Welfare was created.

The creation of the Interstate Highway system is the Eisenhower administration's most effective public works initiative. The forty-one thousand miles of highways built became the backbone of the U.S. highway system.

The president himself concentrated on his search for peace, maneuvering around the "brinks" and over the "summits" of international diplomacy. It was the one area in which he personally took pains to create a novel proposal and to follow it up with his own specific suggestions. "The United States pledges before you," he said in an address to the United Nations in December of 1953, ". . . its determination to help solve the fearful atomic dilemma—to devote its entire heart and mind to find the way by which the miraculous inventiveness of man shall not be dedicated to his death, but consecrated to his life." He proposed a stockpile of atomic materials for peaceful purposes. That proposal, along with his attempts to effect a disarmament treaty, was not achieved. His failure to make headway in what he considered his preeminent task resulted in the most subdued passage in Eisenhower's memoirs: "In the end our accomplishments were meager, almost negligible. . . . the most significant, possibly the only, achievement of the entire effort was the wider education of all civilized peoples in the growing need for disarmament. . . ." In this "bleak" defeat, Eisenhower admitted candidly, "I suffered my greatest disappointment."

Several months after the first of the Geneva Summit Conferences convened in 1955 and failed to produce any easing of Cold War tension, Eisenhower was struck by a massive heart attack. He was hospitalized early on the morning of September 24, 1955, emerged a month later in bright red pajamas bearing the legend "Much Better, Thanks," and finally returned to the White House on November 11. His attack and temporary disability posed the issue of how the business of the president was to be handled when he could not perform his duties. It also raised

Angry Hungarians spit on a giant head of Joseph Stalin during the failed revolt against Soviet rule in 1956. The Eisenhower administration could not intervene to help the Hungarians in their uprising.

the question of whether or not Eisenhower would seek reelection in 1956. On February 29, 1956, he announced that "my answer will be positive, that is, affirmative." Then, on June 7, he suffered an attack of ileitis that required an emergency operation.

Despite these medical problems, Eisenhower's reelection seemed certain. He toyed with replacing Vice President Nixon on the ticket, but Nixon dug in his heels. The Democrats renominated Adlai Stevenson, who made a lackluster race against the popular incumbent. Heading into the fall, Eisenhower's campaign was well ahead of Stevenson.

Then two of the most significant crises of the Cold War occurred. On January 27, 1953, John Foster Dulles had announced by radio to the people of Eastern Europe that they could count on the United States for support in throwing off Soviet domination. In April 1953 Eisenhower again called for "full independence of the East European nations." In June, however, when East Germans rioted, Eisenhower refused to intervene. Afterward the new Soviet leaders began to relax their hold on Eastern Europe, hoping

that by easing the pressure on their captive nations they could avoid an explosion. In 1956 Khrushchev denounced Stalin and Stalinism at the Twentieth Party Congress and called for "greater individual liberty." Poland declared itself a neutral state in October. The Poles attested to their friendship with Russia— but gained some measure of dignity in their stand. In Hungary, meanwhile, all the signals from America and Russia were read incorrectly, and the Hungarians declared their own independence from Russia in November 1956. The Red Army (200,000 troops with 2,500 tanks and armored cars) moved into Budapest in the early morning of November 4 and did not leave until 32,000 people had been killed, more than 195,000 had fled their homeland, and Hungary had been returned to Soviet rule. Washington watched helplessly as these events took place because the president and his advisers had wisely decided that the risk of an encounter with the Soviets outweighed an attempt to help the Hungarians.

At the time that the Hungarian crisis erupted, the Eisenhower administration was also dealing with the fallout from the Israeli, British, and French occupation of the Suez Canal in October 1956. Determined to stop Gamal Abdel Nasser of Egypt from nationalizing the canal and fearful of his ties to the Soviets, the three nations had attacked the Egyptian air force and seized part of the waterway. The United States pressed the British and French to back down and withdraw their forces. The episode was a serious setback to Western unity and the cause of peace in the Middle East.

Neither of these events disrupted Eisenhower's march toward a second term. In fact, they strengthened the case for keeping an experienced president in place. Eisenhower received 457 electoral votes to 73 for Stevenson, and the Republican ticket won more than 57 percent of the popular vote. The Democrats retained control of both houses of Congress. Eisenhower enjoyed a productive working relationship with the two Democratic leaders on Capitol Hill, Speaker of the House Sam Rayburn and Senate Majority Leader Lyndon B. Johnson.

The second Eisenhower term was filled with problems and difficulties. The launching of *Sputnik I*, the first space satellite, by the Russians on October 4, 1957, epitomized for many of the president's critics a sense of drift in his second administration. It was not until 1954 that Eisenhower had had his "first intimation that the orbiting of an earth satellite was either feasible or desirable." Eisenhower could argue with some justification that America's lag in space exploration had begun with Truman. Yet the National Aeronautics and Space Administration (NASA) was not set up until July of 1958—eight months after the Russians had launched two satellites.

The launching of *Sputnik* fostered more criticism of the president. Despite his efforts to assure the nation that *Sputnik* did not represent Soviet technical superiority, which was in fact the case, the public was unpersuaded. America, it seemed, was on the defensive. Its foreign policy was a reaction to Russian initia-tive. Its domestic programs were responses to pressures from such groups as civil rights organizations. Its program for national defense lagged behind that of the

SECOND ADMINISTRATION

INAUGURATION: Jan. 20, 1957; the Capitol, Washington, D.C.

VICE PRESIDENT: Richard M. Nixon

SECRETARY OF STATE: John Foster Dulles; Christian A. Herter (from Apr. 22, 1959)

SECRETARY OF THE TREASURY: George M. Humphrey; Robert B. Anderson (from July 29, 1957)

SECRETARY OF DEFENSE: Charles E. Wilson; Neil H. McElroy (from Oct. 9, 1957); Thomas S. Gates, Jr. (from Jan. 26, 1960)

ATTORNEY GENERAL: Herbert Brownell, Jr.; William P. Rogers (from Jan. 27, 1958)

POSTMASTER GENERAL: Arthur E. Summerfield

SECRETARY OF THE INTERIOR: Frederick A. Seaton

SECRETARY OF AGRICULTURE: Ezra Taft Benson

SECRETARY OF COMMERCE: Sinclair Weeks; Frederick H. Mueller (from Aug. 6, 1959)

SECRETARY OF LABOR: James P. Mitchell

SECRETARY OF HEALTH, EDUCATION, AND WELFARE: Marion B. Folsom; Arthur S. Flemming (from Aug. 1, 1958)

SUPREME COURT APPOINTMENTS: Charles E. Whittaker (1957); Potter Stewart (1958)

85TH CONGRESS (Jan. 3, 1957–Aug. 24 1958): SENATE: 49 Democrats: 47 Republicans HOUSE: 234 Democrats; 201 Republicans

86TH CONGRESS (Jan. 7, 1959–Sept. 1, 1960): SENATE: 64 Democrats; 34 Republicans HOUSE: 283 Democrats; 153 Republicans

STATES ADMITTED: Alaska (1959); Hawaii (1959)

ELECTION OF 1956

CANDIDATES	ELECTORAL VOTE	POPULAR VOTE
Dwight D. Eisenhower (Republican)	457	35,590,472
Adlai E. Stevenson (Democratic)	73	26,022,752
Walter B. Jones (Democratic)	1	—

Russians, allegedly producing a "missile gap." And its sense of adventure, represented by the exploration of space, was thwarted. Peace and freedom, it seemed, were slowly being eroded. Prosperity was shaky at best. (An economic "adjustment," or recession, began in late 1957.) It was the first time most Americans could remember the United States being second best at something. It was a rude realization.

In March 1957, after the Suez Crisis, the president

In the midst of the Cuban Missile Crisis, in 1962, Eisenhower walks with President John F. Kennedy at Camp David in Maryland. The ex-president advised his Democratic successor during foreign policy crises.

promulgated what came to be known as the Eisenhower Doctrine, which stated that America would aid, financially and militarily, any country in the Middle East threatened by any other country "controlled by international communism." Thus in July 1958, President Chamoun of Lebanon requested American forces to fend off an armed rebellion that he said had been instigated by Nasser. Eisenhower sent the 6th Fleet and more than fourteen thousand soldiers and marines to Lebanon, and the crisis abated. In October, American troops were withdrawn, having proved, Eisenhower said, "in a truly practical way that the United States was capable of supporting its friends."

The president dealt with another potential flashpoint in the late summer of 1958 over Quemoy and Matsu, the offshore islands that the Communist Chinese had bombarded in 1954 and chose to shell again that August. The Nationalist Chinese had been building up forces on the islands, and it is likely that the Communists wished only to test American determination in the area. They eventually lost interest and ceased shelling the islands, "except upon unusual or ceremonial occasions," as Eisenhower wrote. They permitted, in this "Gilbert and Sullivan war," the Chinese Nationalists to resupply the islands by convoy on the odd-numbered days of the month.

The 1958 congressional elections brought large gains for the Democrats as the economic recession and voter discontent common in the sixth year of a presidency worked against the Republicans. Internal problems in the administration also eroded Republican morale. The White House faced charges that the chief of staff, Sherman Adams, had taken presents from a business friend who had problems with his income tax. In the resulting furor the president forced Adams out to help Republican election prospects. The gesture did not impress the public. The resurgent Democrats made sweeping gains in the House and Senate.

A few months after the election, Fidel Castro

seized power in Cuba. Convinced that Castro was a Communist, Eisenhower authorized the Central Intelligence Agency to lay plans to drive the new leader out of Havana. A scheme was developed to land anti-Castro rebels at the Bay of Pigs as a way of triggering a general uprising. Eisenhower did not approve the plan while he was in office because of factionalism within the anti-Castro force. The scheme remained in place when Kennedy took office.

Eisenhower made one final attempt at a summit conference, set for May 16, 1960. "From the autumn of 1959 to the spring of 1960," he wrote in his memoirs *Waging Peace*, "most people of the Western world felt that a slight but discernible thaw was developing in the icy tensions . . . between the West and the Soviet Union. This impression resulted partially from Mr. Khrushchev's agreement at Camp David to remove his threat to end the presence of Allied forces in West Berlin." On May 1 a high-flying U-2 reconnaissance plane was shot down over Russia. Five days later Premier Khrushchev informed the Supreme Soviet that crucial parts of the plane were in Soviet hands, that the equipment clearly indicated the U-2 was an espionage plane, and that the pilot, Francis Gary Powers, also captured, had admitted as much. Eventually Eisenhower took responsibility for the U-2 flights, but he did not express regrets.

The Summit collapsed, and the president gradually drew back into his role of elder statesman as Vice President Nixon carried the Republican standard into battle against Kennedy. When reporters pressed him about decisions that Nixon might have made as vice president, Eisenhower responded: "Give me a week and I might think of one." The comment did not help Nixon, who lost narrowly to Kennedy.

Before he retired to Gettysburg, Pennsylvania, with his wife, Eisenhower took upon himself one more important duty, that of warning the nation of the "conjunction of an immense military establishment and a large arms industry," which, he said, was "new in the American experience." "We recognize the imperative need for this development," he said in his farewell address. "Yet we must not fail to comprehend its grave implications. Our toil, resources, and livelihood are all involved; so is the very structure of our society. In the councils of government we must guard against the acquisition of unwarranted influence, whether sought or unsought, by the military-industrial complex. The potential for the disastrous rise of misplaced power exists and will persist. We must never let the weight of this combination endanger our liberties or democratic processes. We should take nothing for granted."

During his retirement, Eisenhower wrote memoirs of his presidential service, played golf, and took some part in Republican politics. His heart problems continued, and he died on March 28, 1969.

During the 1960s Eisenhower's historical standing was low in contrast with Kennedy's and, for a time, even Johnson's. Then, as the effects of Vietnam, social unrest, and Watergate in the Nixon era traumatized the country, Eisenhower's eight years of prosperity and comparative peace grew more attractive in retrospect. Commentators and historians looked into the documentary record at the Eisenhower Library and argued that Eisenhower had been in charge and a forceful executive. His stature rose. Later a reaction against "Eisenhower revisionism" appeared as younger scholars examined with more skepticism his record in civil rights and world affairs. Yet Eisenhower still ranks as one of the most important presidents of the twentieth century.

—CHARLES L. MEE, JR.,
revised by LEWIS L. GOULD

JOHN FITZGERALD KENNEDY

INSPIRING A GENERATION

Few American presidents are seen more differently by scholars and the public at large than John F. Kennedy. In February 2000, almost four decades after his murder, when the Gallup Poll asked Americans who was the greatest president in history, Kennedy won (with 21 percent of the vote). Yet when scholars are surveyed, Kennedy usually ranks no higher than above average or, occasionally, near great.

Among the American people, Kennedy's idealism and martyrdom accounts for some of this high regard, as does his identification with the successful outcome of the Cuban Missile Crisis in 1962, and his endorsement of civil rights in 1963. Mini-series and adoring memoirs have wrapped a tough politician in the Camelot legend. Kennedy's critics harp on his philandering, alleged ties to organized crime, and partial responsibility for drawing the nation into Vietnam.

The thirty-fifth president was born into an aristocracy—that of the Boston Irish. The 1914 marriage of his parents, Joseph Patrick Kennedy and Rose Fitzgerald, united two of the city's most politically prominent families. Rose's father, the affable John F. "Honey Fitz" Fitzgerald, had been mayor of Boston. Joseph's father, Patrick J. Kennedy, was a former state representative and one of Boston's most powerful ward bosses.

Joseph P. Kennedy bypassed politics as a means of gaining power and took a more direct route—high finance. When he had been out of Harvard University for less than two years, he borrowed enough money to win control of a small East Boston bank; at twenty-five he was hailed as the nation's youngest bank president. The home in which he and Rose started their marriage was a gray frame dwelling in middle-class Brookline, Massachusetts. It was in this house that their first two sons were born: Joseph Patrick, Jr., in 1915, and, on May 29, 1917, John Fitzgerald.

During World War I, Joseph Kennedy served as assistant general manager of Bethlehem Steel Company's shipyard in Quincy, Massachusetts, where he had some rather strained dealings with the assistant secretary of the Navy, Franklin D. Roosevelt. When the war ended, Kennedy entered the investment house of Hayden, Stone and Company and started to amass his first million. By the end of the 1920s, the shrewd and ambitious young Irish-American had made his mark in securities, real estate, and the new movie industry. In 1925 he established the first of three trust funds that would make each of his children a multi-millionaire. Joe Kennedy's romantic involvement with the movie star Gloria Swanson contradicted the impression of the Kennedy family's domestic bliss disseminated by his press agents.

In 1926 Joseph Kennedy moved his business operations—and his growing family—to New York. But after 1928, a rambling summer house at Hyannis Port, on Massachusetts's Cape Cod, was the clan's real home. By that time, in addition to Joseph, Jr., and John, there were Rosemary, Kathleen, Eunice, Patricia, Robert, and Jean. With eight children, the proud parents named a sailboat they had acquired the *Tenovus*. The arrival of their ninth and last child, Edward ("Teddy"), in February 1932, coincided with the purchase of a new boat, appropriately called *Onemore*.

In later years much would be made of the influence John Kennedy's father and older brother had exerted on him. His father's often ruthless drive was instilled in most of his children. Even in family sports, such as swimming, sailboat racing, and touch football games on the lawn at Hyannis Port, each Kennedy was taught to play to win.

In his early years, John Kennedy too often found himself in the shadow of Joe, Jr. At Choate, an exclusive preparatory school in Wallingford, Connecticut, Joe won the Harvard Trophy for his combined success in sports and scholarship. Young Jack, a "gentleman C" scholar, finished sixty-fourth in a class of one hundred and twelve. Partly to avoid further competition with his brother, Jack decided not to follow Joe

President Kennedy and his son, John F. Kennedy, Jr., on the steps of the White House on March 28, 1963, playing with a toy.

to Harvard but enrolled instead at Princeton. However, during a summer visit to England, where he studied briefly at the London School of Economics, he contracted jaundice. His illness forced Jack to start late at Princeton, and a recurrence of the ailment caused him to drop out of college during the Christmas recess. In the fall of 1936 he entered Harvard. In his first two years he was again a C student.

Meanwhile, Joseph P. Kennedy had helped his old adversary from the Quincy shipyard days, Franklin Roosevelt, to be elected president in 1932. Two years later Kennedy was appointed to the Securities and Exchange Commission, one of Roosevelt's New Deal reforms, and he served as its first chairman, from July 1934 to September 1935. During the 1936 presidential campaign Joseph Kennedy published a book, *I'm for Roosevelt*, which endeared him to the president. His reward for this campaign support was appointment, in December 1937, as ambassador to the Court of St. James in London.

His father's new position gave Jack access to many of Europe's most influential men. Taking off the second semester of his junior year at Harvard, he traveled across the Continent, including Russia, as the storm clouds of World War II were gathering. Back in London on September 1, 1939, when Hitler's invasion of Poland finally triggered the war in Europe, Jack Kennedy caught his first glimpse of conflict when he went to Scotland to help American survivors of a torpedoed British ship, the *Athenia*.

Sobered by his experiences in Europe, young Kennedy returned to Harvard and in his senior year became a candidate for a degree with honors in political science. His undergraduate thesis, a study of Allied appeasement of Hitler, was later published under the title *Why England Slept* and became a bestseller, in part because his father bought so many copies.

During the winter of 1939–40, Joseph Kennedy grew increasingly pessimistic about Britain's chances of survival, and after the fall of France in June 1940, he began to think of Hitler's triumph as inevitable. He also expressed anti-Semitic sentiments that filtered back to the United States. In December he resigned his ambassadorship after returning to the United States to champion nonintervention. After Pearl Harbor, Kennedy volunteered for service with Roosevelt's wartime administration, but because of the president's bitter feelings toward him, he was never given another government assignment.

During World War II, Jack Kennedy became a war

BIOGRAPHICAL FACTS

BIRTH: Brookline, Mass., May 29, 1917

ANCESTRY: Irish

FATHER: Joseph Patrick Kennedy; b. East Boston, Mass., Sept. 6, 1888; d. Hyannis Port, Mass., Nov. 16, 1969

FATHER'S OCCUPATIONS: Financier; diplomat

MOTHER: Rose Fitzgerald Kennedy; b. Boston, Mass., July 22, 1890; d. Hyannis Port, Mass., Jan. 22, 1995

BROTHERS: Joseph Patrick (1915–1944); Robert Francis (1925–1968); Edward Moore (1932–)

SISTERS: Rosemary (1918–); Kathleen (1920–1948); Eunice Mary (1921–); Patricia (1924–); Jean Ann (1928–)

MARRIAGE: Newport, R.I., Sept. 12, 1953

WIFE: Jacqueline Lee Bouvier; b. Southampton, N.Y., July 28, 1929; d. New York, N.Y., May 19, 1994

CHILDREN: Caroline Bouvier (1957–); John Fitzgerald (1960–1999); Patrick Bouvier (b. and d. 1963)

RELIGIOUS AFFILIATION: Roman Catholic

EDUCATION: Choate School; attended London School of Economics; Princeton University; Harvard University (B.S., 1940)

OCCUPATION BEFORE PRESIDENCY: Writer

MILITARY SERVICE: Ens., lt. (jg), lt., U.S. Naval Reserve (active duty 1941–1945)

PREPRESIDENTIAL OFFICES: U.S. congressman; U.S. senator

AGE AT INAUGURATION: 43

DEATH: Dallas, Texas, Nov. 22, 1963

PLACE OF BURIAL: Arlington National Cemetery, Arlington, Va.

The marriage of John F. Kennedy and Jacqueline Bouvier in 1953 produced one of the most photogenic presidential couples in American history. The strains of their marriage were hidden away from the camera's eye.

hero when his PT boat was sunk in the Pacific and his bravery enabled his crew to survive their ordeal of swimming in shark-infested waters and awaiting help on a deserted island. Meanwhile, his brother Joe died on a bombing mission, and Jack became the heir to his father's political ambitions. As he confided to a close friend, Paul B. "Red" Fay, he would soon be "trying to parlay a lost PT boat and a bad back into a political advantage." After he left the Navy in 1945, Kennedy ran for Congress in Massachusetts and, with

the help of his father's money, the support of other returning veterans, and his own campaigning skills, he was elected in 1946.

Kennedy was a mediocre representative, but his goal was the presidency. To that end, he ran for the Senate in 1952 against the incumbent Republican, Henry Cabot Lodge, Jr. The familiar Kennedy barrage of billboards, tea parties, and reprints of a *Reader's Digest* article about his PT boat exploits was loosed on the state. Kennedy defeated Lodge by more than 70,000 votes, while Eisenhower carried the state for the Republicans by more than 200,000 votes.

Kennedy married the stylish Jacqueline Bouvier in 1953. In the Senate he was not a significant legislator, spending most of his time preparing for a presidential race. To that end, he published *Profiles in Courage,* a book that was substantially ghostwritten, which, thanks in large measure to the assistance of a family friend, Arthur Krock of the *New York Times,* won a Pulitzer Prize for biography in 1957. The book was written during a personal crisis that plagued Kennedy's early senatorial years and which nearly brought a tragic end to his career.

Through his years in Congress, Kennedy continued to be plagued with a bad back and the effects of Addison's disease—a disorder of the adrenal glands — though he kept the latter a secret. By the summer of 1954 he could get about only on crutches. Told that a spinal-fusion operation involved serious risk, he slapped his crutches and said bitterly, "I'd rather die than spend the rest of my life on these things." Twice following an operation that October, Kennedy was close to death, and he survived only to learn that the surgery had not been fully successful. A second operation was performed in February 1955. Kennedy's back condition was never completely cured. At a 1961 tree-planting ceremony in Canada he once more injured his back, and thereafter he never had a day without pain.

During Kennedy's illness in December 1954, the Senate had voted to condemn Wisconsin's Senator Joseph R. McCarthy for his campaign against Communists in government. Kennedy's failure to announce his position on this issue was later the basis for attacks on his own political courage. McCarthy, like Kennedy a Roman Catholic, had a large and vociferous following in Massachusetts, including many Boston Irish.

1956 was a presidential election year. Adlai E. Stevenson, the 1952 Democratic nominee, defeated Senator Estes Kefauver of Tennessee to win renomination. Stevenson dramatically left open to the convention the selection of a vice presidential candidate. Kennedy ignored his father's emphatic advice not to try for the second spot and possibly be tagged a loser. As millions watched on television, Kennedy ran neck and neck with Kefauver for two ballots, only to lose to him on the third. The episode gave Kennedy valuable national exposure as he prepared for a race in 1960.

In 1958 he was reelected to the Senate by a majority of 874,608 votes. Backed by this impressive endorsement, he became the favorite for the 1960 vice presidential nomination. But Kennedy had a different idea. "I'm not running for vice-president anymore," he told one Democrat. "I'm now running for president."

The Kennedy candidacy was launched at a meeting held by sixteen people in Robert Kennedy's house at Hyannis Port on October 28, 1959. The senator and his associates, who included his father and two brothers, plotted strategy about how to conduct a presidential bid. Since Warren G. Harding in 1920, no candidate had gone directly from the United States Senate to the presidency. Curiously, three of Kennedy's rivals for the 1960 Democratic nomination were fellow senators—Hubert H. Humphrey of Minnesota, Stuart Symington of Missouri, and Lyndon B. Johnson of Texas. In the background, waiting for the lightning strike of a third nomination, was Adlai E. Stevenson of Illinois.

To prove that a Roman Catholic could be elected president, Kennedy decided he would have to fight for the nomination in the primaries. When he announced his candidacy on January 2, 1960, he declared his intention of facing the electorate in the New Hampshire primary, the earliest in the nation, the following March. To no one's surprise he rolled up an impressive vote from his fellow New Englanders. The major tests, however, would be in Wisconsin and

West Virginia, in both of which he would be facing the redoubtable Humphrey. Symington and Stevenson remained inactive candidates, each hoping for a deadlocked convention. Johnson said that he was too busy as Senate Majority Leader to campaign, but rounded up support in the Senate for a presidential bid.

The blitz technique, developed in the earlier Kennedy campaigns in Massachusetts, was transferred full scale to Wisconsin in April 1960. An important addition was the Kennedy family airplane, a converted Convair named for the senator's daughter, Caroline, born in 1957. Running against the Kennedys, Humphrey complained, was "like an independent retailer competing with a chain." (Kennedy brushed aside complaints that family money was buying the election by reading at a banquet an imaginary wire from his father: "Dear Jack: Don't buy one vote more than necessary. I'll be damned if I'll pay for a landslide.") On April 5 Kennedy captured 56 percent of the vote in the Wisconsin primary. But the result was not decisive; he would have to meet Humphrey once again on May 10 in West Virginia.

Kennedy had selected the West Virginia battleground with care. The predominantly Protestant state —only 5 percent of its population was Catholic—was also one of the poorest in the Union. If a Catholic and a rich man's son could win there, Kennedy reasoned, he could win anywhere. And so it proved. Jack Kennedy carried the primary with 61 percent of the vote, and Humphrey was forced to withdraw as a candidate. The Kennedy forces spent ample sums of money to help produce this victory.

Led by Robert Kennedy, the senator's campaign staff had been rounding up delegates in states without primaries. Before the July 11 opening of the convention in Los Angeles, Kennedy had 600 of the 761 votes needed to win the nomination. There was still opposition, however. In a withering attack, former President Truman questioned the senator's maturity.

If elected at the age of forty-three, Kennedy would be the second youngest man to serve in the White House. (Theodore Roosevelt, who became president

ROBERT F. KENNEDY

Thirty-six-year-old Robert F. Kennedy, brother of the president-elect, seemed to many Americans a poor choice for attorney general; even Bobby thought the appointment ill-advised, but he gave in to the urgings of his brother and father. "I see nothing wrong," quipped JFK, amid the storm of protest, "with giving Robert some legal experience as attorney general before he goes out to practice law." Educated at Harvard and the University of Virginia Law School, Robert Kennedy had worked as a lawyer in government after completing his education, taking time out to supervise his brother's campaigns. He had been a counsel for the McCarthy committee in 1953, but he later resigned in protest against its excesses and served as counsel for the committee's Democratic minority. He had been counsel for the Senate Rackets Committee and in that capacity had begun a long fight with Teamsters Union boss James Hoffa. Kennedy proved to be an able head of the Justice Department and was his brother's most trusted adviser. After JFK's assassination, Robert Kennedy served in Johnson's cabinet until 1964, when he left to run successfully for the Senate from New York. Kennedy became an outspoken critic of Johnson's Vietnam policies and contemplated a run for the presidency in 1968. Until Eugene McCarthy challenged Johnson and made a good showing in the New Hampshire primary, Robert Kennedy hesitated. He then entered the race and was a major rival to McCarthy and Vice President Humphrey through the spring.

His brief run for the White House ended with his assassination in June 1968. In his death, Robert Kennedy was transformed into a martyr like his older brother, and was seen by many as the man who might have perpetuated Democratic success if not for his untimely passing.

THE KENNEDY ADMINISTRATION

INAUGURATION: Jan. 20, 1961; the Capitol, Washington, D.C.

VICE PRESIDENT: Lyndon B. Johnson

SECRETARY OF STATE: Dean Rusk

SECRETARY OF THE TREASURY: C. Douglas Dillon

SECRETARY OF DEFENSE: Robert S. McNamara

ATTORNEY GENERAL: Robert F. Kennedy

POSTMASTER GENERAL: J. Edward Day; John A. Gronouski (from Sept. 30, 1963)

SECRETARY OF THE INTERIOR: Stewart L. Udall

SECRETARY OF AGRICULTURE: Orville L. Freeman

SECRETARY OF COMMERCE: Luther H. Hodges

SECRETARY OF LABOR: Arthur J. Goldberg; W. Willard Wirtz (from Sept. 25, 1962)

SECRETARY OF HEALTH, EDUCATION, AND WELFARE: Abraham A. Ribicoff; Anthony J. Celebrezze (from July 31, 1962)

SUPREME COURT APPOINTMENTS: Byron R. White (1962); Arthur J. Goldberg (1962)

87TH CONGRESS (Jan. 3, 1961–Oct. 13, 1962):
  SENATE: 64 Democrats; 36 Republicans
  HOUSE: 262 Democrats; 175 Republicans

88TH CONGRESS (Jan. 9, 1963–Oct. 3, 1964):
  SENATE: 67 Democrats; 33 Republicans
  HOUSE: 258 Democrats; 176 Republicans

ELECTION OF 1960

CANDIDATES	ELECTORAL VOTE	POPULAR VOTE
John F. Kennedy (Democratic)	303	34,226,731
Richard M. Nixon (Republican)	219	34,108,157
Harry F. Byrd (Democratic)	15	—

---

wrote the Declaration of Independence, George Washington when he commanded the Continental Army, and Christopher Columbus when he landed in America. A further challenge to Kennedy was posed by the venerable Eleanor Roosevelt, who urged Stevenson's renomination.

Despite these obstacles, Kennedy's nomination came, almost anticlimactically, on the first ballot. His closest rival, Lyndon B. Johnson, was promptly offered, and accepted, the vice presidential nomination. According to some reports, Kennedy had not really expected or wanted the proud and sensitive Johnson to take the second spot, but the choice of the Protestant Texan healed party wounds and gave geographical and religious balance to the ticket.

In one of the early addresses of his campaign, Kennedy moved to eliminate his religion as a political issue. The platform he chose was a daring one, a meeting of Protestant clergy at the Greater Houston Ministerial Association in Texas. There, to a largely hostile audience, he pledged that his Catholicism would in no way hamper the exercise of his presidential duties. He believed, as firmly as they did, he said, in the separation of church and state.

Many political observers felt that the election was won by Kennedy in the series of four television debates held in September and October with his Republican opponent, Richard M. Nixon. Before audiences estimated at sixty-five to seventy million Americans, a relaxed and self-confident Kennedy traded words with an often tired and uncertain Nixon.

On November 8, 1960, John Kennedy was elected president by the narrowest popular margin in the twentieth century. Slightly less than 120,000 votes out of nearly 69,000,000 cast separated Kennedy and Nixon. "So now my wife and I prepare for a new administration, and a new baby," he said in acknowledging Nixon's concession. Sixteen days later, John, Jr., was born.

On January 20, 1961, Kennedy, in one of history's

when he was forty-two, was the youngest.) In a brilliant rebuttal, Kennedy pointed out that his fourteen years in Congress gave him more government experience than all but a few presidents had had at the time of their accession to the office. Kennedy noted that he was older than Thomas Jefferson had been when he

most stirring inaugural addresses, pledged himself to get the country moving again. "Now the trumpet summons us again—not as a call to bear arms, though arms we need—not as a call to battle, though embattled we are—but a call to bear the burden of a long twilight struggle year in and year out, 'rejoicing in hope, patient in tribulation'—a struggle against the common enemies of man: tyranny, poverty, disease and war itself. . . . And so, my fellow Americans: Ask not what your country can do for you—ask what you can do for your country." The address embodied Kennedy's determination to fight the Cold War and set the stage for some of the foreign policy commitments made during his presidency.

As he announced his choices for the cabinet and an expanded White House staff, comparisons began to be made between Franklin Roosevelt's New Deal Brain Trust and Kennedy's New Frontiersmen. Harvard and MIT, it was said, would soon lose all their professors to Washington. For secretary of state he selected Dean Rusk, and he conciliated the business community with the choice of Republican C. Douglas Dillon as secretary of the Treasury. The most controversial appointment was that of his brother, Robert F. Kennedy, as attorney general.

Because of the Kennedy style and wit, his live press conferences were among television's most entertaining shows. The president and his wife held glittering parties at the White House at which artists and intellectuals mingled. Kennedy's reading tastes ran more to James Bond novels than to literature, and his musical preferences were for middlebrow popular songs. But thanks to the sophistication of Jacqueline Kennedy, the White House in the early 1960s seemed a bastion of culture. Her redecoration of the executive mansion in the French style of the early nineteenth century won acclaim, as did her televised tour of the White House in 1962. She became an international celebrity as first lady.

In the White House, Kennedy had an affair with Judith Campbell, an intimate of Chicago organized crime figures, and the names of many other young women have been linked with Kennedy in these years. To help his chronic back pain he took amphetamine shots from a doctor of dubious background. The Federal Bureau of Investigation knew of some of these episodes, and there have been hints that the president was under some forms of pressure from the Bureau's director, J. Edgar Hoover, about his dangerous personal conduct. Such revelations—rumors during his years in office—emerged only a decade or more following Kennedy's death.

Along more executive lines, the Food for Peace program, initiated during Eisenhower's administration, was enhanced during the Kennedy years in an effort to solve the problem of agricultural surplus at home while winning friends abroad. Borrowing an idea from Senators Hubert Humphrey and Richard Neuberger, the president announced on March 1, 1961, the formation of the Peace Corps, which would send volunteer workers to underdeveloped countries. He also launched the Alliance for Progress, an ambitious program for economic cooperation and social development. Political commentators wrote of a Hundred Days that would duplicate or even surpass the accomplishments of Franklin Roosevelt's first three months in office.

Then came the Bay of Pigs. During the closing months of Eisenhower's second term, the Central Intelligence Agency had begun training a force of anti-Castro Cubans in a Guatemalan jungle camp. Between his election and inauguration, Kennedy had been informed of the plans to land this force in Cuba in an attempt to overthrow the Cuban dictator, who had taken his island into the Communist camp. Kennedy let the professional intelligence and military men talk him into endorsing the invasion. In April 1961, the force was put ashore at Cuba's Bay of Pigs—and was easily captured by Castro. The debacle humiliated Kennedy at home and abroad. In the

The Cuban exile community in Miami rallies in support of the Bay of Pigs invasion on April 19, 1961. The collapse of the abortive landing was a foreign policy disaster and decisive setback for the presidency.

wake of the disaster, assassination plots went forward against Fidel Castro which the White House seems to have tacitly endorsed. Some of these ventures involved members of organized crime families.

Another crisis loomed in Southeast Asia, where the United States moved close to intervention in Laos but settled for an international conference that established a neutral country.

Kennedy arranged a rendezvous in Vienna in June with Russia's Premier Nikita Khrushchev. The two days of talks were grim and unproductive, serving only to demonstrate the resolution and inflexibility that separated East and West. Khrushchev threatened to isolate the Western enclave in Berlin by signing a separate peace treaty with East Germany the following December. "It will be a cold winter," President Kennedy warned. That August the East Germans sealed off West Berlin by building their notorious wall.

The 1961 visit to Europe also included stops in London and in Paris, where Jacqueline Kennedy dazzled even the austere General de Gaulle. Noting the press coverage given his wife, Kennedy introduced himself at a Paris luncheon as "the man who accompanied Jacqueline Kennedy to Paris."

At home, Kennedy worked for a trade expansion act and a tax cut to stimulate the economy. He also forced steel magnates to retract a threatened price increase.

During the early autumn, it had become evident to American intelligence that Castro was strengthening his ties to the Soviet Union. Aerial photographs taken by a U-2 reconnaissance plane on Sunday, October 14, revealed that the Russians were installing offensive missiles on the island, only ninety miles off the Florida coast. The choices immediately open to the president were two extremes: an aerial strike that would eliminate the missile threat but would risk nuclear war with Russia, or passive acceptance of the Russian challenge.

In a series of agonizing meetings over the next ten days, Kennedy and his associates reached a compromise: a naval quarantine of the island that would prevent further Soviet supplies from reaching Cuba, and a pledge that the United States would not invade if the Russians promised to dismantle and remove the missiles already there. A formula was found to allow the overextended Khrushchev to save face, and the crisis was resolved in America's favor.

Sensitive to the narrowness of his own victory two years earlier, Kennedy had campaigned exhaustively in the early autumn of 1962 congressional elections. And the Democrats made the best midterm showing since 1934 for a party in power, winning four Senate seats and losing only two in the House. Democrats benefited from Kennedy's mastery of the Cuban Missile Crisis.

In the aftermath of Cuban imbroglio, Kennedy moved rapidly for a new understanding with the Soviet Union. In July 1963 a partial nuclear test ban treaty was concluded with Russia and Great Britain. The "hot line," providing instant communication with the Kremlin, was installed in the White House

JACQUELINE KENNEDY ONASSIS

In the year of her husband's election to the presidency, Jacqueline Kennedy admitted that she had been "born and reared a Republican." Then she added, "But you have to have been a Republican to realize how nice it is to be a Democrat."

For a long while Mrs. Kennedy had not found anything "nice" about politics of any kind: She regarded it, early in her marriage to Senator John F. Kennedy of Massachusetts, as "sort of my enemy as far as seeing Jack was concerned." She had been an inquiring photographer for a newspaper when, in 1951, a married couple "who had been shamelessly matchmaking for a year" invited her and the senator to their home for dinner. In 1952, when Jacqueline was in Paris, she ran into the American art critic Bernard Berenson, who told her, "American girls should marry American boys. They wear better." Heeding his advice, she headed home and on September 12, 1953, married Kennedy.

As first lady, Mrs. Kennedy did not merely have admirers; she had fans and became the first international superstar in the White House. Her hairdos set trends, her clothing was copied, and advertisers sought models who looked like her. Powerless to stop the exploitation, she tried to divert attention from herself to her efforts at redecorating the White House.

The first lady did not often campaign with her husband. However, she was with him on the campaign trail when he was shot in Dallas, and she held his shattered head as he died; she even entered the hospital room while the doctors did everything they could think of to save a life that was already gone. Her incredible bravery during the four days that followed provided Americans with a noble model; like her, they took hold of themselves and controlled their grief.

While insistently maintaining her family's privacy after leaving Washington, Mrs. Kennedy was dedicated to preserving the memory of her husband. She supervised plans for a memorial library and sought to block publication of books that she regarded as sensational or that contained intimate details of her life with the late president. Her marriage to Aristotle Onassis in 1968 changed her image from that of a secular saint, but she retained her appeal as a preeminent world figure until her death in 1994.

In October 1963, after registering for class, James Meredith leaves an administration building at the University of Mississippi escorted by U.S. marshals. The effort by James Meredith to enroll at Ole Miss led to a violent confrontation. Civil rights proved to be one of the thorniest issues for the Kennedy administration.

during that summer; and in October the president authorized the sale of United States surplus wheat to the Russians.

The most persistent problem facing Kennedy was civil rights. Not strongly committed to the issue during his congressional days, Kennedy, as president, saw the demand of African-Americans for equal rights as only one of his many domestic concerns. He made a conscious effort to appoint qualified blacks to federal jobs at high levels. But he did not press for the creation of a federal Department of Housing and Urban Development after it became known that Southerners would oppose the appointment of Robert C. Weaver, an African-American, as the new department's secretary. Courting black votes during the 1960 campaign, Kennedy had said that it would take only the "stroke

of a pen" to issue an executive order against racial discrimination in federal housing; in office, it took him 22 months to make that pen stroke. Some disgruntled civil rights supporters sent the White House "pens for Jack." Feeling that universal suffrage was the key to African-American progress, he urged Attorney General Robert F. Kennedy to intervene throughout the South in voting cases.

In September 1962 Kennedy was compelled to send federal marshals to enforce a court order admitting James Meredith, an African-American, as a student at the University of Mississippi. When violence erupted on the campus, the president federalized the National Guard and moved regular troops into the state. Black demonstrations in 1963 further forced Kennedy's hand. In April local authorities in Birmingham, Alabama, used fire hoses and police dogs to break up civil rights marches, and the president again sent in federal troops to restore order. In the following months he helped achieve the peaceful integration of the University of Alabama, reluctantly endorsed the impressive March on Washington by 250,000 civil rights advocates, and pressed for passage of the most comprehensive civil rights law in the nation's history that had been advocated up to that time. In November 1963 the bill passed its first important hurdle when the House Judiciary Committee reported it favorably. (A year later, after Kennedy's death, the measure became the Civil Rights Act of 1964.)

That same month, South Vietnamese President Ngo Dinh Diem was murdered in a U.S.-backed coup that spiraled out of control. Only the preceding spring Secretary of Defense Robert S. McNamara had announced that the United States had "turned the corner" in its efforts to bolster the South Vietnamese regime against Communism, but it now appeared that the war was entering a dangerous phase. In the years after his death, many of Kennedy's friends and some scholars would claim that the president planned to withdraw from Vietnam during a second term. But the evidence for such an intended departure from the war in Vietnam is ambiguous at best.

As 1963 drew to a close, Kennedy began to lay plans for his reelection in November 1964. Thanks to the civil rights bill, he had lost much of the white support in Southern states he had carried in 1960; he knew he would have to make up these electoral votes elsewhere. In September he had made a highly successful "nonpolitical" tour of several Western states. There was special need for him to repair political fences in Texas, and he scheduled for late November a trip that would take him to San Antonio, Houston, Fort Worth, Dallas, and Austin. The president knew of the possibility of danger. In October, United Nations Ambassador Adlai Stevenson, after being vilified by right-wing demonstrators and hit with a sign

in Dallas, warned Kennedy that he might not be safe in Texas.

In August, Mrs. Kennedy had given birth to a boy who had died of respiratory ailments thirty-nine hours later, and since then she had been convalescing. But she decided to accompany her husband to Texas.

On Thursday, November 21, the Kennedys re-

ROBERT S. McNAMARA

Robert Strange McNamara was one of the stars of the Kennedy administration as secretary of defense. Applying to his job new techniques of management, he brought his department under strict civilian control. He led in the diversification of American weapons and military techniques, which resulted in the abandonment of dependence on nuclear weapons and gave presidents new alternatives to draw upon in times of crisis. Born in 1916, McNamara graduated from the University of California and Harvard Business School, served as a statistician for the Air Force in World War II, and became a Ford Motor Company "Whiz Kid" in 1946. Fifteen years later, having been president of Ford for one month, McNamara was asked to take charge of the Defense Department for President John F. Kennedy. On the New Frontier, and later in the Great Society, his hardheadedness and abilities were much admired. The praise was not, however, universal. Some hawkish critics complained that McNamara had opposed rapid escalation of the war in Vietnam, while some doves held the secretary responsible for the continuance of the fighting there. President Lyndon B. Johnson once said, "I thank God every night for Bob McNamara." That sentiment changed when McNamara began to oppose the war behind the scenes, and Johnson moved McNamara to the presidency of the World Bank in 1968. McNamara's memoirs of his years as secretary of defense and his explanation of his role in Vietnam reopened the controversy about his performance during the 1990s.

ceived warm welcomes at San Antonio, Houston, and, late that night, Fort Worth. Before noon the following day they stepped out of the presidential airplane, *Air Force One*, into warm sunshine at Dallas's Love Field. In an open limousine, the Kennedys rode through the city with Governor and Mrs. John B. Connally. "You certainly can't say that the people of Dallas haven't given you a nice welcome," Mrs. Connally turned to say to the Kennedys. Moments later, at approximately 12:30 P.M., the car passed by the

Jacqueline Kennedy and her children, followed by Robert F. Kennedy and Eunice Shriver, walk down the Capitol steps at President Kennedy's funeral. Mrs. Kennedy's dignity and grace gained her worldwide admiration.

Texas School Book Depository, where Lee Harvey Oswald waited with a rifle at a sixth-floor window.

A first bullet pierced the president's neck; a second shattered his brain. Rushed to Parkland Hospital, Kennedy was declared dead shortly after 1 P.M.

For most of the next horrifying four days, millions around the globe sat in shock by their radios and television sets to listen to and watch the final scenes of the tragedy. Oswald was captured and, on Sunday, November 24, as witnessed by millions of television viewers, was killed by Dallas nightclub owner Jack Ruby.

World leaders and royalty came to Washington for the somber state funeral on November 25. But the most commanding presence that day was the black-shrouded widow, who conducted herself with unflinching dignity during the harrowing hours of the procession from the White House, the funeral mass, the burial on a hillside at Arlington National Cemetery, the lighting of the eternal flame over her husband's grave, and the reception later for the visiting dignitaries. Still Americans continued to wonder who was behind Kennedy's assassination. A majority never accepted the official findings that Oswald had acted alone.

For the first decade after Kennedy's death, his memory remained bright, especially after Jacqueline cited the musical *Camelot* to cast a retrospective glow around her husband and his deeds. In the 1970s, the legend began to crack as revelations about Kennedy's sexual adventures, the murder attempts against Castro, and other personal and political frailties burst into the tabloids. By the eve of the twenty-first century, scholars were struggling to see Kennedy whole. He used tough and even illicit methods to get and keep power and temporized on civil rights and Vietnam. But he was also a leader who guided the world through the most dangerous crisis of the Cold War, who was the architect of the Civil Rights Act of 1964, and who inspired a generation of Americans to think better of themselves, their country, and their political system.

—JOSEPH L. GARDNER,
revised by LEWIS L. GOULD

LYNDON BAINES JOHNSON

SO CLOSE TO GREATNESS

Decades after his death, Lyndon Johnson remains the subject of intense political debate. Admirers laud his support for civil rights and the skills and vision that created Great Society programs like Medicare. Conservative critics blame LBJ's programs for shredding the American social fabric and worsening the problems they were supposed to solve. Detractors on the left cite the Vietnam War and its tragic impact on Americans. With his unquenchable yearning for public affection, LBJ would have preferred to be universally loved but he would probably be grateful not to be ignored.

When Lyndon was born to Samuel Ealy Johnson, Jr., and Rebekah Baines Johnson on August 27, 1908, near Stonewall, Texas, his grandfather is reported to have told neighbors, "A United States senator was born this morning. . . ." Johnson came naturally to a political career. His father had served in the Texas legislature, and his grandfather had sought a legislative seat as a Populist candidate in the 1890s. His mother's father had also served in the legislature and had been secretary of state for Texas.

Lyndon Johnson grew up in the Texas Hill Country. Until he was in his teens, his father was a lawmaker, the publisher of a local newspaper, and an active dealer in real estate. The agricultural depression of the early 1920s reduced Sam Johnson's holdings, but Lyndon's father was never as poor as his son later claimed. The younger Johnson also liked to boast of all the politicians who came through his hometown of Johnson City to see his father. Some of these stories reflected Johnson's lifelong tendency to embroider the truth.

"Thin as a willow fishing pole," Lyndon at fifteen already stood more than six feet tall. He was an indifferent student, and after graduating from high school, he went West. "Up and down the coast I tramped, washing dishes, waiting on tables, doing farmwork," he recalled, ". . . and always growing thinner and more homesick." Back home after several years, he used his father's influence to get work on a road gang where, harnessed to mules, he worked a buck scraper.

Weary of manual labor, Johnson took his mother's advice and entered Southwest Texas State Teachers College, in San Marcos, in February 1927. He majored in history, joined the debating team, and bulldozed his way to political primacy on campus. To finance his way through college, he spent a year in Cotulla, in south Texas, teaching Mexican-American children. The experience shaped his view of the effects of poverty on the nation's minorities. He graduated with a B.S. degree in 1930.

After college, Johnson taught public speaking at Houston's Sam Houston High School. When Richard M. Kleberg, a wealthy South Texas conservative, won election to Congress in 1931, Johnson lobbied for a job as his secretary. Johnson spent four years in Washington, D.C., learning the ropes of national politics. He was elected leader of the Little Congress, an informal group of House secretaries.

On November 17, 1934, after a whirlwind courtship, he married Claudia Alta Taylor (nicknamed Lady Bird by a family cook), the daughter of a well-to-do East Texas landowner. They had two daughters, Lynda Bird and Luci Baines. Living with Lyndon Johnson proved to be, as she put it, "a great adventure," and she became the ideal political partner for the mercurial Johnson.

In the spring of 1935 Johnson returned to Texas as state director of the National Youth Administration, a New Deal program. Under Johnson's efficient leadership, the NYA helped construct roadside parks, created libraries and schools for Texas students, and operated quietly to expand opportunities for black Texans during a segregated era. His tenure as NYA director widened his political base across the state as he prepared to seek elective office.

Early in 1937, the incumbent United States Representative for the Tenth District in Texas died of a

The day after his election victory, in 1964, President Johnson lassoes a Hereford at his Texas ranch.

Lyndon Johnson and his new bride, Claudia Alta "Lady Bird" Taylor Johnson, pose near the Capitol shortly after their wedding in 1934.

of twenty-eight. On May 11, after recuperating from the emergency appendectomy for which he was hospitalized two days before the election, he met with the president and emerged as a Roosevelt protégé. The president helped the young Texan get a seat on the House Naval Affairs Committee. Johnson, a friend recalled, was "a real pusher . . . maybe a little too cocky . . . but he did get things done."

Over the next four years, Johnson worked hard for his new constituency. He obtained millions of federal dollars for local projects and pressed successfully for funds to construct a series of dams on the Colorado River that provided rural electrification for the Hill Country. He was also instrumental in locating a naval air-training base in Corpus Christi and shipyards in Houston and Orange, all outside his district. As Lady Bird said of her tireless husband, "Lyndon behaves as if there were no tomorrow coming and he had to do everything today."

When Vice President John Nance Garner ran for president against Roosevelt in 1940, Johnson took the risky step of supporting the administration and opposing his fellow Texan. He not only backed the president but he also headed the House Democratic Congressional Campaign Committee. Johnson's ability to raise money from Texas oil interests helped the Democrats to retain control of the House.

In April 1941 Johnson made his first bid for a seat in the United States Senate when the incumbent died. Announcing his candidacy from the steps of the White House, Johnson found that his chief opponent would be the popular Texas governor, W. Lee O'Daniel. During the campaign he strongly endorsed Roosevelt's program of military preparedness and an end to isolationism. If war should come, he pledged, and "my vote must be cast to send your boy to war, that day Lyndon Johnson will leave his seat in Congress to go with him." Johnson lost the election by 1,311 votes, amid charges that the O'Daniel forces had manipulated the vote in East Texas.

heart attack. In the special election that followed, Johnson ran as a champion of Franklin D. Roosevelt and the New Deal. He endorsed the president's plan to expand the Supreme Court. Financing his campaign with some of Lady Bird's inheritance, Johnson out-worked and out-spent his opponents, and on April 10, 1937, he was elected to Congress at the age

After the Japanese attack on Pearl Harbor, Johnson made good on his 1941 election pledge and went on active duty in the Navy. In May 1942 Lieutenant Commander Johnson landed on New Caledonia, an island off the east coast of Australia, on a special presidential mission to assess American morale and military strength in the Pacific combat zone. In June, Johnson boarded a B-26 bomber en route from Port Moresby to a mission over the Japanese air base at Lae, near Salamaua. When Japanese fighters attacked, a running fight ensued in which Johnson's plane was badly damaged. General Douglas MacArthur awarded Johnson the Silver Star Medal for showing "marked coolness in spite of the hazard involved."

When Roosevelt ordered all congressmen serving in the armed forces to return home in July 1942, Johnson assumed the chairmanship of a subcommittee of the Naval Affairs Committee. Even with that powerful position and the work he did for Texas, Johnson faced opposition at home from an increasingly conservative Democratic party leadership. As he saw the state swing to the right, he accommodated the new realities. After the end of the war, he supported the controversial Taft-Hartley Act to curb the power of labor unions and voted to override President Harry S. Truman's veto of that legislation.

In 1948 Johnson again sought a Senate seat, facing a conservative former governor of Texas, Coke Stevenson, in the decisive Democratic primary. Johnson emphasized his relative youth and his support for a stronger defense and an American role in the world. He also charged that the "big labor racketeers, the labor dictatorship" opposed him because he had voted for "the anti-Communist Taft-Hartley bill." Johnson—taking a position he would change in later years—attacked Truman's civil rights program as "a farce and a sham—an effort to set up a police state in the guise of liberty." His anti–civil rights position was politically necessary in Texas, but it gave him a reputation for supporting segregation that would limit his presidential chances within the national Democratic party.

The inconclusive result of the first primary in 1948 pitted Johnson and Stevenson in a runoff. In that contest Johnson edged past the former governor by a mere 87 votes. The Stevenson forces charged that ballot boxes in South Texas had been stuffed for Johnson. A bitter series of court battles ensued, but in the end Johnson was certified as the Democratic candidate. He was then easily sent to the United States Senate in the 1948 general election.

BIOGRAPHICAL FACTS

BIRTH: Near Stonewall, Tex., Aug. 27, 1908

ANCESTRY: English

FATHER: Samuel Ealy Johnson, Jr.; b. Buda, Tex., Oct. 11, 1877; d. Austin, Tex., Oct. 11, 1937

FATHER'S OCCUPATIONS: State representative; publisher; landowner

MOTHER: Rebekah Baines Johnson; b. McKinney, Tex., June 26, 1881; d. Austin, Tex., Sept. 12, 1958

BROTHER: Sam Houston (1914–1978)

SISTERS: Rebekah Luruth (1910–1978); Josefa Hermine (1912–1961); Lucia Huffman (1916–1997)

WIFE: Claudia Alta "Lady Bird" Taylor; b. Karnack, Tex., Dec. 22, 1912

MARRIAGE: San Antonio, Tex., Nov. 17, 1934

CHILDREN: Lynda Bird (1944–); Luci Baines (1947–)

EDUCATION: Johnson City High School; Southwest Texas State Teachers College (B.S., 1930); attended Georgetown University Law School

RELIGIOUS AFFILIATION: Disciples of Christ

OCCUPATION BEFORE PRESIDENCY: Teacher

PREPRESIDENTIAL OFFICES: National Youth Administration director in Texas; U.S. congressman; U.S. senator; U.S. vice president

MILITARY SERVICE: Lt. comdr., comdr., U.S. Naval Reserve (active duty 1941–1942)

AGE AT INAUGURATION: 55

OCCUPATION AFTER PRESIDENCY: Retired

DEATH: Stonewall, Tex., Jan. 22, 1973

PLACE OF BURIAL: LBJ Ranch, Stonewall, Tex.

Johnson took to the United States Senate immediately, and his rise in that body was a rapid one. By 1952 he was Minority Whip, in 1953 Minority Leader, and after the Democrats regained control of the Senate in 1954, the Majority Leader in 1955. Throughout, Johnson made it clear that he intended to work with President Dwight Eisenhower. "All of us," he explained, "are Americans before we are members of any political organization."

Johnson was not only leader of the Senate Democrats in voting and in debate; because of the many friendships and alliances he had built and because his position made him chair of three major Democratic caucus committees, he was master of the machinery that ran the Senate. With the agreement of the leader of the conservative Senate Democrats, Richard Russell of Georgia, with whom Johnson had carefully built a close relationship, he broke the seniority rule for committee appointments. This allowed Johnson to win the allegiance of newer senators who were grateful for the chance to have meaningful committee assignments. The historian Louis W. Koenig calls Johnson "one of the most illustrious floor leaders in Senate history," a master architect of political accommodation who commanded "a relentless, overpowering persuasiveness. . . ."

Johnson achieved much in the Senate during his term as Majority Leader. He did so despite suffering a serious heart attack in July 1955. Johnson called the attack "about as bad as you can have, and live." He stopped smoking, lost weight, and was back in the Senate six months later. For the rest of his public career, Johnson and his wife monitored his health and were acutely aware that men in his family rarely lived beyond their mid-sixties.

Two Johnson legislative accomplishments were presiding over the censure of Senator Joseph R. McCarthy of Wisconsin in 1954 while Minority Leader and the passage of the Civil Rights Act of 1957 as Majority Leader. The rebuke to the Commu-nist-hunting McCarthy was a final blow to that senator's demagogic power. The passage of the first civil rights legislation in eighty-two years, which provided new voter registration safeguards for African-Americans, established Johnson's credentials as a national leader and began his transformation into a champion of civil rights. He secured passage of a second civil rights law in 1960 as well.

In foreign affairs, Johnson backed Eisenhower's policies, with one significant exception. When Eisenhower considered sending American planes to aid the beleaguered French forces at Dien Bien Phu in Indochina in 1954, Johnson demanded that the consent of the British be obtained before any intervention occurred. When the British turned down the proposal, the idea was abandoned. However, it was Johnson who would later build up the American presence in Southeast Asia.

Johnson very much wanted to be president but could not on his own overcome the burden of his roots in Texas and the South. He made a favorite son's race in 1956 but gained little support outside of his home state. In 1960 he tried to win the nomination by emphasizing his skills as a Senate leader and his endorsement by fellow senators. These tactics proved ineffective against the shrewder, better financed, and more nationally based campaign of John F. Kennedy. After Kennedy had secured the nomination in July 1960, he asked Johnson to be his running mate in one of the great surprises in the political history of that era. Yet from Johnson's perspective the decision to run with Kennedy made sense. Aware that he could not secure a Democratic nomination on his own, Johnson decided that the vice presidency, for all of its frustrations, offered more promise than being Majority Leader in a Democratic administration. Kennedy needed Johnson to carry the South, and his appearance on the ticket could mean victory.

The vice presidential years were a time of bitterness and frustration for Johnson. He served as a presidential emissary abroad, making several celebrated trips, and worked in a variety of assignments on space and civil rights programs that kept him busy but far away from the centers of real power. Johnson worried that he might not be asked to remain on the ticket in 1964.

Then came the trip to Texas in November 1963 and the sudden tragedy of Kennedy's assassination in Dallas. Lady Bird Johnson remembered seeing in "the president's car a bundle of pink, just like a drift of blossoms, lying on the back seat. It was Mrs. Kennedy lying over the president's body." Two hours after Kennedy's death, Johnson stood solemnly aboard the presidential plane, *Air Force One*, still on the ground at Dallas's Love Field, and took the oath of office as the thirty-sixth president. The transfer of executive power swiftly achieved, he left little doubt of his determination to demonstrate that "our institutions cannot be disrupted by an assassin's bullet."

Johnson got off to an impressive start as president. He told a joint session of Congress, "All I have I would have given gladly not to be standing here today." But John Kennedy's dream, he declared, would not die. Kennedy, Johnson recalled, had said, "'Let us begin.' Today in this moment of new resolve," Johnson told Congress, "I would say to all my fellow Americans, let us continue." Then Lyndon Baines Johnson, son of the South, appealed to Congress: "No memorial oration or eulogy," he declared, "could more eloquently honor President Kennedy's memory than the earliest possible passage of the civil rights bill for which he fought so long." In a subsequent address to the Congress, the new president asked for a declaration of unconditional war on poverty in America.

During his first year in office, Johnson lived up to his reputation as a master of the legislative process. In a rare display of bipartisan unity, the Eighty-eighth Congress passed the Civil Rights Act of 1964— including commands to integrate public accommodations and insure fair employment practices.

After accepting John F. Kennedy's nomination to be on the Democratic ticket, Lyndon B. Johnson holds a newspaper announcing his selection in 1960.

If the Civil Rights Act was the most dramatic, it was by no means the sole achievement of Johnson's first twelve months in the White House. Johnson asked for and got laws authorizing the tax cut requested by Kennedy; federal aid to mass transit facilities; a huge anti-poverty program; and wheat and cotton price support, including a food-stamp program which provided food to the needy in urban areas. The Job Corps, designed to train young Americans and employ them in public projects, was also established.

Despite these legislative successes, from the moment of his accession to the presidency, Johnson labored under a great handicap. He governed in a climate of national grief and in the shadow of a handsome young president who attracted immense popularity in death. Johnson labored, too, under the bitter fact that Kennedy had been killed in his home state during an attempt to bridge a Democratic schism there. As the ballets and recitals gave way to the Johnsons' barbecues on the banks of the Pedernales River, critics concerned more with style than with achievement belittled the president. On at least one occasion, LBJ audibly bridled at his critics' reverence for JFK: "They say Jack Kennedy had style, but I'm the one who got the bills passed."

Foreign policy was an area where Johnson had less visible expertise, and in the first months of his presidency he faced new challenges in the Caribbean. When Fidel Castro demanded the return to Cuba of the United States naval base at Guantanamo and shut off the installation's water, Johnson calmly ordered the base to create its own water supply. Under pressure, Castro turned the water back on.

Johnson acted with similar restraint when President Roberto Chiari of Panama—spurred by nationalist rioting in the Canal Zone—demanded renegotiation of the Panama Canal treaty and severed diplomatic relations with Washington. After tempers on both sides had cooled, Johnson announced that a new treaty would be negotiated.

The one issue that overshadowed Lyndon Johnson's entire presidency was the war for control of South Vietnam. Johnson inherited the situation from not fewer than three previous administrations. In 1950 President Truman had pledged American aid to the French and their Vietnamese friends in fighting the Communists. In 1954, after rebels dealt a catastrophic defeat at Dien Bien Phu, a nineteen-nation conference at Geneva divided French Indochina into Cambodia, Laos, South Vietnam, and Communist-controlled North Vietnam. The Eisenhower administration, while not officially a signatory of the Geneva Accords, issued a unilateral statement supporting them, thus endorsing the conference's call for the eventual unification of Vietnam through free elections and an interdict on foreign military intervention there. Eisenhower made a more specific commitment to South Vietnam's Premier Ngo Dinh Diem in a 1954 letter pledging to "assist the government of [South] Vietnam in developing and maintaining a strong viable state, capable of resisting attempted subversion, or aggression through military means," adding the condition that Saigon make every effort to instigate "needed reforms." When Eisen-

President Johnson consults with Martin Luther King, Jr., in 1966. By then the urban riots and the Vietnam War had already strained their relationship.

hower left the presidency, fewer than one thousand American advisers were present in South Vietnam aiding in the fight against Vietcong guerrillas.

Under the Kennedy administration, the United States commitment to South Vietnam in military advisers and personnel rose to twenty-five thousand. This increase induced a counter-escalation of opposition forces and of activities by the National Liberation Front—the Vietcong's political arm—which had been founded in 1960. Johnson saw himself as carrying out Kennedy's legacy in Vietnam. Kennedy had warned that American withdrawal would be "a great mistake."

From the outset of his administration, Johnson decided that he could not afford to allow Vietnam "to go the way China went." If that happened the Democrats would face Republican attacks from the right. Thus, given his commitment to the premises of containment, Johnson saw no way out of Vietnam through a negotiated settlement and withdrawal from Vietnam. President Johnson maintained, as late as February 1964, that the Vietnam War was "first and foremost a contest to be won by the government and the people of that country for themselves." In August 1964, however, when North Vietnamese torpedo boats allegedly fired twice on United States destroyers cruising eleven miles off-shore in the Gulf of Tonkin, Johnson ordered retaliatory strikes on North Vietnamese installations. On August 5 he sought and received from Congress a resolution authorizing the president "to take all necessary measures to repel any armed attack against the forces of the United States and to prevent further aggression." President Johnson would treat the Tonkin Gulf Resolution as an open-ended authorization for him to do whatever was necessary to achieve success in Southeast Asia.

In the presidential campaign of 1964, Johnson faced the weakest electoral challenger the Republicans could have nominated: Senator Barry Goldwater of Arizona. For his running mate, Johnson selected the liberal Senator Hubert H. Humphrey of Minnesota.

Johnson rejected all attempts to have Robert F. Kennedy, whom he despised, go on the ticket with him. Johnson knew that Vietnam was a potential trouble spot for his reelection campaign, and so in the fall of 1964, he rejected escalation of the war. Of Goldwater, Johnson and the Democrats said that his simplistic military solutions would plunge the nation into nuclear holocaust and that his domestic program would abolish such commonly accepted benefits as Social Security. In city after city, Johnson deplored Goldwater's candid intention to pursue the war in Vietnam toward all-out victory. Repeatedly Johnson assured Americans: "We don't want our American boys to do the fighting for Asian boys. We don't want to get involved in a nation [China] with 700,000,000 people and get tied down in a land war in Asia." Johnson and Humphrey won the election by the largest popular margin in American history up to that time, 43,129,566 votes to 27,178,188. Ominously for the Democrats, however, the Republican candidate carried five Southern states where the Civil Rights Act of 1964 was unpopular.

In accepting the Democratic nomination in 1964, Johnson had said, "This nation, this generation, in this hour has man's first chance to build a great society, a place where the meaning of man's life matches the marvel of man's labor." In January 1965 he pledged new aid to education and to urban renewal, a war on disease and on air and water pollution, aid to depressed areas, and an end to voting restrictions based on color. In the area of the environment, Johnson and his wife were important innovators who set the stage for the heightened interest in ecological issues during the succeeding decades. Under the Johnson administration more than three hundred environmental laws were passed, including the Wild Rivers Act, Clear Water Law, and Clean Air Law.

Again Johnson's leadership of Congress was productive. Outstanding among his achievements were laws authorizing unprecedented, massive federal aid to elementary and secondary schools; Medicare, which provided medical aid to those over sixty-five through the Social Security system; federal aid to the deprived Appalachian states; liberalized immigration; housing; and the creation of a Department of Housing and Urban Development. Under Johnson, too, America surpassed the Russians in the space race, sending one astronaut on a space walk and, in 1968, two men to circle the moon. And under Johnson the states ratified the Twenty-fifth Amendment, which provided for an orderly transfer of presidential power in the event of presidential incapacitation, resignation, or removal from office, and granted the president the power to name—with the approval of Congress—a new vice president in the event of a vacancy.

The president's signal achievement was the passage of the Voting Rights Act of 1965. In a dramatic nighttime personal appearance before Congress, Johnson urged passage of a law authorizing federal voting registrars to assure electoral justice to blacks in areas where they were denied the vote. The African-American cause, he declared, "must be our cause too.

Because it's not just Negroes, but really it's all of us who must overcome the crippling legacy of bigotry and injustice." Then Johnson gave presidential voice to the hymn of civil rights marchers: "And we *shall* overcome."

While the Congress in 1965 was one of the most productive in history, the Great Society began to encounter problems at home and abroad by the time the year closed. A Caribbean crisis erupted in April 1965 when a revolt broke out in the Dominican Republic. President Johnson sent some twenty thousand troops to restore order. He subsequently justified this extreme action by insisting that "we don't propose to sit here in our rocking chair with our hands folded and let the Communists set up any government in the Western Hemisphere." But Communist involvement was questionable, and Johnson's response to the uprising badly damaged United States prestige abroad.

The war in Vietnam, however, posed the major challenge to Johnson's presidential leadership. On February 7, 1965, when the South Vietnamese Communists attacked an American military installation at Pleiku, Johnson ordered air strikes on North Vietnam that, as time passed, increased in intensity. The goal, Johnson said, was to bring the other side to the negotiating table and avoid a humiliating American withdrawal.

If the rationale for the bombing was to force the North Vietnamese and their allies in South Vietnam to negotiate, it did not work, and soon the administration had to introduce ground troops into South Vietnam. A process of escalation had begun that, over the next two years, would see half a million American troops engaged in the Vietnam War. Casualties mounted, and draft calls increased. Soon domestic protests spread as young people resisted involvement in a distant and unpopular conflict. By November 1965 the United States had committed 165,700 troops to Vietnam. Whereas 146 Americans were killed in battle in 1964, 1,104 died in 1965. In 1966,

5,008 Americans were killed and 30,093 wounded.

During 1966 the twin problems of domestic unrest and a foreign war tormented Johnson. At home, riots in cities such as Los Angeles indicated how unhappy African-Americans were with the pace of change. The disturbances alienated white voters and built support for the Republicans. Meanwhile, the war in Vietnam continued.

In that war, Johnson followed a strategy that increased the military pressure on North Vietnam in the hopes that negotiations would ensue. The president found himself criticized on the right for not pursuing the war vigorously enough and on the left for fighting it at all. Aware of the dangers of Soviet or Chinese intervention, Johnson was unwilling to allow the military unlimited support for an elusive victory.

THURGOOD MARSHALL

Thurgood Marshall built a remarkable legal career on his conviction that all forms of racial segregation were unconstitutional. Born in Baltimore in 1908, he was educated in segregated schools. After his graduation from Howard University Law School in 1933, he established a practice and specialized in civil rights cases. In his capacity as special counsel to the National Association for the Advancement of Colored People, Marshall led the assault on state segregation laws, especially in the field of education. He argued thirty-two cases before the United States Supreme Court and won all but three of them. As a result of his efforts, Virginia's law ordering segregated seating in buses was declared to be unconstitutional when interstate travel was involved, and Texas blacks were guaranteed the right to vote in primaries and to serve on juries. His most dramatic success occurred in 1954, when the Court ruled that separate educational facilities were inherently unequal, and that segregated schools were therefore unconstitutional. In 1961 Marshall was appointed by President John F. Kennedy to the United States Court of Appeals. He was named solicitor general five years later, and served in that post until 1967, when President Lyndon B. Johnson selected Marshall to become the first African-American justice of the Supreme Court. Marshall was a leading liberal voice on the Court until his retirement in 1991. He died in 1993.

The result was a stalemate that pleased no one. Without the certainty of ultimate success, Johnson lacked the capacity to persuade his fellow citizens to endure a protracted conflict.

Meanwhile, the political base of the Democratic party deteriorated. Student protests against the war, urban rioting, and a rising crime rate validated the popular impression that the Johnson administration did not fight law-breaking effectively. Underneath these feelings lay white unhappiness with black advances, a sentiment on which the Republicans and Alabama Governor George C. Wallace capitalized. In the 1966 elections, the Republicans gained seats in the House and Senate as the Democrats engaged in factional infighting.

Despite the darkening prospects in Vietnam, Johnson had some successes in 1967. He held a summit with Soviet leader Aleksey Kosygin at Glassboro State College in New Jersey, and he named Thurgood Marshall to be the first African-American on the Supreme Court. But the deadlocked war in Vietnam remained the largest burden on Johnson's presidency. By the end of the year, the president faced a challenge from within his own party as Senator Eugene McCarthy of Minnesota announced his candidacy for the Democratic nomination. For the moment, Johnson's most feared rival, Robert Kennedy, stayed on the sidelines. The news from Vietnam was grim: 9,353 Americans died in 1967 —more than half the total of 15,997 killed in the war up to the end of that year, and nearly twice the number killed in 1966.

Late in January 1968 the Vietcong attacked five major South Vietnamese cities with unprecedented force, assaulting even the American embassy in Saigon in what came to be called the Tet Offensive. In twelve days of fighting, 973 Americans, 2,119 South Vietnamese, and an estimated 30,795 enemy soldiers were killed. The administration was assailed for underestimating enemy strength and will and for overestimating the prospects for an Allied victory. Nor did the seizure of the American intelligence ship *Pueblo* by North Korea bolster American pride or Johnson's prestige. In March, Senator McCarthy won a stunning 42.4 percent of the vote and twenty of the twenty-four delegates in New Hampshire's Democratic primary. McCarthy's showing prompted Senator Kennedy to challenge LBJ for the nomination. Kennedy swiftly took to the campaign trail, condemning the president's war policy as "bankrupt."

But LBJ had a surprise of his own. On March 31 Johnson shocked the world by announcing that he would neither seek nor accept his party's nomination in 1968. He said that he did not wish to permit the presidency to become involved in the partisan divisions of the political year. He also announced the suspension of bombing over 76 percent of North Vietnam and again invited Hanoi to the peace table.

Johnson had set the stage for his departure from politics, but his problems continued. During his last year in office, he faced the assassinations of Martin Luther King, Jr., and Robert Kennedy, and riots in Washington, D.C. In October the long-running negotiations with North Vietnam seemed to offer the prospect of meaningful peace talks. In return, Johnson was ready to offer an end to American bombing. The prospective deal fell through, in part because of Republican encouragement to South Vietnam not to take part in the talks. Without that last-minute help, the Democratic nominee, Hubert Humphrey, lost narrowly to Richard Nixon in the 1968 election.

Johnson retired to his ranch, where he wrote his memoirs, *The Vantage Point*. He began smoking again, put on weight, and suffered from heart problems that plagued his final years. He died at the LBJ Ranch on January 22, 1973.

As Lyndon B. Johnson listens to a tape sent from Vietnam by his son-in-law, Marine Captain Charles Robb, in 1968, he seems to be bearing the full weight of the war in Southeast Asia.

Lyndon B. Johnson was a powerful force for change in race relations and in the way American society was organized. Many of his Great Society programs such as Medicare and Head Start endure. Yet his reputation would always be shadowed by the Vietnam War and the social upheaval that followed in its path. Johnson had hoped to stand in the front rank among all presidents, along with his hero Franklin D. Roosevelt. His failure in Vietnam left him short of greatness. But his passionate convictions about education, health, and poverty, his legislative mastery, and the successes of the Great Society have elevated his reputation with the passage of time.

—*LEWIS L. GOULD*

Richard Nixon once offered an opinion of how best to relate to the American voter: "You've got to be a little evil to understand those people out there." The question of Nixon's own morality divides historical appraisals of the man and his impact on the White House and the country. Opinions are so split about the true nature of Nixon's character that any kind of consensus about his presidency has proven elusive.

Like many modern presidents, Nixon had an inscrutable core that few people, even his family, ever penetrated. His aide, Bryce Harlow, theorized that "as a young person, he was hurt very deeply by somebody he trusted . . . a sweetheart, a parent, a dear friend, someone he deeply trusted. He never got over it and never trusted anybody again." Nixon himself once told an interviewer, "A major public figure is a lonely man. You cannot enjoy the luxury of intimate personal friendships." He lamented that he was "an introvert in an extrovert's profession." Yet despite the stunted quality of his emotional life, Nixon had the capacity to rise to the top of American politics.

He was born in Yorba Linda, California, on January 9, 1913, to Frank and Hannah Milhous Nixon, a Quaker couple. Despite Frank Nixon's best efforts, he never attained economic security from his various money-making endeavors. Richard Nixon overcame the handicaps that life imposed with a combination of a quick mind and dogged hard work. He enrolled in nearby Whittier College, where he made strong grades and was also a fourth-string substitute on the football team. Nixon then was accepted at the Duke University Law School with a scholarship. He received his law degree, finishing third in his class, and wanted to join the Federal Bureau of Investigation but was rejected. He practiced law in Whittier from 1937 to 1942. In 1940 he married Thelma Catherine "Pat" Ryan. They had two daughters, Julie and Tricia.

When World War II began, Nixon worked in the Office of Price Administration where he developed a lifelong distaste for government bureaucracy. Facing the draft and eager to serve as an officer rather than in the ranks, he joined the Navy in the summer of 1942. He spent four years in the service and rose to the rank of lieutenant commander. He did not see combat; stationed in the South Pacific backwaters, he played poker to pass the time.

After the war ended in 1945, local Republicans in southern California asked him to run for Congress against the five-term liberal incumbent, Jerry Voorhis. Nixon responded eagerly that he would wage "an aggressive, vigorous campaign on a platform of practical liberalism." To exploit the fears of Communism then growing in the United States, the Nixon campaign phoned voters and asked: "Did you know that Jerry Voorhis is a Communist?" The Congressman was not a Communist, but the charge hurt his chances. Nixon won the race and in 1950 defeated Helen Gahagan Douglas for the United States Senate. Again, a false connection between Douglas and Communism was alleged. The Republicans called her "the Pink Lady," and Nixon ads exhorted "Fight the Red fear with a fearless man—Dick Nixon."

Congressman Nixon gained national attention when, as a member of the House Un-American Activities Committee, he was instrumental in developing espionage charges against the former Roosevelt-appointed State Department official, Alger Hiss. The 1950 conviction of Hiss on perjury charges associated Nixon with the exposure of Communists, but it also convinced many Democrats and intellectuals that the congressman was unprincipled in his use of the Communist label.

By 1952 Nixon had shaped events leading to the Republican National Convention to make himself attractive to Dwight D. Eisenhower as a potential running mate. Nixon gained a spot on the Republican ticket because his home state of California held a

Vice President Richard Nixon waves to the crowd during a 1960 rally at the Blackstone Hotel in Chicago, Illinois.

had not profited personally from the fund. In the course of the broadcast, he said that he would not return the little dog "Checkers" that "a man down in Texas" had sent the Nixon daughters. He also noted that his wife, unlike some Democrats who had received fur coats from lobbyists, "doesn't have a mink coat. But she does have a respectable Republican cloth coat. And I always tell her that she'd look good in anything." That episode caused the address to become famous as the "Checkers speech." The public response was overwhelmingly favorable. Although skeptical of Nixon's fitness, Eisenhower accepted the inevitable and greeted his running mate during an airport visit with the phrase "You're my boy."

During his eight years as vice president, Nixon solidified his reputation as a tough campaigner by acting as the partisan voice of the administration. He traveled extensively for the White House and gained politically from two episodes abroad. The first was in Caracas, Venezuela, when he showed courage while an angry mob stoned his car. The second was the celebrated "kitchen debate" with Premier Nikita Khrushchev in Moscow when he defended the United States from verbal attack while inside a model of an American house. Nixon brought real substance to the role of vice president, especially when Eisenhower suffered a heart attack in 1955, ileitis in 1956, and a stroke in 1957. As a result of his standing within his own party, Nixon became the front-runner and gained the Republican presidential nomination in 1960.

In the election campaign Nixon faced the young and energetic Democratic nominee, John F. Kennedy. Kennedy did well in their series of four televised debates, while Nixon showed to less advantage in their first encounter. Looking weary from a recent illness and with a heavy beard shadow, Nixon seemed uneasy in front of the camera. Less comfortable than Kennedy with television, Nixon resented the favorable way the press treated his glamorous opponent.

large total of electoral votes, and because his youth offset Eisenhower's age. Nixon's strong credentials as an anti-Communist also appealed to the men around Eisenhower. He was, they agreed, "a man who can stand up and speak."

Almost at once Nixon faced a grave political and personal crisis. He had been the beneficiary of a fund of $18,000 raised to help defray his expenses as a senator. The fund was legal but dubious in the middle of a campaign where the Republicans were charging President Harry S. Truman and the Democrats with corruption. Nixon went on national television to deny allegations of wrongdoing and to show that he

The narrow defeat in the 1960 contest, where he lost by 118,574 popular votes, permanently rankled Nixon. Privately he insisted that the Kennedys had "stolen victory" from him by vote fraud in Illinois and Texas.

Two years after losing the presidency, Nixon ran for governor of California and again went down to defeat. On the day after the election, he went before the press and blamed them for his setbacks and poor public image. He told them that they would not "have Nixon to kick around anymore." He moved his family to New York and engaged in a lucrative law practice. His political career seemed over. But the landslide defeat of Barry Goldwater in 1964, followed by President Johnson's championship of an increasingly unpopular war in Vietnam, revived Nixon's political fortunes. He campaigned for Republican candidates in the 1966 midterm elections, traveled to showcase his knowledge of world affairs, and was once again a leading figure for the Republican nomination in 1968. He beat back challenges by governors Nelson Rockefeller of New York and Ronald Reagan of California and was selected on the first ballot. As his running mate, Nixon chose Spiro T. Agnew, the governor of Maryland, to enhance the ticket's appeal in the suburbs and border states. No investigation of Agnew's past was made at the time.

In the presidential campaign, Nixon faced Democrat Hubert Humphrey and the third-party challenge of Alabama governor George C. Wallace. Nixon indicated that he would be able to end the unpopular war in Vietnam, though he did not say he had "a secret plan." Because of the American people's growing disappointment with the Democrats over the issues of race and war, as well as the rising tide of conservatism in the country, Nixon gained a narrow popular-vote victory over Humphrey. Once elected president, he pledged in his victory speech in New York that his aim would be, as one campaign sign stated, "to bring us together."

In fact Nixon approached the presidency in a quite different spirit. He was convinced that he faced enemies everywhere in Congress, the media, and the Democratic party. In such a hostile environment, he and his associates had to be ready to wage political warfare. A mood of resentment and suspicion pervaded the Nixon White House from its earliest days.

The new first lady, Pat Nixon, was a more genial and gracious figure than her husband. She spent a

President Nixon and his wife, Pat, stroll on the beach near their home in San Clemente, California. The Nixon White House was very adept in creating photo opportunities that showcased the president and his wife.

great deal of time answering personally the letters that people wrote her. In addition, she pursued a redecoration of the White House that rivaled in scope and importance Jacqueline Kennedy's accomplishments.

The cabinet that Nixon assembled included such figures as Melvin Laird, a Wisconsin congressman, as secretary of defense, Nixon's old friend William Rogers as secretary of state, and George P. Shultz as secretary of labor. In foreign policy the real power resided with Nixon's national security adviser, Henry A. Kissinger. Nixon also looked to Democrats and Washington outsiders such as Daniel Patrick Moynihan and John Connally for stimulation and ideas. Inside the White House, the two most powerful men were H. R. "Bob" Haldeman, the White House chief of staff, and John Ehrlichman, who oversaw domestic policy. Haldeman became known as Nixon's "S.O.B." for his strong management of the flow of paper and people to the president. Together the two men, because of their German descent, were described as "the Berlin Wall."

In office, Nixon preferred to run the presidency from a distance. He disliked personal encounters and confrontations, and he strove to minimize conflict in order to retain decision-making powers. Secretive and suspicious, Nixon trusted almost none of his aides and often criticized them behind their backs. There arose within the White House a culture of mutual distrust and a desire to please the president at any cost that laid the foundations for the crimes to come.

Although he had conservative views and believed in Republican doctrines, Nixon has been called "the last liberal president" because of his domestic policies in which he showed a high degree of activism. His goal was to shift power away from the federal government and toward the states, a doctrine he labeled the "New Federalism." At the same time, Nixon enhanced the federal role in welfare and the environment.

In civil rights he sought to conciliate the South while pressing forward with desegregation of schools. He endorsed affirmative action. Nixon named women to high-profile positions and also endorsed the Equal Rights Amendment in 1972. The administration also followed constructive policies toward Native Americans, including increased funding and greater autonomy for individual tribes. The environment was another area addressed by Nixon's domestic policies. The Environmental Protection Agency (EPA) in 1970, the Occupational Safety and Health Administration (OSHA), and the Endangered Species Act (1973) were three Nixon-era measures that dealt with the environment.

One of Nixon's most innovative programs on the domestic side came in welfare reform, where the administration sponsored the Family Assistance Program (FAP). The goal of the initiative was to replace welfare services with cash payments. The legislation to implement payments to the poor encountered opposition in Congress from conservatives who thought it did too much and liberals who considered it too modest. Although this welfare reform was defeated, the Nixon years did see the expansion of Social Security payments for the elderly and the disabled, including the blind. Congress also adopted the system of cost-of-living adjustments for Social Security recipients. Government spending on social programs rose dramatically during the first half of the 1970s. Despite the abolition of some Great Society programs, such as the Office of Economic Opportunity, many other programs initiated under Lyndon Johnson were continued into the Nixon administration.

Nixon's most passionate interests lay in foreign policy, especially the war in Vietnam and relations with the Soviet Union. Henry Kissinger quickly supplanted Secretary of State William Rogers as the key architect of Nixon's foreign policy. Disdaining even his closest counselor, Nixon fretted about Kissinger's influence and once said of him, "There are times when Henry has to be kicked in the nuts. Because

INAUGURATION: Jan. 20,1969; the Capitol, Washington, D.C.

VICE PRESIDENT: Spiro T. Agnew

SECRETARY OF STATE: William P. Rogers

SECRETARY OF THE TREASURY: David M. Kennedy; John B. Connally (from Feb. 11, 1971); George P. Shultz (from June 12, 1972)

SECRETARY OF DEFENSE: Melvin R. Laird

ATTORNEY GENERAL: John N. Mitchell; Richard G. Kleindienst (from June 12, 1972)

POSTMASTER GENERAL: Winton M. Blount (through 1971, when he became director of the U.S. Postal Service, a newly independent agency, ending the cabinet-level status of the postmaster general)

SECRETARY OF THE INTERIOR: Walter J. Hickel; Rogers C. B. Morton (from Jan. 29, 1971)

SECRETARY OF AGRICULTURE: Clifford M. Hardin; Earl L. Butz (from Dec. 2, 1971)

SECRETARY OF COMMERCE: Maurice H. Stans; Peter G. Peterson (from Feb. 21, 1972)

SECRETARY OF LABOR: George P. Shultz; James D. Hodgson (from July 2, 1970)

SECRETARY OF HOUSING AND URBAN DEVELOPMENT: George W. Romney

SECRETARY OF HEALTH, EDUCATION, AND WELFARE: Robert H. Finch; Elliot L. Richardson (from June 24, 1970)

SECRETARY OF TRANSPORTATION: John A. Volpe

SUPREME COURT APPOINTMENTS: Warren E. Burger, chief justice (1969); Harry A. Blackmun (1970); Lewis F. Powell, Jr. (1972); William H. Rehnquist (1972)

91ST CONGRESS (Jan. 3, 1969–Jan. 2, 1971):
SENATE: 58 Democrats; 42 Republicans
HOUSE: 243 Democrats; 192 Republicans

92ND CONGRESS (Jan. 21, 1971–Oct. 18, 1972):
SENATE: 54 Democrats; 44 Republicans; 1 Independent; 1 Conservative
HOUSE: 255 Democrats; 180 Republicans

ELECTION OF 1968

CANDIDATES	ELECTORAL VOTE	POPULAR VOTE
Richard M. Nixon (Republican)	301	31,785,480
Hubert H. Humphrey (Democratic)	191	31,275,166
George Wallace (American Independent)	46	9,906,473

sometimes Henry starts to think he's president. But at other times you have to pat Henry and treat him like a child."

In dealing with Vietnam, Nixon felt that the war had driven Johnson from office, and he wanted to find a way out of the conflict without American defeat. In practice Nixon's program envisioned the gradual withdrawal of American troops and a greater reliance on the South Vietnamese, which went under the general title of "Vietnamization." To press the North Vietnamese to negotiate with the United States, the Nixon White House intended to keep the military pressure on through more intense aerial bombardment. The president ordered secret bombing raids of Cambodia in March 1969 and continued them for some time without informing the Amer-

ican people. In May 1970 the Nixon administration openly launched a massive invasion of Cambodia to find North Vietnamese command facilities. As word spread about the invasion, student protests exploded on campuses around the country. Four students died at Kent State University when Ohio National Guardsmen fired upon them during a demonstration. The campus killings came to be a sad reminder of the growing public disapproval of the war.

For Nixon these military steps in Cambodia were necessary to achieve "peace with honor" for the United States and to show that "the world's most powerful nation" was not "a pitiful, helpless giant." In fact, the pace of American withdrawal was sufficiently slow that stateside protests against the conflict continued through the early years of Nixon's first term.

President Nixon and Premier Chou En-Lai exchange a toast during the president's historic visit to China in February 1972.

The American actions during the next four years included an expansion of the conflict into Cambodia and Laos, the bombing of Hanoi in May 1972, and even more intense bombing of North Vietnam in December 1972. The settlement that Nixon and Kissinger achieved in early 1973 to end troop involvement was very close to the deal that might have been possible with North Vietnam in 1969. During these four years, the lives of twenty thousand Americans and many more Vietnamese were lost. When Nixon and Kissinger signed a pact to end active U.S. involvement in January 1973, the South Vietnamese government was given a slight chance to survive. (That vanished in 1975 when the North Vietnamese swept through the South and Congress prohibited an American counterattack.)

The major achievement of the Nixon administration in foreign affairs was the opening to Communist China in 1971. As a committed and well-known anti-Communist, Nixon could take a step that he would have denounced had Kennedy or Johnson attempted it. The president also regarded normalization of relations with China as a way of putting pressure on the Soviet Union to negotiate more freely and to help bring an end to the war in Vietnam. Nixon and Kissinger called this approach "linkage." It did not accomplish as much as they had hoped.

The diplomacy that led to Nixon's trip to China in February 1972 was intricate and complex. It included an American declaration in April 1971 that ended the two-decade-long embargo on trade with China. Matches between Chinese and American ping pong teams further smoothed the way. In July 1971 Nixon astonished the nation when he declared that he would make a state visit to China. The capstone of his China initiative was the trip itself. Pictures of Nixon and his entourage taken at the Great Wall illustrated the striking change that had occurred in Sino-American relations. The new coverage also reaped publicity benefits for the president in an election year and, he hoped, solidified his reputation as a skilled international negotiator.

In the case of the Soviet Union, Nixon and Kissinger sought a warmer state of relations that became known as *détente*. The president worked out ten agreements with Moscow that provided for greater scholarly and technical cooperation in health and science, an Anti-Ballistic Missile Treaty, and the Strategic Arms Limitation Talks (SALT) which culminated in the SALT I agreement. Nixon did achieve much in cooling tensions between the two superpowers.

President Nixon saw the world from a global perspective in which small developing countries were pawns in the great power game. He was convinced that he and Kissinger were tough-minded negotiators who did not have to bother much with the feelings of lesser states. As a result, Nixon used American power in ways that aroused animosities in the Third World. The White House used the Central Intelligence Agency to bring down the government of Salvador Allende in Chile because he was a Communist, and backed Pakistan in its war with India in 1971. In the Middle East, the administration sought to be even-handed between Israel and its Arab neighbors. Nixon devoted much more time to other parts of the world until the Yom Kippur War of 1973 between Egypt and Israel forced Kissinger and the president to engage the Middle East more directly.

A masterful politician, Nixon sought to build a permanent Republican majority. To that end, he used Vice President Agnew in 1969 and 1970 as a point man to dramatize the cultural divide between Repub-

licans and Democrats. Nixon viewed his Supreme Court appointments in the same light. His nominations of Clement Haynsworth and G. Harold Carswell went down to defeat in the Senate, but he succeeded in adding Chief Justice Warren E. Burger, William H. Rehnquist, and Lewis H. Powell, Jr., to the Court to shift it in what he hoped would be a conservative direction.

Nixon's efforts to insure his second term met a blow in the 1970 congressional races when the Democrats made gains in the House of Representatives and limited the Republican additions in the Senate to two seats. One year before he faced the next election, with

HENRY A. KISSINGER

In the Nixon administration the national security adviser, Henry A. Kissinger, became the celebrity diplomat whose international notoriety rivaled that of his boss. Born in Germany and educated at Harvard, Kissinger liked the way that Nixon focused the making of foreign policy in the White House. Kissinger was the instrument through which Nixon sought to extract the nation from the Vietnam War, practice détente with the Soviet Union, and open up relations with Communist China. Success in these endeavors gave Kissinger a reputation for diplomatic wizardry that made him indispensable to the Nixon White House. As the president became more embroiled in Watergate, he named Kissinger as secretary of state in September 1973. When Gerald Ford took over from Nixon, he retained Kissinger in this post. By the end of his tenure, however, Kissinger's reputation frayed as critics on the right assailed him for being too much the advocate of better relations with the Soviets. On the left, he was seen as the embodiment of a foreign policy of secrecy and trickery who always favored pragmatic realpolitik over human rights concerns. Nonetheless, his multivolume memoirs of his service to two presidents show a consummate politician at work.

the economy experiencing rising prices and unemployment, Nixon imposed temporary wage and price controls and ended the policy of insuring that American dollars could be converted into gold. As he told an interviewer, "I am now a Keynesian." These measures helped the economy a little as 1972 approached.

Determined to secure his own reelection and willing to stretch the Constitution to its limits and beyond, Nixon pursued tactics toward his political opponents that went beyond the accepted limits of partisan warfare. There was wiretapping of govern-

A Watergate-era "Wanted" poster shows President Nixon as the only figure in the scandal still at large while all his associates have been apprehended. Nixon received a pardon from President Gerald Ford in September 1974 for his role in the Watergate break-in and thus escaped the fate of his colleagues.

ment employees to plug security leaks, the use of the Internal Revenue Service to hound potential critics, and even burglaries to gain evidence against those suspected of transmitting classified documents to the press. The White House compiled an "enemies list" of opponents whose tax returns should be examined and whose reputations should be tarnished. These tactics, and others, later became known as "dirty tricks."

In 1971 the *New York Times* published secret documents about the origins of the war in Vietnam that came to be known as the "Pentagon Papers." Angry at divulgence of sensitive foreign policy information, the White House fought the *Times* and other newspapers in court but lost when the Supreme Court ruled that the publication of the documents could not be blocked. To stem the tide of leaks, the Nixon people created the "plumbers," a unit designed to prevent future disclosures. This activity soon spilled over into illegal conduct. Out of this climate of fear and potential repression came the Watergate scandal that brought Nixon down.

The actual events that opened the scandal involved a break-in at the headquarters of the Democratic National Committee on June 17, 1972. It happened in the Watergate complex in Washington and was conducted by a team of burglars employed by the White House to conduct political espionage. Discovered by a security guard, the men were arrested and their links with the White House revealed. A major question of the Watergate scandal was whether Nixon had any knowledge of the break-in before it occurred. He always maintained that he was unaware of it. However, it was known that Nixon placed few limits on what his aides could do to produce his reelection.

The break-in was the brainchild of White House operatives such as G. Gordon Liddy whose activities were financed through the Committee to Reelect the President. What they were searching for in the Democratic headquarters remains obscure more than a quarter of a century later.

Ironically, by the time the Watergate scandal began to unfold, it was evident that Nixon would be easily reelected. The Democrats chose Senator George S. McGovern of South Dakota, who campaigned against continued U.S involvement in the Vietnam War. His liberal views made him an ideal target for Nixon's conservative rhetoric, and the president's success seemed assured. Despite these favorable signs for the Republicans, Nixon's men wanted to guarantee his reelection, even if it meant committing criminal activity.

When press reports of the Watergate break-in appeared, however, Nixon and his men were confronted with the prospect that their other misdeeds—burglary, illegal campaign contributions, sabotage of other campaigns—could come to light. Knowing what had happened at least as early as June 20, 1972, Nixon authorized on June 23 a cover-up that would forestall a probe by the Federal Bureau of Investigation of the break-in by demand of the CIA. With that action, Nixon became part of an effort to obstruct justice that would in time lead to his ouster. Despite the president's instructions, the CIA did not comply with the White House directive and the FBI continued to investigate the break-in.

The Watergate issue simmered throughout the remainder of 1972. In the election, Nixon defeated McGovern by carrying every state except Massachusetts and the District of Columbia. With America on the verge of withdrawal from Vietnam, Nixon seemed in a very strong position to begin his second term. However, the Watergate scandal was already eroding the foundations of his presidency.

The early months of 1973 produced revelations about the Watergate cover-up. The public and the press demanded to know whether Nixon had been involved. On April 30, 1973, still claiming that he knew nothing about the cover-up, the president accepted the resignations of his White House counsel John Dean, Haldeman, and Ehrlichman. Testifying before a Senate committee established to investigate

SECOND ADMINISTRATION

INAUGURATION: Jan. 20, 1973; the Capitol, Washington, D.C.

VICE PRESIDENT: Spiro T. Agnew; Gerald R. Ford (from Dec. 6, 1973)

SECRETARY OF STATE: William P. Rogers; Henry A. Kissinger (from Sept. 22, 1973)

SECRETARY OF THE TREASURY: George P. Shultz; William E. Simon (from May 8, 1974)

SECRETARY OF DEFENSE: Melvin R. Laird; Elliot L. Richardson (from Feb. 2, 1973); James R. Schlesinger (from July 2, 1973)

ATTORNEY GENERAL: Richard G. Kleindienst; Elliot L. Richardson (from May 25, 1973); William B. Saxbe (from Jan. 4, 1974)

SECRETARY OF THE INTERIOR: Rogers C. B. Morton

SECRETARY OF AGRICULTURE: Earl L. Butz

SECRETARY OF COMMERCE: Peter G. Peterson; Frederick B. Dent (from Feb. 2, 1973)

SECRETARY OF LABOR: James D. Hodgson; Peter J. Brennan (from Feb. 2, 1973)

SECRETARY OF HEALTH, EDUCATION, AND WELFARE: Elliot L. Richardson; Caspar W. Weinberger (from Feb. 12, 1973)

SECRETARY OF HOUSING AND URBAN DEVELOPMENT: George W. Romney; James T. Lynn (from Feb. 2, 1973)

SECRETARY OF TRANSPORTATION: John A. Volpe; Claude S. Brinegar (Feb. 2, 1973)

93RD CONGRESS (Jan. 3, 1973–Dec. 20, 1974):
SENATE: 56 Democrats; 42 Republicans; 2 Others
HOUSE: 242 Democrats; 192 Republicans; 1 Independent

ELECTION OF 1972

CANDIDATES	ELECTORAL VOTE	POPULAR VOTE
Richard M. Nixon (Republican)	520	47,169,911
George S. McGovern (Democratic)	17	29,170,383
John Hospers (Libertarian)	1	—

Watergate, chaired by Democratic Senator Sam Ervin of North Carolina, Dean insisted that Nixon had masterminded the cover-up.

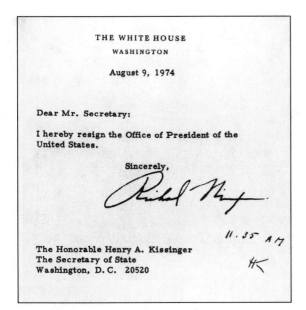

THE WHITE HOUSE
WASHINGTON

August 9, 1974

Dear Mr. Secretary:

I hereby resign the Office of President of the
United States.

Sincerely,

Richard Nixon

11.35 A M

HK

The Honorable Henry A. Kissinger
The Secretary of State
Washington, D. C. 20520

Nixon's official letter of resignation to Secretary of State
Henry A. Kissinger completed his removal from office in
the face of certain impeachment and conviction by
Congress in August 1974.

Then in July 1973, Alexander Butterfield, a White House aide, told the Ervin Committee that Nixon had a voice-activated taping system in the White House. That revelation meant that it would be possible to determine from the tapes whether Nixon had been criminally involved in the Watergate scandal. John Dean's testimony could be confirmed or refuted. A subpoena was drawn up to demand access to the tapes. Nixon did not destroy the tapes because he realized their historical value, and he wanted to avoid possible charges of destroying evidence; he made broad claims of executive privilege to justify retaining control of the tapes.

While the issue of the tapes troubled the president during the summer and fall of 1973, a fresh scandal, this one involving Vice President Agnew, added to the woes of the administration. Investigators learned that Agnew had received money as kickbacks from gov-

ernment contractors while he was governor of Maryland. These payoffs had continued while he was vice president. In return for his resignation, he was allowed to plead no contest to a charge of tax evasion on the corrupt income. To replace him, using for the first time the Twenty-fifth Amendment on presidential succession, Nixon nominated House Minority Leader Gerald Ford of Michigan, out of eagerness to have his choice quickly confirmed.

Public pressure had compelled the special prosecutor in charge of the Watergate probe, Archibald Cox, to threaten to subpoena the tapes from the president once their existence became known. Efforts to work out a compromise short of this constitutional precedent failed, and when Cox insisted on having the tapes in October 1973, Nixon ordered that he be fired. Attorney General Elliot Richardson and one of his deputies refused to do so. They resigned, and Robert Bork, the solicitor general, carried out the order. The press called the expulsion of the Justice Department officials the "Saturday Night Massacre," and cries for Nixon's impeachment grew much louder.

In the wake of the public outcry, the president turned over some tapes to the courts; one of them contained an unexplained eighteen-minute gap. During this period, in a statement to the press and public, Nixon announced, "I am not a crook." The House Judiciary Committee began a preliminary investigation, which led in turn to the start of an impeachment inquiry in April 1974. Efforts to obtain the tapes from the president went on throughout the first half of 1974. Nixon made some selected portions of the tapes available as a public relations gesture in April. The editing omitted Nixon's frequent profanity, substituting the phrase "expletive deleted." The battle in the courts went on as the president appealed to the Supreme Court over his right to preserve the tapes from scrutiny.

Finally, in the case of *United States v. Nixon,* in July 1974 the Supreme Court ruled that the president had to release the tapes. The Court said that the judiciary had the power to decide when a claim of executive privilege was appropriate. Three days later the Judiciary Committee voted to approve the first article of impeachment. Votes to approve a second and third article followed on July 29 and July 30, 1974. When Nixon turned over the tapes, and the contents of the June 23, 1972 conversations were disclosed, it was evident that Nixon had been part of the cover-up from its very beginning. Even Republicans who had supported him now called for his removal from office.

By early August 1974 Nixon's hold on the presidency was weakening. He could count on no more than 10 or 15 votes for acquittal in the Senate. Nixon knew that resignation was his only chance to avoid impeachment. His chief of staff, Alexander Haig, tried to feel out Vice President Ford about a possible pardon, but Ford would not commit himself before Nixon's resignation.

President Nixon resigned on August 9, 1974, and Ford pardoned him for his Watergate crimes a month later. That action effectively forestalled any further criminal inquiry into the conduct of the former president.

During the next twenty years until his death in 1994, Nixon wrote a number of books and articles in an effort to rehabilitate his historical image and establish himself as an elder statesman. He also traveled to China and Russia for the same purpose. In the campaign to regain public credibility he was more successful than one might have thought possible when he resigned. He and his attorneys also waged a dogged legal battle to keep the remaining Watergate tapes from being made public. (After Nixon's death, his family made a deal with the government to allow the controlled release of the tapes.) A private Nixon presidential library opened in California, but it lacked Nixon's tapes and presidential papers, still held by the National Archives. When Nixon died of a stroke on April 22, 1994, the Watergate episode received less attention in the media than his achievements as president

Nevertheless, Richard Nixon remains the only American president to resign. He did this to avoid certain impeachment and conviction after the worst presidential scandal in American history. In retrospect, it is clear that Nixon regarded politics not as a democratic profession to be carried out within agreed-upon rules, but as an all-out venture in which only victory mattered. When he saw enemies breaking rules large and small, he became convinced that he must play the game the same way with even more intensity. Thus a talented politician stretched the limits of American politics to the breaking point and beyond.

Historians and the American people continue to grapple with how to weigh all of this against Nixon's high intelligence and political skills, innovations like the Environmental Protection Agency and his creativity in foreign policy—especially his diplomatic opening to China. While revisionist scholars find many of Nixon's accomplishments in the White House praiseworthy, his reputation will never escape the Watergate scandal. Had his abuses of presidential authority not been revealed as a result of Watergate, later presidents would have been emboldened to use, as Nixon did, the FBI, IRS, CIA, and an alarming array of dirty tricks against their political enemies. Thanks to the Watergate investigations, new laws, and public expectations, subsequent presidents would find it far more difficult to repeat Nixon's abuses of power.

—LEWIS L. GOULD

On August 9, 1974, Richard Nixon's helicopter took off from the White House lawn and the new president, Gerald R. Ford, was sworn in. Referring to Nixon's Watergate scandal, he said, "My fellow Americans, our long national nightmare is over." Someone observed, "People are smiling. It's been a long time since I've seen anyone smile in the White House."

Ford gained a lasting place in the nation's history when he managed successfully the transition of power after the trauma of Richard Nixon's tumultuous last two years in office. Ford's twenty-nine months as president did not produce earth-shattering events, but his low-key moderation seemed to be just what the United States needed. Ford lost the 1976 election to Jimmy Carter in part because of his pardon of Richard Nixon and in part because of his own limitations as a leader. "A Ford, not a Lincoln," he said of himself. But Ford had other more subtle skills to bring to the job.

Born in 1913, Ford grew up in Grand Rapids, Michigan, where his mother settled after her first marriage, to Leslie King, failed. Her son was called Leslie Lynch King, Jr., but he became Gerald R. Ford, Jr., when his mother remarried and he took his stepfather's name. After high school young Ford attended the University of Michigan, where he starred as a center on the football team. He graduated from Yale Law School in 1941 with a strong academic record.

During World War II, Ford was a Navy officer in the Pacific. Like many in his party and from his region, Ford had held isolationist views before Pearl Harbor. The experience of the war persuaded him that internationalism was necessary for the future. "It was clear to me, it was inevitable to me, that this country was obligated to lead in this new world. We had won the war. It was up to us to keep the peace." In 1948 he ran in the Republican primary for a seat in the House of Representatives against the isolationist incumbent, Bartel J. Jonkman. As a young war veteran who favored a greater role for the United States in the world, Ford campaigned hard and won the primary easily. Shortly after his defeat of Jonkman, he married Elizabeth "Betty" Warren, whom he had been courting for some time. In the solidly Republican Fifth District, Ford had no trouble winning his House seat in the fall election.

Ford took naturally to the masculine fellowship of the House of Representatives, and he rose rapidly within the Republican party. By late 1964 he was ready to challenge the Republican leader, Charles A. Halleck, following Lyndon B. Johnson's landslide victory over Barry Goldwater. Ford won the contest for the minority leadership and then began dreaming of becoming Republican Speaker of the House. He and Senate Minority Leader Everett Dirksen became familiar performers on televised news conferences in what reporters entitled the "Ev and Jerry Show." As Dirksen put it, "Minority Leader Ford is the sword; I am the oilcan." Although the Republicans made gains throughout the rest of the 1960s, it was evident by 1972 that the party would not take over from the Democrats in the foreseeable future. Following his reelection to a thirteenth term in 1972, Ford decided that he would make one more race in 1974 and then retire from politics.

In the House, Ford's easygoing nature, gift for friendship, and open honesty made him a popular figure on both sides of the aisle. He sometimes exhibited a strong partisanship, as when he called for the impeachment of Justice William O. Douglas in 1970. But he had close friends in both parties. One political foe was Lyndon B. Johnson, who quipped to his aides that "Jerry played football too many times without a helmet" and was unable to "walk and chew gum at the same time." But even LBJ and Ford could work amiably together.

Freshman congressman Gerald Ford, in front of the Capitol in March 1955, places a tag touting Michigan apples on the back of his car.

On October 10, 1973, Ford's life abruptly changed. Richard Nixon's vice president, Spiro T. Agnew, resigned in disgrace to avoid prosecution on bribery and corruption charges. Nixon himself was enmeshed in the Watergate scandals, and the prospect of impeachment loomed. In selecting a successor for Agnew, Nixon wanted to designate his former secre-tary of the Treasury, John Connally, the former Democratic governor of Texas, and position Connally to succeed him in 1976. But congressional Democrats warned that a bruising confirmation fight would be invited by so political a choice. Nixon thus turned to Ford, who was well liked on Capitol Hill and would easily be confirmed.

The first part of the scenario went as Nixon had anticipated. Ford was indeed confirmed without difficulty and his swearing-in as vice president occurred on December 6, 1973. Assured by men close to Nixon that the president was not personally involved in the Watergate scandal or cover-up, Ford defended Nixon against the growing chorus of attacks on his administration. Nixon found, however, that the Ford selection actually undermined the president's chances of staying in office. As the months passed and Nixon's situation worsened, his vice president began to seem more and more of a decent alternative to Nixon's corruption and untruths. Ford's pleasant personality contrasted sharply with Nixon's darker side and the growing suspicion of his guilt of Watergate crimes.

After serving only eight months as vice president, Ford knew by August 1974 that Nixon's days as president were coming to an end. The revelation of a crucial Watergate tape recording that placed Nixon at the center of the cover-up meant that impeachment and conviction had become inevitable. Ford quietly prepared for as smooth a transition as possible. On August 9, 1974, Richard Nixon resigned and Gerald R. Ford succeeded him as the thirty-eighth president. He was the first president to enter office as a result of the Twenty-fifth Amendment, and Ford's nonelected status meant that he had to wage a constant battle to establish the legitimacy of his presidency. In his initial remarks to the nation, President Ford said, "I am acutely aware that you have not elected me as your president by your ballots. So I ask you to confirm me as your president with your prayers."

The first month of the Ford presidency produced

a national honeymoon for the new occupants of the White House. The president's early approval ratings in the polls reached 71 percent. The Fords appeared to be an idyllic American family. Admiring essays appeared in the national newsmagazines about the change in atmosphere and tone from the beleaguered Nixon days.

For Ford, the question of what to do about his disgraced predecessor dominated the early weeks of his administration. Nixon still faced possible legal jeopardy from the Watergate prosecutors, who had previously named him as an unindicted coconspirator in the cover-up. Before Nixon left office, the men around him had talked about the possibility of a presidential pardon from Ford, but the then vice president had carefully stayed away from a commitment. Contrary to the claims of some skeptics, no deal to pardon Nixon had been made prior to Ford's accession to the presidency.

In the first weeks of the new administration, however, the issue of Nixon's legal fate dogged the White House. At Ford's first news conference, reporters pressed him on whether he would consider granting Nixon a pardon. Ford became convinced that the controversy over Nixon and the pardon would drag on and overshadow his presidency. (There was also the question of Nixon's uncertain health, which would become apparent when he had a serious attack of phlebitis in the fall.) As Ford told Secretary of State Henry Kissinger, "Henry, we've got to put this behind us, and get on with all the other things we have to do." The president decided to pardon the former president so that the issue would be resolved well before the 1976 election. Still to be settled were the issues of timing and the conditions under which Nixon would be pardoned.

The announcement came on Sunday, September 8, 1974, following the Ford family's regular attendance at a church service. The president appeared on national television to announce that Nixon had been granted "a full, free, and absolute pardon for all offenses" he had committed in the White House. Ford called the fate of Nixon an "American tragedy [that] could go on and on and on, or someone must write an end to it. I have concluded that only I can do that, and if I can, I must."

Ford's motives in pardoning Nixon were laudable. Nonetheless, it seemed to many Americans as if Ford were trying to short-circuit the legal process, and the pardon of Nixon smacked of politics as usual. The conjunction of the pardon with an amnesty for Vietnam draft evaders did not help. To an extent, his pres-

The cover of the August 1974 issue of the French magazine *L'Express* depicts the new president from the American Midwest sewing up rips in the American flag from the Watergate scandal.

idency never recovered from the pardon. Some complained that Ford had not even forced Nixon to issue an admission of guilt. The public reaction was vehement. Editorials denounced the move. The president's standing in the public opinion polls dropped more than twenty points. Ford's press secretary, Jerald terHorst, resigned in protest, saying that the pardon was an unethical action. No longer a refreshing example of new political leadership, Ford at once seemed to become a symbol of the old ways of doing things in Washington. To counter suspicions that he had made a secret deal with Nixon, trading a pardon for a presidency, Ford took an unprecedented step for a sitting president, and testified personally before a House committee about the reasons for his decision, such as Nixon's health and the desire to put the controversy behind the country. He was nevertheless unable to counteract the damage that the pardon had done to his administration.

One asset for the new president in the early days of his term was his wife. Betty Ford became one of the most popular first ladies of her era. She held a press conference to tell reporters that she supported both the Equal Rights Amendment and the recent Supreme Court decision upholding abortion rights. When she was diagnosed with breast cancer and had to undergo surgery, she spoke openly about her condition and encouraged women to see their doctors for checkups regularly. In 1975 she became controversial when she told an interviewer on *60 Minutes* that she would counsel with but not condemn her daughter, Susan, if she had an extramarital affair or smoked pot. Conservatives were outraged; the general public was delighted with Mrs. Ford's frankness.

Mrs. Ford's popularity for her independence and sophistication hid a more somber reality. During Ford's political rise, his wife had dealt with the demands of four growing children and her husband's frequent absences. In grappling with her loneliness and frustration, she developed an addiction to painkillers and other drugs she kept hidden from all but family members. Her dependence on these substances continued throughout her White House years.

In the organization of the White House staff, President Ford encountered problems from the outset with holdovers from the Nixon team. He eased Alexander Haig out as chief of staff and replaced him with Donald H. Rumsfeld. Ford endeavored to put men loyal to him into the White House structure. That process was never fully achieved during the brief administration, and infighting among Ford and Nixon staffers plagued the operational side of the presidency.

One key appointment was Ford's selection of Nelson A. Rockefeller as his vice president. The choice was controversial because Rockefeller, the wealthy governor of New York State and a symbol of liberal Republicanism, had been a target of conservatives during the divisive battles of the 1960s. Although

Rockefeller had not sought the post, he agreed to it when Ford assured him that he would have a substantive role in shaping domestic policy. Congress confirmed Rockefeller in December 1974 following protracted hearings into his financial affairs.

After a year in office, Ford shook up his cabinet. He gave Rumsfeld the post of secretary of defense, made George Bush director of the Central Intelligence Agency, and named Richard Cheney as the new chief of staff. Facing a potential challenge to his renomination from Ronald Reagan, Ford had to conciliate the conservative wing of the party and thus asked Nelson Rockefeller to step off the ticket for 1976.

Before the public, Ford encountered difficulties that enhanced the popular impression of him as bumbler. Exiting an airplane, he slipped on the steps and fell to the ground. Comedians such as the popular Chevy Chase from *Saturday Night Live* began doing sketches that featured Ford falling all over himself. Erratic presidential golf shots that hit spectators became part of the caricature of Ford that spread across the country. Although a superb athlete and graceful in his movements, Ford became fixed in the popular mind as an oaf.

From the outset of his term, Ford faced a difficult political environment in Washington. The 1974 midterm elections saw a demoralized Republican party encounter heavy losses at the hands of a Democratic party that cried "Watergate." When the House Democrats were united, they had enough votes to pass measures over Ford's veto. The president had more leverage with the Senate, where the Democratic majority was below the two-thirds level. While Ford benefited from the cordial relations he enjoyed with his old friends in the House and Senate, removing much of the rancor of the Nixon years, strong partisan divisions still made Ford's leadership difficult.

In the midst of the partisanship on the Hill, the domestic economy showed signs of weakness. Unemployment was increasing, and inflation was approaching double digits. The nation faced a serious economic threat from the mounting inflation rate, some of it the result of the Arab oil embargo of 1973 that had hiked energy prices rapidly. Ford told Congress in October that the country should adopt a 5 percent tax surcharge on individual and corporate taxes and substantially reduce government spending. He also proposed that Americans contribute to the anti-inflation fight by sporting buttons with the letters WIN—Whip Inflation Now. The latter proposal gave television comedians a lively topic for jokes, and suggested that Ford was not able to confront a serious issue.

The economic problems persisted as a recession

NELSON A. ROCKEFELLER

"I never wanted to be vice president of *anything*," Nelson Rockefeller once remarked, but when Gerald Ford nominated him to fill the position in August 1974 Rockefeller took a final chance at national office. A four-term governor of New York State, the sixty-six-year-old Rockefeller was the embodiment of liberal Republicanism in a party whose conservatives had frustrated his races for the presidency in 1960, 1964, and 1968. Now, with Ford in office as president after the resignation of Richard Nixon, Rockefeller became the first unelected vice president in the nation's history. He faced a difficult and prolonged confirmation process, and was not confirmed in the position until December 19, 1974. He never got to play the vital role that Ford had promised him, and Republican conservatives pressured Ford to drop him from the ticket. In November 1975 Rockefeller said he would not run for the post again in 1976 after receiving strong signs from the Ford campaign that he should bow out. In the end his experience proved the correctness of Rockefeller's remark in 1960, after Richard Nixon had offered him the chance to be his running mate, that he was not "standby equipment."

replaced inflation as a primary concern for the White House. Early in 1975 Ford told the country that "the state of the union is not so good." With the recession gaining in intensity, the president proposed tax cuts and further reductions in domestic spending. The Democrats wanted more spending and deeper tax cuts, and the president used his veto power to push Congress toward his position. That impasse continued for most of the remainder of Ford's term. He vetoed more than fifty bills, and the Democrats were able to override only nine of them. Ford and his advisers believed that the president's emphasis on economic restraint helped to hold down spending and slow the impact of inflation on the economy.

In foreign policy, Ford relied on the Nixon-appointed secretary of state, Henry A. Kissinger, during the early months of his presidency. Ford's initial dependence on Kissinger attracted criticism, especially from conservatives. As Ford became more comfortable in the job, he took a greater part in formulating his own decisions about world matters.

Ford presided over one of the most painful

moments in American history with the fall of South Vietnam. The formal American role had ended in 1973, but considerable equipment and personnel remained in South Vietnam. When the North Vietnamese occupied South Vietnam in April 1975, the president had to order the withdrawal of all military personnel. A month later, when the American merchant ship *Mayaguez* was seized by Khmer Rouge Cambodians in the Gulf of Thailand, Ford used military force to free the crew members. The reassertion of American power gave Ford a temporary boost in the polls. To promote the healing of domestic wounds caused by Vietnam, Ford advanced his program to allow Vietnam-era draft evaders and military resisters to gain amnesty in return for two years of public service. The plan pleased neither those who had resisted nor the conservatives who believed that harsher penalties were appropriate.

In relations with the Soviet Union, Ford encouraged Kissinger's negotiation of a Strategic Arms Limitation Treaty (SALT II) but deferred action on it when conservatives within and outside the admin-

South Vietnamese civilians try to leave Saigon with personnel evacuations after the collapse of the South Vietnamese government in April 1975. During the last terrible hours of the American departure from the aftermath of the nation's longest war, some Vietnamese even tried to cling to the runners of helicopters.

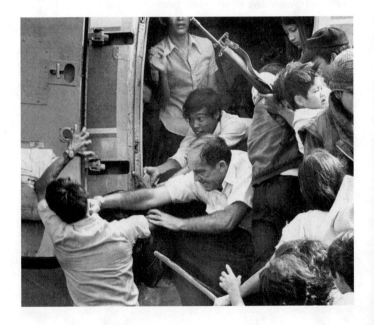

istration assailed it for having conceded too much to the other side. Ford participated with the Soviet leaders and other Western European leaders in signing the Helsinki accords, which ratified the boundaries established after World War II and pledged the signatory nations to the free movement of people and ideas. Ronald Reagan and others criticized the Helsinki Pact as a concession to the Soviets.

As for the Middle East and Africa, Ford followed the broad lines of policy established by his predecessor. In the case of Angola, in southern Africa, the existing policy included using the Central Intelligence Agency to fund one of the three factions contending for power after the Portuguese had departed from their former colony. The deepening American involvement during the Ford administration led to congressional hearings about the war and eventually a decision to stop financing the conflict. By 1976 Kissinger and Ford had repudiated the policies of supporting white governments in Rhodesia and South Africa as difficulties with the earlier approach became clear.

While Ford was a conservative Republican who hewed largely to the domestic policies that his party had established, he was not conservative enough to satisfy the right wing among Republicans. The cultural moderation of Mrs. Ford, especially her endorsement of the Equal Rights Amendment, was one source of suspicion. The presence of moderate Republicans in the White House also aroused unease on the right. Ronald Reagan announced his candidacy for the presidency on November 20, 1975. The contest proved to be bitter. One of Ford's aides described the situation: "Ford thought Reagan was a phony, and Reagan thought Ford was a lightweight, and neither one felt the other was fit to be president."

Ford had the advantages of incumbency and the White House on his side. Reagan had the fervor of his true believers. At first it looked as if Ford might lock up the nomination early after the president scored an

---

THE FORD ADMINISTRATION

INAUGURATION: Aug. 9, 1974, in the East Room of the White House
VICE PRESIDENT: Nelson A. Rockefeller
SECRETARY OF STATE: Henry A. Kissinger
SECRETARY OF THE TREASURY: William E. Simon
SECRETARY OF DEFENSE: James R. Schlesinger; Donald H. Rumsfeld (from Nov. 20, 1975)
ATTORNEY GENERAL: William B. Saxbe; Edward H. Levi (from Feb. 7, 1975)
SECRETARY OF THE INTERIOR: Rogers C. B. Morton; Stanley K. Hathaway (from June 13, 1975); Thomas S. Kleppe (from Oct. 17, 1975)
SECRETARY OF AGRICULTURE: Earl L. Butz; John A. Knebel (from Nov. 4, 1976)
SECRETARY OF COMMERCE: Frederick B. Dent; Rogers C. B. Morton (from May 1, 1975); Elliot L. Richardson (from Feb. 2, 1976)
SECRETARY OF LABOR: Peter J. Brennan; John T. Dunlop (from Mar. 18, 1975); Willie J. Usery, Jr. (from Feb. 10, 1976)
SECRETARY OF HEALTH, EDUCATION, AND WELFARE: Caspar W. Weinberger; F. David Mathews (from Aug. 8, 1975)
SECRETARY OF HOUSING AND URBAN DEVELOPMENT: James T. Lynn; Carla A. Hills (from Mar. 10, 1975)
SECRETARY OF TRANSPORTATION: Claude S. Brinegar; William T. Coleman, Jr. (from Mar. 7, 1975)
SUPREME COURT APPOINTMENT: John Paul Stevens (1975)
93RD CONGRESS (Jan. 3, 1973–Dec. 20, 1974):
  SENATE: 56 Democrats; 42 Republicans, 2 Independents
  HOUSE: 242 Democrats; 192 Republicans; 1 Independent
94TH CONGRESS (Jan. 14, 1975–Oct. 1, 1976):
  SENATE: 61 Democrats; 37 Republicans; 2 Independents
  HOUSE: 291 Democrats; 144 Republicans

---

upset hairbreadth win in the New Hampshire primary. Ford carried Florida and Illinois, and seemed to have Reagan on the ropes. Then the challenger bounced back in the primary in North Carolina, where his main supporter, Senator Jesse Helms, remarked that "Ultra-liberals in this country hate Ronald Reagan like the devil hates holy water."

Reagan won the North Carolina contest and swept through a series of victories. The two men fought it out grimly in the remaining states. Reagan even tried to win the nomination by shaking up the convention with the surprise announcement of a liberal running mate, Senator Richard Schweiker of Pennsylvania, but that gesture angered conservatives and failed to put him over the top.

When the Republicans held their convention in Kansas City, Ford held a narrow lead in delegates which he maintained through the intense maneuver-

President and Mrs. Ford comfort each other as they watch the election returns showing the president's defeat in the 1976 presidential election.

ing that ensued. With control of the convention machinery securely in his hands, Ford won a first-ballot victory. He selected Senator Robert Dole of Kansas as his running mate to help him hold the Midwest and placate conservatives. Dole's acid campaign style alienated moderates of both parties. Ford prepared for a race against the Democratic nominee, Jimmy Carter, of Georgia, a former one-term governor who had startled pundits by sweeping to victory in the primaries.

Ford began the 1976 campaign well behind Carter in the polls and had to defend a Reaganite platform imposed on him at Kansas City. Carter, a moderate Democrat who promised to return morality to Washington after what he called the "Nixon-Ford" era, had a huge early lead after the summer conventions. The Republicans had excellent political operatives, and the manager of Ford's campaign, James A. Baker, was a gifted tactician. They capitalized on the American Bicentennial and other patriotic appeals to depict Ford as a man who deserved to have another term in office. Doubts about the Democrat's ability to lead the country brought a narrowing of the polls in Ford's favor. Ford's solid performance in the first televised debate made the race even tighter.

The second debate, however, gave Carter a large boost. In response to a question about the Helsinki accords and the status of the nations of Eastern Europe, Ford asserted that "there is no Soviet domination of Eastern Europe and there never will be under a Ford administration." What Ford was trying to say was that he did not accept, nor did the peoples of Eastern Europe, the principle of Soviet domination. But he sounded as if he was ignorant of even the basics of foreign policy. The president sagged in the polls. Jokes about his intelligence reappeared, and Carter bounced back into the lead.

Despite all of Ford's problems and Carter's advantages, the president came very close to winning a term on his own. Carter's total in the popular vote on November 2, 1976, was 50.1 percent to 48 percent for Ford. The margin in the electoral college was wider but still relatively close; Carter had 297 electoral votes, Ford had 240, and one elector cast a vote for Ronald Reagan. The president was deeply disappointed at the outcome. "Considering the mess I inherited," he later said, "I was convinced I had done a good job and should have won on the merits."

The transition from Ford to Carter went smoothly, and he and Mrs. Ford retired to private life in Rancho Mirage, California, and Avon, Colorado. In 1980 he briefly considered another run for president, but discarded the idea. At the Republican convention, Ronald Reagan approached Ford as a possible running mate on a "dream ticket," but efforts to work out a satisfactory sharing of power between the two men collapsed when Ford suggested a kind of copresidential status. Reagan turned instead to George Bush. Although the two men had pledged to bury their old antagonisms, after Reagan became president he virtually ignored his Republican predecessor. Indifferent to this, the popular Ford played in celebrity golf tournaments, served on numerous corporate boards, including American Express and Twentieth Century-Fox, gave speeches for large honoraria, and raised money for his presidential library and museum in Michigan. In 1989, when Soviet satellites fled Moscow's orbit, Ford joked that he had been right to say that there was no Soviet domination of Eastern Europe—just a decade too soon. In 1998, when President Bill Clinton faced a Senate impeachment trial, Ford offered a compromise proposal to defuse the controversy, which his own party did not accept.

After the presidency, Mrs. Ford's alcoholism and drug dependence became an intense problem, and her husband and children staged an intervention to persuade her to face her addictions. The result was a long course of treatment and a reclaimed sobriety. She also founded and devoted much of her time and energy to the Betty Ford Center for Alcoholism and Drug Abuse. Both Fords remained popular figures in the public eye. Ford said that he was "pleased to carry a card in what Herbert Hoover called 'my exclusive trade union' of former presidents."

A generation after he left the presidency, Gerald Ford had the satisfaction of seeing the American people come around to the view that pardoning Richard Nixon was the right thing to do. With the fall of Saigon, he helped Americans to accept the first military defeat in their history with a minimum of recriminations and poison. Ford's decency and simple virtues helped to restore Americans' faith, in the wake of Watergate, that their political leaders were not all liars or crooks. Had Nixon been succeeded by a different kind of human being, the history of the 1970s could have been different. One reason Gerald Ford was so underrated by his contemporaries was that he made it all look so easy.

—LEWIS L. GOULD

It began with brilliant hopes. On January 20, 1977, the newly inaugurated President Jimmy Carter, his wife, Rosalynn, and their daughter, Amy, walked a mile hand in hand down Pennsylvania Avenue, from the Capitol to the White House, waving and smiling. The break with precedent and protocol brought cheers from the crowds that lined the avenue. After the national traumas of the Vietnam War and the Watergate scandal, perhaps this fresh face from the South could deliver on his campaign promise of a government as good as the American people. Carter relished his persona as a nonpolitician. As his vice president, Walter F. Mondale, remarked, "Carter thought politics was sinful. The worst thing you could say to Carter if you wanted to do something was that it was politically the best thing to do."

The Carter presidency, despite some signal successes, never fulfilled the expectations of the inaugural. Four years later, Americans abandoned him. Nevertheless, thanks to many of the ideals that also marked his first presidential campaign and his term in office, Carter came to have the consolation of being hailed as the best former president in American history.

Born in Plains, Georgia, to James Earl, Sr., and Lillian Gordy Carter in 1924, young Jimmy sold peanuts in town even as a preschooler. After graduating from high school in 1941, he attended college in Georgia before entering the U.S. Naval Academy where, according to a classmate, "a big man on campus he was not." He graduated in 1946. Carter then spent several years working with Admiral Hyman Rickover on the nuclear submarine project. He married Rosalynn Smith on July 7, 1946. The couple had three sons and one daughter.

In 1953 Carter's father died and, despite Rosalynn's misgivings, Jimmy returned to Plains to revive his family's peanut business. The episode strained the marriage. "She almost quit me," Carter remembered.

In the 1960s, Carter reexamined the Baptist faith of his youth, reaffirmed his commitment to it, and felt himself "born again." As he put it, "When we accept Jesus as our savior, it's new life. That's what 'born again' means."

Carter served two terms in the Georgia Senate from 1963 to 1966. He then made an unsuccessful race for the Georgia governorship, losing to the segregationist Lester Maddox. Four years later Carter was elected governor of Georgia in a campaign that used racial code language to win the white vote against his liberal foe, former governor Carl Sanders. But in his inaugural address Carter said that "the time for racial discrimination is over." This statement gave Carter a national reputation as one of the new breed of racially moderate Democratic governors.

Although he could be a tough and effective politician, Carter saw governing as a process in which partisan issues should rarely intrude. Decisions should be based on rational calculations of the national interest in which party considerations took a back seat. "Carter's antipolitical attitudes used to drive me nuts," Mondale said later, "because you couldn't get him to grapple with a political problem."

As Georgia's governor, Carter devoted most of his energies to reorganizing the state government. His emphasis on thrift and efficiency put him in the long line of business progressives who governed Southern states during years when racial issues were not at the forefront of regional concerns. Carter encountered difficulties, however, with the legislature, where his frequent veto threats did not endear him to lawmakers. His gubernatorial term was reasonably successful, but he was already gaining a reputation for stubbornness and determination. "Carter reminds me of a South Georgia turtle," said one Georgian. "He doesn't go around a log. He just sticks his head in the middle and pushes and pushes until the log gives way." None of this seemed to add up to a presidential bid in 1976.

That goal Carter reached on his own. He had not

Jimmy Carter, governor of Georgia, in his hometown of Plains, Georgia, in 1974.

JAMES EARL CARTER ☆ 465

When Jimmy Carter announced his candidacy for president in 1974, he seemed an unlikely aspirant in the Democratic field. But he and his advisers had framed a shrewd strategy to win the nomination.

been impressed with such national Democrats as George S. McGovern or Morris Udall when he met them, and he reasoned that he was as well qualified for the White House as they were. He knew that the nominating process would be wide-open since there was as yet no single leading Democrat. Carter and his advisers also perceived that a candidate who could build up early momentum in the Iowa caucuses and the New Hampshire primary could attain a standing in the public opinion polls, and with delegates that would make him difficult to overtake.

Carter was at his political best during the 1976 campaign for the Democratic nomination. In the post-Watergate climate of 1975–1976, the nation was receptive to the idea of a little-known leader untainted by Washington scandals or insider deals. Carter depicted himself as a maverick from the heart of America. He said he was not a lawyer, not from Washington, not a politician. He promised his audiences that "I will never lie to you," and he declared that what the country needed was "a government as

good as the American people." Delivered with his engaging smile and open face, these comments seemed a breath of fresh air after the deception and wrongdoing of the Watergate episode. Carter also used his Southern Baptist background to appeal to evangelicals, an untapped voting bloc of impressive size. His statements about being "born again" resonated with them as few presidential candidates' words had done before. He grasped that a moderate Southern Democrat had a chance to defy the political pundits and win.

Carter's strategy, worked out by his adviser Hamilton Jordan and the pollster Pat Caddell, functioned almost exactly as they hoped. The Georgian won the Iowa caucuses on January 19, 1976, with nearly 28 percent of those who designated a candidate, well ahead of the other four main Democratic contenders in the state. He then did well in other caucus states leading up to the critical New Hampshire primary. On February 24, Carter secured 28 percent of the total vote to around 24 percent for Congressman

Morris Udall of Arizona. The victory established Carter as the clear front-runner for the Democratic nomination.

During the remainder of the primary season, Carter held on to the lead that he had established at the outset. As the public and the party got to know him better, his novelty wore off and some of the reservations about his style began to appear. As a result, he suffered some late primary defeats at the hands of Governor Edmund G. (Jerry) Brown of California and Senator Frank Church of Idaho, but the Carter campaign had won so many delegates that he could not be denied the nomination. At the Democratic National Convention in New York City, Carter selected Senator Mondale of Minnesota, a liberal with close ties to Hubert Humphrey, as his running mate. The Democrats came out of the convention united, and Carter had built up a huge lead in the public opinion polls over President Gerald Ford. The advantage was illusory since the Republicans were split between Ford and California Governor Ronald Reagan. Meanwhile, Carter was an unknown quantity to the American people. Once the campaign started in earnest, the race was bound to get much closer.

That happened because the Republicans began to unite after Ford beat back the Reagan challenge at their convention in Kansas City. The president enjoyed a surge in the polls coming out of his convention, and the Republicans planned to drive home Carter's lack of experience with the voters. Carter stumbled when he gave an interview to *Playboy* magazine in which he said, "I have looked on a lot of women with lust; I've committed adultery in my heart many times." While such comments would seem innocuous a generation later, in 1976 they generated searing comment about the sincerity of Carter's religious beliefs.

As the campaign tightened, the televised debates offered Carter an opportunity to establish himself on an equal footing with President Ford. Ford was thought to edge out Carter in the fisrt debate, but in the second one on October 6, 1976, the president, in response to a question, asserted that "there is no Soviet domination of Eastern Europe and there never will be under a Ford administration." Ford was trying to say that the Soviet Union had not won the hearts and minds of the people of Eastern Europe and that the United States would not recognize Soviet domination, but his turn of phrase seemed to confirm the notion that the president was not sharp.

Still, the presidential race was very close as the election approached. The Republican campaign had used advertising very effectively to cast doubt on Carter's record in Georgia, and Ford was fast closing

BIOGRAPHICAL FACTS

BIRTH: Plains, Ga., Oct. 1, 1924
ANCESTRY: English
FATHER: James Earl Carter, Sr.;
  b. Arlington, Ga., Sept. 12, 1894;
  d. Plains, Ga., July 23, 1954
FATHER'S OCCUPATIONS: Farmer; storekeeper
MOTHER: Lillian Gordy Carter; b. Richland,
  Ga., Aug. 15, 1898; d. Americus, Ga.,
  Apr. 30, 1983
BROTHER: William "Billy" Alton Carter, III (1938–1988)
SISTERS: Gloria (1926–1990); Ruth (1929–1983)
MARRIAGE: Plains, Ga., July 7, 1946
WIFE: Rosalynn Smith; b. Plains, Ga., Aug. 18, 1927
CHILDREN: John William (1947–); James Earl (1950–);
  Donnel Jeffrey (1952–) ; Amy Lynn (1967–)
RELIGIOUS AFFILIATION: Baptist
EDUCATION: Plains High School; attended Georgia
  Southwestern College; Georgia Institute of Technology;
  U.S. Naval Academy (B.S., 1946); attended Union
  College
OCCUPATIONS BEFORE PRESIDENCY: Farmer; businessman
MILITARY SERVICE: U.S. Navy, ens.; lt. (jg); lt.; lt. comdr.
PREPRESIDENTIAL OFFICES: Georgia State senator;
  governor of Georgia
AGE AT INAUGURATION: 52
OCCUPATIONS AFTER PRESIDENCY: Writer; humanitarian

the gap in the polls as November began. On election night, Carter ran well in the South and the Northeast, with Ford holding the traditional Republican bastions in the Midwest and Far West. Carter moved ahead decisively in the electoral college vote and went over the top when Mississippi fell into the Democratic column. The final result had Carter with 297 electoral votes and almost 41 million popular votes. Ford trailed with 240 electoral votes and just over 39 million popular votes.

The victory in 1976 became the high point of Jimmy Carter's political career. He saw the opportunity that existed for the right kind of Democratic candidate from the South, and he capitalized on it. Carter and the men around him were understandably elated, but they read many of the wrong lessons from their triumph. They believed that they did not need to court Washington, D.C., or the nation's political establishment. To them, Congress was part of the problem with how government worked.

In a conversation with House Speaker Thomas P. "Tip" O'Neill in December, the president-elect said that if Congress gave him difficulty, he would go over their heads and appeal to the American people as he had done in Georgia, with the state legislature. O'Neill later recalled that "I tried to explain how important it was for the president to work closely with the Congress; he didn't seem to understand." Carter knew that Congress was important, but he also believed that as president he could summon public opinion as he desired. That task would prove more difficult than he anticipated.

The issue of congressional relations was just one indicator that Carter would approach the presidency as if partisan considerations mattered little in deciding how issues were to be handled. Coming from a state long-dominated by one party, he had little sense of how Republicans and Democrats interacted in Washington. The new president also believed that the White House did not need a strong chief of staff to serve the administration as in the Nixon presidency. Instead, Carter organized his administration without clear lines of authority, much as John F. Kennedy had. The idea was to prevent a single individual from wielding power over presidential options. In practice, it meant that Carter's White House was often fragmented and confused in its daily operations.

Two areas where Carter innovated as president involved his vice president, Walter Mondale, and the first lady, Rosalynn Carter. In the case of Mondale, Carter departed from the usual practice of keeping the vice president away from power. Instead, he gave Mondale an office in the West Wing and put one of Mondale's aides on the presidential staff. The two men shared a close working relationship, and Carter's restructuring of the vice presidency became a precedent for later presidents.

In the case of the first lady, the Carters had been political partners from the outset of his career. It was thus natural for Rosalynn Carter to play a prominent role in the new administration. She made a diplomatic tour of Latin America for her husband, persuaded him to establish a presidential commission on mental health, and campaigned for Democratic candidates as a surrogate. Her presence at cabinet meetings aroused criticism, even though she simply listened and took notes. Mrs. Carter's use of her staff and her personal activism made her an important figure in the evolution of the institution of the first lady.

Carter appointed more women to top positions than any president before him, endorsed the National Women's Conference in 1977, and threw his prestige behind an effort to extend the time limit for ratifying the Equal Rights Amendment. Most feminists, however, bridled at Carter's reluctance to support federal funding for abortions, and said that he showcased Rosalynn and his daughter, Amy, instead of campaigning for women's issues himself.

Carter's cabinet was a mix of individuals with Washington experience, such as Secretary of State

Cyrus R. Vance, Secretary of Defense Harold Brown, and Secretary of the Treasury W. Michael Blumenthal. Other posts went to what became known as the "Georgia Mafia," including Budget Director Bert Lance and Attorney General Griffin B. Bell. The heavy presence of Georgians limited the amount of outside advice that Carter received and used.

Although he did not court members of Congress, Carter nonetheless expected them to enact an ambitious program during his first year in the White House. He wanted authorization to reorganize the government and to address the nation's energy needs. The president's decision to strike nineteen water projects from the budget in February 1977, however, alienated members on Capitol Hill by imperiling one of their favorite pork-barrel endeavors.

Compounding the problems with Congress was the president's decision at the outset of his administration to pardon those who had evaded the draft during the Vietnam War. Aimed at healing the wounds from the conflict, the action outraged the right wing in American politics who believed that draft dodgers deserved punishment, not a pardon. The nomination of Theodore Sorensen to be director of the Central Intelligence Agency also caused a political furor. The selection had to be withdrawn because Sorensen had once registered for the draft as a conscientious objector and had taken classified documents from the White House without permission after the Kennedy presidency.

The first year in office was a difficult one for Carter. His appointment of so many Georgians to his staff attracted unfavorable comment. The clamor grew louder in the summer of 1977, when the press and political opponents began raising questions about Budget Director Bert Lance's banking practices in Georgia before he came to Washington. While the president believed that Lance had not done anything wrong, the intensity of the attacks made the budget director a political liability. Within a few weeks, the

---

THE CARTER ADMINISTRATION

INAUGURATION: Jan. 20, 1977; the Capitol, Washington, D.C.

VICE PRESIDENT: Walter F. Mondale

SECRETARY OF STATE: Cyrus R. Vance; Edmund S. Muskie (from May 8, 1980)

SECRETARY OF THE TREASURY: W. Michael Blumenthal; G. William Miller (from Aug. 7, 1979)

SECRETARY OF DEFENSE: Harold Brown

ATTORNEY GENERAL: Griffin B. Bell; Benjamin R. Civiletti (from Aug. 16, 1979)

SECRETARY OF THE INTERIOR: Cecil D. Andrus

SECRETARY OF AGRICULTURE: Robert S. Bergland

SECRETARY OF COMMERCE: Juanita M. Kreps; Philip M. Klutznick (from Jan. 9, 1980)

SECRETARY OF LABOR: Fred R. Marshall

SECRETARY OF HEALTH, EDUCATION, AND WELFARE (became Health and Human Services in 1979): Joseph A Califano, Jr.; Patricia Roberts Harris (from Aug. 3, 1979)

SECRETARY OF HOUSING AND URBAN DEVELOPMENT: Patricia Roberts Harris; Moon Landrieu (from Sept. 25, 1979)

SECRETARY OF TRANSPORTATION: Brock Adams; Neil E. Goldschmidt (from Sept. 24, 1979)

SECRETARY OF ENERGY: James R. Schlesinger; Charles W. Duncan, Jr. (from Aug. 24, 1979)

SECRETARY OF EDUCATION (department created Dec. 1, 1979): Shirley M. Hufstedler

95TH CONGRESS (Jan. 4, 1977–Oct. 15, 1978):
SENATE: 61 Democrats; 38 Republicans; 1 Independent
HOUSE: 292 Democrats; 143 Republicans

96TH CONGRESS (Jan. 15, 1979–Dec. 16, 1980):
SENATE: 58 Democrats; 41 Republicans; 1 Independent
HOUSE: 277 Democrats; 158 Republicans

ELECTION OF 1976

CANDIDATES	ELECTORAL VOTE	POPULAR VOTE
James E. Carter (Democratic)	297	40,830,763
Gerald R. Ford (Republican)	240	39,147,793
Ronald W. Reagan (Republican)	1	—

president had to cut his losses and accept Lance's resignation.

Despite these problems, Carter pressed ahead with his ambitious set of initiatives. He asked Congress to address welfare reform, Social Security, medical care, and government ethics. The lawmakers reacted tepidly, and most of the president's program became bogged down in committees. Much of it was never enacted. The economy lagged as the year ended, and mounting unhappiness with Carter was evident in the polls.

Carter also wanted to be an activist in foreign policy to repair what he saw as the mistakes of the Vietnam War and the overemphasis on the Cold War mentality. Secretary of State Cyrus Vance was often an implementer of presidential directives, while the main architects of the Carter program were the president and his national security adviser, Zbigniew Brzezinski. Their foreign policy emphasized human rights and the pursuit of détente with the Soviet Union. Carter also wanted to advance peace in the Middle East.

Carter's foreign policy was not easy to put into practice. His outspoken advocacy of human rights for nationalities and dissenters within the Soviet empire angered the men in the Kremlin. Leonid Brezhnev, the Soviet leader, said that the effort to emphasize human rights was in "direct opposition to further improvement of Soviet-American relations." At the same time, Republicans attacked the policy as being too weak toward the Soviet Union, and they circulated leaked intelligence estimates that showed a growing threat from Moscow.

Another of Carter's foreign policy initiatives outraged his critics on the right even more. The president believed that the United States should negotiate an end to the treaty that gave his nation a dominant role over the Panama Canal. An important international waterway, the canal retained great significance as a symbol of the era of Theodore Roosevelt, gunboat diplomacy, and American supremacy in Latin America. Carter signed a pact with Panama in September 1977 which relinquished control of the canal to Panama in 1999. Ronald Reagan, already the front-runner for the Republican presidential nomination in 1980, charged that Carter was "giving away the canal," and he had made the issue one of the centerpieces of his campaign throughout 1976. The president, using his influence with the Republican leader in the Senate, Howard Baker, lobbied successfully to gain the two-thirds vote needed to approve the treaty in April 1978.

Carter's greatest foreign policy success came in September 1978 when he brokered the Camp David

ROSALYNN CARTER

She was called "the Steel Magnolia" for her role in the Carter White House, where she sat in on cabinet meetings, went on diplomatic missions, and campaigned as a presidential surrogate. Rosalynn Carter was approaching her nineteenth birthday when she married Jimmy Carter in July 1946, and her years as a Navy wife taught her independence and self-reliance. Although she disapproved of the move from the Navy to the peanut business, she adapted quickly to the rigors of keeping the books and watching the accounts. They were a close couple who depended on each other. "I've never had time for friends," Rosalynn Carter once remarked, "I've always worked too hard."

She campaigned hard for her husband in 1976 and intended to be a working first lady. The president said that they were "full partners in every sense of the word," and they pursued that course during his presidency. She became a champion of the mentally ill, conducting lobbying efforts out of her office, and became the most visible first lady on the campaign trail. Out of office, she was a vital force in the positive contributions that marked the Carters' post-presidential years.

President Carter smiles at Egyptian President Anwar Sadat, left, and Israeli Prime Minster Menachem Begin, right, during the Camp David summit, in 1978, one of the diplomatic triumphs of the Carter presidency.

accords between Egypt and Israel. The situation in that troubled region had been explosive since the Yom Kippur War of 1973. In its wake the Ford administration and Secretary of State Henry A. Kissinger had promoted negotiations between Israel and its Arab enemies. Issues relating to the possibility of Israeli withdrawal from the territories it had conquered in 1967 and the future status of the Palestine Liberation Organization (PLO) made Carter's task a delicate one. The president acted imaginatively in inviting the Egyptian president, Anwar Sadat, and the Israeli prime minister, Menachem Begin, to the presidential retreat at Camp David for thirteen grueling days of talks. At the end of the protracted discussions, an

agreement had been reached for the eventual signing of a peace treaty between the two countries. That ceremony occurred in March 1979 after Carter himself went to the Middle East to see that the negotiations did not fall apart.

Despite his success in the Middle East and the enactment of his energy plan in Congress at the end of 1978, the Carter presidency was in deep trouble. Economic growth had slowed, unemployment stood at 6 percent, inflation had increased, and popular confidence in the president's leadership had eroded. The Republicans gained in the congressional elections of 1978, and they looked expectantly at a Reagan candidacy in 1980. Among the Democrats, many of whom were impatient with Carter's centrist leanings, support grew for Senator Edward M. Kennedy of Massachusetts as a liberal challenger to Carter's renomination. The president remarked that if Kennedy ran, "I'll whip his ass."

The fortunes of the administration worsened in 1979. As oil prices continued to rise because of the actions of the Organization of Petroleum Exporting Companies (OPEC), the president decided in July 1979 to speak to the nation on the energy problem. The speech was postponed, and the president spent eleven days closeted at Camp David. He then delivered televised remarks in which he asserted that the nation faced "a crisis of confidence." Every citizen would have to pull together to bring the nation through the energy problem. Although the remarks did not contain the word malaise, it soon became known as the "malaise speech" for Carter's pessimistic interpretation of the American character. Beyond the impact of the address, his demand for the resignations of a number of his cabinet members contributed to a sense of a White House adrift.

The situation darkened abroad for President Carter during the rest of 1979 as interest rates rose to dizzying levels near 15 percent. In Iran, where the shah had been overthrown in January, the new revolutionary regime of Ayatollah Ruhollah Khomeini seized the American embassy in Tehran and took fifty-two Americans hostage. The fate of the captives became a staple of the nightly television news programs. Walter Cronkite on *The CBS Evening News* announced each night how many days the Americans had been imprisoned.

A month after the Iran hostage crisis began, the Soviet Union invaded Afghanistan. Carter slapped a grain embargo on Moscow and pulled the United States out of the 1980 Olympic Games. He also delayed action on the SALT II disarmament treaty. While these were forceful actions, they did not placate the critics on the right wing of American politics who charged that the nation's defenses were in shambles and the country's future in peril. The embargo also angered farmers and other voters in rural areas.

Had Carter been able to solve the hostage crisis, he might have saved his presidency. But an effort to extract the hostages by a military raid ended in disastrous failure on April 25, 1980, and the outcome contributed to the public sense of presidential ineptitude. Secretary of State Vance resigned in protest because his warnings about the mission had not been heeded. The administration's foreign policy seemed in utter disarray.

Carter turned back the insurgency of Senator Kennedy, who had announced his run for the White House in November 1979. Although Kennedy had once enjoyed a large lead in the polls over Carter, his campaign got off to a fumbling start, and the president was able to sew up the nomination. Nonetheless, the primaries indicated pervasive voter unhappiness with Carter's leadership, especially among traditional Democratic constituencies.

The president faced a grim prospect in the general elections. The economy had gone into the tank with inflation approaching 20 percent annually and unemployment rising above 8.2 million in July 1980. The president's approval rating hovered at 22 percent, which was lower than Nixon's standings during Watergate. Meanwhile, Republican nominee Ronald Reagan opened up a substantial lead in the polls over the president. Carter also faced a third-party independent challenge from Congressman John Anderson of Illinois, who seemed certain to divert more votes from the incumbent.

The fall campaign did not go as badly for Carter in its initial phases as the polls had predicted. The president's brother, Billy Carter, had been involved with the Libyan government as a kind of lobbyist. The press charged that there was a "Billygate" scandal. When the younger Carter testified before Con-

Televised images, like this one of hostage Barry Rosen on December 26, 1980, convinced the public that Carter had not dealt effectively with Iran. The hostage crisis involving American diplomats in Iran was a crippling problem for the Carter presidency.

gress in the autumn of 1980, he laid the major charges to rest, and the controversy ebbed away. At the same time, Reagan's campaign got off to a shaky start because of the candidate's propensity for erratic statements, such as "Fascism was the real basis for the New Deal." By late September the economy showed some signs of improvement, and Reagan's huge lead in the polls, which had stood at 28 points in July, had narrowed to just 4 percentage points. While the American people liked Reagan's manner and affability, they had questions about his capacity to lead. Their feelings for Carter included respect for his dedication as president but doubts about his personal qualities and competence. The televised debate seemed likely to have a great influence on the outcome of the election.

The confrontation occurred on October 28, 1980, and Reagan emerged as the clear winner. At one point Carter said that Reagan would attack the Social Security system. Reagan gave one of his trademark smiles, shrugged, and said, "There you go

again." The line seemed to take the air out of Carter. Then, in his closing statement, the challenger said that voters should ask themselves before casting their ballots "Are you better off than you were four years ago?" It was a question to which Jimmy Carter and had no good riposte by November 1980.

One imponderable was the fate of the hostages in Iran. Negotiations with Tehran continued down to the eve of the election, but the terms that the Iranians wanted, including unfreezing their assets and selling them some arms, were unacceptable to the White House. Republicans warned that Carter might pull "an October surprise" to extricate the hostages for political effect. When Carter gave a televised address days before the election indicating that the hostage stalemate was still unbroken, his political fate was sealed. Undecided voters broke heavily for Reagan in the last days of the campaign.

In the presidential election, Reagan achieved an electoral college landslide with 489 votes to 49 for Carter, who carried only five states and the District of

Former President and Mrs. Carter observe elections in Nigeria on February 27, 1999, as voters line up at a polling station.

Columbia. In the popular vote, Reagan polled 51 percent to 41 percent for Carter and 7 percent for John Anderson. While the overall turnout was low, at 52 percent of the registered voters, the import of the election was clear: The American people had decided that Jimmy Carter was not up to the job of being president, and they wanted the positive, upbeat qualities that Ronald Reagan promised them.

Carter had suffered in office in part from circumstances beyond his control, such as the energy crisis and the revolution in Iran. But he also left the prom-

ise of his presidency unfulfilled because he tried to be a nonpartisan figure in a position that, by its very nature, required consummate political skills.

Despite his defeat, Carter managed the transition to the Reagan administration with impressive grace and skill. On the last day of his presidency, minutes after Reagan had been sworn in, the hostages were released. Reagan sent his predecessor to greet them in Germany. Then the Carters returned to Georgia and private life.

While his presidency became an object of historical study, Jimmy Carter enjoyed an unexpected renaissance after his administration ended. He and his wife wrote their memoirs (hers sold much better than his) and made a living with other writings. Carter did not cash in on his presidential reputation. Instead, he and Rosalynn established the nonprofit Carter Center in Atlanta to address issues of conflict resolution, international health, and democracy, mostly in developing countries. The former president also became involved with Habitat for Humanity. He and Mrs. Carter spend one week each year building low-cost homes in poor neighborhoods throughout the country.

Carter also became increasingly visible on the international scene as he monitored elections and carried on peacemaking missions in Haiti, Korea, and Africa. These activities enhanced Carter's reputation for the disinterested pursuit of a more peaceful world. By the mid-1990s his standing with Americans had risen dramatically and he had achieved the status of respected elder statesman that might have seemed improbable when he left the White House a rejected president.

His post-presidency had succeeded where his presidency had faltered because it allowed Carter full scope for his nonpolitical propensities. He remained aloof from partisan activities and was not identified with the Democratic party or its inner workings. His ability as a world figure to approach problems from a neutral posture enabled him to be a much more constructive force than many other former presidents. In that way, the years after the White House became a redemptive experience for the religious Carter.

Despite his successes (getting the Panama Canal treaties through the Senate, achieving the Camp David agreement on the Middle East) Carter may prove to be a cautionary example of the hazards of approaching the presidency with limited national experience and a puritanical attitude toward Congress. Yet as time goes on, Americans are likely to admire the same qualities in Carter's presidency that they admired in his ex-presidency: high ethical standards, a core of political convictions rooted—more than most Americans realized at the time—in his religion, and a willingness to do what seemed to him right even when it jeopardized his political future.

—*Lewis L. Gould*

RONALD WILSON REAGAN

THE GREAT COMMUNICATOR

For most Americans who remember his presidency, the indelible image of Ronald Reagan is of a tall, handsome man delivering a speech with practiced ease. Whether it was on the Normandy beach, before the Statue of Liberty, or in an address to Congress, he would be there with a modest turn of the head and an effective phrase. He told religious broadcasters that Soviet Communism was "the focus of evil in the modern world." In Berlin he declared, "Mr. Gorbachev, tear down this wall!" When twitted about his light schedule, he retorted that long hours were the sign of a bad executive. (He quipped, "It's true hard work never killed anybody, but I figure, why take a chance?") After a generation of failed presidents, Reagan seemed to be in charge.

Reagan's passionate defenders assign him credit for reviving the presidency after the damage of Vietnam and Watergate, for restoring prosperity after 1982, for winding down the Cold War, and for turning the nation in a conservative direction. To many in the Republican party, he is a totemic symbol of past political greatness. Critics of Reagan, on the other hand, point to the huge budget deficits, which escalated during his watch. They contend that he ignored social problems and allowed the Iran-contra scandal to happen. Some deprecate him as a deft reader of a prepared script.

Ronald Wilson Reagan was born in Tampico, Illinois, on February 6, 1911, to John Edward Reagan and Nelle Wilson Reagan. Reagan's father was Roman Catholic in religion and alcoholic in his personal life; his mother belonged to the Disciples of Christ and imparted conservative values to her son. She also introduced him to acting by entering him in church skits. From the start, he responded to the applause of audiences. Because of his alcoholic father's "week-long benders," the family moved around a good deal and had to endure the embarrassment of a drinking parent. After high school, young Ronald went to Eureka College, a Disciples of Christ school in Illinois. He played football, acted in college plays, and was a popular figure on campus. Years later he remarked upon a return to Eureka, "Everything good that has happened to me—everything—started here on this campus."

Young Reagan graduated in 1932 and then managed, in the depths of the Depression, to find a job as a part-time sports announcer. He spent several years in radio in the Midwest. During a spring training trip to California in 1937, he took a screen test and went to work at Warner Brothers studios. Reagan was a solid, talented movie actor but not a major star. His capacity to memorize dialogue quickly made him easy for directors to work with. This dramatic training and his natural affinity for the camera gave him a valuable background for a political career later in life.

Reagan's most memorable role was as the ill-fated Notre Dame football player George Gipp in *Knute Rockne: All American*. The dying Gipp tells Rockne (Pat O'Brien) that if Notre Dame is ever losing an important game, the coach should tell the players to go out and "win one for the Gipper." The episode became a trademark of Reagan's career, and he was even known to some as "the Gipper." In January 1940 Reagan married the actress Jane Wyman. They had a daughter, Maureen, born in 1941, and a son, Michael, whom they adopted in 1945.

During the 1930s and 1940s Reagan was a liberal Democrat, like his father. He supported a number of New Deal causes and was active in movie politics in the Screen Actors Guild. During World War II, he served in the Army Air Force with duties in the Hollywood area at Culver City. He never left the country and never saw combat. In fact he slept most nights in his own bed at home. Because films were so real to Reagan, however, during his political career he

Ronald Reagan's nationwide appeal was enhanced from 1954 to 1962, when he hosted the live television show, *General Electric Theater.*

often invoked memories of the war as if he had experienced them.

After his military service ended, Reagan returned to films and began moving toward the conservatism that would mark his later political career. Part of his change of mind came from his anger at the high tax rates he and other movie stars paid. In addition, as president of the Screen Actors Guild, he encountered Communists there and in other Hollywood unions. He testified before the House Un-American Activities Committee in 1947 against the tactics of the Communists in Hollywood and cooperated with the widespread blacklist against suspected subversives in the motion picture industry. Meanwhile, his first marriage ended in divorce. Reagan's second marriage, to Nancy Davis, in 1952, linked him to a conservative wife from a strongly Republican background. The Reagans had two children, Patricia and Ronald.

Through the 1950s Reagan hosted a television series for General Electric and became their corporate spokesman. He refined his speech about conservative values in countless appearances before business audiences. Although a Democrat, he campaigned for Richard Nixon in 1960 and attacked John F. Kennedy as a socialist. By the early 1960s he had registered as a Republican, and he campaigned for Barry Goldwater against Lyndon Johnson in 1964.

During that campaign Reagan's televised speech for Barry Goldwater, "A Time for Choosing," delivered on October 27, 1964, galvanized conservatives. Largely a distillation of the remarks he had made to audiences at General Electric plants, the presentation was described by journalist David Broder as "the most successful national political debut since William Jennings Bryan electrified the 1896 Democratic Convention with his 'Cross of Gold' speech."

The triumph of Reagan's address led to talk that he too should seek public office. His friends in California urged him to run for governor in 1966 against the incumbent, Edmund G. "Pat" Brown. Although given little chance against Brown, Reagan proved to be a superb campaigner and a popular figure with Californians. He won nearly 58 percent of the vote. There were soon demands for a Reagan presidential bid. But with a late-starting campaign in 1968, Reagan could not defeat Nixon's better-organized effort for the Republican nomination.

As governor of California, Reagan proved to be a strong executive, but he did not achieve the conservative program he had promised in the campaign to pursue. Despite Reagan's pledge to lower taxes and reduce the size of government, the California budget and the

Reagan and his second wife, Nancy Davis Reagan, during the early years of their marriage.

tax burden on its citizens rose because of a growing population and the state's need for enhanced services. None of these developments hurt Reagan's popularity. When he left office in early 1975, Reagan began preparing for a presidential bid in the coming year.

Reagan challenged President Gerald Ford for the nomination with a conservative critique of the president's performance in foreign policy and the economy. One key Reagan proposal was a ninety billion dollar cut in government spending, a move so radical that it backfired against the challenger. Nonetheless, Reagan gave Ford an intense race, and he was defeated very narrowly at the Kansas City convention. Once Ford lost to Jimmy Carter in the presidential contest, Reagan became the front-runner for the nomination in 1980. He would be sixty-nine in 1980, and thus the oldest man from a major party to seek the presidency. But his popularity among the Republican rank and file was deep.

Reagan easily turned back the challenge of George Bush and others in the Republican primaries in 1980 because of his strength with the party's conservative base in the South and West. Reagan sailed to a first-ballot nomination and, after a flirtation with former President Ford, chose Bush as his vice presidential candidate. Although some argued that Reagan's extremism made him a weak candidate, the political tides were running in his direction. The American people were disenchanted with Carter over his handling of the Iran hostage crisis and the Soviet invasion of Afghanistan. More important, runaway inflation and a troubled economy cast strong doubts on Carter's competence. With his promises of lowered taxes, decreased spending on domestic programs, and a more robust national defense, Reagan proved attractive and presidential. He defeated Carter in their one televised debate. When Reagan asked viewers on that occasion if they were "better off" in 1980 than they had been four years earlier when Carter was elected, he posed the question that turned the race decisively

BIOGRAPHICAL FACTS

BIRTH: Tampico, Ill., Feb. 6, 1911
ANCESTRY: Irish and Scotch-English
FATHER: John Edward Reagan, b. Fulton, Ill., July 13, 1883; d. Los Angeles, Calif., May 18, 1941
FATHER'S OCCUPATION: Shoe salesman
MOTHER: Nelle Clyde Wilson Reagan; b. Fulton, Ill. July 24, 1885; d. Santa Monica, Calif., July 25, 1962
BROTHER: John Neil (1909–1996)
FIRST MARRIAGE: Los Angeles, Calif., Jan. 26, 1940
FIRST WIFE: Jane Wyman, b. St. Joseph, Mo., Jan. 4, 1914
SECOND MARRIAGE: Los Angeles, Calif., Mar. 4, 1952
SECOND WIFE: Nancy Davis, b. New York, N.Y., July 6, 1921
CHILDREN: (by first wife) Maureen Elizabeth (1941–); Michael (adopted in 1945); (by second wife) Patricia Ann "Patti" (1952–); Ronald Prescott (1958–)
RELIGIOUS AFFILIATION: Episcopalian
EDUCATION: Eureka College (B.A., 1932)
OCCUPATIONS BEFORE PRESIDENCY: Broadcaster, film actor
MILITARY SERVICE: U.S. Army, 2d lt., capt.
PREPRESIDENTIAL OFFICE: Governor of California
AGE AT INAUGURATION: 69
OCCUPATION AFTER PRESIDENCY: Public speaker

in his favor. He trounced Carter in the electoral college vote and gained a strong plurality of the popular vote against the president and the third-party challenger, Congressman John B. Anderson. Reagan had a Republican majority in the Senate as well, and the promise of a working coalition of Republicans and Southern Democrats in the House of Representatives.

In his inaugural address Reagan argued that government was not the solution to the nation's difficulties; it was the major cause of those problems. He promised a vigorous foreign policy against the Soviet Union and international communism. A conservative president with a conservative agenda had taken over in Washington. On the day of the inauguration, the Iran hostages were released, and Reagan's presidency began on a high note.

After 444 days in captivity in Tehran, the American hostages were released on January 20, 1981—thirty minutes after Reagan was inaugurated—providing the new administration with a promising start.

To run the White House the new president relied on a trio of advisers who managed his priorities with great skill. The chief of staff, James A. Baker, was a good administrator who coordinated the activities of the White House and dealt well with Congress. Reagan appointed his old gubernatorial aide Edwin Meese as counselor to the president. Media efforts fell to Michael Deaver, an expert in television and staged events. The "troika," as it was called, presented Reagan in his most favorable light. All three of the men understood the importance of a positive presidential image. As Reagan's press secretary, Larry Speakes,

once joked to a reporter, "You don't tell us how to stage the news, and we don't tell you how to cover it."

As chief executive, Reagan showed modest interest in the day-to-day operations of the presidency. He set broad priorities and left the implementation to others. As a vestige of his movie days, he found it comforting to have a precise schedule of events to follow, from which he rarely deviated. He sought to restore the dignity and majesty of the office after the informality of the Carter years, and the sounds of "Hail to the Chief" echoed throughout the Reagan presidency.

A leading personality in the Reagan administration was the new first lady. Nancy Reagan was determined to protect her husband from influences that she distrusted and insisted on overseeing his work schedule. She played a key role in the selection of White House personnel and administration appointments. Her opulent clothes and expensive tastes caused talk of "Queen Nancy" which she defused by making fun of herself to the press and endorsing an anti-drug campaign built on the slogan "Just Say No." She was one of the most powerful of the modern first ladies.

The president's performance in two crises set the tone for the new administration in its early months. On March 31, 1981, an assassination attempt in Washington, D.C., by John Hinckley, Jr., left the new president more seriously wounded than the public was told. Reagan's bravery in the face of death, including a quip to his doctors to "Please tell me you're Republicans," enhanced his strong standing with the American people, endowing him with elements of legend and myth. Behind the scenes Reagan's recovery proceeded slowly, and his actual involvement with policy-making in this period diminished.

The second event that helped Americans to understand the depth of Reagan's resolution came in early August 1981 when the Professional Air Traffic Controllers Association (PATCO) staged a walkout from their posts. The president fired all thirteen thousand of the air traffic controllers. Reagan observed that his action "convinced people who might have thought otherwise that I meant what I said." The stern response to a union that had supported Reagan in 1980 showed Americans (and the Soviets) that he was a decisive, no-nonsense executive.

One of the key aspects of Reagan's economic program was what became known as "supply-side" economics. Reagan had promised to cut taxes, raise de-fense spending, and balance the budget, all within his first term. The president and his advisers, especial-

FIRST ADMINISTRATION

INAUGURATION: Jan. 20, 1981, the Capitol, Washington, D.C.

VICE PRESIDENT: George Bush

SECRETARY OF STATE: Alexander M. Haig, Jr.; George P. Shultz (from July 16, 1982)

SECRETARY OF THE TREASURY: Donald T. Regan

SECRETARY OF DEFENSE: Caspar W. Weinberger

ATTORNEY GENERAL: William French Smith

SECRETARY OF THE INTERIOR: James G. Watt; William P. Clark (from Nov. 21, 1983)

SECRETARY OF AGRICULTURE: John R. Block

SECRETARY OF COMMERCE: Malcolm Baldrige

SECRETARY OF LABOR: Raymond J. Donovan

SECRETARY OF HEALTH AND HUMAN SERVICES: Richard S. Schweiker; Margaret M. O'Shaughnessy Heckler (from Mar. 9, 1983)

SECRETARY OF HOUSING AND URBAN DEVELOPMENT: Samuel R. Pierce, Jr.

SECRETARY OF TRANSPORTATION: Andrew L. Lewis, Jr.; Elizabeth H. Dole (from Feb. 7, 1983)

SECRETARY OF ENERGY: James B. Edwards; Donald P. Hodel (from Dec. 8, 1982)

SECRETARY OF EDUCATION: Terrel H. Bell

SUPREME COURT APPOINTMENT: Sandra Day O'Connor (1981)

97TH CONGRESS (Jan. 25, 1981–Dec. 23, 1982):
  SENATE: 53 Republicans; 46 Democrats; 1 Other
  HOUSE: 242 Democrats; 192 Republicans; 1 Other
98TH CONGRESS (Jan. 3, 1983–Oct. 12, 1984):
  SENATE: 54 Republicans; 46 Democrats
  HOUSE: 269 Democrats; 166 Republicans

ELECTION OF 1980

CANDIDATES	ELECTORAL VOTE	POPULAR VOTE
Ronald W. Reagan (Republican)	489	43,904,153
James E. Carter (Democratic)	49	35,483,883
John B. Anderson (Independent)	—	5,720,060

ly the budget director, former Congressman David Stockman, contended that if taxes were cut sufficiently, economic activity would be spurred, revenues

restore the nation's defense, the Pentagon budget increased dramatically. The result was an even greater federal deficit and an expanding national debt. Although Reagan was committed to reducing the role of the government in economic life, the budget deficits actually increased the importance of the federal sector in shaping the nation's future.

The Reagan administration pushed through its financial program with the aid of a conservative coalition in Congress composed of Republicans and "boll weevil" Democrats (conservatives from the West and South). The main feature of the Reagan approach was a reduction in tax rates of 25 percent over a three-year period. As the legislation moved through the House of Representatives, the Democrats and Republicans engaged in a war to see who could provide more incentives for their members. Reductions and benefits for special interests piled up. Budget Director David Stockman observed that "the hogs were really feeding."

The upshot of the Reagan program was a sharp rise in the budget deficit to $113 billion in 1982. This red ink continued throughout the Reagan presidency. The president's pledge to balance the budget by 1984 quietly disappeared. One result of what occurred was that little money existed for additional government spending on social programs. It seemed evident that this was what the White House had intended all along. The first year of the Reagan administration saw the economy fall into a severe recession with growing trade deficits and mounting unemployment.

In keeping with Reagan's belief that "in this present crisis, government is not the solution to our problem, government *is* the problem," the administration sought to push a policy of government deregulation wherever possible. For the environment, Reagan's secretary of the interior, James G. Watt, opened up new sections of government lands to oil drilling, reduced purchases of national park land,

would rise, and the budget would be balanced. Reagan also believed that there was enough "fraud, waste, and abuse" in the federal budget that spending cuts could be made without affecting important or popular government services. As it turned out, however, the cuts that were necessary to achieve a balanced budget brought with them serious political risk.

The resulting economic package brought some cuts in federal spending for such programs as Medicaid, Aid for Dependent Children, and food stamps, but left the largest part of domestic government expenditures, Social Security and Medicare, untouched as part of the social safety net. Meanwhile, to

and staffed agencies with officials determined to cut the number of environmental regulations in place.

Another long-term crisis that confronted the Reagan administration was Social Security. By the early 1980s the cost of paying benefits to increasing numbers of elderly Americans was rapidly rising. In the spring of 1981 Reagan proposed that there be a cut in benefits for those who retired early at age 62. The reaction from the Democrats was overwhelming opposition, and the White House rapidly retreated from any effort to limit benefits for such a potent voting bloc. Several years later, however, a presidential commission worked out a compromise set of Social Security proposals that Congress adopted to save the system into the twenty-first century.

While he sought to trim social programs and an activist government, Reagan wished to confront in foreign policy what he perceived to be an aggressive Soviet Union. For Reagan, the Cold War was a battle between "right and wrong and good and evil." The president believed that the United States could outspend the Soviets in an arms race, and he favored a massive buildup in American defenses. At a time when the leadership in Moscow was aging and inept, he shied away from summit meetings. The early 1980s saw a distinct chill fall over Soviet-American relations. Reagan made it clear that he was appalled by the imposition of martial law by the Polish government to crush the challenge from the trade-union group Solidarity.

Reagan was flexible in some respects toward the Soviet Union. He lifted the grain embargo that President Carter had imposed after the Soviets had invaded Afghanistan. Distrustful of the SALT II Treaty that Carter had worked out, Reagan still observed the provisions of the pact. Nonetheless, it was a time of growing East-West tension.

The initial architect of Reagan's foreign policy was Secretary of State Alexander Haig, who had been Richard Nixon's chief of staff during the Watergate period. Haig soon proved with his turf-consciousness that he could not work amiably with the president. His most memorable gaffe occurred shortly after the

As this cartoon suggests, the covert operations of the Reagan administration in Nicaragua and elsewhere in Central America were anything but silent and discreet.

assassination attempt on Reagan. He erroneously told reporters that he was second in line of presidential succession and added, "I am in control here in the White House," prompting many to think him eager to grab power. Haig gave way in 1982 to George P. Shultz, who was a more competent spokesman for the Reagan policies. The president ran through a number of national security advisers during the first term as well.

One area of crisis was Central America. To the men around Reagan, the victory of the Sandinista rebels in Nicaragua in 1979 brought a significant threat to United States interests in the region. To meet this danger, Washington funded a rebellion against the Sandinistas led by the so-called "contras." The president said that these men were in the mold of the patriots of the American Revolution. Congress did not agree. It adopted the Boland Amendment in 1982, which endeavored to stop funds from being used to throw out the Sandinistas.

Reagan's first four years produced a mixture of successes and failures in foreign policy. In the Middle East efforts to broker a lasting peace between Israel and its neighbors did not prosper. The White House saw Israel invade Lebanon in June 1982 to strike at bases of the Palestine Liberation Organization. The attack was carried out against the overt wishes of Washington, and the United States later sent in Marines as part of a multinational peacekeeping contingent. The involvement led to a tragedy when a terrorist bomb blew up a barracks and killed 241 Marines in 1983. The United States withdrew its forces in early 1984. This kind of attack would become more frequent during the 1980s as radical states, such as Libya under Muammar Gadhafi, used the weapon of terror against the West.

In October 1983 the United States invaded the Caribbean island of Grenada to forestall what the White House believed was a potential Cuban attempt to turn the island into a Soviet base. After a quick struggle, the United States seized control of the situation. The episode reinforced Reagan's image as a powerful leader.

Reagan announced the most important defense policy of his first term in October 1983 when he proclaimed the Strategic Defense Initiative (SDI). The president spoke of a system of space-based laser weapons that could shoot down Soviet missiles before they reached the United States. It would serve, said Reagan, as "a defensive screen that could intercept those missiles when they came out of the silos." Critics promptly dubbed the program "Star Wars" and warned that it would involve a dangerous escalation in the arms race with the Soviets. Fears about a nuclear exchange nourished a popular movement in the United States for the abolition of nuclear weapons. The leaders of the Soviet Union found the prospect of SDI especially ominous. They knew that their economy would never be able to reciprocate such an expenditure. This was just what Reagan intended.

A severe recession persisted throughout 1982. Reagan urged the American people to "stay the course," but on Election Day the Republicans suffered defeats. The Democrats picked up twenty-seven House seats while the Republicans retained control of the Senate. Still, Reagan argued that his economic policies would soon pay off.

Shortly after the votes were counted, the economy began to improve and the president's poll numbers started to climb. By early 1984 he had reached 55 percent. Republican commercials proclaimed that it was "Morning in America" and that under Reagan the country was "stronger, prouder and better." With a strong base in the South and the West, the Republicans saw a promising electoral map when they looked to the 1984 contest.

The only potential problem was Reagan's age: He was now seventy-three. He often seemed detached from the problems of the administration, and his physical stamina was in doubt. (After his presidency,

The president enjoys a whistle-stop tour through Ohio on October 12, 1984, waving to the crowds that lined up to see him. His reelection campaign in 1984 was a triumphal procession over the Democratic ticket of Walter Mondale and Geraldine Ferraro.

the public learned that he had Alzheimer's disease; with no serious evidence, some later charged that the effects of his illness might have started while Reagan was president.) Still, unless he faltered because of his age, he was clearly the favorite over any prospective Democratic rival.

The Democrats picked the stolid former Vice President Walter Mondale. Even Mondale's dramatic selection of Representative Geraldine Ferraro as the first female vice presidential candidate could not disrupt the Reagan lead. When Mondale said that tax increases would be necessary, he handed the Repub-

licans a winning issue. During the first of two debates with Mondale, the president was slow and uncertain. But two weeks later, after being carefully prepared, Reagan bounced back when one of the reporters asked him about his age. Reagan quipped that he would not allow age to be an issue: "I am not going to exploit for political purposes my opponent's youth and inexperience." Even though Reagan stumbled toward the end of the debate, the media emphasized his witty comment and declared him the winner.

The election was a landslide. President Reagan

carried 49 of the 50 states, losing only Mondale's home state of Minnesota and the District of Columbia. He took 58.8 percent of the popular vote. The American people liked Ronald Reagan and wanted to see him stay in office. This was despite the fact that Republicans in 1984 had provided few guidelines for the country's course over the next four years. The Reagan Revolution was running out of gas.

In the second administration, staff changes diminished the dynamic and efficiency of the Reagan White House. James Baker replaced Secretary of the Treasury Donald Regan, who moved over to become the White House chief of staff. Baker was interested in the more challenging job at the Treasury Department, and Regan fancied himself the kind of astute manager who could make Reagan do even better in a second term. The president approved the shift without much thought, and Regan began aggregating power and attention in an effort to make himself Reagan's "prime minister."

The Reagan administration sought little domestic legislation during the second term. The president got credit for the Tax Reform Act of 1986, which produced lower rates and less complexity, but that law owed at least as much to Senators Robert Packwood and Bill Bradley. The deficits continued to mount despite the adoption by Congress of a plan to reduce the red ink, called the Gramm-Rudman-Hollings Act.

The Soviet-American tension of the first term began to ease after Mikhail Gorbachev came to power in Moscow in March 1985. Eager to pursue reform in the creaking Soviet system and to forge a new, more harmonious relationship with the United States, Gorbachev tried to restructure his nation's economy, calling it "perestroika." At the same time, he demanded greater openness within Soviet society which he called "glasnost." Gorbachev announced cuts in Soviet missiles and proclaimed that his nation should be part of Europe. The two leaders met amiably in Geneva in

November 1985. At Reykjavík, Iceland, in October 1986, the two men surprisingly came close to agreement on a plan to sharply reduce their nuclear arsenals, but they failed when Gorbachev insisted that research for Reagan's SDI be confined to the laboratory. Reagan still wanted to cap off his second term with an arms control treaty that would give him a historical reputation as a peacemaker and encourage concessions from Gorbachev that would wind down the Cold War.

Before that could be done, however, a major foreign policy scandal erupted that cast a shadow over the remainder of Reagan's presidency. In November 1986 the news broke that the United States had sold arms to the Islamic government in Iran to secure the release of several western hostages held by radical groups in the Middle East. The nation soon also learned that money received from these arms sales had been secretly and illegally diverted to support the Nicaraguan contras in their battle against the Sandinista government. The Iran-contra scandal, as it came to be called, involved people in the White House including the national security adviser, Rear Admiral John Poindexter, and Lieutenant Colonel Oliver North, a Marine officer assigned to the staff of the National Security Council. President Reagan had approved trying to use the arms sales to persuade Middle Eastern terrorists to release hostages. What he knew or understood about the diversion of funds to the contras remains unclear.

When the scandal broke, Reagan insisted, "We did not, repeat, did not, trade weapons or anything else for hostages, nor will we." Reagan's insistence on this point in the face of the clear factual record to the contrary undermined his credibility with the American people. Those involved in Iran-contra left the government and were later prosecuted for their part in the scheme. Reagan's relaxed leadership style came under fire from a special commission, chaired by Senator John Tower of Texas, which Reagan himself named, as well as from a joint Senate-House Committee. The highly publicized congressional hearings opened up a covert world of White House independent foreign policy initiatives about which even the Central Intelligence Agency and the Defense Department were not well informed. The resulting confusion did serious damage to American interests in the world.

With only a year and a half left for Reagan's administration, there was, however, little disposition to pursue impeachment proceedings against the president. Many in Congress worried that the country would suffer if, so soon after Nixon, another president was driven from office by scandal. Encouraged by his wife, Reagan fired Donald Regan from the White House staff.

In his first term, Reagan had named the first woman to the Supreme Court—Sandra Day O'Connor. When Chief Justice Warren Burger retired, the president named Justice William H. Rehnquist to succeed him and Antonin Scalia, a federal appeals court judge, to take the vacant seat. Then in June 1987, when Justice Lewis Powell resigned, Reagan nominated Robert Bork. A prominent legal conservative, Bork encountered a firestorm of liberal and feminist opposition and his candidacy was rejected.

The administration and Congress had agreed early in the decade to deregulate the nation's savings and loan industry. Freewheeling lending practices cost the taxpayers hundreds of billions of dollars. Similar problems were becoming apparent in the Department

President Reagan and Soviet Union General Secretary Mikhail Gorbachev pose for photographs in Moscow's Red Square during their summit on May 31, 1988. Soviet-American relations had warmed considerably by the end of Reagan's presidency, opening the way for the end of the Cold War.

of Housing and Urban Development. Attorney General Edwin Meese and other presidential advisers were charged with ethical violations. A stock market crash in October 1987, while causing little permanent damage to the economy, became a symbol of the slowing down of the economic successes of the Reagan years.

But relations with the Soviet Union were improving dramatically. By late 1987 the two sides had decided to remove intermediate range missiles from Europe. Gorbachev came to Washington in December 1987 to sign that agreement. The following year, Reagan went to Moscow to meet with his Soviet counterpart. There was an atmosphere of East-West hope that would have seemed inconceivable at the beginning of the 1980s.

Reagan took no public position on who should win the Republican nomination in 1988, but he was pleased when Vice President Bush defeated Democrat Michael Dukakis, governor of Massachusetts, to win the presidency. When Reagan left the White House in January 1989, his poll ratings stood at 70 percent, the highest ever for a retiring chief executive. On the day the Reagans departed Washington, the former president said to his wife as they gazed down on the White House from their airplane: "Look, honey, there's our little shack."

As an ex-president, Reagan gave speeches, published his memoirs, and dedicated the Reagan Library in 1991. Then in November 1994 he released a poignant letter to the American people disclosing that he had Alzheimer's disease. "I now begin the journey that will lead me into the sunset of my life," he said. "I know that for America there will always be a bright dawn ahead." In the years that followed, his condition sharply worsened. He no longer recognized old friends or even many family members. For Nancy Reagan, her husband's experience of Alzheimer's became a tortuous "long goodbye."

Ronald Reagan's presidency is still the subject of

much argument. His defenders assign him credit for victory in the Cold War, the revival of the presidency and national spirit, and the economic prosperity that marked the last six years of his administration. Detractors contend that the Soviet Union collapsed because of its own internal weaknesses and that Reagan's defense policies and budget deficits imposed an intolerable burden of debt on the American people. To liberal critics, Reaganism meant profits for the well-to-do and hardship for the poor and underprivileged, moving the country backward on issues such as race relations and the environment.

Until Reagan's papers become fully available and we gain greater hindsight, many of these questions will remain unresolved. Reagan himself was a very difficult person to understand. Was he "an amiable dunce," as the Democratic leader Clark Clifford called him, or a shrewd operator who knew how to have other people do what he wanted? There is no doubt that Reagan had the internal fortitude to pursue controversial goals in the certainty that the American people would agree with him. While president, he was loved as no president had been since Eisenhower. Whether or not people approved of his policies, they responded to his optimism and unabashed patriotism in a manner that made him seem a Republican counterpart to his own political idol, Franklin D. Roosevelt. Whatever history's verdict, it is probable that Reagan will be seen as one of the most important leaders of the twentieth century. In his farewell letter to the nation, announcing his diagnosis of Alzheimer's disease, he thanked his fellow citizens "for giving me the great honor of allowing me to serve as your President."

—LEWIS L. GOULD

THE FORTY-FIRST PRESIDENT ★ 1989–1993

GEORGE HERBERT WALKER BUSH

THE LAST COLD WARRIOR

On Christmas Day 1991, at the presidential retreat at Camp David, George Bush took a call from Mikhail Gorbachev, the man with whom Bush had presided over the end of the Cold War. The Soviet leader told him that he would be resigning his job and declaring the Soviet Union dead.

Afterwards, Bush dictated into his private diary, "There was something very moving about this phone call—a real historic note. I mentioned to him Camp David and wanting him back up here. . . . I didn't want to get too maudlin or or too emotional, but I literally felt like I was caught up in real history with a phone call like this. . . . God, we're lucky in this country—we have so many blessings."

That moment captures one of Bush's two major historical achievements—the end of the Cold War on essentially American terms and his leadership in the Persian Gulf War against Iraq. Bush could not know it at Christmas 1991, but in these victories were the seeds of his defeat for reelection eleven months later, when Americans turned away from foreign policy.

Bush was born in 1924 in Massachusetts to a wealthy investment banker, Prescott Bush, and his wife. George grew up in Greenwich, Connecticut, and vacationed at the family home in Maine. He attended private schools and, after graduating from Phillips (Andover) Academy in 1942, joined the Navy. Bush became the youngest Navy pilot. After he was sent to the Pacific, he was shot down on a bombing mission in September 1944 but was rescued by an American submarine. Upon his return home, he married Barbara Pierce in January 1945. (The couple had met during Bush's last year at Andover, and their romance continued while he served in the Pacific.) They had six children; their daughter, Robin, died of leukemia when she was three. As adults, two of their sons became governors: George Walker Bush of Texas and John Ellis "Jeb" Bush of Florida.

After the World War II, George Bush went to Yale. There he played baseball and joined the secret society Skull and Bones; he was, as a friend later said, "not among Yale's young activists or its intellectuals." He graduated in 1948. Rather than following his father's path into investment banking in the East, Bush moved to West Texas where family friends, an expanding postwar economy, and his own hard work, exuberance, and ingenuity assisted him in making a small fortune in the oil business.

Meanwhile, his father had become a United States Senator from Connecticut. Mindful of that example, George Bush was ambitious to forge a career in Republican politics in Texas. When the family moved to Houston in the early 1960s, George Bush served as Republican chairman in Harris County and then announced his candidacy for the United States Senate in 1964. He won the Republican primary easily but lost in the general election to the Democratic incumbent, Ralph Yarborough, in the Lyndon B. Johnson landslide of that year.

Two years later Bush was elected to the House of Representatives, where he spent four years. He was interested in family planning and population control, which earned him the nickname "Rubbers." He voted for the Fair Housing Act of 1968, an act of courage in his conservative district. In 1970 he planned to make another try for the Senate against Yarborough. Foiling the Republican's plans, a more moderate Democrat, Lloyd M. Bentsen, Jr., upset the liberal Yarborough in the Democratic primary and then went on to defeat Bush in the fall. After two failed senatorial races, Bush's political career was at a crossroads.

President Richard Nixon named him as United States ambassador to the United Nations, and then, after the 1972 elections, as chairman of the Republican National Committee. In the latter role he had to face the fallout for the party of the Watergate scandal. When Gerald Ford succeeded Nixon, Bush was his

George Bush, a World War II fighter pilot in the Pacific, looks out from the cockpit of his TBM Avenger—named *Barbara III* for his future wife.

second choice (after Nelson Rockefeller) for vice president. Bush instead became the United States envoy to China and then director of the Central Intelligence Agency. The series of appointive assignments in the 1970s helped raise Bush's visibility within the Republican party and fed his own interest in presidential politics. He positioned himself, in the words of a reporter, to gain the "support of the moderate, Gerald Ford wing of the party."

In 1980 Bush emerged as the main challenger to Ronald Reagan in the race for the presidential nomination. His ads claimed that he would be "a president we don't have to train." He won the Iowa caucuses in an upset over Reagan and seemed to be heading toward a victory because his campaign had "momentum." In describing Reagan's tax-cutting proposals, Bush later coined the term "voodoo economics." In New Hampshire, however, Reagan's natural strength with the Republican rank and file reasserted itself; he soon eclipsed Bush and won the nomination. Reagan picked Bush as his running mate, and the Republican ticket defeated Jimmy Carter and Walter Mondale in the 1980 presidential contest.

Bush served Reagan as a loyal vice president for eight years. He refrained from any public criticism of the president and accepted the assignments of foreign travel and standing in for the president. Bush went to so many state funerals that he joked his motto was: "You die, I fly." In 1984 he debated the Democratic vice presidential candidate, Congresswoman Geraldine Ferraro. Facing the first woman candidate of a major national party, Bush emphasized his experience and knowledge, saying at one point in a discussion of the Middle East: "Let me help you with the difference, Mrs. Ferraro, between Iran and the embassy in Lebanon." Ferraro responded, "I almost resent your patronizing attitude that you have to teach me about foreign policy." After the event he told reporters, "We tried to kick a little ass last night." Bush himself later remarked, "I was too testy."

The vice president eagerly embraced most of the accomplishments of the Reagan administration, but one aspect proved to be a political problem for him. When the debacle known as the Iran-contra scandal emerged in 1986, the question arose of how much Bush knew about selling arms for hostages to Iran and diverting funds to the contra rebels in Nicaragua. Bush argued strongly that he was not "in the decision-making loop." Critics charged that Bush should have known what was taking place and even that he was involved in the wrongdoing. Though Bush had a general sense of what arms-for-hostages entailed, his personal participation in the scandal was peripheral.

As he prepared to enter the presidential race after eight years as vice president, the biggest problem Bush faced was the perception that he had become too deferential to Ronald Reagan and his administration. The cartoonist Garry Trudeau jibed that Bush had put his manhood in "a blind trust." The columnist George Will wrote that "the unpleasant sound Bush is emitting as he traipses from one conservative gathering to another is a thin, tinny arf'—the sound of a lapdog." Bush saw his major task as establishing himself as a presidential candidate on his own political terms.

Bush announced his candidacy for the Republican nomination in 1987. His strongest challenge rose from Senate Republican leader Robert Dole of Kansas. In the Iowa caucuses Dole led Bush, who finished third, after evangelist Pat Robertson, and they faced each other in a definitive struggle in the New Hampshire primary. Largely because of the strong endorsement of Governor John Sununu and his organization, Bush won the primary and then went on to capture the nomination by winning primaries in the South and West. In return, Bush was to name Sununu as his White House chief of staff. For his running mate, Bush selected Senator J. Danforth Quayle of Indiana. Quayle's youth and good looks were supposed to complement Bush's age and experience, but a furor ensued over Quayle's qualifications and his efforts to join the National Guard, which kept him from going to Vietnam. Bush remained loyal to his choice and the storm blew over, but doubts about Quayle's stature persisted.

The defining moment of the convention week was Bush's acceptance speech. At the climax of his remarks, he predicted that when he was president, Democrats in Congress "will push me to raise taxes, and I'll say no. And they'll push and I'll say no." When they pushed again, "I'll say to them: read my lips, *no new taxes!*"

The crowd roared. Bush surged ahead of the Democratic nominee, Massachusetts Governor Michael Dukakis, who had enjoyed a seventeen-point lead in the polls. But the speech proved to be curse as well as blessing. Once Bush was in office with the reality of a Democratic Congress, the pledge would present him with an excruciating choice. Keep it, and face a stalemate on Capitol Hill. Break it, and break the confidence of conservatives in his devotion to their principles.

During the campaign, experienced Republican political operatives, led by a take-no-prisoners Southerner named Lee Atwater, unleashed negative advertising that eroded Dukakis's position with the voters. They depicted the Massachusetts governor as an extreme liberal without any experience in foreign policy. Dukakis was an uninspiring candidate, and he did little to rebut the Republican assault on his character and record. One signature moment was a television spot known as the "Willie Horton" ad. Horton, an escaped African-American convict from a Massachusetts furlough program that Dukakis supported, had raped a woman in Maryland before his recapture. An independent group, sympathetic to the Bush campaign, ran the ad. Democrats charged racism, but the image stuck with the electorate.

Bush proved to be a reasonably capable debater in his two confrontations with Dukakis. The Democrats hurt their own cause in the second debate when

BIOGRAPHICAL FACTS

BIRTH: Milton, Mass., June 12, 1924
ANCESTRY: English
FATHER: Prescott Bush; b. Columbus, Ohio, May 15, 1895; d. Greenwich, Ct., Oct. 8, 1972
FATHER'S OCCUPATIONS: Investment banker; U.S. senator
MOTHER: Dorothy Walker Bush; b. Kennebunkport, Me., Jan. 1, 1901; d. Greenwich, Ct., Nov. 19, 1992
BROTHERS: Prescott Sheldon (1922–); Jonathan James (1931–); William Henry Trotter (1938–)
SISTER: Nancy (1926–)
MARRIAGE: Rye, N.Y., Jan. 6, 1945
WIFE: Barbara Pierce; b. Bronx, N.Y., June 8, 1925
CHILDREN: George Walker (1946–); Robin (1949–1953); John Ellis "Jeb" (1953–); Neil Mallon (1955–); Marvin Pierce (1956–); Dorothy Pierce (1959–)
RELIGIOUS AFFILIATION: Episcopalian
EDUCATION: Private schools; Phillips (Andover) Academy; Yale University (B.A., 1948)
OCCUPATION BEFORE PRESIDENCY: Co-founder of Zapata Petroleum and Zapata Off-Shore (drilling in Gulf of Mexico)
MILITARY SERVICE: Pilot, U.S. Navy (active duty from June 12, 1942–Sept. 18, 1945)
PREPRESIDENTIAL OFFICES: U.S. congressman; U.S. ambassador to UN (1971–73); chairman of the Republican National Committee (1973–74); U.S. liaison to China (1974–75); director of CIA (1976–77); U.S. vice president
AGE AT INAUGURATION: 64
OCCUPATION AFTER PRESIDENCY: Writer; speaker

Dukakis responded tepidly to a question about whether he would change his views on the death penalty if his wife "were raped and murdered." Dan Quayle did less well in his confrontation with the Democratic vice presidential nominee, Lloyd Bentsen. When Quayle claimed that he had "as much experience in the Congress as Jack Kennedy did when he sought the presidency," Bentsen pounced. "Senator," he responded, "I served with Jack Kennedy. I knew Jack Kennedy. Jack Kennedy was a friend of mine. Senator, you are no Jack Kennedy."

Bush's "Read My Lips" speech gave cartoonists endless inspiration. This one, by Pat Oliphant, appeared on December 7, 1988.

The election went Bush's way in the end. Bush carried 53 percent of the popular vote and forty states. But the Republicans lost seats in both the House and the Senate. Bush named James A. Baker as secretary of state, and he sought to have former Senator John Tower become secretary of defense. The latter selection failed when senators raised questions about Tower's reputation as a drinker and womanizer. Congressman Richard Cheney of Wyoming proved to be an able substitute. The chairman of the Joint Chiefs of Staff, General Colin L. Powell, the first African-American to hold the post, also proved a strong figure in the Bush foreign policy team. While asserting that the new administration would be an extension of Ronald Reagan's, Bush was concerned to put his own stamp on the presidency. That stance did not please Reagan loyalists who still eyed the chief executive with suspicion.

Bush relished being president. He held regular press briefings, chatted for hours with foreign leaders by phone, and enjoyed wielding the levers of power. His cryptic phrases became known as "Bushisms," as when he said a person in trouble was "in deep doo-doo." He raced through work and vacations at the same hectic pace. In domestic policy he lacked what

he called, in his own verbal shorthand, "the vision thing." His goal, he said, was "first, do no harm," and then to pursue "a kinder, gentler nation." He emphasized volunteerism and private charitable acts that created "a thousand points of light" for the nation. The Bush White House supported the Clean Air Act (1990) and the Americans with Disabilities Act (1990). He told the public, "In case you haven't noticed, I really love my job."

The preoccupying interest of the new president was in foreign policy, where the United States faced both challenges and opportunities as the Cold War receded. As his national security advisor, Bush selected General Brent Scowcroft, who worked well with Baker, General Powell, and the president. At home the economy seemed strong and the need for new domestic legislation appeared relatively modest. As a result, the president could devote ample time to his first love, foreign affairs.

The Bush team faced complex problems arising from the growing difficulties under which the Soviet Union was laboring by 1989. Despite the best efforts of the Soviet leader, Mikhail Gorbachev, at introducing reform (perestroika) and greater openness (glasnost), the economic troubles of the Soviet empire were mounting. Apprehensions about the future of the Soviet bloc grew intense. Bush sought "a thorough review of our policy toward the Soviet Union, in terms of arms control, in terms of everything." In a speech at Texas A&M, the new president said that it was propitious "to move beyond containment" as a national policy. By the time that Bush first met Gorbachev, in Malta during December 1989, the Soviet empire had begun to disintegrate. Eastern European nations such as Hungary and Czechoslovakia were breaking away from the Communist bloc. Bush was careful not to embarrass Gorbachev as these momentous changes, including the destruction of the Berlin Wall and the unification of Germany within NATO (which Bush's careful diplomacy had encouraged), went forward.

This process continued until 1991, when old-line Communists attempted a coup against Gorbachev in Russia. Because of the leadership of Boris Yeltsin, the head of the Russian Republic, the uprising failed and with it the Communist party. The republics of the Soviet Union broke away from each other, and by the end of the year the Soviet Union had disappeared. Yeltsin emerged as the new leader of Russia. Bush and Yeltsin pushed through a series of measures to provide aid to Russia and to reduce the number of nuclear weapons in both countries. Managing the transition from the Cold War to a new international arrangement represented one of the striking foreign policy achievements of Bush's presidency. However, not all the Eastern European nations experienced a smooth exit from the Cold War era. The former Yugoslavia broke up into its component parts, and ethnic and religious tensions soon produced long-lasting violence in the region.

In other areas of the world, the Bush administration encountered a mixture of success and difficulty. In Panama, the country's leader, General Manuel Noriega, had been both a paid American agent and a drug trafficker with the Colombian cartel. On the basis of some social encounters, Noriega boasted:

THE BUSH ADMINISTRATION

INAUGURATION: Jan. 20, 1989, the Capitol, Washington, D.C.

VICE PRESIDENT: J. Danforth "Dan" Quayle

SECRETARY OF STATE: James A. Baker, III; Lawrence S. Eagleburger (from Dec. 8, 1992)

SECRETARY OF THE TREASURY: Nicholas F. Brady

SECRETARY OF DEFENSE: Richard B. Cheney

ATTORNEY GENERAL: Richard L. Thornburgh; William P. Barr (from Nov. 20, 1991)

SECRETARY OF THE INTERIOR: Manuel Lujan, Jr.

SECRETARY OF AGRICULTURE: Clayton K. Yeutter; Edward Madigan (from Mar. 7, 1991)

SECRETARY OF COMMERCE: Robert A. Mosbacher; Barbara H. Franklin (from Feb. 27, 1992)

SECRETARY OF LABOR: Elizabeth H. Dole; Lynn M. Martin (from Feb. 22, 1991)

SECRETARY OF HEALTH AND HUMAN SERVICES: Louis W. Sullivan

SECRETARY OF HOUSING AND URBAN DEVELOPMENT: Jack F. Kemp

SECRETARY OF TRANSPORTATION: Samuel K. Skinner; Andrew H. Card (from Jan. 22, 1992)

SECRETARY OF ENERGY: James D. Watkins

SECRETARY OF EDUCATION: Lauro F. Cavazos, Jr.; Lamar Alexander (from Mar. 14, 1991)

SECRETARY OF VETERANS AFFAIRS: Edward J. Derwinski

SUPREME COURT APPOINTMENTS: David H. Souter (1990); Clarence Thomas (1991)

101ST CONGRESS (Jan. 3, 1989–Oct. 28, 1990):
SENATE: 55 Democrats; 45 Republicans
HOUSE: 260 Democrats; 175 Republicans

102ND CONGRESS (Jan. 3, 1991–Oct. 9, 1992):
SENATE: 56 Democrats; 44 Republicans
HOUSE: 267 Democrats; 167 Republicans

ELECTION OF 1988

CANDIDATES	ELECTORAL VOTE	POPULAR VOTE
George Bush (Republican)	426	48,886,097
Michael S. Dukakis (Democratic)	112	41,809,074
Lloyd M. Bentsen, Jr. (Democratic)	1	—

President Bush eats Thanksgiving dinner with American troops in Saudi Arabia on November 22, 1990, in the midst of the buildup toward the Gulf War. The victory in the war would be the high point of Bush's years in office.

"I've got Bush by the balls." In December 1989 the president and his men saw things differently. When the Panamanians roughed up American soldiers and then killed one serviceman, Bush ordered an invasion that led to Noriega's capture, trial, and imprisonment in the United States.

Because of his work in China during the 1970s, Bush felt a special affinity for that country. In the spring of 1989, students demonstrating for democracy in Tiananmen Square were crushed by the authorities. In protest, the administration had to take steps to reduce contact between the two nations. Bush believed that strong economic sanctions against the Chinese would not help in curbing human rights abuses in that country. He thought that changes toward free market capitalism would in time break down China's isolation and commitment to Commu-

nism. Behind the scenes the negotiations continued, and discord with Beijing persisted.

The greatest foreign policy crisis of the Bush presidency came in the summer of 1990 when Iraq, led by Saddam Hussein, invaded its small neighbor, Kuwait. Until that time the Reagan and Bush administrations had courted Iraq as a counterweight in the Persian Gulf against the threat from Iran. Many elements went into shaping American policy in that area of the world. The United States had a vital stake in Mideast oil supplies. Iraq was a key player in preserving the balance of power against Iran, and there had long been the sense that Washington could do business with Saddam Hussein. In the spring of 1990 the American ambassador had indicated to Iraq that the United States was not overly concerned about the fate of Kuwait. However, when Saddam Hussein invaded

Kuwait and imperiled the crucial oil reserves of Saudi Arabia, Bush told the nation, "This will not stand, this aggression against Kuwait." He and his administration assembled a coalition against Iraq that enabled the United States to build a military force to oust the invader from Kuwait.

The Gulf War saw Bush's personal diplomacy and international contacts enable the United States to assemble an allied force large enough to confront and then overwhelm the Iraqi army. The initial goal was to protect Saudi Arabia from Iraqi invasion under the code name Operation Desert Shield. With the Soviet Union supporting Iraq's withdrawal from Kuwait, the president told Congress that "Out of these troubled times . . . a new world order can emerge."

Bush believed that economic sanctions would not compel Saddam's withdrawal, and his administration obtained United Nations approval for military action to eject Hussein from Kuwait. American action in Kuwait required the assent of Congress, which the Bush administration secured by a narrow margin in January 1991. Within days an air war (Operation Desert Storm) against Iraq was underway, and then in late February came the ground assault that after a few days of combat had driven the Iraqi forces out of Kuwait and back into their native country.

So powerful was the allied force that the administration worried that continuation of the war might draw charges of atrocities and slaughter. The issue of pursuing Saddam Hussein to Baghdad to remove him from power was considered but abandoned as likely to disrupt the coalition. The liberation of Kuwait had been achieved, and the outright expulsion of Hussein was not part of the administration's strategy, nor that of the multination coalition formed to fight Iraq. In the aftermath of the war, when Hussein rebounded, this decision came under criticism. Bush's argument had merit since the American public, while euphoric over victory, had little appetite for a protracted war in Iraq. The problem of Hussein persisted throughout

the remainder of Bush's term and the presidency of Bill Clinton.

The success in the Gulf War lifted Bush's personal popularity ratings near the 90 percent range. Commentators argued that Bush was now unbeatable for reelection in 1992. Major Democratic contenders decided to sit out the presidential race. The president had always preferred governing to running for office. He wanted to delay active campaigning for reelection for as long as he could. His advisers worried about this decision since they suspected that Bush's domestic situation was more perilous than it seemed in the heady days of victory in Iraq. With foreign policy in such good shape, the voters were now inclined to judge presidential candidates on their performance at

COLIN L. POWELL

General Colin L. Powell personified the military image of the Bush administration as the chairman of the Joint Chiefs of Staff from 1989 to 1993, the first African-American to hold the post. Entering the Army as a second lieutenant in 1958, he rose through the officer grades to general and by the 1970s was serving in a variety of posts in the Pentagon that brought his abilities to the attention of his political superiors. He became the presidential assistant for national security during the last two years of the Reagan administration. As chairman of the Joint Chiefs under President Bush, Powell was intimately involved in the planning for the operation to capture Panama's leader, Manuel Noriega, and was even more prominent in the Gulf War. He became, with General H. Norman Schwarzkopf, the embodiment of American power in the world. After the Bush term, Powell was much talked of for the Republican presidential nomination in 1996. Although he declared himself a Republican, Powell decided not to run, instead throwing himself into causes that emphasized young people and voluntarism. His political future was still bright as the 1990s ended.

home, an area where Bush was having difficulties.

Bush's troubles began in earnest in May 1990 when he faced the problem of getting a budget through the Democratic Congress. It became clear that the Democrats would not accept a budgetary agreement that rested solely on cuts in spending. Some increases in revenues would be necessary to accomplish a budget deal. The White House announced the end of Bush's "no new taxes" position. This raised a furor among many Republicans. The president's endorsement of a capital-gains tax cut that would benefit wealthier taxpayers suggested to critics where his priorities lay. During the fall of 1990 the White House negotiated a budget agreement that called for some revenue increases and cuts in government spending. Conservatives were further outraged

that Bush had repudiated his earlier pledge on the eve of the congressional elections. Although the policy was probably unworkable from the outset, many Americans never recovered their faith in Bush after his change of heart. Within the Republican party, conservatives such as Patrick Buchanan, a television commentator and former aide to Presidents Nixon and Reagan, planned on mounting a challenge to Bush's renomination.

In 1991, Bush nominated Clarence Thomas, an African-American federal court judge, to succeed Thurgood Marshall on the Supreme Court. When Anita Hill, a former colleague of Thomas, charged him with sexual harassment, a nationwide controversy erupted. Thomas was eventually confirmed as the debate over the issue galvanized women.

The economy worsened during the first half of 1992 as Bush's political troubles grew. Buchanan entered the race for the Republican nomination. He never got more than about one third of primary votes, but he pushed Bush to the right and forced the president to expend resources in the pre-nomination period. Many Americans managed to be convinced that Bush did not understand their problems or needs.

In the search for a political alternative, the voters found two credible candidates seeking their votes. Bill Clinton was the potential Democratic nominee. A youthful governor and gifted campaigner, Clinton had surmounted charges against his personal integrity to clinch the Democratic nomination. The lagging economy became one of Clinton's main themes. As his political adviser James Carville put it, Democrats should never forget the central issue: "It's the economy, stupid." Meanwhile, Texas billionaire Ross Perot, who had fallen out with Bush in the late 1980s, announced an independent candidacy for president. Soon Perot led both Bush and Clinton in many public opinion polls. For Bush the problems multiplied when Perot pulled out of the race just after Clinton's nomination, insisting that the Democratic party had been "revitalized," and Clinton built up a large lead in the polls over the president. Compounding the difficulties that Bush faced was the Republican National Convention in Houston, where many delegates, led by Buchanan, cheered for divisive cultural themes that alienated middle-class voters.

To beat Clinton, Bush persuaded Secretary of State Baker to leave his post and run a presidential campaign once again, as he had done for Ford in 1976 and Bush in 1988. The Republicans attempted to make an issue of Clinton's opposition to the Vietnam War but did not have much success. As the election neared, Perot reentered the race and appeared in the televised debates with Bush and Clinton. In those encounters, Bush often came across as detached and distant, at one point glancing at his watch as if he were waiting for another appointment.

Although the gap in the polls narrowed as election day approached, it widened again when, on the eve of the election, in a move whose timing was hotly debated, the Iran-contra special prosecutor, Lawrence Walsh, released information suggesting that Bush might have known more about the scandal that he had insisted. Clinton received 43 percent of the popular vote to Bush's 38 percent. The Democrat won thirty-two states to eighteen for Bush. Perot took 19 percent of the vote but did not gain any electoral votes. "It hurts," Bush told Colin Powell. "It really hurts to be rejected."

In the months that remained of his presidency, Bush carried forward on some policies that his successor would bring to fruition. In December 1992 he met with President Carlos Salinas de Gortari of Mexico and Prime Minister Brian Mulroney of Canada to sign the North American Free Trade Agreement. In the war-ravaged African nation of Somalia, where there was chaos and famine, the administration sent in troops to relieve suffering and starvation. Just before his term ended Bush pardoned some of the participants in the Iran-contra scandal.

Following the end of his term, Bush returned to Texas and devoted himself to writing a diplomatic history of his administration (with General Scowcroft), and organizing the Bush Presidential Library at Texas A&M University. The election of his sons George (in 1994) and Jeb (in 1998) as governors represented a degree of political vindication for the elder Bush. So did George W. Bush's nomination for president by Republicans in Philadelphia in August 2000, which opened the possibility that the two Bushes might become the first father and son elected president since John Adams and his son John Quincy.

George Bush managed the end of the Cold War on terms that few Americans could ever have dreamt of. Though problems remained in Central Europe, especially with the breakup of the former Yugoslavia, he had succeeded, as he had often promised, in creating a Europe that was "whole and free." Bush's Gulf War coalition-building in 1990 was very skillful, and the war itself produced a sweeping victory. As a war leader, Bush will likely enjoy favorable evaluations from future historians for his conduct of diplomacy and combat.

Bush's difficulties lay in domestic policy. He supported Reagan's policies but without his predecessor's fervor. By 1992 the administration had largely run out of domestic innovations. With the Cold War over, American voters opted for a leader whom they considered to be more engaged by the economy and social issues. Nevertheless, historians of the future are likely to find that Bush approached his presidency with responsibility and dedication. As he noted in his diary on his last day in office, "I've tried to serve here with no taint or dishonor; no conflict of interest; nothing to sully this beautiful place and this job I've been privileged to hold."

—LEWIS L. GOULD

THE FORTY-SECOND PRESIDENT ★ 1993–

WILLIAM JEFFERSON CLINTON

PROSPERITY AND TURMOIL

Bill Clinton was one of the most talented and intelligent men ever to serve as president. His complicated personal life and much-questioned moral character brought him to the brink of ouster from office when he became the first elected president to be impeached and tried by the United States Senate. At the same time, under Clinton's leadership, the United States enjoyed the greatest peacetime economic boom in its history. Because of these paradoxes, Bill Clinton seemed likely to be one of the most written about and debated American presidents for years after the close of his second term on January 20, 2001.

During most of his presidency Clinton was a "New Democrat" who governed from the center of the political spectrum. His policies and good economic times combined to lift his personal popularity to great—and sustained—heights. He prospered politically by adopting the goal of a balanced budget, reforming welfare, and providing small, incremental changes that appealed to Americans already basically happy with their lives. Abroad, he sought to be a peacemaker in Northern Ireland, Haiti, the Middle East, and the Balkans.

Although Clinton was usually cautious in his politics, he drove his enemies to spasms of denunciation and hatred, and they pursued his removal from office with greater intensity as their quarry eluded them time after time. As Clinton brought out the worst in his foes, they brought out the worst in him. Decades after he left office, historians were likely to still be arguing whether he or the Clinton haters were right.

He was born William Jefferson Blythe IV in Hope, Arkansas, on August 19, 1946. His father died in an automobile accident before he was born, and his mother remarried into an abusive relationship with his alcoholic stepfather. Despite these problems, young Bill took his stepfather's surname, Clinton. He was always close to his mother Virginia. He grew up

in Hot Springs, Arkansas, a racetrack and gambling town where his mother, an enthusiastic gambler, loved the bright lights. The twin aspects of Southern evangelism and a high-rolling lifestyle that Clinton saw all around him helped to form his character.

In 1963, as a delegate to Boys' Nation, Clinton shook hands with President John F. Kennedy during a White House visit. The moment reinforced Clinton's desire for a life of public service. A year later he won a scholarship to Georgetown University, where he plunged into campus politics and became president of the freshman class. Clinton's brilliance and ambition helped him win a Rhodes Scholarship to Oxford. During his two years in England, he formed a number of crucial friendships with future political advisers and also participated in some demonstrations against the Vietnam War.

While he was in England in 1969, the Arkansas draft board sent him a notice to report for a preinduction physical. Opposed to the war and determined to avoid going to Vietnam, Clinton explored all of his options, including service in a Reserve Officers Training Corps detachment at the University of Arkansas. Clinton pulled some of the strings possible to avoid the draft until the lottery system was instituted and he drew a high enough number to be sure that he would not be called. The actions of the young Rhodes scholar were typical of those taken by many men determined to evade service in an unpopular war, but his tactics returned to plague him when he ran for president in 1992.

Clinton then went to Yale Law School, where he met his future wife, Hillary Rodham, whom he married on October 11, 1975. A native of Illinois who had once supported Barry Goldwater, Rodham had delivered a fiery speech at her 1969 commencement at Wellesley College that criticized the establishment and the Vietnam War. After their move to Arkansas, Hillary Rodham (she continued to use her maiden

President Clinton joins men dressed as soldiers from the American Revolution at Battlefield Monument in Freehold, New Jersey, on September 24, 1996.

name until 1982) worked in the Rose Law Firm and was voted one of the hundred best lawyers in the nation. Their daughter, Chelsea, was born in 1980. The relationship of the Clintons seems to have been one of mutual admiration and passion, but within two years of his marriage, Clinton pursued extramarital affairs. After completing law school he returned to Arkansas and ran unsuccessfully for Congress in 1974. In 1976 he was elected attorney general of Arkansas. Two years later he made his first victorious race for governor of his state.

During his first term, Clinton alienated the voters of Arkansas with a number of controversial policies, including a hike in car license fees, and was defeated for reelection in 1980. Two years later, having apologized to the people of Arkansas for his errors, he was returned to the governorship, and he governed as a moderate Democrat. He remained governor for the next ten years.

By the mid-1980s, Clinton was a rising star in the party nationwide, heralded as a "New Democrat" not tied to the liberal programs of the past. He thought

The Clintons hold their daughter, Chelsea, on March 5, 1980, one week after her birth. Her upbringing is one Clinton activity that has never drawn criticism.

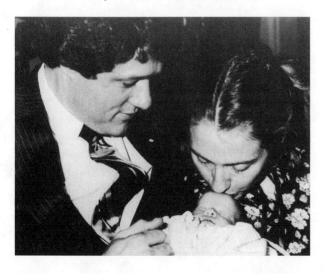

about running for president in 1988 but decided not to do so, in part because of the youth of his daughter and in part because of fears of press inquiries into his private life. At the 1988 Democratic National Convention he gave a lengthy nominating speech for Michael Dukakis that bored the delegates, evoked jeers, and turned into a public relations disaster. As he had done so often, Clinton bounced back with an amusing critique of his own performance on late night television. Running for his sixth term as governor in 1990, Clinton promised Arkansans that he would not be a presidential candidate, but he was already contemplating a race in 1992.

His presidential candidacy did not seem plausible in early 1991. President George Bush was at the height of his popularity after the Gulf War, and other Democratic contenders withdrew from the competition, citing the conventional wisdom that Bush was a shoo-in. Clinton recognized, however, that the weakening economy and Bush's vulnerabilities made the Democrats' chances better than most people realized. By this time, the Friends of Bill (FOBs) were scattered across the Democratic party. Clinton's charm and allure made him seem to many the best of the potential candidates among the baby boomers. He announced for president in October 1991.

Clinton encountered obstacles in the early going. During the New Hampshire primary, he confronted revelations from a Little Rock nightclub singer and television reporter named Gennifer Flowers about their relationship. The draft-dodging issue also surfaced. At the same time, his one-time business partner James McDougal alerted the press to the Whitewater project. This venture was a controversial land deal in which Clinton and his wife had been involved during the 1980s. McDougal's leaks began a sequence of news stories that lasted for years.

When Flowers disclosed their relationship, Clinton had responded with carefully phrased denials, including an appearance on *60 Minutes* during which he and Mrs. Clinton acknowledged past problems in their marriage. Clinton was able to survive and achieve a second-place finish in New Hampshire. He dubbed himself "the Comeback Kid." In the weeks that followed, he piled up delegates on the way to a first-ballot nomination.

Other events conspired in Clinton's favor. Billion-aire computer magnate Ross Perot entered the race as an independent candidate and he sapped votes from Bush. Then, during the Democratic National Convention, the quirky Perot pulled out of the race, and Clinton inherited much of his support. For his running mate, Clinton selected Albert "Al" Gore, Jr., of Tennessee. The team of two youthful Southerners proved attractive to the electorate. In the fall Perot reentered the race and participated in three-way debates with Bush and Clinton. The Democratic candidate scored well in these encounters, and the Clinton-Gore ticket swept to victory in November 1992. They garnered 370 electoral votes to 168 for Bush and none for Perot. Clinton won 43 percent of the popular vote to 37 percent for President Bush and almost 19 percent for Perot.

Clinton had little time to ease into the role. The president-elect stirred things up immediately by advocating a lifting of the ban on homosexuals serving in the armed forces. Eventually the new administration adopted what became known as the "Don't Ask, Don't Tell" policy in which gay servicemen and -women would not be interrogated about their sexual orientation as long as they were not openly homosexual. Adding to the troubles of the new president, efforts to appoint a female attorney general met difficulties until Janet Reno was named to the post. Then in February 1993 an armed struggle occurred between members of the Branch Davidian religious community and agents of the Bureau of Alcohol, Tobacco and Firearms, near Waco, Texas. The episode added to the discontent with Clinton on the far right wing of national politics.

BIOGRAPHICAL FACTS

BIRTH: Hope, Ark., Aug. 19, 1946, born as William Jefferson Blythe IV

ANCESTRY: English

FATHER: William Jefferson Blythe III; b. Sherman, Tex., Feb. 27, 1918; d. Sikeston, Mo., May 17, 1946

FATHER'S OCCUPATION: Traveling salesman

STEPFATHER: Roger Clinton; b. July 25, 1909; d. 1967

STEPFATHER'S OCCUPATION: Car salesman

MOTHER: Virginia Cassidy Clinton Kelley; b. Bodcaw, Ark., June 6, 1923; d. Hot Springs, Ark., Jan. 6, 1994

MOTHER'S OCCUPATION: Nurse anesthetist

HALF BROTHER: Roger Clinton, Jr. (1956–)

MARRIAGE: Fayetteville, Ark., Oct. 11, 1975

WIFE: Hillary Diane Rodham; b. Chicago, Ill., Oct. 26, 1947

CHILD: Chelsea Victoria (1980–)

RELIGIOUS AFFILIATION: Baptist

EDUCATION: Georgetown University (B.S., 1968); attended Oxford University; Yale University Law School (J.D., 1973)

OCCUPATION BEFORE PRESIDENCY: Law professor

PREPRESIDENTIAL OFFICES: Attorney general of Arkansas; governor of Arkansas

AGE AT INAUGURATION: 46

When a White House lawyer and former Rose Law Firm partner of Hillary Clinton, Vincent Foster, committed suicide in July 1993, conspiracy theorists publicly claimed that the death was a murder in which the president and Mrs. Clinton had been involved. The charges were groundless but were an example of the passions that the presidential couple had aroused in their adversaries. Some opponents of the president and the first lady contended that the Clintons would stop at nothing, not even murder, to retain power. President Clinton and his wife also faced the unprecedented assault of probes into their pre–White House business affairs. Stemming from their investment in the Whitewater land deals, these investigations came to be in the hands of an independent counsel named Kenneth Starr, a well-known

FIRST ADMINISTRATION

INAUGURATION: Jan. 20, 1993; the Capitol, Washington, D.C.

VICE PRESIDENT: Albert "Al" Gore, Jr.

SECRETARY OF STATE: Warren M. Christopher

SECRETARY OF THE TREASURY: Lloyd M. Bentsen, Jr.; Robert E. Rubin (from Jan. 11, 1995)

SECRETARY OF DEFENSE: Les Aspin; William J. Perry (from Feb. 7, 1994)

ATTORNEY GENERAL: Janet Reno

SECRETARY OF THE INTERIOR: Bruce Babbitt

SECRETARY OF AGRICULTURE: Mike Espy; Daniel R. Glickman (from Mar. 30, 1995)

SECRETARY OF COMMERCE: Ronald H. Brown; Mickey Kantor (from Apr. 12, 1996)

SECRETARY OF LABOR: Robert B. Reich

SECRETARY OF HEALTH AND HUMAN SERVICES: Donna E. Shalala

SECRETARY OF HOUSING AND URBAN DEVELOPMENT: Henry G. Cisneros

SECRETARY OF TRANSPORTATION: Federico F. Peña

SECRETARY OF ENERGY: Hazel R. O'Leary

SECRETARY OF EDUCATION: Richard W. Riley

SECRETARY OF VETERANS AFFAIRS: Jesse Brown

SUPREME COURT APPOINTMENTS: Ruth Bader Ginsberg (1993); Stephen G. Breyer (1994)

103RD CONGRESS (Jan. 5, 1993–Dec. 1, 1994):
  SENATE: 57 Democrats; 43 Republicans
  HOUSE: 258 Democrats; 176 Republicans; 1 Other

104TH CONGRESS (Jan. 4, 1995–Oct. 4, 1996):
  SENATE: 52 Republicans; 48 Democrats
  HOUSE: 230 Republicans; 204 Democrats; 1 Other

ELECTION OF 1992

CANDIDATES	ELECTORAL VOTE	POPULAR VOTE
William J. Clinton (Democratic)	370	44,909,326
George Bush (Republican)	168	39,103,882
H. Ross Perot (Independent)	—	19,741,657

Republican attorney and former federal judge who had been appointed by a three-judge panel in 1994 that many Democrats felt was out to get the president. Starr pursued charges of wrongdoing against President and Mrs. Clinton with intensity during the years that followed. At one point the president erupted about all the suspicion and incessant questioning, exclaiming to his close aide, George Stephanopoulos, "No president has ever been treated like I've been treated."

Adding to the legal troubles for Clinton was the lawsuit filed by Paula Corbin Jones in April 1994, alleging that, while governor of Arkansas, he had sexually harassed her. The suit gave Clinton's enemies a means to unearth damaging information about his private life. Their ideological motivation combined with Clinton's own propensity for serial philandering made the Jones case a time bomb for the presidency. Clinton's attorneys began proceedings to delay the suit until after he left office. They succeeded in doing so for his first elective term.

Some policy victories were recorded, but the president and his party paid a stiff price politically. With a slim margin in the House and a one-vote triumph in the Senate, Clinton obtained the enactment of an economic package that included tax increases and spending cuts to lower the budget deficit to $255 billion in 1993 and to $203 billion in the following year. Republicans denounced what they called "the largest tax increase in history" and predicted economic ruin for the nation. Clinton noted that wealthy taxpayers would bear the brunt of the new levies. The economy grew more prosperous, but many voters heeded the Republican charges.

Another Clinton success came when he campaigned for the North American Free Trade Agreement in late 1993. Ross Perot was a notable opponent. He predicted that there would be a "giant sucking sound" as jobs left the United States for Mexico. But when Perot debated Vice President Gore about the issue on television, he did poorly. Despite the opposition of much of organized labor and many Democrats, NAFTA cleared Congress with help from many Republicans and proved economically beneficial to both the United States and Mexico.

The centerpiece of the first Clinton administration was an attempt to reform the nation's healthcare system. Led by Hillary Rodham Clinton, which angered critics who felt that a first lady should not have a prominent role in policy, the White House wanted to expand coverage to all Americans through a system of health alliances that stressed managed care. Well-to-do Americans would have had to pay higher rates to consult a private doctor. When the initiative went to Capitol Hill, there was strong public support for some kind of reform.

As Republicans and their allies in the insurance industry turned their fire on Mrs. Clinton's plan, the public's attitude quickly changed. Commercials depicting a mythical couple named "Harry and Louise" attacked it as too costly, intrusive, and bureaucratic. Mrs. Clinton lobbied hard for her brainchild, but the movement for healthcare reform stalled. Republicans asserted that there was no problem in need of fixing. By the middle of 1994 the healthcare initiative was all but dead on Capitol Hill, and it finally expired in the autumn.

The first Clinton term did accomplish some notable results in foreign policy after a very wobbly start. For a president with no military background and little interest in world affairs beyond economic and trade concerns, initiation into the demands of world leadership was painful. In Somalia a rescue operation, began by President Bush, ended in the deaths of eighteen American servicemen and televised pictures of the body of an American pilot being pulled through the streets. In Haiti a peacekeeping force was turned back by an angry mob. There was also the dilemma of Bosnia, the former Yugoslav republic, where lightly-armed United Nations troops were trying to keep the peace against Serb forces bent on what was known as "ethnic cleansing."

Then Clinton's foreign policy began to register some results. Russian troops withdrew from Estonia in 1994. Clinton acted as a broker for peace negotiations among Ireland, Great Britain, and the Irish Republican Army. In the Middle East, spurred by a handshake between Yasir Arafat and Yitzhak Rabin on the White House lawn, the administration pushed along talks between Israel and the Palestine Liberation Organization. (The accord was signed in September 1995.) In Haiti a threatened American military intervention in 1994 helped to oust an authoritarian regime.

The political tide turned against the Democrats in 1994. The Republicans, led by Representative Newt Gingrich of Georgia, pushed "the Opportunity Society" that would replace the Great Society of Lyndon B. Johnson. In the fall 1994 campaign, Gingrich and his allies unveiled the "Contract with America" that

President Clinton shares a light moment with Palestine Liberation Organization leader Yasir Arafat after the signing of the Middle East peace accord with Israeli Prime Minister Yitzhak Rabin on September 28, 1995. The president pursued peace in the Middle East during both his terms.

promised conservative answers to pending national problems, defining Clinton as a left-liberal.

Rather than making the election a series of local contests, Clinton and the Democrats accepted the Republican challenge and fought the election on the issues raised in the contract and the accomplishments of the Clinton presidency. Many Republican candidates tried to tie Clinton around their opponents' necks. As a result, the Republicans regained control of the House of Representatives for the first time since 1954, and also regained control of the Senate. Gingrich became Speaker of the House. Pundits predicted that Clinton would not win a second term in 1996.

Through the spring of 1995 that forecast seemed accurate. At one point Clinton even reminded a press conference that he remained "relevant" in Washington. But an unexpected tragedy transformed the political equation and gave Clinton an opportunity to recover. When the Alfred P. Murrah Federal Building in Oklahoma City was blown up on April 19, 1995, Clinton responded to the shock of the awful event by going to the scene and comforting the victims.

The president's speech about the bombing enabled him to identify himself with the center of the political spectrum. Clinton worried that his public profile had gotten too far left during his first two years. He rehired an old political adviser, Dick Morris, who now worked mainly for conservative Republicans. With Morris's help, he co-opted many Republican positions on issues like crime and welfare, and steered clear of both liberal Democrats and the Gingrich right to cast himself as a centrist in a process that Morris dubbed "triangulation."

As would happen so often to Clinton, his enemies did him the most good. A reporter quipped that Clinton "makes the Republicans crazy," and the president did seem to goad his enemies into self-destructive tactics. After adopting the easy and popular parts of the contract, the Republicans went after environmental laws and government regulation of business. That allowed the White House to assail them for insensitivity about the environment. When the Republicans passed a bill that would have reduced spending on education by more than a billion dollars, Clinton issued his first veto to stop the congressional action. The political opposition also pursued the Clintons over the Whitewater investment issue throughout 1995 but did not turn up any substantial charges. Meanwhile, the independent Starr investigation continued with periodic leaks to the press about the legal perils for the president and the first lady.

Despite Starr's inquiries, 1995 proved to be a period of political success for Clinton. For the Balkans, American negotiators worked out a peace agreement at Dayton, Ohio, that led to a cease-fire guaranteed by the presence of NATO troops, with American peacekeepers playing a key role. The economy continued to be strong at home, and Clinton seemed more forceful as an international leader. Budget negotiations between the White House and the Congressional Republicans were stalled, with most of the public inclined to blame the Republicans for the problem.

By the end of 1995, the more conservative wing of Republicans in the House argued that it would be better to shut down the government than to compromise with Clinton. That tactic worked against Gingrich and his troops. Two government shutdowns in November and December saw the president's ratings rise and those of the Republicans fall. Although the world did not yet know it, with his prospects improving, Clinton began an intimate affair with a twenty-two-year-old White House intern named Monica Lewinsky. The young woman soon informed friends about these trysts, and Clinton's vulnerability increased. Clinton's political future was now headed toward what became a potentially career-ending crisis.

The political current continued to run toward Clinton in early 1996. The Republicans yielded on the budget. At the same time, the White House began a saturation advertising campaign to dominate the issues debated in the 1996 presidential race. So successful did that strategy prove that Republicans were down in the polls even before they nominated their front-runner, Senator Robert Dole, during the summer. A poor campaigner with a weak organization, Dole never found a way to dent Clinton's lead. Even the entry of Ross Perot as an independent candidate again did not hurt Clinton's chances.

To keep his hold on the middle ground of American politics, Clinton pursued his effort to make many Republican issues his own. A notable example of this skill was his support for welfare reform during the summer of 1996. Having promised in 1992 "to end welfare as we know it," Clinton endorsed the bill that ended the federal responsibility for welfare policy in favor of block grants to the states. For Clinton it represented the "New Democrat" approach that he had once campaigned on.

The presidential campaign went Clinton's way almost to the very end of the election season. He handled Dole easily in the debates, and the Democrats seemed on their way to retaking the House from the Republicans behind Clinton's momentum. Then newspaper stories appeared about possible scandals in Clinton's fund-raising. Some of the money seemed to have come from Chinese sources, and the disclosures cast a cloud over the campaign. During the last days of the race between Clinton and Dole, it appeared as if the president and his party were stumbling toward the finish line.

The result was a victory for Clinton as he captured 379 electoral votes and 49 percent of the popular vote to 159 electoral votes and 41 percent for Dole. Perot trailed with 8 percent of the vote and no electoral votes. However, the Democrats did not regain control of the House, and Clinton faced a Republican Congress for the duration of his second term. Pundits noted that once again, despite a vigorous economy,

ALBERT "AL" GORE, JR.

Albert Gore, Jr., was an important player in the successes and failures of the Clinton presidency—probably the most influential vice president in history. The vice president's debate with Ross Perot in 1993, in which he soundly defeated the Texas computer billionaire, turned the tide in favor of the North American Free Trade Agreement. Yet Gore's fund-raising visit to a Buddhist temple in 1996 became a metaphor for the administration's problems with campaign contributions. Gore also pursued the Reinventing Government initiative that involved reforms to streamline the way government worked. The program pursued a laudable goal without always reckoning the political costs.

Although often wooden in public, Gore was thought by friends and aides to be lively and funny in private. Clinton gave Gore real authority as vice president and the two men worked closely together. When the Monica Lewinsky scandal erupted, Gore strongly defended him. On the day of Clinton's impeachment, Gore publicly predicted that Clinton would be considered one of the greatest presidents in history. Out of gratitude and the knowledge that being succeeded by a friend could be helpful in all sorts of ways, Clinton broke the usual precedent by endorsing Gore for the 2000 Democratic nomination. There was one serious challenger in former Senator Bill Bradley, who campaigned as a Democrat willing to make a clean break with Clinton and Gore, but he won not a single primary.

Clinton had proved unable to get a majority of Americans to vote for him.

During 1997 the Clinton presidency benefited from the economic boom that was taking the stock market to dizzying heights. The problems with the budget deficit faded away as the prospect of an actual surplus loomed invitingly on the horizon. In foreign policy, the White House expanded NATO to include Hungary, Poland, and the Czech Republic.

That step took NATO beyond its Cold War mandate of defending Europe against invasion and set the stage for a more assertive role on the part of the Alliance. The Balkans remained volatile, as ethnic tensions bubbled throughout the region. But Clinton could declare, "The sun is rising on America again."

Clinton's persistent personal problems continued throughout 1997. The Supreme Court ruled in the Paula Jones case in May 1997 that the plaintiff could pursue her lawsuit against the president while he was in office. The justices asserted that the proceedings would not unduly burden the presidency, a forecast that proved to be inaccurate. The Starr investigation also continued, but without major indictments or probes aimed at the president and Mrs. Clinton. Republican inquiries into the Chinese fund-raising scandals did not implicate Clinton. The president's political enemies had to face the prospect that the man they called "Slick Willie" might elude them.

Clinton's sexual indiscretions, however, caught up with him in January 1998. Monica Lewinsky had spoken of her relationship with the president to a number of her friends, including a fellow executive branch employee named Linda Tripp. Tripp had secretly taped her phone calls with Lewinsky and then turned the recordings over to Kenneth Starr and his office as well as the lawyers for Paula Jones. In January 1998, confronted with questions about Lewinsky in a deposition for the Jones lawyers, Clinton gave answers that seemed to Starr and others to have been dishonest. Soon the scandal burst into public view. Talking to the nation from the Roosevelt Room of the White House, Clinton angrily insisted, "I did not have sexual relations with that woman, Miss Lewinsky."

The legal inquiry turned on the question of whether the president had committed perjury in his testimony and obstruction of justice by lying to his secretary, Betty Currie, having her retrieve presents from Lewinsky, and by asking his friend Vernon Jordan to find a job for Lewinsky. Hillary Clinton attributed the episode to a "vast right-wing conspiracy," and a media feeding frenzy erupted. Washington pundits predicted Clinton's resignation or impeachment at an early date.

The president was able to blunt the attack for months, but that summer, Lewinsky struck an immunity deal with prosecutors and gave them a dress stained with the president's DNA. Clinton was soon compelled to testify before Kenneth Starr's grand jury

"Zippergate," a Jim Borgman cartoon published in February 1998, when the news broke of Clinton's affair, vividly encapsulates a new view of the White House. The scandal over the president's relationship with White House intern Monica Lewinsky led to his impeachment in 1998.

investigating the Lewinsky affair as an expansion of its original probe into the Whitewater matter. In his testimony, Clinton admitted to "inappropriate" conduct with Lewinsky but denied wrongdoing. In September, Starr sent a report to the House of Representatives charging that there was "substantial and credible evidence" that Clinton had committed impeachable offenses under the Constitution. To make the case, Starr and his prosecutors delivered an abundance of salacious and sexually explicit information about Clinton's relationship with Lewinsky. To the extent that the material was intended to outrage the American people, it had the opposite effect, arousing sympathy for Clinton and animosity toward the prosecutors. The House Judiciary Committee took up consideration of whether charges should be sent to the Senate.

Before that could occur, however, the congressional elections of 1998 intervened. At the time Starr's report was sent to Congress, it was widely assumed that the Republicans would make large gains, especially in the House, because of public disgust with Clinton. Instead, the president's popularity remained high as the public reacted against the media's intense preoccupation with the Clinton scandal. As a result, the impeachment drive worked against the Republicans. In a stunning reversal of political fortunes, the Democrats gained five seats in the House. More important for Clinton, the Senate produced no change in the 55–45 Republican margin. That meant that any impeachment effort would have to obtain the votes of twelve Democratic senators to be successful. That prospect seemed unlikely in the wake of the Democratic triumph and Clinton's high poll numbers.

Nonetheless, the Republicans in the House pressed ahead with impeachment. The Judiciary Committee, under Chairman Henry Hyde of Illinois, adopted four articles of impeachment in December 1998 on a strict party-line vote. All twenty-one Republicans voted for three of the four articles; one

SECOND ADMINISTRATION		

INAUGURATION: Jan. 20, 1997; the Capitol, Washington, D.C.

VICE PRESIDENT: Albert Gore, Jr.

SECRETARY OF STATE: Madeleine K. Albright

SECRETARY OF THE TREASURY: Robert E. Rubin; Lawrence H. Summers (from July 2, 1999)

SECRETARY OF DEFENSE: William S. Cohen

ATTORNEY GENERAL: Janet Reno

SECRETARY OF THE INTERIOR: Bruce Babbitt

SECRETARY OF AGRICULTURE: Daniel R. Glickman

SECRETARY OF COMMERCE: William M. Daley

SECRETARY OF LABOR: Alexis M. Herman

SECRETARY OF HEALTH AND HUMAN SERVICES: Donna E. Shalala

SECRETARY OF HOUSING AND URBAN DEVELOPMENT: Andrew M. Cuomo

SECRETARY OF TRANSPORTATION: Rodney E. Slater

SECRETARY OF ENERGY: Federico F. Peña; Bill Richardson (from Aug. 18, 1998)

SECRETARY OF EDUCATION: Richard W. Riley

SECRETARY OF VETERANS AFFAIRS: Jesse Brown

105TH CONGRESS (Jan. 3, 1997–Dec. 19, 1998):
  SENATE: 55 Republicans; 45 Democrats
  HOUSE: 227 Republicans; 207 Democrats; 1 Other

106TH CONGRESS (Jan. 6, 1999–):
  SENATE: 55 Republicans; 45 Democrats
  HOUSE: 222 Republicans; 211 Democrats; 1 Other

ELECTION OF 1996

CANDIDATES	ELECTORAL VOTE	POPULAR VOTE
William J. Clinton (Democratic)	379	47,401,054
Robert J. Dole (Republican)	159	39,197,350
H. Ross Perot (Reform)	—	8,085,285

Republican defected on one article. All sixteen Democrats opposed impeachment. The Republicans could impeach Clinton with their House majority, but no strategy seemed likely to attract Democratic votes for conviction of the president.

Later in December the House adopted two articles of impeachment charging Clinton with lying under oath to the grand jury in his testimony in the Starr inquiry, and with obstructing justice in his efforts to keep prosecutors from learning of his relationship with Lewinsky. Although five Democrats voted with the House Republicans and five Republicans supported the president, the basic division fell along partisan lines.

The Senate began the trial of the president in early January. The House managers warned that failure to remove Clinton would endanger the nation and imperil "the rule of law." Their arguments were not crafted in a way that would have swayed any potential Democratic defectors, and it became obvious from the outset that the votes to remove Clinton from office were unlikely to be obtained. When the president made an effective State of the Union speech on January 19, 1999, his poll ratings went even higher.

The Senate acquitted Clinton on both impeachment counts when the vote occurred on February 12, 1999. On the count charging perjury, 45 Republicans voted for conviction while 10 Republicans and all 45 Democrats voted for acquittal. On the obstruction of justice count, the Senate split evenly with 50 Republicans voting for conviction and 45 Democrats and 5 Republicans voting for acquittal. On neither count was a majority reached. Clinton had been acquitted, if not vindicated.

The impeachment case was an example of the degree to which the nation had polarized around President Clinton during his years in the White House. To his opponents, Clinton was guilty of committing crimes in office and should have been removed at once. To the rest of the country, some 60 percent or more, Clinton was guilty of deplorable private behavior, but nonetheless a competent president who should serve out his term.

A foreign policy crisis added to the complexity of the last years of his presidency. The Balkans, where ethnic hatreds had exploded since the breakup of Yugoslavia, again became a flash point as the government of Serbia conducted "ethnic cleansing" (the murder and forced displacement of minority populations) of Albanians in the province of Kosovo. In March 1999, convinced that Serbia and its leader Slobodan Milosevic would respond only to armed force, Clinton and NATO commenced a series of air strikes against Serbia and Serbian forces in Kosovo. The success of the NATO campaign vindicated Clinton's strategy, but polls showed that the public gave him little credit.

HILLARY RODHAM CLINTON

Few first ladies in history have attracted more criticism than Hillary Rodham Clinton. To her admirers she was the embodiment of what it meant to be a modern woman, especially her courage and resolve in the face of her husband's failings. Among her detractors, she was either a coconspirator with the president in nefarious doings or his pliant dupe. She was the only wife of a president subpoenaed to testify before a federal grand jury. That happened to Mrs. Clinton early in 1996 when Kenneth Starr's Whitewater grand jury probed her personal and business affairs. By that time, she had become a lightning rod within the administration for conservative criticism. Her role in pushing a national healthcare program—she was criticized for arrogance, amateurism, and secretiveness—had resulted in one of the major defeats for the administration in President Clinton's first term. During the Lewinsky scandal, Mrs. Clinton withstood the firestorm with a high degree of grace and personal courage. As a result, by mid-1999 she emerged from these trials as an independent political figure in her own right and a candidate for the United States Senate from New York. Whatever her political future holds, Hillary Rodham Clinton seems fated to be a symbol of American ambivalence about the place of women in politics.

President Clinton, dining with troops at Ramstein Air Force Base, Germany in May 1999, gives a thumbs-up sign expressing his appreciation for the efforts of all involved in the NATO air strikes in Kosovo. The strikes provoked much controversy at home but ultimately resulted in a victory for the West.

There is no question that Bill Clinton will be deemed one of the most controversial of our presidents. More books were written about him during his presidency than about many of his long-dead predecessors. More books are promised, and the flood of interpretations about Bill and Hillary Clinton is only gathering force.

Clinton was clearly one of the most intelligent, articulate, and politically agile, presidents of the twentieth century. He took the Democrats from minority status and made them competitive in presidential elections. He had less success in restoring their fortunes in Congress. Few presidents have been more adroit in adopting the ideas of their political enemies. Above all, he presided over America's longest economic expansion.

Despite these skills, Clinton lacked a moral compass, a sense of mature responsibility, the capacity for self-denial, that might have allowed him to live up to the standards of the presidency at its best. George Stephanopoulos captured the dilemma Clinton presents for historians when he wrote in his memoirs, "If only this good president had been a better man."

—*Lewis L. Gould*

☆ SELECTED BIBLIOGRAPHY ☆

Brinkley, Douglas. *American Heritage History of the United States.* New York: Viking, 1998.

Burner, David. *Herbert Hoover: A Public Life.* New York: Alfred A. Knopf, 1979.

Cooper, John Milton, Jr. *The Warrior and the Priest: Woodrow Wilson and Theodore Roosevelt.* Cambridge, Mass.: Belknap Press, 1983.

Dallek, Robert. *Flawed Giant: Lyndon Johnson and His Times, 1961–1973.* New York: Oxford University Press, 1998.

Dangerfield, George. *The Era of Good Feelings.* Boston: Harcourt Brace Jovanovich, 1963.

De Voto, Bernard. *The Year of Decision: 1846.* Boston: Little, Brown, 1943.

Doenecke, Justus D. *The Presidencies of James A. Garfield and Chester A. Arthur.* Lawrence, Kans.: The Regents Press of Kansas, 1981.

Donald, David Herbert. *Lincoln.* New York: Simon & Schuster, 1995.

Ellis, Joseph J. *American Sphinx: The Character of Thomas Jefferson.* New York: Alfred A. Knopf, 1997.

Ferrell, Robert H. *The Presidency of Calvin Coolidge.* Lawrence, Kans.: University Press of Kansas, 1998.

Ferrell, Robert H. *The Strange Deaths of President Harding.* Columbia, Mo.: University of Missouri Press, 1996.

Fischer, Roger A. *Tippecanoe and Trinkets Too: The Material Culture of American Presidential Campaigns, 1828–1984.* Urbana, Ill.: University of Illinois Press, 1988.

Freidel, Frank. *Franklin D. Roosevelt: Rendezvous with Destiny.* Boston: Little, Brown, 1991.

Gould, Lewis L. *1968: The Election That Changed America.* Chicago: Ivan R. Dee, 1993.

Gould, Lewis L. *Lady Bird Johnson: Our Environmental First Lady.* Lawrence, Kans.: University Press of Kansas, 1999.

Graff, Henry F., ed. *The Presidents: A Reference History,* 2nd ed. New York: MacMillan, 1997.

Greene, John Robert. *The Presidency of Gerald R. Ford.* Lawrence, Kans.: University Press of Kansas, 1995.

Greenstein, Fred I. *The Hidden-Hand Presidency: Eisenhower As Leader.* Baltimore: Johns Hopkins, 1994.

Guelzo, Allen C. *Abraham Lincoln: Redeemer President.* Grand Rapids, Mich.: W. B. Eerdmans Publishing Co., 1999.

Hamby, Alonzo. *Man of the People: A Life of Harry S. Truman.* New York: Oxford University Press, 1995.

Harbaugh, William H. *Power and Responsibility: The Life and Times of Theodore Roosevelt.* New York: Farrar, Straus and Cudahy, 1961.

Hoogenboom, Ari. *Rutherford B. Hayes: Warrior and President.* Lawrence, Kans.: University Press of Kansas, 1995.

Israel, Fred L. *Student's Atlas of American Presidential Elections: 1789–1996.* Washington, D.C.: Congressional Quarterly Books, 1997.

Kane, Joseph Nathan. *Presidential Fact Book.* New York: Random House, 1999.

Kaufman, Burton I. *The Presidency of James Earl Carter, Jr.* Lawrence, Kans.: University Press of Kansas, 1993.

Koenig, Louis W. *The Chief Executive,* 6th ed. New York: Harcourt Brace, 1995.

Leech, Margaret. *In the Days of McKinley.* New York: Harper, 1959.

Link, Arthur S. *Wilson: The Road to the White House.* 5 vols. Princeton, N.J.: Princeton University Press, 1947.

Malone, Dumas. *Jefferson and His Time.* 6 vols. Boston: Little, Brown, 1993.

McFeely, William S. *Grant: A Biography.* New York: W. W. Norton, 1981.

Melder, Keith. *Hail to the Candidate: Presidential Campaigns from Banners to Broadcasts.* Washington, D.C.; Smithsonian, 1992.

Nevins, Allan. *Grover Cleveland: A Study in Courage.* New York: Dodd, Mead, 1966.

Oates, Stephen B. *With Malice Toward None: The Life of Abraham Lincoln.* New York: Harper & Row, 1977.

Parmet, Herbert S. *George Bush: The Life of a Lone Star Yankee.* New York: Scribner, 1997.

Parmet, Herbert S. *JFK: The Presidency of John F. Kennedy.* New York: Dial Press, 1983.

Pemberton, William E. *Exit with Honor: The Life and Presidency of Ronald Reagan.* Armonk, N.Y.: M. E. Sharpe, 1997.

Pringle, Henry F. *The Life and Times of William Howard Taft.* 2 vols. New York: Farrar & Rinehart, Inc., 1939.

Reeves, Thomas C. *The Life and Times of Chester Alan Arthur.* New York: Alfred A. Knopf, 1975.

Remini, Robert V. *Martin Van Buren and the Making of the Democratic Party.* New York: W. W. Norton, 1959.

Rutland, Robert A. *James Madison: The Founding Father.* Columbia, Mo.: University of Missouri Press, 1997.

Schlesinger, Arthur M., Jr. *The Age of Jackson.* Boston: Little, Brown, 1953.

Smith, Richard Norton. *Patriarch: George Washington and the New American Nation.* Boston: Houghton Mifflin, 1993.

Trefousse, Hans L. *Andrew Johnson: A Biography.* New York: W. W. Norton, 1989.

Trefousse, Hans L. *Lincoln's Decision for Emancipation.* Philadelphia: Lippincott, 1975.

Walker, Martin. *The President We Deserve: Bill Clinton: His Rise, Falls, and Comebacks.* New York: Crown Publishers, 1996.

Wicker, Tom. *One of Us: Richard Nixon and the American Dream.* New York: Random House, 1995.

☆ RELATED WEBSITES ☆

America Votes: Presidential Campaign Memorabilia from the Duke University Special Collections
(http://scriptorium.lib.duke.edu/americavotes)

American Presidents: Life Portraits
(http://www.americanpresidents.org)

The First Ladies of the United States of America
(http://www.whitehouse.gov/WH/glimpse/firstladies/html/firstladies.html)

Grolier Online's The American Presidency
(http://gi.grolier.com/presidents)

The History Place™
(http://www.historyplace.com)

Presidential Campaign Button Collection and Election History: 1940 to 1980
(http://www.sddt.com/features/convention/buttons.html)

Presidential Libraries
(http://www.nara.gov/nara/president/address.html)

Presidents of the United States
(http://www.ipl.org/ref/POTUS)

Project Whistlestop: Harry S. Truman Digital Archive on the Web
(http://www.whistlestop.org)

Time and the Presidency
(http://www.presidentsonline.com)

U.S. Presidential Ancestor Tables
(http://www.rootsweb.com/~rwguide/presidents)

The White House Historical Association
(http://www.whitehousehistory.org/whha/default.asp)

☆ PICTURE CREDITS ☆

FRONTISPIECE
2 1941 photograph of Mount Rushmore © Charles E. Rotkin/CORBIS.

GEORGE WASHINGTON
16 The Gilder Lehman Collection on deposit at the Pierpont Morgan Library, New York. GLC 1855. The Pierpont Morgan Library, New York, N.Y., U.S.A. **18** Courtesy of The Mount Vernon Ladies' Association. **21** *MHQ: The Quarterly Journal of Military History*/MapQuest. **25** ©Collection of The New-York Historical Society. **30** The Metropolitan Museum of Art, Gift of Edgar William and Bernice Chrysler Garbisch, 1963. (63.201.2). **33** Library of Congress, neg. #USZC4-724.

JOHN ADAMS
34 Architect of the Capitol. **39** Courtesy, Winterthur Museum. **45** Huntington Library/SuperStock. **46** White House Collection, courtesy White House Historical Association.

THOMAS JEFFERSON
48 White House Collection, courtesy White House Historical Association. **53** Architect of the Capitol. **57** Huntington Library/SuperStock. **59** Missouri Historical Society, St. Louis. **63** Monticello/Thomas Jefferson Memorial Foundation, Inc.

JAMES MADISON
64 Bowdoin College Museum of Art. **69** Library of Congress, Rare Book Collection. **73** Maryland Historical Society, Baltimore, Maryland. **75** Painting ca. 1817, by Bass Otis ©Collection of The New-York Historical Society.

JAMES MONROE
76 James Monroe Museum and Memorial Library. **81** Architect of the Capitol. **86** Culver Pictures.

JOHN QUINCY ADAMS
88 The Metropolitan Museum of Art, Gift of I. N. Phelps Stokes, Edward S.

Hawes, Alice Mary Hawes, and Marion Augusta Hawes, 1937. (37.14.34). **90** Library of Congress, neg. #USZ62-14438. **93** ©Collection of The New-York Historical Society. **96** The Connecticut Historical Society, Hartford, Connecticut.

ANDREW JACKSON
98 The Hermitage: Home of President Andrew Jackson, Nashville, TN. **101** The Hermitage: Home of President Andrew Jackson, Nashville, TN. **103** Stock Montage/SuperStock. **106** Library of Congress, neg. #USZ62-43901. **112** Library of Congress, neg. #USZ62-1562.

MARTIN VAN BUREN
114 Library of Congress, neg. #USZ62-13008. **118** ©Collection of The New-York Historical Society. **121** Library of Congress, neg. #USZ62-8844. **123** Broadsides Collection, CN00690, The Center for American History, The University of Texas at Austin.

WILLIAM HENRY HARRISON
124 The Metropolitan Museum of Art, Gift of I. N. Phelps Stokes, Edward S. Hawes, Alice Mary Hawes, and Marion Augusta Hawes, 1937. (37.14.44). **127** ©Collection of The New-York Historical Society. **128** The Granger Collection, New York. **130** Indiana Historical Society.

JOHN TYLER
132 Courtesy of the Tyler Family. **136** Courtesy of J. Tyler Griffin.

JAMES KNOX POLK
140 Library of Congress. **142** Collection of the James K. Polk Memorial Association, Columbia, Tennessee. **145** Oregon Historical Society, neg. #OrHi 791. **147** © Bettmann/CORBIS. **148** The Granger Collection, New York.

ZACHARY TAYLOR
152 The Metropolitan Museum of Art, Gift of I.N. Phelps Stokes, Edward S.

Hawes, Alice Mary Hawes, and Marion Augusta Hawes, 1937. (37.14.32). **155** The Granger Collection, New York. **156** Library of Congress, neg. #USZ62-5220.

MILLARD FILLMORE
160 Library of Congress, neg. #USZ62-13013. **163** The Library of Virginia. **165** Library of Congress, neg. #USZ62-1283. **166** Library of Congress, neg. #USZC4-4588. **168** Buffalo and Erie County Historical Society.

FRANKLIN PIERCE
170 Library of Congress, neg. #USZ62-13014. **172** The Pierce Brigade. **174** From *AMERICA: A Narrative History,* Fourth Edition by George Brown Tindall and David E. Shi. **176** Kansas State Historical Society.

JAMES BUCHANAN
178 National Archives (NWDNS-111-B-4157). **182** Library of Congress, neg. #USZ62-14827. **184** Courtesy Mrs. John Steuart Curry. **187** Library of Congress, neg. #USZ6-695.

ABRAHAM LINCOLN
188 Library of Congress. **193** Library of Congress, neg. #USZ6-300. **197** Courtesy of the Illinois State Historical Library. **200** Library of Congress, neg. #B8171-0602. **205** Library of Congress, neg. #USZ62-8286. **206** Courtesy of the Illinois State Historical Library.

ANDREW JOHNSON
208 Library of Congress, neg. #B8184-10690. **211** Library of Congress, neg. #USZ62-31177. **214** Library of Congress, neg. #USZ62-9962. **217** New York Public Library.

ULYSSES SIMPSON GRANT
220 Library of Congress, neg. #BH82501-42. **224** New York Herald. **229** Rutherford B. Hayes Library. **232** Library of Congress.

RUTHERFORD BIRCHARD HAYES
234 Rutherford B. Hayes Library.
236 Rutherford B. Hayes Library.
239 Museum of American Political Life, University of Hartford, West Hartford, CT. **260** Library of Congress, neg. #USZC2-1239.

JAMES ABRAM GARFIELD
262 Library of Congress, neg. #USZ62-209. **264** Lake County Historical Society. **266** Library of Congress, neg. #USZ62-4915.

CHESTER ALAN ARTHUR
270 Library of Congress, neg. #USZ62-23233. **274** Library of Congress, neg. #USZ62-25794. **277** Culver Pictures.

GROVER CLEVELAND
280 Library of Congress, neg. #USZ62-7618. **284** New York Public Library. **288** Library of Congress, neg. #USZ62-93406. **291** Library of Congress, neg. #USZ62-96526.

BENJAMIN HARRISON
292 Benjamin Harrison House. **295** Benjamin Harrison House. **297** The Granger Collection, New York. **301** National Archives (NWDNS-FL-FL-22)

WILLIAM MCKINLEY
304 Library of Congress. **307** Museum of American Political Life, University of Hartford, West Hartford, CT. **311** Library of Congress, neg. #USZ62-105703. **313** Library of Congress, neg. # USZ62-99204.

THEODORE ROOSEVELT
314 Theodore Roosevelt Collection, Harvard College Library. **316** Library of Congress, neg. #USZ62-32238. **320** Grey Towers USDA Forest Service. **323** Theodore Roosevelt Collection, Harvard College Library. **326** Theodore Roosevelt Collection, Harvard College Library.

WILLIAM HOWARD TAFT
328 Library of Congress, neg. #USZ62-38780. **331** Library of Congress, neg. #USZC4-6430. **335** Library of Congress, neg. #USZ62-32716.

WOODROW WILSON
336 AP/Wide World Photos.
338 Brown Brothers. **343** AP/Wide World Photos. **346** AP/Wide World Photos. **348** New York Public Library.

WARREN GAMALIEL HARDING
350 Library of Congress, neg. #USZ62-106243. **355** *The Commercial Appeal.*

CALVIN COOLIDGE
356 Culver Pictures, Inc./SuperStock. **359** Boston Public Library. **361** Miguel Covarrubias Foundation. **365** AP/Wide World Photos.

HERBERT CLARK HOOVER
366 Herbert Hoover Presidential Library. **368** The University of Iowa Museum of Art, Gift of Edwin B. Green. **373** Franklin D. Roosevelt Library. **375** Franklin D. Roosevelt Library.

FRANKLIN DELANO ROOSEVELT
376 Archive Photos.
378 Franklin D. Roosevelt Library.
381 Franklin D. Roosevelt Library.
385 Franklin D. Roosevelt Library.
387 Franklin D. Roosevelt Library.

HARRY S. TRUMAN
390 U.S. Navy, courtesy Harry S. Truman Library. **395** Library of Congress, neg. #USZ62-75597. **399** © Hulton-Deutsch Collection/CORBIS. **400** National Archives (306-PS-50-10828). **403** Harry S. Truman Library.

DWIGHT DAVID EISENHOWER
404 Union Pacific Museum Collection, Image Number 38. **406** New York *Daily News.* **412** Archive Photos. **414** George Tames/NYT Pictures.

JOHN FITZGERALD KENNEDY
416 Photo No. ST-C63-1-63 in the John F. Kennedy Library. **419** Photo No. 81-32:65 in the John F. Kennedy Library. **424** AP/Wide World Photos. **426** AP/Wide World Photos. **428** Photo No. AR8255-2B in the John F. Kennedy Library.

LYNDON BAINES JOHNSON
430 AP/Wide World Photos. **432** LBJ Library Collection. **435** Archive Photos. **436** Yoichi R. Okamoto, LBJ Library Collection. **441** Jack Kightlinger, LBJ Library Collection.

RICHARD MILHOUS NIXON
442 New York *Daily News.*
445 Nixon Presidential Materials Staff. **448** National Archives (8555-9A). **450** Library of Congress, Prints and Photographs Division. **452** National Archives (NWCTC-59-PI15E767-NIXON).

GERALD RUDOLPH FORD
454 Courtesy Gerald R. Ford Library.
457 Courtesy Gerald R. Ford Library.
460 © Bettmann/CORBIS. **462** Courtesy Gerald R. Ford Library.

JAMES EARL CARTER
464 Library of Congress, neg. #USZ62-91316. **466** Courtesy Jimmy Carter Library. **471** Courtesy Jimmy Carter Library. **473** AP/Wide World Photos. **474** Emma Seimodei.

RONALD WILSON REAGAN
476 Courtesy Ronald Reagan Library. **478** Courtesy Ronald Reagan Library. **480** AP/Wide World Photos. **483** Dan Wasserman/*Los Angeles Times* Syndicate. **485** Courtesy Ronald Reagan Library. **488** Courtesy Ronald Reagan Library.

GEORGE HERBERT WALKER BUSH
490 George Bush Presidential Library. **494** Library of Congress, neg. #USZ62-120044. **496** George Bush Presidential Library.

WILLIAM JEFFERSON CLINTON
500 AP/Wide World Photos. **502** AP/Wide World Photos. **505** AP/Wide World Photos. **508** Reprinted with special permission King Feature Syndicate. **511** Archive Photos.

A CAMPAIGN PORTFOLIO
241 Top: Gift of Edgar William and Bernice Chrysler Garbisch, © 2000 Board of Trustees, National Gallery of Art, Washington; bottom: National Museum of American History, Smithsonian. **242** Top: The Granger Collection, New York; bottom left: National

Museum of American History, Smithsonian; bottom right: ©Collection of The New-York Historical Society. **243** Top: From the collections of the Dallas Historical Society; bottom: Library of Congress, neg. #USZC4-2713. **244** The Saint Louis Art Museum. **245** Top left: Rare Book, Manuscript, & Special Collections Library, Duke University; top right: The Granger Collection, New York; bottom: Museum of American Political Life, University of Hartford, West Hartford, CT. **246** The Granger Collection, New York. **247** Top: Museum of American Political Life, University of Hartford, West Hartford, CT; middle: Rutherford B. Hayes Library; bottom: The Granger Collection, New York. **248** Top: American Heritage Picture Collection; bottom: Library of Congress, neg. #USZC4-824. **249** Top left, middle, and right: © Bettmann/CORBIS; bottom left: The Granger Collection, New York; bottom right: National Museum of American History, Smithsonian. **250** Top: Theodore Roosevelt Collection, Harvard College Library; bottom: The Granger Collection, New York. **251** Top left: © Bettmann/CORBIS; top right: The Eugene V. Debs Foundation, Terre Haute, Indiana; bottom left: Museum of American Political Life, University of Hartford, West Hartford, CT; bottom right: Ohio Historical Society. **252** Top: Franklin D. Roosevelt Library; left: © Estate of Ben Shahn/ Licensed by VAGA, New York, NY; middle: Franklin D. Roosevelt Library; bottom right: © Bettmann/CORBIS. **253** Top: Rare Book, Manuscript, & Special Collections Library, Duke University; right: Mamie Doud Eisenhower Birthplace, Boone, Iowa; bottom: © Bettmann/CORBIS. **254** Top: Copyrighted Chicago Tribune Company. All rights reserved used with permission; middle: LBJ Library Collection; bottom: AP/Wide World Photos. **255** Top: © Bettmann/CORBIS; middle: National Archives (NLNP-WHPO-MPF-C0868); bottom: National Museum of American History, Smithsonian. **256** Top left (buttons): Rare Book, Manuscript, & Special Collections Library, Duke University; top left (poster): Rainbow/PUSH Coalition; top right: Rare Book, Manuscript, & Special Collections Library, Duke University; middle: Forbes Magazine Collection; bottom left and right: AP/Wide World Photos.

☆ ABOUT THE AUTHORS ☆

John Milton Cooper, Jr., is E. Gordon Fox Professor of American Institutions at the University of Wisconsin, Madison. He has taught at Wisconsin since 1970 and previously taught for five years at Wellesley College. He is the author of four books, including *The Warrior and the Priest: Woodrow Wilson and Theodore Roosevelt* and *Pivotal Decades: The United States, 1900–1920.*

Lewis L. Gould is Eugene C. Barker Centennial Professor Emeritus in American History at the University of Texas at Austin. He is the editor of the Modern First Ladies series published by the University Press of Kansas. Among his recent books are *1968: The Election that Changed America* and *Lady Bird Johnson: Our Environmental First Lady.*

Louis W. Koenig is professor emeritus of political science at New York University and visiting distinguished professor at C. W. Post, Long Island University. His book on the presidency, *The Chief Executive*, is in its sixth edition. He is also the author of *The Truman Administration* and *The Invisible Presidency*, a study of presidential advisers, and has received grants from the National Endowment for the Humanities to conduct seminars on the presidency for college teachers.

Robert A. Rutland is Research Professor in American History at the University of Tulsa. He is also professor emeritus in American History at the University of Virginia, where he was editor-in-chief of the *James Madison Papers* from 1971 to 1987.

Hans L. Trefousse, a distinguished professor of history emeritus at Brooklyn College and the Graduate Center of the City University of New York, is a specialist in the history of the Civil War and Reconstruction. The author of biographies of Benjamin F. Butler, Benjamin Franklin Wade, Carl Schurz, Andrew Johnson, and Thaddeus Stevens, Trefousse has also written accounts of the radical Republicans and Lincoln's decision for emancipation, as well as books on American foreign policy.